TADAO ANDO

TADAO ANDO
COMPLETE WORKS
FRANCESCO DAL CO

Phaidon Press Limited
Regent's Wharf
All Saints Street
London N1 9PA

Published by
Phaidon Press Limited, 1995

© 1994, Electa, Milano
Elemond Editori Associati

© English edition
Phaidon Press Limited, 1995

Reprinted 1996

A CIP catalogue record for this book
is available from the British Library

ISBN 0 7148 3471 8

All rights reserved. No part of this
publication may be reproduced, stored
in a retrieval system or transmitted, in
any form or by any means, electronic,
mechanical, photocopying, recording or
otherwise, without the prior permission
of Phaidon Press Limited.

Translations
Sabu Koso and Judy Geib: pp 509–512
translated from Japanese;
Thomas Muirhead: pp 7–30, 476–481,
484, 492–494, 507–508; all translated
from Italian.

Printed in Italy

A number of people have contributed to
the realization of this book, and I would
like to acknowledge them here collectively
before thanking them each as they deserve
to be. I must especially thank Yumiko Ando
for her patience in gathering together the
material which provided the basis of our
work and to Masataka Yano, who carefully
followed each step in organizing this
book. Giovanna Crespi helped me in
every moment; this book owes much to
her helpfulness and kindness. *F D C*

Contents

7 The Architecture of Betrayal
Francesco Dal Co

31 **Buildings and Projects**

Writings by Tadao Ando
444 A Wedge in Circumstances
445 The Wall as Territorial Delineation
446 From Self-Enclosed Modern Architecture towards Universality
449 Interior, Exterior
450 Facing up to the Crisis in Architecture
451 Mutual Independence, Mutual Interpenetration
453 Shintai and Space
454 Representation and Abstraction
455 From the Church on the Water to the Church of the Light
456 Materials, Geometry and Nature
457 Spatial Composition and Nature
458 Light, Shadow and Form
460 Nature and Architecture
461 The Traces of Architectural Intentions
462 From the Periphery of Architecture
466 The Power of Unrealized Vision
467 Sensibility and Abstraction
468 In the Japanese Pavilion at Expo 92, Seville
470 Light
472 The Agony of Sustained Thought: The Difficulty of Persevering
474 The Eternal within the Moment
476 Interview with Tadao Ando
Hiroshi Maruyama

Critical Anthology
484 Tadao Ando
Vittorio Gregotti
485 Tadao Ando: Heir to a Tradition
Kiyoshi Takeyama
488 Tadao Ando's Critical Modernism
Kenneth Frampton
489 The Story AND O
Peter Eisenman
490 Tadao Ando and the Cult of Shintai
Kenneth Frampton
492 Infinitesimally Small and as Palpable as Silence
Giordano Tironi
495 Dormant Lines
Darell Wayne Fields
496 Indicencies: in the Drawing Lines of Tadao Ando
Peter Eisenman
498 'Brutalizing' History and the Earth
François Chaslin
500 The Architecture of Tadao Ando – Predicated on Participation
Tom Heneghan
501 Tadao Ando and the Enclosure of Modernism
Fredric Jameson
503 Three Houses by Tadao Ando
Vittorio Magnago Lampugnani
507 Minimalism and Architecture
Vittorio Gregotti
509 Reflections on the Architecture of Tadao Ando
Yuzuru Tominaga

Appendices
514 Biography
515 Bibliography
519 Bibliography of Works
523 Index of Works
524 Photographic Credits

The Architecture of Betrayal
Francesco Dal Co

'The Japanese word for *discourtesy*,' wrote Ananda K Coomaraswamy, 'can be translated as *unexpected behaviour*; there are ceremonies for living which, like the layout of a cultivated garden, cannot be allowed to run out of control; similarly, architectural form, when it is correctly conceived, must also take account of the need to respond to its surroundings. The self-effacing Oriental conceals himself in the mass, intimately belonging to it whilst his personality blossoms forth free of restriction.' In the West, our models of the cosmos assume it operates by conflict within an original Chaos. In the East (according to Elémire Zolla), it is thought that 'hermitage and ecumene, Order and Chaos' are closely linked one to another. The difference between these two approaches to life offers us some illumination as we investigate the architecture of Tadao Ando. Ando reveals the inadequacies of western criticism more in his built work than his writings, and more clearly than others working in the Japanese milieu. Western architectural writing, incapable of distinguishing the subtle differences between ourselves and the East, tends to adopt a competitive attitude, 'westernizing' whatever aspects of oriental culture seem amenable to the formation of tangible working relationships. It fails to see how today, as always, Japanese art and architecture are innately disdainful and detached, with a tension of their own which derives from this aloofness. In his more thoughtful work, Ando expresses this in ways it would be quite wrong to reduce to our own dichotomous vision of how we think the world is made.

Here and there in his œuvre there is a deliberate monotony and repetitiveness designed to induce stillness, timelessness and quietude. In such moments he is able to express this rarefaction with an architecture of the utmost simplicity, and it is up to us not to miss these rare and unfamiliar experiences. Even in Japan, Ando's architecture is often and too easily seen as mere nostalgia, a commonplace which Ando himself does not seem inclined to refute. His cool style is seen as carrying forward a certain kind of Japanese tradition which cultivates a particularly charming relationship with nature.

Partly because of Ando himself (there are significant differences between what he says and what he does) it is all too easy for some to see him as one who has found a way around the crisis of Modernism towards a great restatement of its moral positions; but only by totally ignoring the things which have been happening in architecture elsewhere is it possible to really believe this, as so many seem to. For them, Ando's buildings show that Modernism will march on somehow, as able as it ever was to make places in which modern man can look forward to 'living poetically' in some sort of re-pacified coexistence between technology and transition, nature and artifice, poetry and utility. Ando, the self-taught innocent of Osaka, shows the way as he consoles and encourages us to carry on believing that 'Full of merit, yet poetically, man Dwells on this earth'. That line from Hölderlin, borrowed by Heidegger, has been responsible for so many banalities of contemporary criticism. The architectural poetic of Ando 'the minimalist' (one can hardly recall it and not squirm with embarrassment) is supposed to be able to resolve the conflict between earth and world, no less; the 'being' of one and the 'becoming' of the other, to paraphrase Heidegger.

Obviously, these critics find it impossible to say anything at all about the complex and contradictory meanings which make up the very nerve-system of Ando's so-called minimalist architectural language: the intertwined truths and sleights of hand, the conciseness and the echoing allusiveness, the occasional gravity and the frequent severity, the fastidiousness and (at times) the imprecision. In the middle of all this Ando, just occasionally, with 'the candour of the fox and the cunning of the dove' hits on something that reaches the very highest level of serious and tragic discourse, crossing the line beyond which there is nothing but life itself, in all its emptiness.

In such moments when truth is able to get the better of trickery and he is able to acknowledge how precarious and painful it is to exist, Ando does return to tradition, but only to make a helpless and disconsolate architecture which sets out precisely how irreconcilable the distance is that separates tradition from

Watanabe Kazan, portrait of Ichikawa Beian, 1837 (Kyoto National Museum).

real life. Hence the complete absence of anything playful in his architecture and his fondness for Piranesi's *Le Carceri*; it is only the dark side of Piranesi's mind that interests Ando. To salute him as the Messiah of a newly re-pacified Modernity is to strip his work of all its significance and nobility. Tadao Ando, at his most sincere, expresses only the devastation which marks the greatest moments in Japanese art, says how remote and inaccessible tradition is and demonstrates how pointless it is to think that simply to live in a beautiful house could in any way bring peace to the world.

Ando's architecture, if it renews anything, has the great merit of once again laying bare for us the deepest disturbances of the Japanese soul: the idea that existence is a hopeless struggle that has to be suffered to the extreme and unthinkable limit. Those who chat so comfortably about Ando and his charming allusions to Japanese tradition (oh, the details, the spatial configurations, the poetry of the Zen garden, the perfect measures of the Sukiya, the tea houses of Kobori Enshu, Shuko, Sen no Rikyu!) forget, or do not know, how ghastly and threatening this tradition is for the cultured Japanese. What Ando expresses of this tradition is nothing more than vague, elusive sensations and memories with only the consistency of shadows; but whoever glimpses these shadows may see that in some of his work he might deservedly be called noble. There are certain works of art made during the late Edo epoch (the remarkable portrait paintings by Watanabe Kazan, *The Nobility of Defeat* by the Japanologist Ivan Morris), which express in countenances or descriptions what it feels like to stare into the maelstrom of a wrecked life, a story which has ended in disaster, a lost hope, a tempest which has washed up nothing but a heap of flotsam from which civilization can expect nothing that might offer any comfort at all. Tadao Ando knows this world where hope has gone and life is shut in on all sides by defeat and solitude. Writing about Ivan Morris, Marguerite Yourcenar concludes with these words of a Roman emperor: 'Every man's life is a defeat to which he can only submit.' Whether Ando himself fully realizes it or not, this, paradoxically, is the moment

Views of the Katsura Palace and a minka interior.

of a man's greatest happiness. Sometimes his architecture seems to acknowledge it.

In 1817 Commander Perry, at the head of a US Navy squadron, dropped anchor off Uraga and required Japan to open its doors to trade with the West. When the last of the shogun handed back his power to the Emperor, ending the Edo epoch, those 'heroes' (described in *The Nobility of Defeat*) must have been as sombre as the faces in Kazan's portraits. Their anguish then still speaks to us of the futility of the efforts which contemporary civilization believes will lead to something. The same anguish dominates the written novel after the unthinkable act this civilization perpetrated at Hiroshima and Nagasaki. Forced to concede utter defeat, Yukio Mishima, like Watanabe Kazan 130 years before, publicly took his own life according to the strict rules of *seppuku*.

It may be that those cuts and lacerations explain something about the architecture with which the Japanese Metabolists astonished the world in the late 1950s and early 1960s: entire cities, audaciously suspended from giant structures, but hanging pointlessly in the empty air. The old anguish, the void once again. The Tokyo projects by Tange, Kikatake, and Kurokawa, or Isozaki's photomontages 'City of the Future', and then 'Destruction of the City of the Future' confirm that twenty years after Hiroshima, Japanese architects were anything but looking forward to Japan's new personification, this time as a world economic power. Projects by the Japanese Brutalists (such as Isozaki's Medical Centre and Library at Oita, 1959–66) are wild with hyperbole about the new materialism and seem to be gesturing desperately for some sort of new relationship with western architecture. Quieter architects like Kiyoshi Seike and Kazuo Shinohara (the latter especially elegant and profound) were looking for integration with prewar European reductivism such as that of Bruno Taut, so though it may seem that the two modes were poles apart, they touched tangentially and in this scenario, Tadao Ando began his work.

His Soseikan–Yamaguchi House for two brothers (Hyogo, 1974) set out some themes which, unchangingly, were to

Tadao Ando, Soseikan–Yamaguchi House, 1974–5, conceptual sketch and exterior view.

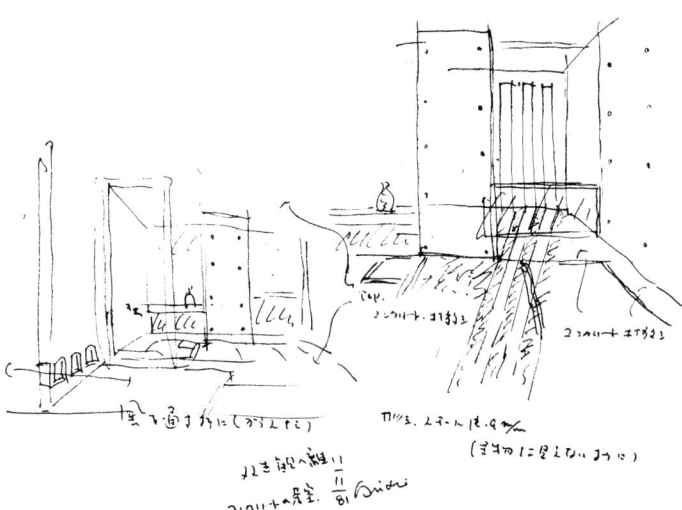

dominate his domestic architecture for the next twenty years. Here in Hyogo we have two parallel blocks placed end to end and connected by a bridge. Each block is cut back on the diagonal to give the project a modishly Brutalist appearance. The elevations are dramatized by double square-framed 'Corbusian' windows (no doubt inspired by Isozaki's most recent work) and large openings looking out over the garden show that inside, there are internal double-height spaces each with a view straight up towards the sky. The formal references may be traceable to Brutalist and Metabolist experimentalism, but Ando's use of materials is spare and rigorous and the abrasive elegance of the concrete is handled with a care which seems to nod more in the direction of Louis Kahn than to the postwar *béton brut* of Le Corbusier.

His project for what he called the Twin Wall house (1975) shows that the debt to Kahn is not only about concrete. Another double box is pierced by arched openings cut down vertically to make the entrances, and bearing in mind such Kahn projects as the United States Embassy in Luanda (1959–61), it is not difficult to trace the probable source of this somewhat awkward version of the thermal window. As in Soseikan–Yamaguchi, the short-end elevations have the same pairs of projecting square windows. Ando allows himself to look in two directions, to the Master of Chaux-de-Fonds and the other Master, of Philadelphia. The stiff linearity of this house is relieved (as before) by including a central full-height space which, because of its size and position, emphasizes how symmetrical the general arrangement is intended to be. Once again, the first-floor rooms at the ends of the building are connected by a bridge. The concrete, inside and out, is relieved by nothing but the beams of light which happen to fall across its surfaces.

The Twin Wall project leads straight on to one of Ando's more unsettling and challenging buildings, the little Azuma House in the Sumiyoshi district of his native Osaka (1975–6). It stands on a tight urban plot and as before, has a long, thin and absolutely symmetrical layout on plan. It is not that Ando feels no need to re-invent what he had already done before; the

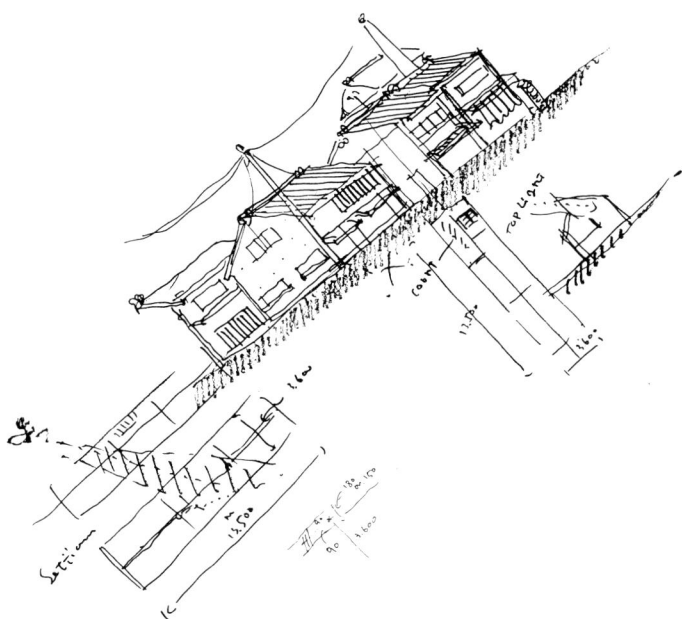

Tadao Ando, Azuma House, 1975–6, conceptual sketch and exterior view.

notion of reiteration, as we shall see, is far more important to him than that. Once again, he arranges blocks at the front and rear ends of the site and connects them by the now-familiar bridge, this time crossing a central space which is left open as a little courtyard. All these arrangements are by now part of the architect's repertoire. The facade is ruthlessly minimal: a taut wall in concrete, which ignores the urban scene of the street and concentrates on its own perfection. Thanks to the care taken by his workmen, Ando's concrete is carefully graded, densely mixed, painstakingly cast, tamped inch by inch, evenly drained and when struck leaves a meticulously fine finish carefully punctuated by the marks of the formwork fixings. Grey and leaden in colour and bereft of any other relieving gestures, with a tiny black hole for an entrance, this facade turns towards the light as a flat plane which, perhaps, vaguely recalls something of the *nijiriguchi* (entrances to tea ceremony rooms) or the *torii* (the gateways which stand in front of Shinto temples). But there is no room for overt citation here; these are merely the shadows of suggestions, the vaguest of remote echoes, just possibly a kind of traditional order which might underlie Ando's already totally irreducible essentialness. The interior spaces are uncompromising to the point of anti-domesticity. They reorganize living into a tremendously strict ritual which is not domesticity at all but its simulacrum; such dissimulation restricts the patterns of living in this house to a series of deliberate movements written out beforehand and performed in complete seclusion, away from external disturbances. This play-acting is to be carried out in a space which, as is still preferred generally in Japan, cuts out all awareness of the city. Thus Ando's basic house-plan comes to perfection in this Osaka street, quite deliberately suppressing all possible awareness that there is anything outside at all. The simple, uniform concrete is its logical corollary and leitmotif.

These houses know nothing (and do not wish to know) about the tensions with which western architects struggle to bring architectural form out of the flux of history. Coomaraswamy says 'the aim of Oriental art is to represent a state of

Tadao Ando, Twin Wall, 1975, view of the model.

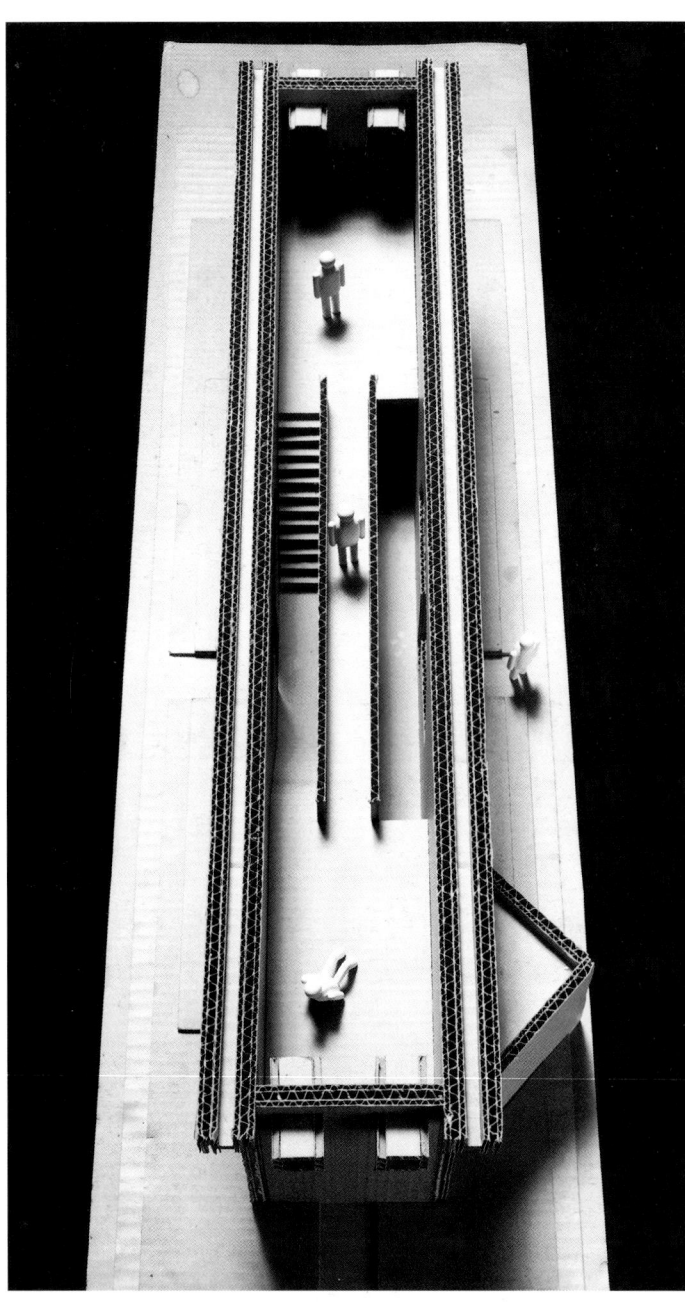

continuum', and so it is with Ando. His houses are self-sufficient, closed, and completed sequences of primordial stillness (which, whatever people may say, has very little to do with western minimalism). The only continuity Ando's minimal language hopes to achieve is the endless murmur of the mantra, deliberately monotonous and desiring only that there be stillness and composure. Static and absolutely empty, Ando's houses offer the chilliest of welcomes, inviting all activity to cease. If stasis of this kind can indeed eliminate conflict by simply excluding everything that might interfere, that may be a kind of order that depends on keeping itself aloof and shut away, but it cannot guarantee that there be either peace or renunciation. All the houses offer the physical withdrawal of the traditional shoji or paper house, in which there is, indeed, a sense of *suki*, being far away from life, engaged in purposeless contemplation of nothing.

So Ando's houses cannot really be places of refuge at all because they are filled with this absence, this deafening emptiness which is almost palpable. As in the tea ceremony, the void itself becomes the raw material for knowing the possibilities of being. Compared with its chaotic site, the Azuma House is the most remote and secluded of places and has a beauty as lonely as must be the inner pain of the man who lives in it. Arriving home, he squeezes through the hole in the concrete facade, is received into the implacability of his concrete womb and in a continuous, endless essentialness, hopes that the space will make possible what Ezra Pound called, 'harmonization of perception and association'; this is what Ando intends.

In 1977 Ando completed his Manabe House which, like the Azuma House, is intended to intensify repetition until complete immobility is achieved. The design of the house is based on a continuous modular grid which measures out a rhythm of interspersed solids and voids. The columns and beams are all deliberately made the same size (ignoring structural logic) simply so that their elongated shadows will all be of the same width. Lost in the haphazard parcelling out of land which is

Tadao Ando, Kidosaki House, 1982–5, view of the courtyard and conceptual sketch.

typical of the Japanese city, the orderliness of this building and its grid is totally arbitrary, referring to nothing external at all. Order and arbitrariness become the opposed extremes which give it whatever life it has. An open concrete frame envelops some parts of the house, shifting them slightly off the main axis – a paradox, because the movement induced by this rotation means absolutely nothing, being based only on the grid which is itself no more than a metaphor for its own abstract and self-referential order.

After this, grids become a constant in Ando's compositional strategy, as in the Matsumoto House in Hyogo (1976–7). Four years before Ando started work on this project Louis Kahn had finished the Kimbell Art Museum in Fort Worth, Texas. In attempting to reproduce the delicate atmosphere of Kahn's building, Ando not only reiterates some of its formal aspects, but also tries to recreate the experience of light falling into the interior by attempting to make a contrast (as Kahn put it) between the reflected 'green light' of nature and 'the silver light of the sky'. Kahn achieved the contrast by placing three inner courtyards between his buildings. Ando attempts the same thing by doubling up the enclosure of the house to create two overlapping skins (one thick, one thin). The house turns its back on the street and opens towards its garden through a kind of double-skinned portico. The open space-frame slithers skeleton-fashion through the house, where its oversized concrete columns and beams (far thicker than they need to be) give the interiors a sense of ever-present repetitive marching. The rooms are grouped (as ever) in two extremities of the building separated by a courtyard, and there are double-circulation corridors through the narrow passages between the grid and the envelope.

The blind wall to the street further intensifies the work Ando had carried out on the external elevation for the Azuma House (though one would have not thought it possible to make that experience any more intense than it already was). Here the openings are concealed behind concrete screens and nothing is allowed to interrupt the elevation which, ruthlessly, cuts into

Tadao Ando, Matsumoto House, 1976–7, view of wall, and Ishihara House, 1977–8, perspective of the courtyard with plan.

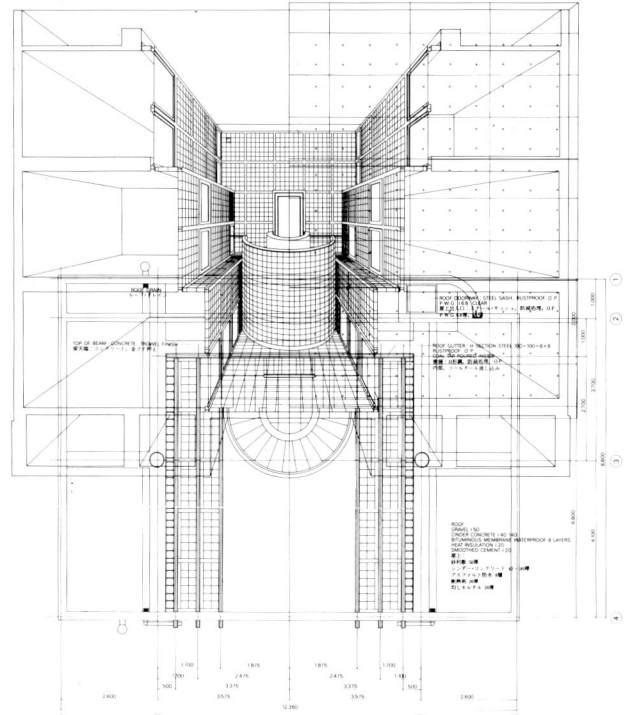

the earth as sharply as the edge of a hand or, perhaps more appropriately, a ceremonial blade which opens a wound that may never heal again. Whatever Ando may tell critics to keep them happy, walls like this have very little to do with the delicate task of 'separating and uniting' as he would have it. This is violence of the roughest kind which threatens anyone who even dares to think there might be anyone inside this place; and yet on the far side there is indeed a totally unexpected domestic space, ordered and structured by the grid, arranged around a little courtyard and looking towards a garden.

The wall is an interruption that first separates the house totally from its context and then breaks down on the garden side, towards nature, before completely dissolving into infinite space. As in traditional Japanese painting, the extreme formality of Ando's architecture, as in this wall, creates the necessary formal break. Stylization is a way of interposing a moment or a gesture which has the effect of stopping, excluding, eliminating, and only then making possible the configuration of static, quieted spaces which, as they silently contemplate their own essentialness, are similar to *Noh* drama. That most formal of all Japanese rituals moves the soul 'only when all representation, singing, dancing, mime and movement have been brought to a stop', and emotion can then flow out of 'pure stillness'.

Such purity and essentiality (one might be forgiven for thinking) must surely have called for an unusual degree of truth to principles and therefore very few opportunities to work, but that is not what comes to mind when we consider the enormous amount of work Ando has done since the mid-seventies. Now we find him at the top of his profession, completing building after building with astonishing speed but only able to do so by falling back on the design and conceptual procedures he had worked out in earlier researches. Thus, perhaps inevitably, we discern the gradual emergence of a Mannerist streak. In the Step Commercial Complex in Kagawa (1977–80) or the piece of virtuoso bravura which is the Ishihara House (Osaka, 1977–8) or the very self-conscious Horiuchi House (Sumiyoshi,

Tadao Ando, Ishihara House, 1977–8, interior view.

Tadao Ando, Manabe House, 1976–7, view of the principal elevation, and Horiuchi House, 1977–9, view of the courtyard.

1977–9), no amount of Ando's skill and polish can disguise a certain over-indulgence and hesitancy.

Of his buildings completed at the end of the 1970s it is worthwhile to stop and look at the Okusu House in Tokyo. This most ambiguous and unresolved of buildings is planned on an unusual L-shape whose narrower and longer arm has a facade which shows what a difference there is between this building and something so evocative and essential as the Azuma House. Here the *torii* motif is an obvious and literal citation. A concrete arch, placed in front of the real facade in the most direct way, makes its bow to tradition and deprives the elevation of any significance it might otherwise have had. The interiors are better, with a more careful articulation which moves through complex sequences of the now-familiar alternations between solid and void. The linear progression of the plan, enriched as it goes by a series of unexpected twists and turns, in the end does not give any impression of essentialness or clarity but creates the effect of walking through a labyrinth. The interior space is interrupted by a procession of walls placed to take advantage of this or that source of light. This gives a foretaste of the kind of attention which, later, he dedicates to the definition of pedestrian routes through much more complex buildings. The stylistic ability of this Mannerist period reaches its high point at Rokko Housing in Kobe. Of its three phases, the first and smallest (1983) is perhaps the most interesting. A central axis, marked by the ramps of external access stairs, climbs up and terminates in a sort of 'apse' which makes the building look as though it is leaning against the hillside. This curving protruberance is Ando's rather unexpected way of terminating what would otherwise be an entirely orthogonal and modular arrangement. The same motif reappears, slightly modified, in the later phases of the project as well as in the Step Commercial Complex which (despite the very different setting) has some analogies with Rokko. In the Okamoto Housing (Kobe, 1976) cylindrical volumes are used to interrupt the grid and the superimposition of geometric figures (square and circle) shifts it off axis. At Step

Tadao Ando, Raika Headquarters, 1986–7, exterior and interior views.

a circle breaks out of the grid and emerges on the central axis as part of a cylinder. Such procedures are intended to create interference between discrete geometric shapes and repetitive grids, creating tensions which offer compositional opportunities. After Rokko this has become a trait even in the more thoughtful parts of Ando's enormous output, such as the Raika Headquarters (Osaka 1986–9) or the Hyogo Children's Museum (1987–9). These two works lead to one of the most mature expressions of this period, the Museum of Literature at Himeji, completed in 1991.

Rokko is a residential complex consisting of repeating cells which adapts itself to the steeply sloping site around a central spine of services. Each dwelling is accessed from outside and uses the roof of the apartment below as a terrace. The grid's decisiveness renders the building's general layout easy to understand. Its regularity contrasts with the somewhat self-indulgent sculptural form of the external staircases, no doubt a way of breaking the monotony but tending towards something vaguely Brutalist and expressionistic. (The architect might justify himself by saying he had to meet some requirement or other of the notorious Japanese fire regulations.) Despite the stereometrical configuration of its grid, Rokko exhibits a number of tensions: the curving terminal at the top of the external stairs submits the grid to a certain exertion, and the reductivism of the one and the superabundance of the other confront each other in an area of attrition around the composition's central axis. The precision of the building's construction only emphasizes how it sets artifice against nature, adapting to the site by conserving the slope and stepping back as necessary, but not in any self-effacing way. Indeed it shows off all these conflicts and collisions as a grand spectacle, with a brutality which Ando does not seem in the least inclined to conceal. As Vittorio Gregotti says, 'Rokko is profoundly rooted in the discussion about site, architecture, and geography. It establishes a way of its own of existing on this rock-face; all the thinking which proceeds therefrom, constantly bears that mark, in its very language'.

Tadao Ando, Rokko Housing I and II, 1978–89, conceptual sketches and aerial view.

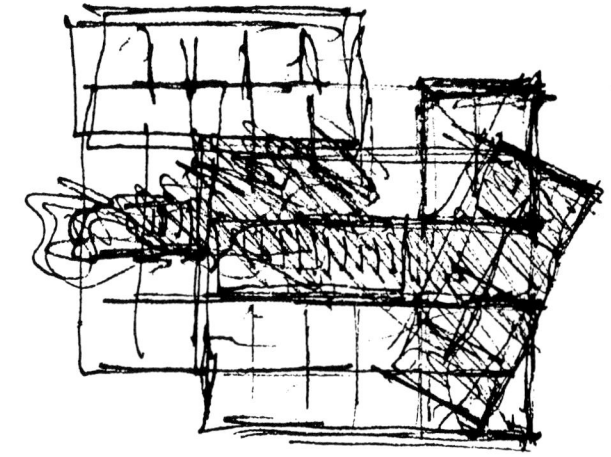

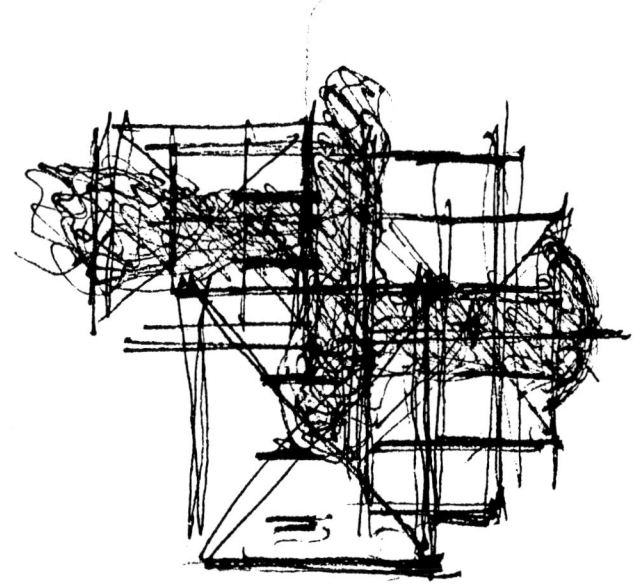

Although Rokko II and III are bigger, their general characteristics are the same. The experience of designing Rokko enabled Ando to work out fully the problems he had set himself and to perfect compositional approaches which were then to inform his more important work of the late 1980s.

Further exploring the effects obtainable with grids, Ando's experiments continued with the Festival Commercial Complex in Naha (1980–84) and the Jun Port Island Building (Kobe, completed 1985). Introverted, closed in on themselves, these buildings have a rigorously geometric order of their own. They assert their presence, undecorated and intransigent, amidst the chaotic urban noise, ignoring the particularities of the context and following the method worked out at Rokko I. The order given by grids (montage as the expression of formal discipline, repetition as the synonym for order, reproducibility made possible by constructional precision), is by now a prime concern in Ando's work and the expertise he has acquired in manipulating them is manifest in these projects, as moments of possible meaning in the formless, seething Japanese metropolis.

We can pass quickly over the 'Old/New' restaurant complex at Hyogo (1985–6). The complex, four restaurants connected by a shared service space, is too mannered a building, which goes too far in demonstrating all of Ando's standard tricks. His malls are altogether more interesting because of the confrontations they seek with their setting. The two blocks of Time's in central Kyoto (1983–4 and 1986) occupy a narrow plot overlooking the River Takase and contain three floors of shops with a small plaza on the river side. They overlook the water with an elevation of superimposed walls which rise straight up from the bank to a curving metal roof, an apparently simple shell which stands in contrast to the jumbled panorama of the commercial district. Despite its modesty and small size, the expanding and contracting interior spaces turn out to be surprisingly complex, whilst at the Collezione Complex in Tokyo (1986–9) the complexity is taken so far that it actually disorientates. It is laid out on a uniform square grid which emerges here and there as freestanding fragments of concrete frame. The layout is

Tadao Ando, Hyogo Children's Museum, 1987–8, view showing pools.

determined by two rectangular blocks, shifted in response to the diverging site boundaries and enclosing a large cylinder which protrudes through an opening in the rather elegant freestanding facade. The interior circulation starts from here and penetrates inwards through spaces which are never the same twice. One shop leads to another in the most fortuitous and unexpected way while cuts and views offer surprise glimpses of the outside. Collezione is a vertical labyrinth in which one can very easily get lost and this, one supposes, is intentional; Ando is in the habit of defining his work as 'the architecture of betrayal'. The complicatedness, the disorder, the unpredictability of this building leave the visitor feeling he has been in something much bigger and this is an effect achieved (to borrow an analogous term from linguistics) by a technique called hyperbaton. When a continuum of undifferentiated grammatical units is separated out by inserting other words, the flow of the discourse is broken up. One part comes to seem more noticeable than another, taking space to expand its own particular meaning and potential. This is not unlike Ando's technique of superimposing a circle, or parts of circles, onto a grid as in the characteristically elegant Iwasa House in Hyogo (1982–4) and the Kidosaki House in Tokyo (1982–6) where the curves, convex in the former and concave in the latter, interrupt the grid so that the space seems to expand.

The uniformity of appearance and absence of any detail (other than that given by the perfect construction and the repetitiveness of its typological arrangements), means that Ando's architecture does not readily communicate and his buildings demand our careful attention; in exchange (on their terms and in their time) the buildings begin to reveal how intimately they live in complete symbiosis with nature and light. Light is the protagonist of the Koshino House (Hyogo, 1979–81), the Izutsu House (Osaka, 1981–2) the Iwasa and Yoshida Houses (Osaka, 1986–8), the Ito House (Tokyo, 1988–90) and the Miyashita House (Kobe, 1989–92).

'In the game of light and shade,' writes Ernst Jünger 'things acquire spiritual existence as they are unveiled. They reach a

Exterior views of the Hyogo Children's Museum.

Tadao Ando, Time's, 1983–6, exterior view and river elevation.

higher sphere in which they never decay and which is an inherent part of their own project for themselves. They seem to be immaterial yet, at the same time, more imposing.' Thus Ando's concrete reacts to light; illuminated, it reveals that it exists, 'returning again' to the base materials of which it was made. The toil required to shape it now no longer conceals its mineral origin, which seems to come to the surface. Light reveals the truth which is in things and at the same time gives them new meanings. The more it penetrates them, the more these things become weightless, pure and simple, and acquire the definitive characteristics attributed to them by the project. When they reach perfect attunement with luminosity, thus bringing to reality their 'desire for disclosure' (as one might say paraphrasing De Bruyne), Ando's buildings encounter the form they were destined to assume and conquer the essentialness to which they aspire. Light reinforces their motionless monotony. If, as Hans Sedlmayer has written, 'in forms, light shows that it possesses a static component whilst in colours, it reveals that is also has a dynamic component', we may find it easier to understand how the state of immobility, in which Ando's spatial continuities come together, is unable to exist without the consistent monochromatism of concrete.

In the Church of the Light at Osaka (1987–9) luminosity is obliged to perform a symbolic function. In those circumstances, even if in a context of rarefied abstraction, it is made use of for contingent purposes; a giant cross of light is incised into the wall behind the altar to articulate an otherwise hermetic space. In his houses Ando succeeds in using light without making such compromises; in this church, however, light is supposed to be an allegory for spirituality and therefore an expression of the function of a space of which it is merely the decoration. In the Koshino House, on the other hand, it is a constituent part of the luminosity of the architecture itself, a fundamental component of the spirituality of *all* things, an expression of their 'desire to disclose themselves'; not an add-on but the very essence of how materials and forms are perceived. Light devoid of compromises, with no purpose in mind nor meanings to

Tadao Ando, Collezione Commercial Complex, 1986–9, exterior view showing the entrance and axonometric.

elucidate, reveals the relationship between its own clarity and the geo-numeric *claritas* of Ando's architecture, in those few isolated works in which the architecture manages to free itself of conditioning to pursue its own purpose. It is not by chance that there is no colour in Ando's spaces because as Goethe reminds us, colours are evidence of, 'the campaigns and sufferings to which light has been subjected', and could thus only disturb the intimate quietness which this house seeks to achieve.

Between the two wings of the Koshino House, on the inner surfaces and outside walls of its external court, there is a continuous alternation of light and shadow emanating from all points of the compass. Like rain streaming down the shining walls of the open parts of Ando's houses, or the wind which blows across the terraces of the Miyashita House, light is both an abstract image of nature and a figurative representation of the passage of time. In Ando's houses time is measured against the endless activity of nature while nature transforms time in a series of palpable manifestations. This mutual belonging can only really be perceived in spaces designed to offer total seclusion and protection; enclosed gardens whose prototypes derive from Ch'an-Zen art. They are indistinctly recalled in the outside *niwa* spaces in front of some rooms in Ando's houses and can only really be explored visually. Paradoxically, it is the sense of remoteness in these gardens which brings intimately close the perceived phenomena of Zen tradition, implying the most extreme abstraction and requiring that we pay attention to their essentialness. This abstraction enables us to participate in perfection and to become aware of nature; time makes itself manifest as the source of knowing, symbol of the sentiments. Mircea Eliade reminds us that the whole body must participate in this vision of perfection or, as Ando would call it, *shintai*. Every resource must be mobilized, intellect and senses must respond in unison, and grasp that instant in which a comprehension of reality is spontaneously offered, provided we know how to be aware of the instant in which time stops, 'projecting us into *nunc stans*, the eternal present'. The rules of the tea ceremony or *chanoyu* were laid down in the fifteenth

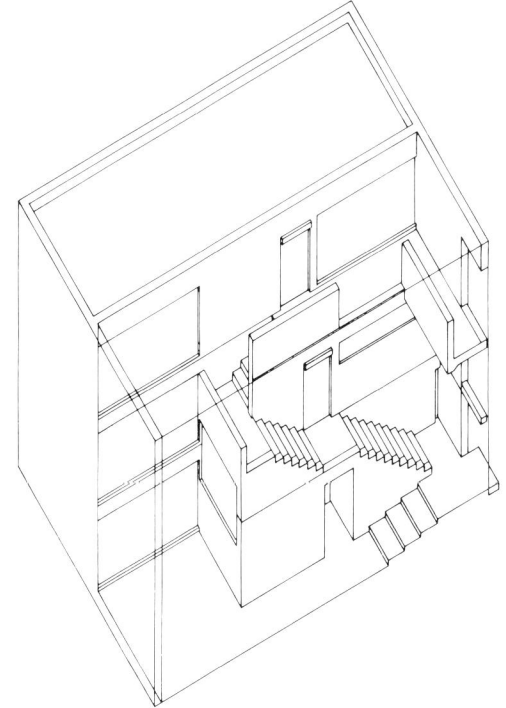

Tadao Ando, Koshino House, 1979–81, interior view, conceptual sketch and view from the garden.

century as the highest expression of Zen. Chanoyu is carried out within the restricted and essential space of the Sukiya, which connects to the *roji*, an alternative route leading across a garden linking the *yoritsuki* (waiting room) to the tea room itself, the *chahitsu*. Nothing must interfere with the ritual carried out in these places of absolute privacy. Nothing must get in the way of direct perception of a meticulously designed nature offered to the senses. There must be no detail of architecture which could take anything away from it and no work of art to interfere with the state of pure abstraction in which shintai can only be experienced. Nothing, in fact, could be good enough for the 'manifestation' which takes place here because this is simply the phenomenon of life itself, expressing its own existence as the highest art form of all. 'The forms which are taken on by life are not empirically determined in any way but are designed according to a metaphysical tradition: on the one hand the search for conformity to a divine order and on the other, the intention to facilitate in each individual, according to his or her nature, the achievement of an approximate perfection to be realized in the whole of the being'. (Ananda K Coomaraswamy). In such places, according to Chuang-Tzu, 'the mind of the sage, quiet and at rest, reflects the universe and all Creation'. Time ceases to pass. The intimate coexistence of nature and time, directly experienced, does not protect the shintai from pain and suffering any more than could the paper walls of the Sukiya, but does offer shelter from anguish and anxiety in a place as far away from the world as it is possible to be, even though the world is close by, separated only by an interval whose suspended time ignores the anxieties of the world and in which the world has nothing it could offer, if not the power of abstraction which shintai brings about.

A trace of this tradition is discernible in Ando's designs for lonely gardens. In his more serious house designs the tradition reverberates as an awareness of the intimacy between light and nature, as something that happened far away, a long time ago, a faded sense which renews itself in the monotony of his spaces but which offers no consolation in what they evoke,

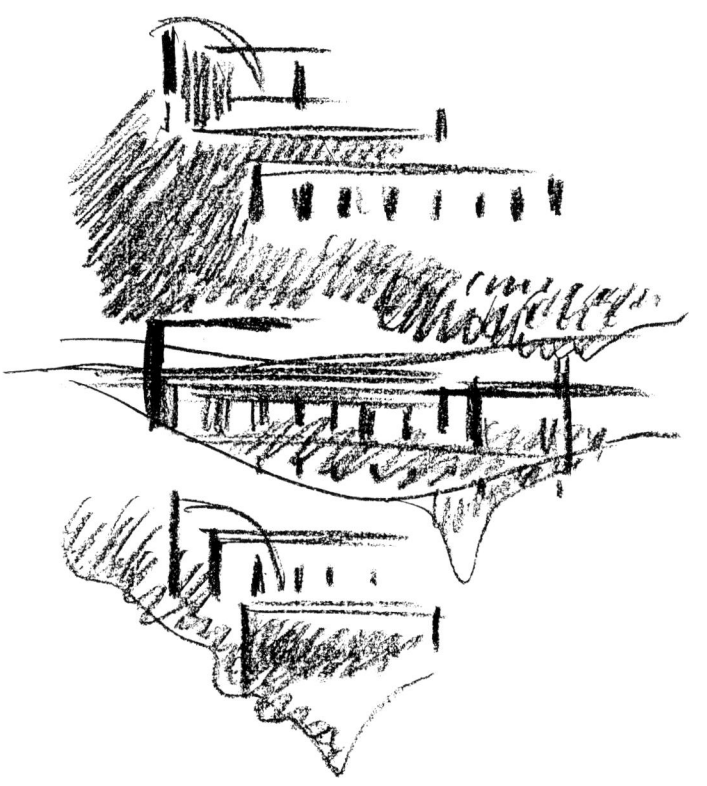

Tadao Ando, Ito House, 1988–90, exterior view.

recounting only something that has been lost and forgotten. But these are only fleeting moments – as we were saying. As he hurries undecided from one siren call to another, through an opus which seems to be intensifying at an alarming speed, it must be difficult for Ando to resist temptation. How complicated to not just exhibit one's personal anguish but to take the responsibility for making something which might also console others!

In considering his frenetic production of the late 1980s one must therefore take note of oscillations which are not always purposeful. This shows clearly when we compare two buildings which have the same programme: the Church on Mount Rokko near Kobe and a second Church at Tomamu. The Mount Rokko Chapel (1985–6) has all the characteristics typical of Ando's most successful projects. It is composed of three parts, clearly identified: a courtyard isolating the garden from nature, the church itself, and a long understated colonnade leading to the entrance. These parts are brought together in the simplest way imaginable, without clever superimpositions or intermixings, as a collage of pure geometric signs. All excess is spurned, and frugality is exercised in making the composition. The nonchalance of the plan contrasts with the sophistication of the interior daylighting. The church is lit by slits where the perimeter walls meet each other and where the roof sits on the end wall; the concrete surfaces are animated with shafts of light and shadow, giving a richness of effect one would not have imagined possible when looking at the rigorously geometric exterior. These shafts of light articulate the box, cutting through the connections between its sides and top while a giant window, divided into four by heavy concrete frames, permits 'green light' from the courtyard to add an extra 'unexpected dimension' to this little *boîte à miracles*.

Located in a recently-opened holiday resort, the Church on the Water at Tomamu (1985–8) rises from a vast expanse of water and is delimited to one side by a long wall which obstructs a free view of the landscape. The completely open and empty facade of a low building standing at the water's edge is framed by a

Tadao Ando, Miyashita House, 1989–92, views of the courtyard.

Tadao Ando, Japanese Pavilion, Expo 92, Seville, view of the entrance.

freestanding open structure which extends further beyond; a mechanically operated window in this opening is held up by a very large frame which takes the form of a cross. The church is approached by a tortuous route from the back, leading to a strange glazed cage with no roof. Behind these sheets of glass are four uncompromising-looking crucifixes made out of concrete. Another crucifix, of steel, stands further away, in the water. Compared with the carefully-considered arrangement of the church the access route is not so much a rite of passage as just a convoluted path, and the heavy symbolism which the various crucifixes are supposed to embody make this building merely sepulchral, and far too ingratiating.

Ando's project for the Japanese Pavilion at the Seville Expo (1992) received wide acclaim at the time and certainly, compared with the dreary architectural histrionics on show elsewhere at the Expo this was hardly surprising. Unfortunately, as at the Church on the Water, Ando once again fell into the trap of trying to create a deliberate effect using easily-assimilated suggestions, rather than designing with true integrity. Adopting materials of obviously 'traditional' character he showed off his usual constructional brilliance and went straight for monumental effect, shamelessly succumbing to the vulgarity which seems to typify all such occasions, playing to please the crowd by whipping up nostalgia in a scenario which could only be described as 'techno-idiocy'. Clowning for the amusement of his public, juggling with the most facile architectural signs fished straight out of 'history' his centrepiece, placed under the central opening of the Pavilion, was a far too obviously 'evocative' timber structure, meant to evoke the details of real Japanese temples. These concessions to a supposedly popular taste, for whatever reason, seem so self-consciously 'exotic' and 'primitive' that it is hard to imagine that this is the same Ando who at other times, in other places, has such a sophisticated dialogue with the genuine tradition.

Ando's naivety at Seville is even more perplexing when one considers that at the same time he was building the Water Temple at Hyogo, one of his most poetic and original works.

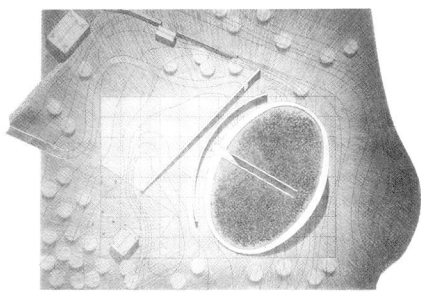

Tadao Ando, Water Temple, 1989–90, site plan and view of the lotus pond.

Tadao Ando, Church on the Water, 1985–8, view of the lake and site plan.

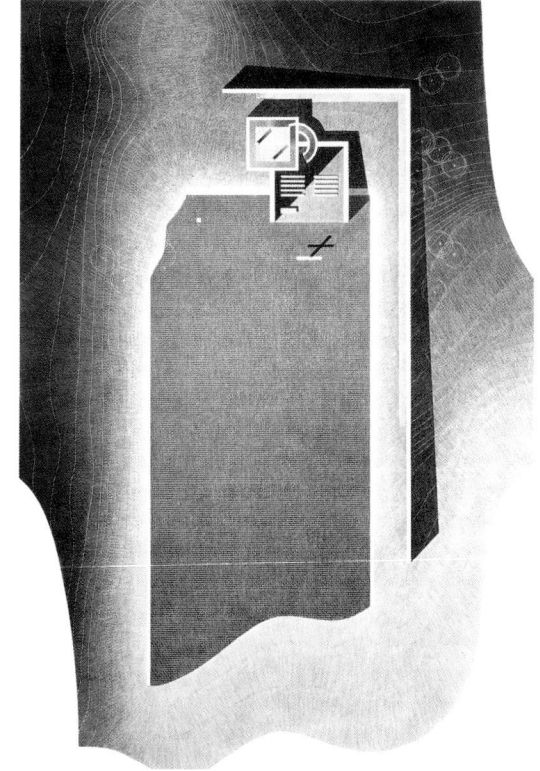

This temple stands in hilly country where the valleys have been re-made many times as basins for collecting rainwater. It stands at the top of one of these hills, beyond a traditional temple that one passes on the way up. It is approached by a path which climbs through lush greenery, suddenly coming out into an open area of white gravel which stops against the backdrop of a long, low, concrete wall which stands out sharply against the sky and is pierced by a single opening. This, once again, is possibly an abstracted and subtle allusion to the traditional *torii*. Walking through this opening one enters a narrow space where another curving wall leads away. Following the curve, the visitor's feet crunch on the white gravel. At the end of this curve is a flight of steps which leads to the shrine. It dives down into the ground, across the middle of an oval pool full of water descending as it goes and passing almost unnoticed below the surface of the water. The visitor, descending, looks straight across the pool through the floating lotus-blossoms before losing sight of far-off hills and lakes which seem to murmur to the temple in a language only they know. The light, blindingly white, reflects off the gravel; coming down the steps it gradually becomes shady and, in the vermilion shrine, there is complete darkness. By using the most restrained gestures and signs Ando evokes emotions and impressions, inciting the senses and the mind to resist a seduction that disconcerts with its purity. The finest qualities of modern architecture only manifest themselves when the architect stays true to the request Hamlet's mother made to Polonius: 'More matter, with less art'.

Buildings and Projects

List of Works

Osaka Station Area Reconstruction Project 34–35

Tomishima House 36–37

Hiraoka House 38–39

Tatsumi House 40–41

Shibata House 42–43

Port Island Project 44–45

Soseikan–Yamaguchi House and Extension 46–53

Twin Wall Project 54–55

Azuma House 56–61

Hirabayashi House 62–65

Bansho House and Extension 66–71

Tezukayama Tower Plaza 72–73

Rose Garden 74–77

Manabe House 78–81

Koto Alley Project 82–83

Okamoto Housing Project 84–85

Matsumoto House Project 86–91

Kitano Alley 92–95

Art Gallery Complex 96–97

Step 98–101

Ishihara House 102–109

Okusu House 110–111

Horiuchi House 112–117

Matsumoto House 118–119

Onishi House 120–121

Kitano Ivy Court 122–123

Matsutani House and Extension 124–127

Ueda House and Extension 128–131

Fuku House 132–133

Rokko Housing I 134–141

Rin's Gallery 142–143

Koshino House and Extension 144–151

Sun Place 152–153

Atelier in Oyodo I 154–155

Nakanoshima Project I – Osaka City Hall 156–157

Festival 158–163

Kojima Housing 164–167

Ishii House 168–171

Bigi Atelier 172–175

Akabane House 176–179

Umemiya House 180–183

Fukuhara Clinic 184–185

Izutsu House 186–189

Doll's House Project 190

Festival 0 191

Iwasa House 192–195

Melrose 196–197

Kidosaki House 198–203

Kaneko House 204–205

Ogura House 206–209

Time's I 210–213

Time's II 214–217

Jun Port Island Building 218–221

Yoshie Inaba Atelier 222–225

All buildings located in Japan unless otherwise stated.

Nakayama House 226–229

Mon Petit Chou 230–231

Hata House 232–235

Sasaki House 236–237

Guest House for Hattori House 238–239

Taiyo Cement Headquarters 240–241

TS Building 242–245

Church on Mount Rokko 246–251

Old/New Restaurant 252–255

Tanaka Atelier 256–257

Shibuya Project 258–259

Noguchi House 260–261

Oyodo Tea Houses 262–267

Kitayama Apartment Block 268–269

Kara-za Mobile Theatre 270–273

I House 274–277

Rokko Housing II 278–281

Church on the Water 282–287

Theatre on the Water 288–289

Galleria Akka 190–293

Bigi 3rd 294–295

Collezione 296–301

Kaguraoka Apartment Block 302–303

Morozoff Studio 304–305

Yoshida House 306–309

Raika Headquarters 310–315

Shinto Shrine Project 316

Mount Rokko Banqueting Hall Project 317

Church of the Light 318–321

Children's Museum 322–327

Natsukawa Memorial Hall 328–331

Izu Project 332–333

Nakanoshima Project II – Space Strata and Urban Egg 334–337

I Gallery Project 338–339

Ito House 340–343

Naoshima Contemporary Art Museum 344–349

Garden of Fine Arts, Expo 90, Osaka 350–351

Museum of Literature 352–355

Ishiko House 356–357

Vitra Seminar House 358–361

Gallery for Japanese Screens, Art Institute of Chicago 362–363

Rokko Island 364–365

Sayoh Housing 366–369

Minolta Seminar Building 370–371

Otemae Art Center 372–373

Atelier in Oyodo II 374–377

Rockfield Factory 378–379

Japanese Pavilion, Expo 92, Seville 380–383

Water Temple 384–387

Forest of Tombs Museum 388–391

Miyashita House 392–393

Temporary Theatre for Photography 394–395

College of Nursing 396–399

The Modern Art Museum and Architecture Museum, Stockholm, Project 400–401

Chikatsu-Asuka Historical Museum, Osaka 402–405

YKK Seminar House 406–407

Children's Seminar House 408–409

Garden of Fine Arts, Kyoto 410–411

Kyoto Station Reconstruction Project 412–413

Oyamazaki Museum 414–415

Konan University Student Centre 416–417

Nara Convention Hall Project 418–419

Church in Tarumi 420–421

Suntory Museum 422–423

Lee House 424–427

Museum of Wood 428–431

Gallery Noda 432–433

Rokko Housing III 434–435

'Fabrica', Benetton Research Centre 436–439

Installation for 'Tadao Ando Architectural Works' Exhibition 440–441

Osaka Station Area Reconstruction Project

Conceptual sketches.

This design is a two-part proposal for the redevelopment of the area in front of Osaka Station, following a request by the city of Osaka in 1969. A dense forest of towering buildings, both homogeneous and highly efficient, the area is a symbol of Japan's rapid economic growth. The project is an attempt to reintroduce nature into this space and enable people to enjoy an environment that affords them spiritual richness, even in a large overcrowded city.

The first part of the proposal suggests covering the top of the existing buildings with greenery and the various rooftops would be connected by escalators. This would effectively create an undulating landscape in the middle of the air. The second part would be to connect the rooftops of the group of buildings with slabs of artificial ground to create a verdant public garden plaza. Besides the introduction of these gardens, the extended rooftop area would incorporate libraries, art museums, theatres and other public facilities; in effect, elevating people from the ground level which is governed by economic principles.

These ideas were developed and given more concrete shape twenty years later in the proposal for the design competition of Kyoto Station in 1990.

Location Osaka
Design 1969

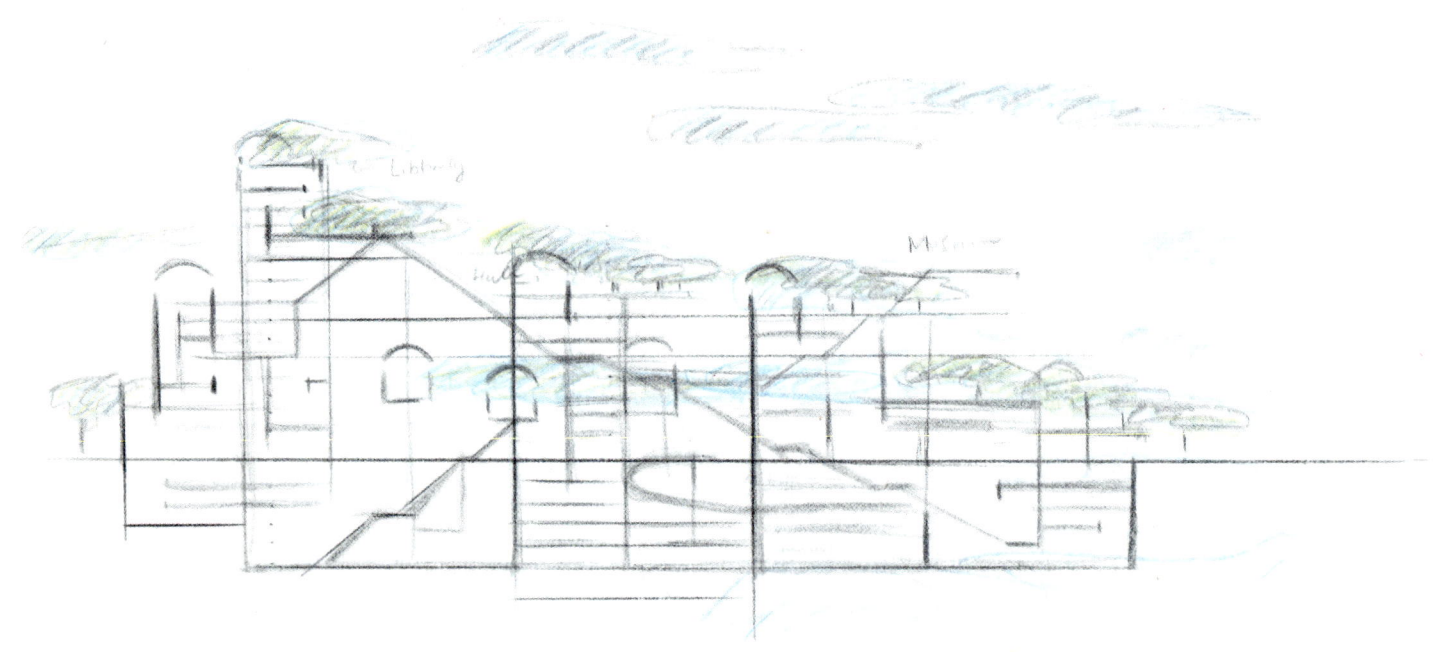

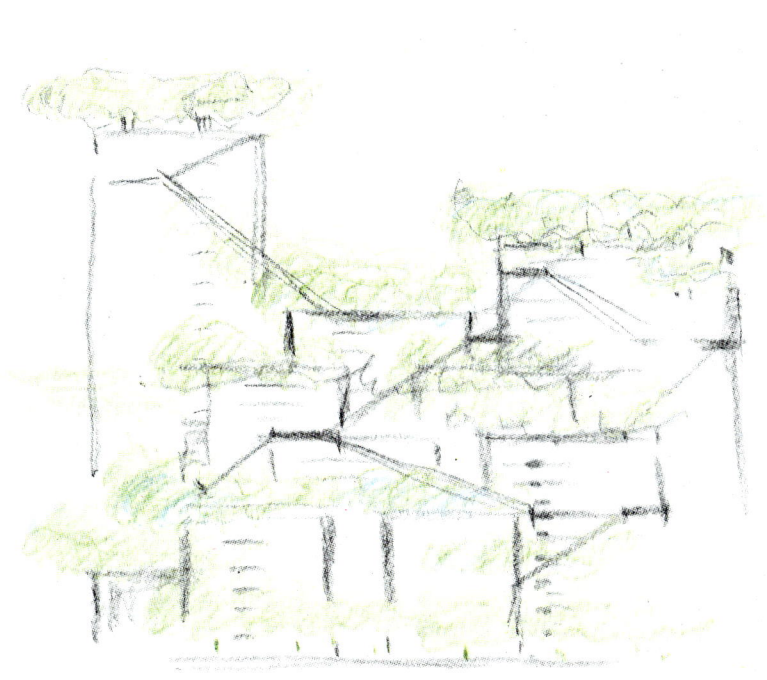
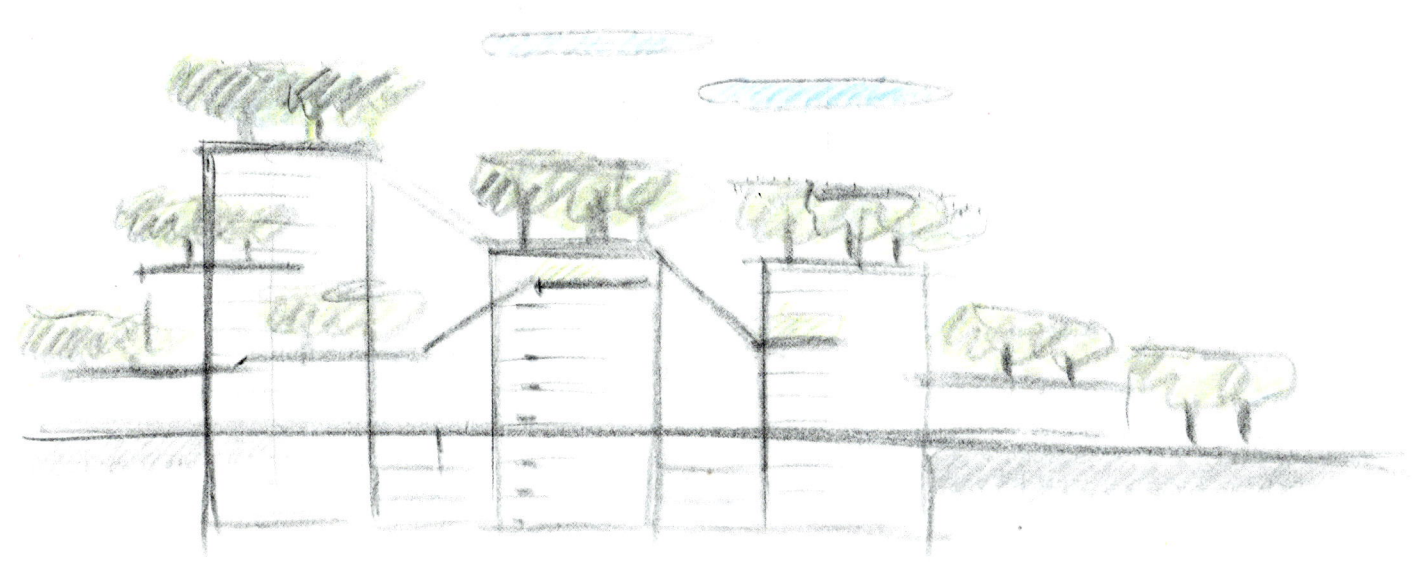

Tomishima House

Floor plans, longitudinal section and axonometric.

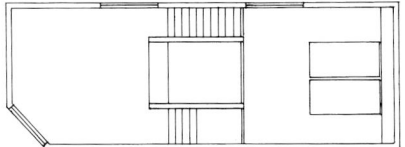 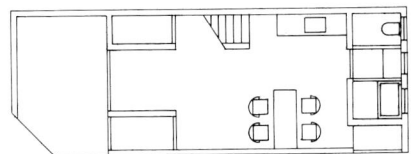

This project was Tadao Ando's first after opening his own design office in 1969. The site is in the centre of Osaka, a narrow 47 square metres of land adjoining the end of a line of wooden row houses erected before the war. The building was created as a house for the family of a friend of the architect. Walled in along its periphery to create an inner sanctuary undisturbed by the noise of the surroundings, the sunlight penetrates the interior of this three-storey void through a skylight.

The apertures into this house are the minimum required for illumination, direct sunlight and ventilation; it is the quality of light that is explored, not the quantity. The interior space interacts with the outside solely through the light which enters from a skylight and illuminates each level of the house by means of the central atrium. This direct light softens as it descends through the staggered floor levels – accommodating bedroom, living room and dining room – giving a natural rhythm to life within the sanctuary of the building's blank enclosing walls.

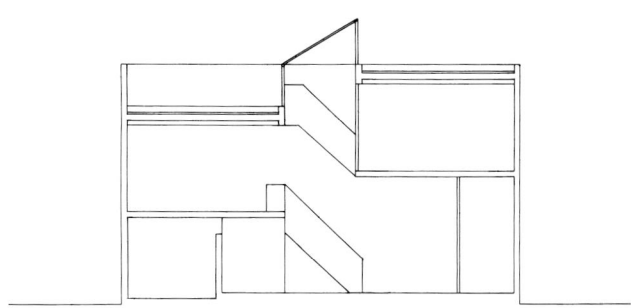

Location Osaka
Design 1972
Construction 1972–3
Structure Reinforced concrete
Site area 55.2 m^2
Building area 36.2 m^2
Total floor area 72.4 m^2

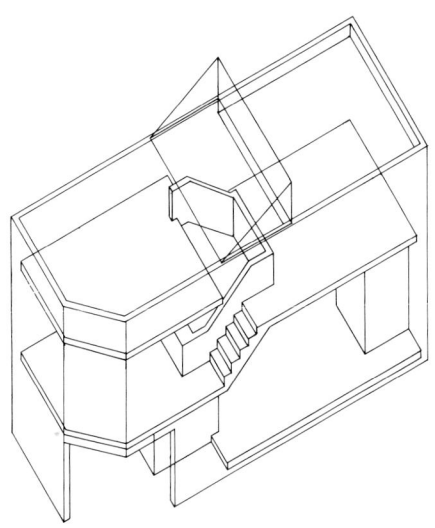

View showing the building in its city context, the entrance and interior view.

Hiraoka House

Floor plans and axonometric.

The site is located in a stepped residential tract that has been carved from a mountainside – a way of dealing with the rapid advance of urban sprawl in Japan. One of a series of subdivided lots, it is surrounded by prefabricated houses whose superficial diversity create, conversely, a landscape of barren monotony.

Within this environment of restrictive order and monotony, the architect has introduced an 'alcove' of space at the building's juncture with the road. From here one proceeds, through a rich sequence of changes, to the house which contains an interior space of an entirely unexpected character. By enclosing a wooden box within a simple box of concrete, a highly varied space has been produced, a part of which projects out towards the city.

Location Takarazuka
Design 1972–3
Construction 1973–4
Structure Reinforced concrete
Site area 238 m^2
Building area 58 m^2
Total floor area 87.9 m^2

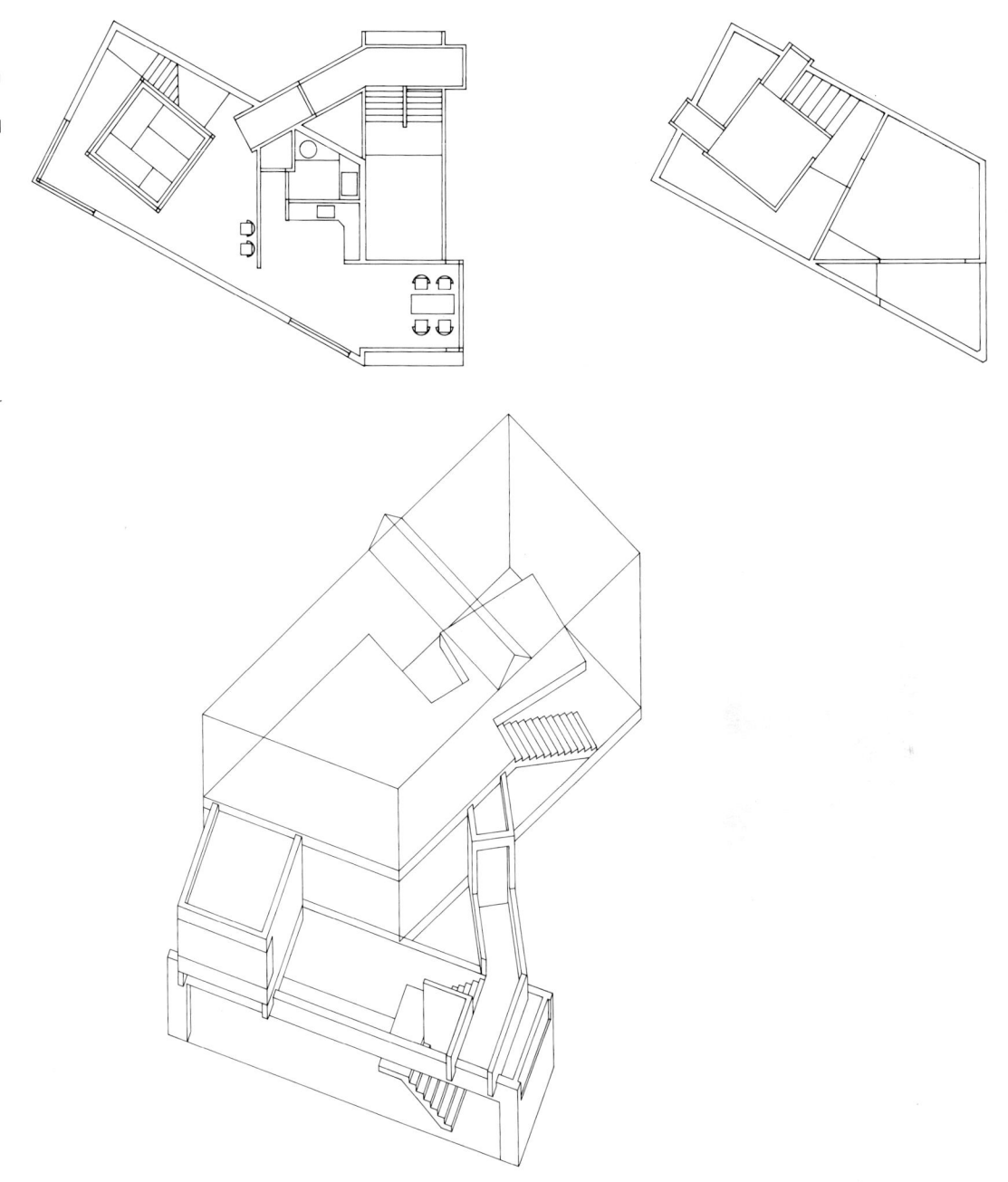

View showing protruding volume of the dining room and general view of the building.

Tatsumi House

Axonometric and floor plans.

This building is sited within a chaotic concentration of residences, shops and factories. A complex building, it accommodates a coffee shop on the ground floor, a boutique on the first and a private residence on the second. The internal functions are packed within concrete walls – much like a condensed version of the chaotic surroundings. A void passes through all three floors, however, imparting unity to the interior. The void, which narrows as it rises, expresses the drama of a vertically-oriented space, reaching upwards to the sky for light.

Location Osaka
Design 1972–3
Construction 1973–4
Structure Reinforced concrete
Site area 61.7 m²
Building area 56.1 m²
Total floor area 135.5 m²

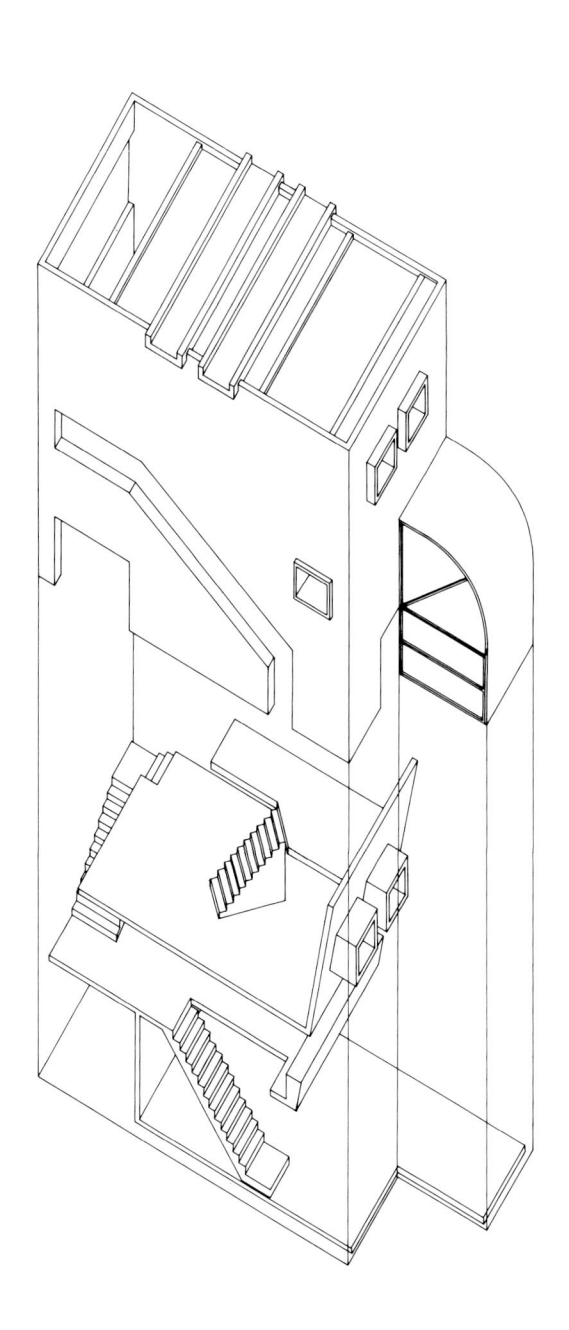

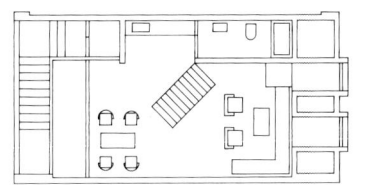

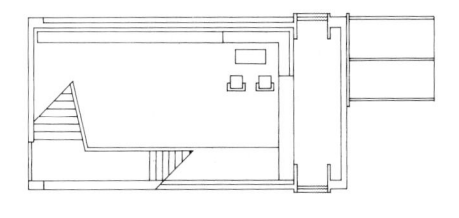

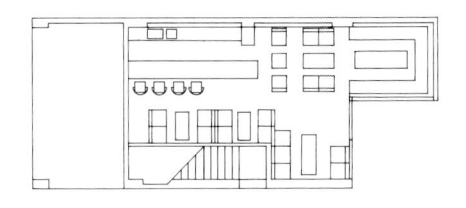

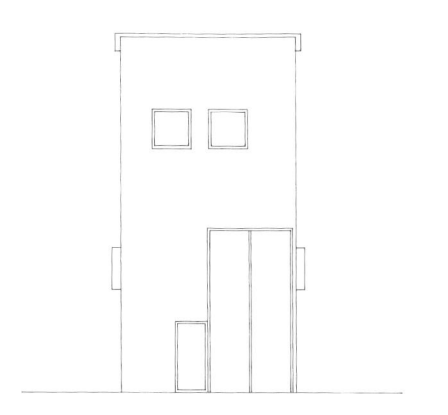

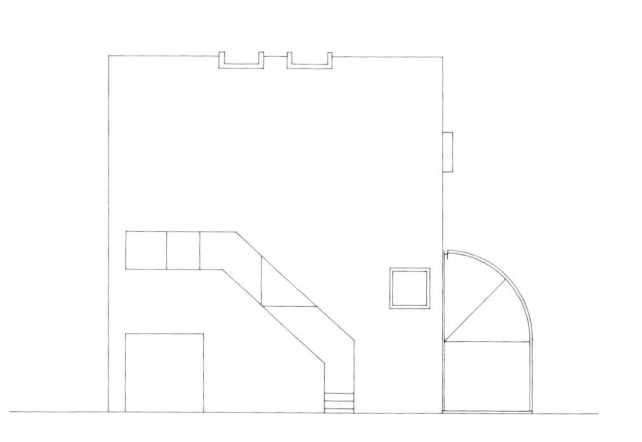

Views showing the street elevation and interior, and side and street elevations.

41

Shibata House

Exploded axonometric and floor plans.

The intimate living environment of this prestigious residential district has gradually deteriorated under the advance of urban sprawl, bringing gridiron road patterns and prefabricated houses of various colours. Walls have therefore been used to insulate this residence from its surroundings and to create a rich interior space.

The building is composed of a rectangular and a cylindrical volume. The functions for daily life are contained in the rectangular form, while the cylinder houses a multi-purpose hall to accommodate the domestic functions that, while important, are not strictly practical. It has a single symbolic pillar and light flows around the thick circular wall creating a reflective interior space.

Location Ashiya
Design 1972–3
Construction 1973–4
Structure Reinforced concrete
Site area 186.9 m²
Building area 73.8 m²
Total floor area 144.6 m²

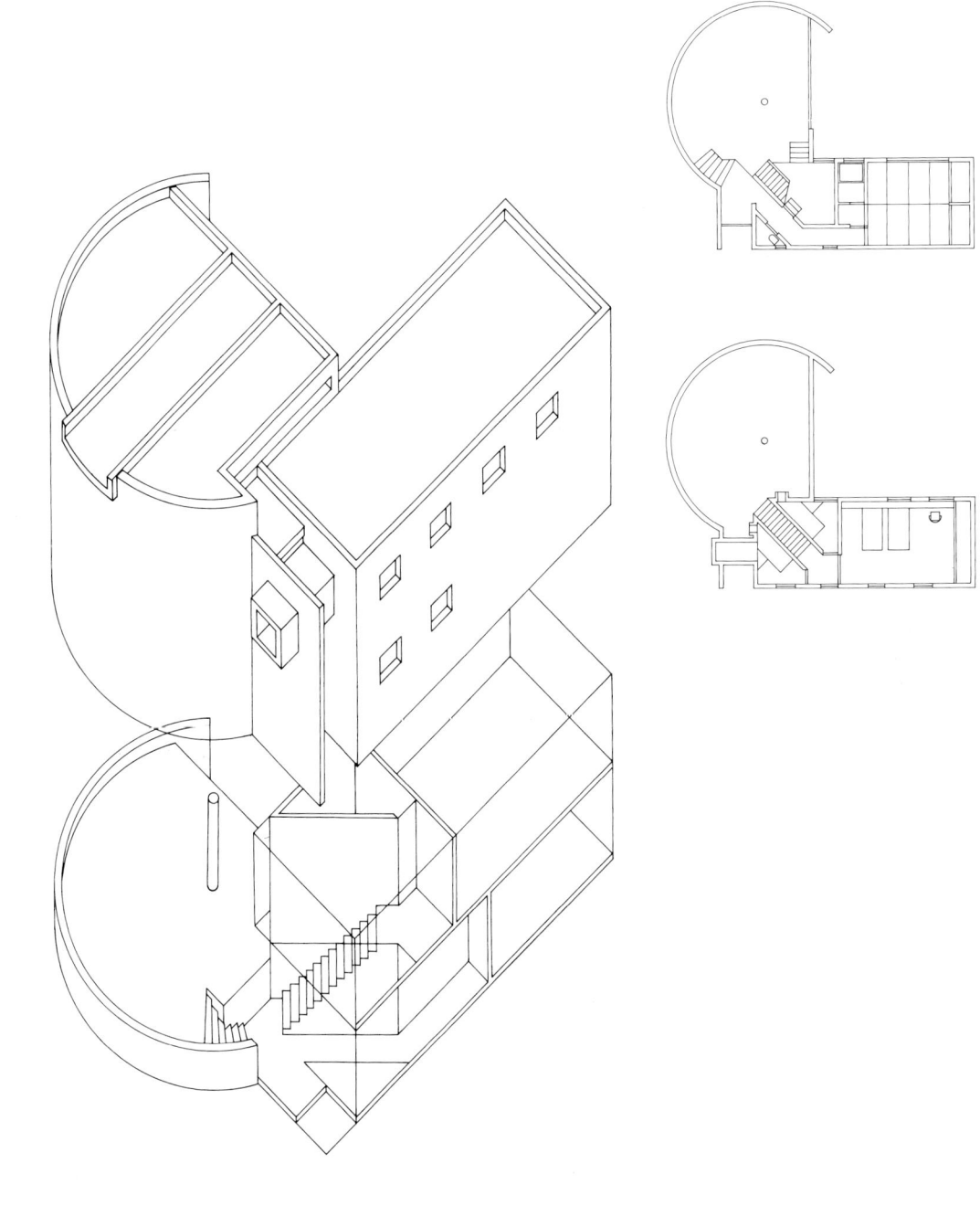

View showing the two compositional volumes, and interior views of the building.

43

Port Island Project

Conceptual sketches.

This project was a study in the landscaping of Port Island, a man-made island located off the harbour of Kobe. The aim was to create four 20-metre-high hills at the centre of the island and a stream which would flow between them. The project would therefore reclaim and recreate features of the natural landscape in an artificial environment.

Location Kobe
Design 1973

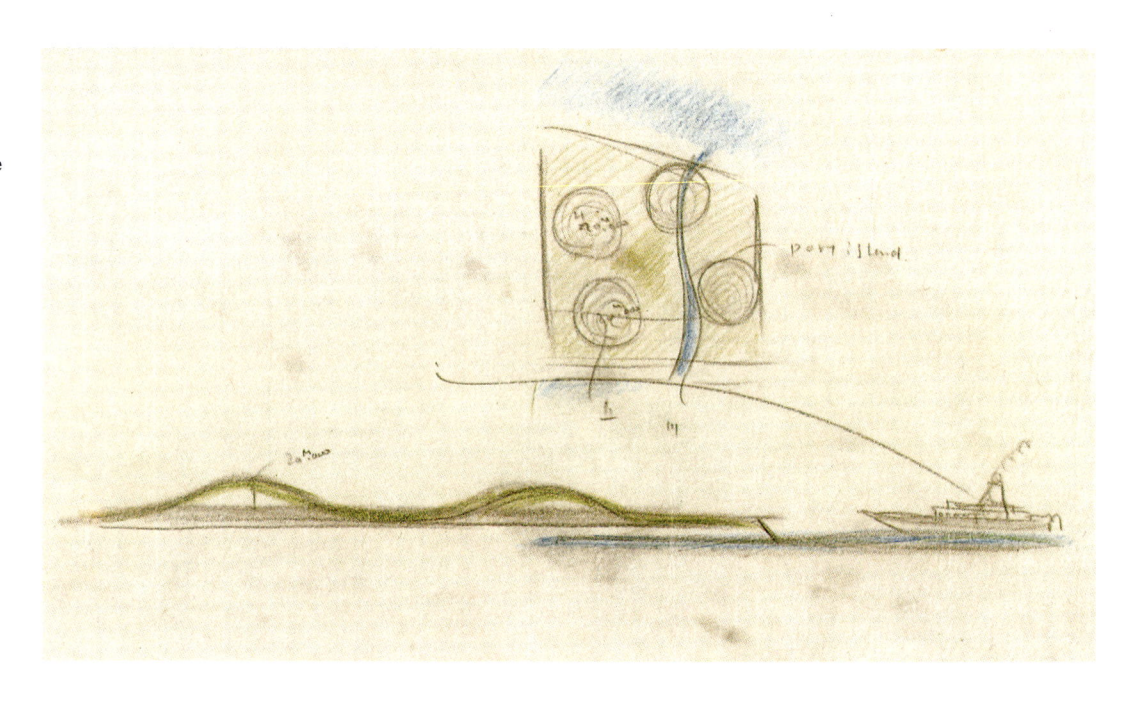

TADAO ANDO

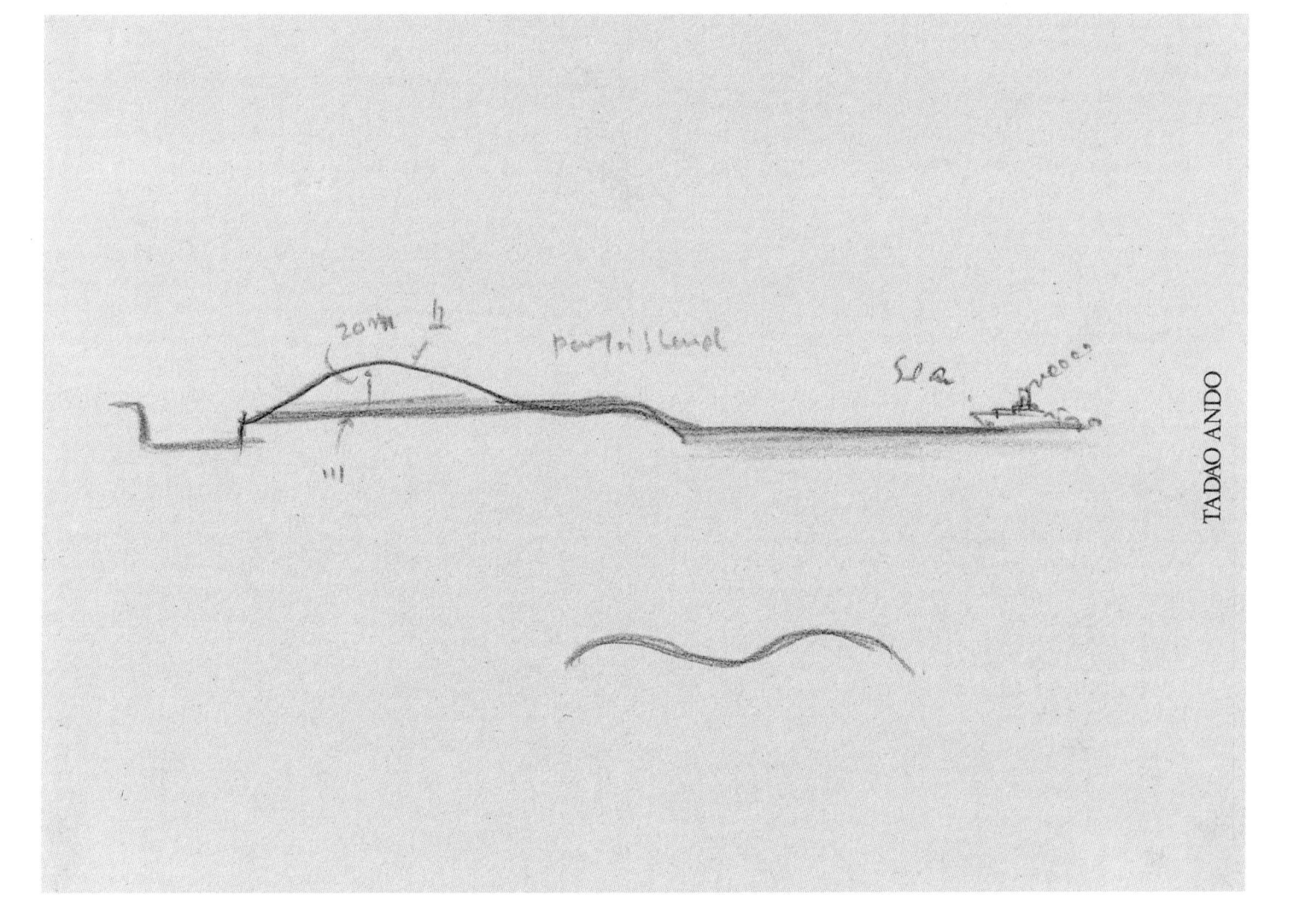

Soseikan–Yamaguchi House and Extension

Floor plans, longitudinal section and axonometric.

Located on what was once a verdant hill, now developed into housing lots, this house was designed for two brothers. There are two blocks, similar in shape and each possessing a highly enclosed space. By staggering them and connecting them with a deck, an independent exterior space was created between the blocks.

Inside, the intention was to close off the south side with a wall and to create a space that made full use of the various visual effects of a wall. The light that penetrates the vault-shaped toplight passes through a three-storey space and illuminates each floor. This joins the light from a clerestory on the ground-floor living room and is transformed from a strong, direct light into a softer light.

Six years after the completion of the house, the addition of a tea house was requested. In contrast to the existing building, which is a strongly assertive, concrete mass, the tea house has a simple exterior composed of smoothly-finished concrete walls. A traditional style was not employed, but the aim was to revive the true character of tea houses through the three-dimensional composition of spaces, details and distribution of light and darkness.

The walls surrounding the tea room form an approach and also serve to limit the light entering the interior. One enters through a large steel door and is confronted by a concrete wall, behind which is a window of frosted glass. The faint light introduced by the window illuminates the floor while a deep darkness gathers in the ceiling.

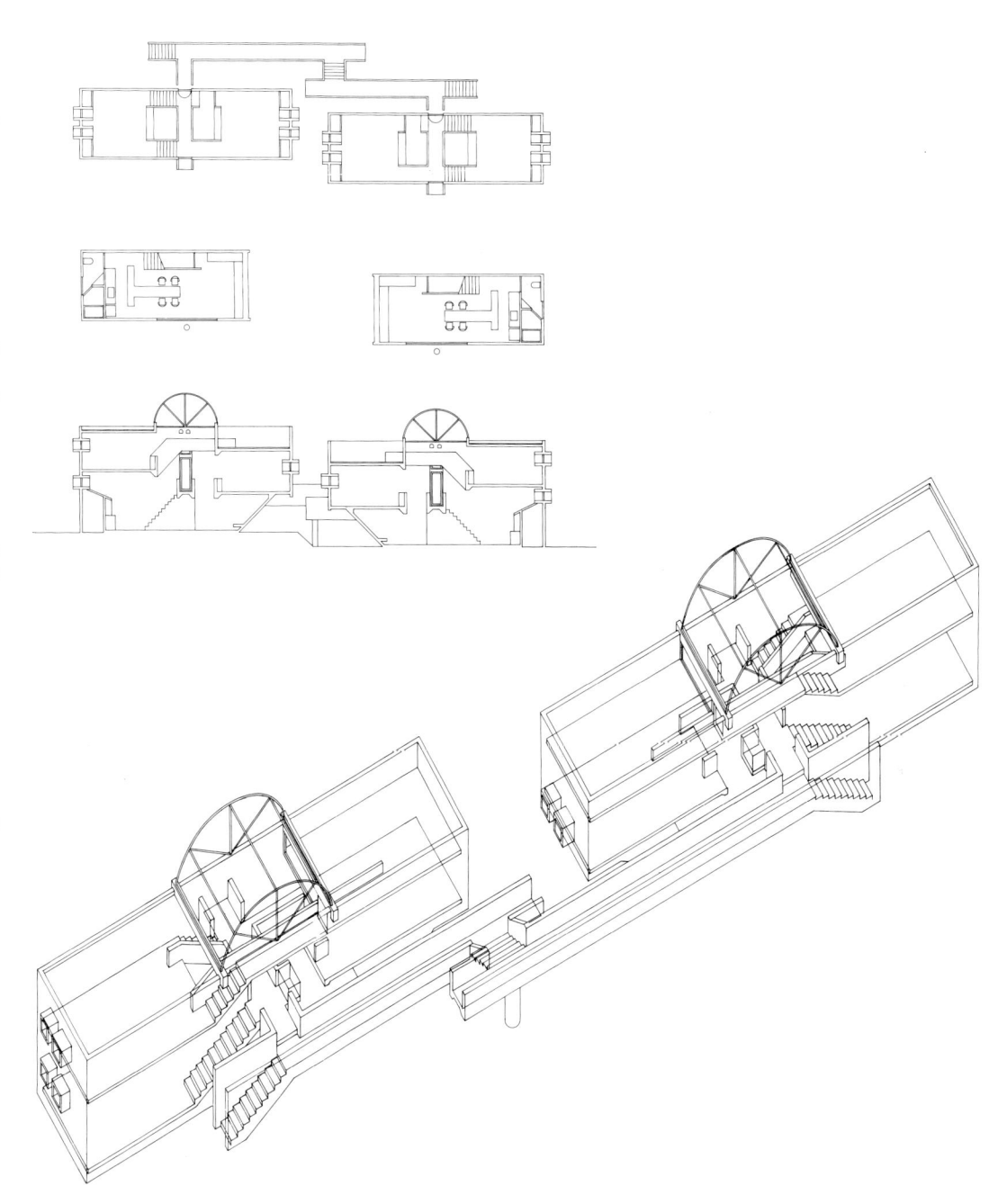

View and drawing of the principal elevation.

Conceptual sketches of the tea house.

Location Takarazuka
Design 1974–5
Construction 1975
Structure Reinforced concrete
Site area 523.6 m²
Building area 97.5 m²
Total floor area 161.9 m²

Extension
Design 1981–2
Construction 1982
Structure Reinforced concrete
Building area 15.5 m²
Total floor area 12.8 m²

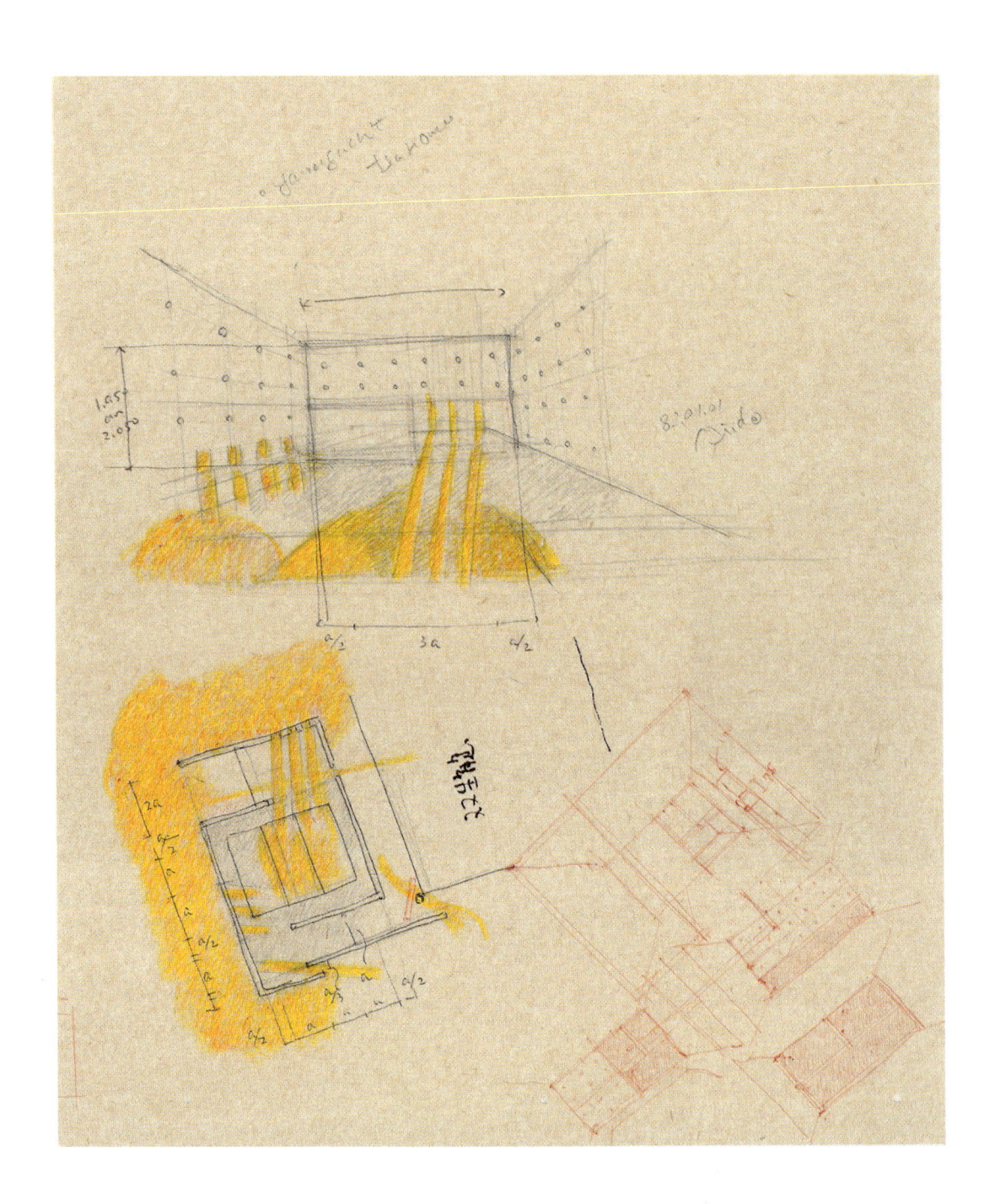

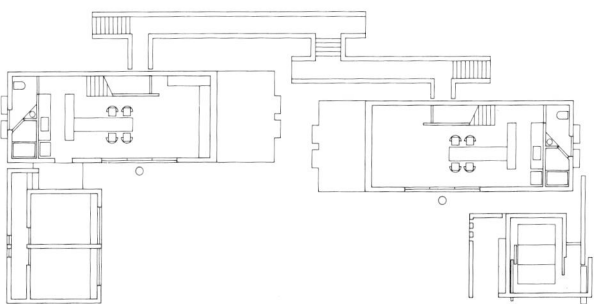

View and plan of the main building with the tea house extension.

49

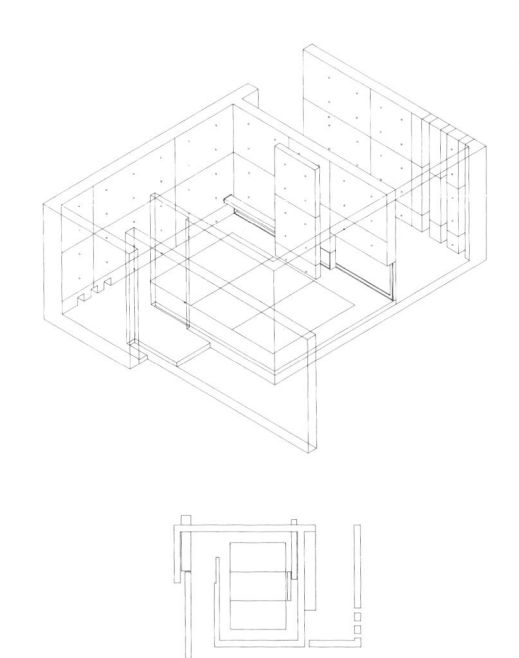

Axonometric and plan, and interior views of the tea house.

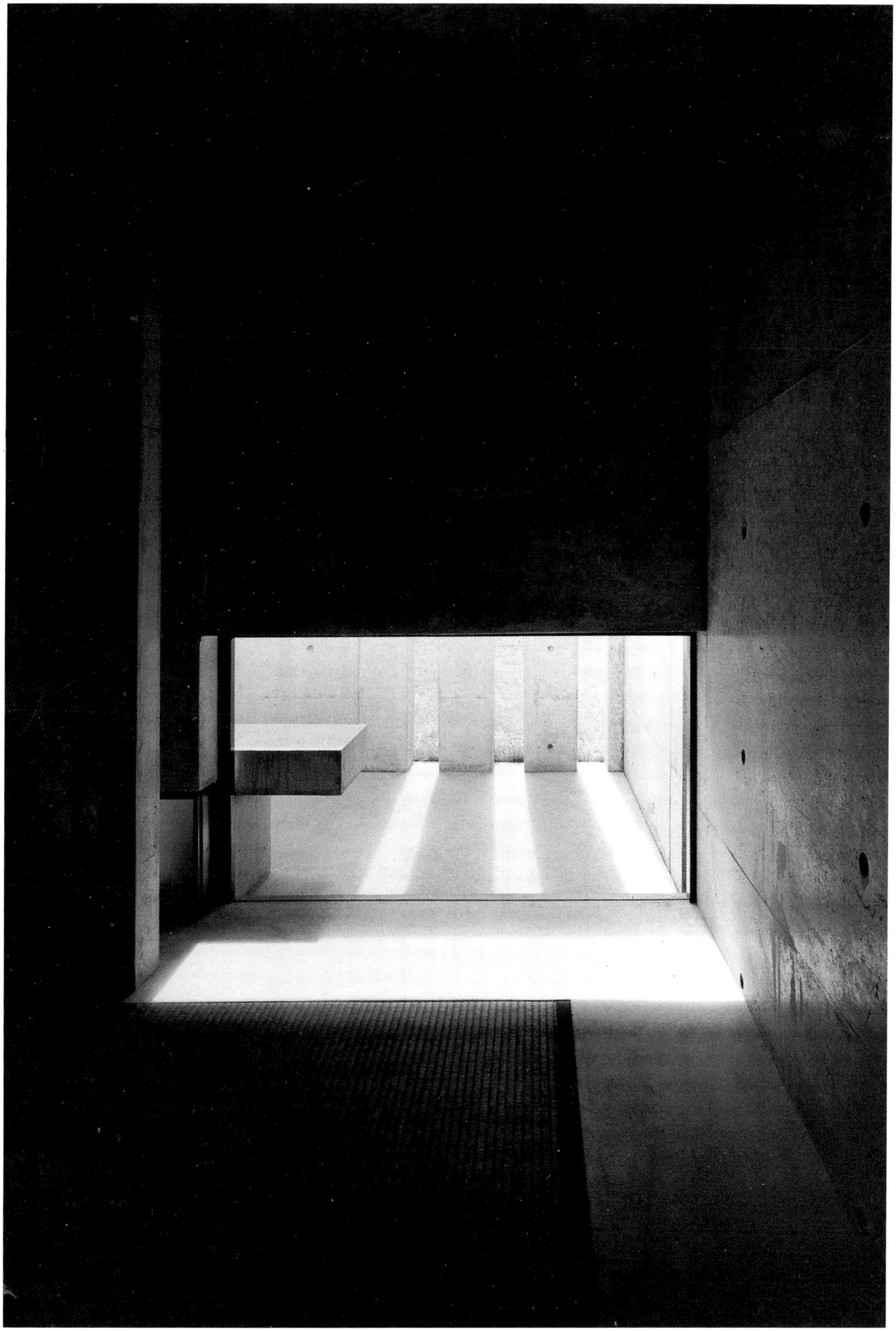

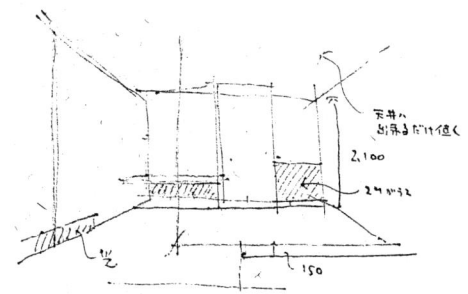

Interior views and conceptual sketches of the tea house.

53

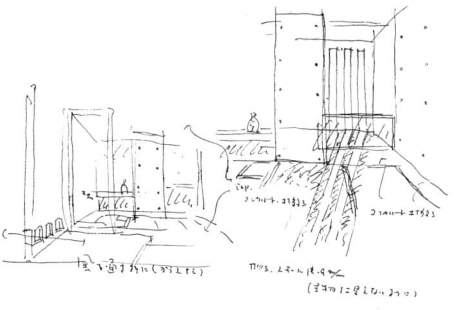

Twin Wall Project

Aerial view of the model and perspective.

Faced with harsh, overcrowded conditions, city dwellers tend to build thick enclosing walls to protect their own territories. This house makes use of such a wall to forcibly create a place to live in the city. This is not so much two walls as one thick wall in which a fissure has been introduced. Inside this fissure are the appurtenances necessary for everyday life.

The entire composition consists of two walls, penetrated by an offset cube. On the ground floor, a bedroom and the dining room face each other across a hall. Ascending the symmetrically-branching stairway to the first floor, there are two more rooms flanking a deck. The toplight running along the fissure throws light onto the deck below.

Design 1975
Structure Reinforced concrete
Site area 85.1 m^2
Building area 70.6 m^2
Total floor area 107.2 m^2

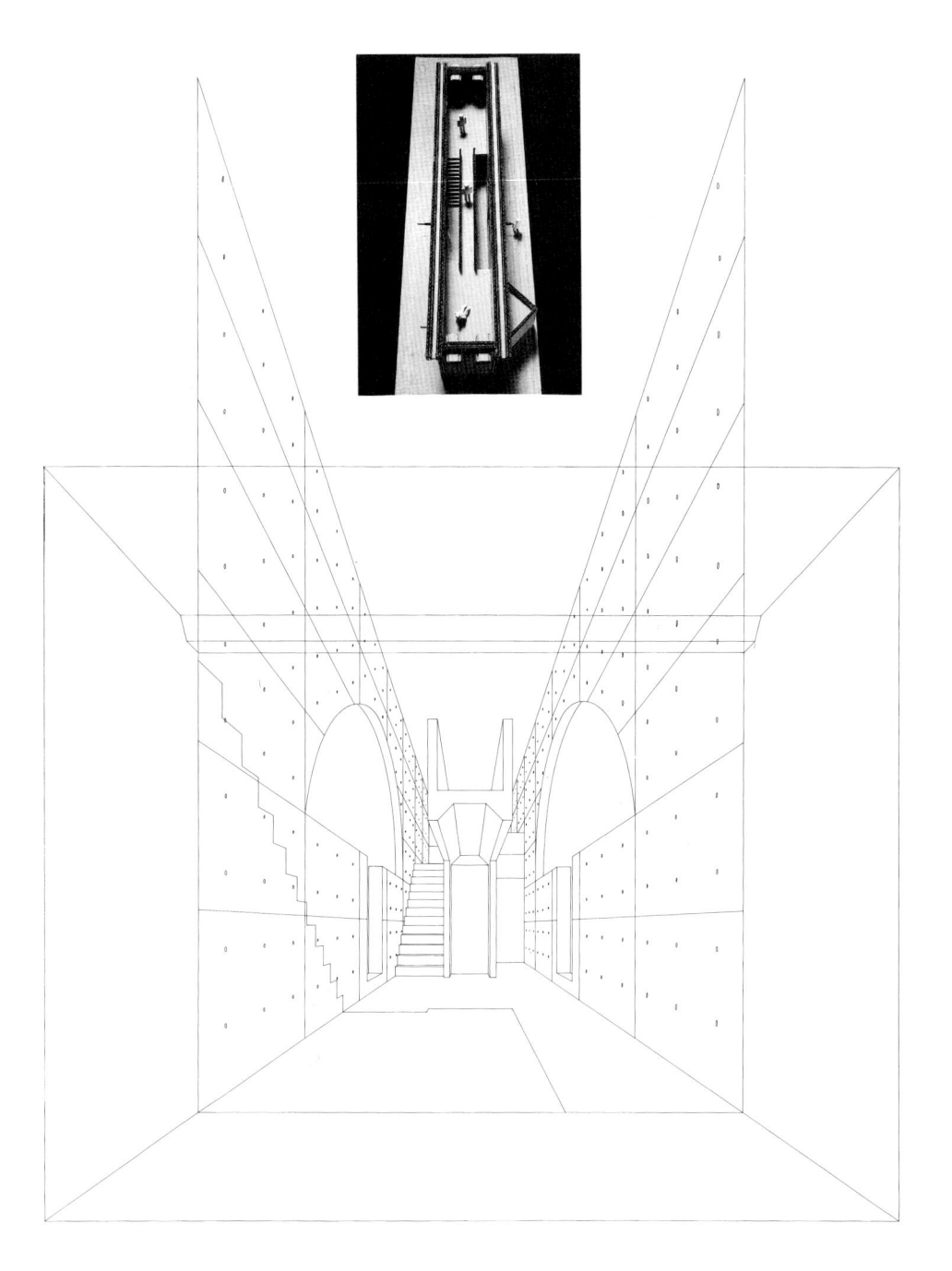

Main elevational view of the model and plans.

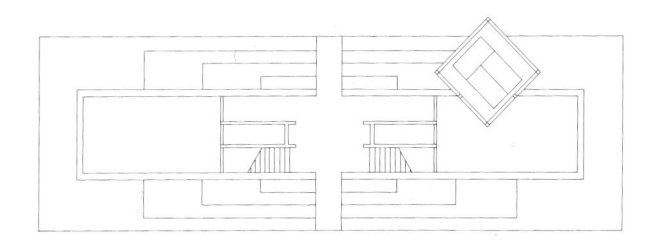

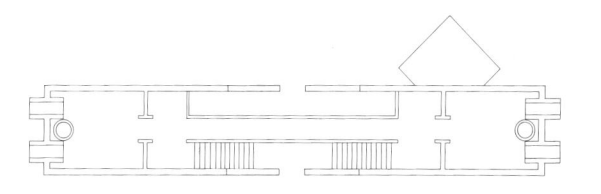

Azuma House

Conceptual sketch, view showing the roof, plans, section and axonometric.

In the central part of Osaka, the wooden row houses that survived the war can still be seen, and this row house in the Sumiyoshi district replaced the middle portion of three such houses. The intention was to insert a concrete box and create a microcosm within it; a simple composition, closed but dramatized by light.

The spatial organization is centripetal with a courtyard occupying the middle portion of the tripartite plan. This courtyard is the centre of everyday life and each room is accessed from the courtyard. On the ground floor, the courtyard is flanked by the living room on one side and the kitchen, the dining room and the bathroom on the other. On the upper level, the courtyard separates the master bedroom from the children's room. By means of this composition the courtyard assures privacy for all four rooms.

The house completely closes itself off from the street except for the entrance opening where daylight enters and illuminates the entrance floor. This light, which is reflected onto the street by the vertical and horizontal planes of the recess, acts as the mediator in relating the inward-looking house to the street.

Location Osaka
Design 1975
Construction 1975–6
Structure Reinforced concrete
Site area 57.3 m^2
Building area 33.7 m^2
Total floor area 64.7 m^2

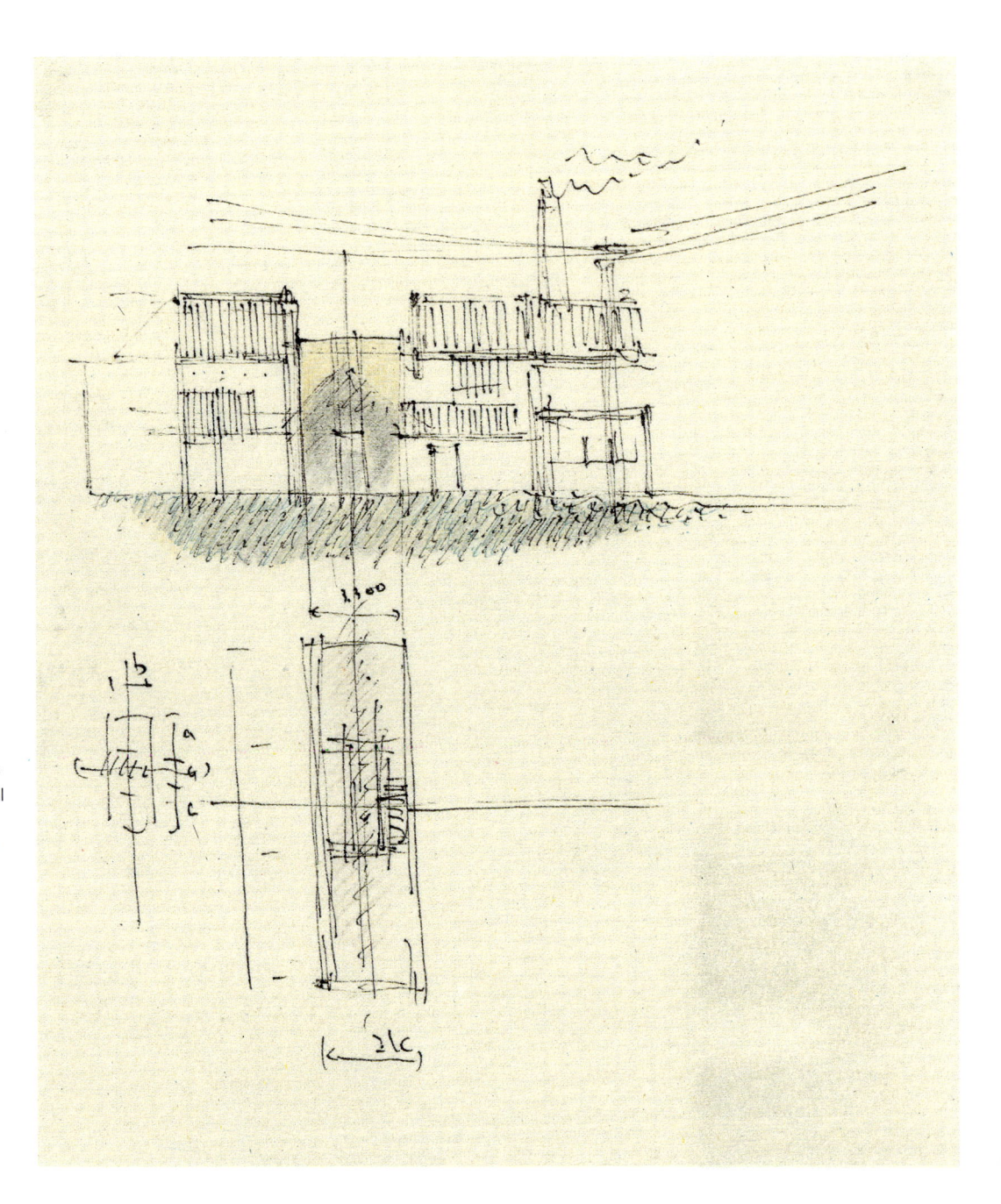

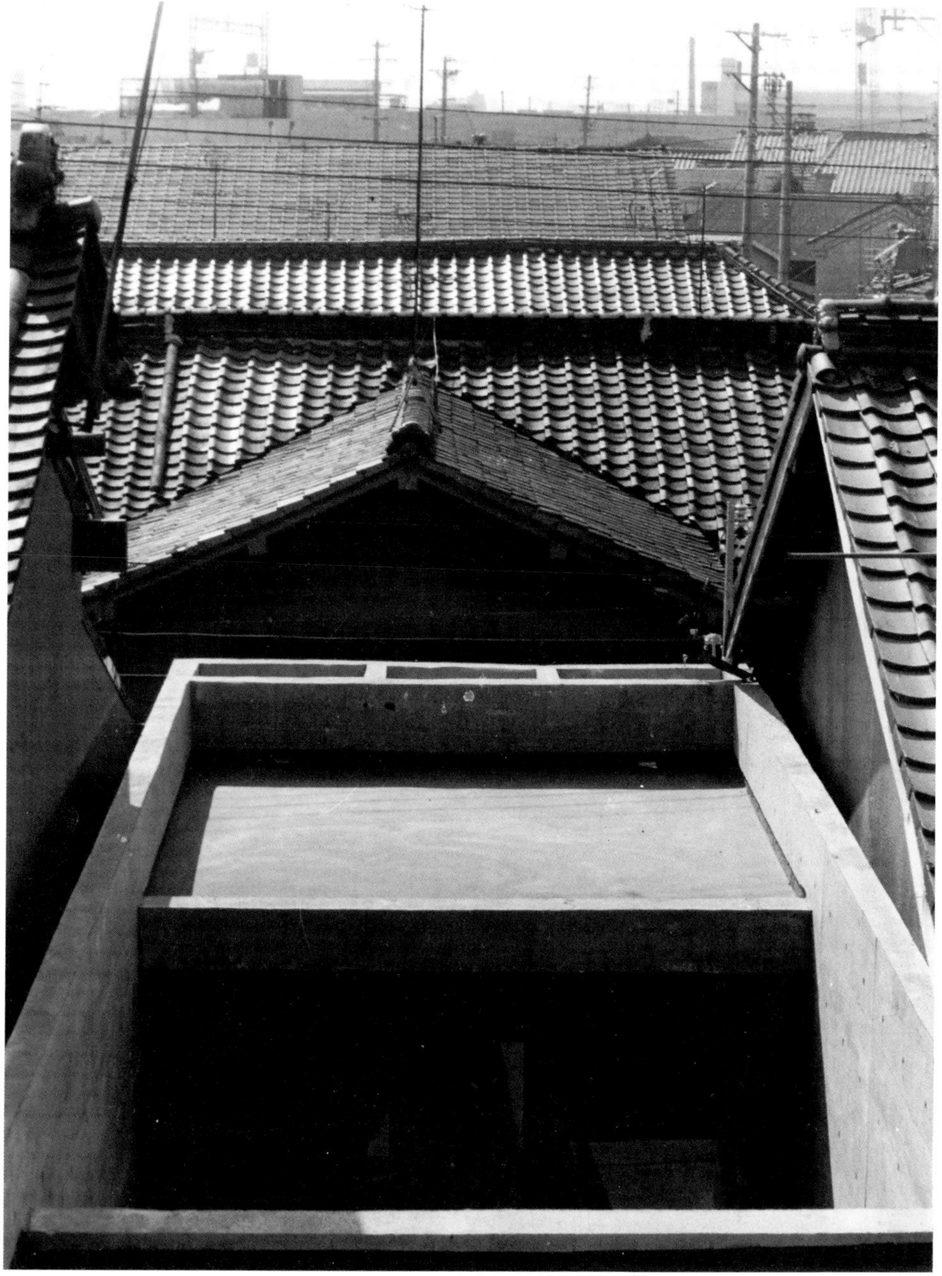

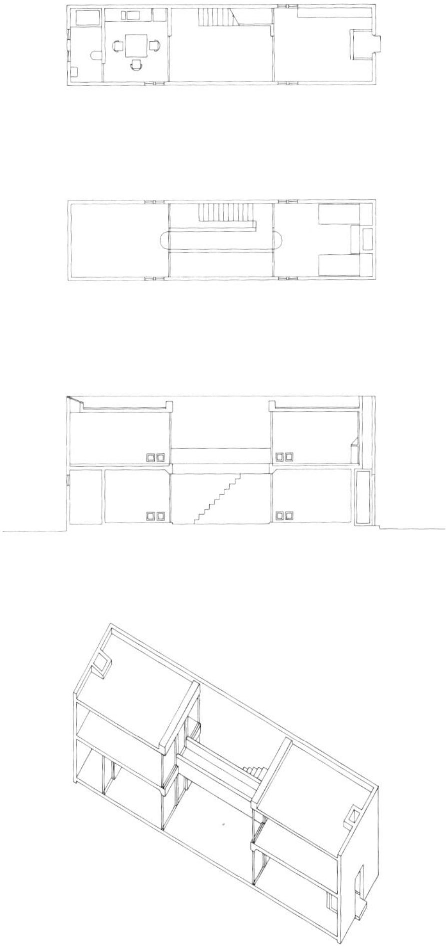

Oblique view and main view of entrance.

Floor plans and sectional perspective.

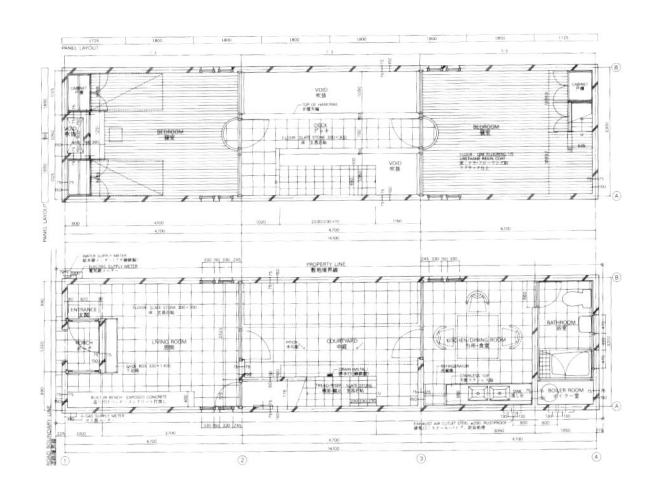

Entrance walkway and interior perspective.

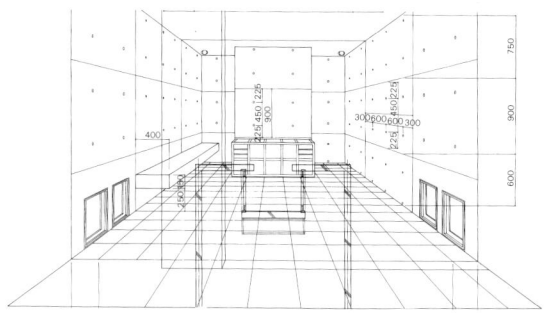

View and perspective of the courtyard.

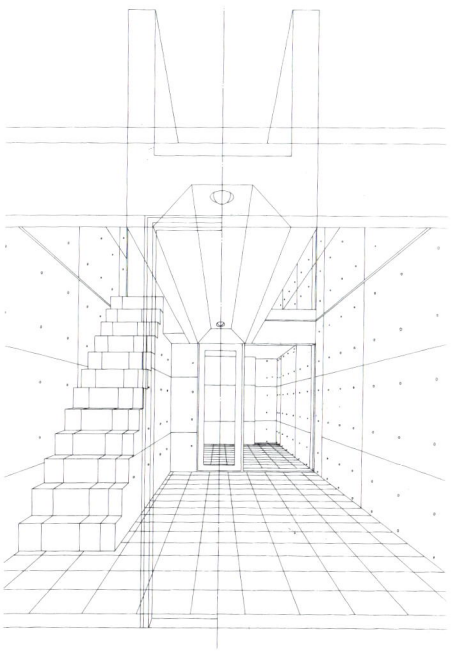

Hirabayashi House

Floor plans, longitudinal section and view of the building.

The building is composed of an interpenetration of thick walls and uniform frames. The walls stand by the edge of the site, attempting to perfect the geometric form; the frames, on the other hand, stand by themselves. These two modes of structure are extremely simple and direct.

The semi-cylindrical double-height hall is animated by the minimal amount of light entering through the slit openings at the intersection of the walls and the frames. The filtered light from the ceiling clerestory as it falls on the furniture also creates a spatial drama.

The independent wall on the south side provides for the spatial integrity of the frames which enclose the guest room and the children's bedroom. The straight wall running along the site generates a narrow space between it and the frames in which the service functions, such as the corridor and the staircases, are housed.

Location Osaka
Design 1975
Construction 1975–6
Structure Reinforced concrete
Site area 394.4 m^2
Building area 143.3 m^2
Total floor area 211,7 m^2

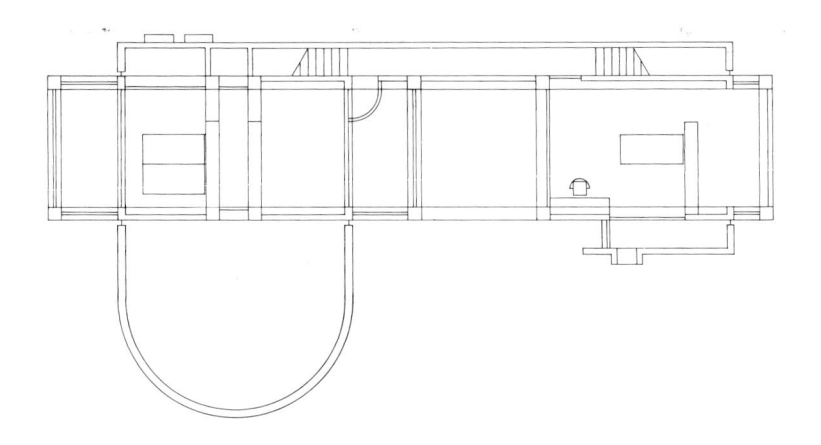

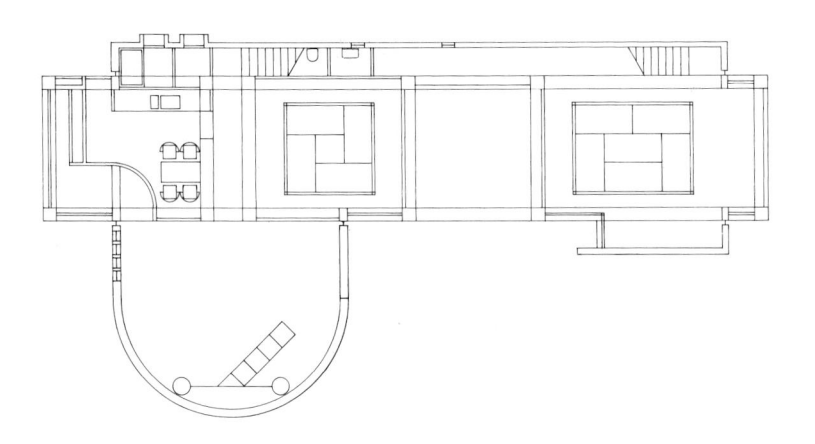

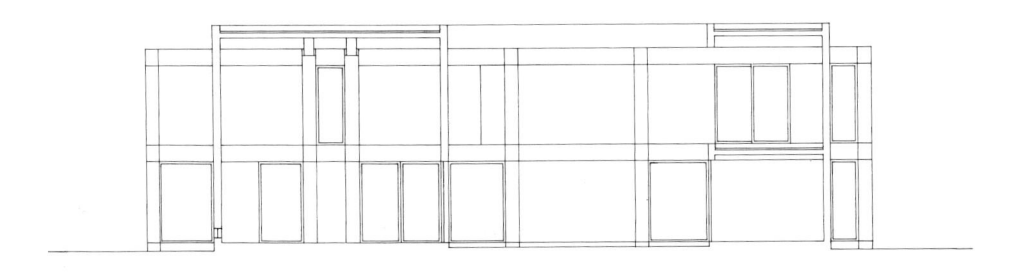

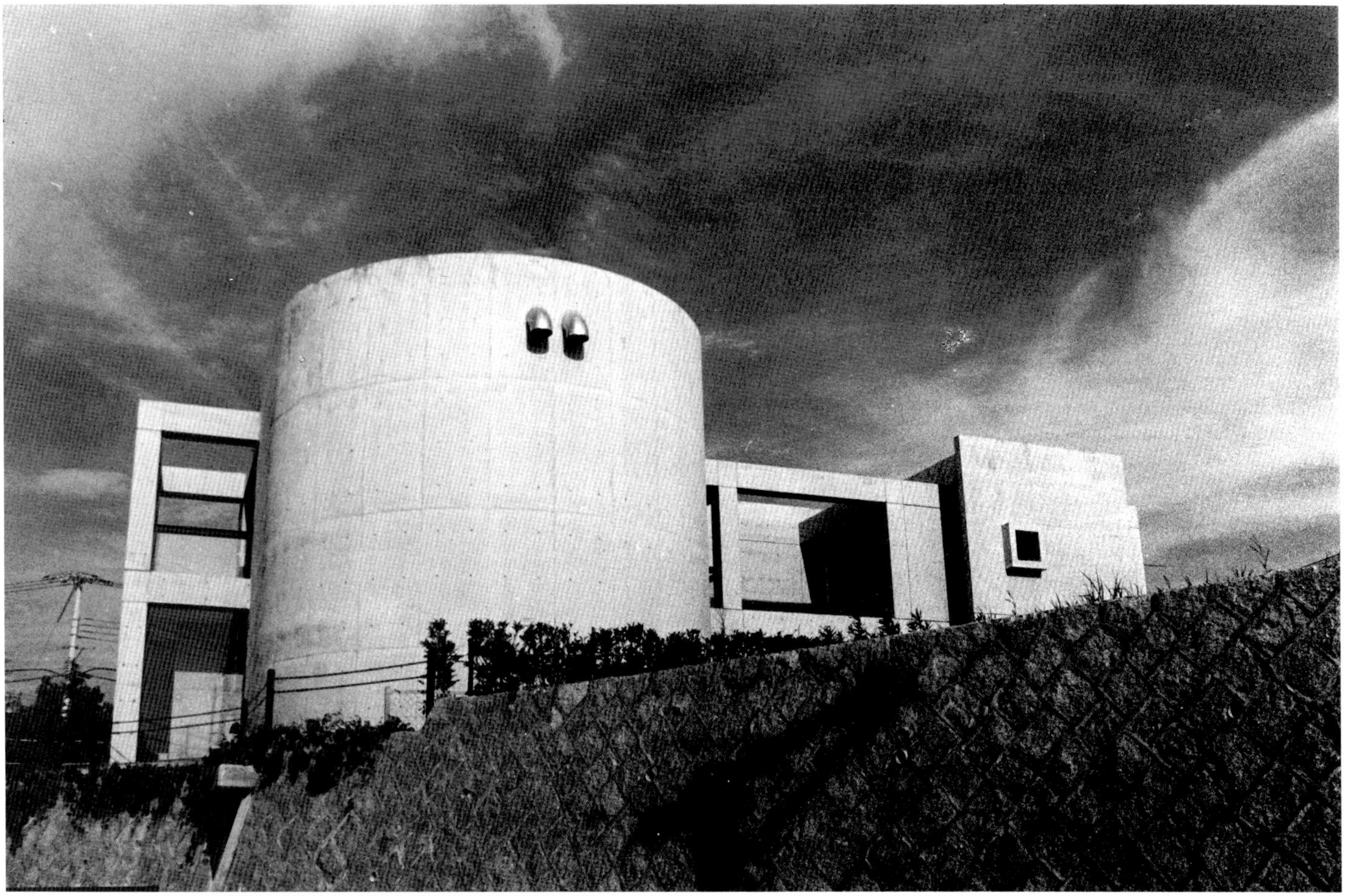

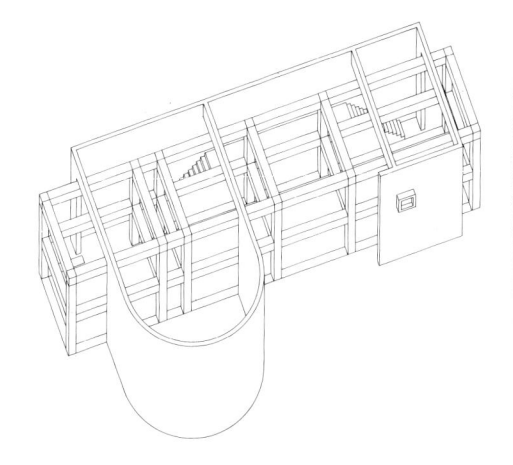

Axonometric showing the structural frames and views of the semi-cylindrical double-height hall.

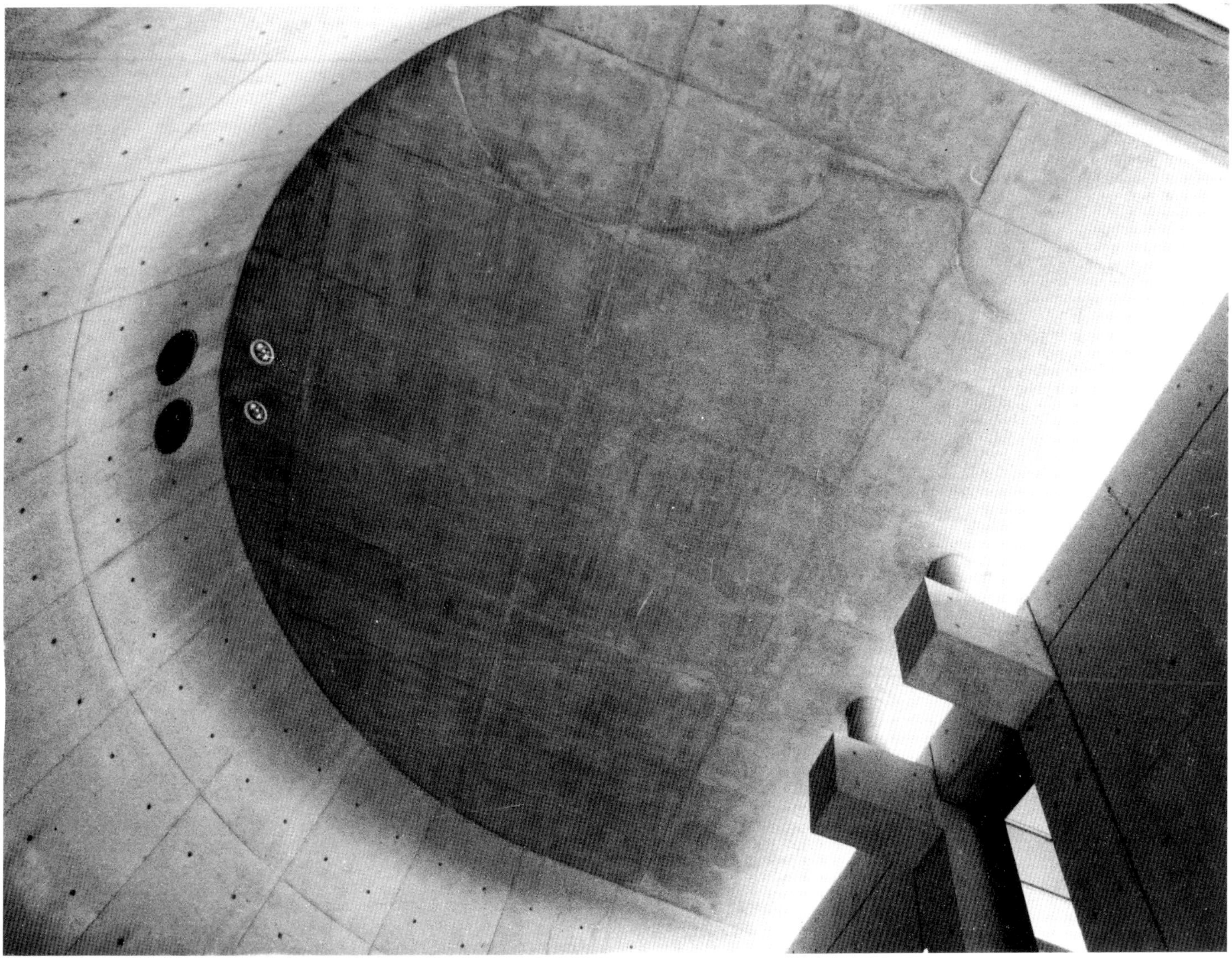

Bansho House and Extension

Floor plans and longitudinal section.

In this project light is treated as a symbolic representation of the living space. The building consists of a rectangular prism colliding into a cube made of exposed concrete. The cube contains the public space, such as the living room and a roof garden. The rectangular prism contains the dining room, the kitchen and utility room, and the bathroom on the ground floor; the bedroom and a closet room are on the first floor.

The clerestory at the juncture of the two forms is the only one that is south-facing. Light entering from the other openings filters into the undifferentiated space, imbuing it with a quality and accentuating the spatial functions.

Four years after the completion of the original building, a studio was added onto the north of the living room. Being set parallel to the rectangular prism, it faces south carrying deep eaves. The smoothly-finished concrete floor extends from the inside of the studio to the outdoor terrace. The only light admitted inside by the deep eaves is that which has been reflected off the terrace. In the studio, the two slits opened to the north deny the spatial directionality produced by the abundant light pouring in from the south.

Location Aichi
Design 1975–6
Construction 1976
Structure Reinforced concrete
Site area 168.3 m²
Building area 63.5 m²
Total floor area 85.7 m²

Extension
Design 1980
Construction 1980–81
Structure Reinforced concrete
Building area 35.4 m²
Total floor area 28.2 m²

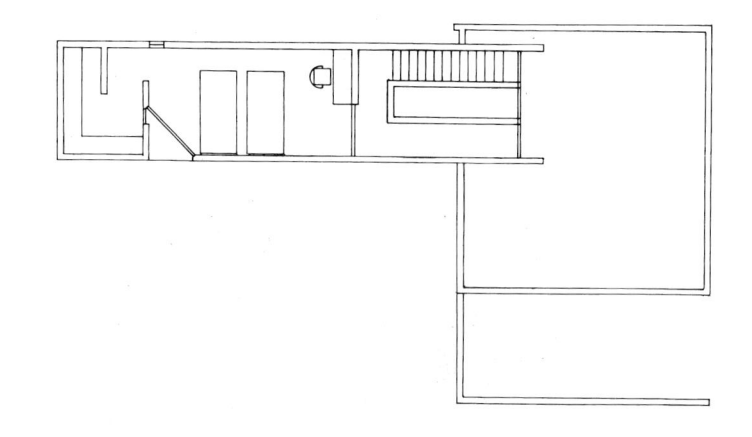

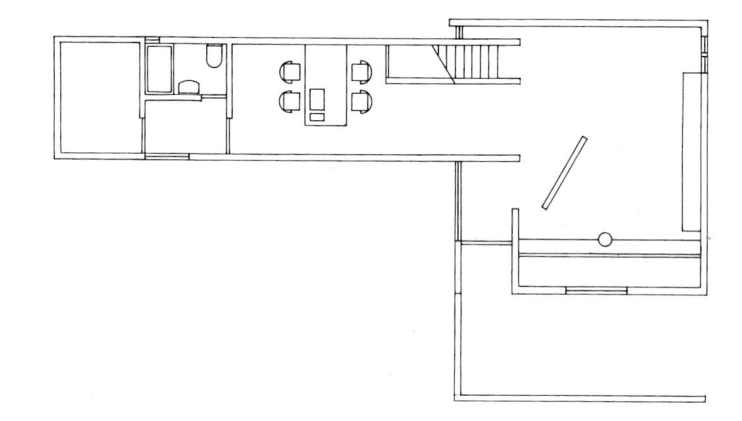

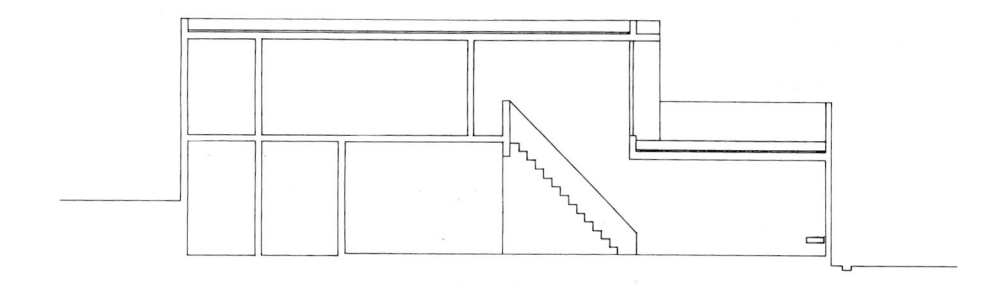

Conceptual sketch.

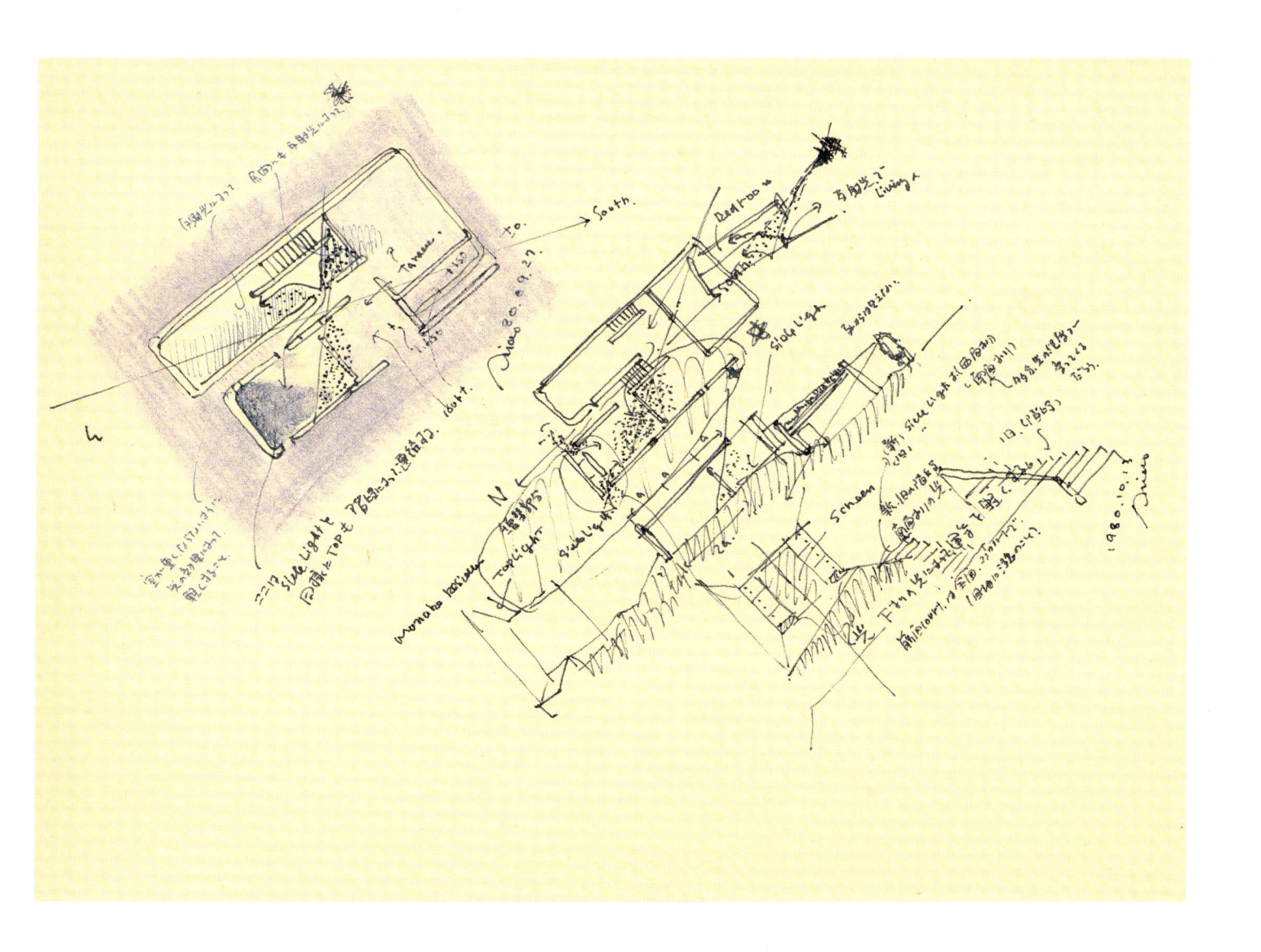

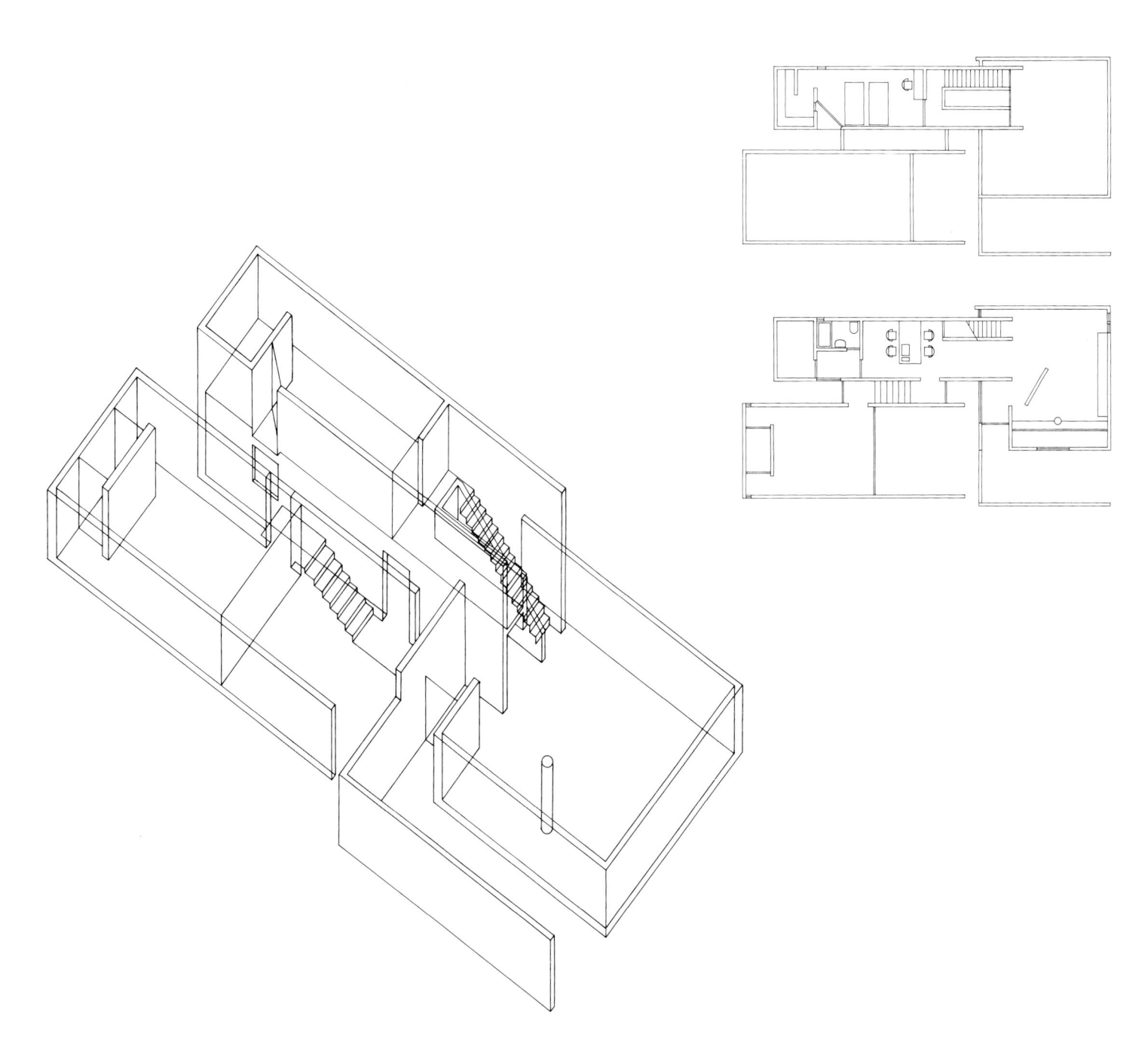

Axonometric and plans of the house and the extension.

68

Interior and exterior views and axonometric.

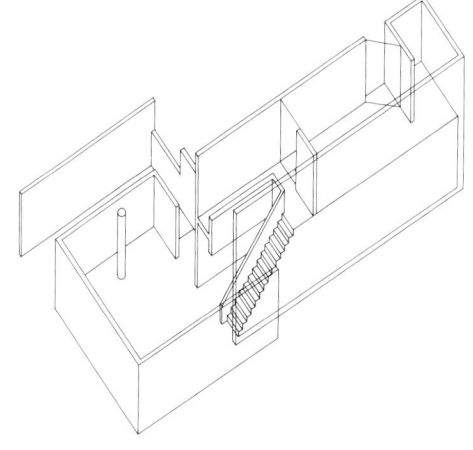

Views showing the roof of the extension.

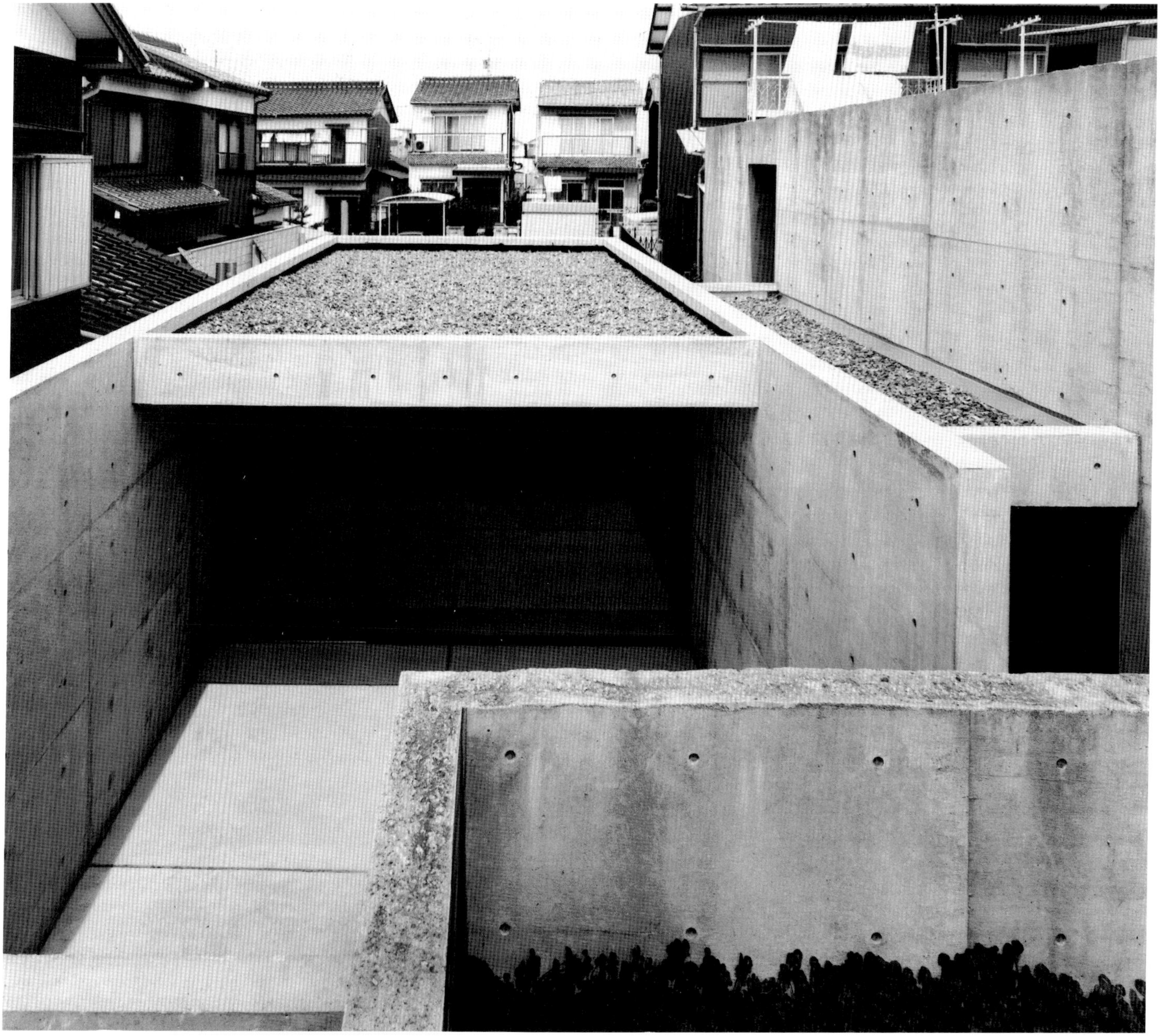

Tezukayama Tower Plaza

Floor plans.

This mixed-use building consists of four towers of identical shape and volume, with decks bridging the towers. The basement and ground floor are for commercial use, and the first and second floors are maisonette units. The towers are independent of each other ensuring privacy, and each unit is also made independent by the provision of a multi-storey space within. The toplight on each tower hints at the presence of this space, which serves as a buffer zone. However, at the ground and basement levels a plaza and decks bring the four towers together.

Location Osaka
Design 1975–6
Construction 1976
Structure Reinforced concrete
Site area 376.2 m²
Building area 161.4 m²
Total floor area 754.4 m²

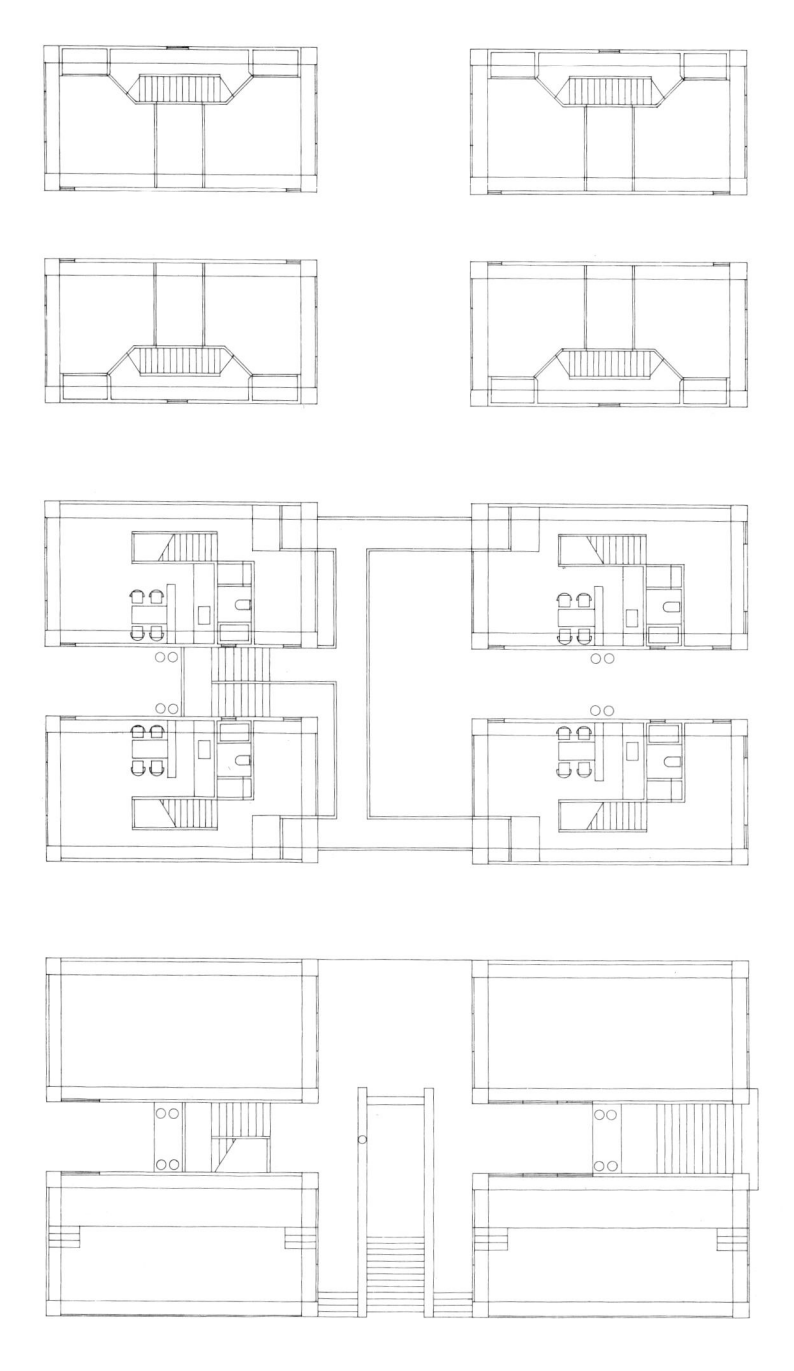

Views from the street, aerial view and section.

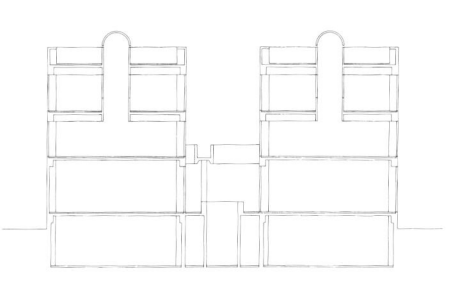

73

Rose Garden

Floor plans, section and view showing entrance.

Kitanocho, Kobe, located between the Rokkosan mountains in the north and the Seto Inland Sea to the south, is blessed with greenery and a view of open water. Since the opening of the Kobe port to foreign trade in the nineteenth century, foreigners have lived and built western-style residences in this part of the city.

The wall on the street side of this commercial complex is split in three places and the resulting pieces are staggered irregularly to open up views to the sea. A steel-frame roof is placed over the spaces between the two walls, leaving a plaza open in the middle. The sloping topography is an element in the surrounding architectural environment and, in many instances, it determines the building volume. Taking the topography into consideration was a way of reflecting the characteristics of the region. The two blocks of the building are placed in what amounts to a split-level arrangement because of the slope of the land. The resulting level differences between the decks of the two blocks eliminates the sense of height differential in the plaza, which acquires a human scale.

Location Kobe
Design 1975–6
Construction 1976–7
Structure Reinforced concrete
Site area 410.2 m²
Building area 270.9 m²
Total floor area 933.1 m²

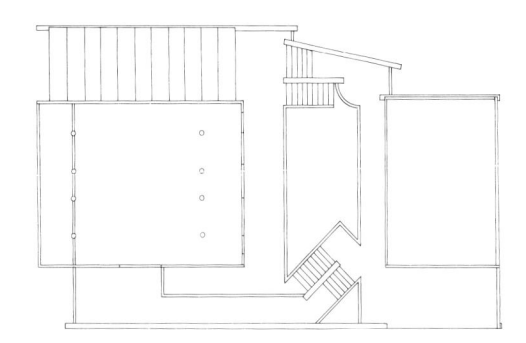

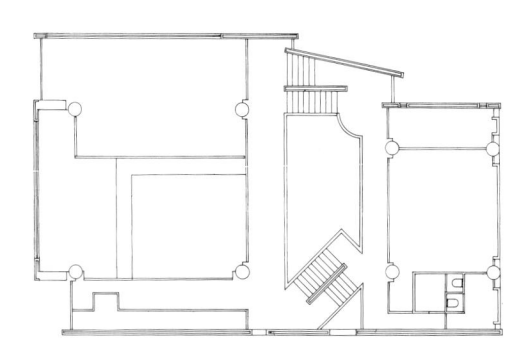

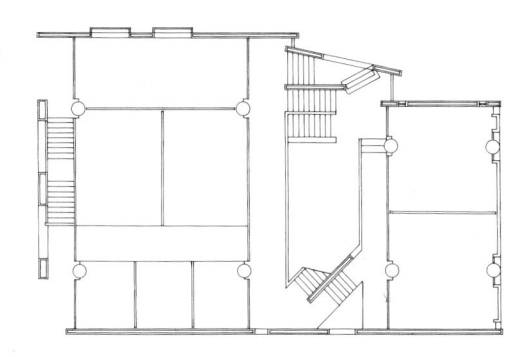

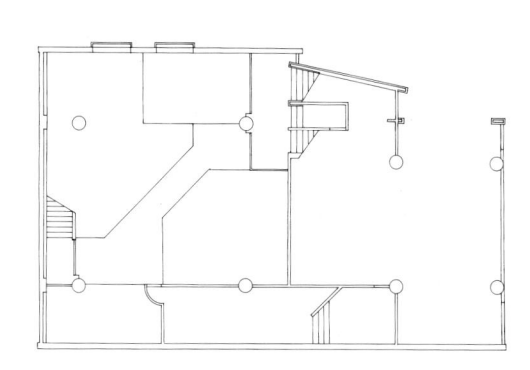

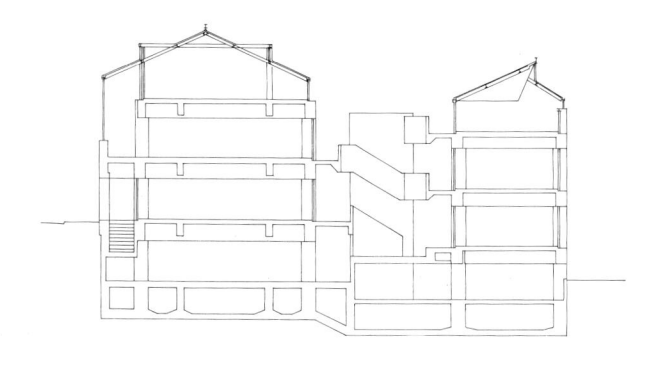

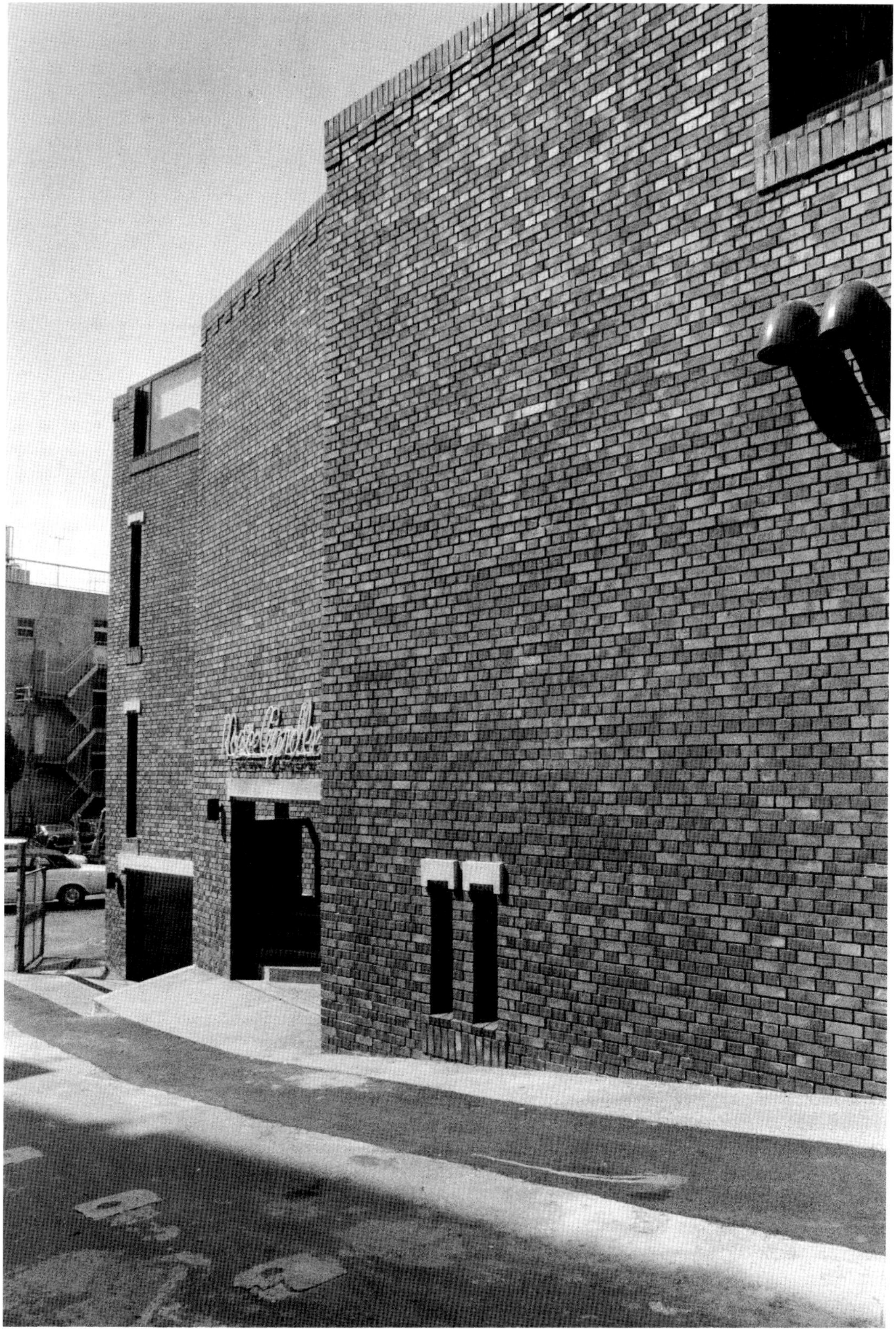

Views showing the main facade and the interior courtyard.

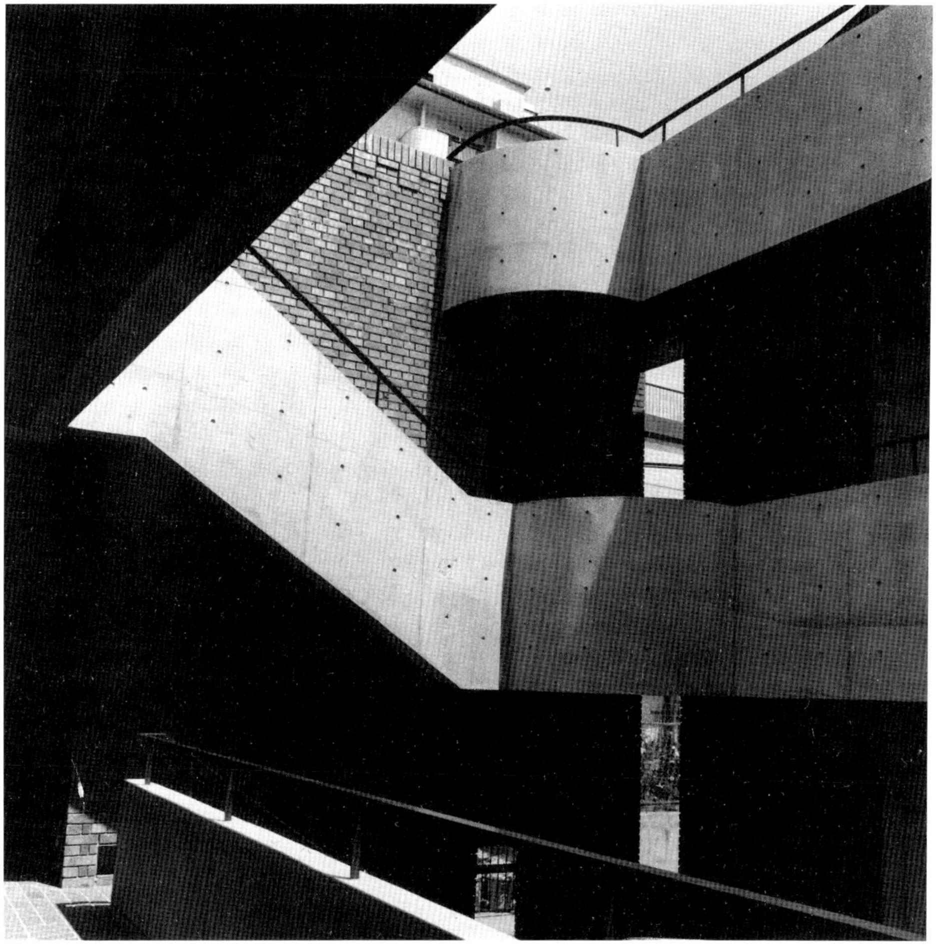

Manabe House

Plans and longitudinal section.

Located on a moderate slope, in the Tezukayama district of Osaka, this structure is composed of a reinforced concrete frame creating square bays, a protective wall bounding the property, and a freestanding wall that cuts through the body of the frame. The protective wall absorbs the irregular outline of the site while the concrete frame accommodates the uneven slope. The freestanding wall, interrupting the frame at a 45-degree angle, not only disrupts the homogeneity of the space, but also articulates the different functional elements by diffracting light.

The north block is recessed behind a sloping courtyard and contains the principal elements of this residence – entrance, living and dining rooms and bathroom on the ground floor, and guest room and children's room upstairs. The south block houses the master bedroom.

Location Osaka
Design 1976–7
Construction 1977
Structure Reinforced concrete
Site area 273.3 m^2
Building area 108.8 m^2
Total floor area 147.3 m^2

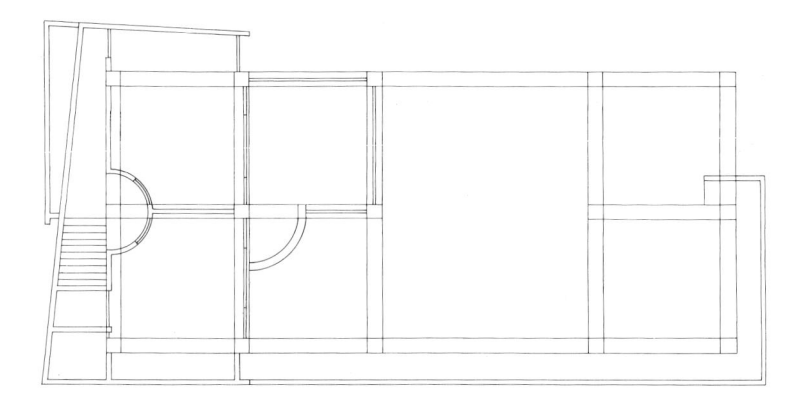

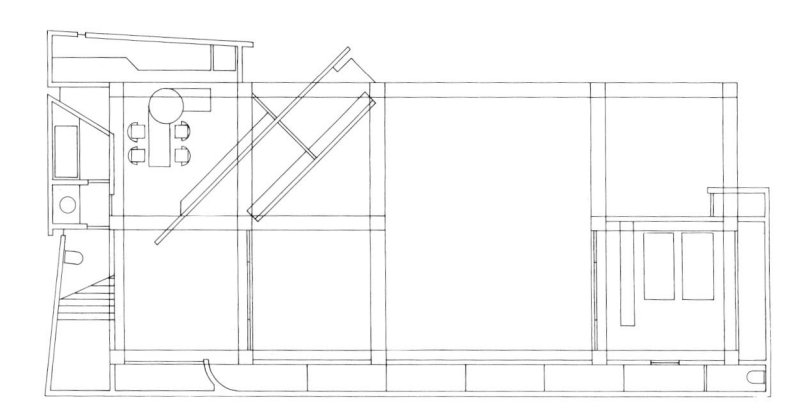

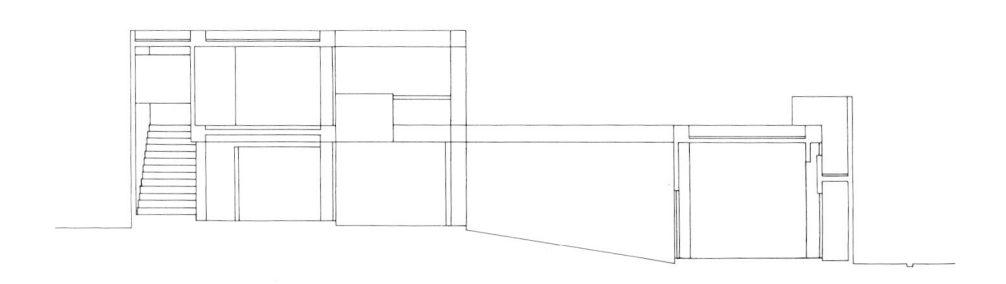

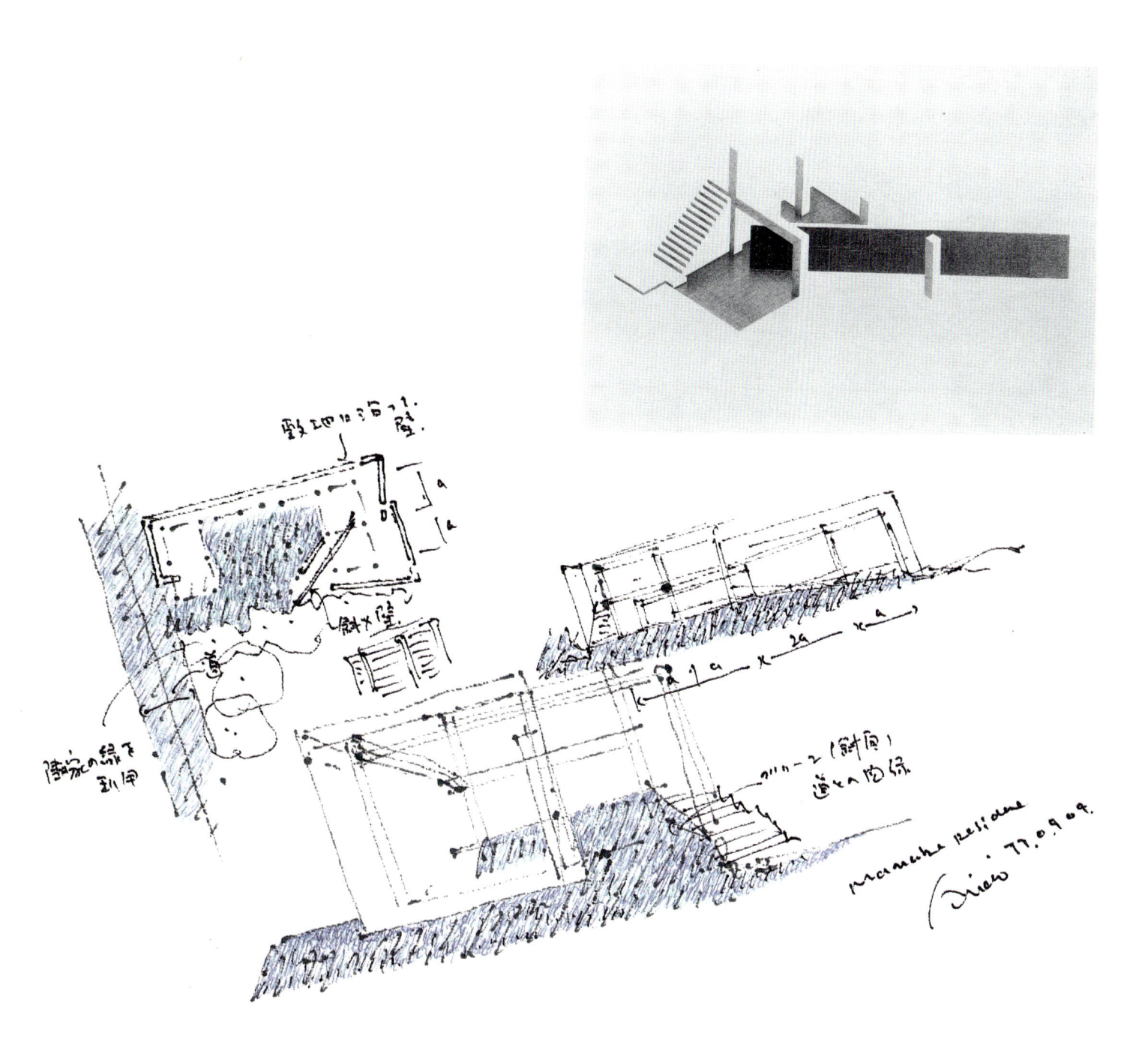

Drawing showing intersection of the wall with the structural elements, and conceptual sketch.

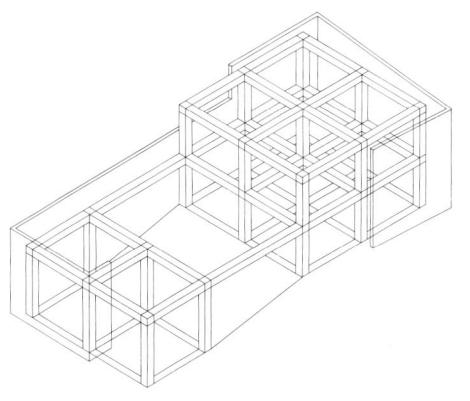

View of the roof, axonometric showing the structural frame, and views of the building.

81

Koto Alley Project

Axonometrics and views of the model.

This project, which is for a commercial and residential centre consisting of shops, ateliers and apartments, is located on the outskirts of the city, close to the railway station. A street, which has a small plaza located at its centre, cuts through the complex, and thus draws the commercial centre out onto an open public space.

Location Nishinomiya, Hyogo
Design 1976

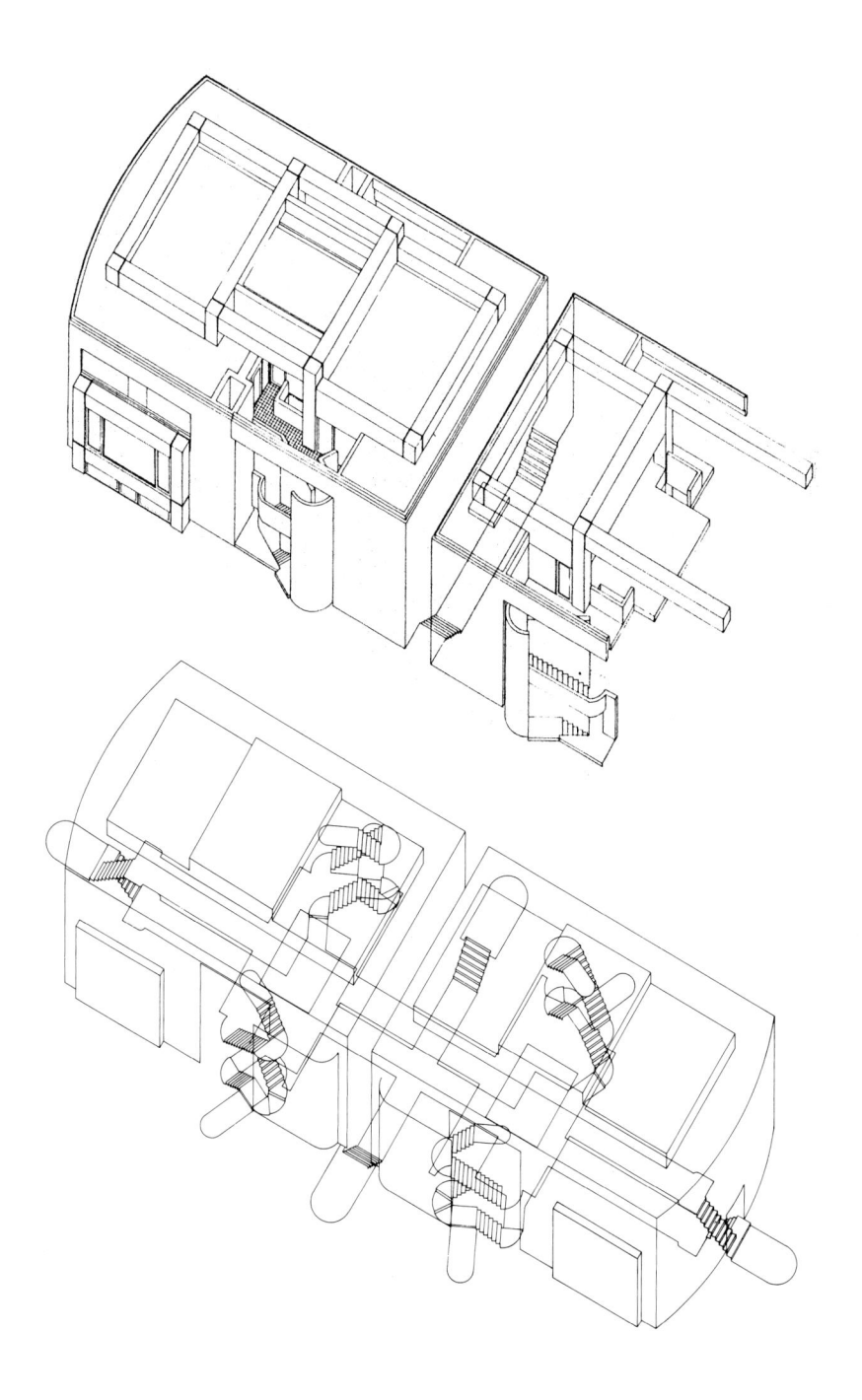

83

Okamoto Housing Project

Axonometric showing the structural grid and unit composition.

This housing scheme is based on a three-dimensional grid in the form of an exposed concrete frame with six-metre spans. A succession of seventeen cubic units are arranged among the greenery of a south-sloping site, conforming to the topography and, in the process, becoming staggered and creating flowing spaces.

Each unit is composed of two or three grids and is designed to provide both privacy and views of the ocean. The basic type is a maisonette, but there are many variations. The shifting of the grids as a result of the topography generates two-storey spaces inside and roof gardens outside, as well as producing a stepped plaza. A large frame unifies the separate buildings of the project.

Although this project was not executed because of functional and financial problems, the ideas were subsequently realized in the Rokko Housing schemes.

Location Kobe
Design 1976
Structure Reinforced concrete
Site area 1,774.9 m²
Building area 556.4 m²
Total floor area 1,404.7 m²

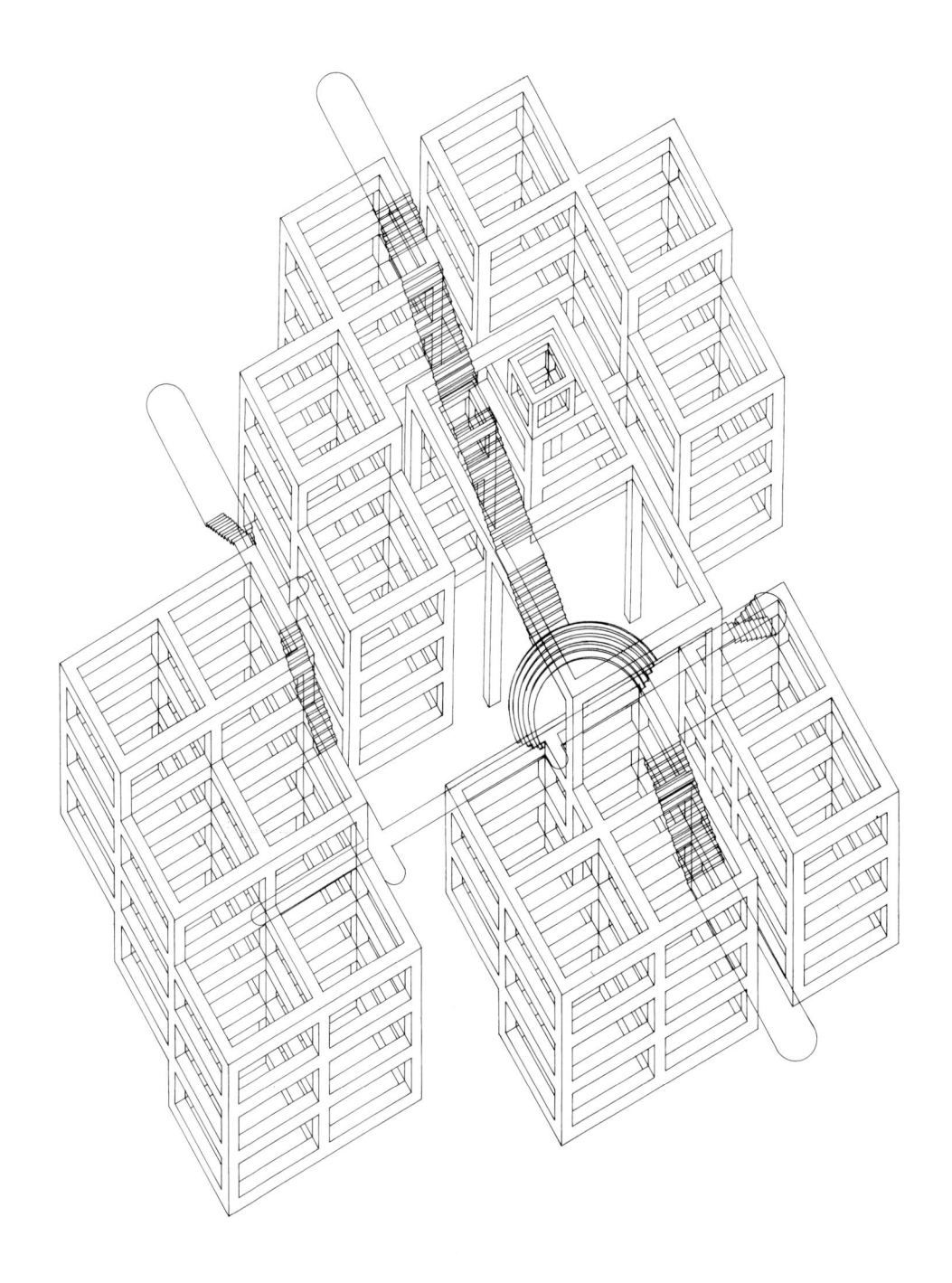

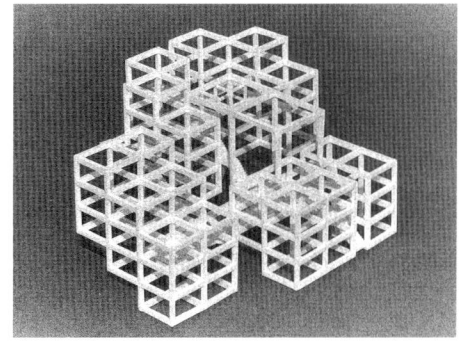

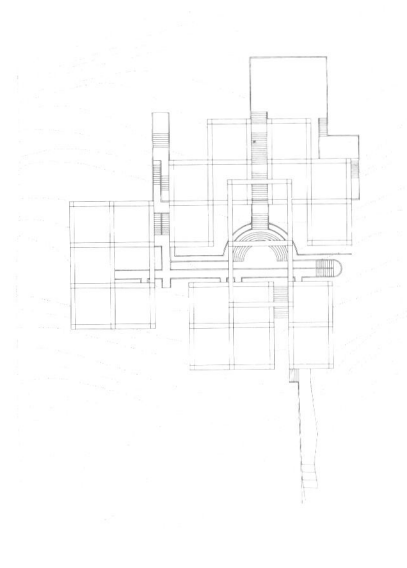

Aerial view of the study model, drawing of the structural scheme and plan.

Matsumoto House Project

Conceptual sketches.

The geometric frames and walls of this building are inserted into the wooded hillside of a ravine in a national park. The walls stand by themselves and define a territory while the frames regulate the space containing separate functions. The stepped courtyard set in the middle of the continuous frames opens out towards the rest of the site.

This courtyard divides the building into two distinct blocks – the house and an atelier – reiterated by the two independent vaults. The light admitted by the vaults clarifies the relationship between the freestanding walls and the frames. In this way, the continuous frames become a colonnade and cast shadows against the walls.

Location Ashiya
Design 1976–7
Construction 1977
Structure Reinforced concrete
Site area 1,082.1 m^2
Building area 128.4 m^2
Total floor area 237.7 m^2

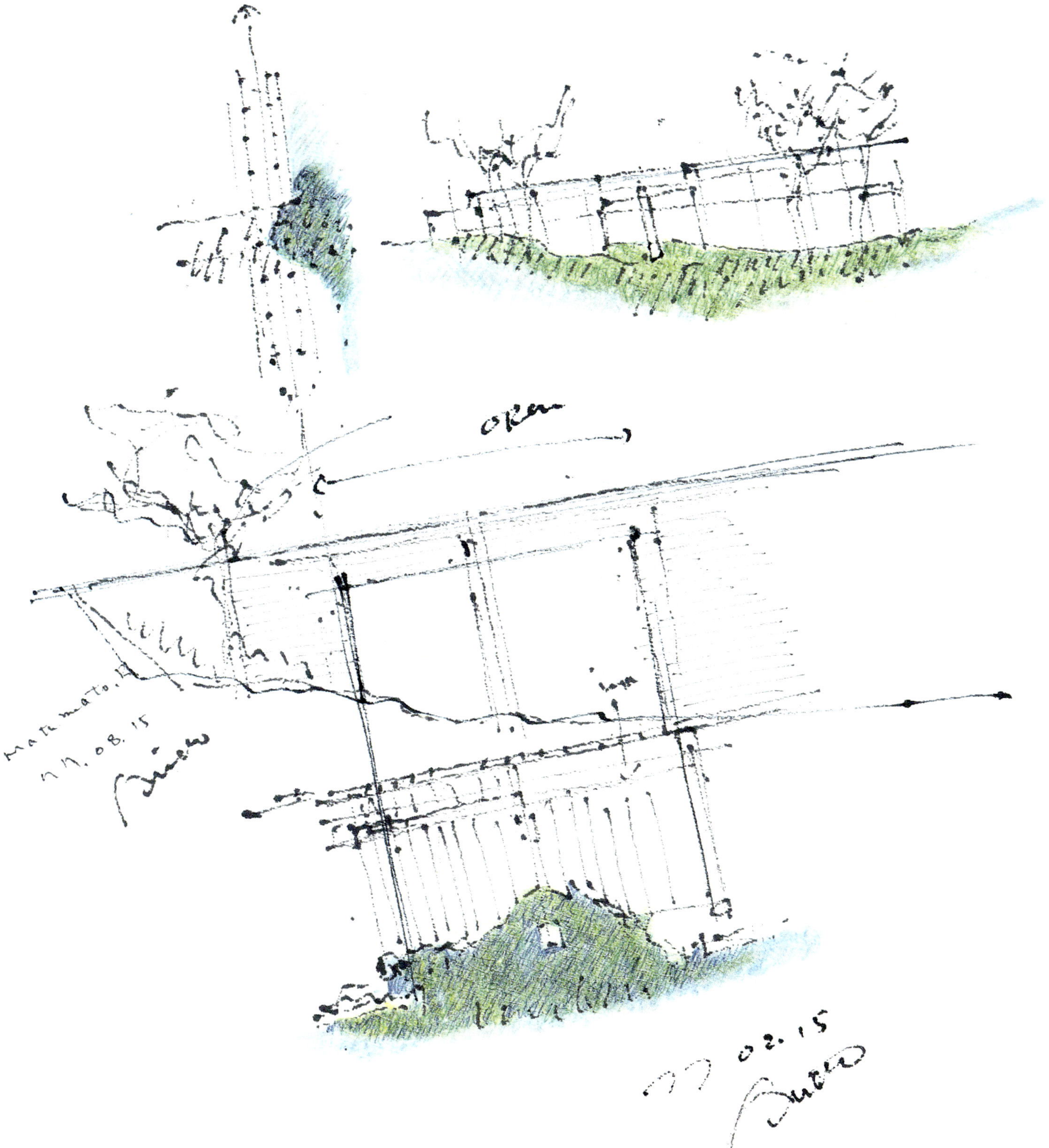

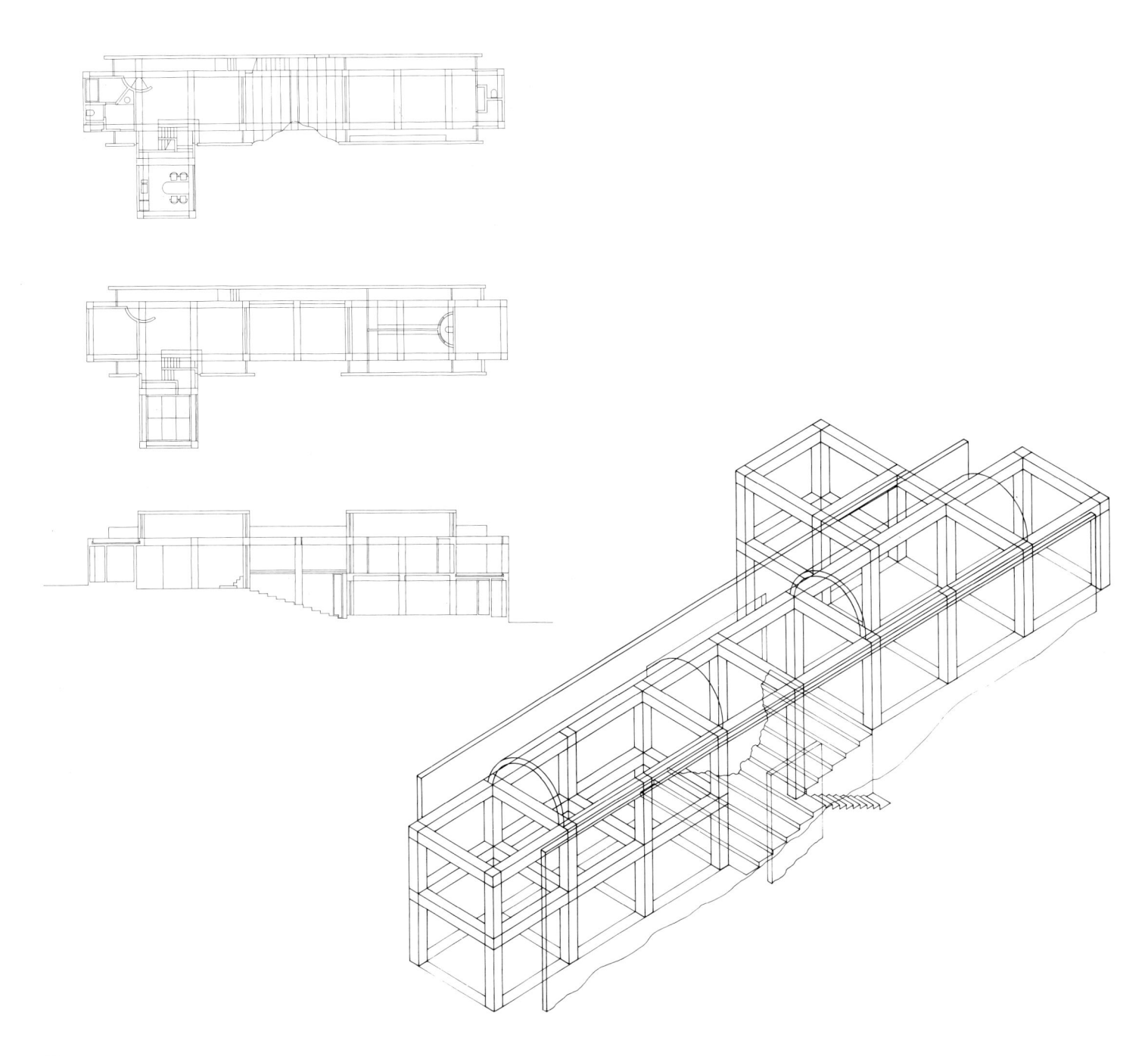

Floor plans, longitudinal section and axonometric.

View from the street showing the freestanding walls.

Perspective, view of the courtyard and oblique view from the street.

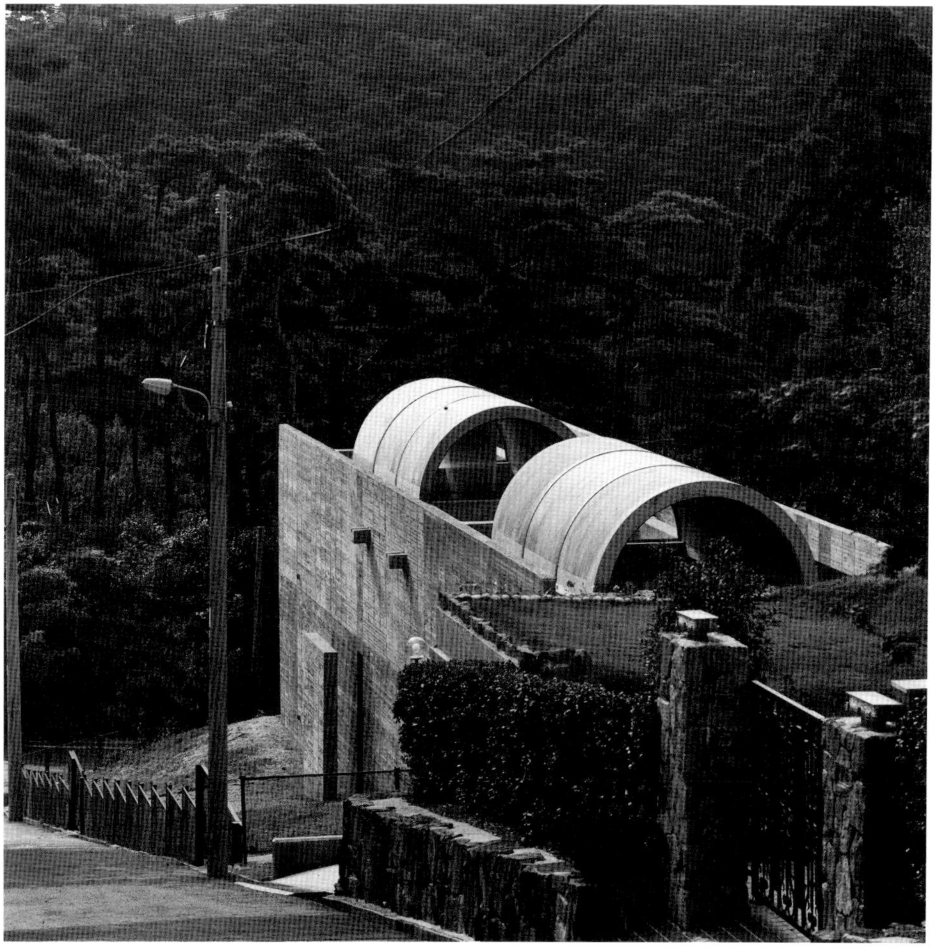

Kitano Alley

View of the entrance walkway, plans and aerial view.

The design approach for this building, a commercial centre in Kobe, was an attempt at a new kind of spatial transformation through an interpretation of the environment. Here two identical rectangular forms and the semi-cylinder joining them were the starting point. These pure geometric solids generated a blank space on the irregular site and thus established a clear zone structure. The two rectangular concrete solids are topped with steel-frame roofs and have shops at the basement and ground floor levels and a studio on the first floor.

As long as a blank space has its own theory, it too can exert its own personality in relation to its surrounding site. When a blank space is controlled by a building, and is architecturalized so that it has its own structure, the site and the architecture set up a mutability that, by means of the mediation of the street, preserves the individuality of the site and responds to the district.

Location Kobe
Design 1976–7
Construction 1977
Structure Reinforced concrete and steel
Site area 345.4 m^2
Building area 190.4 m^2
Total floor area 427.4 m^2

93

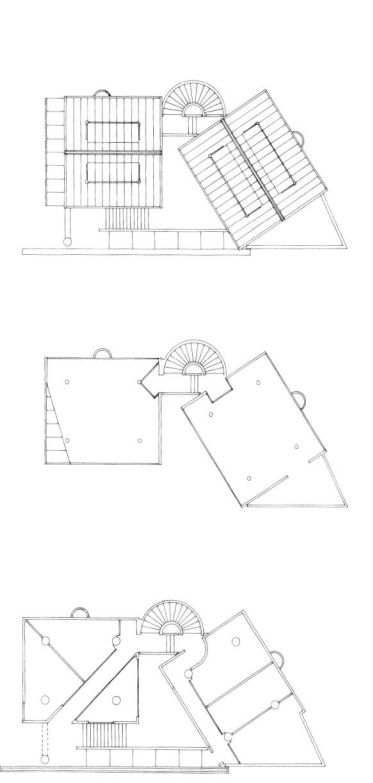

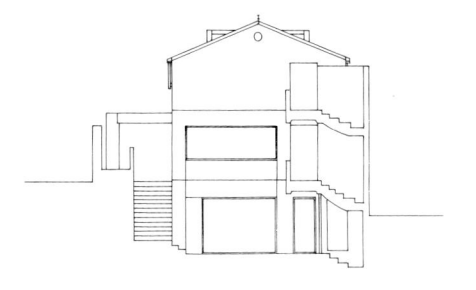

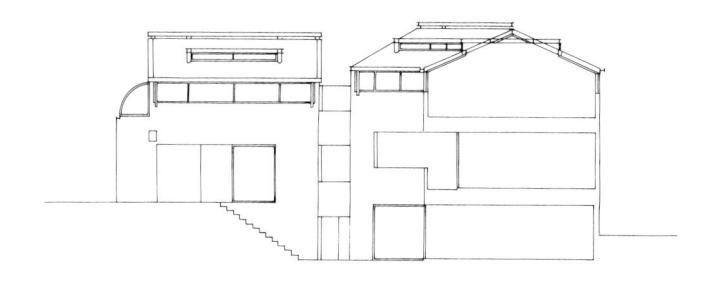

Oblique view of the corridor, sections and view from the stairs.

94

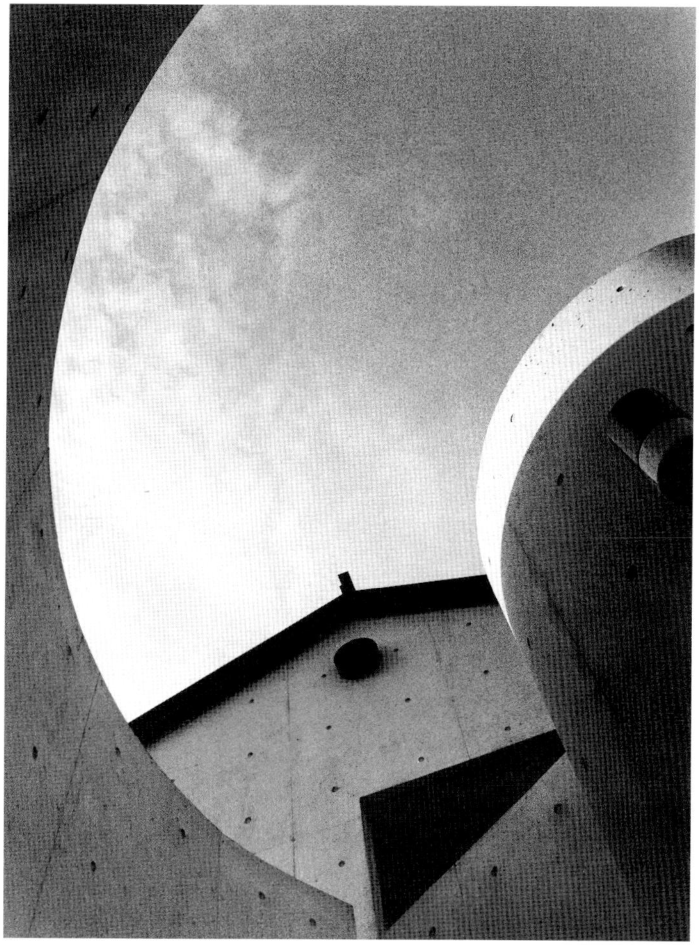

Art Gallery Complex

Floor plans, sections and views of the model.

This project was planned as a complex accommodating a gallery for contemporary art, a small theatre for avant-garde experiments, and offices, primarily in the design field. The building is made up of three blocks with frames of exposed reinforced concrete, and a curved wall of glass block forms a circle intersecting the three blocks.

Inserting a frame into the irregularly-shaped site produced gaps that create a variety of spaces and stepped terraces, linked by the frames overhead. These terraces are spectator seats, stages and galleries. The stairs not only link different levels but serve as interior plazas where people can meet and designers and artists can communicate – creating a forum for unexpected drama.

Location Tokyo
Design 1977

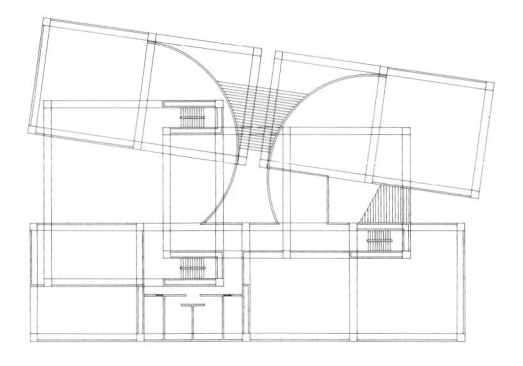

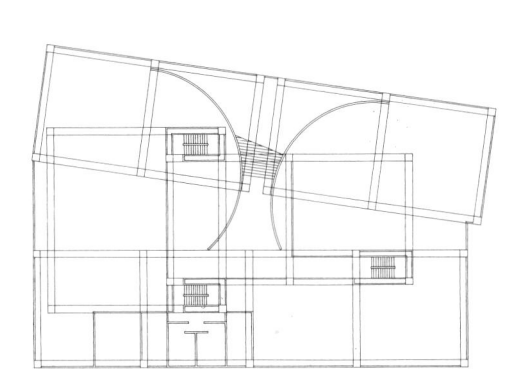

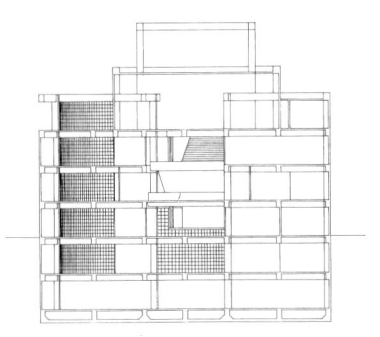

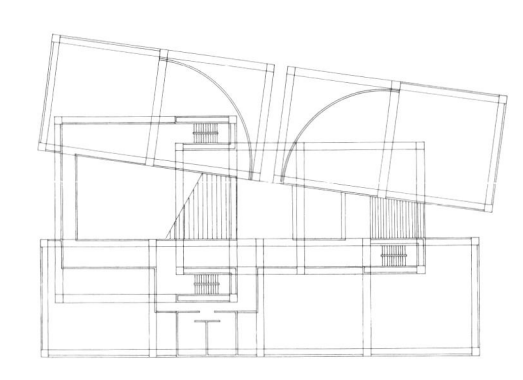

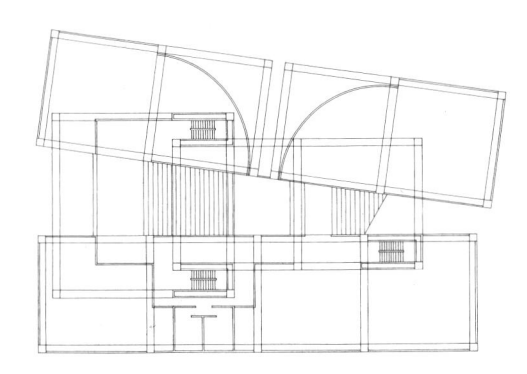

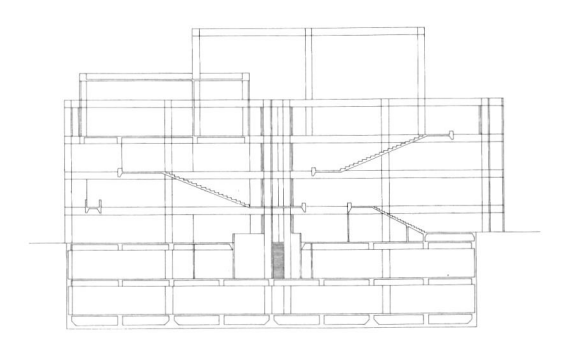

97

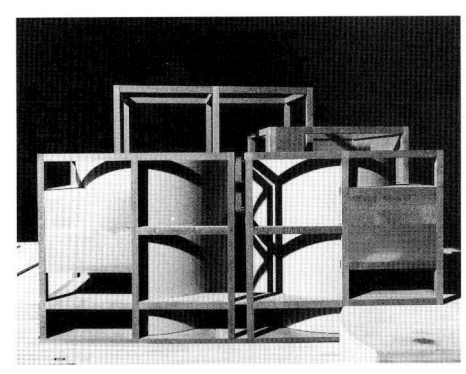

Step

Axonometric showing the structural grid.

Set in a typical commercial arcade in a local city centre, the design proposal for this commercial complex was to introduce a space which had a vertical dimension, related to the city three-dimensionally, and which would draw in light from the sky, re-establishing the sense of nature which has been lost in urban life.

The four-storey building consists of rigid frames with a basic unit of five metres, three staircases dissimilar in form, and walls enclosing the site. Interior scenes unfold along the length of an axis defined by an exterior staircase which leads from the arcade to the plaza on the top floor. The exterior spaces of the building, including the angled stairway on the east side, can thus be seen as streets that draw in activity from the city.

Location Takamatsu
Design 1977–8
Construction 1979–80
Structure Reinforced concrete
Site area 466.4 m^2
Building area 365.1 m^2
Total floor area 1,142 m^2

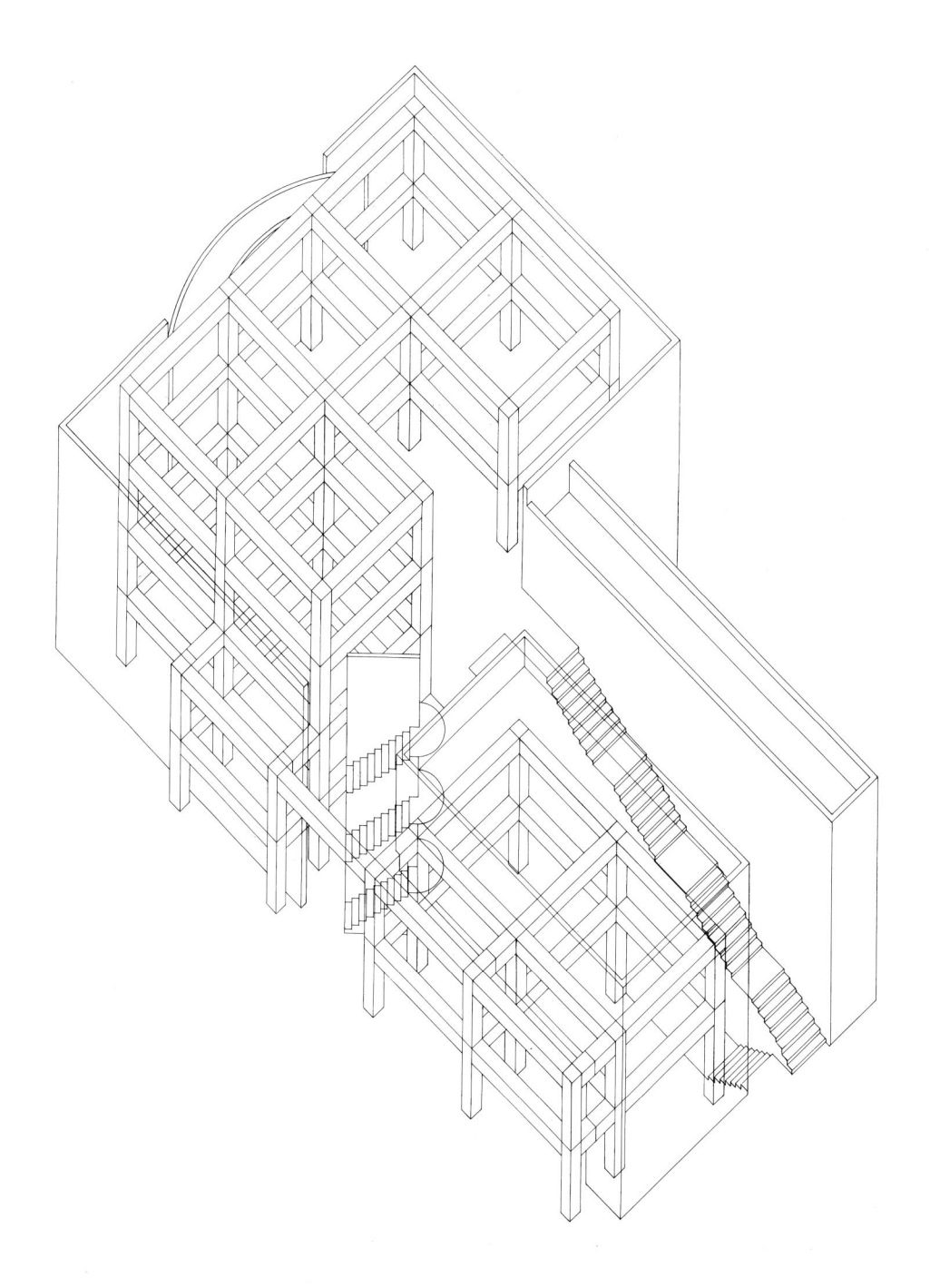

View of the exterior staircase and floor plans.

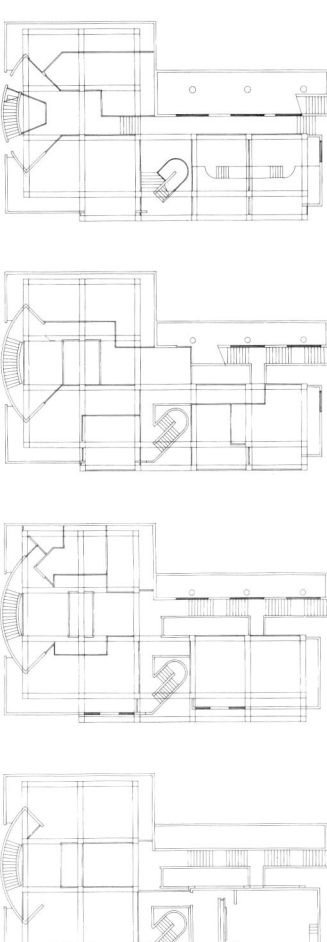

99

Views of the staircase and roof.

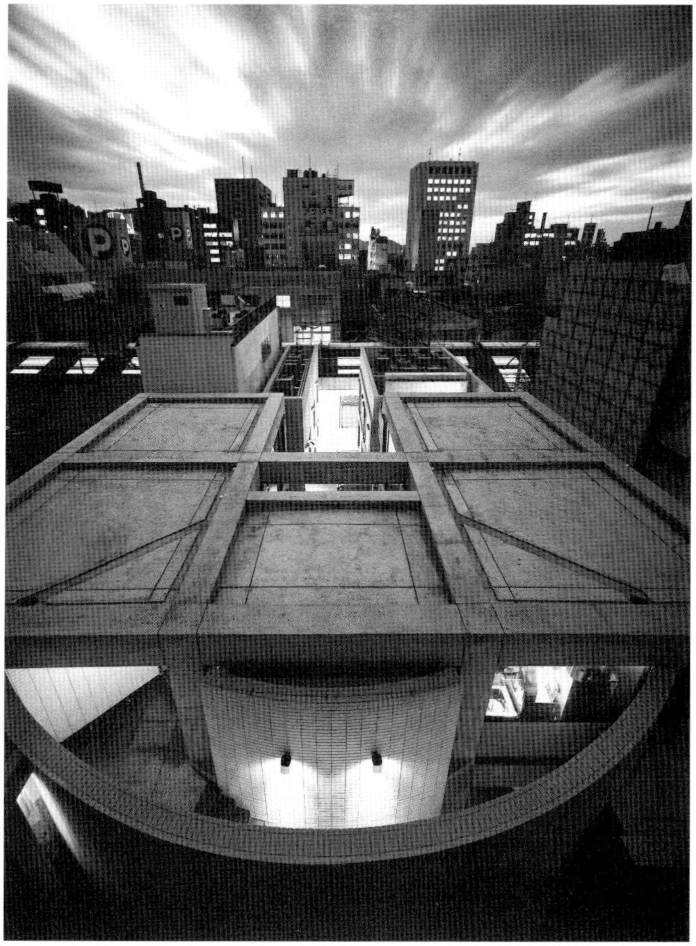

Ishihara House

Conceptual sketches.

By sealing this house within concrete walls and installing a central light court, a microcosm is generated whose privacy is undisturbed by the din of Osaka's old downtown quarter. The building has three levels and achieves clear articulation of zones from its axial symmetry in plan and the stepped recessing of its upper levels in section.

The essential component in this design is an interior membrane of glass block. This translucent membrane divides the building's rectangular form into equal void and solid volumes and distributes the natural light filling the court to six recessed rooms. The dual character of glass block, at once translucent and opaque, allows diffusion of sufficient light into the residence and renders palpable the outside world's presence, while, at the same time, obstructing vision and guarding the privacy of the occupants.

Soft natural light from the light court permeates the rooms for daytime activities, and at night this is reversed, as artificial light from the rooms illuminates the exterior space of the light court and transforms it into a box of light.

Location Osaka
Design 1977–8
Construction 1978
Structure Reinforced concrete
Site area 458.4 m^2
Building area 92 m^2
Total floor area 221.5 m^2

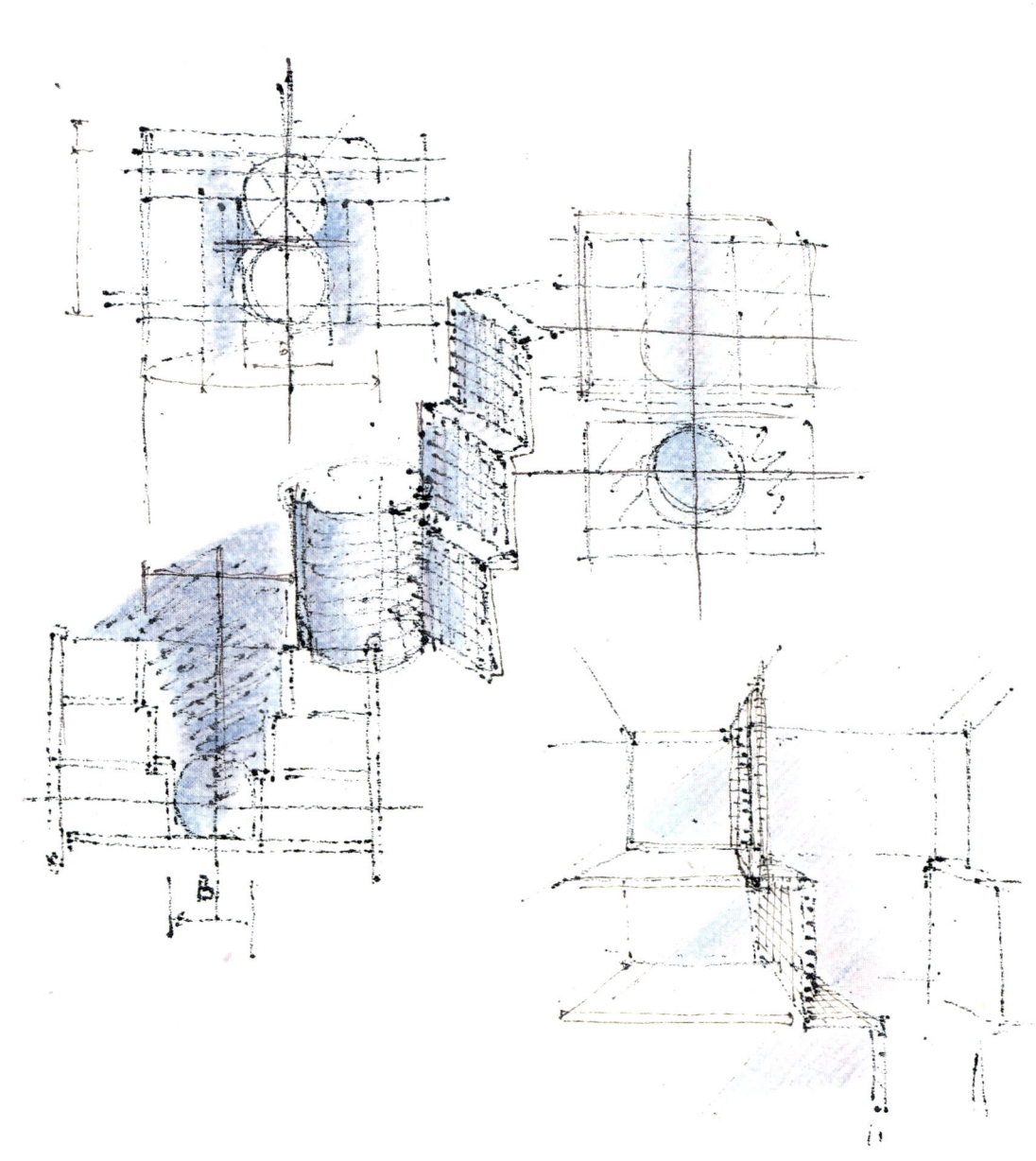

Top Light.

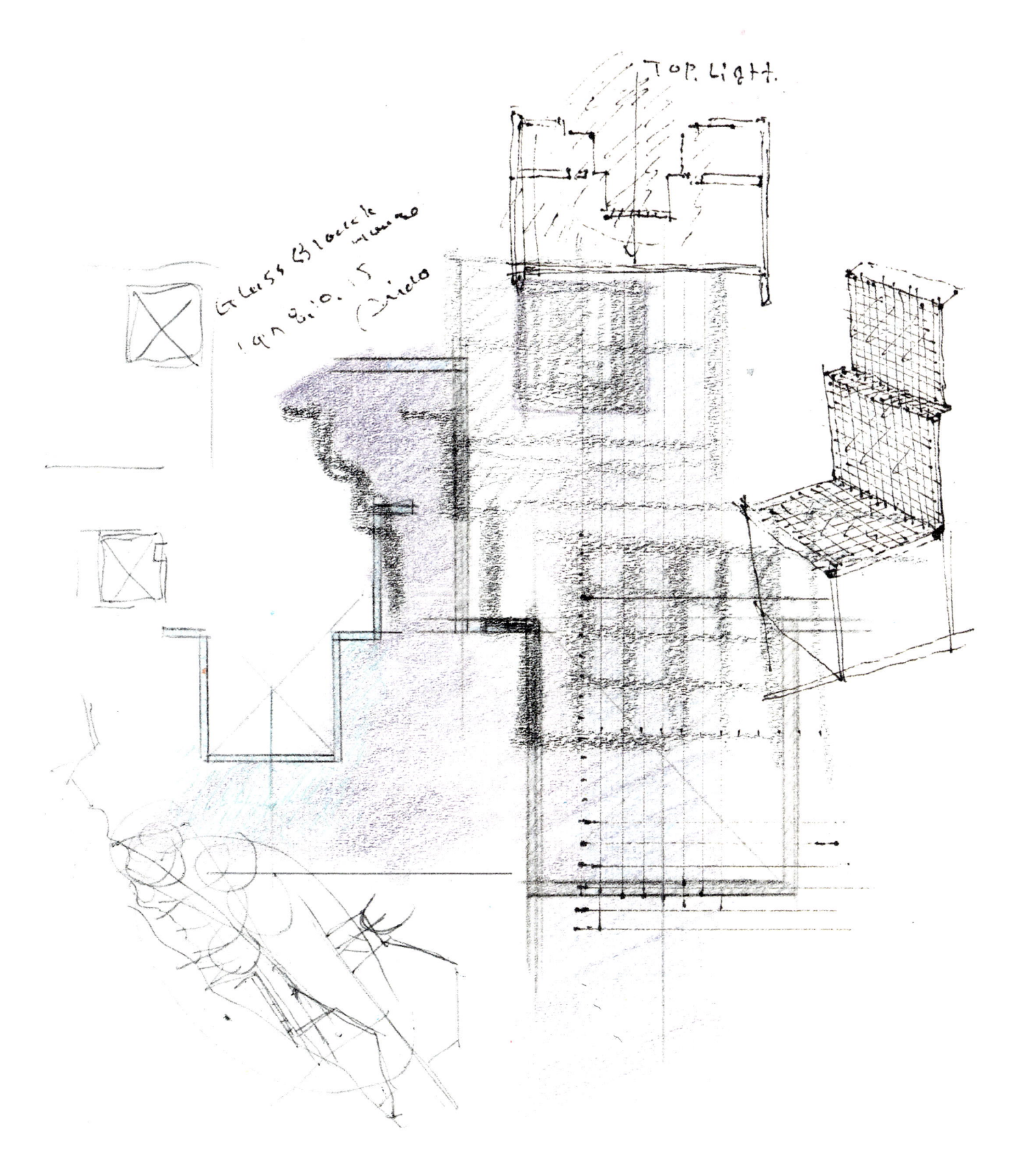

Glass Block muro
in gio. 15
Cielo

Floor plans, section and view from the street.

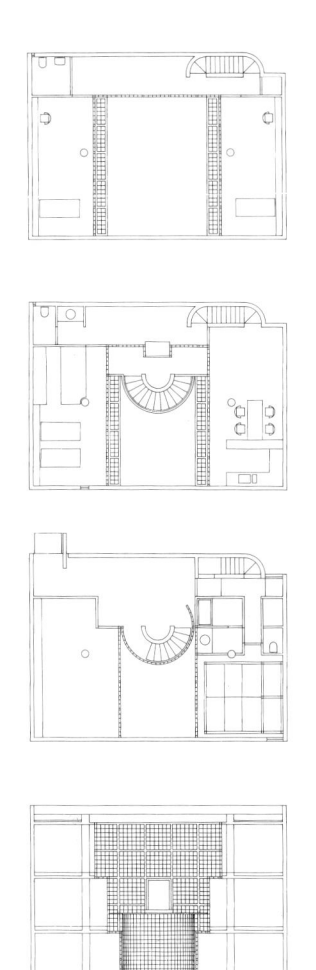

Aerial view and axonometrics of the courtyard.

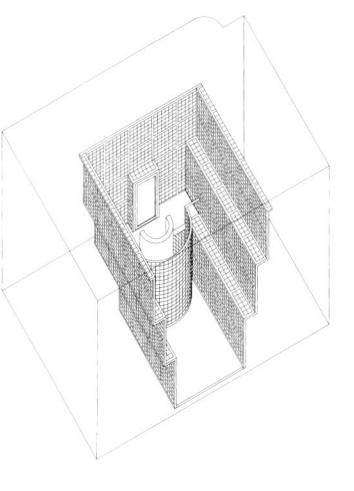

105

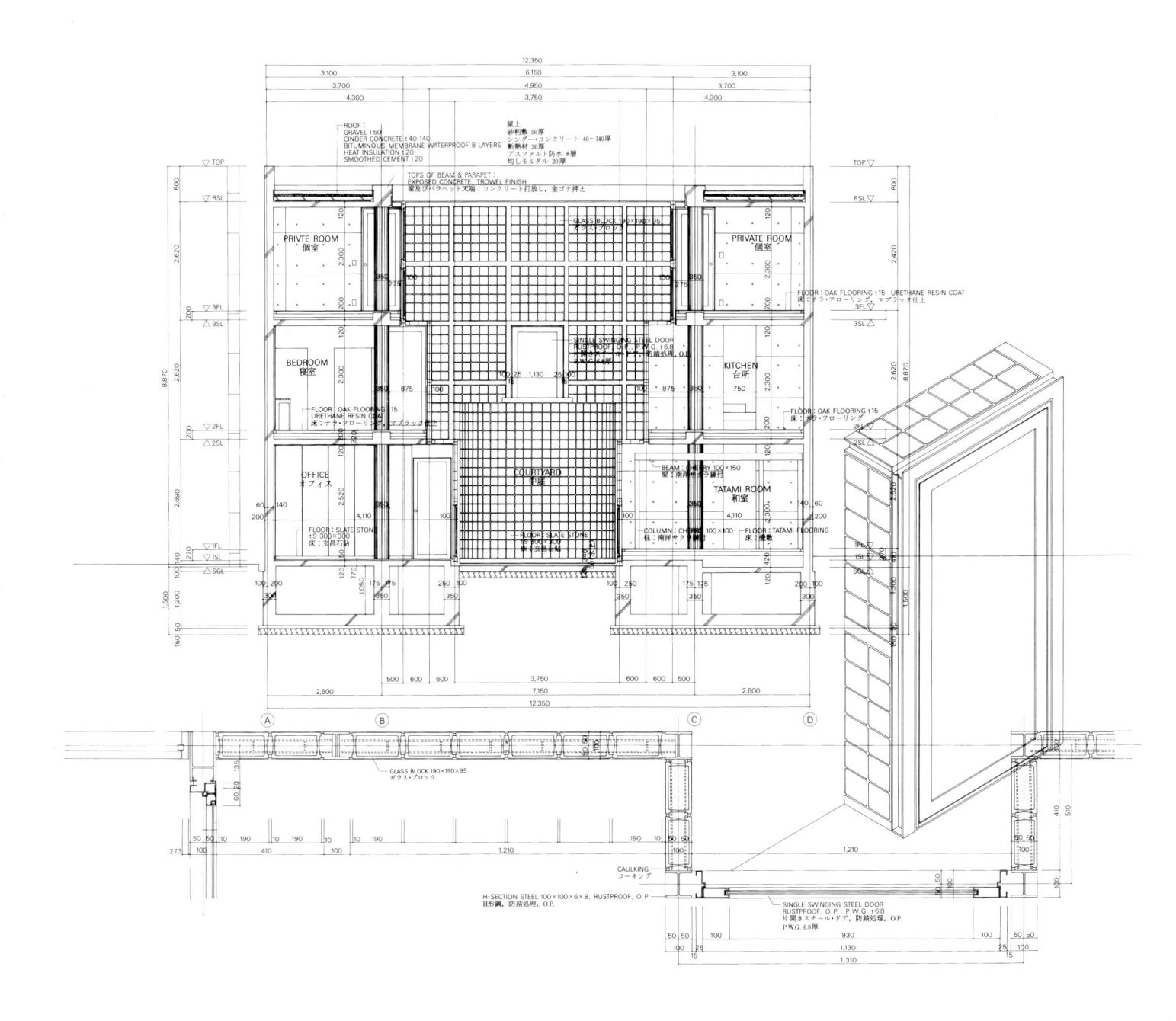

Section and construction details, and view of the courtyard from the roof.

106

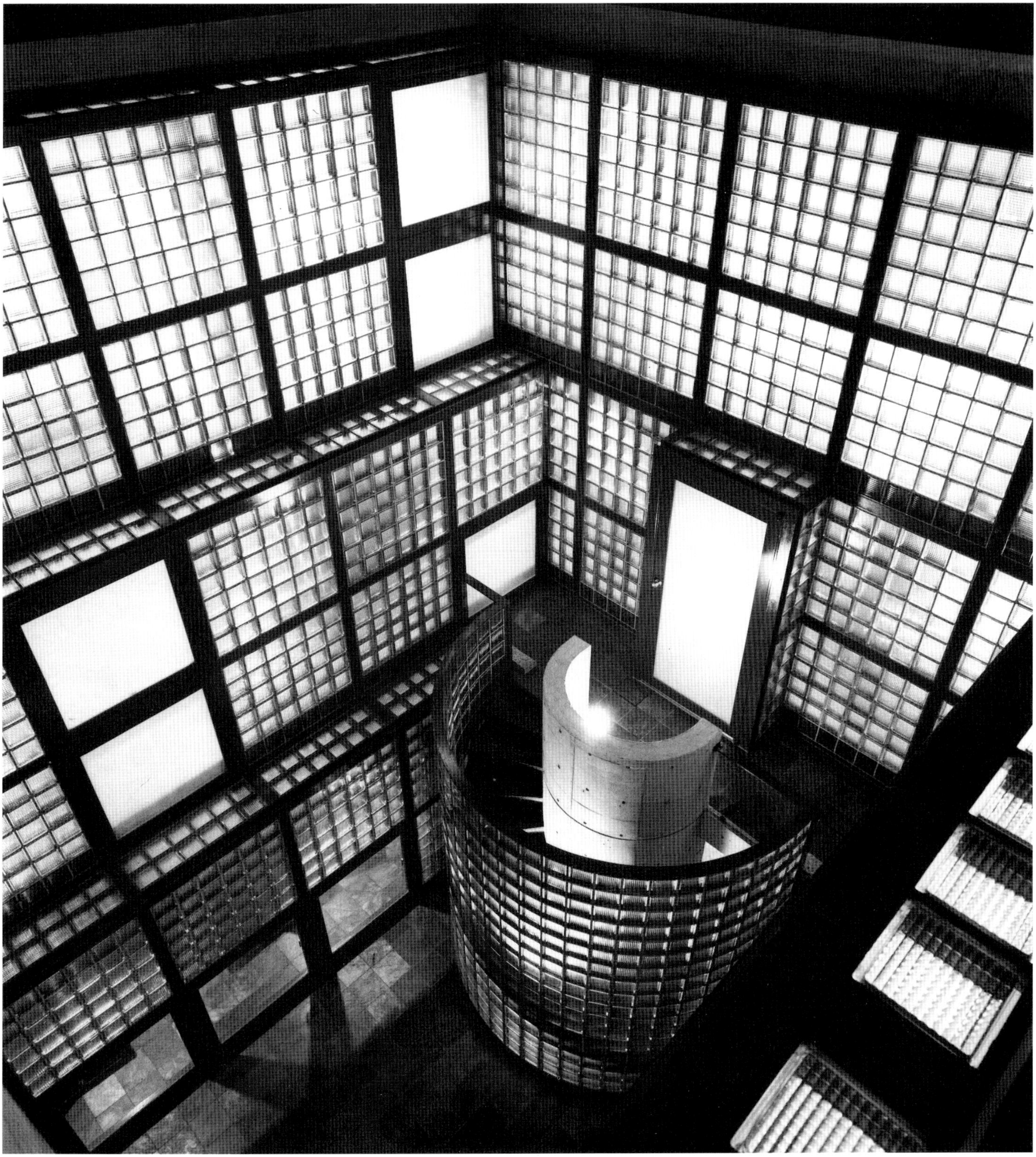

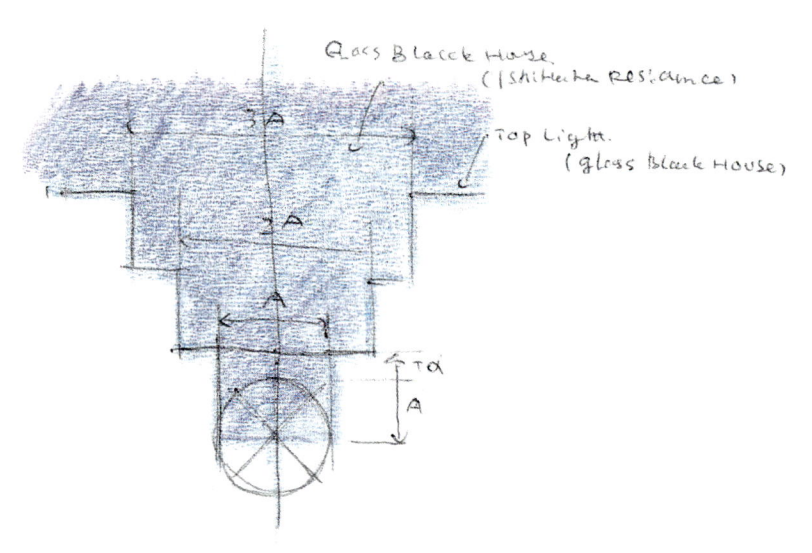

Interior views, conceptual sketch and view showing the glass-block walls.

108

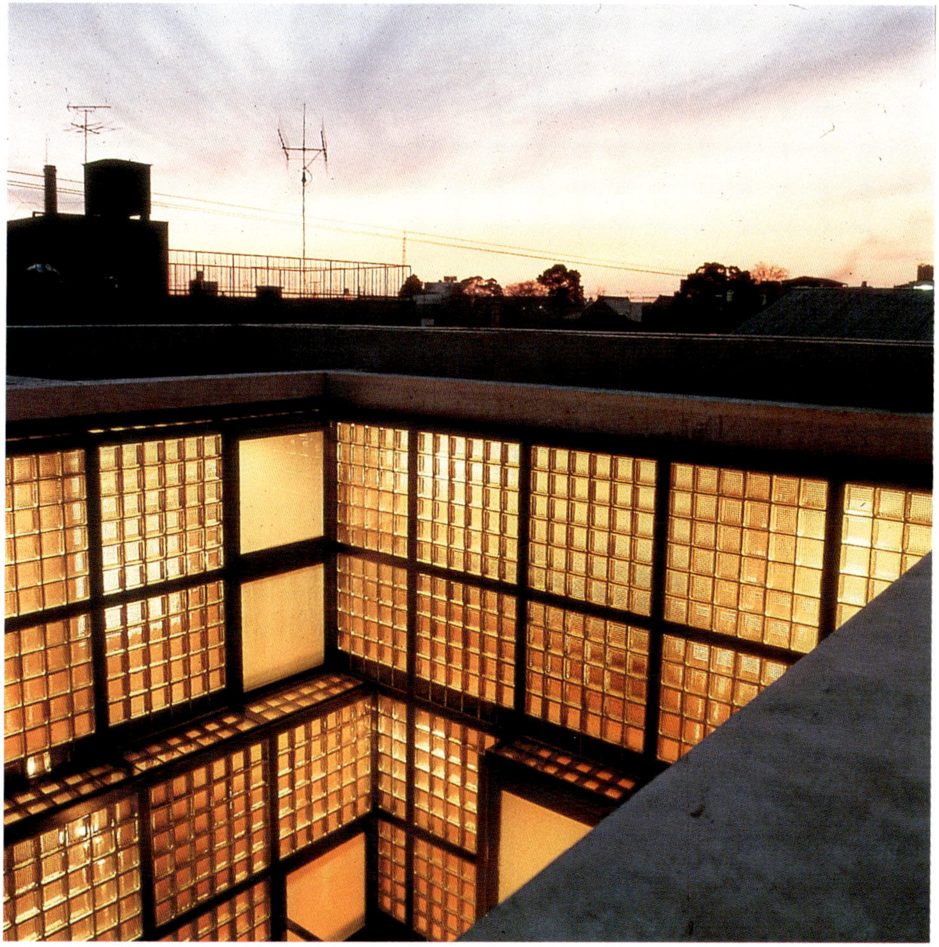

Okusu House

Floor plans, section showing the principal staircase and axonometric of the entrance area.

This irregular L-shaped site, set in a wealthy, established suburb of Tokyo, resulted when a large estate was carved up into smaller parcels. The building conforms to this shape, consisting of two long, narrow concrete boxes that intersect. The one close to the street is devoted to the reception of guests and contains a guest hall, entrance hall and guest room. The other is given over to family spaces.

Two freestanding concrete frames define the approach from the street, which has only a few metres of frontage; these suggest depth and lead the visitor into the structure. The darkened entrance approach is followed by a gently rising stairway that is brightly lit and leads to the second-floor entrance hall. The separation and integration of reception spaces and private spaces have resulted in a number of very distinctive stairs and multi-storey spaces. The broad stairway of the entrance approach and the guest room deck, and the way they interact with the concrete walls, sky and wind, lights and shadows, make one aware of the spatial extension in all directions.

Location Tokyo
Design 1977
Construction 1978
Structure Reinforced concrete
Site area 531.1 m^2
Building area 194.2 m^2
Total floor area 288.4 m^2

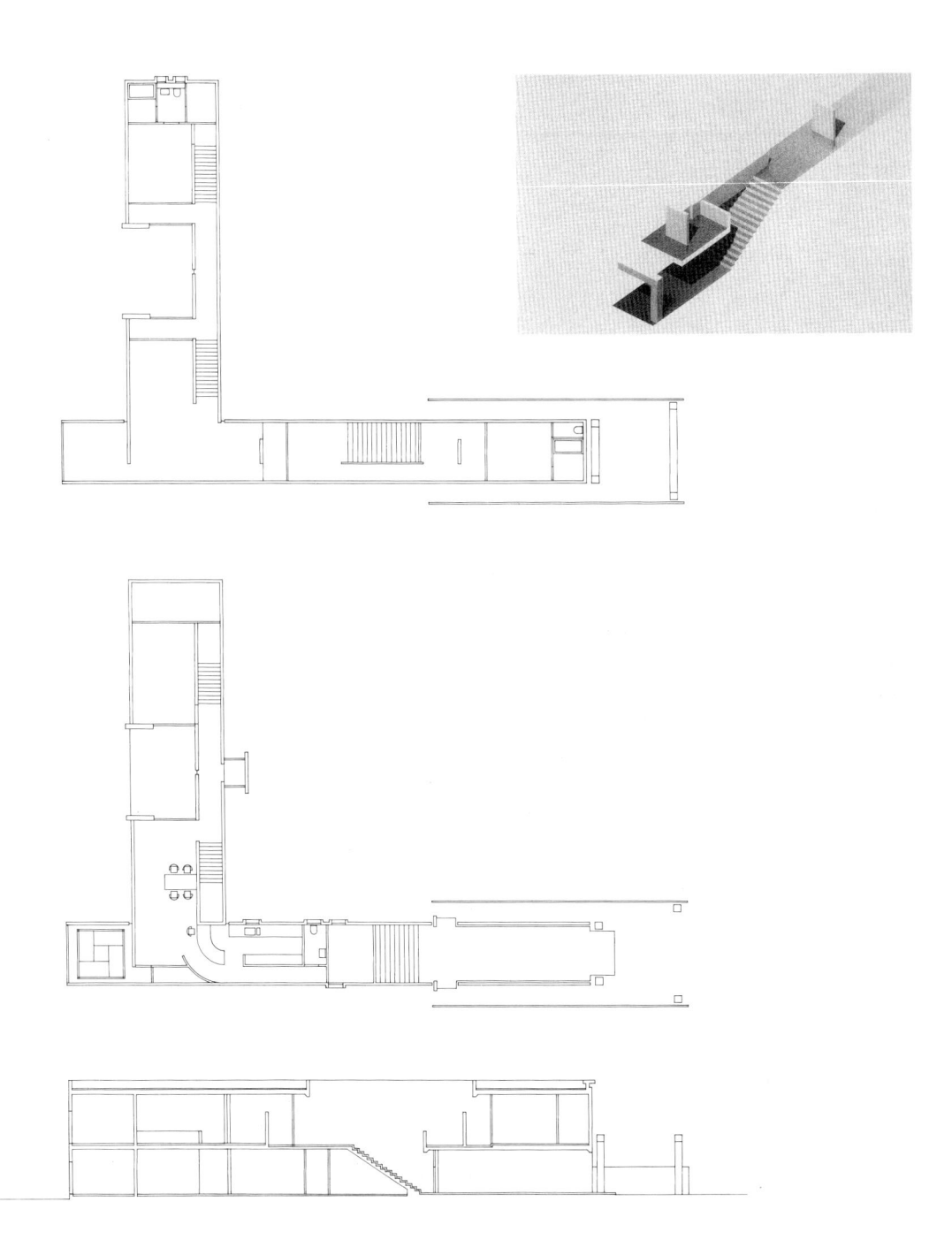

Views showing the interior and entrance.

111

Horiuchi House

Conceptual sketches.

The building consists of an exposed concrete wall enclosure and a freestanding glass wall. There are three storeys and the courtyard separates the building into north and south parts in plan. The living room and main bedroom are arranged around the atrium on the south side and on the north side the kitchen occupies the middle floor, with children's rooms and a tatami room above and below respectively.

The freestanding wall defines the domain of the house within the city and is a basic element of the landscape within the house. The light that penetrates the glass-block wall causes transformations in the landscape with the passing of time, and suggests a relationship between the architecture and the city. The dual characteristics of glass blocks – their translucency and obstruction of vision – assure privacy and permit the screen to serve as a medium of communication between the landscape outside and the landscape within the house. As a result, the house and its environment are linked solely by light.

Location Osaka
Design 1977–8
Construction 1978–9
Structure Reinforced concrete
Site area 237.9 m²
Building area 95 m²
Total floor area 243.7 m²

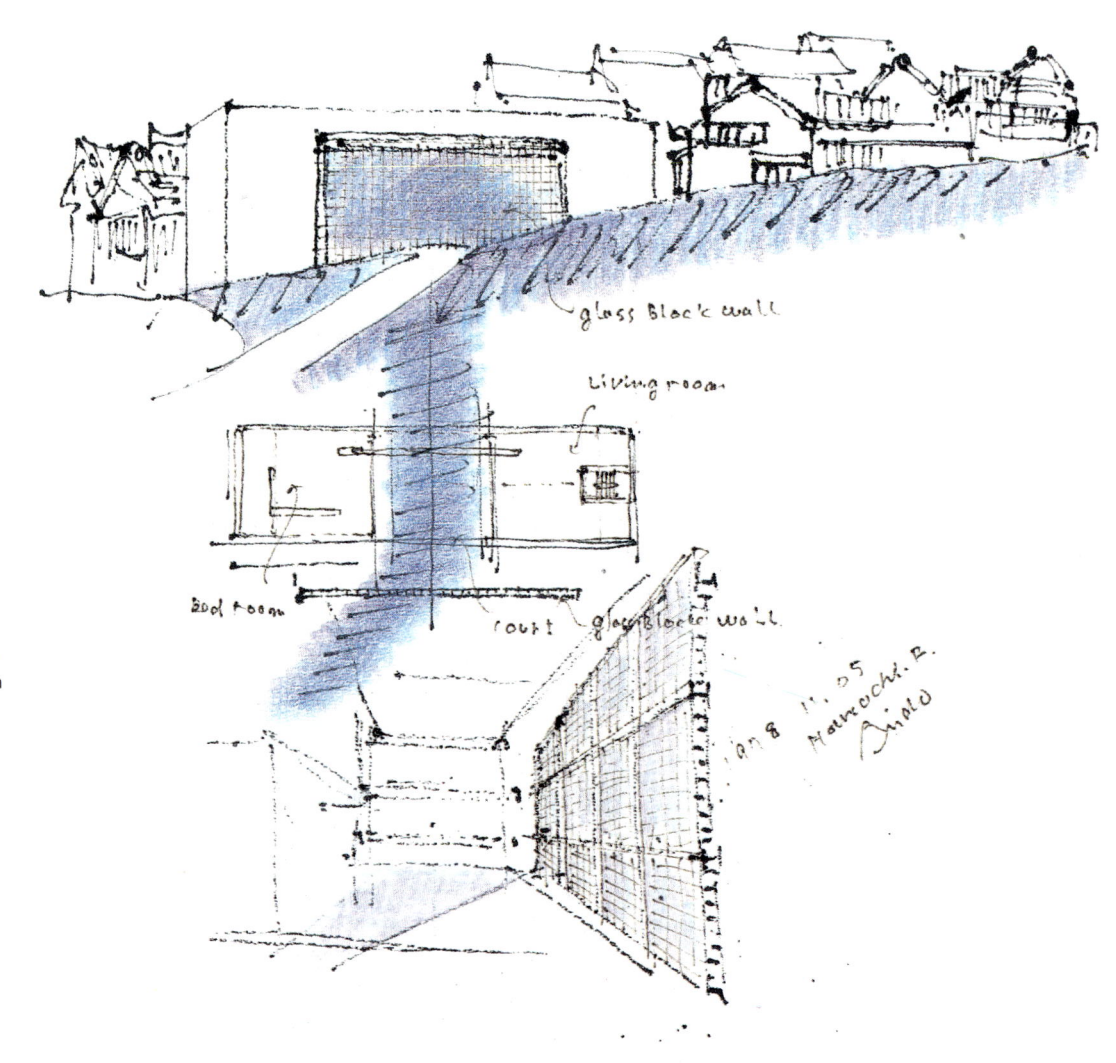

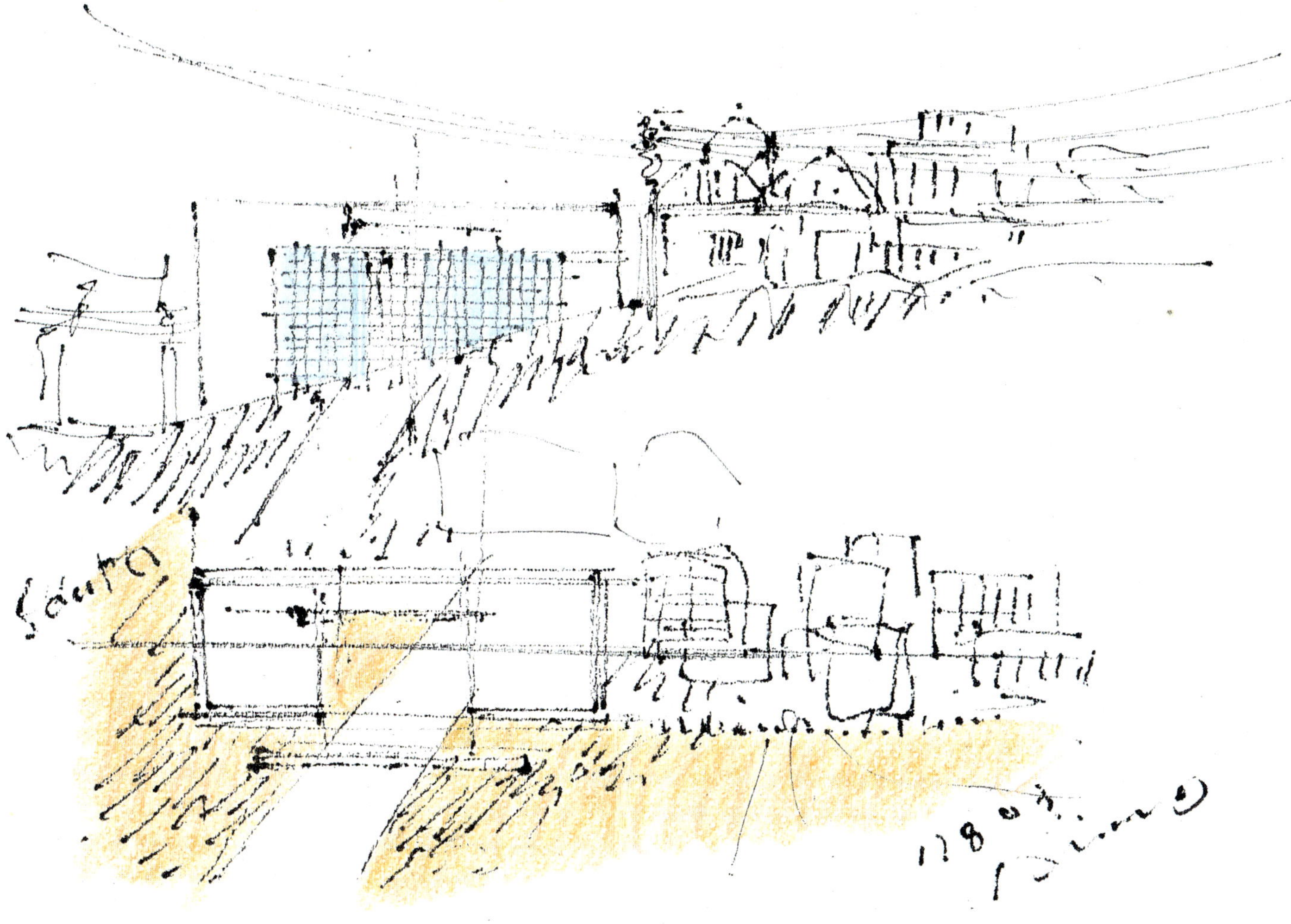

Floor plans, section, axonometric and oblique view from the street showing the glass-block wall.

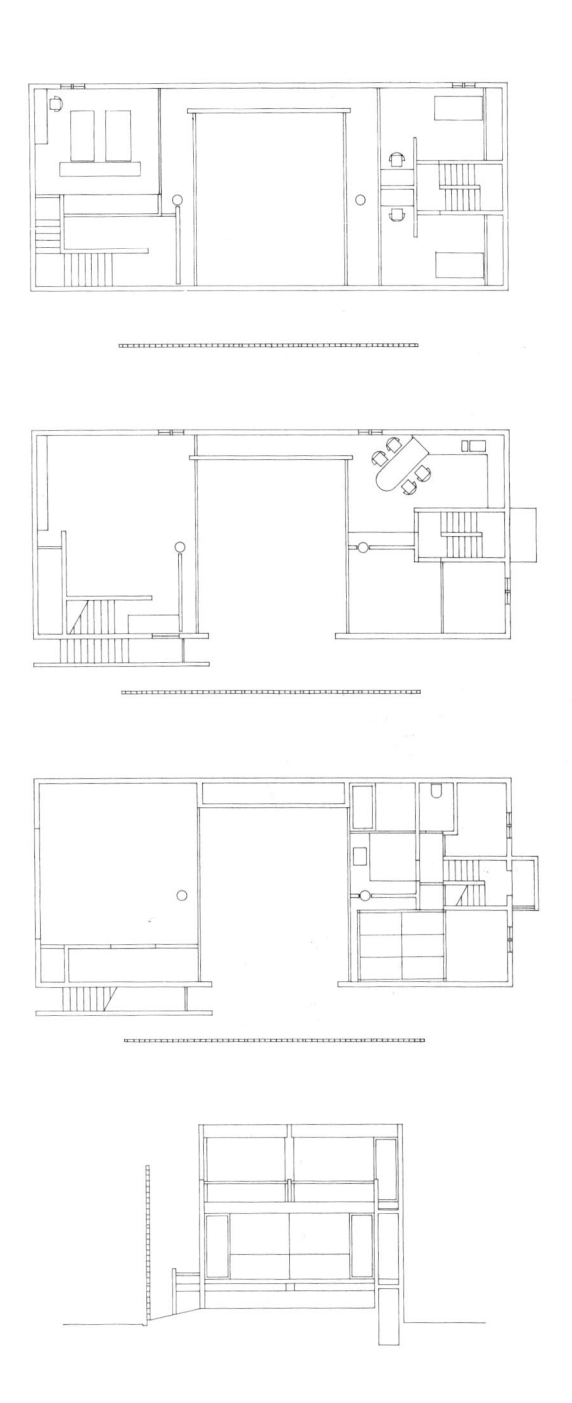

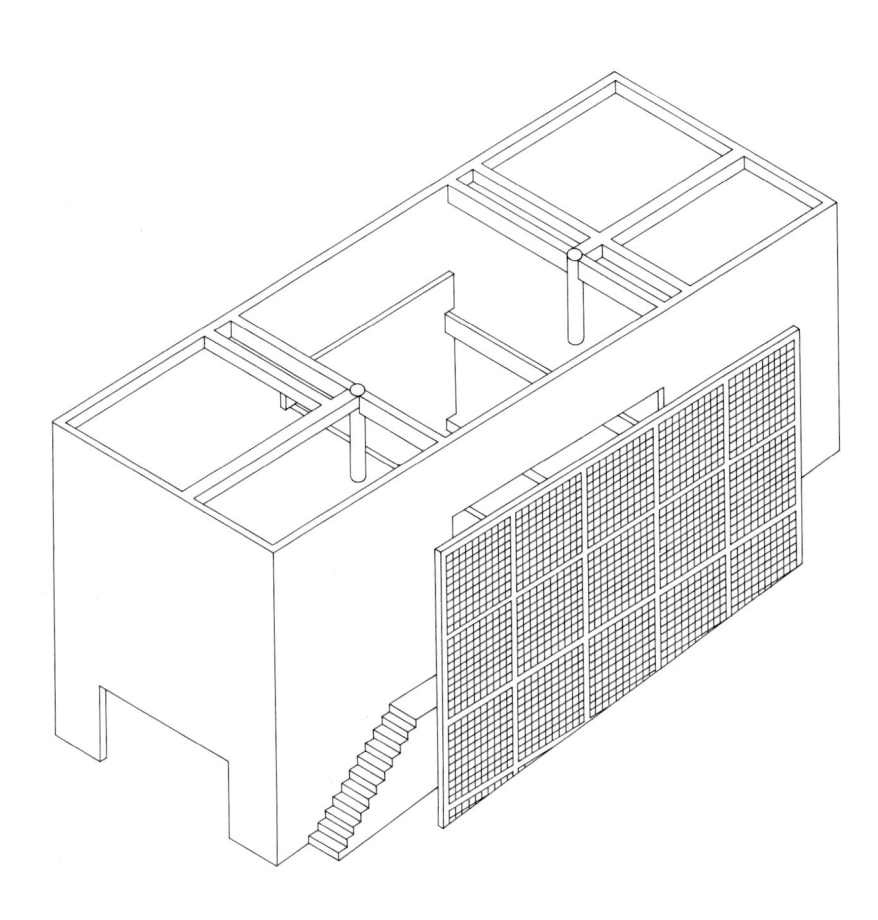

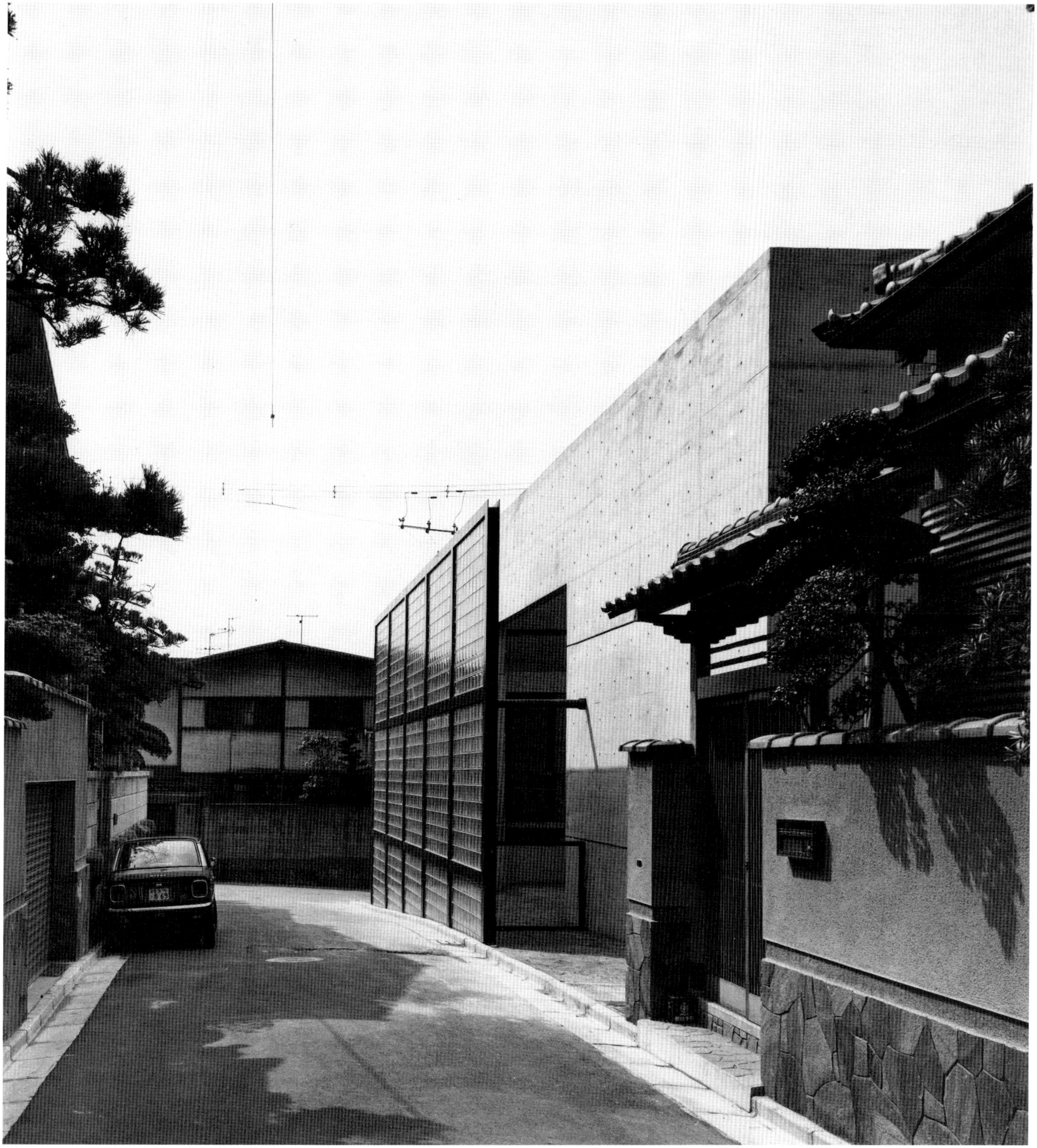

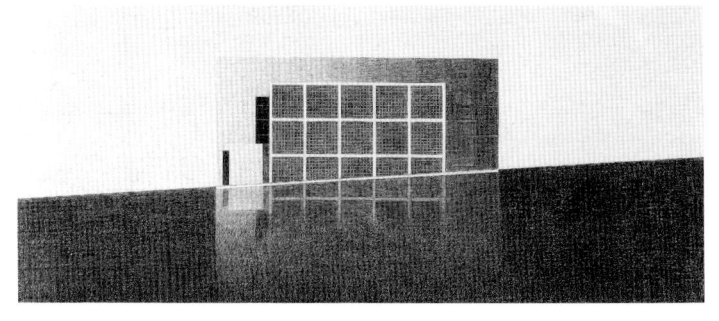

Views and perspective showing the glass-block wall.

116

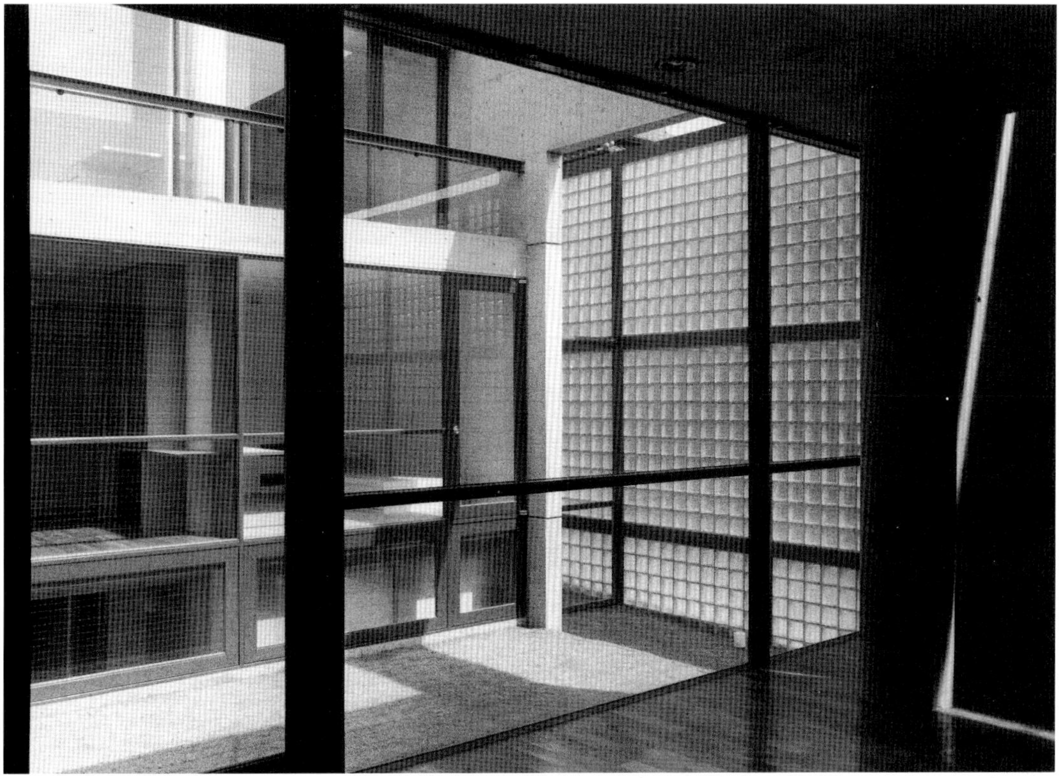

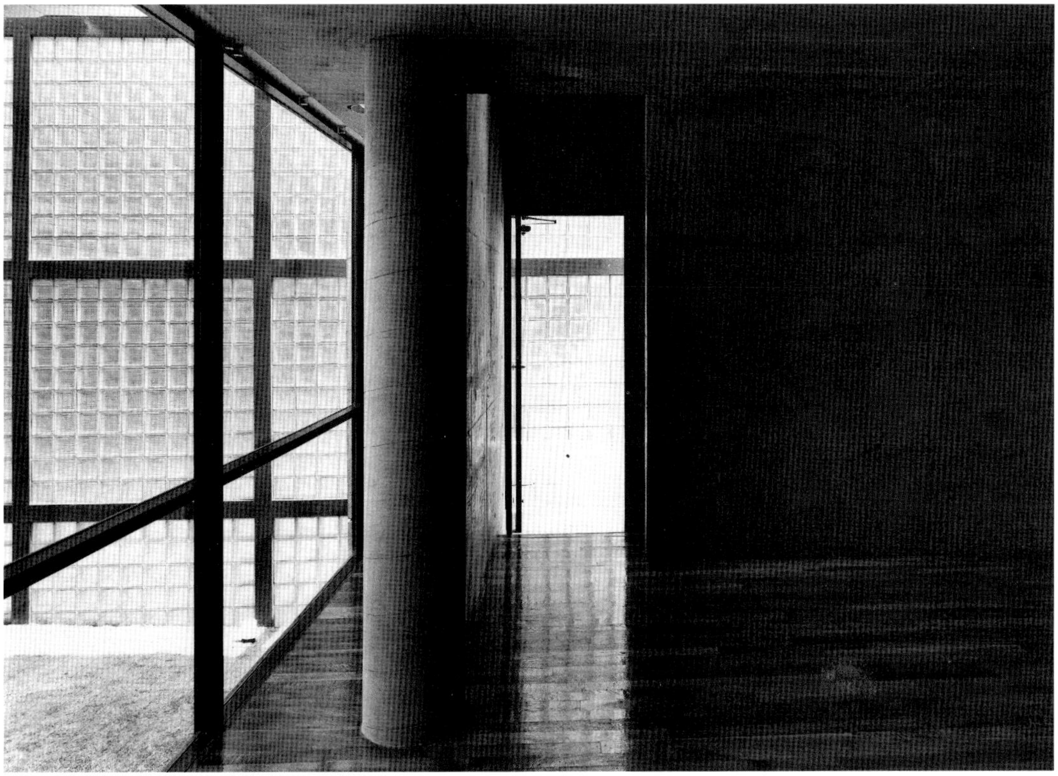

Matsumoto House

Plans and conceptual sketches.

The aim of this design was to produce architecture independent from the noisy setting and possessing its own private scenery. The abstract exemplification of this intent is the hallway which, enclosed in glass-block walls, becomes the central feature of the house. The building consists of two wings of rough concrete frames designed on a module of 5.2 x 5.2 metres plus a double row of frames connecting the two wings.

The hall is an interiorized exterior with a gentle, tender mood evoked by the directionless light admitted through the glass blocks fitted into the concrete framework. Colouring it lightly eliminates the sense of actuality, volume and dimensionality of the framework. The deck passing overhead intensifies the extraordinary mood of the space.

Location Wakayama
Design 1978–9
Construction 1979–80
Structure Reinforced concrete
Site area 952.1 m²
Building area 317.4 m²
Total floor area 484.1 m²

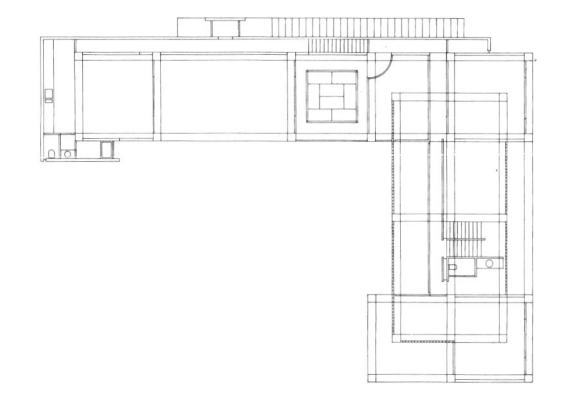

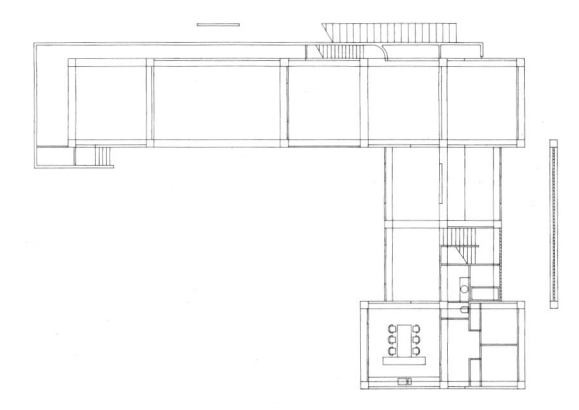

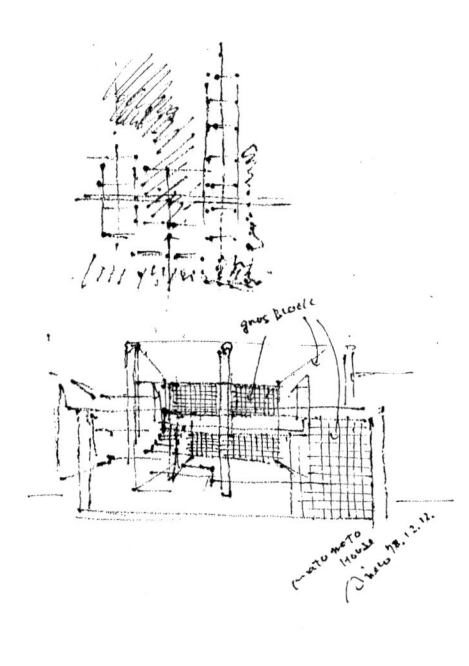

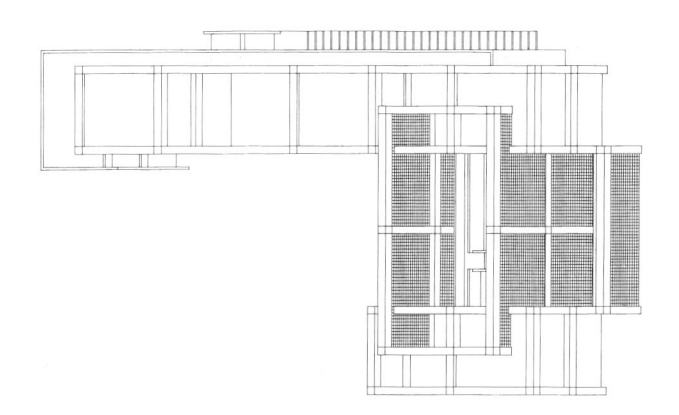

Partial, aerial and interior views of the building.

Onishi House

Axonometric and plans.

This house was built on a site approximately 165 square metres, facing a five-metre road. The legal building regulation known as the 'exterior wall setback' is strictly enforced in Japan, regardless of the size of the site, and makes a small site even more restrictive.

The building consists of exposed concrete frames and a sloping garden. The frames are composed of three levels of a stacked grid which, in turn, is made up of four rectangles. The sloping garden starts from the bottom-most grid sunk half a level below ground level, and it rises gradually towards the street. The frontage, a response to building regulations, has an overhang to serve as a parking space. This space is also utilized as a children's play area and thus it produces varied scenes in the cityscape.

Location Osaka
Design 1978–9
Construction 1979
Structure Reinforced concrete
Site area 165.2 m^2
Building area 60.5 m^2
Total floor area 144.3 m^2

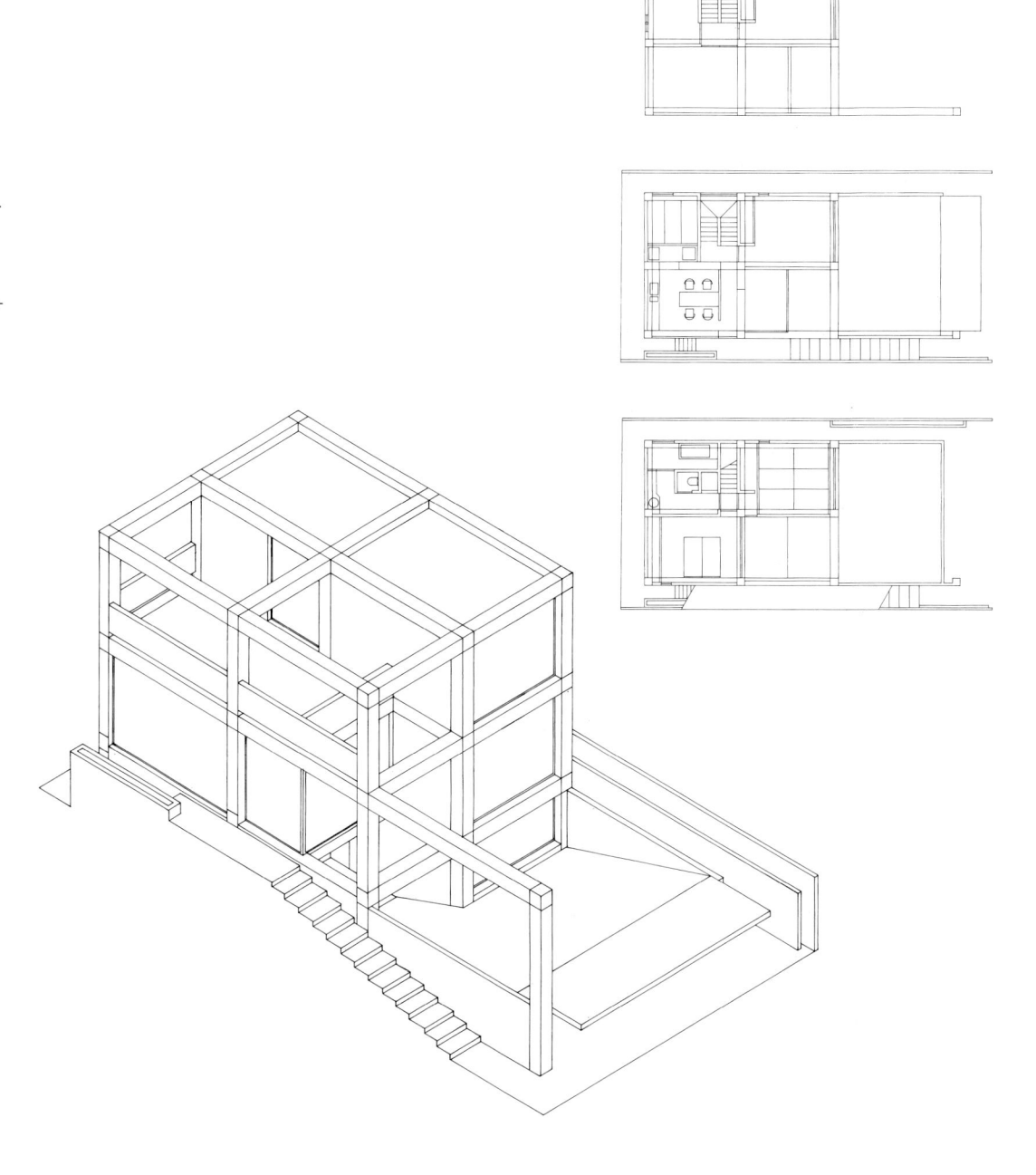

Views of the entrance and detailed view of the side of the building.

Kitano Ivy Court

View from the street and section.

The building is located on a street on a slight slope. Its two volumes which make up the commercial complex are each four floors high and are separated by an exterior stairway; the roof of the building, however, allows the building an identity of its own. Brick walls face the sides of the complex and serve to hide the balconies and the large structural columns in reinforced concrete which are visible from the upper levels of the building.

Location Kobe
Design 1978–9
Construction 1979–80
Structure Reinforced concrete
Site area 575.7 m^2
Building area 344.8 m^2
Total floor area 1,211.9 m^2

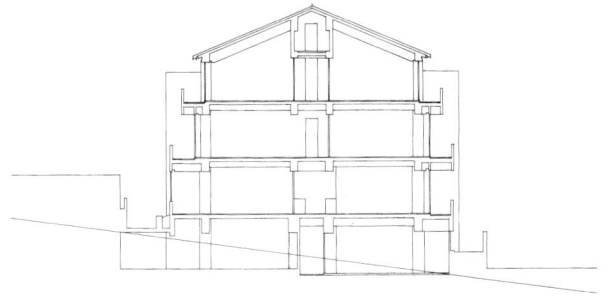

View showing the balcony and floor plans.

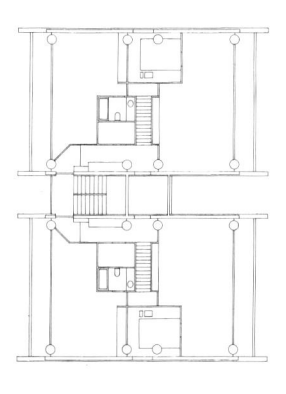

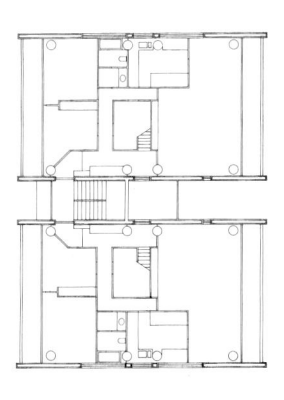

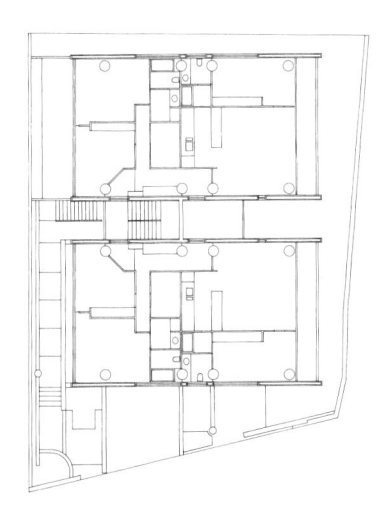

123

Matsutani House and Extension

Overall view of the building, plans, longitudinal section and view from the bedroom.

This small house for a family of four is an attempt to create pure architectural space. All materials, including the concrete of the floors, walls and ceilings, have been simplified as much as possible. The materials enclose a space where nothing but the apertures and the volumes enclosed are stressed. The sizes of the apertures were determined by the relation between floor area and height and between floor area and total volume.

The whole composition consists of two blocks separated by a courtyard. The blocks are composed of cubical basic units 4.2 metres to a side. On the first level is an open space for studio work plus a veranda and, across the courtyard, the dining room and master bedroom. Both the living room and the children's room on the second floor face south. The pounded-earth (*tataki*) area found in traditional Japanese farmhouses and town houses is hinted at in the rough-concrete floor extending from the dining room into the courtyard.

Ten years after the completion of the building, the client, an art teacher, wanted to add a studio. As Ando's buildings are always intended to be formally complete, designing an extension means transforming one complete form into a different one. Here, a new form was achieved by contrasting the extension with the original house.

A studio of steel-frame construction with a two-storey void has been introduced on the east side of the courtyard. As a result, the courtyard which used to be half-enclosed, is now completely enclosed, which allows for a more centralized scheme.

125

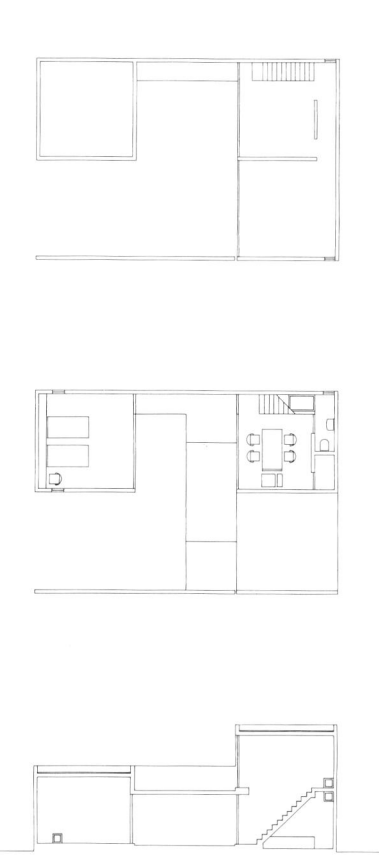

View from the studio to the courtyard, and conceptual sketches.

Location Kyoto
Design 1978–9
Construction 1979
Structure Reinforced concrete
Site area 143.1 m²
Building area 56.6 m²
Total floor area 91.9 m²

Extension
Design 1989–90
Construction 1990
Structure Steel
Building area 16.4 m²
Total floor area 16.4 m²

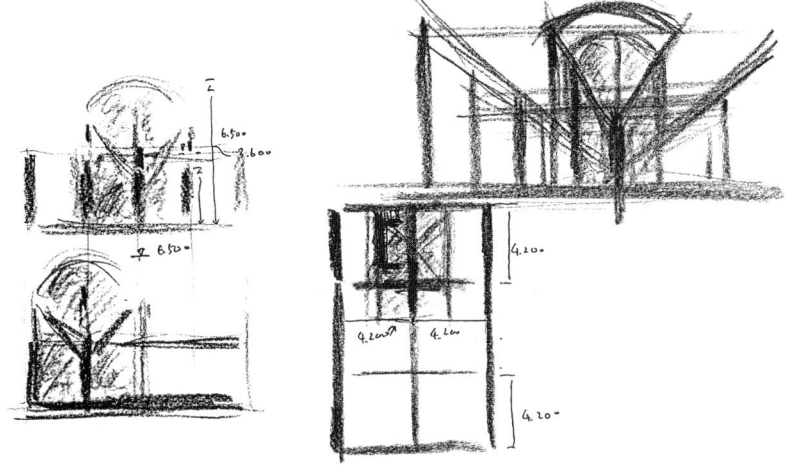

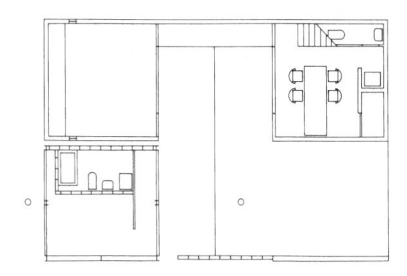

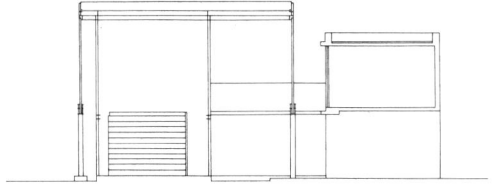

Detail of the window, plan and section of the main building and the extension.

Ueda House and Extension

Plans and section showing the stairs, and exterior and interior views.

The owner of the house is a musician, and the brief was for the building to accommodate an area for piano lessons. This was done by dividing the house into two spaces, each 5.5 metres wide x 4.4 metres deep x 3.8 metres high, placed in axial symmetry and separated by walls. The openings in the walls further subdivide the spaces; these are limited to windows facing each other, but light coming through them articulates daily life spaces in different ways in each of the two main blocks. The high window at the mezzanine level admits soft northern light, which falls down onto the first-floor zone. Strong light from the window on the south side of the first storey illuminates the concrete floor. These two kinds of light – northern and southern – combine to expand the sense of spatial volume visually. Wind passing southward from the north and northward from the south expands the volume in a tactile sense.

Eight years after the completion of the house, an extension was built at the client's request. The existing music room was changed into a living room and dining room, and a new music room was provided in the new building. The materials were kept as simple as possible in order to make the intention behind the spatial composition clear. The extension halves the existing courtyard and faces the original house across a green courtyard, enclosing it and making the scheme more centralized. The composition is based on the ratio 2:1 in terms of the number of floors and the span. For the sake of privacy, the extension was half-buried, and its openings were shifted so that they do not look into the openings of the original house.

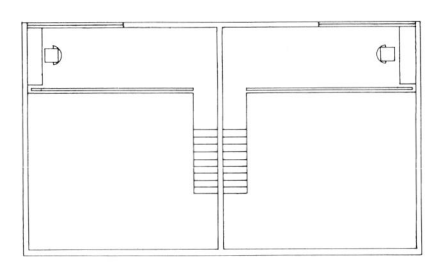

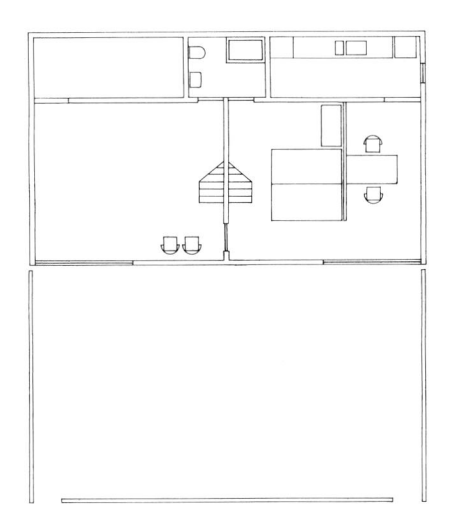

Location Soja
Design 1978–9
Construction 1979
Structure Reinforced concrete
Site area 180.4 m^2
Building area 70.1 m^2
Total floor area 94.4 m^2

Extension
Design 1986–7
Construction 1987
Structure Reinforced concrete
Building area 37.5 m^2
Total floor area 37.5 m^2

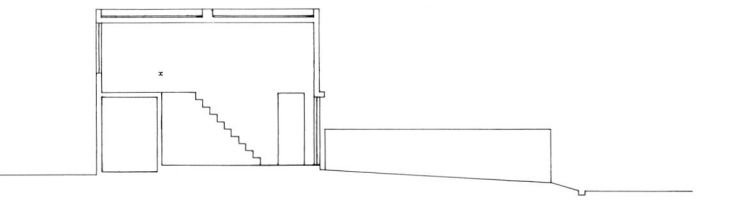

129

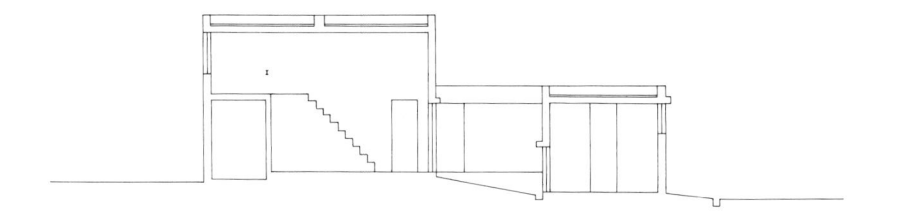

Exterior view and section showing the music room.

Plan of the main building and the extension, and interior view.

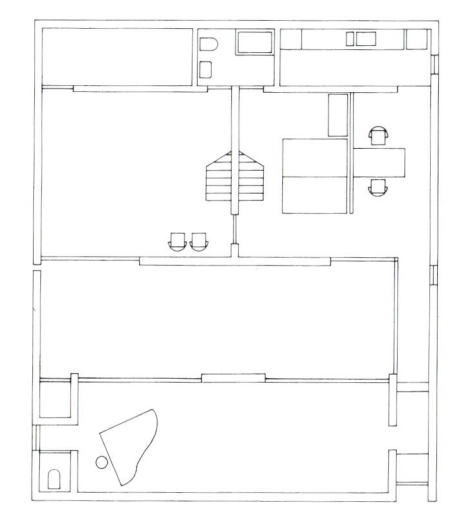

131

Fuku House

Conceptual sketch and perspective.

The complex consists of two identical concrete wings placed in parallel, two glass-block walls, and an unfinished-concrete wall surrounding the site. The two wings, designed on a module of 4.2 x 4.2 metres, are two-storeys high and contain private spaces. They employ frames divided into four equal squares.

The innermost of the two glass-block walls is flat and delineates one side of the courtyard. The curved outermost one is actually a series of concrete frames into which glass blocks are set. The space between the two is the hall. The courtyard, which shows further geometric treatment, is cut off from the environment. Parking space is located beneath this zone, where it contributes to the multi-level nature of the house and serves a practical function.

Location Wakayama
Design 1978–9
Construction 1979–80
Structure Reinforced concrete
Site area 800 m^2
Building area 345 m^2
Total floor area 483.6 m^2

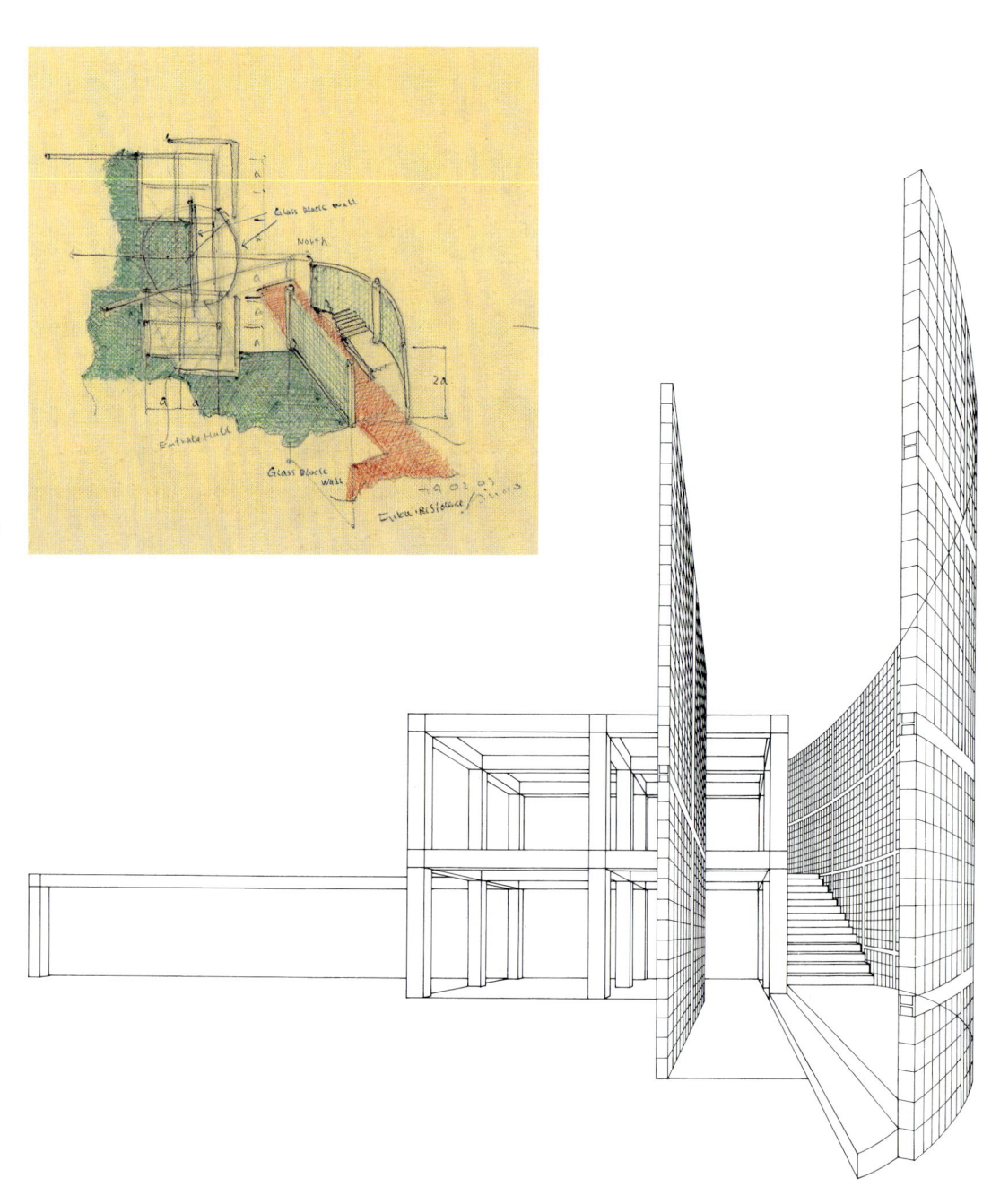

Floor plans, section, aerial view of the building and detail of the ceiling of the curved wall.

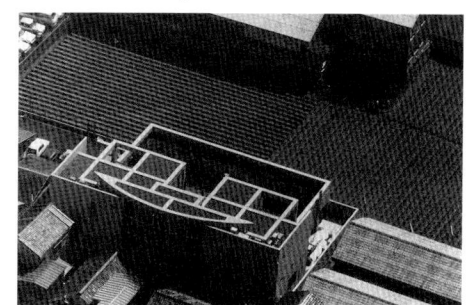

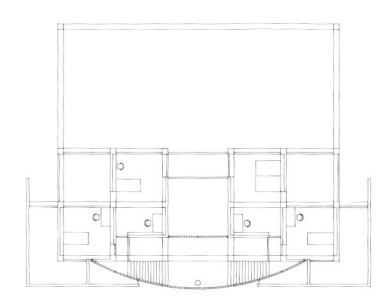

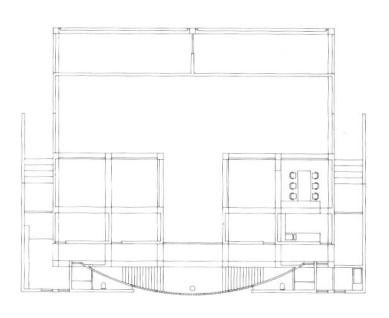

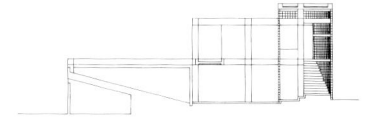

Rokko Housing I

Conceptual sketch, section, axonometric and site plan.

This building is located in a residential district at the foot of Kobe's Rokko Mountains, and its site is a south-facing 60-degree slope from which there is a panoramic view from Osaka Bay to the port of Kobe. To avoid the havoc wrought on nature by cutting out stepped building lots, it was determined to take a fresh approach to the relationship between building and nature. In order to merge the structure into its verdant surroundings, it was necessary to dig it into the ground and restrain its height.

The building is composed of a group of units, each measuring 5.4 x 4.8 metres. In section it follows the slope and in plan it is symmetrical. In stepping up the slope, gaps are intentionally created to relate to each other and serve as a plaza. The dry areas at the edges of the buildings serve as mechanical spaces and promote ventilation and insulation. The twenty units piled up on the face of the slope are all different in type and size, although each one has a terrace affording many different views. Variety is introduced among the dwellings by the asymmetry occurring in the structure as a result of the irregular topography.

A new feature for housing complex life has been introduced with this project; each unit has direct access to the outer road. Running within the building itself, the outer road becomes the axis around which the dwellings are assembled. The surrounding green plants invade the architecture, whose concrete geometric forms emphasize artifice and render nature more conspicuous, its beauty more intense.

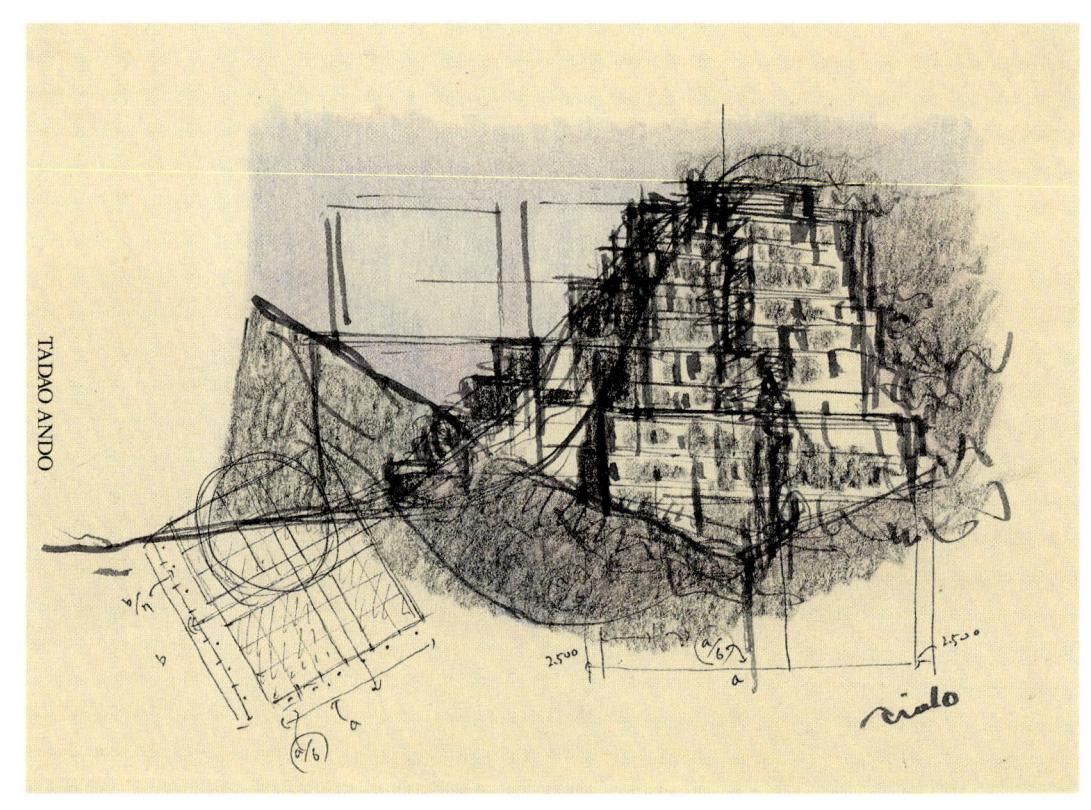

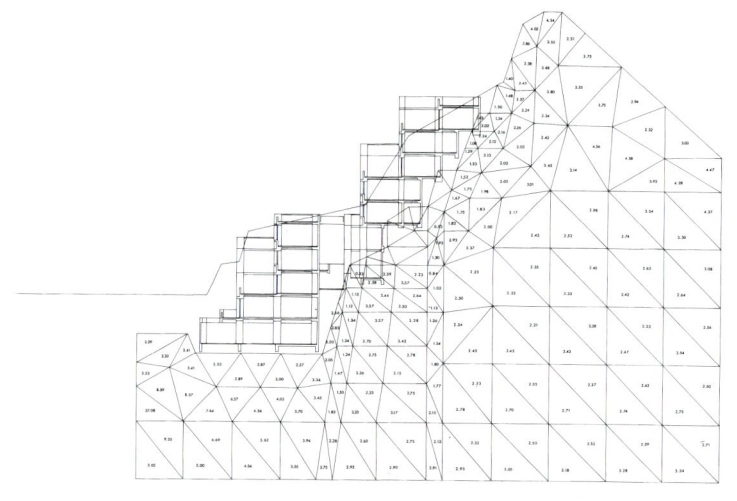

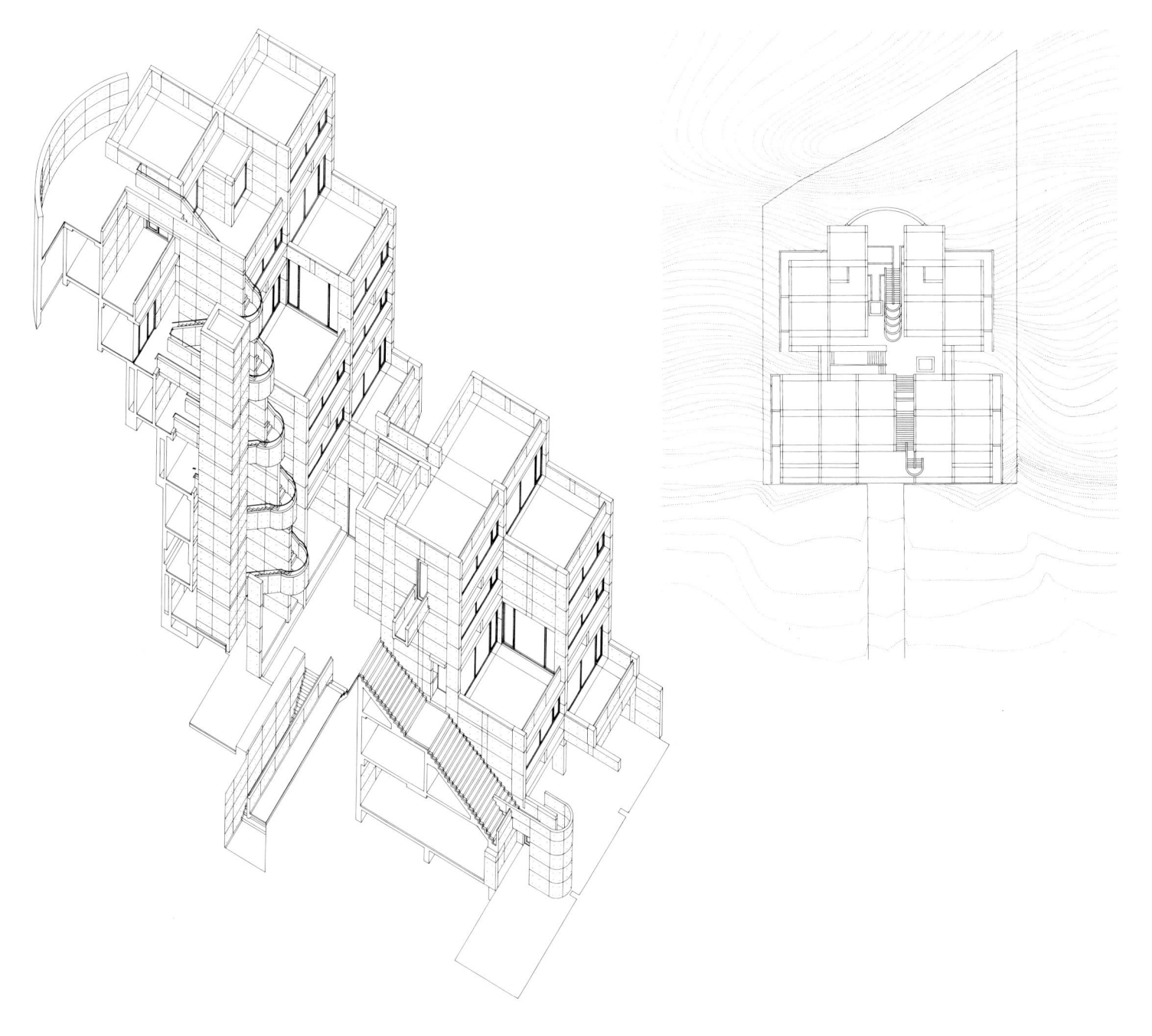

Overall and aerial views of the building, and axonometric showing its relation to Mount Rokko.

Location Kobe
Design 1978–81
Construction 1981–3
Structure Reinforced concrete
Site area 1,852 m²
Building area 668 m²
Total floor area 1,779 m²

137

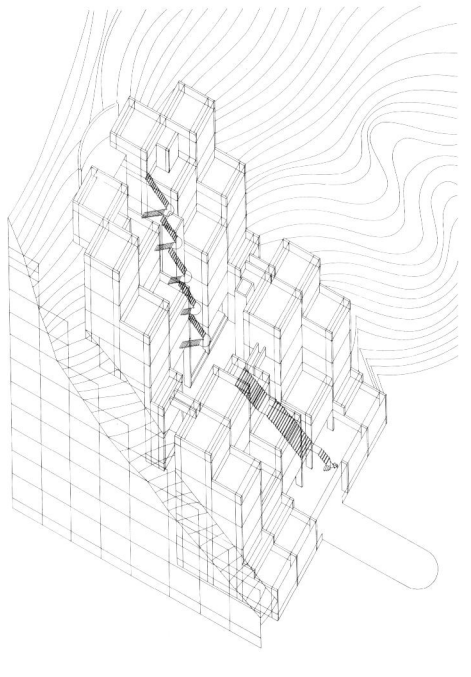

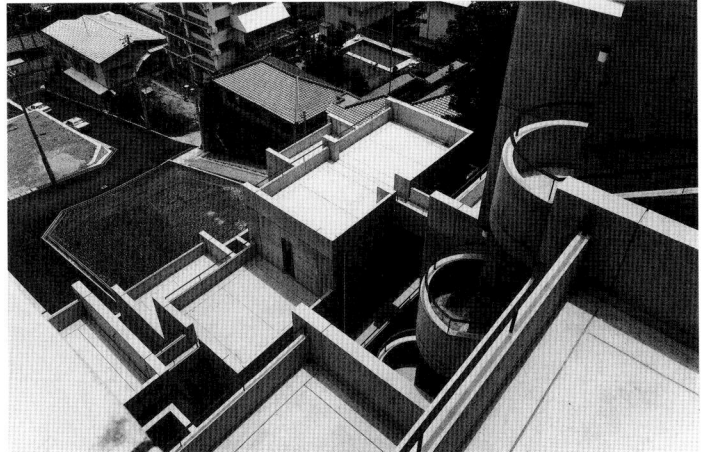

Views of the housing complex.

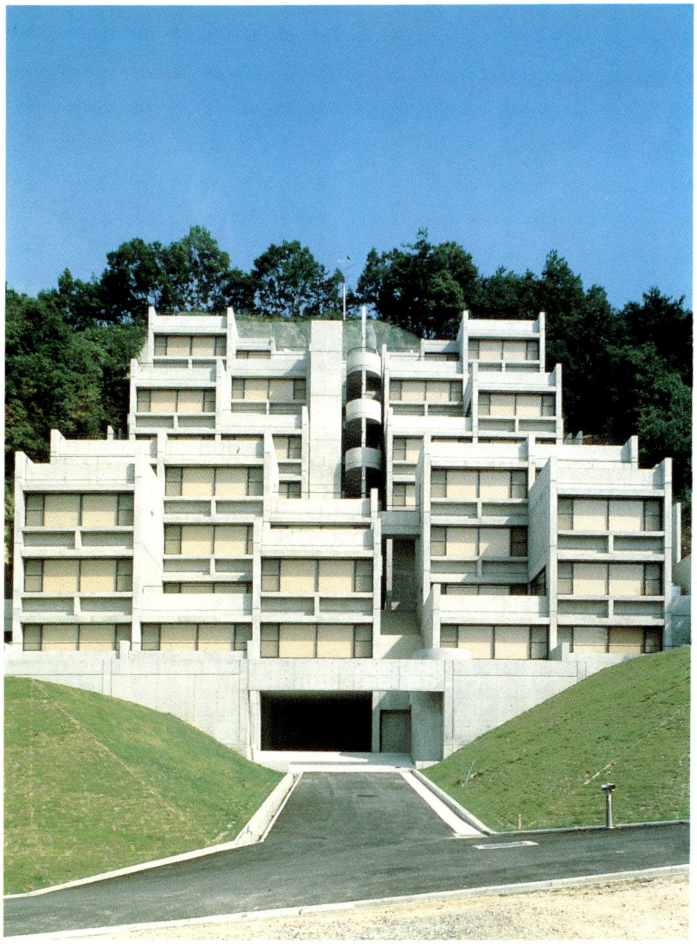

Views showing the interior and circulation space, and detail of the principal elevation.

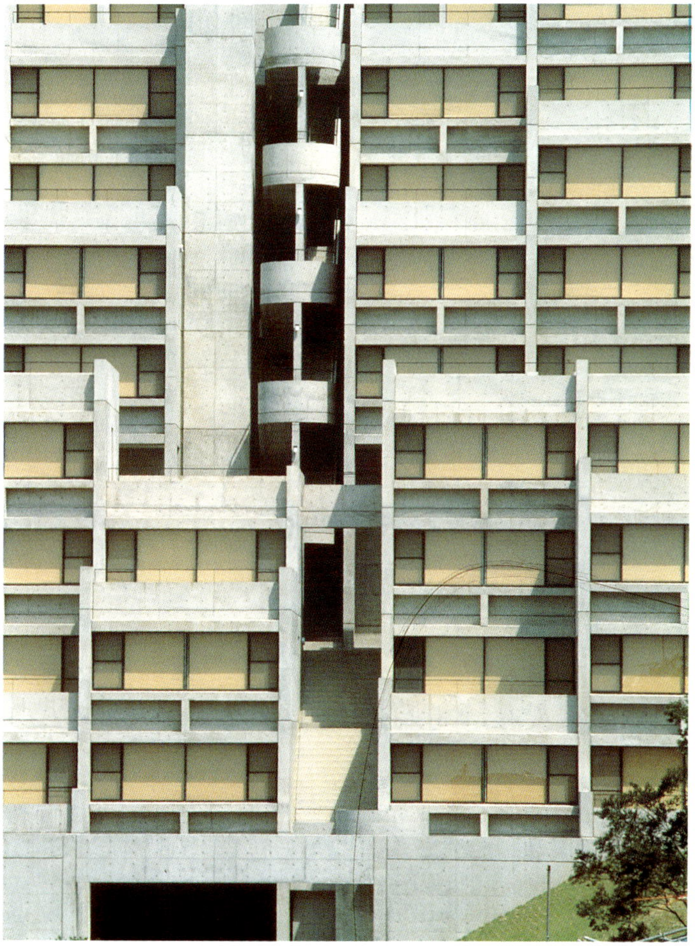

Rin's Gallery

Views of the building from the street and of the main staircase, plans and section.

The twin rectangular buildings of this commercial complex sit on a square site. They are faced in brick and are distinguished by their askew sloping roofs. Exterior stairways and circulation spaces link the two structures which themselves are in reinforced concrete. Inside each building, the interior spaces are organized around four thick columns which form the four corners of a square in plan.

Location Kobe
Design 1979
Construction 1980–81
Structure Reinforced concrete
Site area 703.7 m²
Building area 361.6 m²
Total floor area 1,594.9 m²

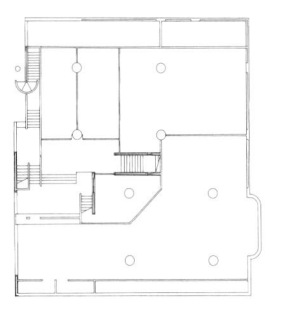

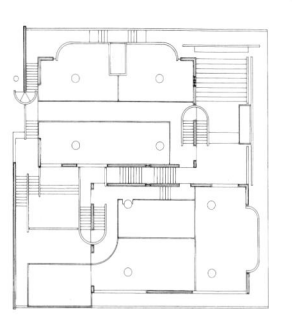

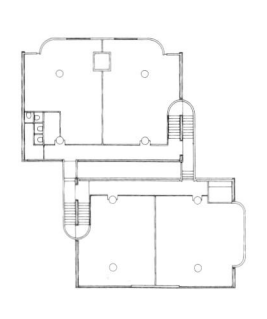

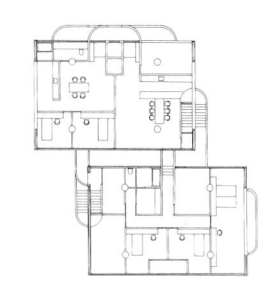

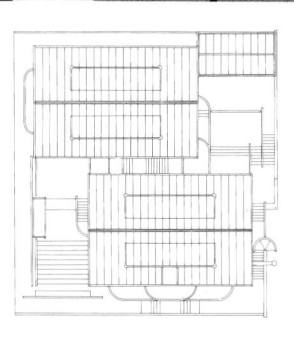

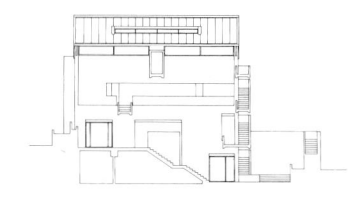

Detail of the entrance.

Koshino House and Extension

Conceptual sketches, view of the exterior wall and plans.

Two concrete boxes are located on a verdant slope in a national park, and placed side by side so as to respect the surrounding trees. Although the house seems to be an autonomous structure, it responds to its natural surroundings. The two boxes are linked by an underground corridor which is adjacent to a courtyard. Of the two buildings one is two floors high, consisting of, at one level, a double-height living room, kitchen and dining room. The upper level houses the master bedroom. The second building is longer and flatter and contains a row of six rooms (children's bedrooms and a tatami room), an atrium and a bathroom. The smooth concrete around the stepped courtyard seems to float effortlessly, open to the sky, while the openings to the house along the wall facing the courtyard create points of intersection between light and shadow.

Four years after the house was built an atelier extension was added. This fan-shaped building introduces a curvilinear volume into a previously rectilinear scheme. The extension is located at the higher part of the slope and is half-buried into the ground, separated from the main building by a lawn. A narrow opening along the curved wall allows light to enter from above and casts patterns of shadows which contrast with the sharper effect of the main building. The extension completes the composition and allows for a more articulated and architectural landscape.

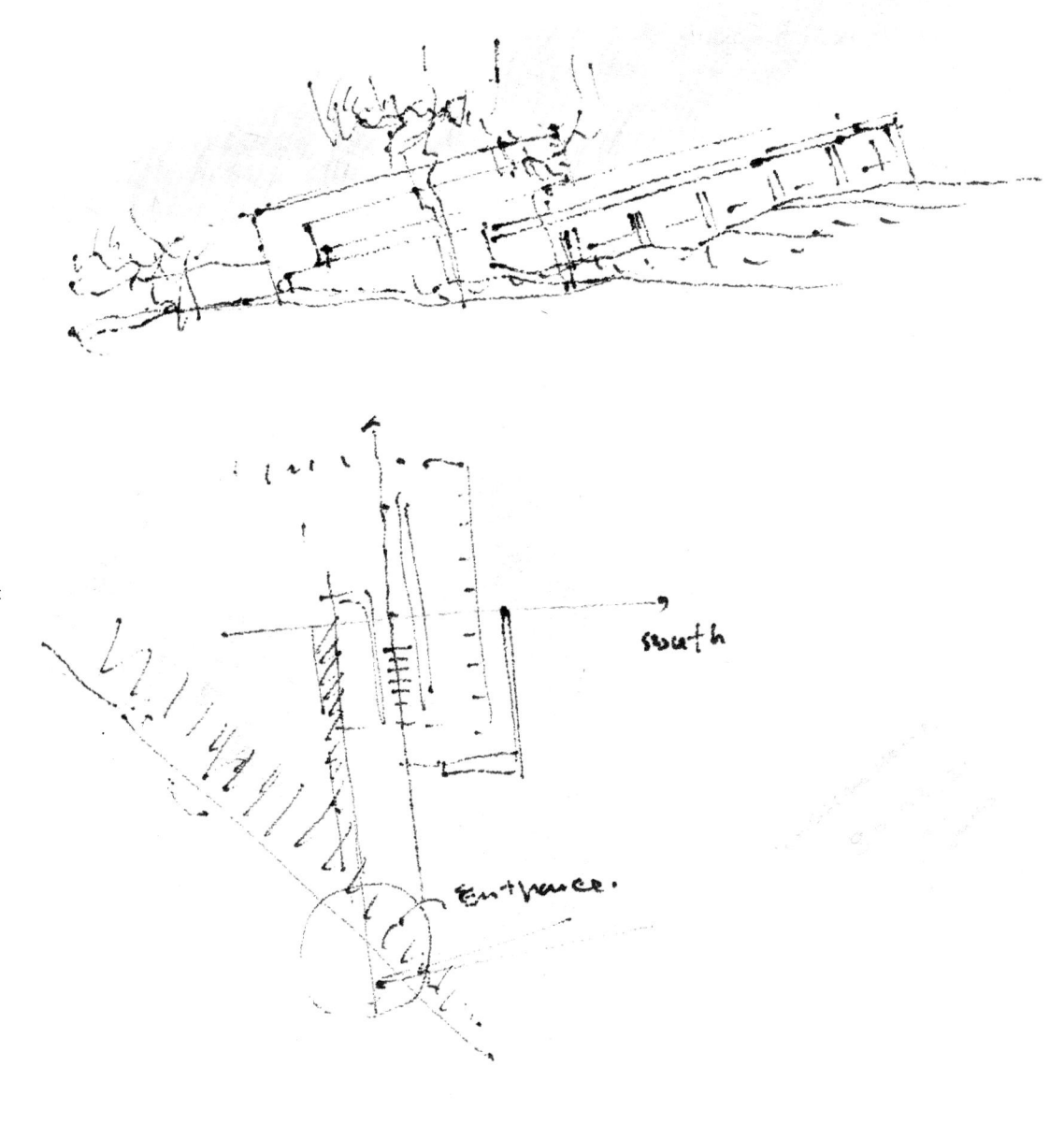

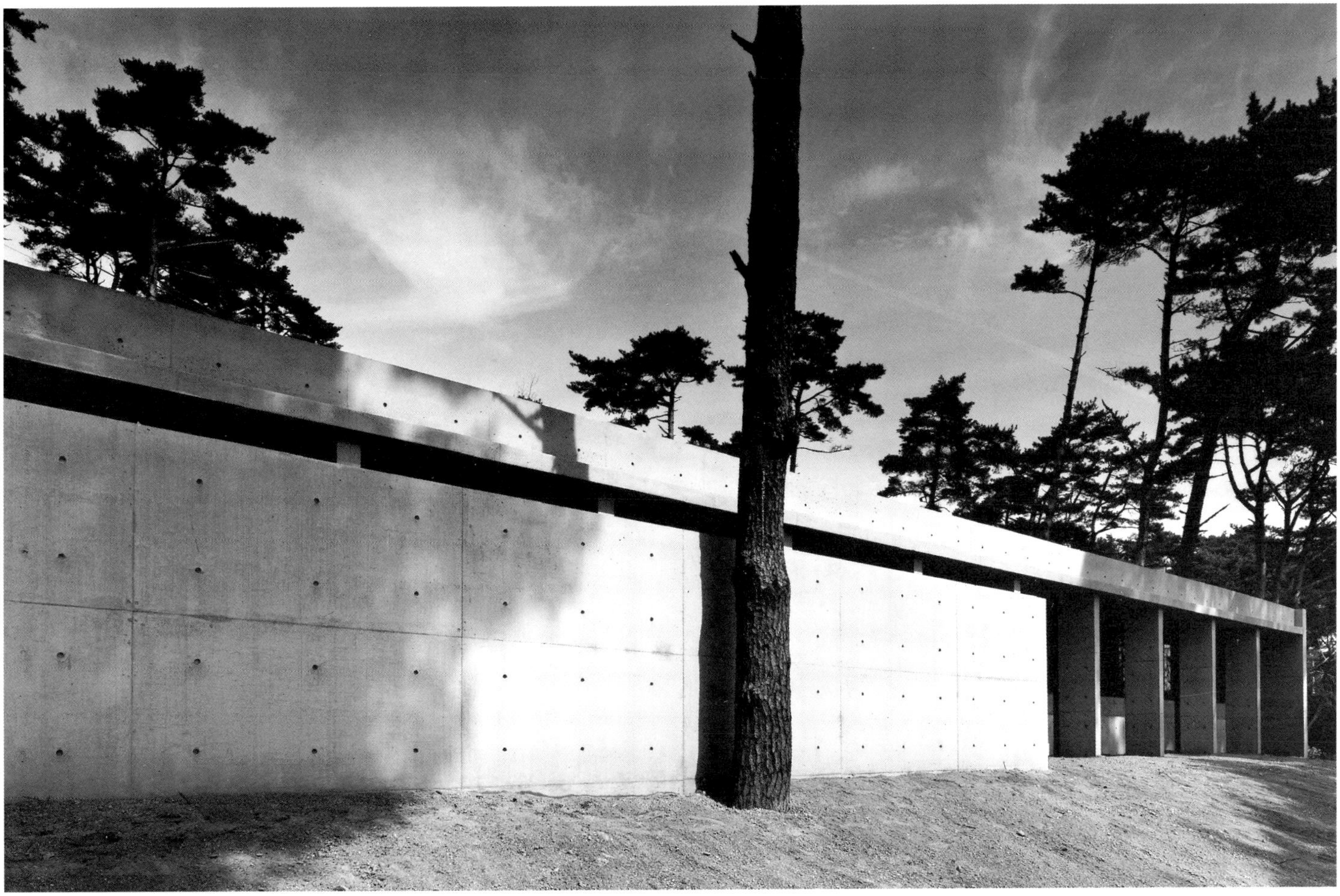

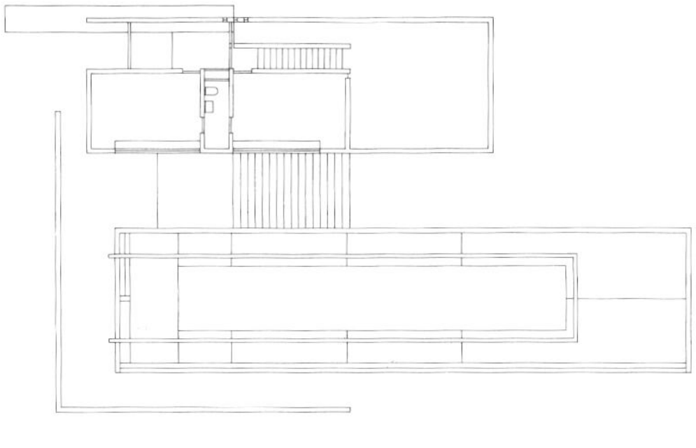

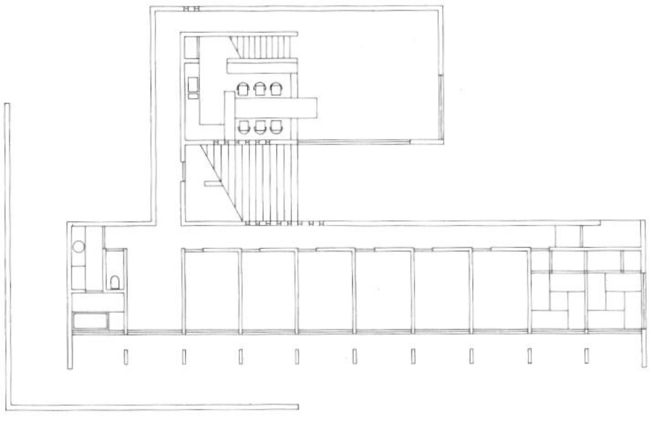

View showing the main staircase, interior view and conceptual sketches.

Location Ashiya
Design 1979–80
Construction 1980–81
Structure Reinforced concrete
Site area 1,141 m²
Building area 227.8 m²
Total floor area 241.6 m²

Extension
Design 1983
Construction 1983–4
Structure Reinforced concrete
Total floor area 52.7m²

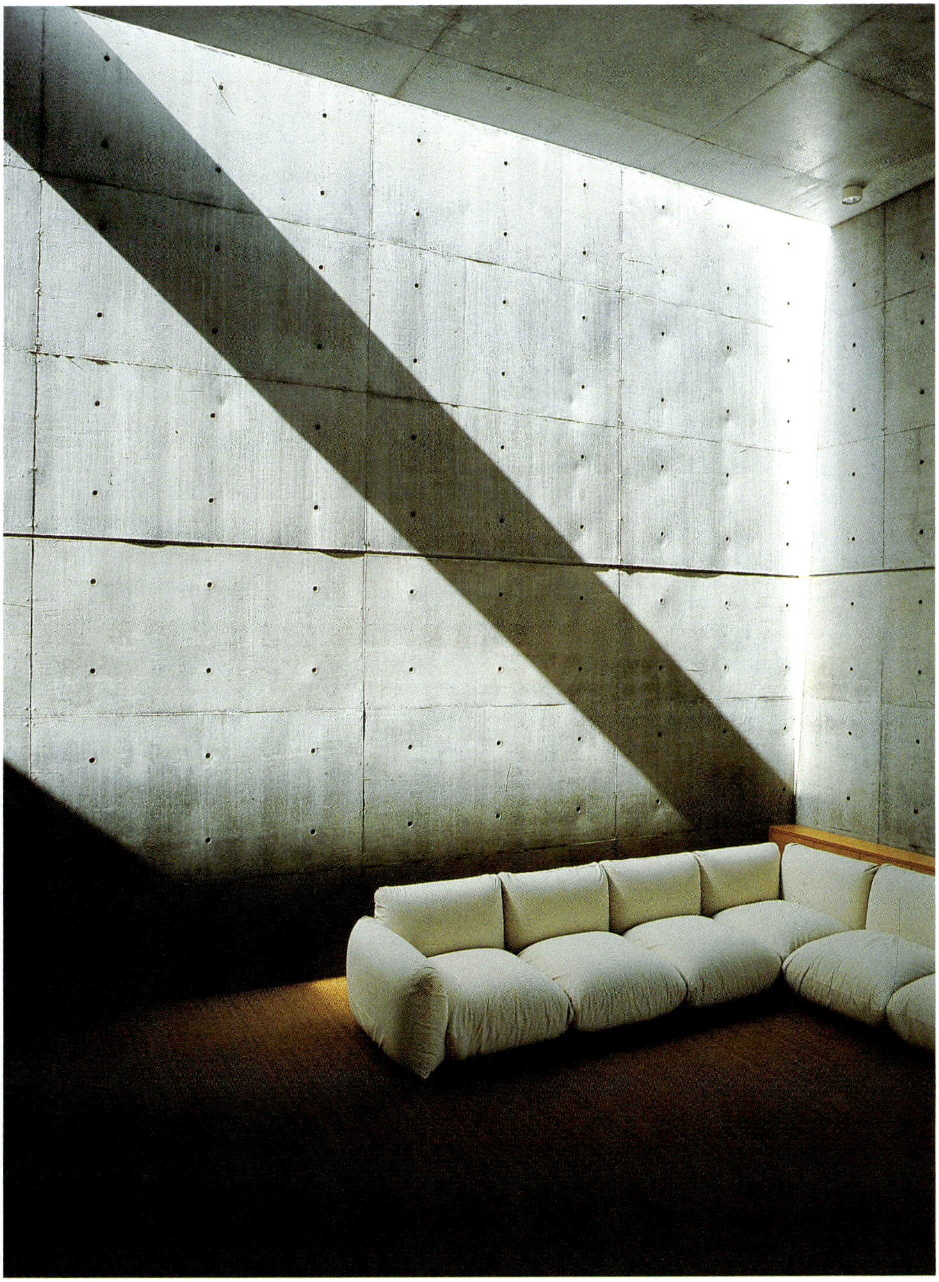

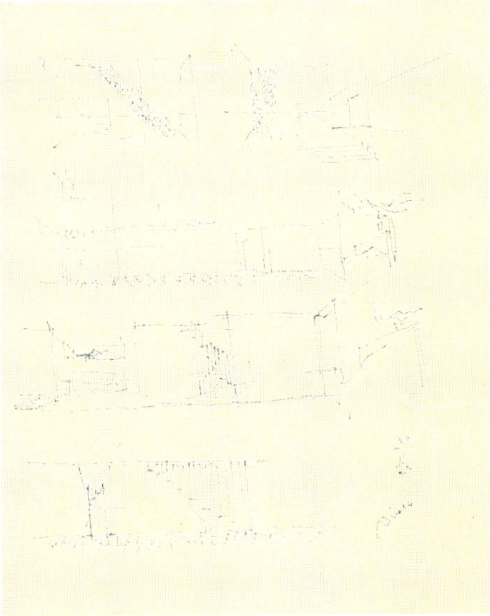

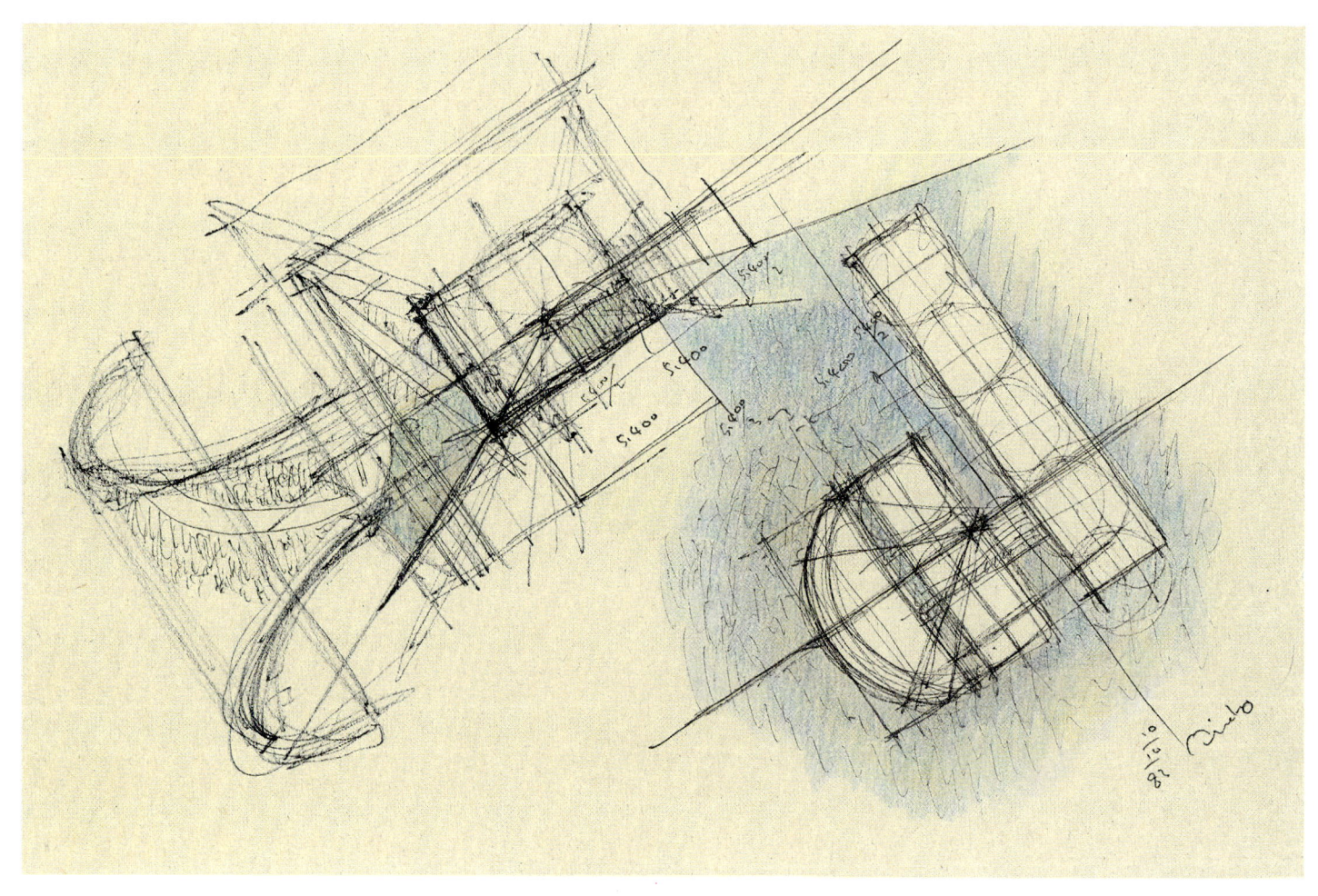

Conceptual sketches, aerial view and axonometric of the house and the extension.

148

149

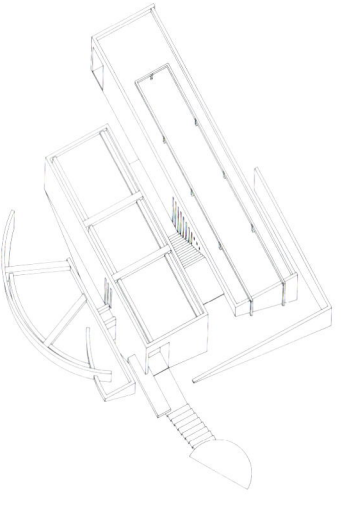

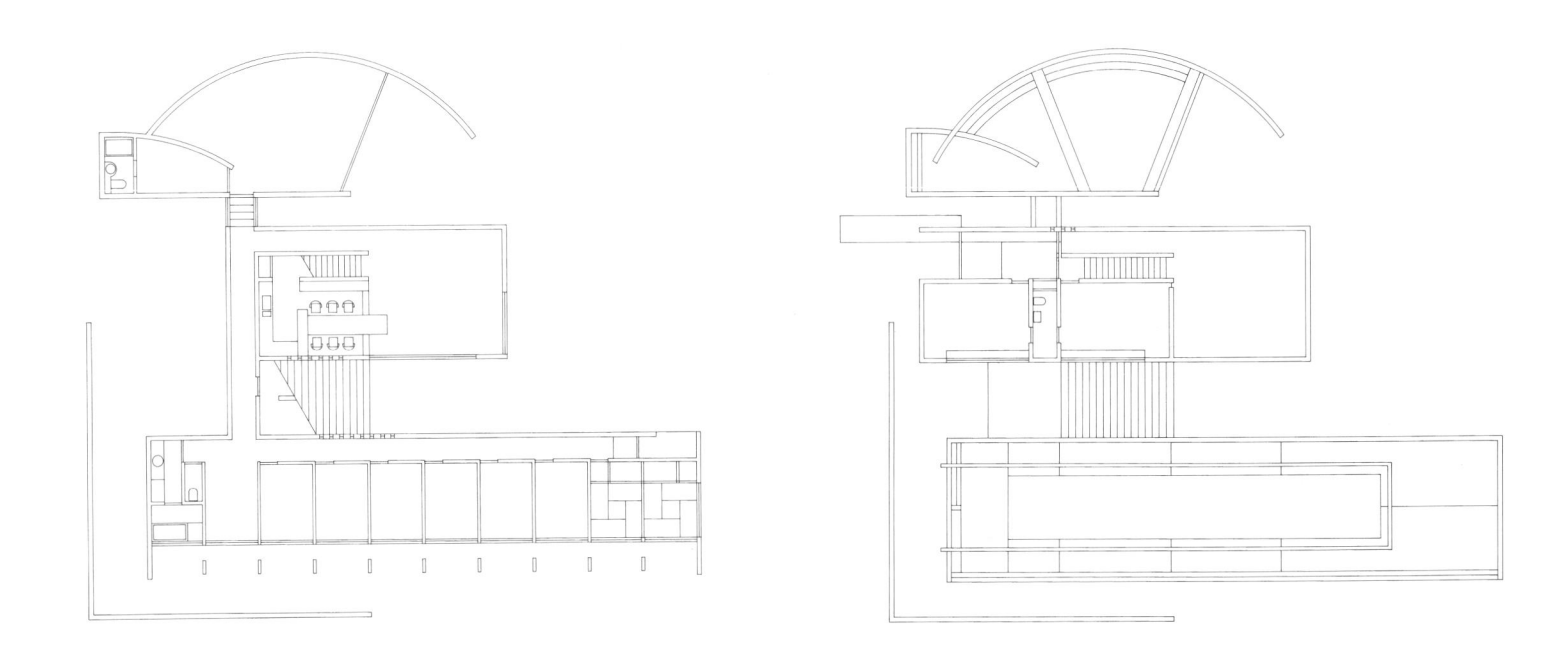

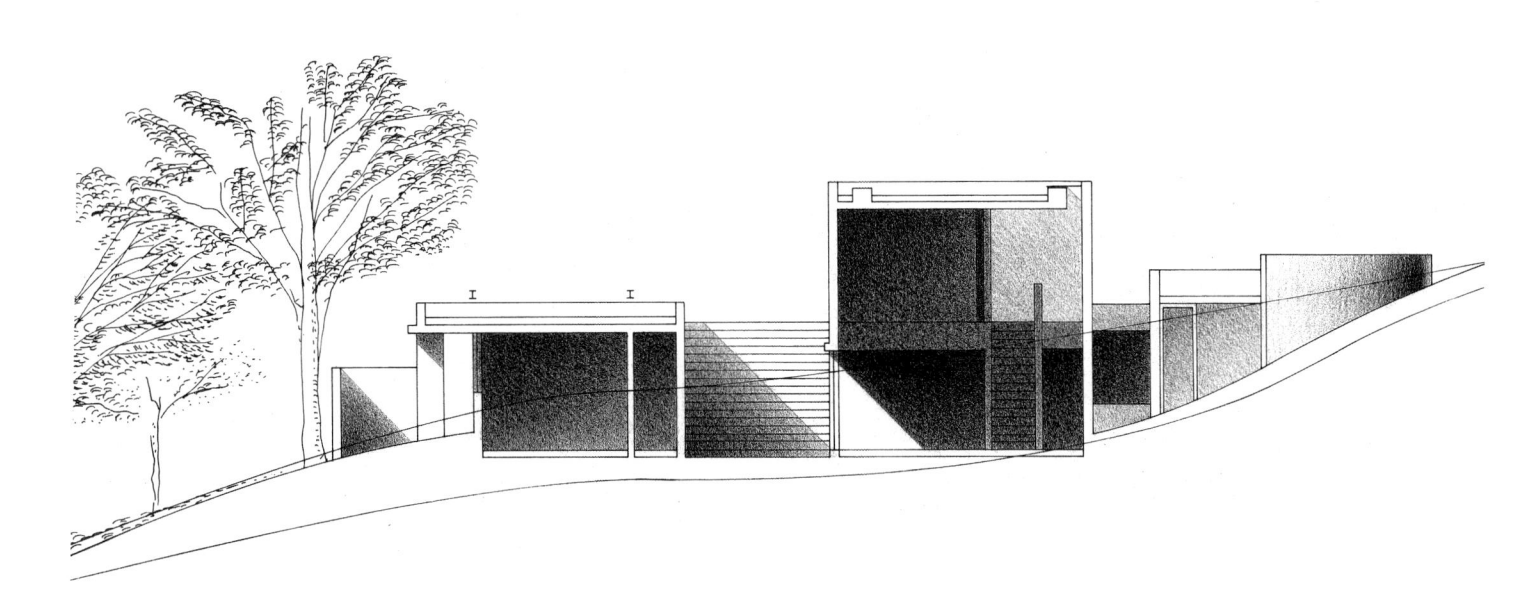

Plans showing the building and the extension, and longitudinal section.

150

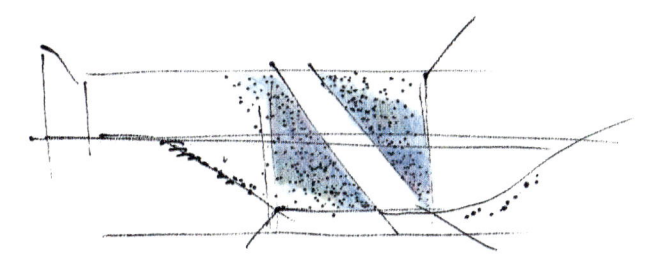

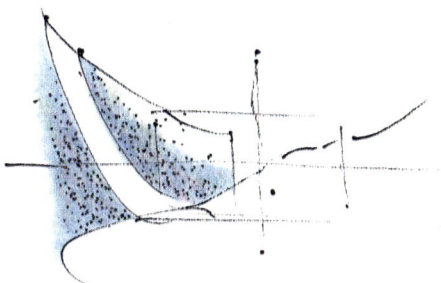

Interior view and sketches showing light in the space.

Sun Place

View of the entrance.

This project re-examines the influences of a bank's semi-public function in the city. As with most banks, this one is located in a typical shopping arcade in the city centre, but not open to the public during the busy hours of the evening. In order to redress the balance, a multi-purpose hall and two shops have also been incorporated into this scheme; the former above the bank and the latter intervening between a covered passage and the bank proper. Thus new relationships between people and the building, and between the building and the city, are encouraged.

The building consists of a uniform concrete frame, which is the skeletal frame of the spatial organization, the wall and the aluminium panel which serves as an external definer. Forming an independent arc, the aluminium panel encloses a common space inside the building and is designed as part of the cityscape. The whole building is so composed as to welcome the externality of the passage into its interior.

Location Takamatsu
Design 1979–80
Construction 1981–2
Structure Reinforced concrete
Site area 663.7 m^2
Building area 551.2 m^2
Total floor area 1,793.2 m^2

Plans, axonometric and view of the skylight.

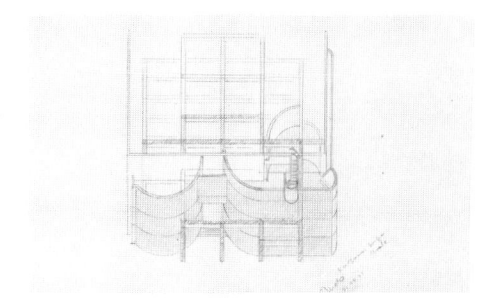

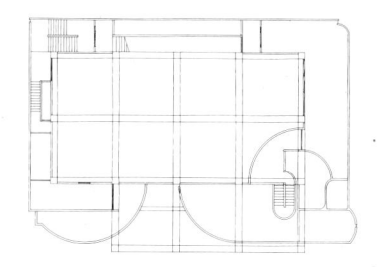

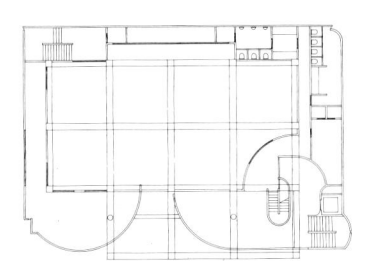

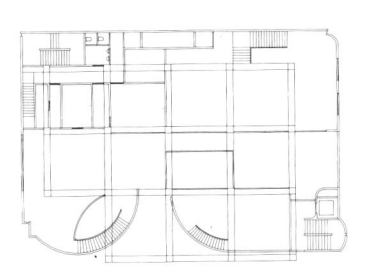

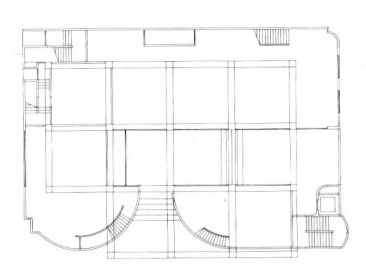

153

Atelier in Oyodo I   *Conceptual sketches and axonometric.*

This building in the centre of Osaka was originally designed in 1972 for a family of four. It was built on a narrow 47-square-metre strip of land next to a wooden tenement house erected before World War II. A three-storey volume, it was organized around an atrium that stretched the full height of the building. Sunlight penetrated through a skylight. However, it was the quality rather than the quantity of light that was explored here. Ten years after it was built Tadao Ando bought the building and converted it into his studio. He enlarged it by expanding onto a neighbouring site and by adding to it in height.

Location Osaka
Design 1980
Construction 1981
Structure Reinforced concrete
Site area 115.6 m^2
Building area 79 m^2
Total floor area 194.54 m^2

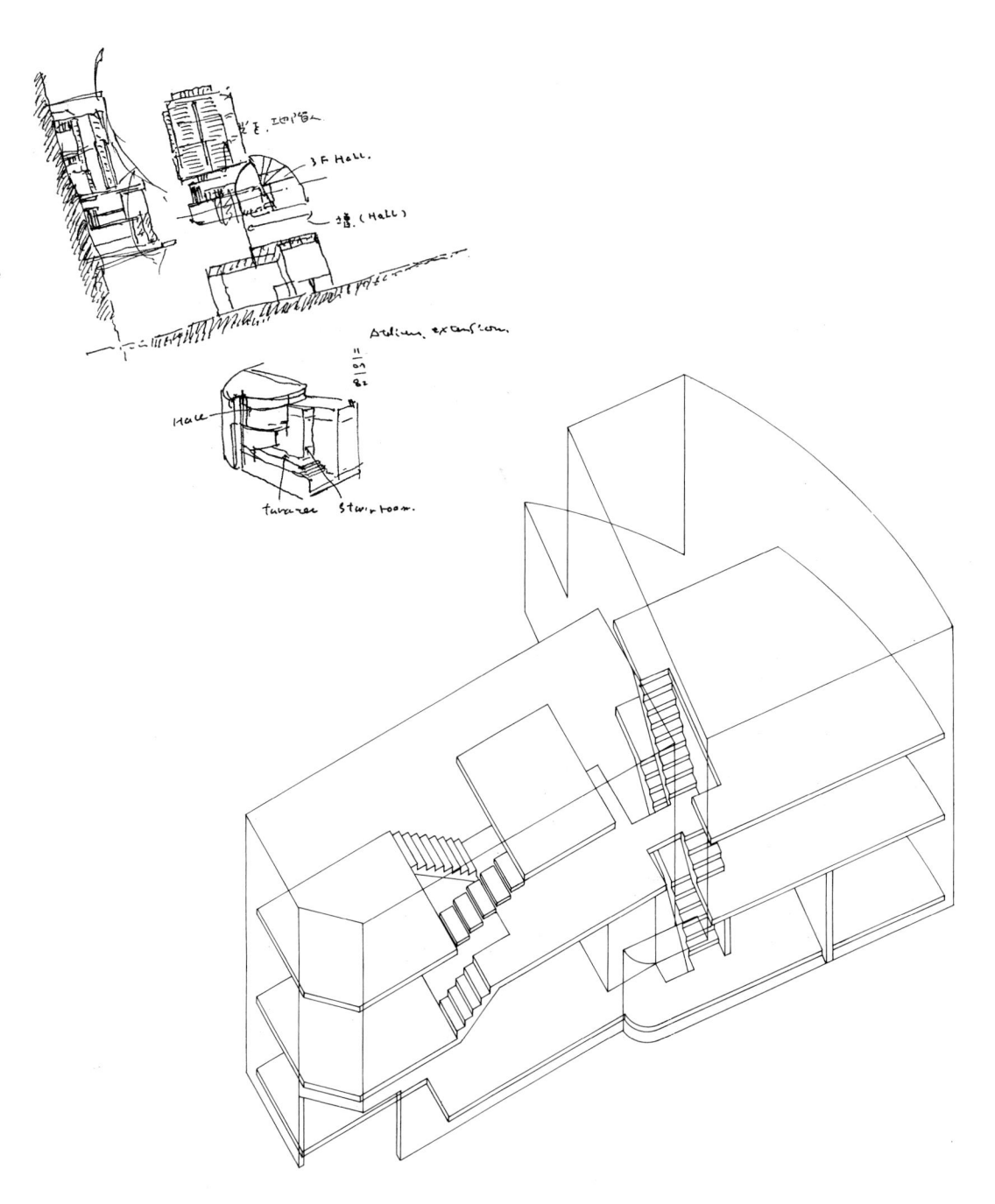

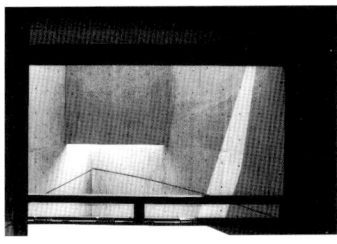

View of the entrance and interior views at different times of the day.

155

Nakanoshima Project I – Osaka City Hall

Sectional elevation and view showing the roof volumes.

This project addresses the question of how Osaka City Hall, completed in 1921, might be preserved and restored. A historical building can only effectively be revitalized when its environment, and even the city structure, are also protected and clarified. The proposal calls for preserving the Hall's facade, as well as that of the Bank of Japan opposite the building.

The original concept of the building's interior – an innovative one being Japan's first public building to organize the various functions around the entrance hall – must also be brought to life and reinforced. The new structure was envisaged as responding to the city around it by enveloping and, at the same time, liberating its interior space. It would therefore produce an internal exterior both in plan and section.

Within the colonnaded frame of the new hall, the historical facade and hall stand independently. Enclosing this richly historical structure within a simple, modern, uniform grid frame brings the dichotomy of old and new to the fore and stimulates a dialogue with events of the past.

Location Osaka
Design 1980

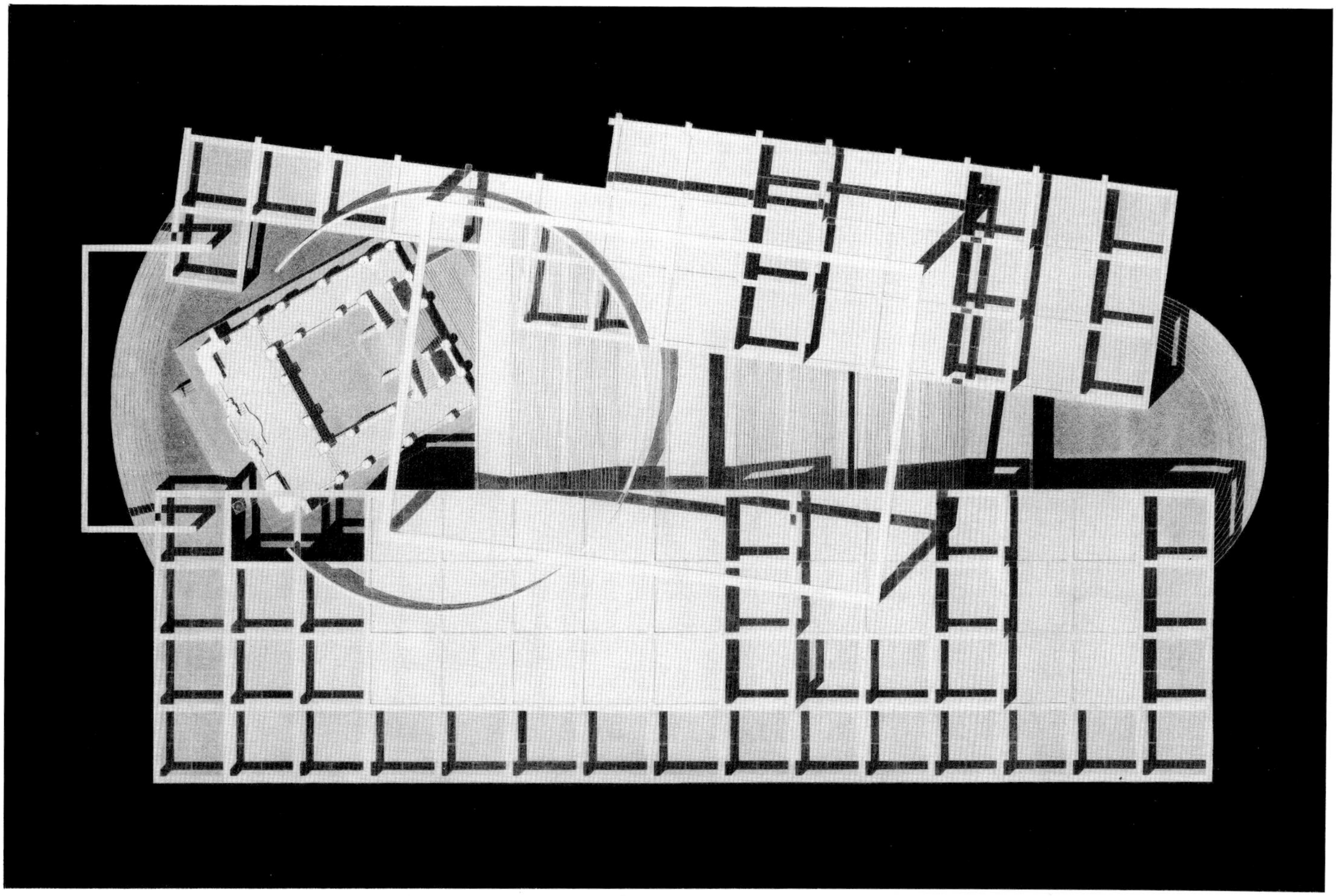

Festival

Conceptual sketches, view showing the building in its urban context, and axonometric.

This commercial complex stands in the heart of Naha City in Okinawa, located at the southernmost extremity of the Japanese archipelago. The building composition is that of a cube, the sides of which are 36 metres and follow the boundaries of the site. This cube is composed of an eight-storey, exposed concrete frame of equal spans, infilled by bearing walls and 200mm square perforated block screens. The atrium takes up one-fifth of the width of the building and extends from the front to the back of the structure. On the top two levels is an open court, spatially articulated by the concrete frame, and a planted banyan tree which is native to Okinawa.

The atrium space, extending the full height of the building, can be glimpsed from the street through a perforated concrete-block screen. Although the building is externally simple in its geometry, inside it has its own complex landscape. It is an urban 'alcove' – an active environment with a distinctive ambience that opens itself to the city.

Location Naha
Design 1980–83
Construction 1983–4
Structure Reinforced concrete and steel
Site area 1,658.1 m²
Building area 1,510.7 m²
Total floor area 7,936.4 m²

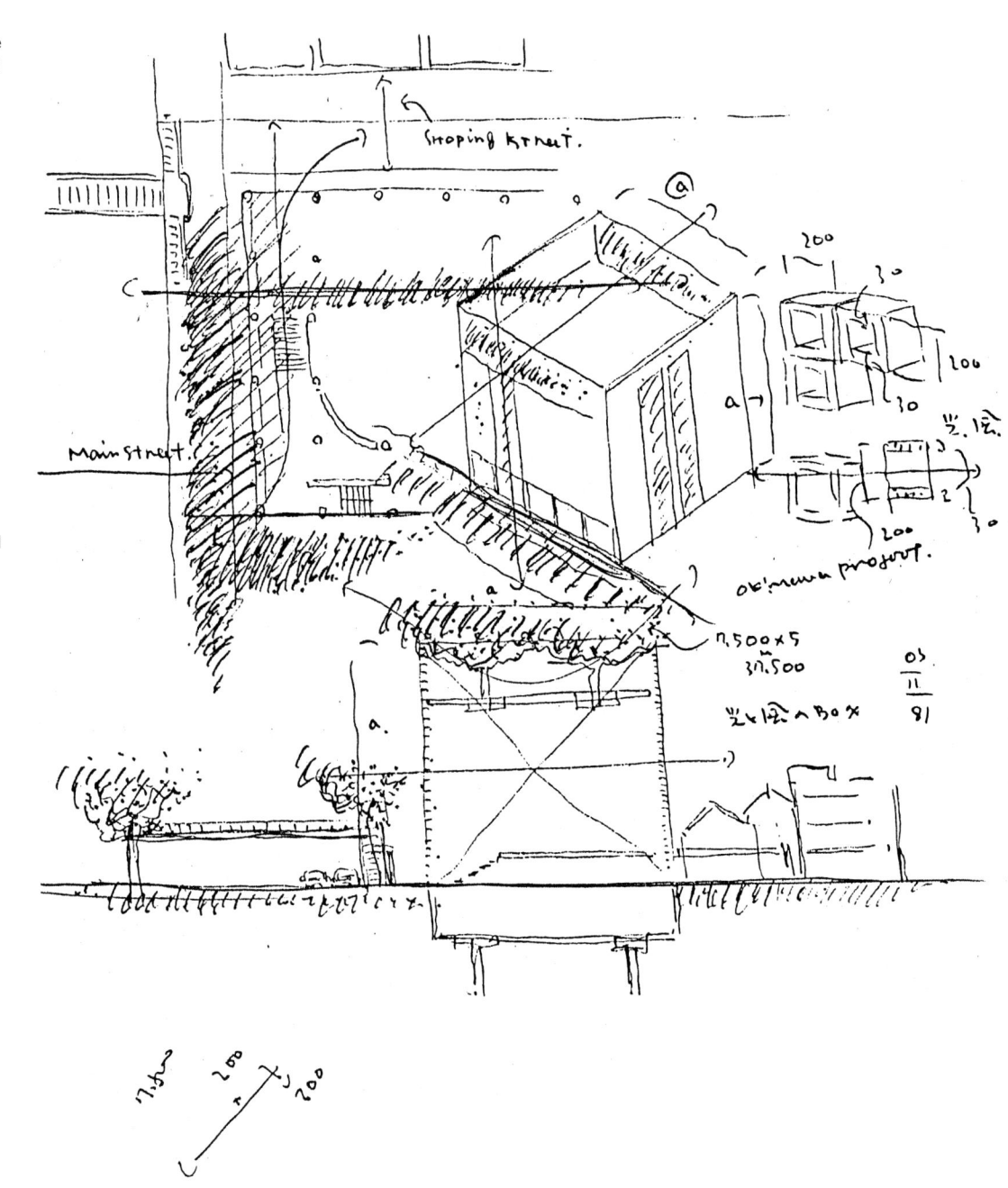

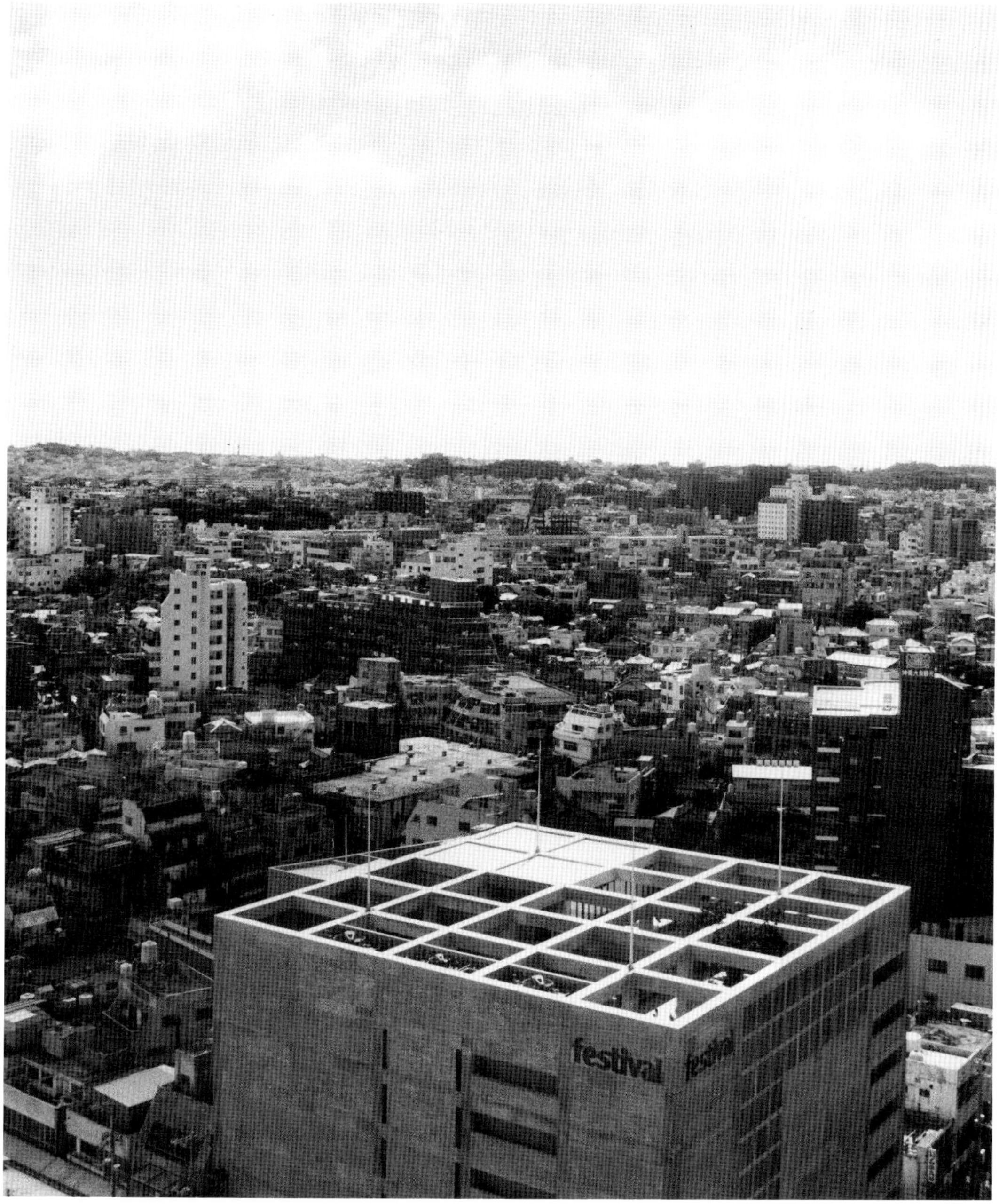
festival
festival

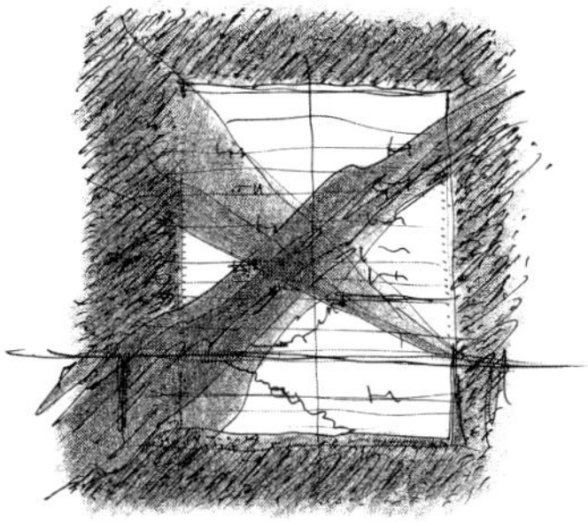

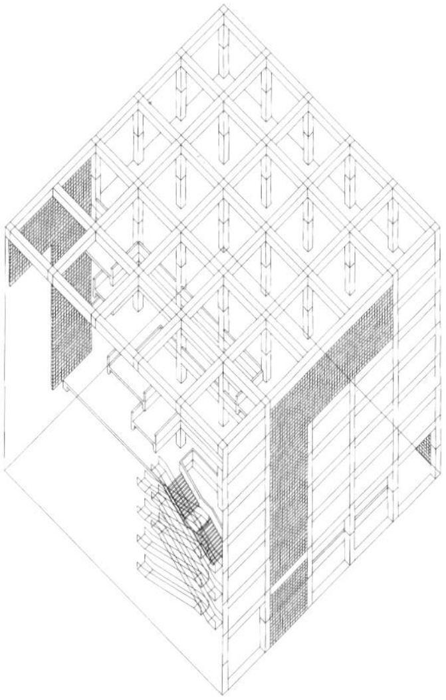

Views and perspective of the circulation spaces and the atrium.

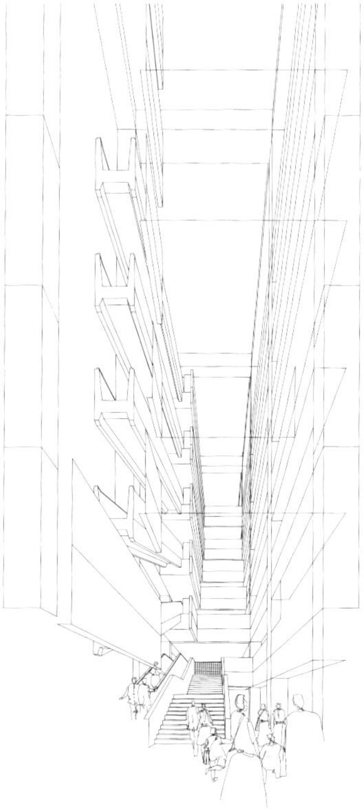

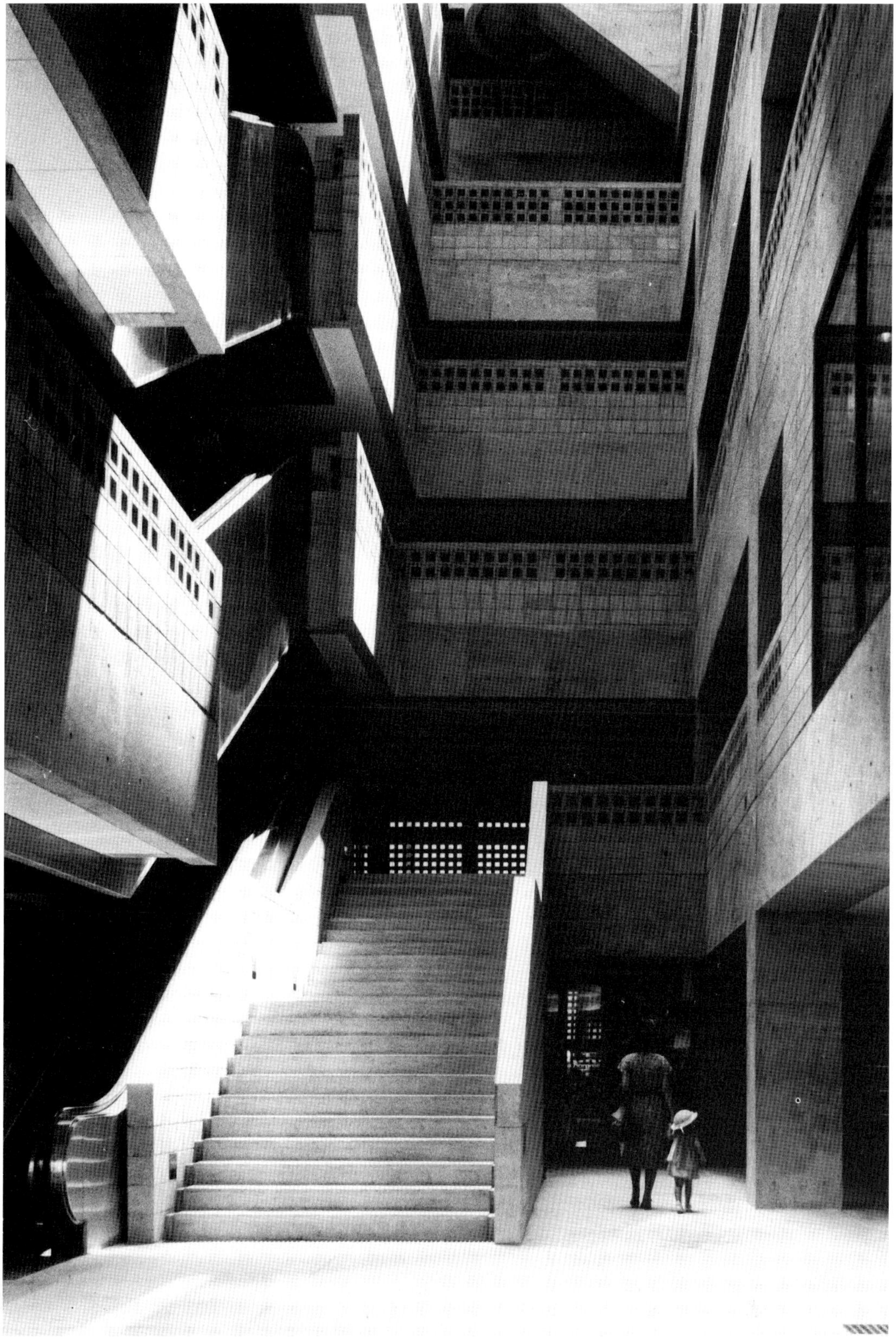

Conceptual drawing and view of the circulation spaces and the atrium below.

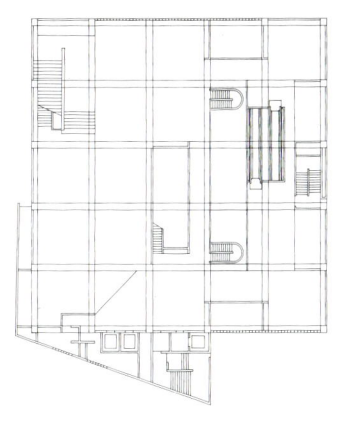

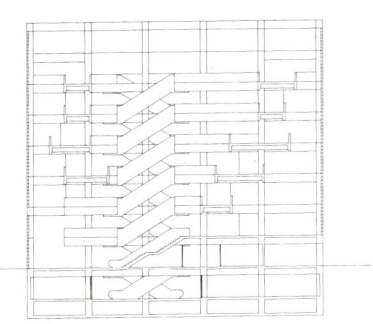

View of a meeting room, plan and section showing the stairs.

163

Kojima Housing

Overall view showing the building in its urban context, conceptual sketches and view of the entrance.

The main theme of this design was to connect three units while ensuring privacy for three households, each with its own lifestyle. The basic layout is two square-plane blocks staggered to generate spaces between them serving different public functions. The public space on the north is a two-level approach and the one on the south is a common-use courtyard.

The western block houses the owner's residence, while the eastern one contains the two rental apartments. The freestanding wall, which extends to connect with the east block, makes the approach more conspicuous and sets the complex area apart from its surroundings. The concrete walls facing the common-use court, however, are pierced with openings. Articulating between the private and the public, they simultaneously create restricted-use, void spaces for each block while leading to the common-use court, which is the focal point of the complex. Like the exterior surfaces, the interior walls, floors and ceilings are rough concrete.

The aim of this design was to see to what extent a simple space, full of varied possibilities, could be made to interweave with the residents' lifestyles through the mediation of abstracted light and wind.

Location Kurashiki
Design 1980
Construction 1981
Structure Reinforced concrete
Site area 655.3 m^2
Building area 145.6 m^2
Total floor area 238.3 m^2

165

Views of the interiors and floor plans.

167

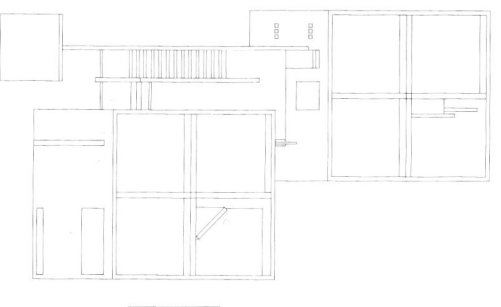

Ishii House

View of the entrance, conceptual sketch and view showing the courtyard.

An L-shaped wall is partially wrapped around the site while inside the building is a freestanding cylindrical wall. The two-storey, south-facing wing is a private zone of bedrooms. In the other wing, a gently descending stairway leads to a living room on the mezzanine level, parallel to the street. At its end, this wing faces the private wing. The different levels create a tension in the entrance, which is located where two overlapping walls slide past each other. Once past the low-ceilinged vestibule, the visitor sees the freestanding cylinder, inside which is the dining area, and a deep overhang controlling sunlight. A toplight is situated in the gap between the cylinder and the L-shaped wall, and here a second 'exterior space' unfolds within the building.

Location Hamamatsu
Design 1980–81
Construction 1981–2
Structure Reinforced concrete
Site area 371.2 m^2
Building area 154.1 m^2
Total floor area 253.3 m^2

169

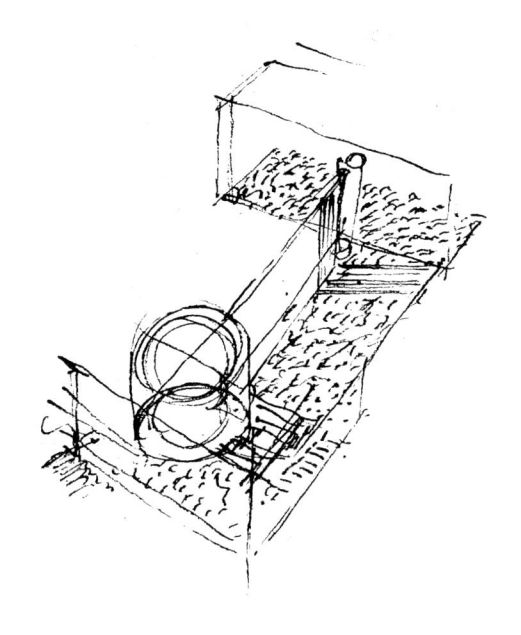

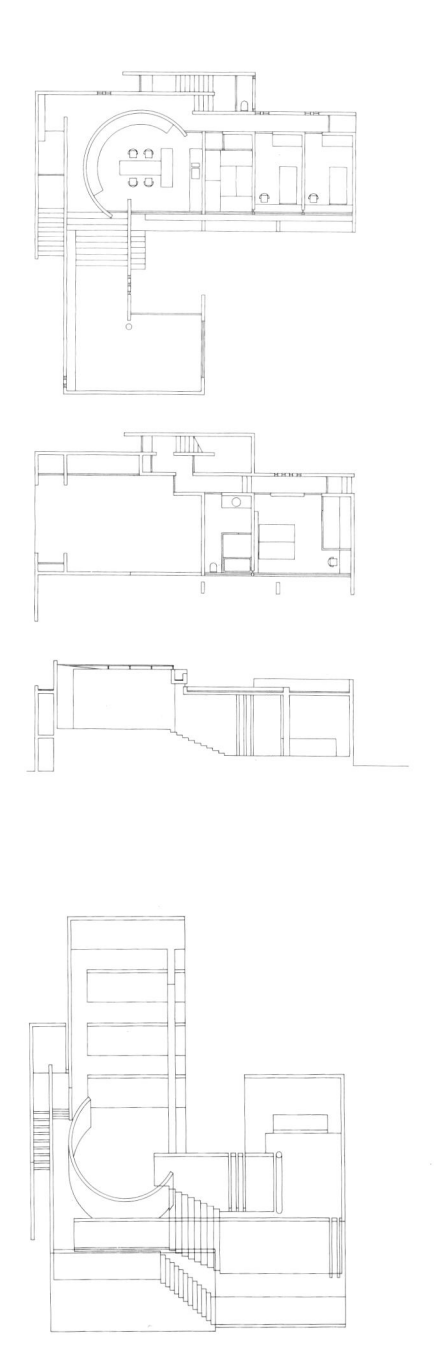

Floor plans, section and axonometric, interior view of the hallway and detail of the exterior.

170

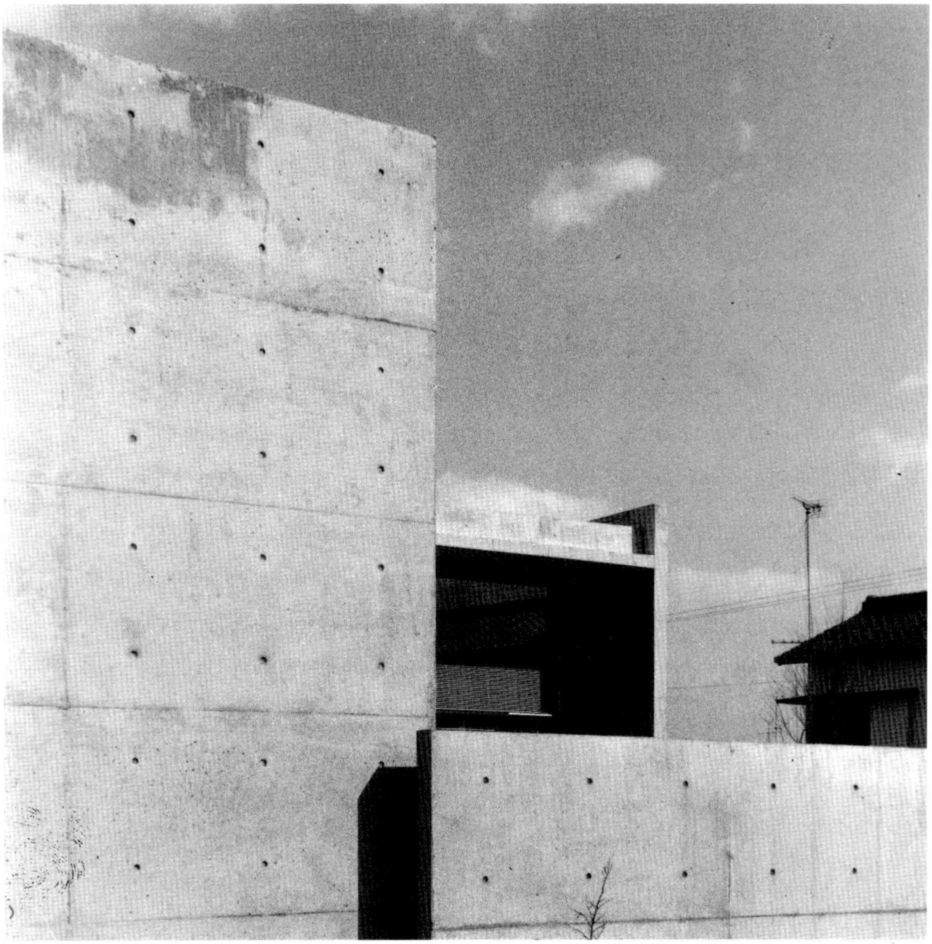

Bigi Atelier

Aerial view of the building and site plan.

The main function of this building is as an atelier for a fashion designer. Due perhaps to the hilly topography, there are, unusually, many trees left in this district, a quiet upper-income residential area with a sprinkling of embassies and fashion-related showrooms.

The building, therefore, is as restrained as possible and is integrated into its surroundings by half its volume being buried under the ground. At the same time, it creates a pure, geometrical configuration that is self-sufficient and in sharp contrast to its context. The materials used are exposed concrete and, for the curved wall, thick frosted glass.

The functional organization is centred around two multi-purpose ateliers which are large double-height spaces. The lower-floor atelier faces a sunken garden, while the upper-floor atelier is closed off on one side by the curved wall; the diffused light that penetrates it gives the interior an atmosphere of tranquility and other-worldliness.

Location Tokyo
Design 1980–82
Construction 1982–3
Structure Reinforced concrete
Site area 742.7 m^2
Building area 286.3 m^2
Total floor area 998.5 m^2

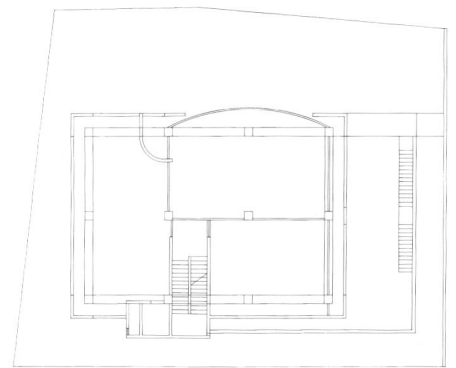

Floor plans and view showing glass wall.

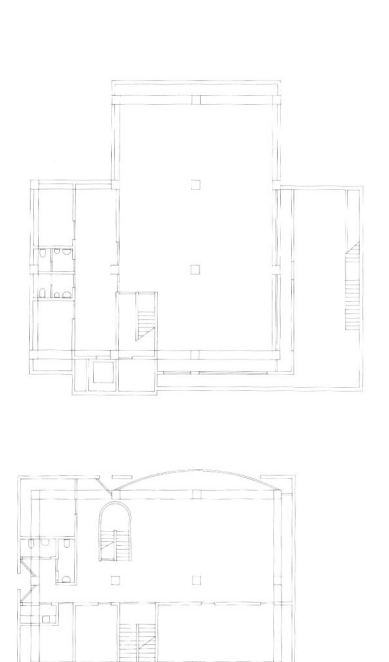

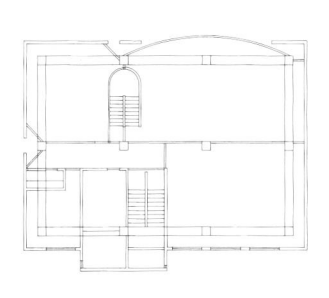

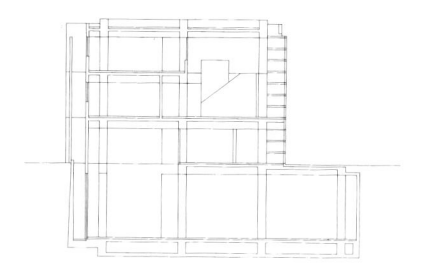

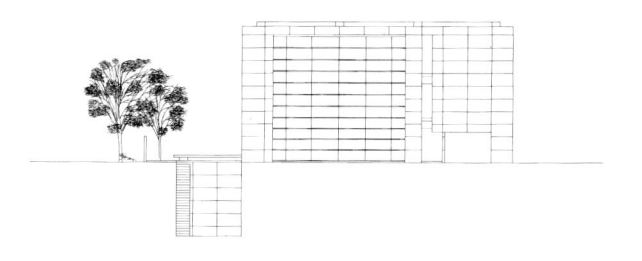

View of the garden stairs, section, elevation and interior view showing glass wall.

174

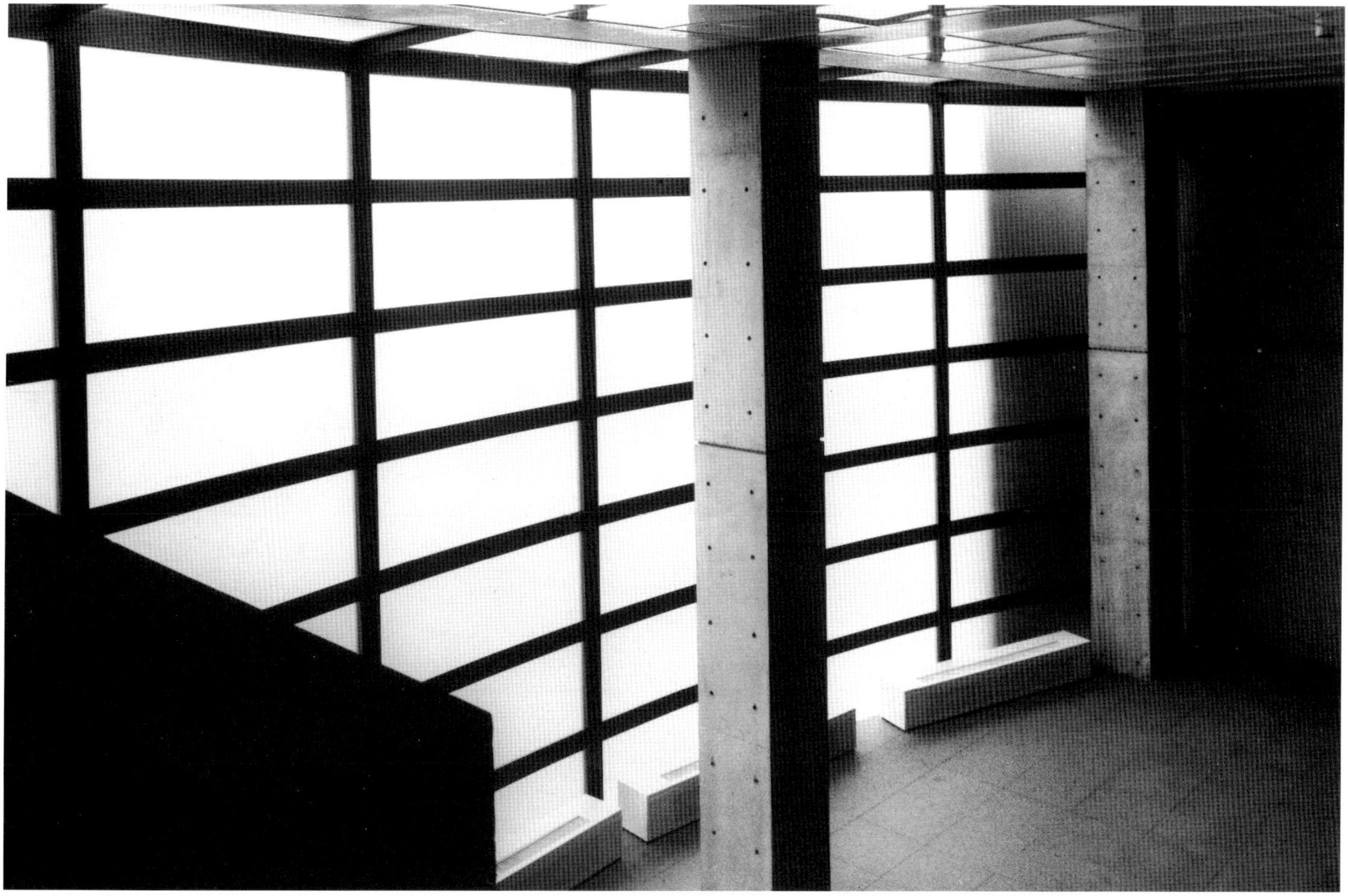

Akabane House

Conceptual sketch, view of the garden and axonometric.

Enclosed within a cubic volume, this one-family house is distinguished by the presence of an imposing stairway contained in a large rectangular reinforced concrete building. The stairs are at the centre of the composition around which are located all the spaces of the house. On the basement are the service areas and a tatami room, and on the other floors are the bathroom, kitchen and living room and bedrooms, all of which have a view onto the courtyard. The exterior walls are punctuated by long, narrow windows which both allow light to filter into the building and permit a view to the courtyard.

Location Tokyo
Design 1981–2
Construction 1982
Structure Reinforced concrete
Site area 240.8 m²
Building area 61.1 m²
Total floor area 119 m²

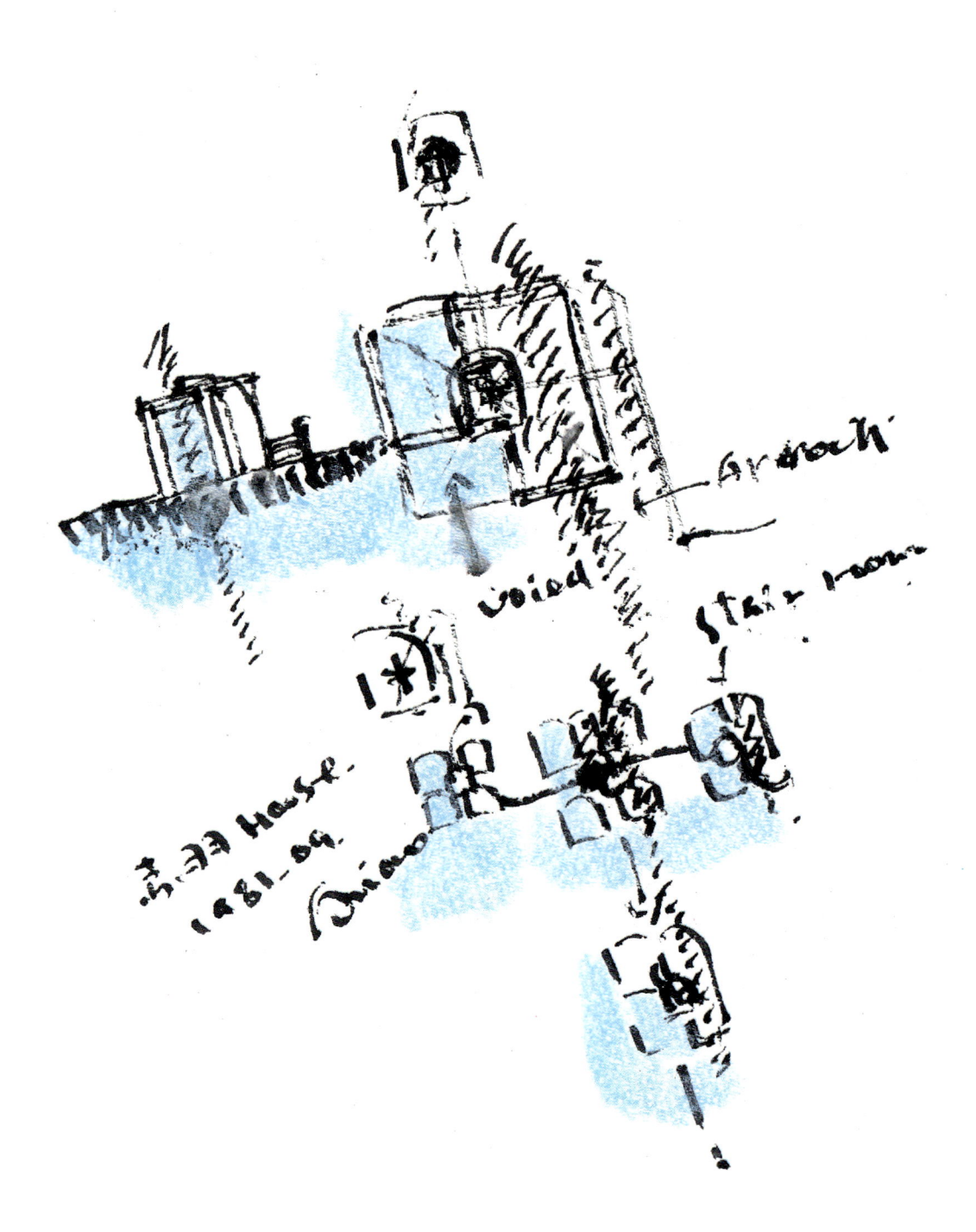

177

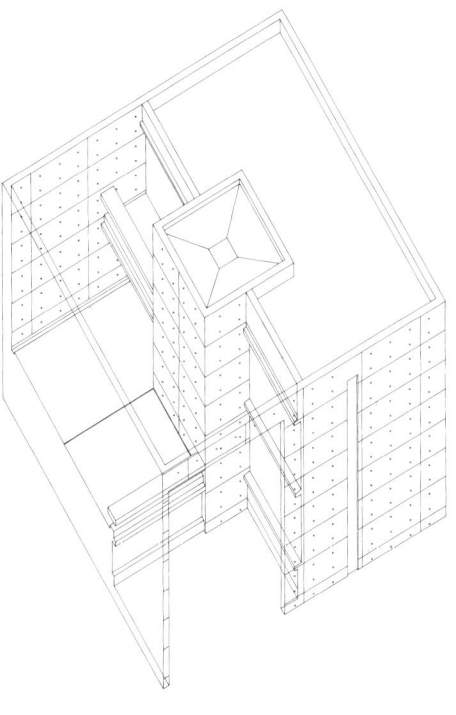

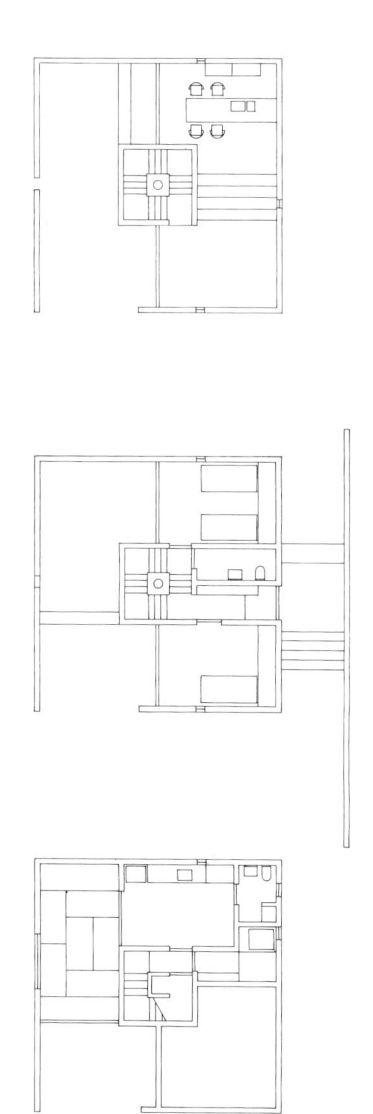

Floor plans, views of the dining area and courtyard.

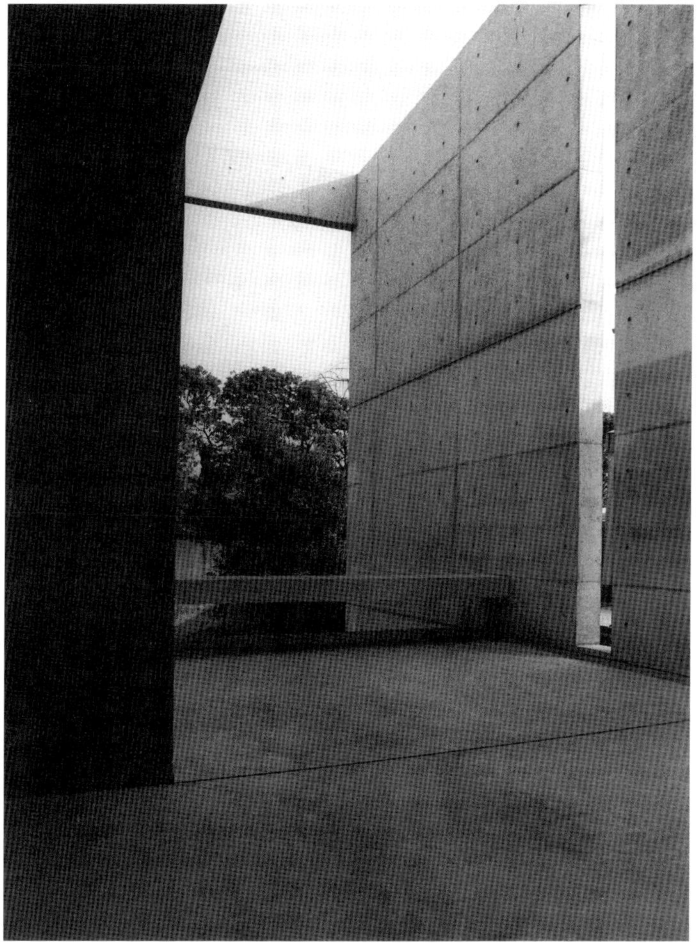

Umemiya House

Conceptual sketch, section and site plan.

This detached extension to an older house stands at the top of a southern slope overlooking the Seto Inland Sea. The overall plan is composed of two overlapping squares and accommodates a studio and dwelling rooms. In order to take advantage of the views, the dining room, which is at the centre of daily life activities, is on the second floor and has a balcony which is, in fact, the roof over the outer square and the part of the plan shared by both squares. From the dining room it is possible to look across the balcony and see the greenery of Awajishima island in the near distance.

The staircase in a corner of the inner square leads down to the first floor, to a bedroom and a studio. Because of the slope of the site, it was possible to drop the studio a level lower than the rest of the first floor and thus increase its ceiling height. Blind walls are used in the studio to restrict light and preserve a dim mood. The only sources of natural illumination are two staggered rectangular windows whose light creates varying patterns as the hours go by.

Location Kobe
Design 1981–2
Construction 1982–3
Structure Reinforced concrete
Site area 681.7 m^2
Building area 68 m^2
Total floor area 119.7 m^2

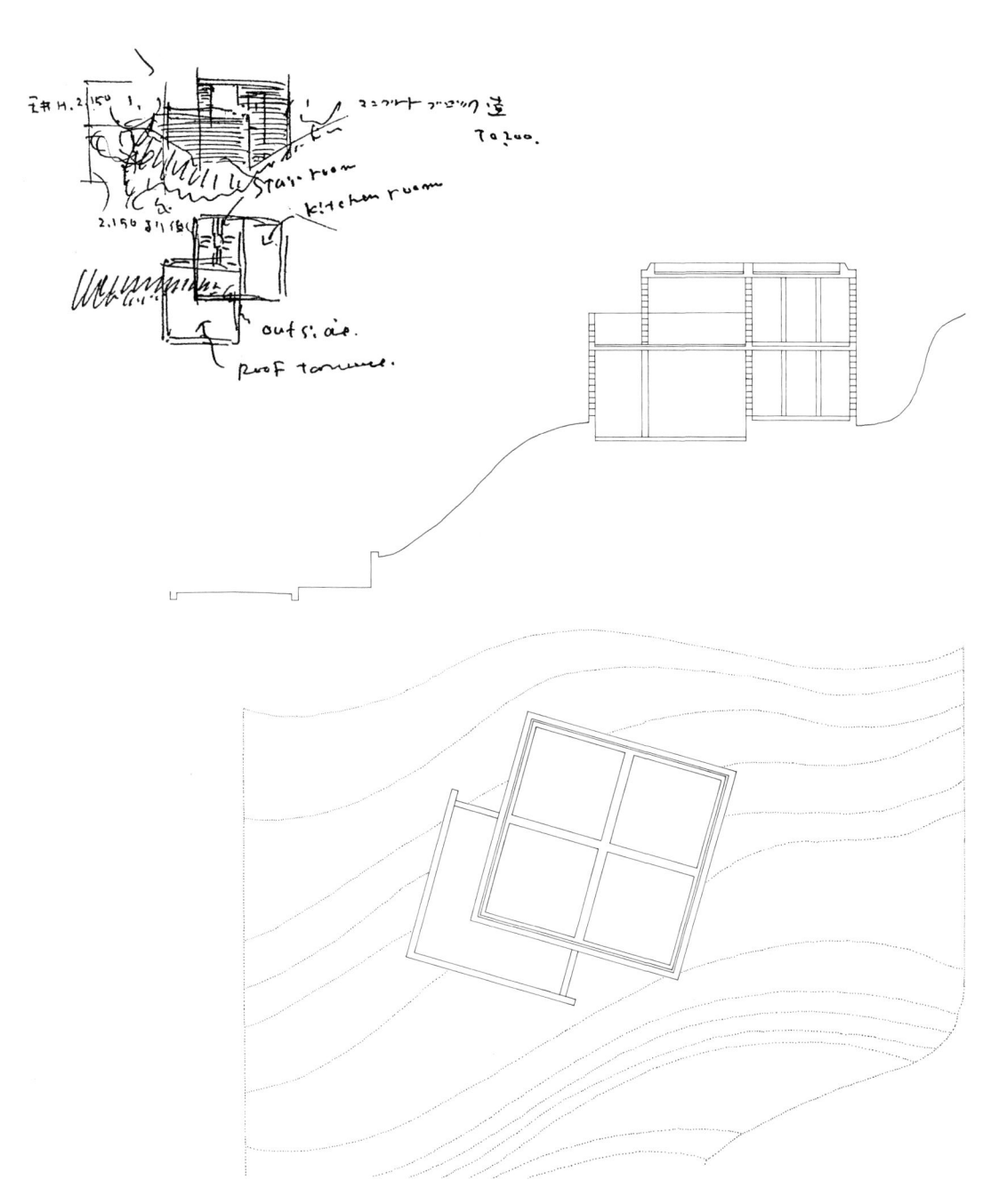

View of the roof and axonometric.

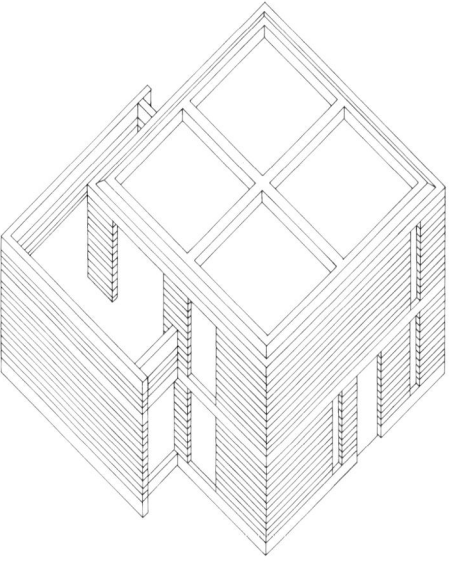

181

Floor plans, view from the street and interior view.

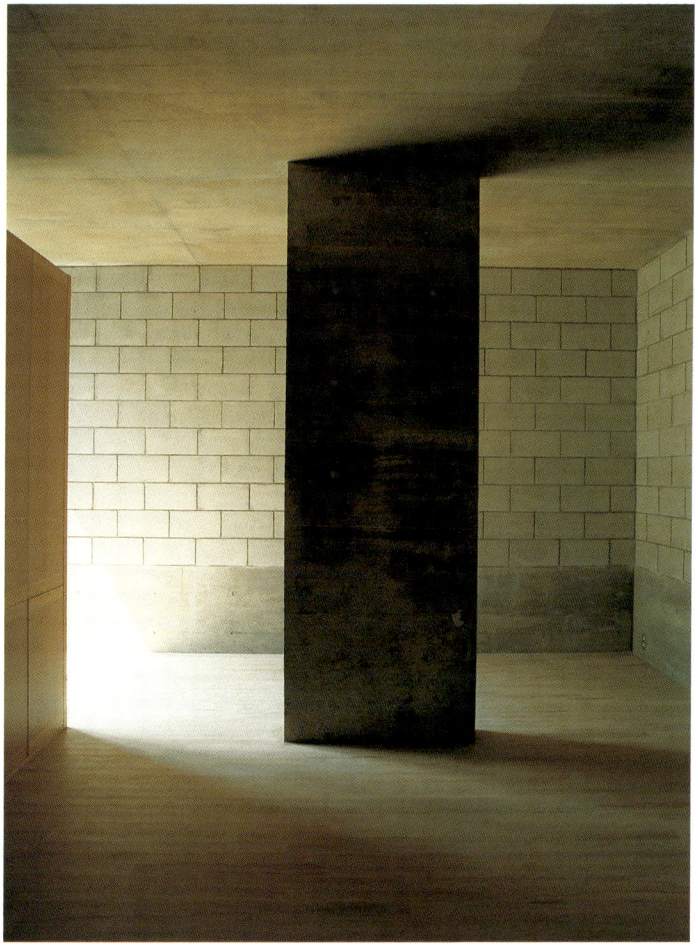

Fukuhara Clinic

Floor plans, overall view showing the building in its urban context, and axonometric.

This clinic was planned from the start as a facility that would provide therapy based on rehabilitation. The architectural design reflects the medical and social demands by making the entire building a rehabilitative facility; even the stairways and corridors are used for this purpose.

The plan is basically a combination of circles and rectangles. At either end of the building is a service core containing a stairway, a lift and mechanical systems. To the rear of the site is an open space that rises the full height of the building. This introduces nature in the form of light and air into every floor. At the bottom of this space is a sunken court with greenery. The basement level which faces this sunken court is given over to a heated pool, sauna and bathroom. The diagnostic section is on the ground floor, and the entire first floor is used as a physical therapy room. The in-patients' rooms and cafeteria are on the second, third and fourth floors. The cafeteria's openness is characterized by a gently curving wall of glass and is filled with light. The quarters for the director of the clinic are on the top floor and face a terrace.

Location Tokyo
Design 1981–5
Construction 1985–6
Structure Reinforced concrete
Site area 627 m^2
Building area 434.2 m^2
Total floor area 2,638.7 m^2

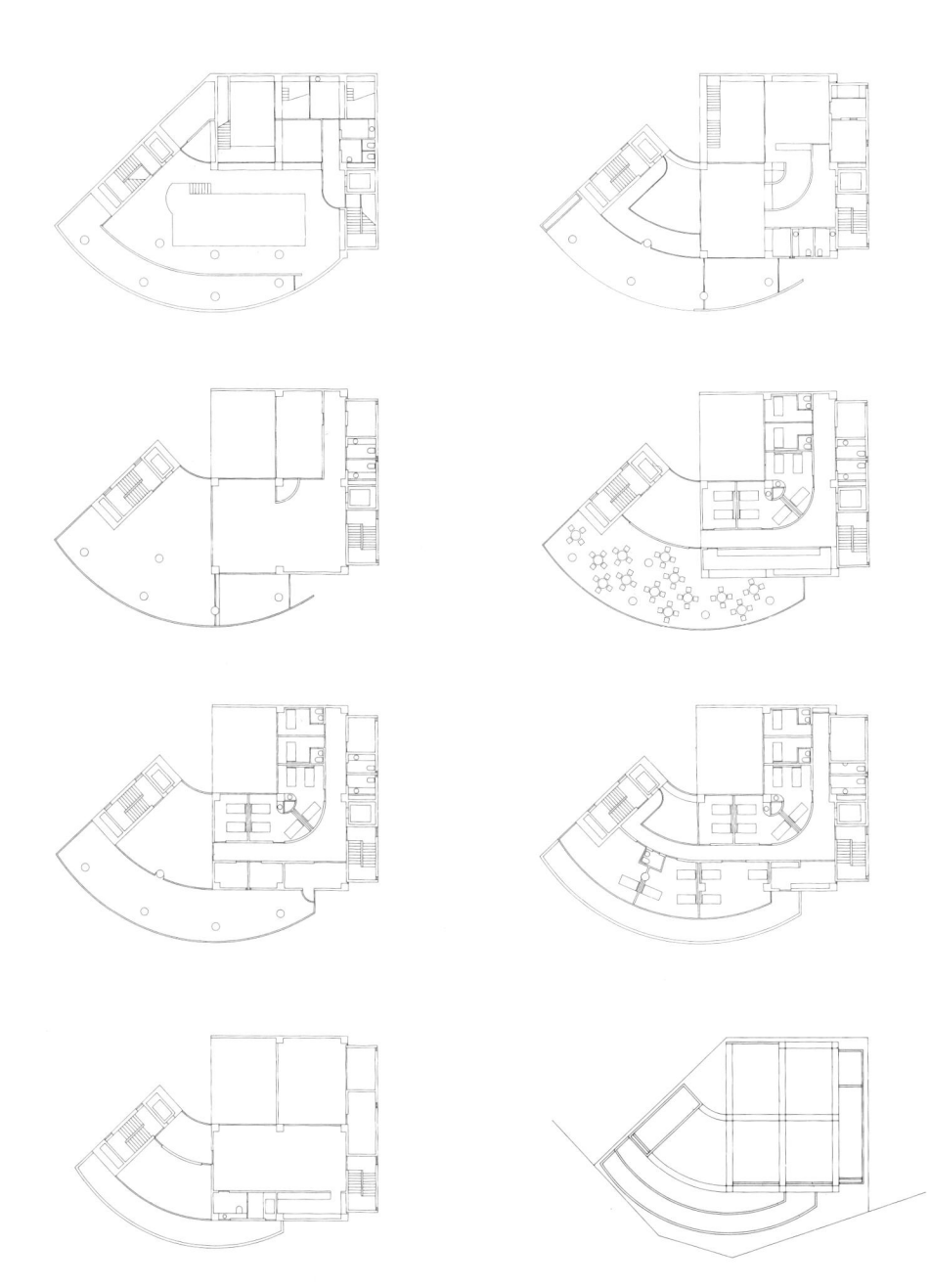

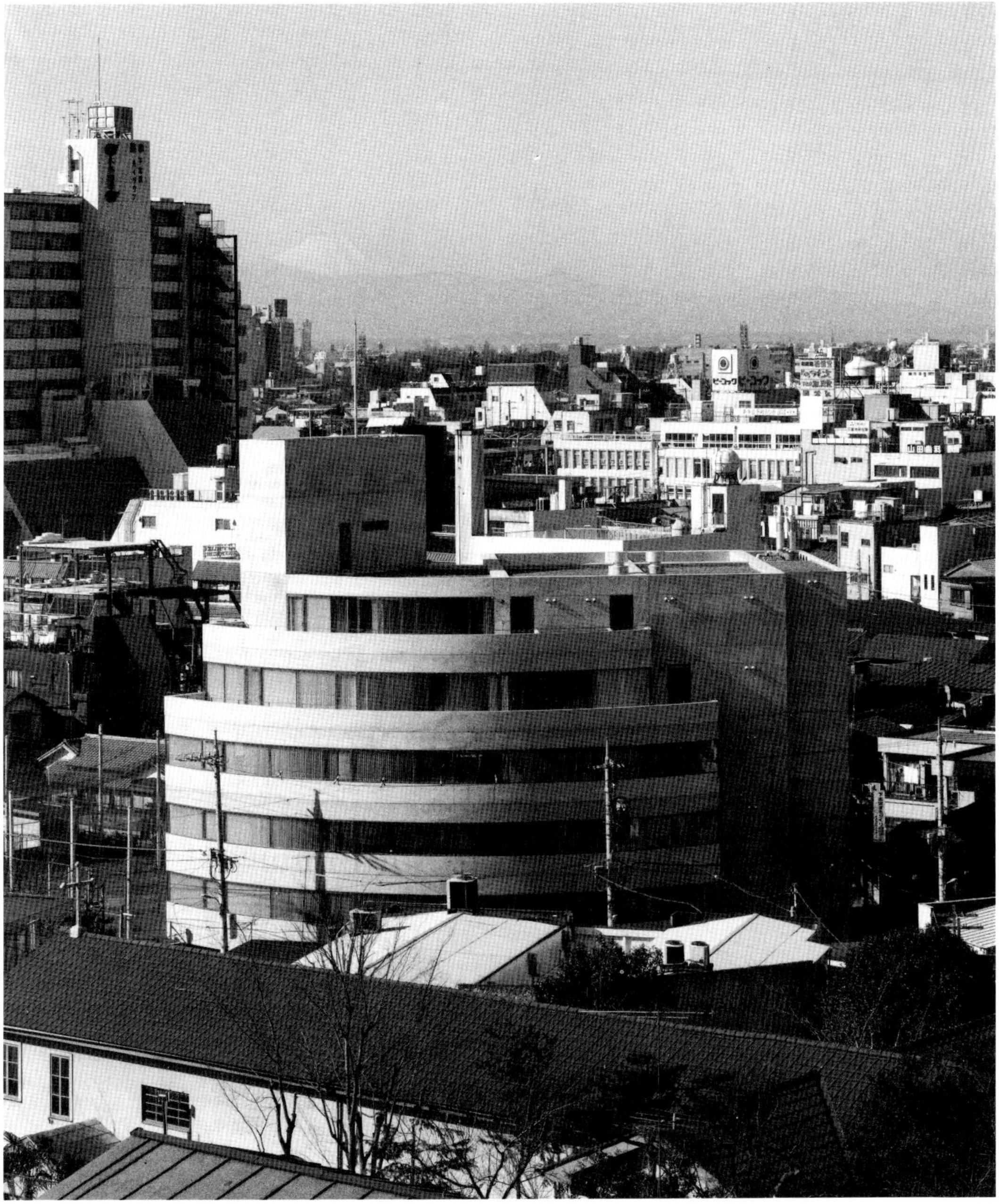

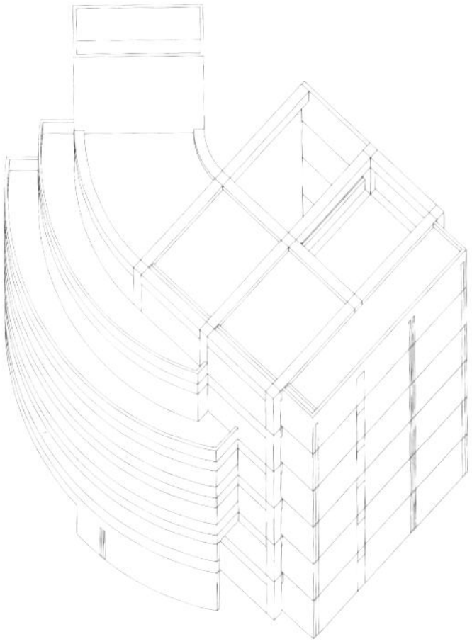

Izutsu House

View showing the building among the neighbouring rooftops.

This building is on a typical Osaka street where houses, factories and stores crowd together. On the floor half a level below the street are the dining room and bedroom for a young couple, and a bathroom, lavatory and workroom. The floor above, reached by an open stairway, accommodates a dining room with a large window, a study below the stairway, and a tatami room. The tatami room is lit only by a high window. The main bedroom is on the second floor.

The volume of the domain defined by the concrete box is divided in two, into the everyday living spaces and the exterior space which is like an extension of the street. A passageway leading from the street to the courtyard and then up the stairway to the deck occupies the exterior space which accounts for half the total building volume.

The stairway, a central feature of everyday life, is located where these two spaces come together, and there is direct access from the courtyard to each room. This courtyard was provided to make natural elements a part of everyday activities.

Location Osaka
Design 1981–2
Construction 1982
Structure Reinforced concrete
Site area 71.2 m^2
Building area 46 m^2
Total floor area 114.5 m^2

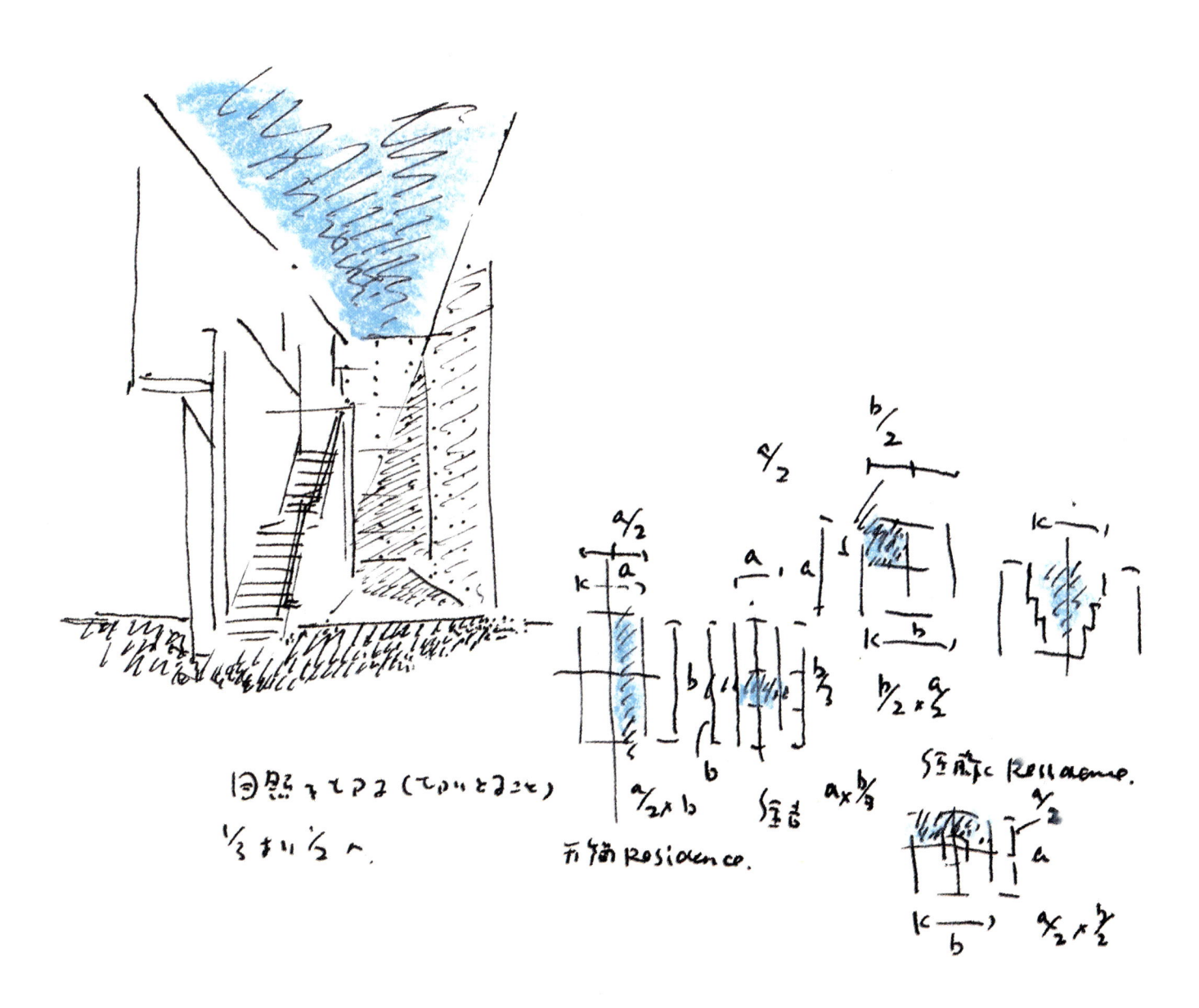

Perspective sketch and sketches showing dimensions of the plan.

Floor plans and oblique view of the building.

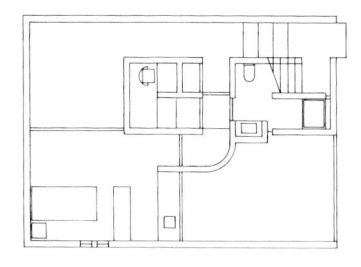

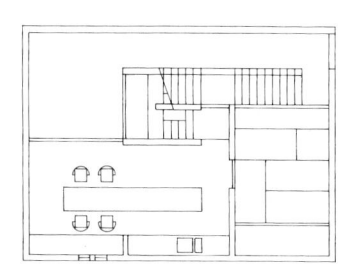

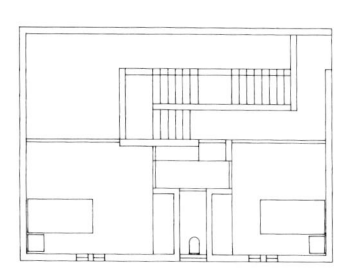

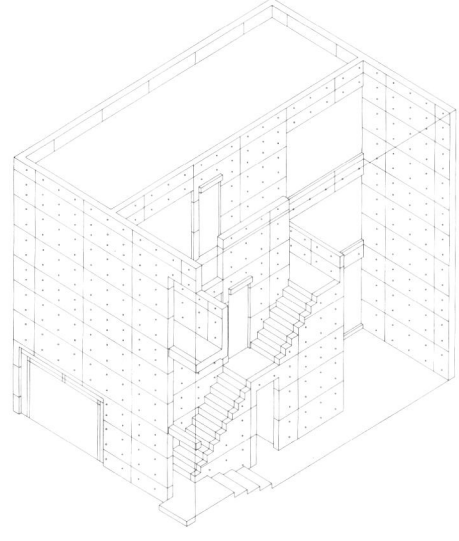

Aerial view showing main stairs and axonometric.

189

Doll's House Project

View of the model, plan and axonometric.

This is a three-storey building, two floors of which are below ground. The composition is based on the continuous subdivision of squares, and suggests movement between the infinitely large and infinitely small. Three of the lowest-level volumes, which correspond to three squares in plan, give onto an internal courtyard.

Design 1981–2

Festival O

Longitudinal section and plan.

The project is for a commercial complex for Naha city centre. The building's grid is derived from a 20-centimetre-square module, equivalent to the dimensions of a concrete block, and gives form to successive cubic volumes the sides of which are 36 metres. A large cylindrical volume for an auditorium is introduced into the square plan.

Location Naha, Okinawa
Design 1982

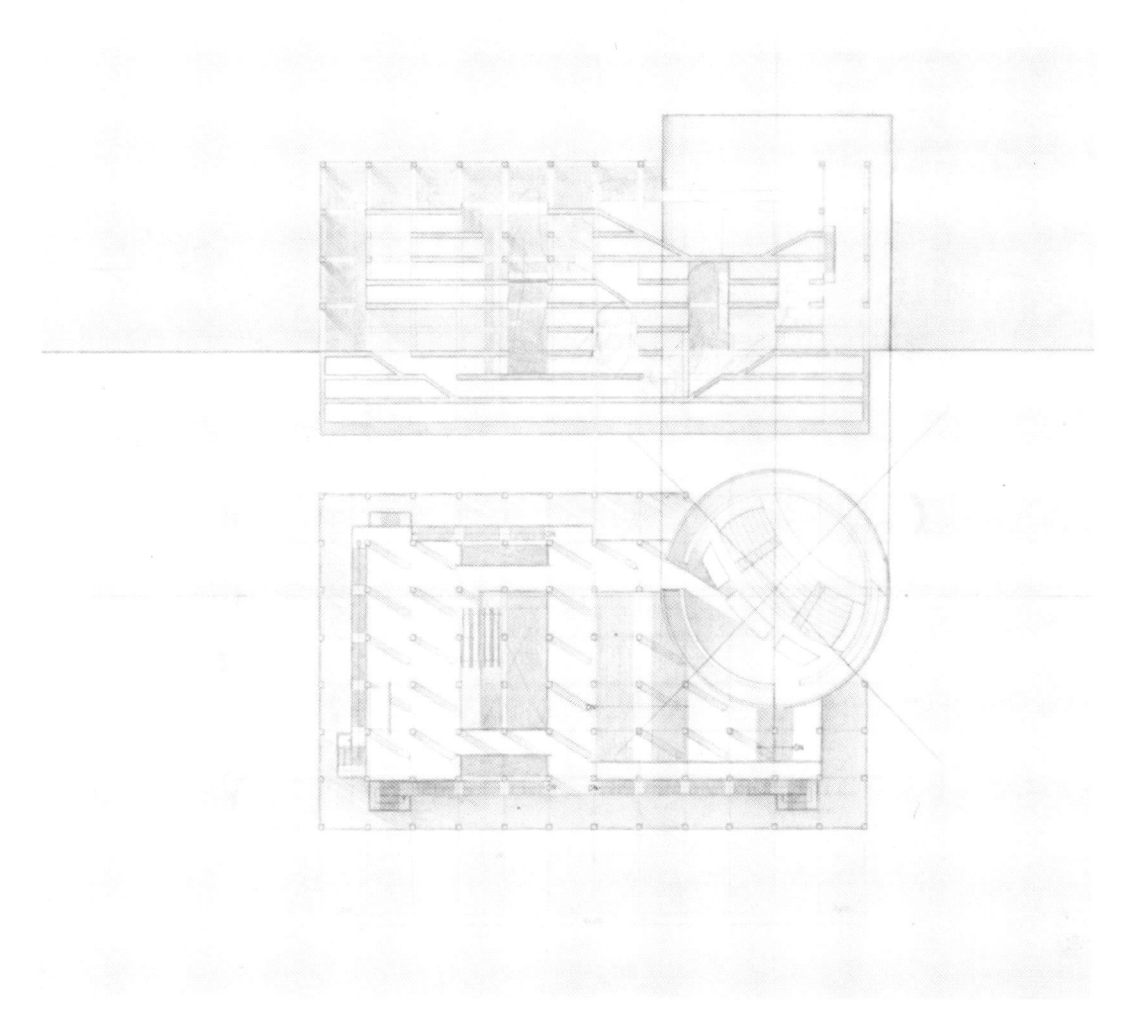

Iwasa House and Extension

View of the building and elevation.

This large house is half-buried on a gentle slope in a national park between Osaka and Kobe. It has two storeys and is 5.4 x 27.4 metres in plan. The composition is structured around two multi-storey spaces of different character.

The building, in the form of a rectangular prism, is oriented in the east–west direction and open to the south. On the north side, a curved wall has been inserted which encloses an interior space. The multi-storey space to the south is the point of contact between inside and outside, and the multi-storey space to the north is the centre around which the interior landscape unfolds.

You are led downwards in a spiral, past the upper-storey deck and the lower-storey slope, to the multi-storey space on the south side. There is a terrace on the top level with views of the distant ocean. The east side of the house, which is screened off by a central wall, has a two-storey space framing the hillside.

The dining and living rooms are on the west side of the upper storey, and public rooms, such as the tatami room, are on the east side. On the lower storey, the atelier is to the west and the bedrooms to the east. The multi-storey space enclosed by the curved wall is a node linking the upper storey with the lower storey, the east side with the west side.

Six years after the building's completion, the owner had a guest room added. Since the site is within the national park, this extension, like the existing house, is recessed into the ground to balance with the scale of the surroundings. The extension has a curved wall opposing the curved wall at the centre of the existing building,

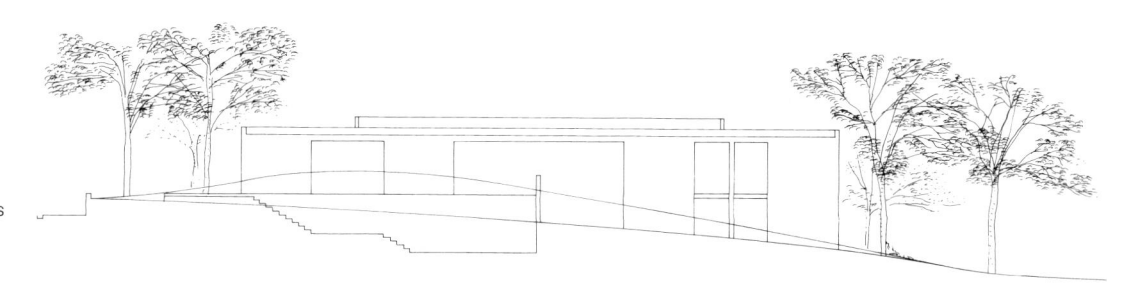

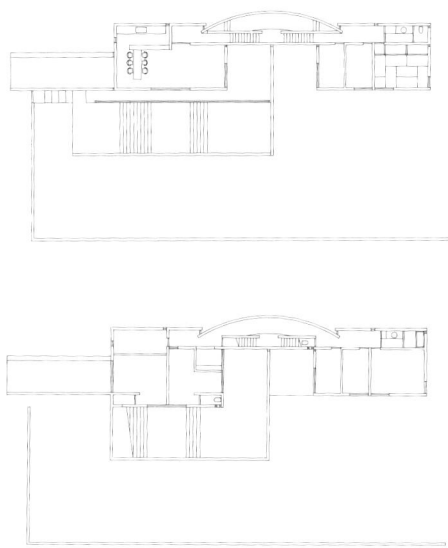

View showing circulation space and floor plans.

Floor plans, section and view showing the building with its extension.

but with the same radius. The guest room is placed below ground level, with a terrace on its roof. At the lower level, the curved wall guides the approach to glazed doors on the east side of the guest room through which nature is called into the interior. The original building and the extension, each autonomous, stand in opposition, yet coexist as a single composition.

Location Ashiya
Design 1982–3
Construction 1983–4
Structure Reinforced concrete
Site area 821.4 m^2
Building area 188 m^2
Total floor area 235.6 m^2

Extension
Design 1989–90
Construction 1990
Structure Reinforced concrete
Total floor area 34.2 m^2

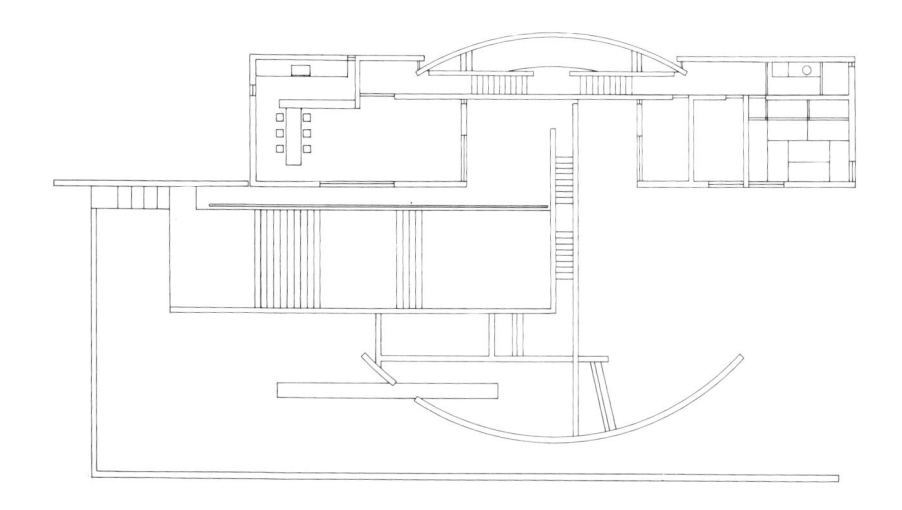

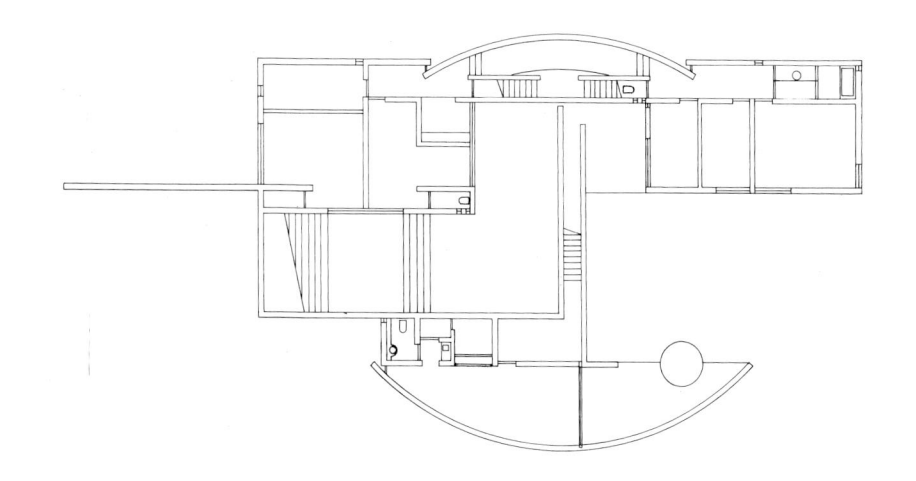

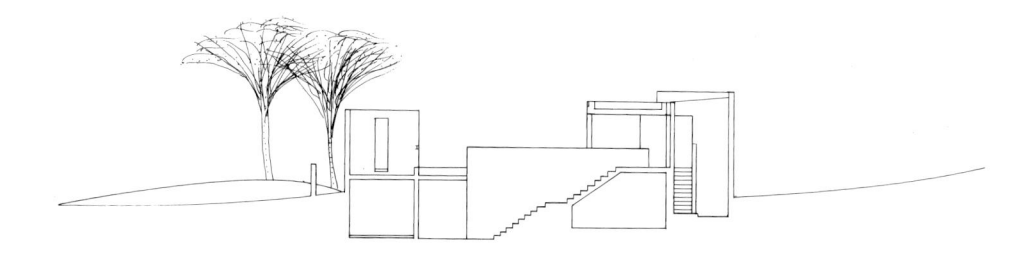

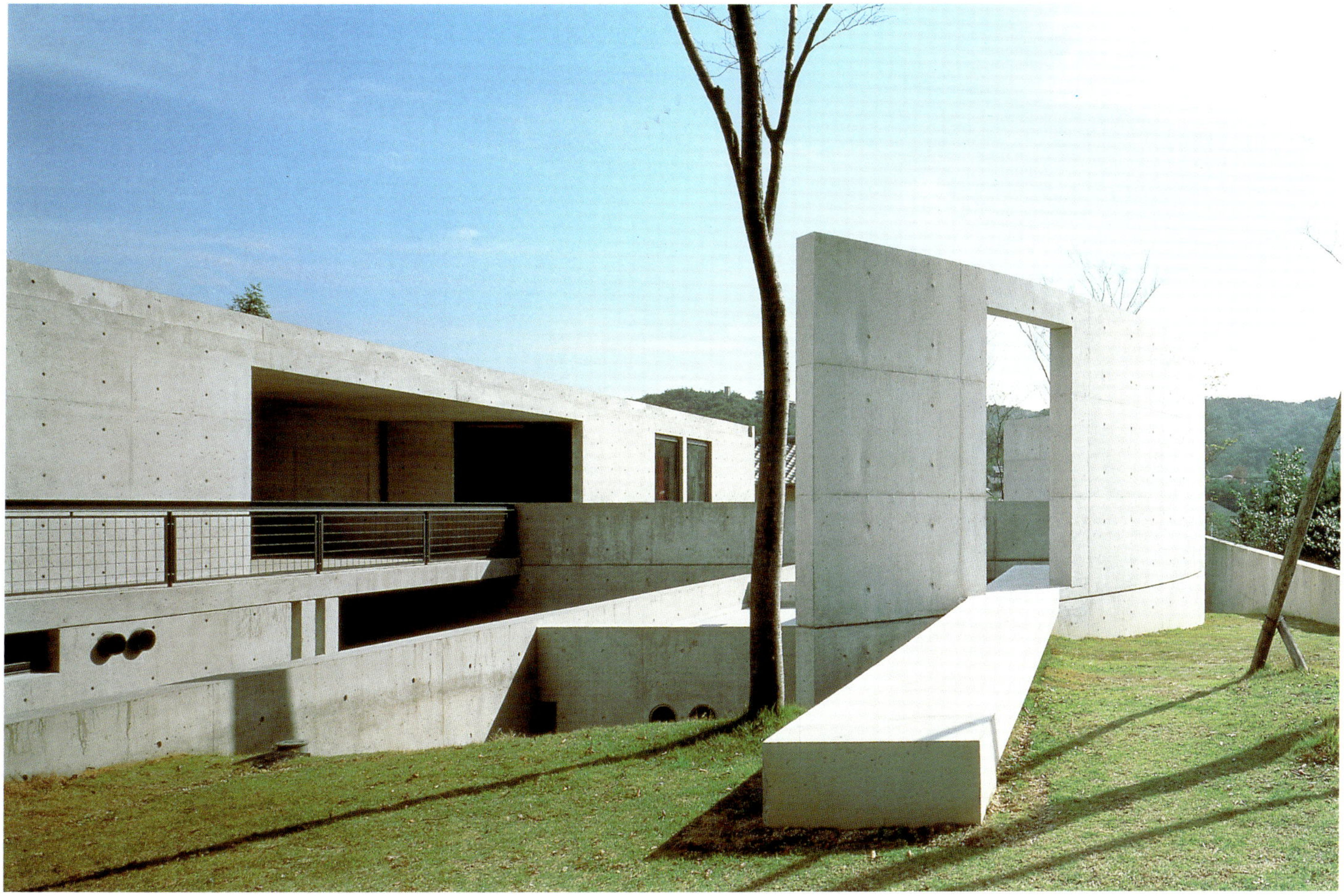

Melrose

View of the entrance and section.

This is an office and atelier for a fashion designer in Tokyo. The structure is composed of a seven-storey block and a four-storey block, each of differing functions, connected by a common space with a plan in the shape of a quadrant. The two blocks have exposed concrete frames, of equal 5.8 metre spans, with the wall wrapped around them. They are connected to form an L-shaped plan. A curved wall of frosted glass, the same height as the lower block, defines a common space at the corner of the L.

The tall block is given over to offices. The low block is primarily an atelier. The storage is in the basement. On the first floor of the low block is a showroom and the despatch area; on the second floor is the atelier with a roof garden. Mechanical spaces including a lift are in the portion where the two blocks connect.

Location Tokyo
Design 1982–3
Construction 1983–4
Structure Reinforced concrete and steel
Site area 1,659.9 m^2
Building area 839.1 m^2
Total floor area 3,531.8 m^2

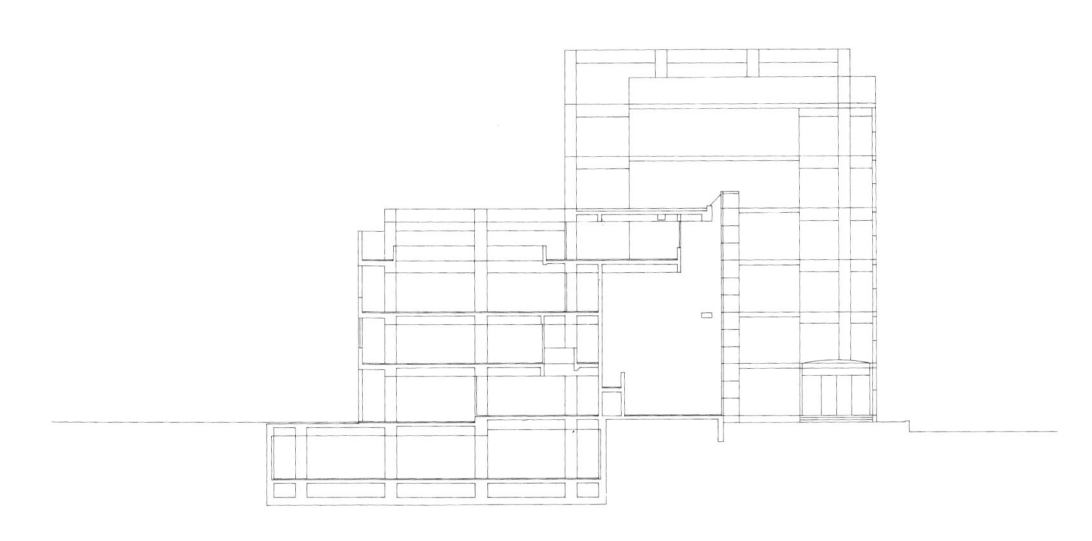

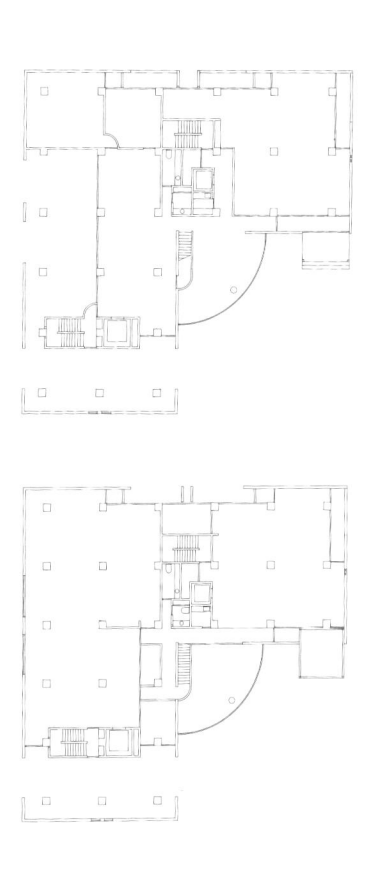

Interior view showing the curved window and floor plans.

Kidosaki House

Aerial view of the site, conceptual sketch and floor plans.

In a quiet residential suburb, this house was built for three families: a couple and their parents. Designed as a multi-dwelling unit, it affords the occupants privacy in their living quarters yet companionship in their daily activities through the insertion of common courtyards and terraces.

The building consists of a cubic volume with a protective wall along the property line. The cubic volume's almost central position on the site gives the peripheral spaces a three-dimensional character. This arrangement creates a buffer zone around the lives of the families, while also providing a sense of communal territory.

Location Tokyo
Design 1982–5
Construction 1985–6
Structure Reinforced concrete
Site area 610.9 m^2
Building area 351.5 m^2
Total floor area 556.1 m^2

199

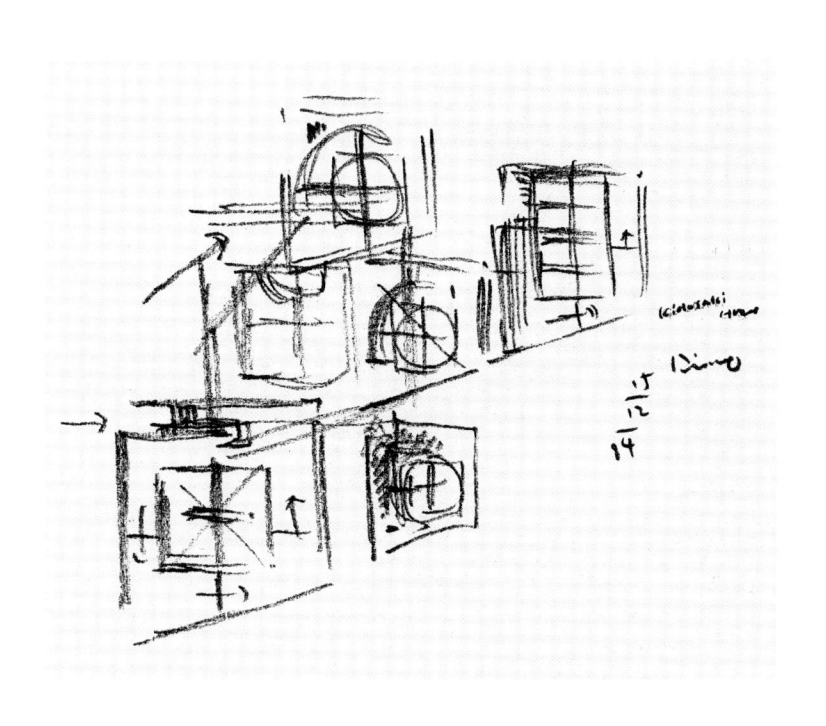

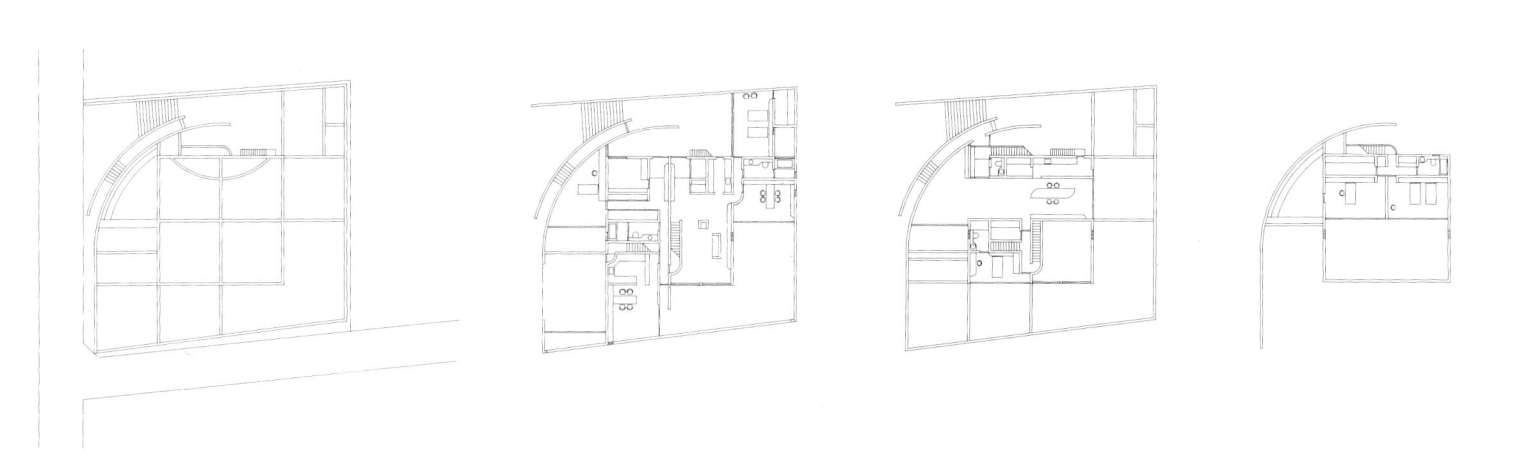

View of the curved wall and conceptual sketch.

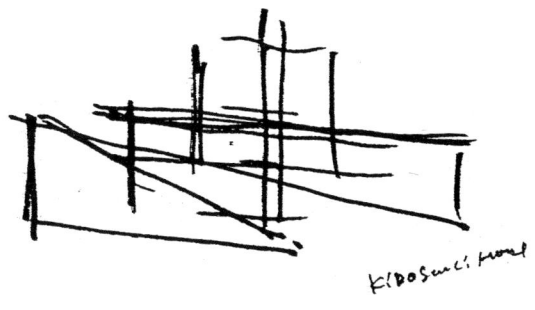

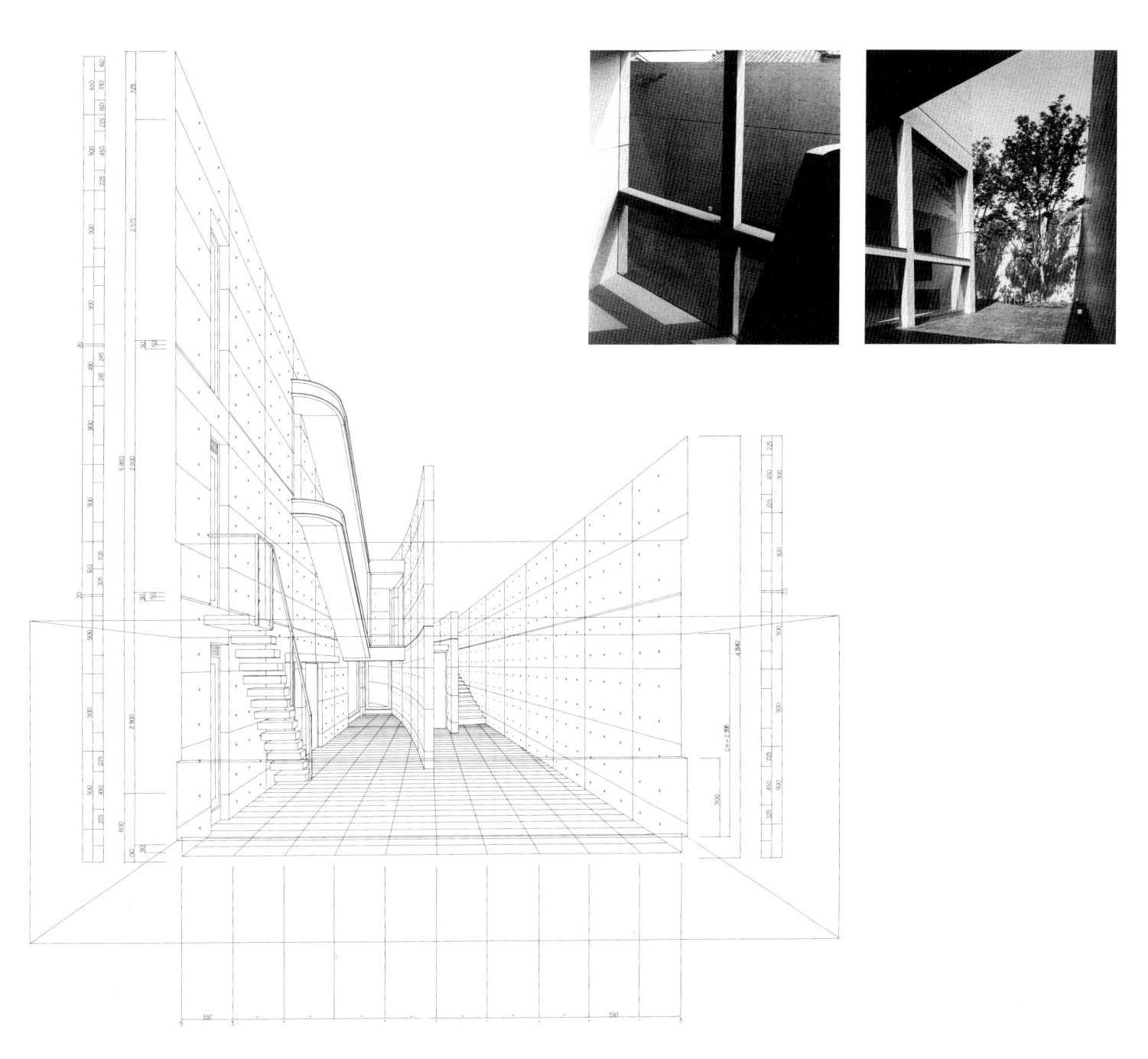

Perspective of the entrance, view from the interior and view of the garden.

201

Axonometric and interior views.

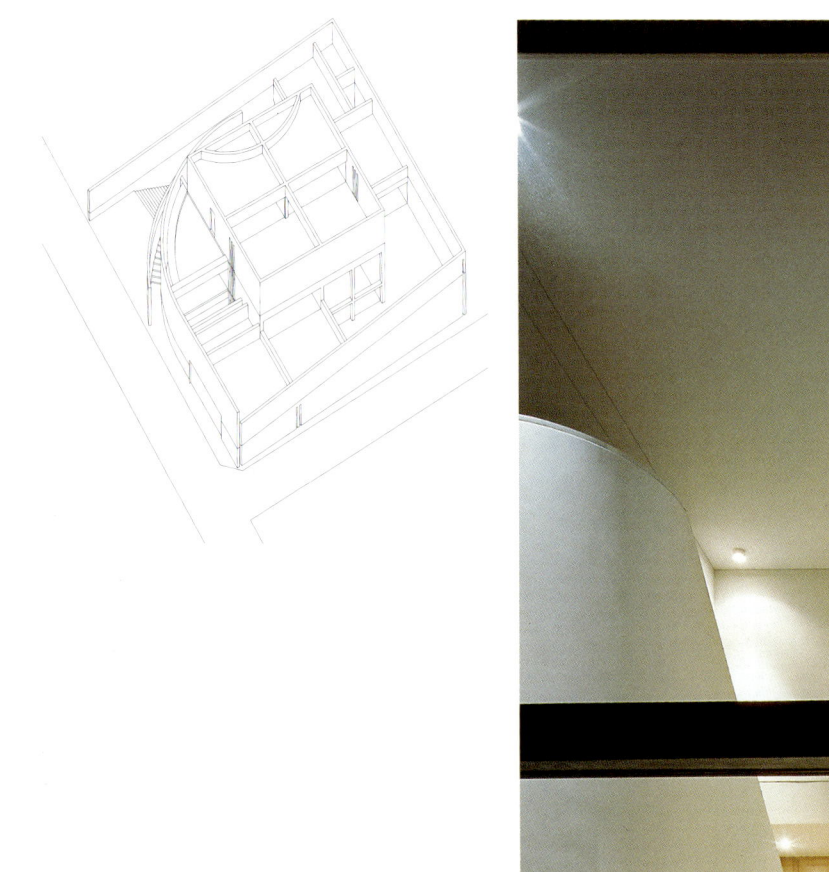

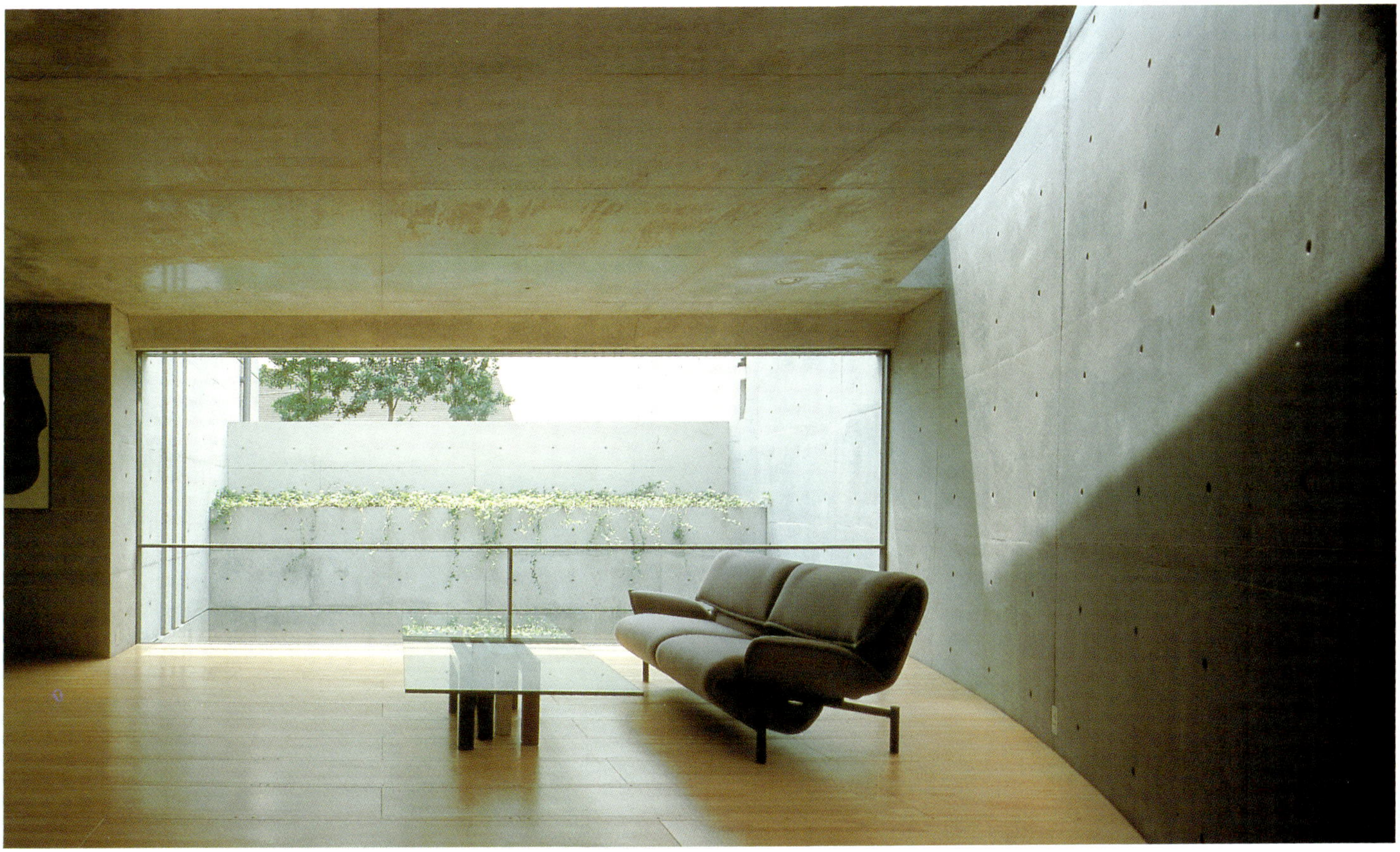

Kaneko House

Oblique view of the entrance and axonometric.

This building is in a quiet residential neighbourhood – a rare phenomenon in the centre of the city. It was necessary to build a compact structure on a limited site, and this was achieved by linking the rooms, not by a corridor but by stairs.

The house has four levels, connected at half-storey intervals by a top-lit stairway. You pass through an opening in the freestanding wall facing the street, and the entrance is a half-storey above the street. You climb a stairway to reach the living room. A half-storey above is the dining room and a half-storey below is the children's room. Another half-storey below the children's room is the main bedroom. This house has two courtyards, the larger one on the south side is a brightly lit, open space, surrounded by a wall independent of the building. The small courtyard on the north side is a very enclosed space with more limited light. The four rooms on separate levels overlook the large courtyard. The entire composition was planned so that one of the two courtyards is visible from every room. The space of the small courtyard, which serves as a lightwell, continues up the stairway to the roof.

Location Tokyo
Design 1982–3
Construction 1983
Structure Reinforced concrete
Site area 172.9 m²
Building area 93.6 m²
Total floor area 169 m²

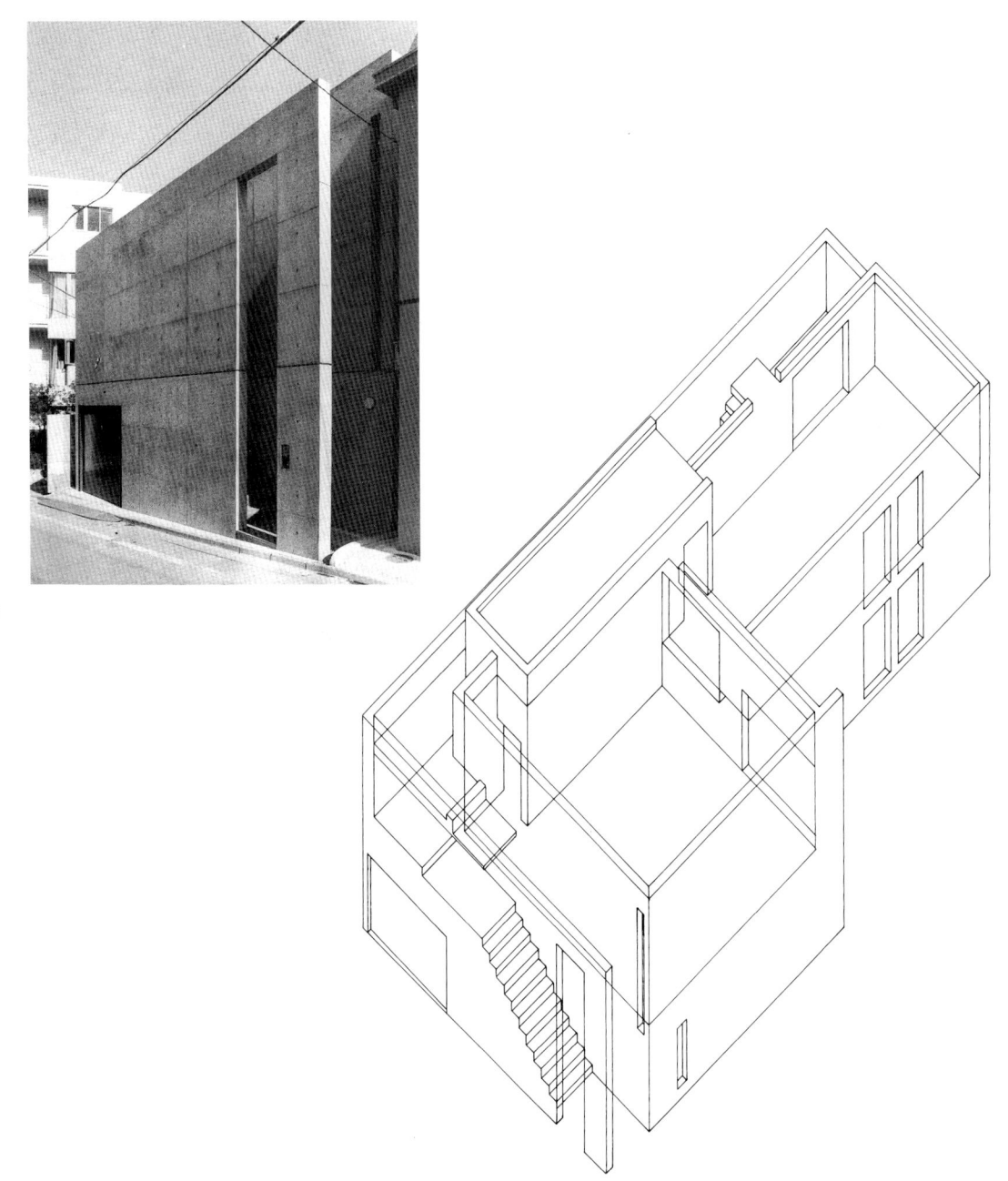

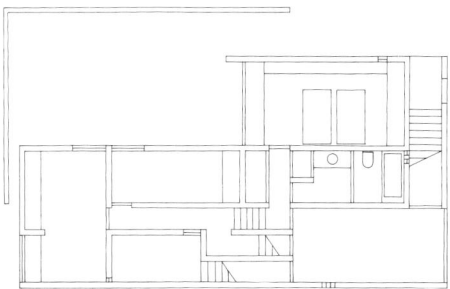

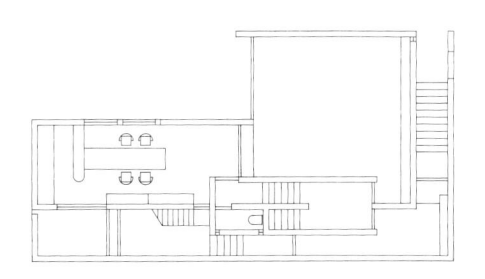

Detailed view of the skylight from the stairs, and floor plans.

Ogura House

Conceptual sketch and view of the building from the street.

This house is a three-storey rectangular volume horizontally divided into three equal parts – two of these, at the north end, are devoted entirely to the exterior space of the site. The rooms are able to open out towards their natural surroundings, yet each room relates to the exterior space in its own unique way. The beam that spans the opening in the east wall frames the nearby hill, and cuts across the sky visible over the building's exterior void, thus inviting the green landscape and blue sky into the building.

Location Nagoya
Design 1983–7
Construction 1987–8
Structure Reinforced concrete
Site area 214.9 m^2
Building area 106.6 m^2
Total floor area 189.4 m^2

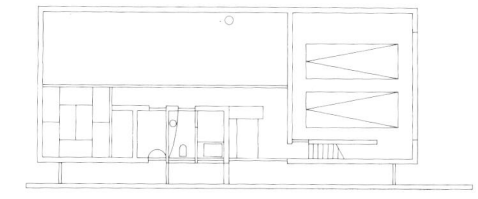

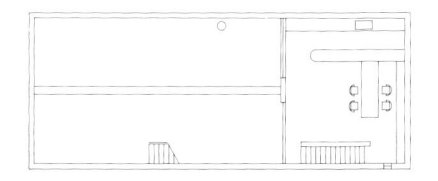

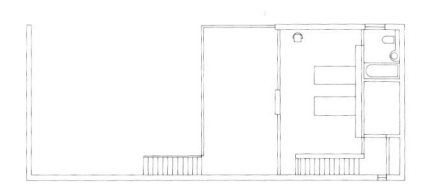

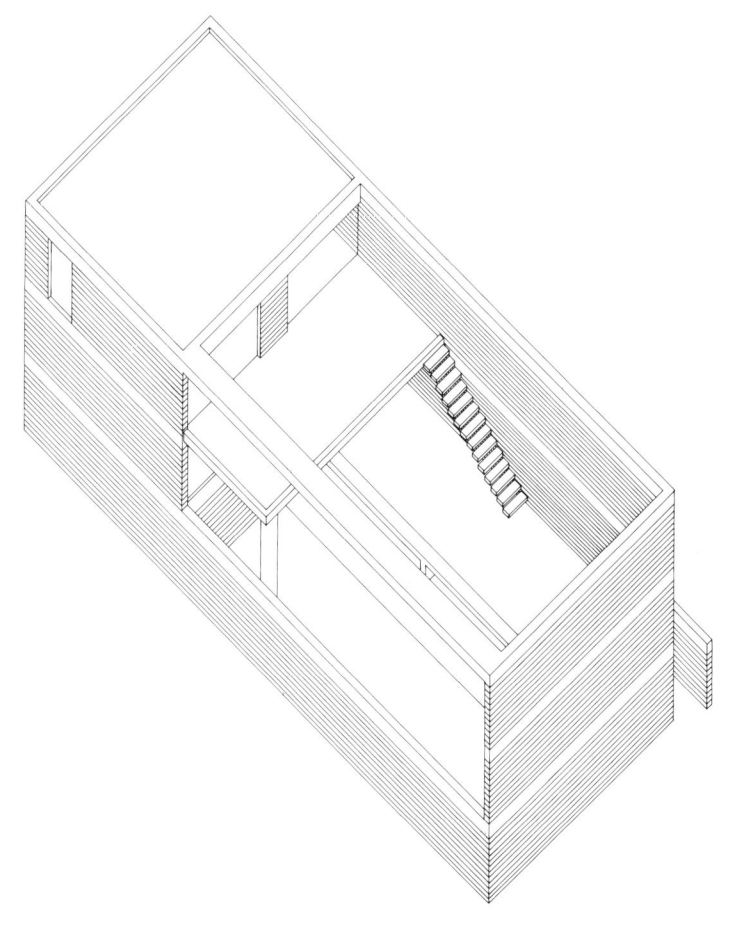

Floor plans, axonometric and view of the terrace.

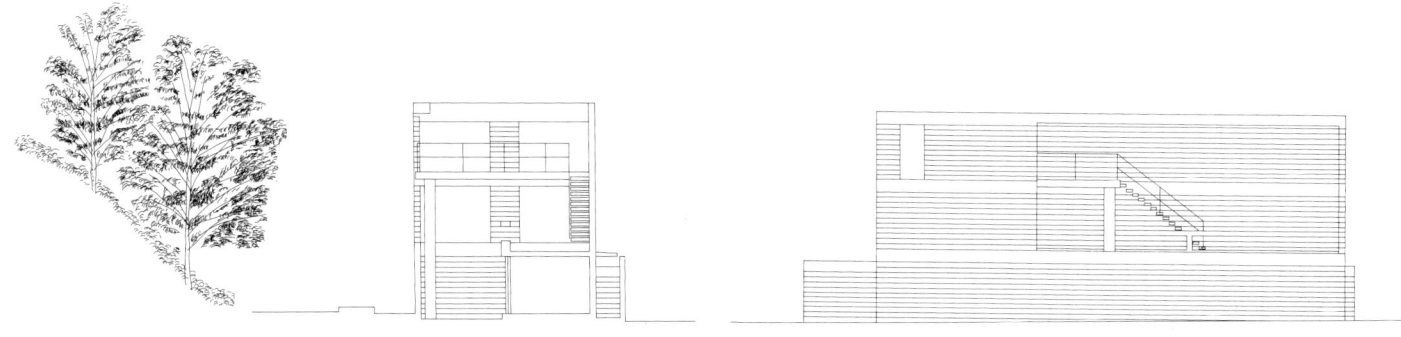

Detail view of the terrace, section and garden elevation.

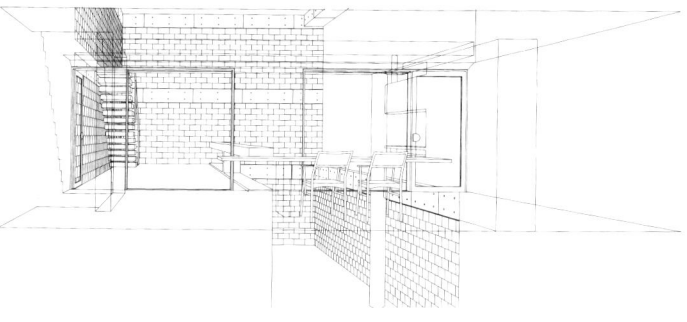

View of the terrace and perspective of the interior.

209

Time's I

View showing the building in its urban context and on the river, and site plan.

Located next to the Sanjo-Kobashi Bridge on the Takase River, a historically illustrious river weaving through the heart of Kyoto, this building was intended to focus attention on the river's history by relating the architecture to it. By putting people back in touch with the water it would give the city something new while at the same time protecting its scenery. Connecting the building directly to the public street above and the river below produced a complex space. As a result, city, nature and building – each autonomous and yet existing harmoniously – come together in complete equilibrium. Views of the river's current orchestrate the building's interior spaces, and a dialogue between man and water can be revived.

Location Kyoto
Design 1983
Construction 1983–4
Structure Reinforced concrete
Site area 351.3 m^2
Building area 289.9 m^2
Total floor area 641.2 m^2

211

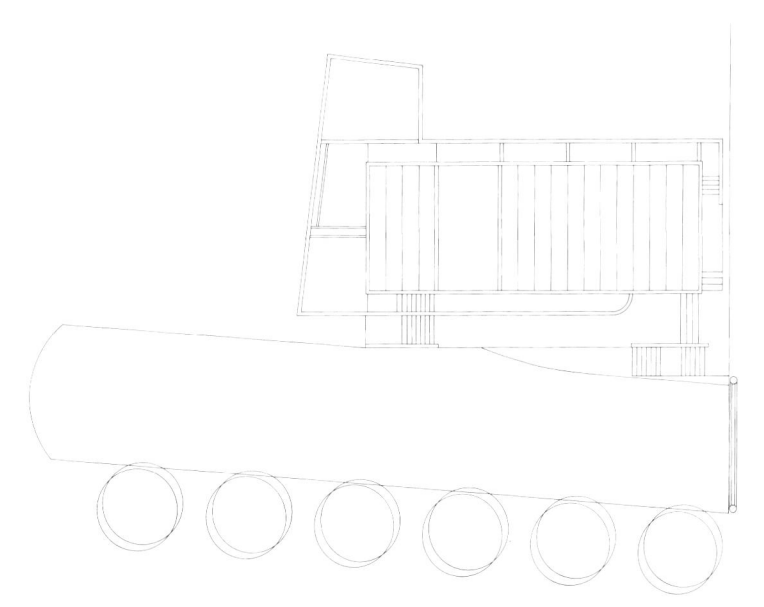

View showing river bank and elevation.

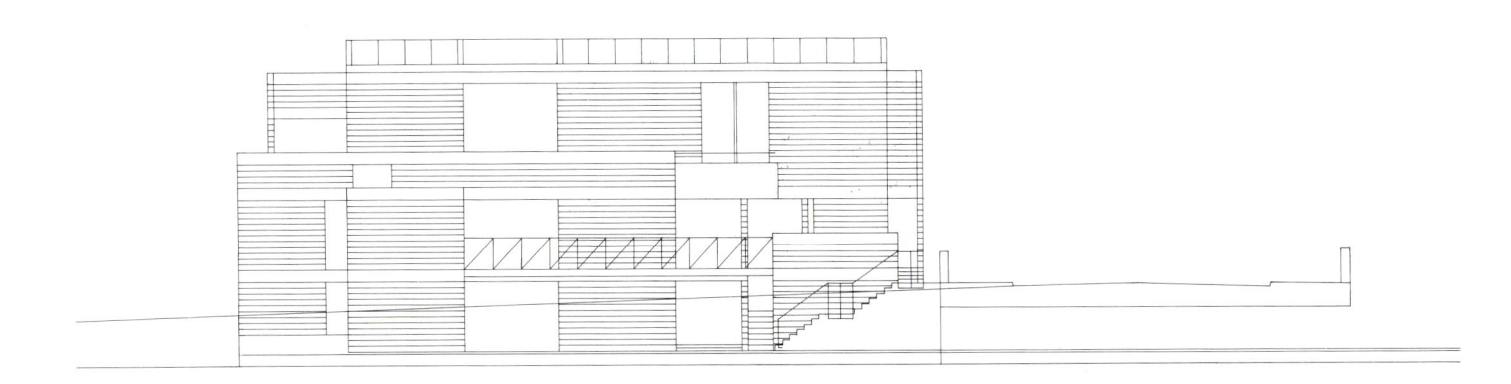

212

View showing the steps to the river and section.

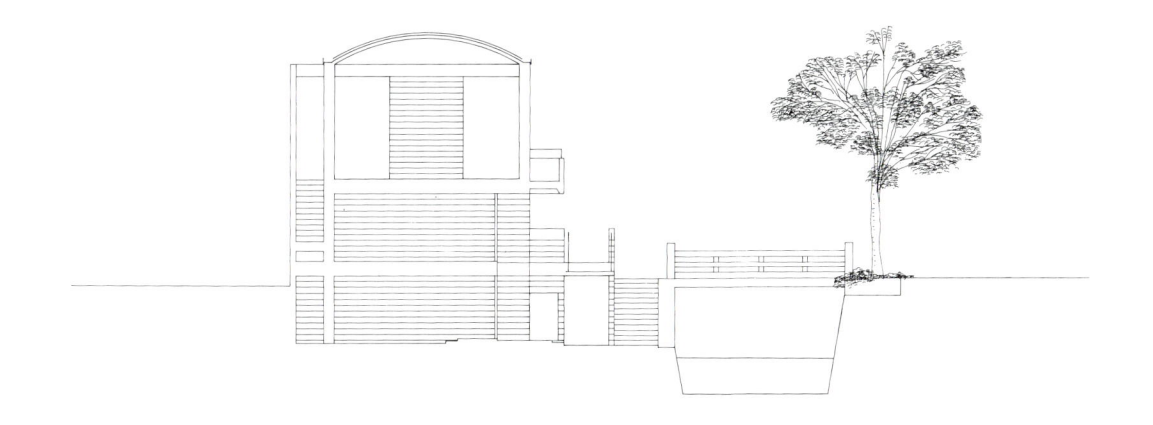

Time's II

Aerial view showing both buildings, I and II, site plan and conceptual sketch.

This is an extension to the Time's building completed in 1984. In Time's I, the relationship binding city, site and building was examined, while the building emphasized the interrelation of people and river. The building's surroundings were evoked in its interior spaces. Time's II explores this concept further and endeavours to extend the plaza along the river. Its plazas connect with those in Time's I, though set at different levels, and its vantage points are scattered more variously throughout the building. The result, in these combined projects, is a path of movement that is dramatically more complex and circuitous.

Location Kyoto
Design 1986–90
Construction 1990–91
Structure Reinforced concrete
Site area 485.8 m^2
Building area 107.9 m^2
Total floor area 274.2 m^2

215

View of the extension and plans.

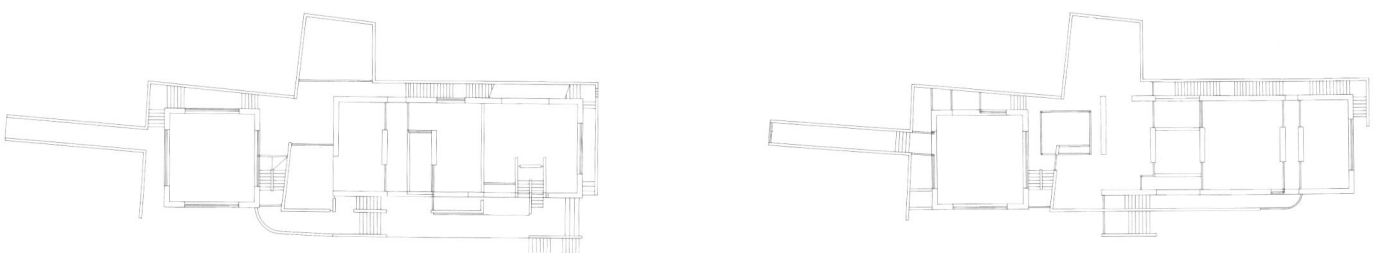

Detailed views of the river elevation and the roof, and conceptual sketch.

217

Jun Port Island Building

Floor plans, aerial view and section.

This building is on Port Island, a man-made island jutting out from the port of Kobe into the sea. It includes a reception space, a multi-purpose hall and storage.

A four-storey, medium-rise block and a low-rise block that stretches north–south along one of the longer sides of the site, form an L in plan and take up half the site, leaving the other half to a lawn. The lawn is not flat but bulges upwards in the middle to form a hillock. The intention was to create a distinctive interior landscape that was not simply open to the outside but was open yet closed.

The compositional elements of the building consist of a grid based on a square 6.4 metres to a side and a screen of frosted glass that absorbs infrared rays. The grid bestows order on the homogeneous land; walls enclose places, and openings carefully frame the exterior landscape.

There is extensive office space on the first floor which itself is on three levels. Stairs and decks link the levels three-dimensionally. At the end of the low-rise block there is an enclosed garden, separated from the hillock by a single wall. This is partly linked to the outside by an opening, but from inside the building you can only see the expanse of green and the exposed concrete wall, which establish a restrained atmosphere.

Location Kobe
Design 1983–4
Construction 1984–5
Structure Reinforced concrete
Site area 6,238.9 m^2
Building area 2,114.3 m^2
Total floor area 5,361.2 m^2

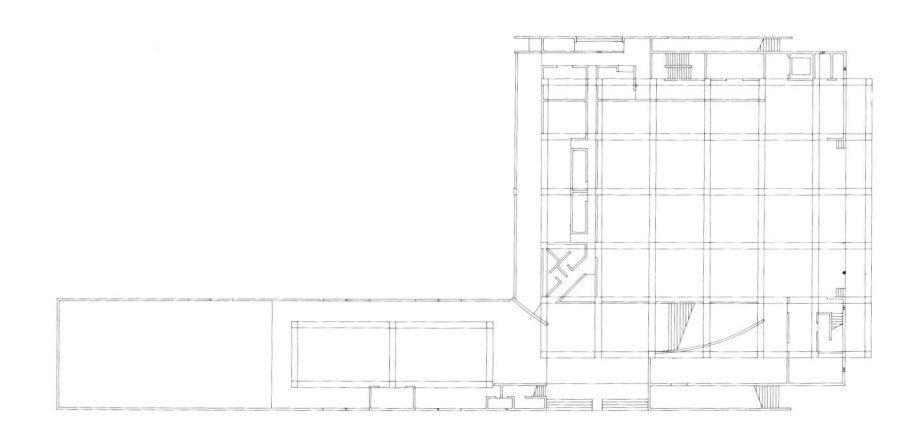

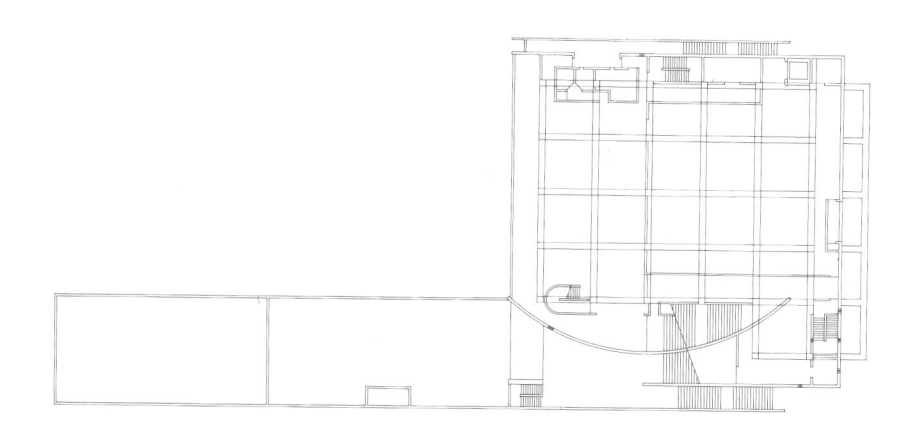

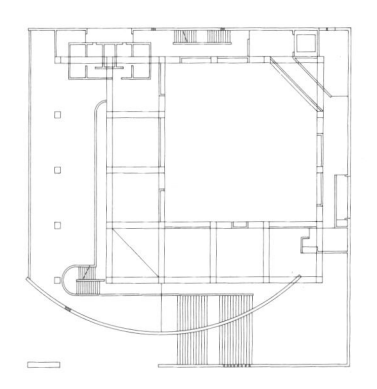

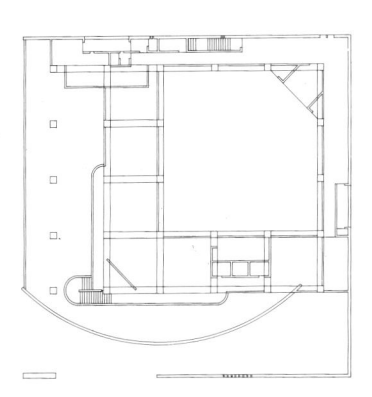

219

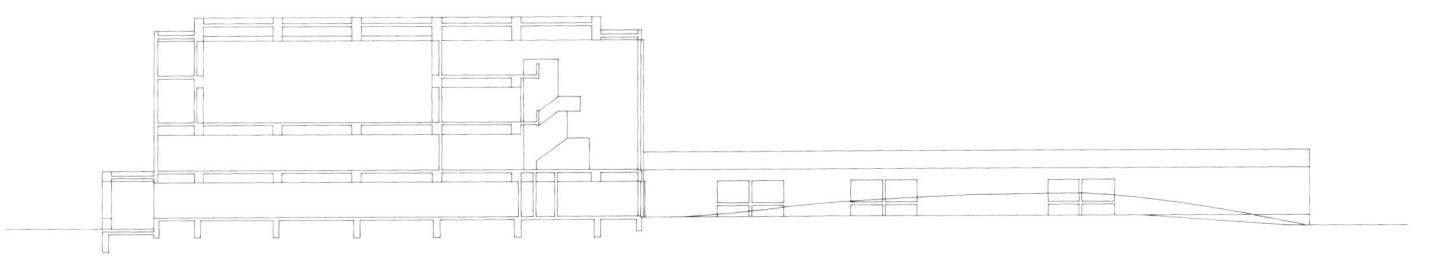

Oblique view of the low-rise block, axonometric and interior view showing the offices.

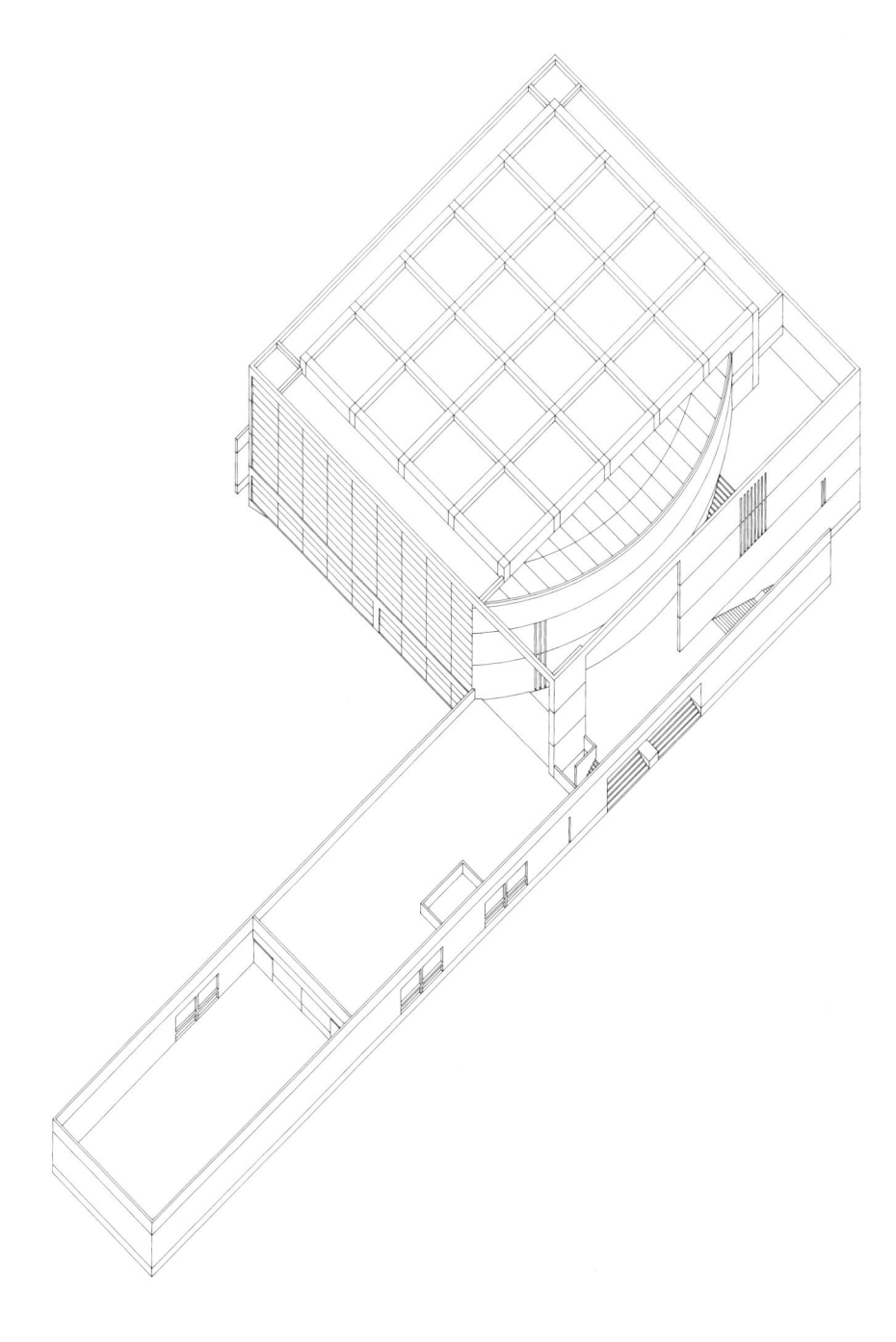

220

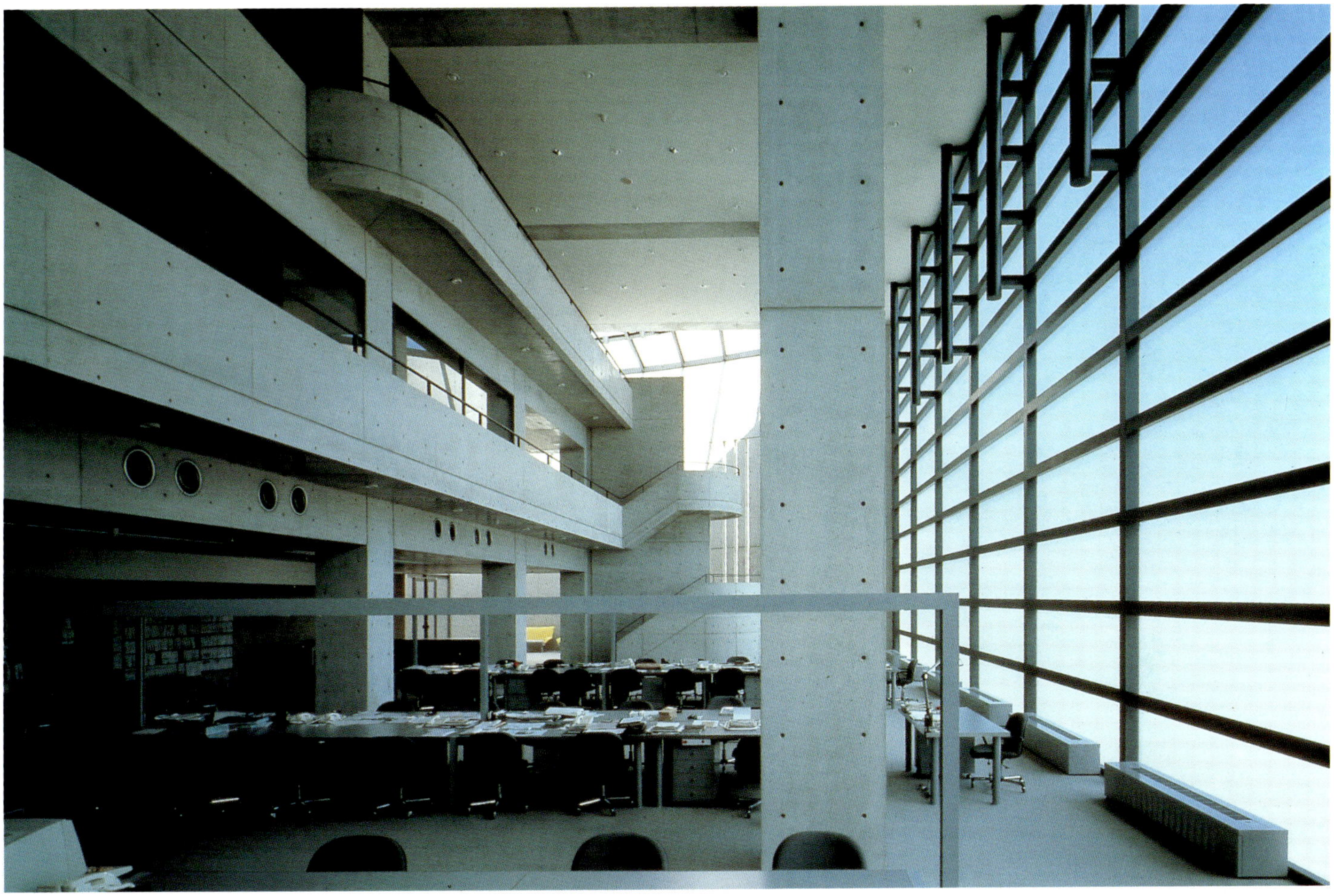

Yoshie Inaba Atelier

Floor plans, view of the entrance and section.

This atelier for a fashion designer is in a neighbourhood where houses are on relatively large lots, around 650 square metres in size, punctuated by numerous stone walls and trees. Care had to be taken not to destroy the quiet surroundings, so the building was given a simple exterior form and half the building volume was buried underground in a basement. Three- and four-storey exterior spaces are the key features in the design.

In front of the atelier is a frosted glass screen open at the bottom. This creates a sense of greater depth in the building and eases the relationship between building and street. Passing by the service core in an open corner of the front courtyard, you come to a four-storey space. A wide stairway leads to the second basement floor, and a parallel, narrower stairway leads upwards. At the top is access to the service core and a deck area. From the deck built over the front courtyard, a stairway leads to the terrace on the roof.

The frosted glass screen on the outside of the L-shaped public space dramatizes the interior of the building. It selectively introduces natural light and creates contrasts of light and shadow, cuts off the western sun and shows just the shadows of moving branches of the trees outside.

Location Tokyo
Design 1983–4
Construction 1984–5
Structure Reinforced concrete
Site area 374 m^2
Building area 181.9 m^2
Total floor area 756.2 m^2

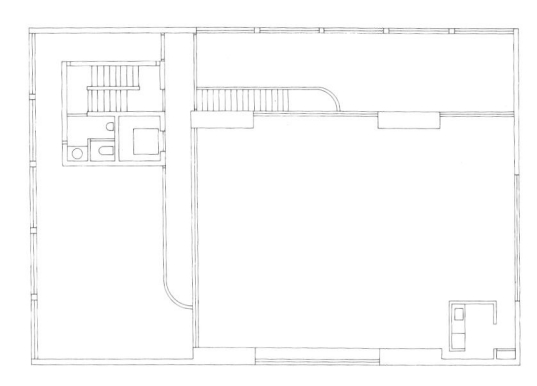

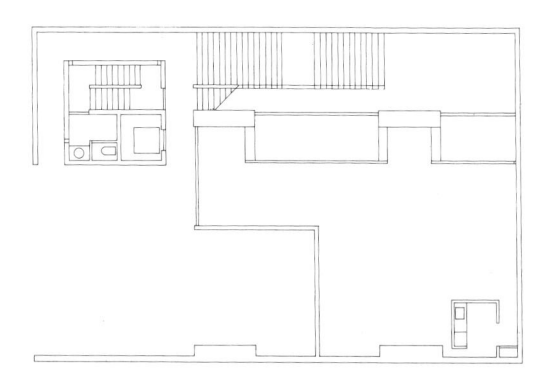

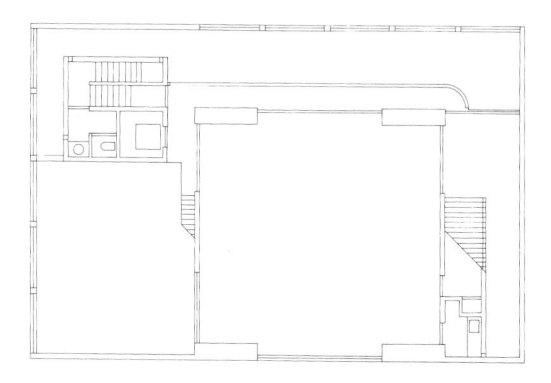

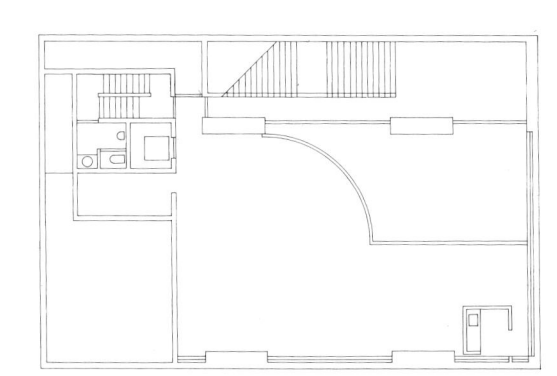

223

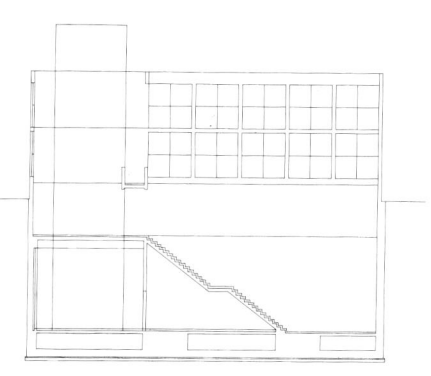

Interior views, axonometric showing circulation spaces and oblique view of the glass screen.

225

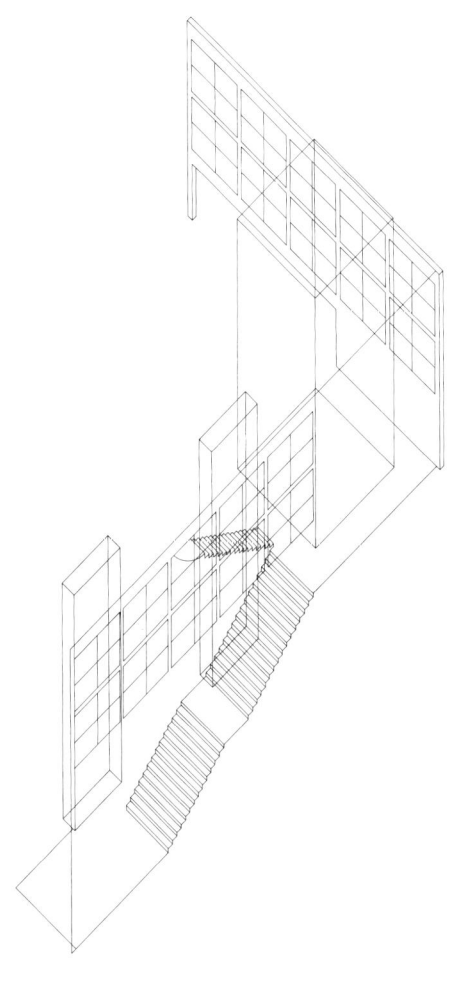

Nakayama House

View of the courtyard and aerial view, and conceptual sketches.

The Nakayama House is in a residential area under development on the border of Nara and Kyoto prefectures. Placed in this landscape is a concrete rectangular prism, with a plan 7 x 19 metres and a height of two storeys. The building is divided in two along its length, with one half given over to a courtyard and the other to the living spaces. The dining room and living room are on the first floor; and on the second floor are the bedroom, a Japanese style room, and a terrace which takes up half the floor area. This terrace is linked by an open stairway with the first-floor courtyard and is part of a three-dimensional outdoor space.

You enter the house along a narrow passageway squeezed between the building and a wall along the property line. The outdoor landscape is completely shut out. A single material was deliberately chosen for the whole composition in order to purify the character of the space. Each room opens out on the courtyard and faces the wall opposite, so becoming a part of the courtyard.

Location Nara
Design 1983–4
Construction 1984–5
Structure Reinforced concrete
Site area 263.3 m^2
Building area 69.1 m^2
Total floor area 103.7 m^2

227

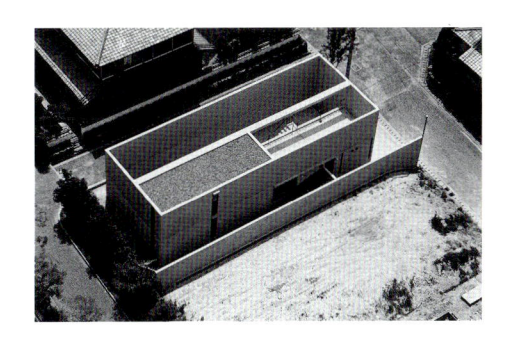

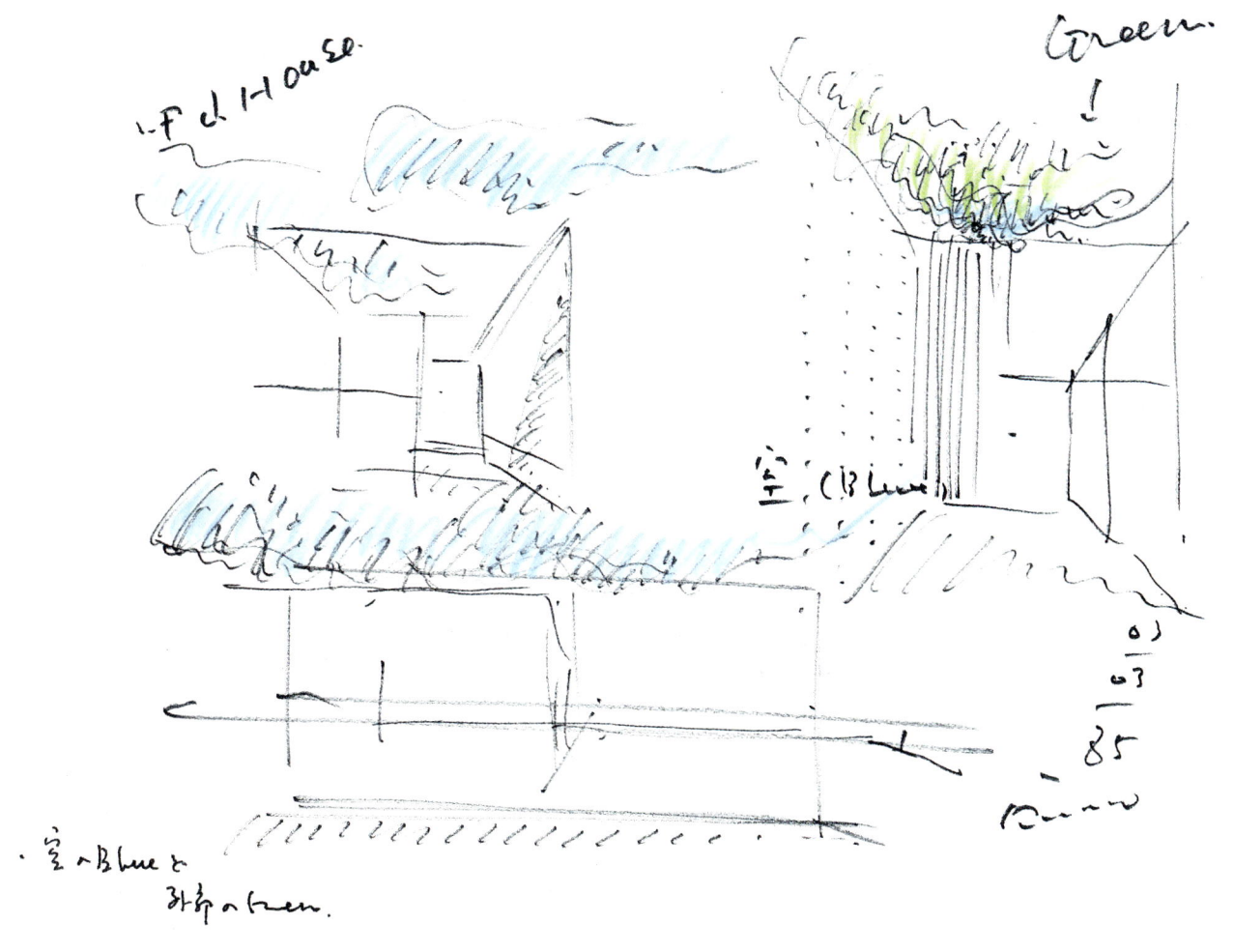

View of exterior stairs and floor plans.

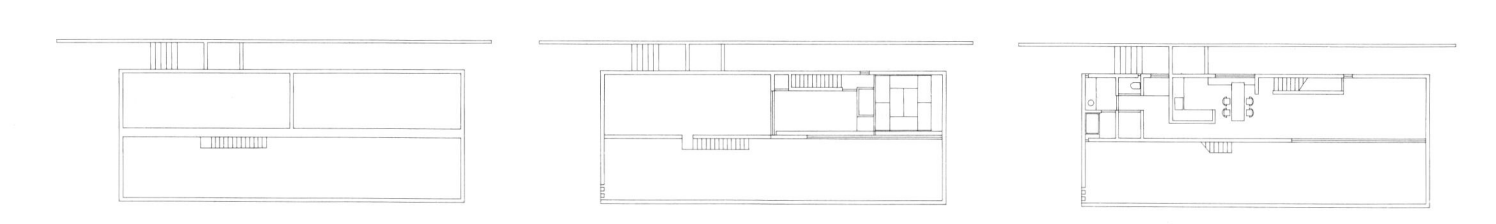

Interior and exterior views.

Mon Petit Chou

Exterior and interior views, plans and axonometric.

This café and cake shop is in a quiet residential district of northern Kyoto. It is two-storeyed but half-buried in the ground to harmonize with the low houses in the neighbourhood. The overall composition consists of a long, narrow box measuring 7 x 21 metres and topped by a vault with a cross section of one-sixth of a circle, and a curved wall a quarter of a circle in plan introduced into the box. The circle appears both in plan and section, lending movement to the space.
The vault suggests a horizontal, axial movement that is met by a curved wall which redirects the movement along its surface to the outside. The plan is simple, but the introduction of a two-storey space adds dynamism. On the ground floor are an area for tables and a take-away space, and in the basement are more tables and a kitchen. The basement dining area is a multi-storey space and is open to a sloping area of greenery. In place of the open sky this area is enhanced by a toplight along the curved wall, light from the courtyard, and the greenery.

Location Kyoto
Design 1983–4
Construction 1984–5
Structure Reinforced concrete
Site area 516.8 m^2
Building area 180.4 m^2
Total floor area 322.9 m^2

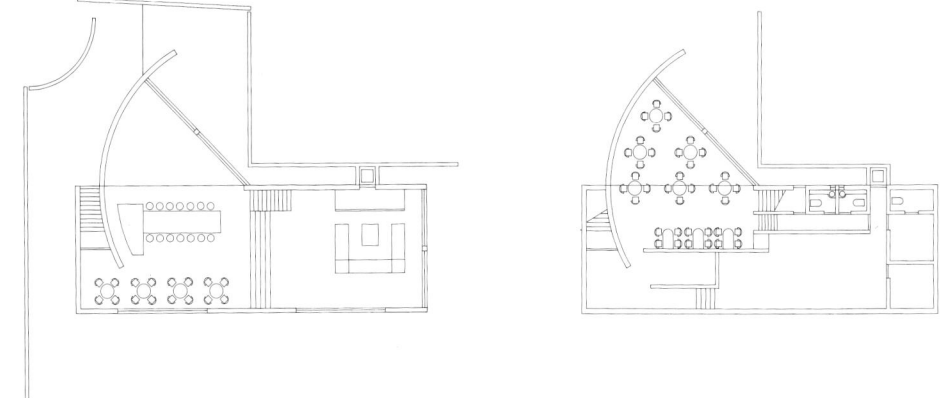

231

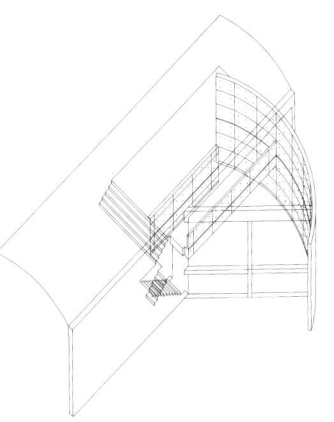

Hata House

Aerial view of the building, conceptual sketch, axonometric and detailed view of the terrace.

This three-storey house stands on a suburban hillside with a stream flowing nearby and with a forest as backdrop. Its compositional arrangement draws from the Japanese gardening technique *shakkei*, 'borrowed scenery'. Conceived as having two outlooks, part of the house is open and the other closed. The open part of the house faces south towards the forest, and has an outdoor stepped terrace; and on the first floor is the hall, a multi-storey space, a dining room and a tatami room. The green hillside beyond the terrace can be seen from the dining room.

On the ground floor, there is a bedroom facing a sunken court. This is the closed aspect of the house, where the landscape is shut out to allow a more intense experience of nature in the guise of sunlight, wind and rain.

Location Nishinomiya
Design 1983–4
Construction 1984
Structure Reinforced concrete
Site area 441.5 m^2
Building area 118.7 m^2
Total floor area 207.2 m^2

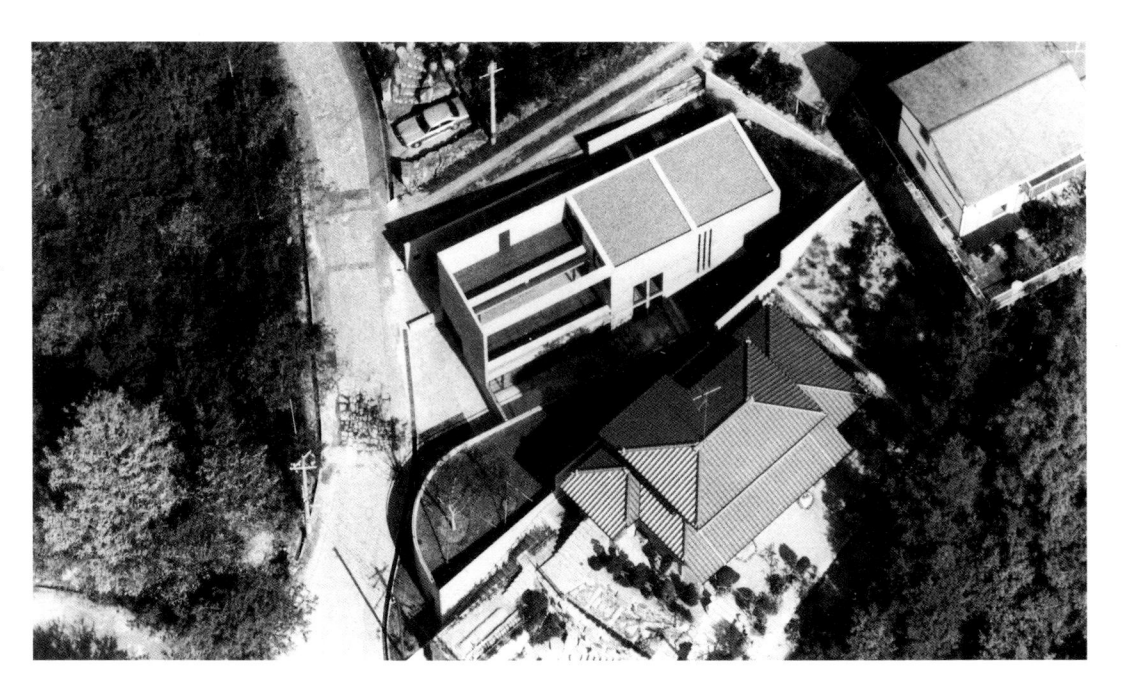

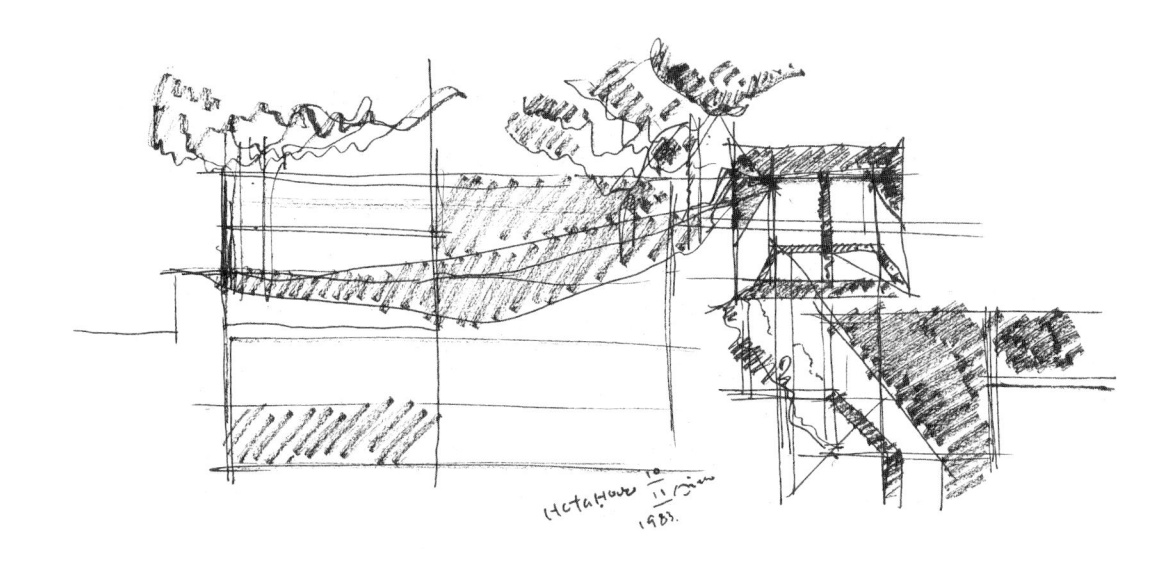

233

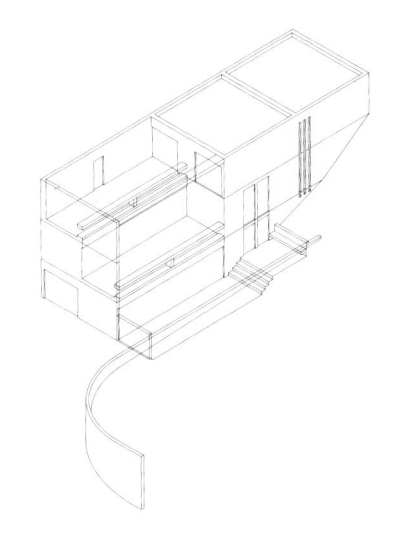

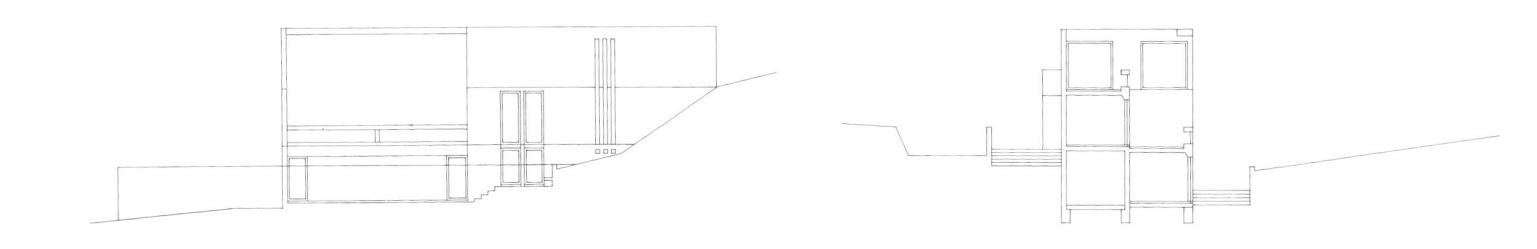

Principal elevation, section and view onto the terrace.

Floor plans, oblique view of the building and view showing the glazed wall of the dining room.

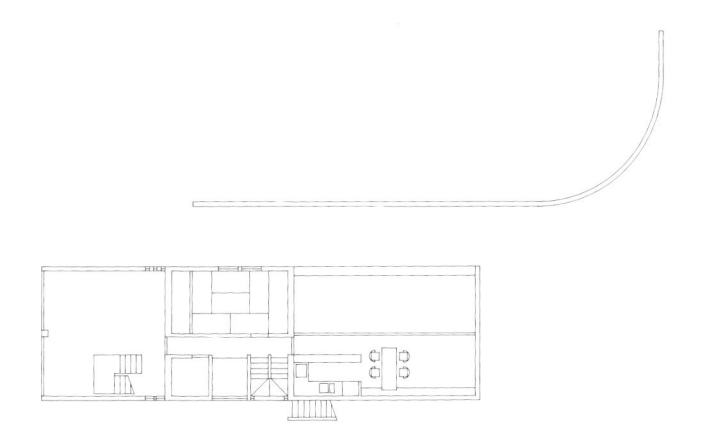

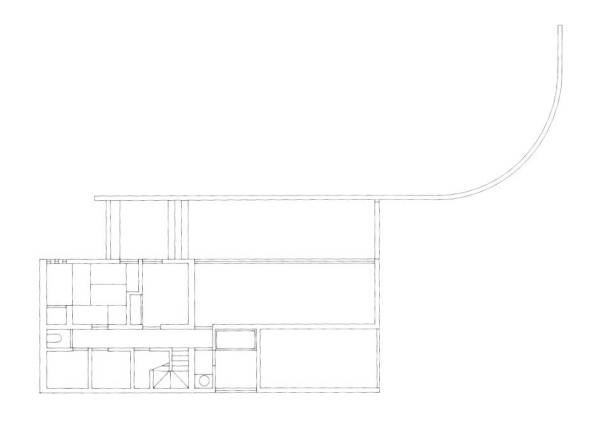

Sasaki House

Detail of the facade and floor plans.

This house is at the corner of a Y-shaped intersection in an old, upper-income residential district of Tokyo. To maintain privacy and to keep out noise, a curved wall of concrete block has been built along the street.

The plan is composed of a square, 12 x 12 metres, and a quadrant of a circle with a radius of nine metres. These two parts are staggered. The curved wall extends along the property line and draws visitors in from the street. There is a two-storey entrance in the space between the square and the curved wall.

Light is introduced by a slit along the top of the curved wall. The dining room, living room and main bedroom are on the ground floor facing the garden to the south. On the first floor are a bedroom in the quadrant portion and the hall in the square portion. A diagonal wall that corresponds to the north–south axis divides the hall and the terrace. The interior and exterior, separated by the 45 degree wall, are very different living spaces and form the nucleus of the house.

Location Tokyo
Design 1984–5
Construction 1985–6
Structure Reinforced concrete
Site area 382.1 m^2
Building area 227.1 m^2
Total floor area 373.1 m^2

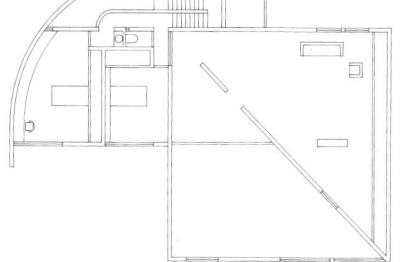

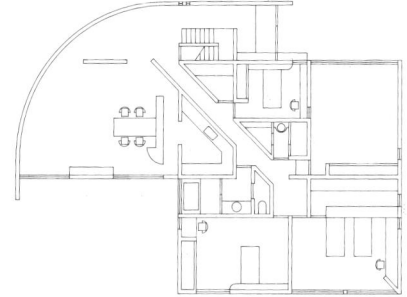

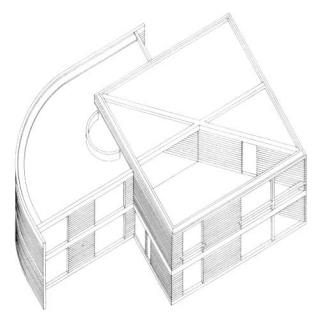

View onto the terrace, view of the curved wall and axonometric.

237

Guest House for Hattori House

Longitudinal section, floor plans and view of the entrance walkway.

This guest house, an extension built next to an existing wooden house, was to be used as a communal space by neighbours. The plan is a rectangle 3.3 metres wide and 28 metres long, and approximately two-thirds of this area is given over to outdoor space. The compositional elements consist of a guest room, the long approach to that room and a long wall. The approach serves as a buffer zone between the new and older buildings.

The entrance and parking space are on the ground floor. You approach by way of stepping-stones – which also lead to the entrance to the house – and go along the long wall, ascend steps, and after crossing an 11-metre long deck, arrive at the guest room. This is a square, 3 metres to a side, in its transverse section. The room is located at about mezzanine level relative to the house and offers a new way of looking at the by now familiar house and garden.

Location Osaka
Design 1984–5
Construction 1985
Structure Reinforced concrete
Building area 32.3 m²
Total floor area 68.3 m²

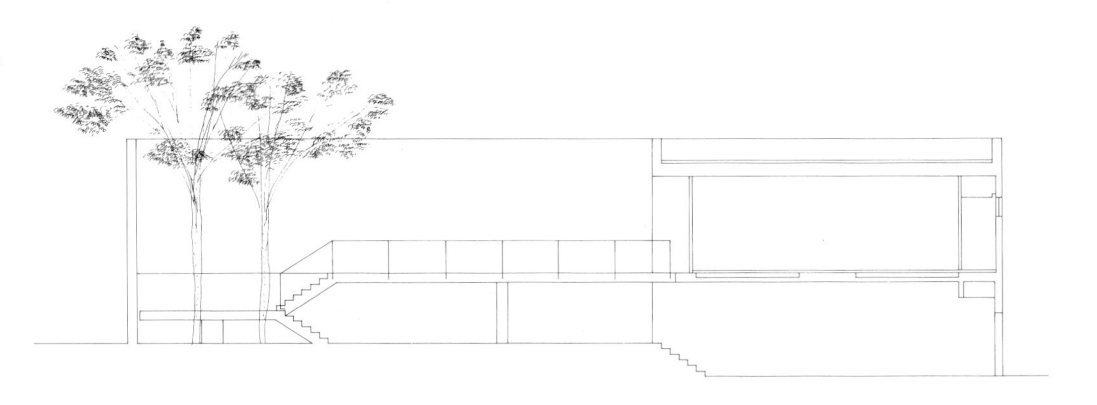

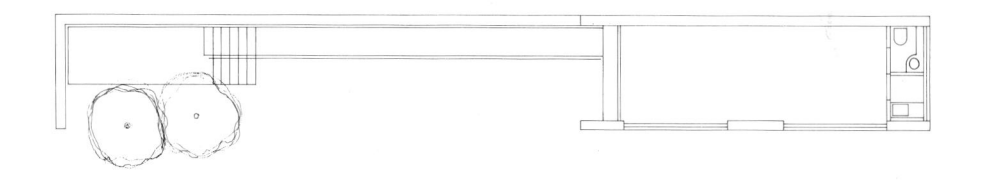

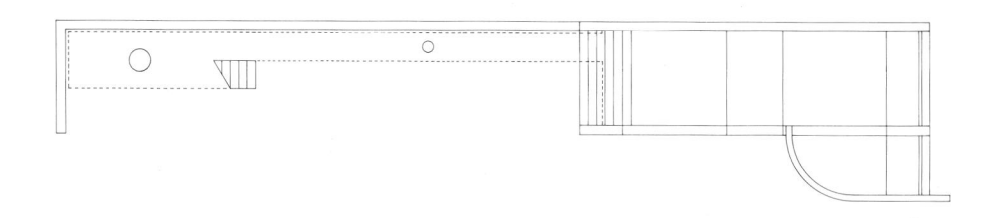

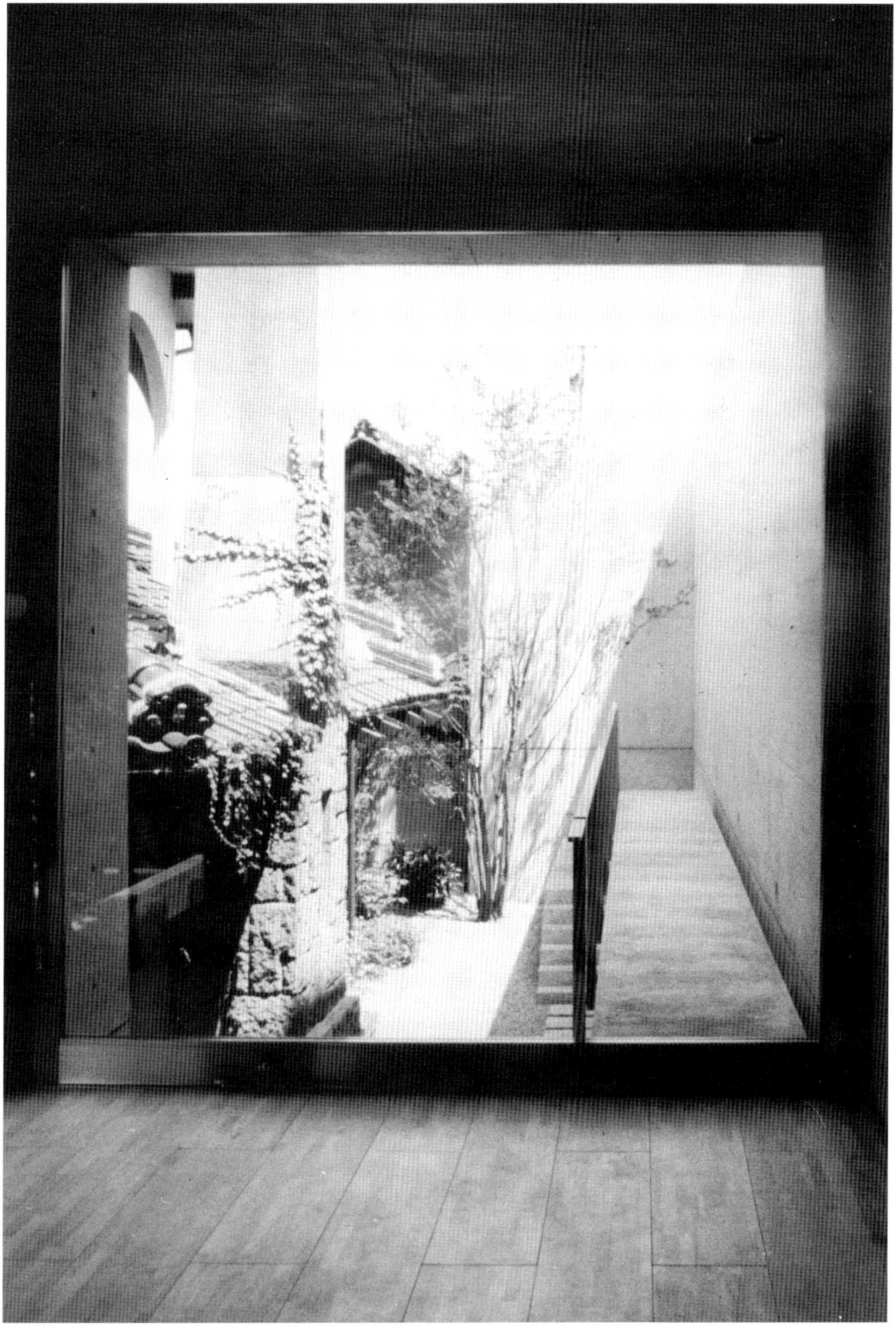

Taiyo Cement Headquarters

Axonometric, views showing the entrance walkway and interior of the building, and floor plans.

Amidst the complex cityscape of Osaka, the concrete-block wall has created an architectural domain that enables a building to cut itself off from the outside world. In this building new forms of spatial expression were explored, and the durability, use and composition of concrete blocks were also analysed.

In wet concrete-block construction, joints are usually 10 mm thick; here the construction method, using the blocks as forms, is dry and the joints are 3 mm thick. The blocks measure 197 mm x 397 mm x 240 mm, and the design module is 200 mm x 400 mm. Every part of the building is dimensioned according to this module. Working within such structural constraints, the intention was to construct a large, framed space with a simple expression.

Office spaces, separated into different zones for different departments, are on the ground and first floors, and a conference room that can also serve as a multi-purpose hall, with a 3.6 metre ceiling height, is on the second floor. The building is centred around a three-storey outdoor space that extends from the street to the far end of the building; all circulation between floors is contiguous to this space.

Location Osaka
Design 1984–5
Construction 1985–6
Structure Reinforced concrete
Site area 1,069.3 m^2
Building area 300.6 m^2
Total floor area 742.6 m^2

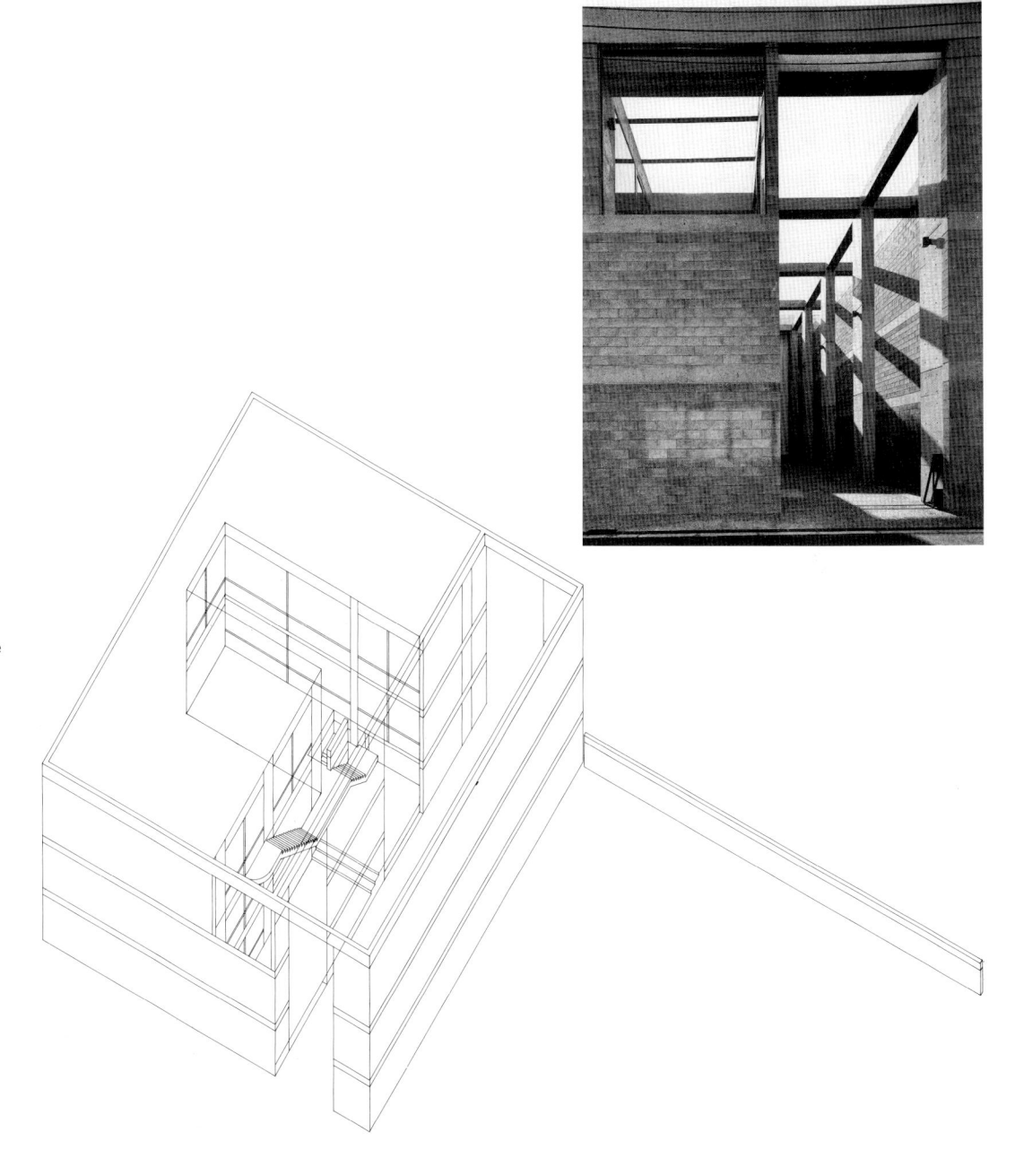

241

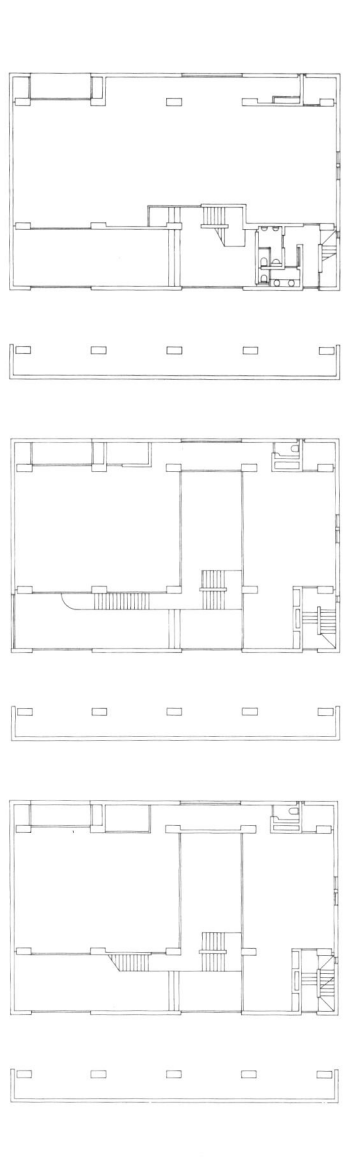

TS Building

Axonometric and section.

The site is near Nakanoshima, the central district of Osaka. Across the street is a park full of greenery and beyond that is Dojima River, the stage for the 'Tenjin-matsuri', one of the three major Japanese festivals.

The building has six floors. The windows on the south side, facing Dojima River, are full height and pivoted to provide a complete opening, so that one is able to view the 'Tenjin-matsuri' from inside the building. The ground level is used as a furniture showroom visible from the street across the central multi-storey space. Offices are on the first, second and third floors and are arranged around the multi-storey space which has a ceiling of glass blocks.

The guest house on the fourth and fifth floors is divided into two zones separated by the central lightwell. A bedroom and a tatami room occupy the two zones on the fourth floor, while on the fifth floor a lobby is separated from the bedroom and kitchen.

Location Osaka
Design 1984–5
Construction 1985–6
Structure Reinforced concrete
Site area 160.7 m^2
Building area 158.1 m^2
Total floor area 665 m^2

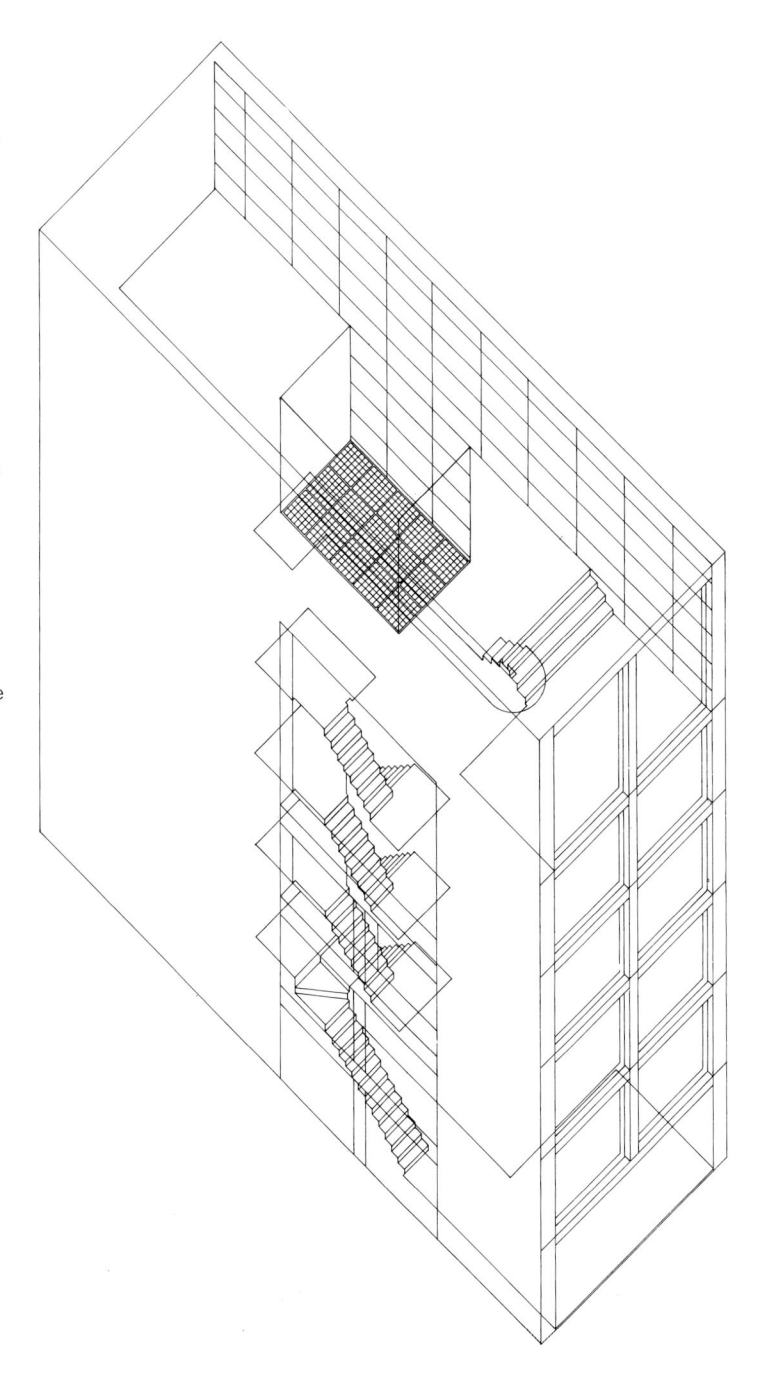

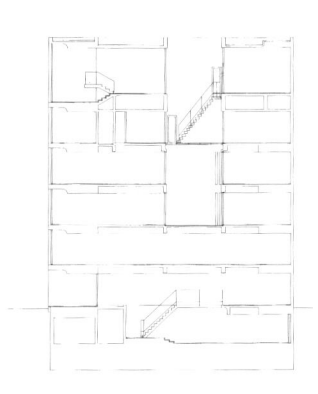

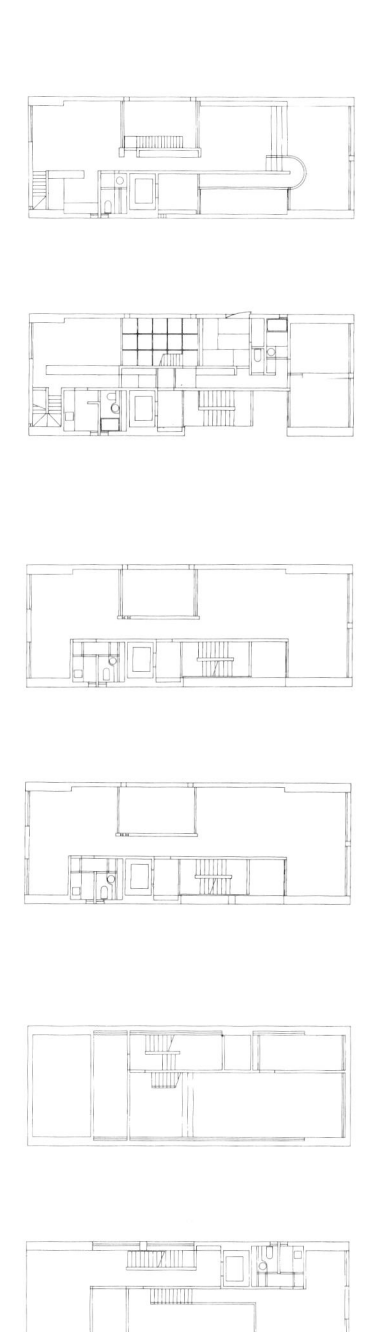

View from the street, ground-level showroom and floor plans.

Interior views and conceptual sketch.

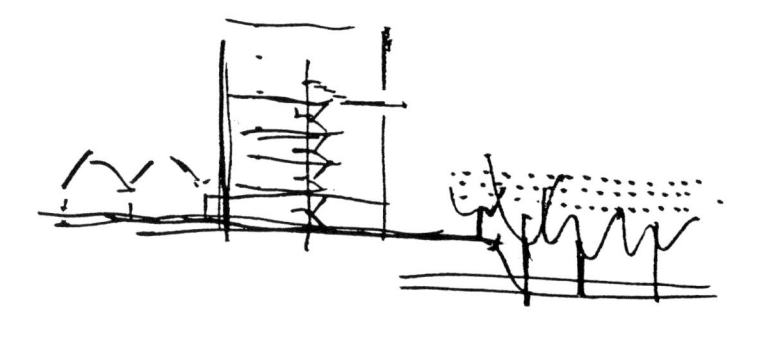

244

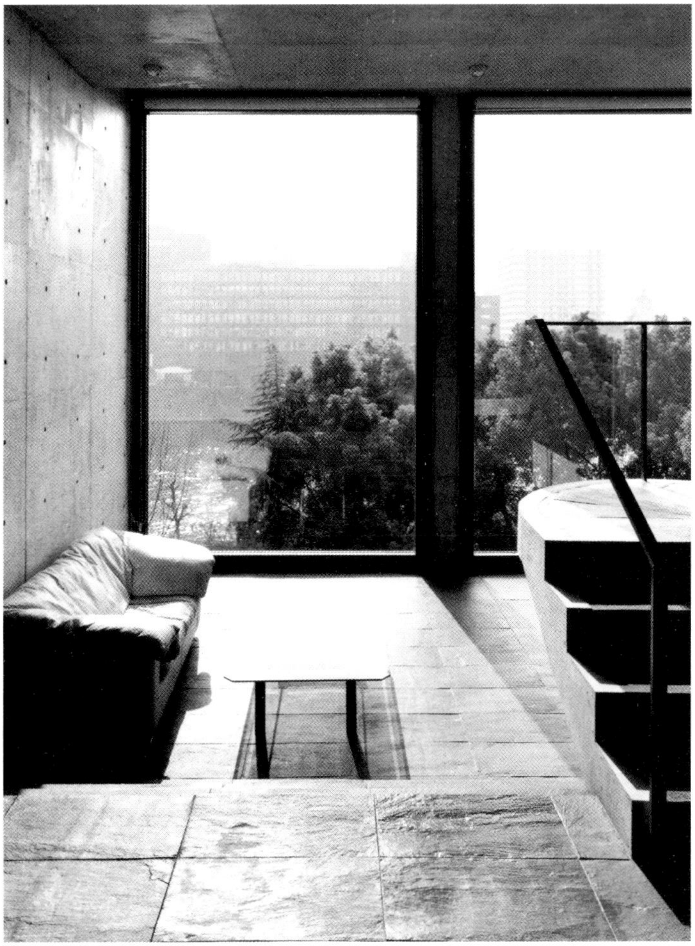

Church on Mount Rokko

View of the roof, site plan and view showing bell tower.

On a verdant slope of Mount Rokko, this small church enjoys sweeping ocean views. The building has a chapel and bell tower, a covered colonnade and a freestanding wall, which partially encloses the landscape.

While the chapel is a concrete mass, the long colonnade is a glazed promenade. At the end of the colonnade, the visitor is led from a light-infused space into the sharply contrasting dark chapel. The altar is straight ahead and, to the left, a large window – divided by a cross-shaped post and beam which cast a distinct cruciform shadow on the floor – looks out onto the mountainside.

Location Kobe
Design 1985
Construction 1985–6
Structure Reinforced concrete
Site area 7,933.3 m^2
Building area 220.3 m^2
Total floor area 220.3 m^2

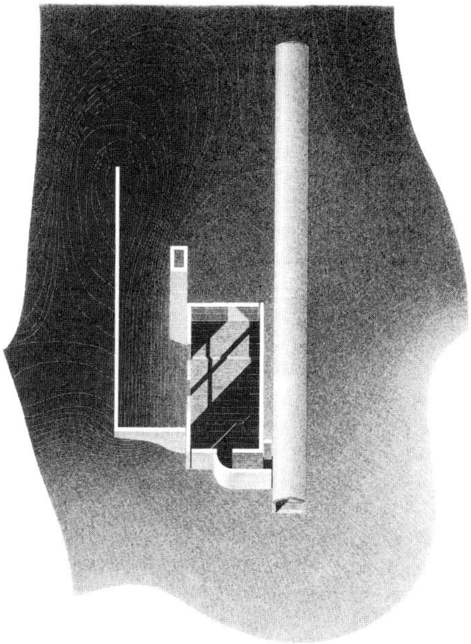

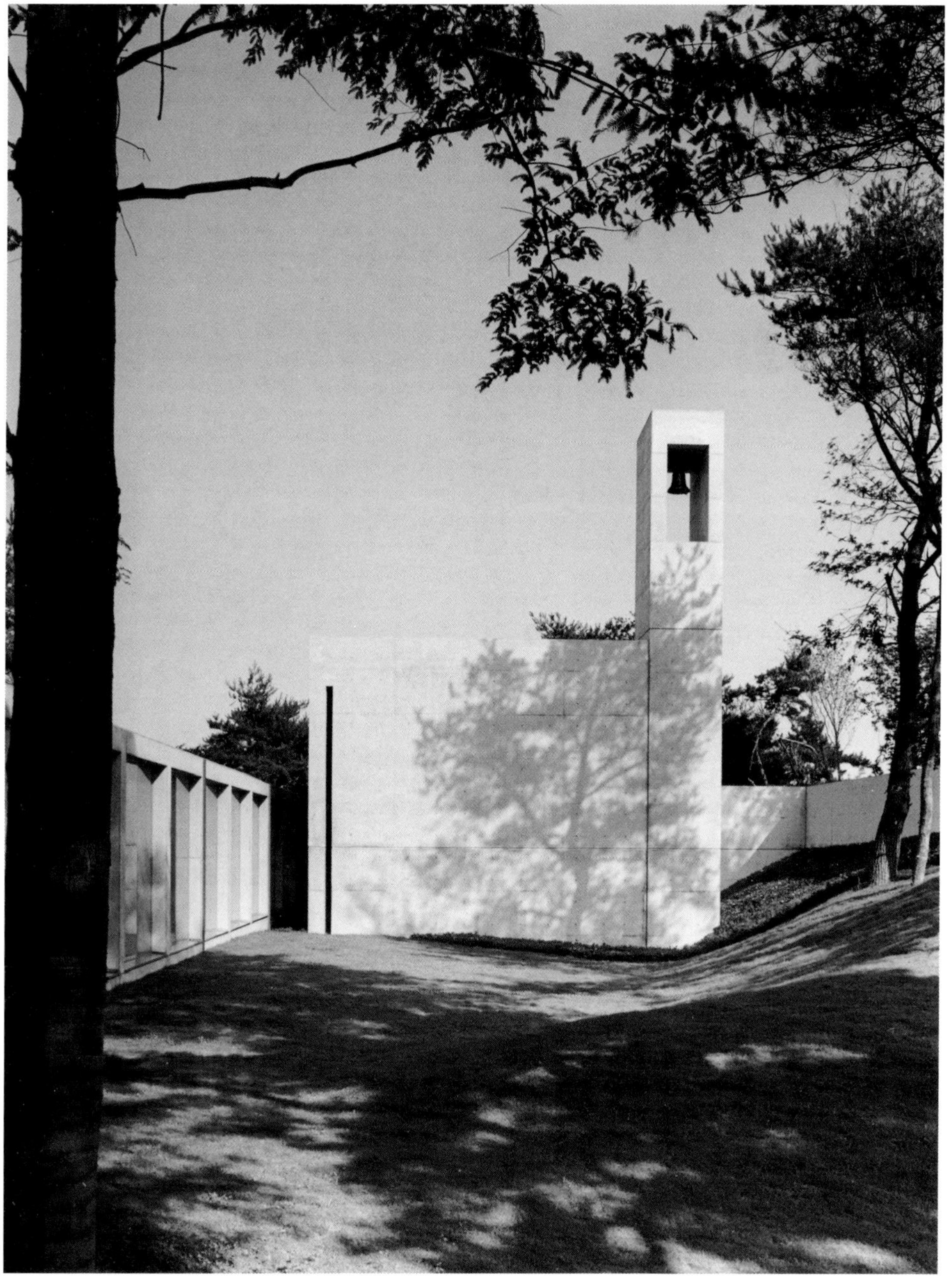

Construction drawing and view of the church.

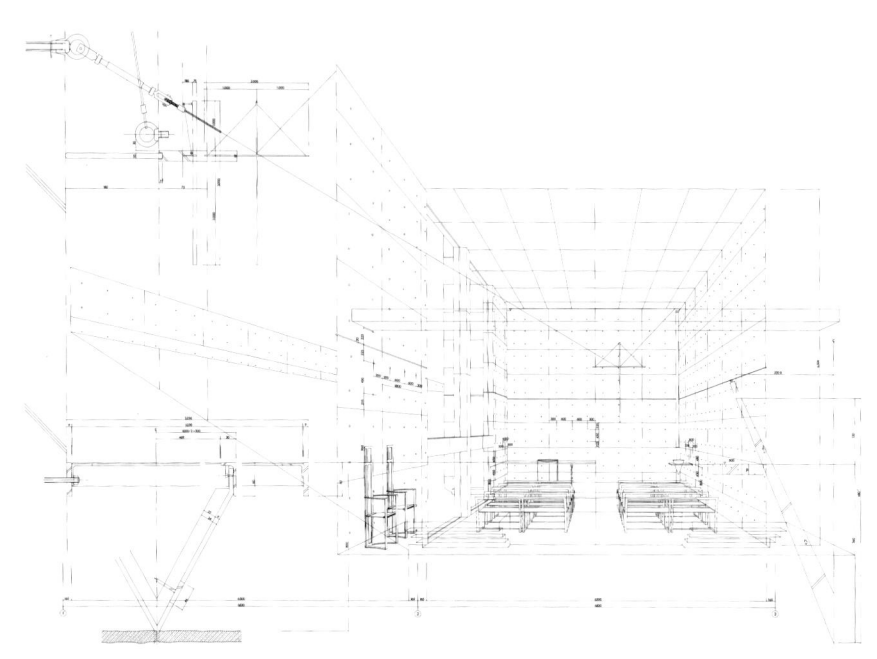

Construction drawing and view of the portico.

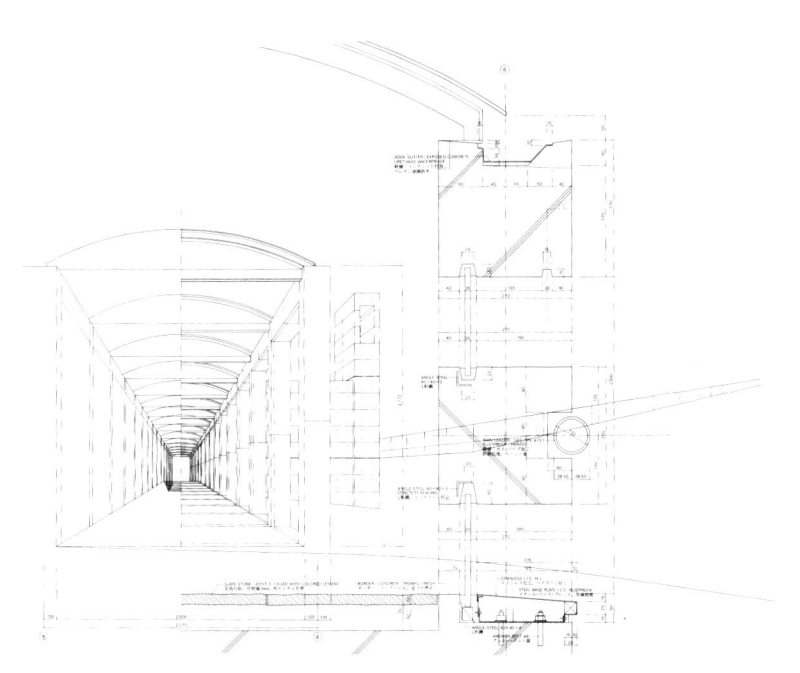

Interior views of the chapel and view looking out to the garden.

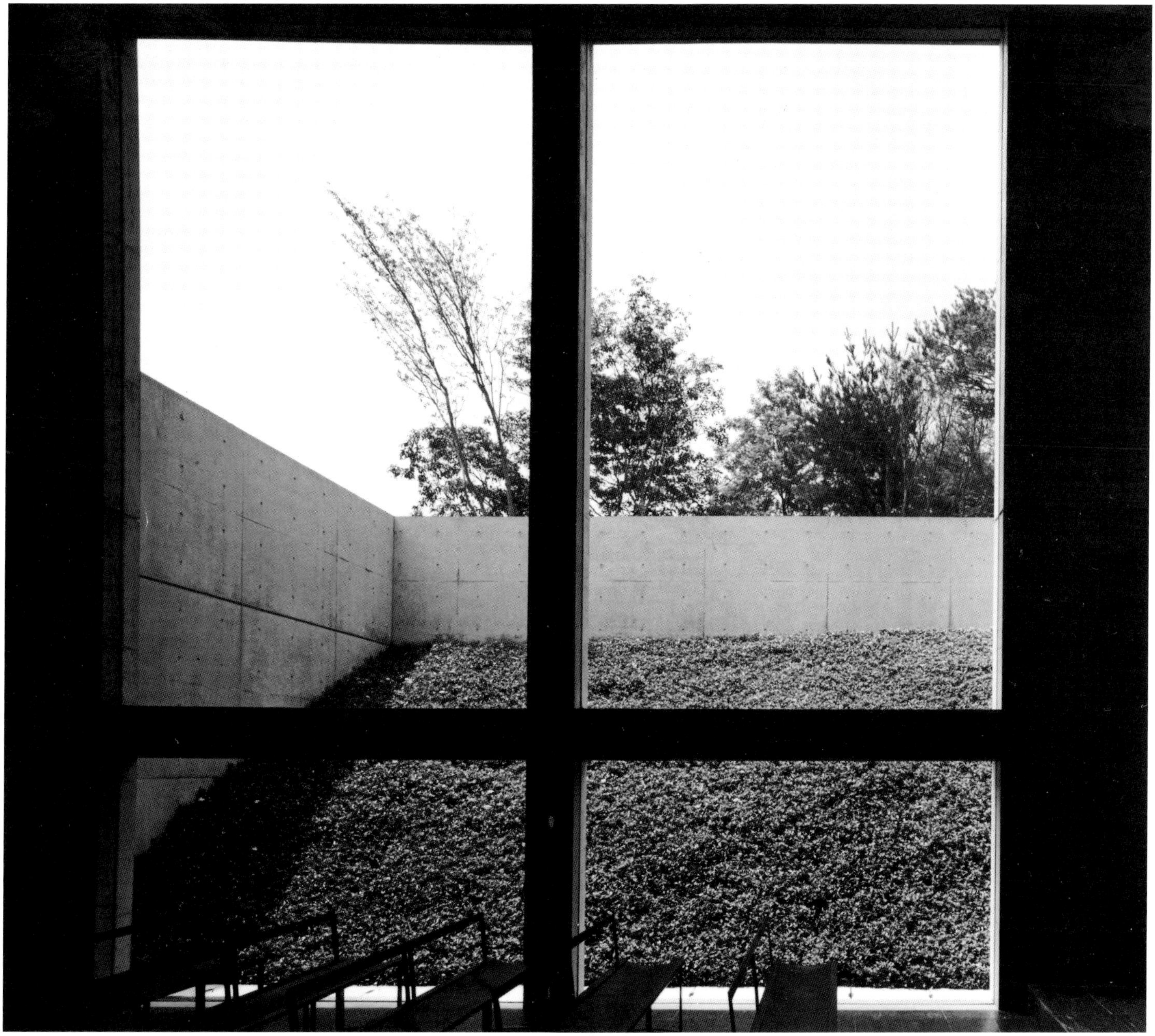

Old/New Restaurant

Axonometric, conceptual sketch, floor plans and oblique view of the stone wall.

The Old/New Rokko restaurant complex is built on a steep gradient of over 1:8, affording distant views of the ocean from the second-floor bar. A multi-storey entrance hall separates, and at the same time links, the four eating areas, which include Japanese and western restaurants. The whole building was composed around three 200-year old camphor trees. The perimeter retaining walls use the locally quarried Mikage granite that is a feature of traditional residences in this area.

Location Kobe
Design 1985
Construction 1985–6
Structure Reinforced concrete
Site area 1,283 m^2
Building area 481.1 m^2
Total floor area 806.5 m^2

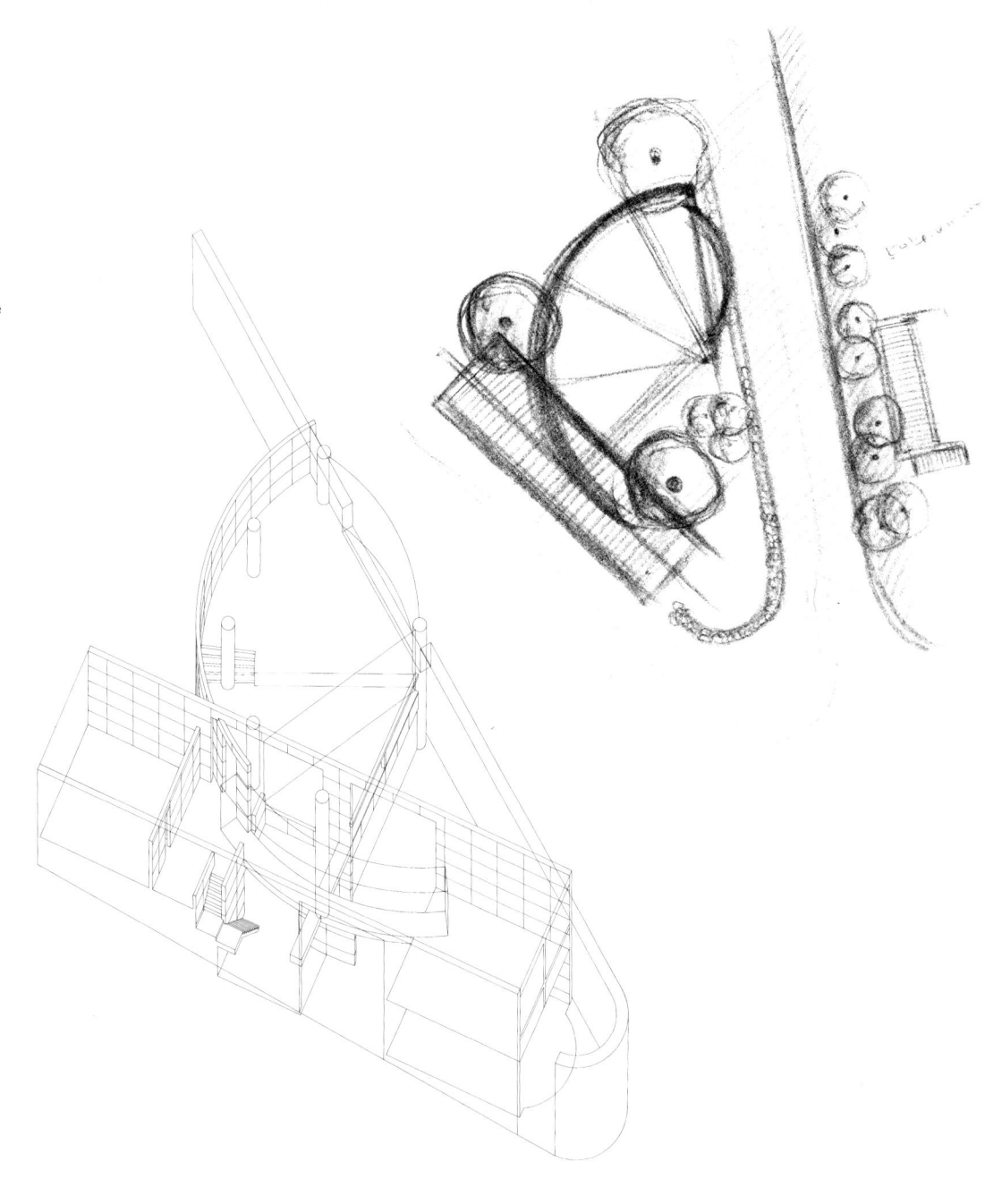

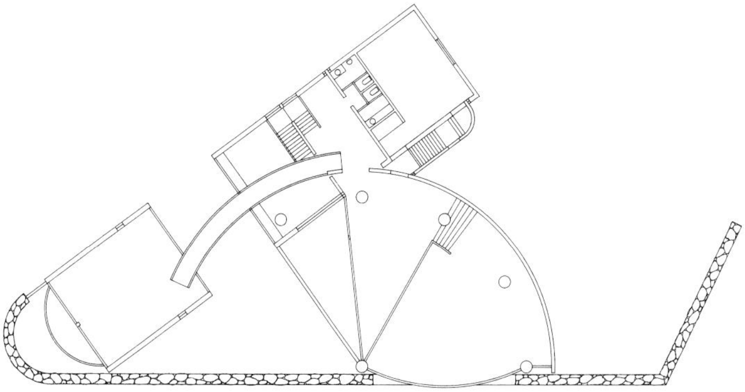

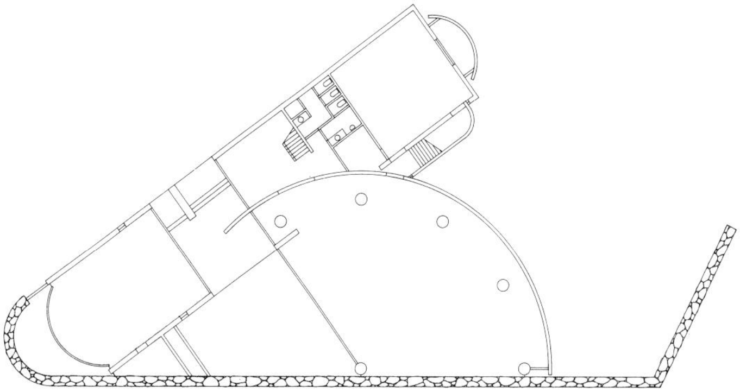

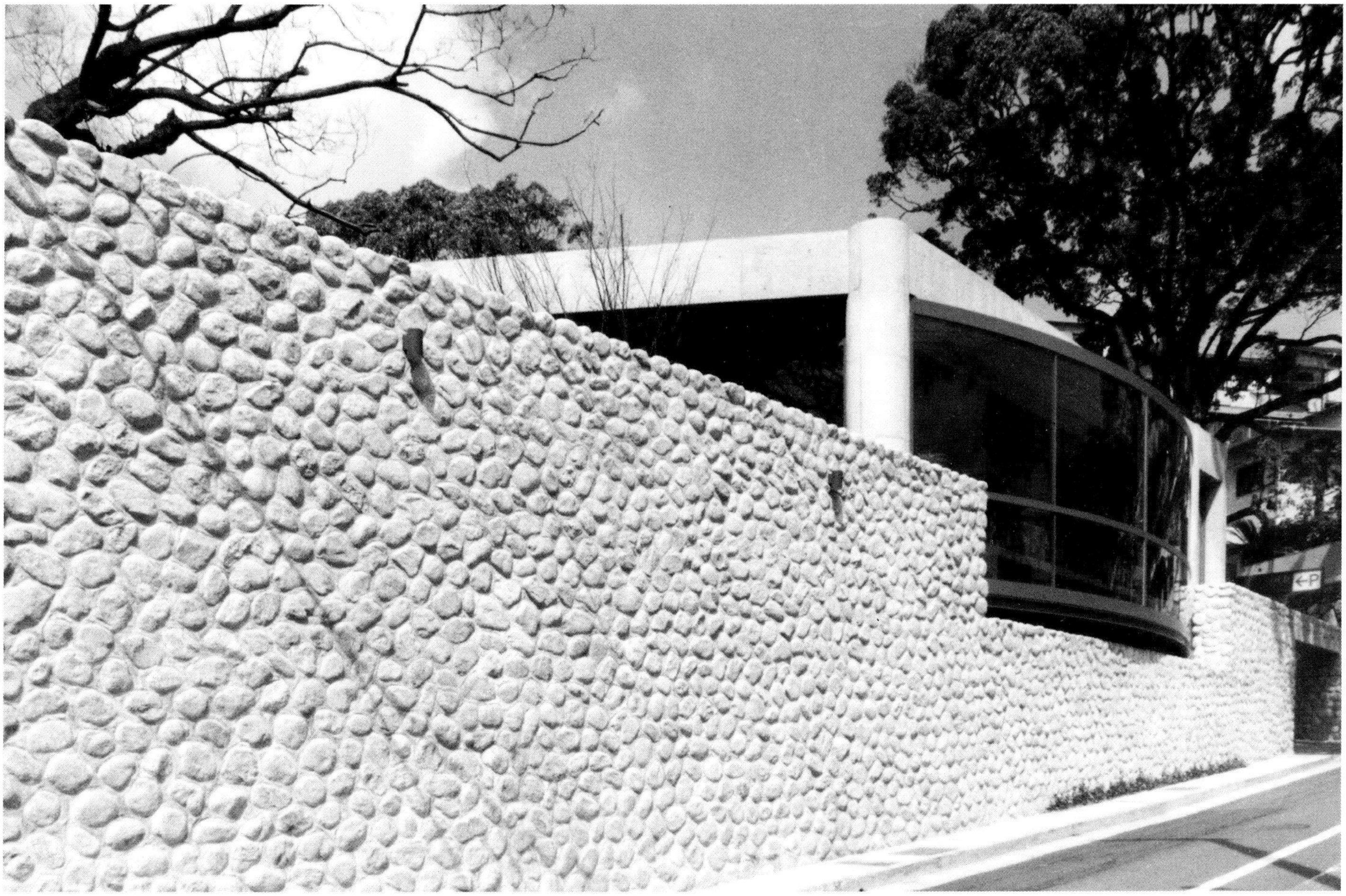

View from the street and oblique view.

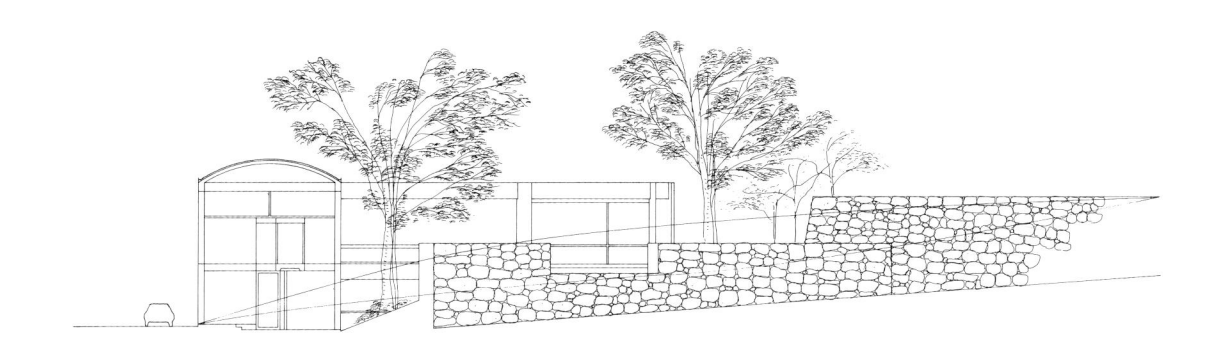

254

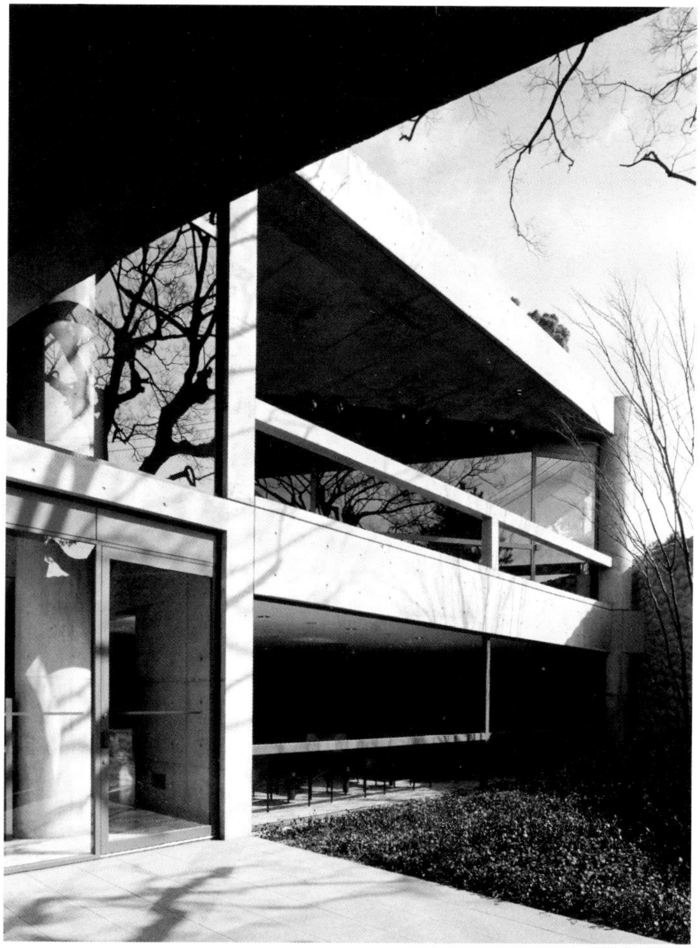

Tanaka Atelier

Exterior and interior views, and section.

This long and narrow building is topped by an arc-shaped ceiling. The basement level contains the service areas; the ground floor houses the atelier itself; while the level of the semi-circular form accommodates the terraces of the building. The ceiling bestows uniformity and fluidity to the space overall, and the exterior roof is steeply sloping with overhanging eaves.

Location Yamanashi
Design 1985–6
Construction 1986–7
Structure Reinforced concrete and steel
Site area 693.6 m^2
Building area 71.9 m^2
Total floor area 100.5 m^2

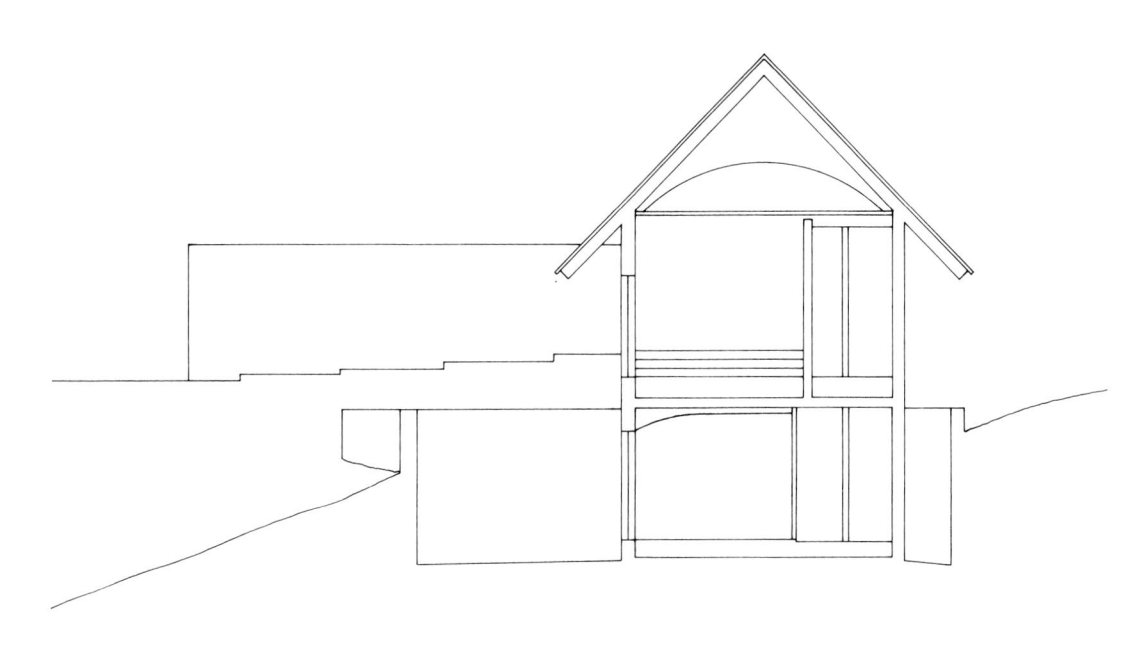

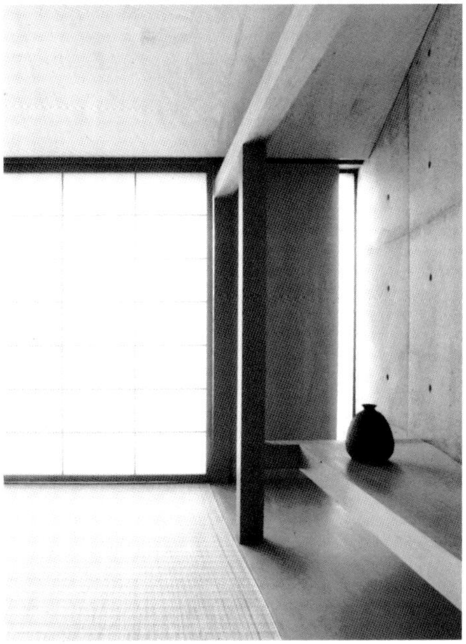

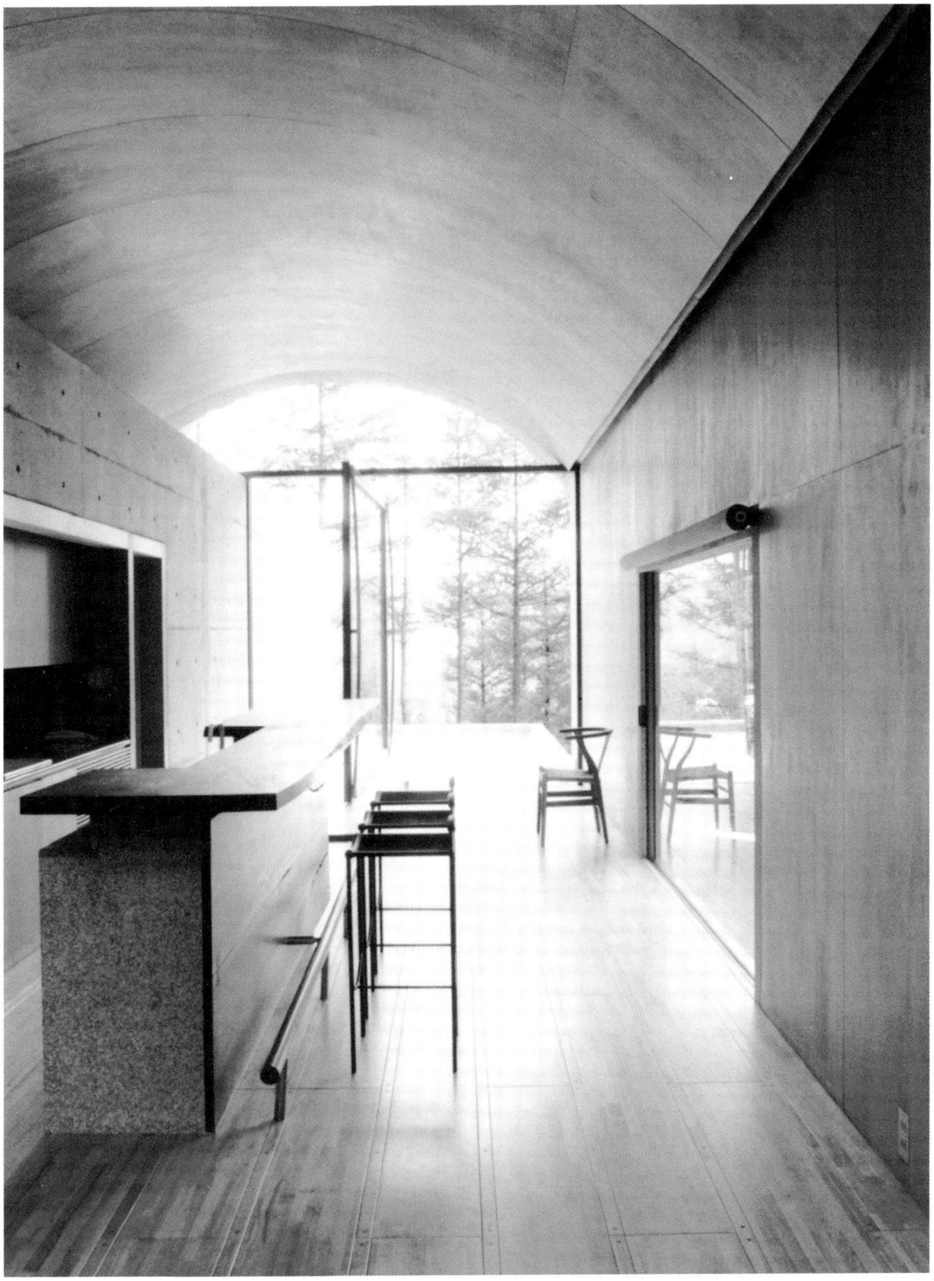

Shibuya Project

Conceptual sketch, site plan, axonometric and sectional view of the model.

This commercial complex planned for a site in the middle of the Shibuya area in Tokyo will house twenty different stores, restaurants and cafés of various sizes.

There are four above-ground floors and ten basement floors, due in no small measure to the abnormally high land prices in Japan. The setback from the street, determined by law, restricts the above-ground floors to four and also sets a limit to the ceiling height at each level. So exterior space is used to the full and pedestrians relate to the architecture three-dimensionally.

A screen stands along the street, and the building proper is at a 15-degree angle to it. The gap between the screen and the building is a public space in the nature of an 'urban alcove'. This gap is to be used for vertical circulation, in the form of an open stairway leading to the third basement floor.

A cylindrical volume sits in the centre of the building, and stairs leading upwards coil around this volume. The screen, facing south, consists of glass blocks arranged in orderly fashion within a concrete grid and introduces light deep into the basement.

Location Tokyo
Design 1985–7
Structure Reinforced concrete
Site area 1,130.7 m^2
Building area 867.1 m^2
Total floor area 6,210.1 m^2

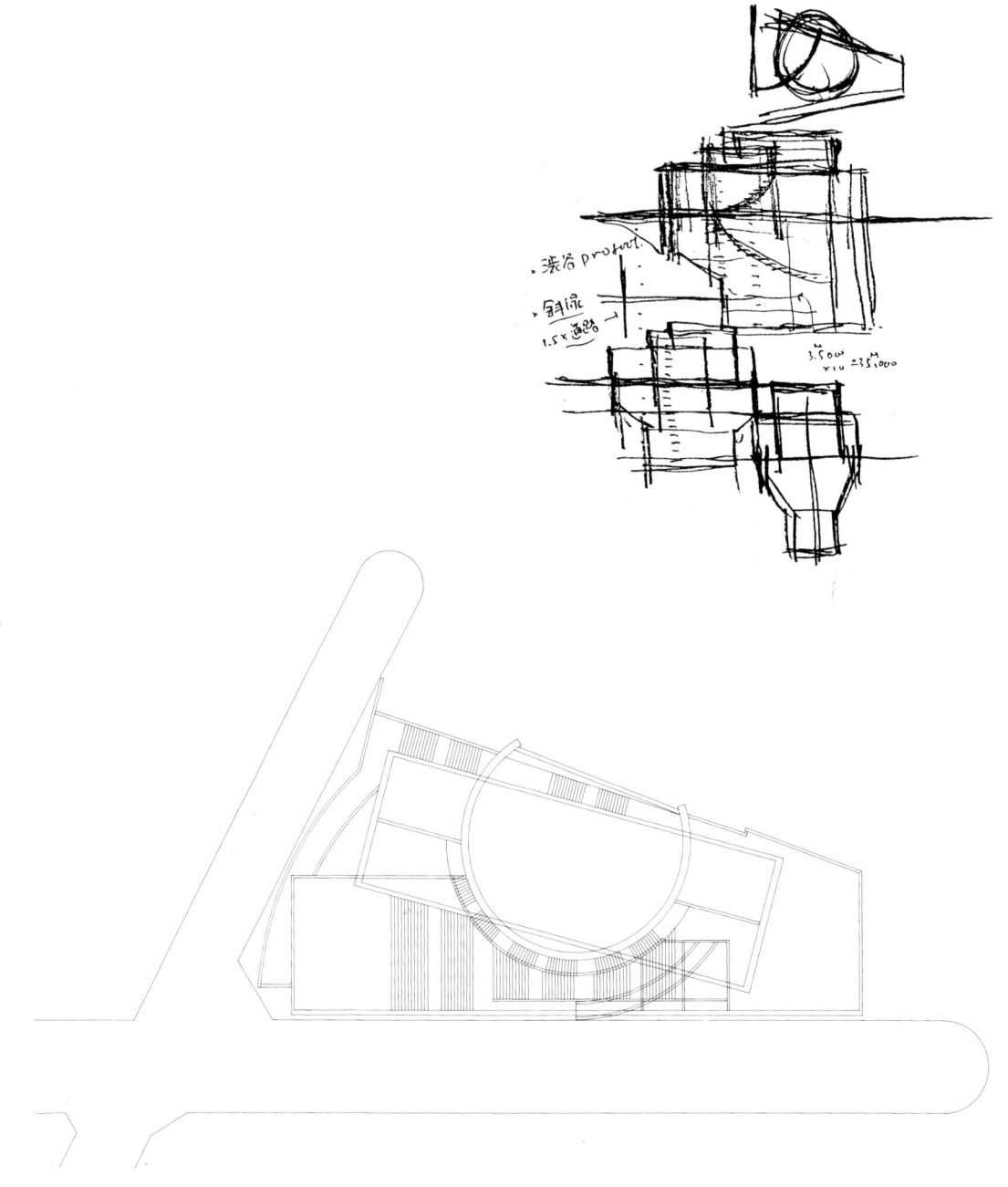

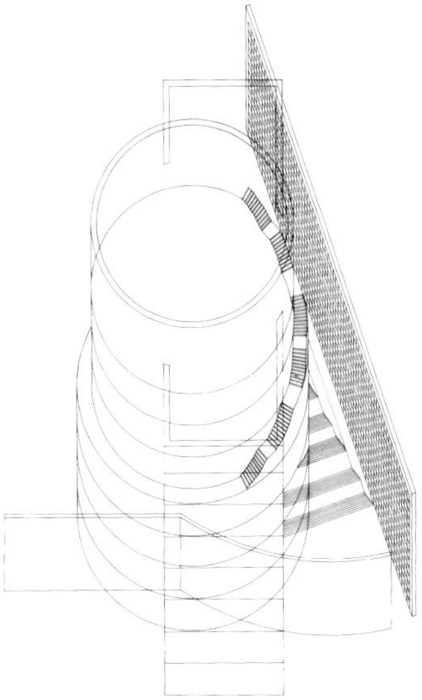

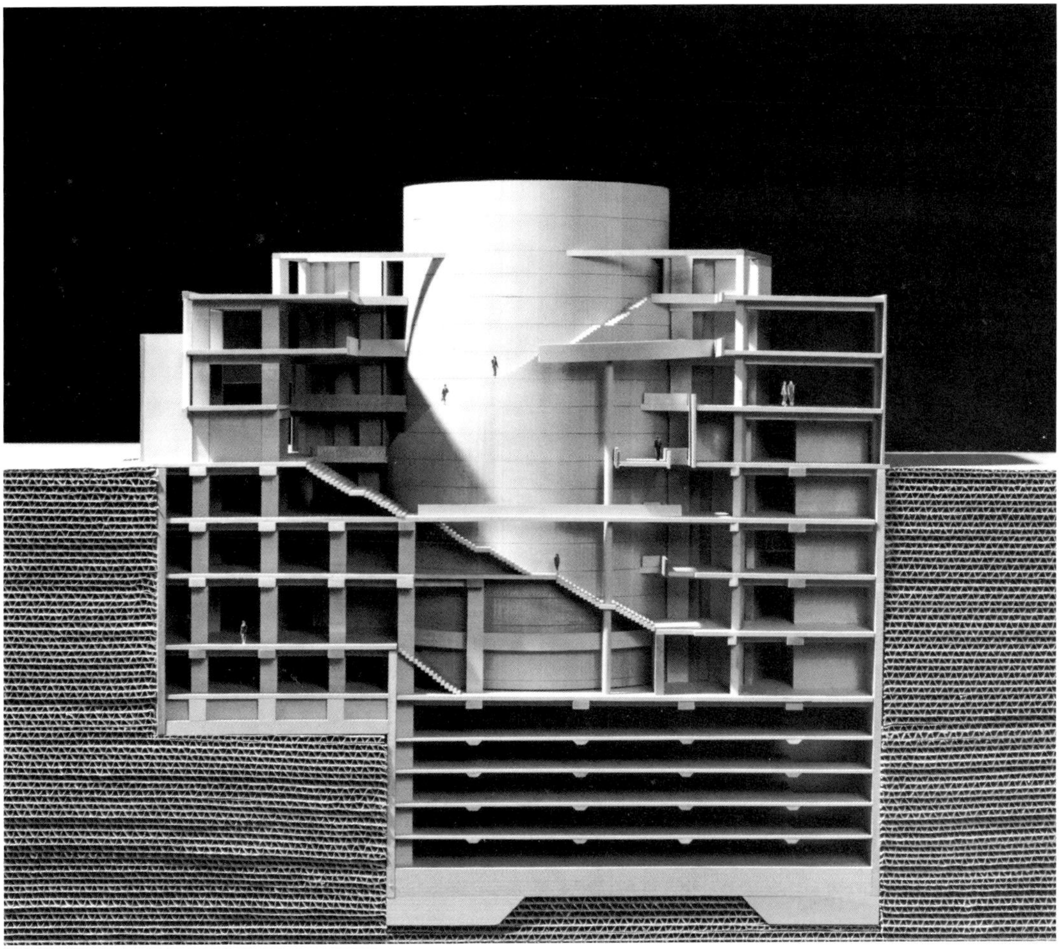

Noguchi House

Conceptual sketches.

The house occupies a long, narrow lot in a densely-populated area on the outskirts of Osaka. The street elevation is only a few metres wide and is in line with those of the neighbouring houses. Despite the lack of surrounding free space, a light well, located at the centre of the building, permits light to penetrate and air to circulate all around the house. The rooms are at the extreme ends of the building, with the ground floor consisting of the living room and kitchen, while bedrooms and auxiliary rooms are on the floors above.

Location Osaka
Design 1985
Construction 1985–6
Structure Reinforced concrete
Site area 68.5 m^2
Building area 40 m^2
Total floor area 106.3 m^2

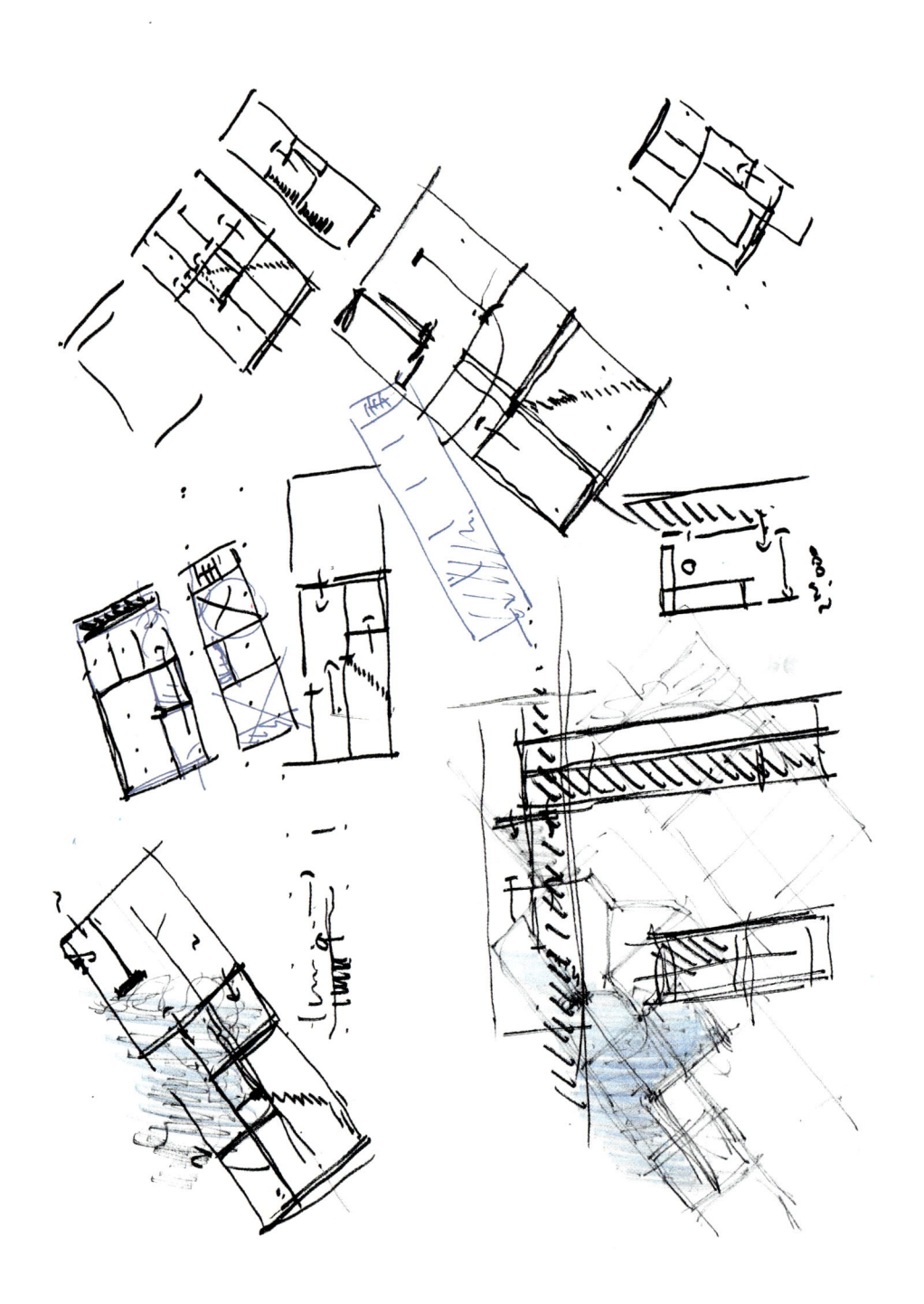

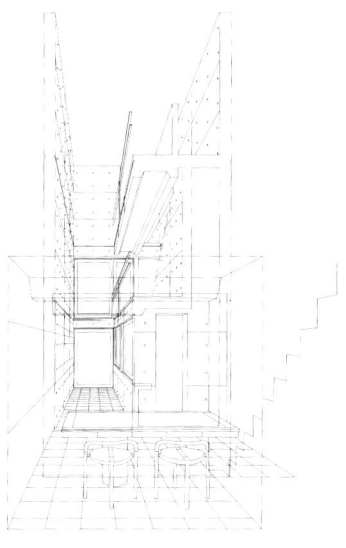

View of the roof, perspective of the entrance and view of upper-level walkway.

Oyodo Tea Houses

Floor plans and section.

The first of the three Oyodo tea houses, the veneer tea house, is an extension to a wooden row house. The exterior gives no hint of its existence. You approach through the older building which acts as a passageway to the separate world of the tea house and which serves the same function as the *roji*. In this process of passage, you experience a number of reversals of expression. The various devices installed in the entrance to the tea house and the six sides of the tea house proper – ie the floor, walls and ceiling – are intended to bestow a deeper significance to very simple functions. The aim is to give infinite depth to a minimal space. A veneer of Japanese linden is the main material used on the floor, walls and ceiling of the interior.

The scale was determined with the Myokian tea house in mind. You enter the Oyodo tea house by way of a steep, interior stairway. The interior is a cube of 2,390 mm sides, and there is a suspended ceiling that is a vault representing one-sixth of a cylinder. The space is determined by columns and beams, and the beams are 100 mm lower than those at the Myokian tea house, because there you enter via a *nijiri-guchi* at floor level whereas here you enter at a level lower. A blind is hung on one wall surface, and with twilight complex shadows are cast. The warm quality of the Japanese linden gives the space a very different character from that of the block tea house.

The block tea house was created by renovating the first floor of an old wooden row house. It consists of a rectangular orthogonal space, 1,400 mm wide, 2,800 mm long and 2,000 mm high, with polished concrete blocks of 200 mm x 400 mm as the sole material in the space. Used not only for the walls, but also for the floor, they have a hard-looking finish.

Light passing through the milky white glass, inscribed with a ginkgo tree leaf pattern, is reflected onto the blocks. Although small, a certain order emerges in this restrained space. The materiality of the blocks is neutralized and visitors are invited into a cold, but solemnly spiritual world.

Finally, the tent tea house is evocative of a square balloon which has softly landed from the sky above. It appears so small and fragile that it looks as if the slightest breeze would carry it away. However, it is a space filled with intimate intention. Composed of steel supports, a glass floor and ceiling, it has a tent roof and screen, which can be rolled up and down to provide temporary space.

The freedom of the tent tea house lies in the materials. From the outset, those commonly used in traditional Japanese buildings were intentionally excluded. But the traditional Japanese module, 5 *Shaku* 8 *Sun* (175.4 cm), was adapted for the interior dimensions and for the height of the ceiling. It is this module for square space, alone, that gives the structure a sense of tradition.

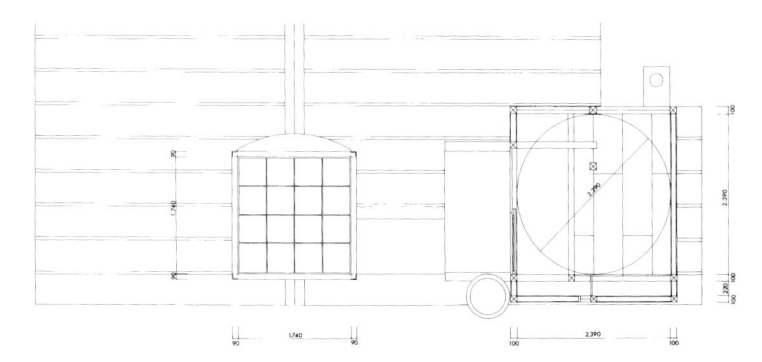

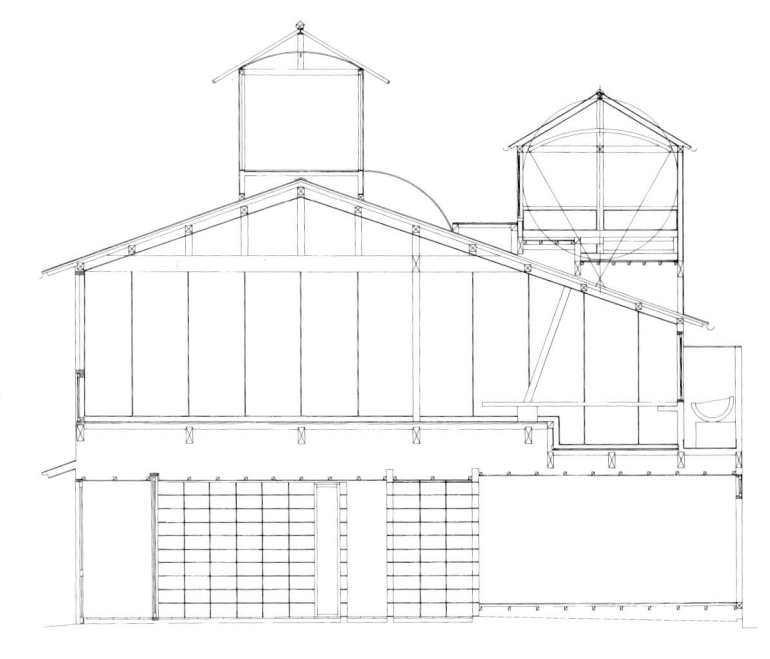

Conceptual sketches.

Veneer tea house
Location Osaka
Design 1985
Construction 1985
Structure Wood
Total floor area 7.0 m²

Block tea house
Design 1985–6
Construction 1986
Structure Concrete
Total floor area 4.4 m²

Tent tea house
Design 1987–8
Construction 1988
Structure Steel
Total floor area 3.3 m²

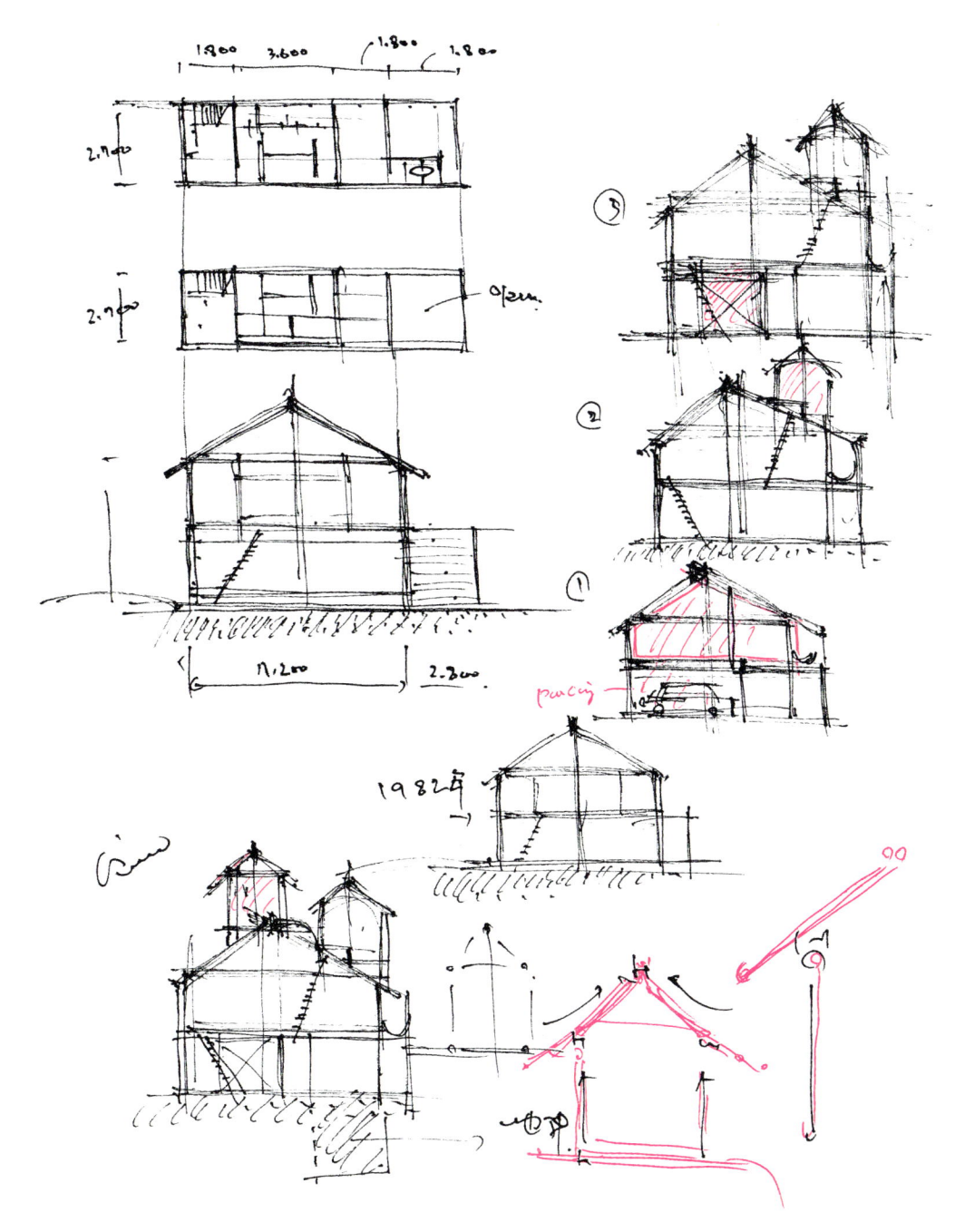

263

Perspective and view of the block tea house.

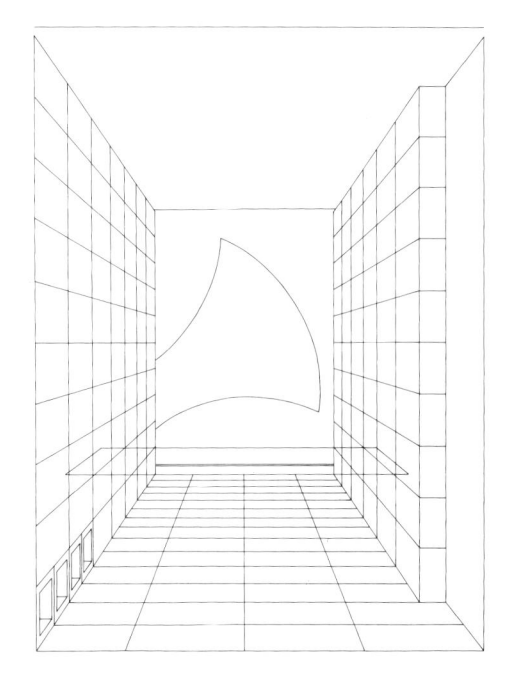

264

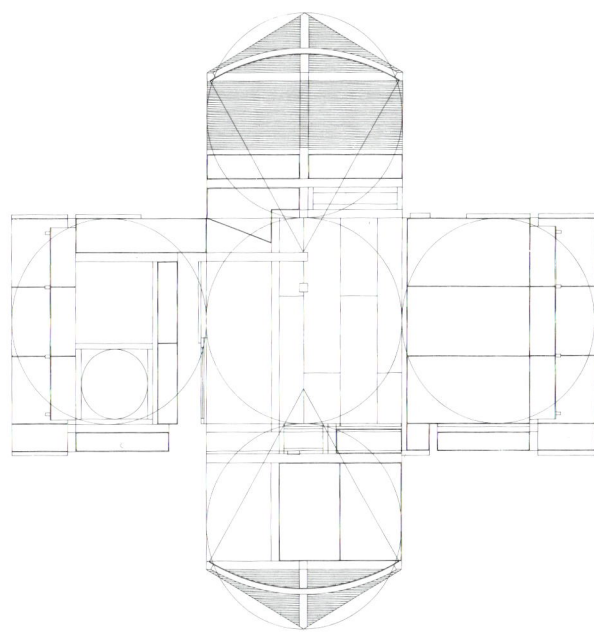

Interior views of the tent and veneer tea houses, and plan of the veneer tea house.

265

Interior view of the veneer tea house, conceptual sketches and detail view of the tent tea house.

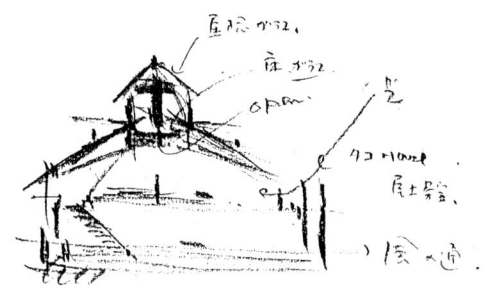

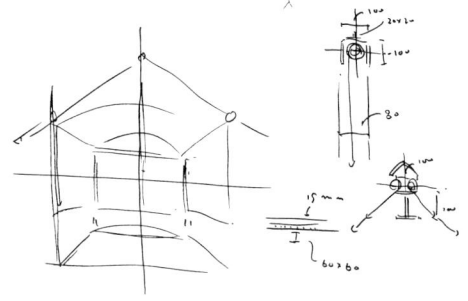

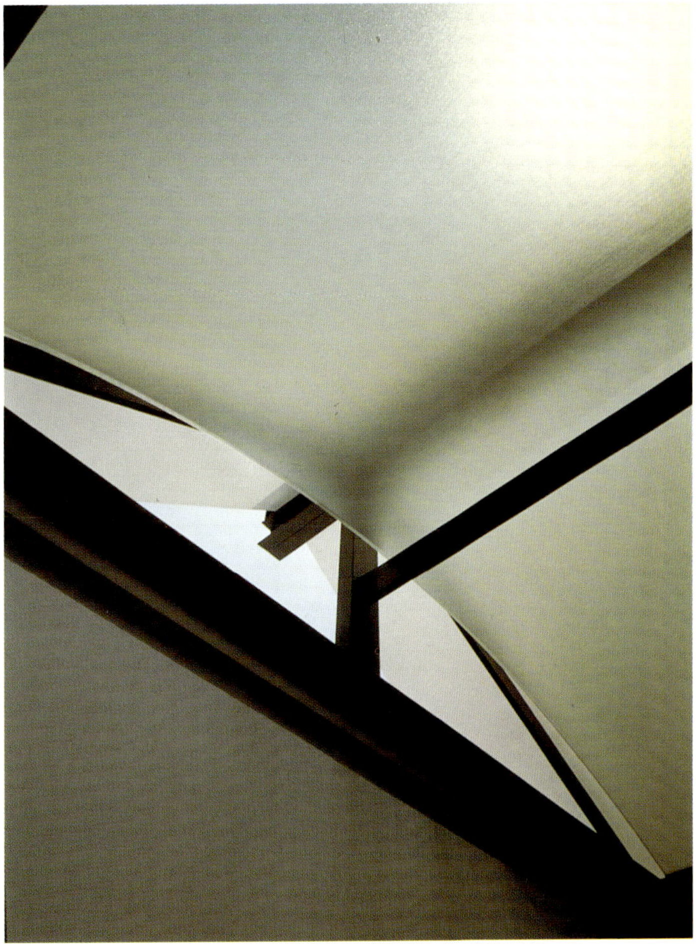

Kitayama Apartment Block

Overall and detail views of the entrance of the building and axonometric.

The building is constructed entirely of concrete blocks. The volume itself is a result of the interpenetration of four elements: a curvilinear wall, punctuated by long and narrow apertures; a structure made up of partially enclosed cubic modules (one side of which supports the vault of a long hall); a rectilinear wall enclosing the complex on three sides; and, finally, a long stairway which extends the length of one side and crosses the various levels of the building.

Location Kyoto
Design 1985–8
Construction 1988–90
Structure Reinforced concrete blocks
Site area 564.2 m^2
Building area 377.7 m^2
Total floor area 1,117.6 m^2

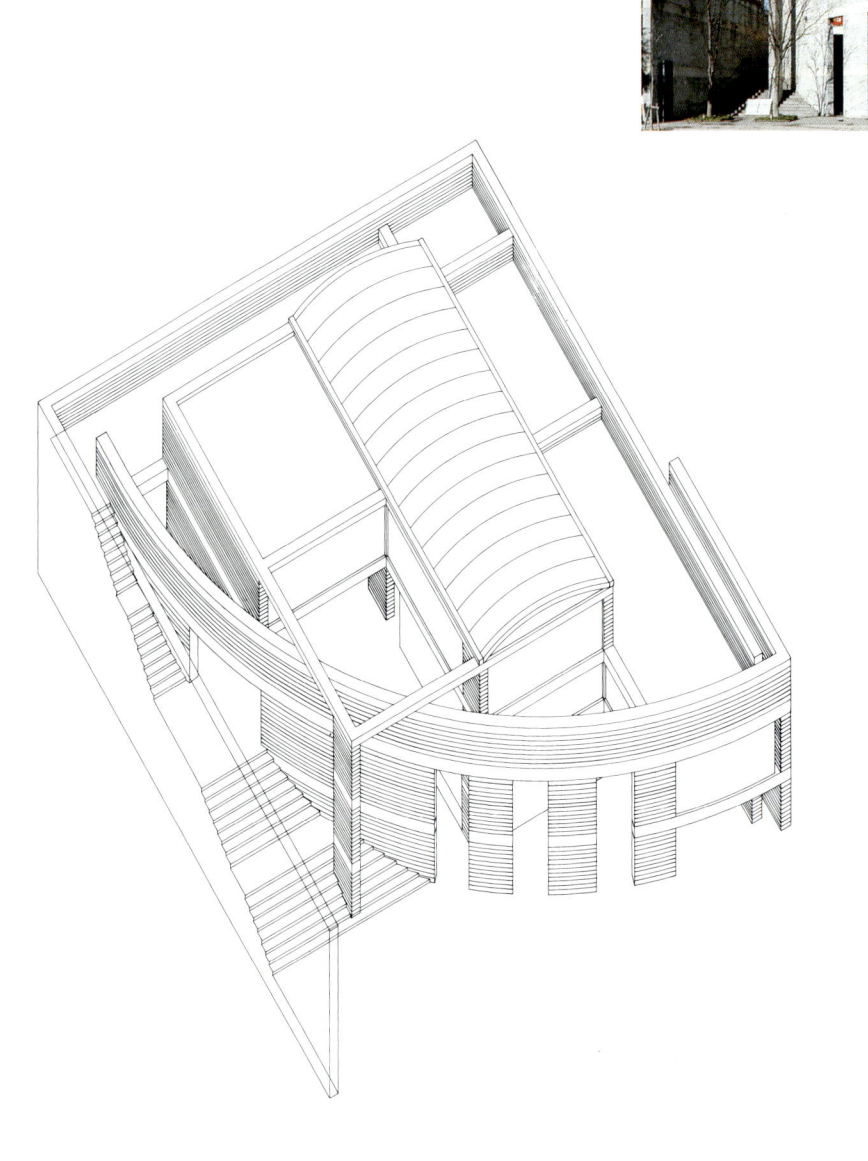

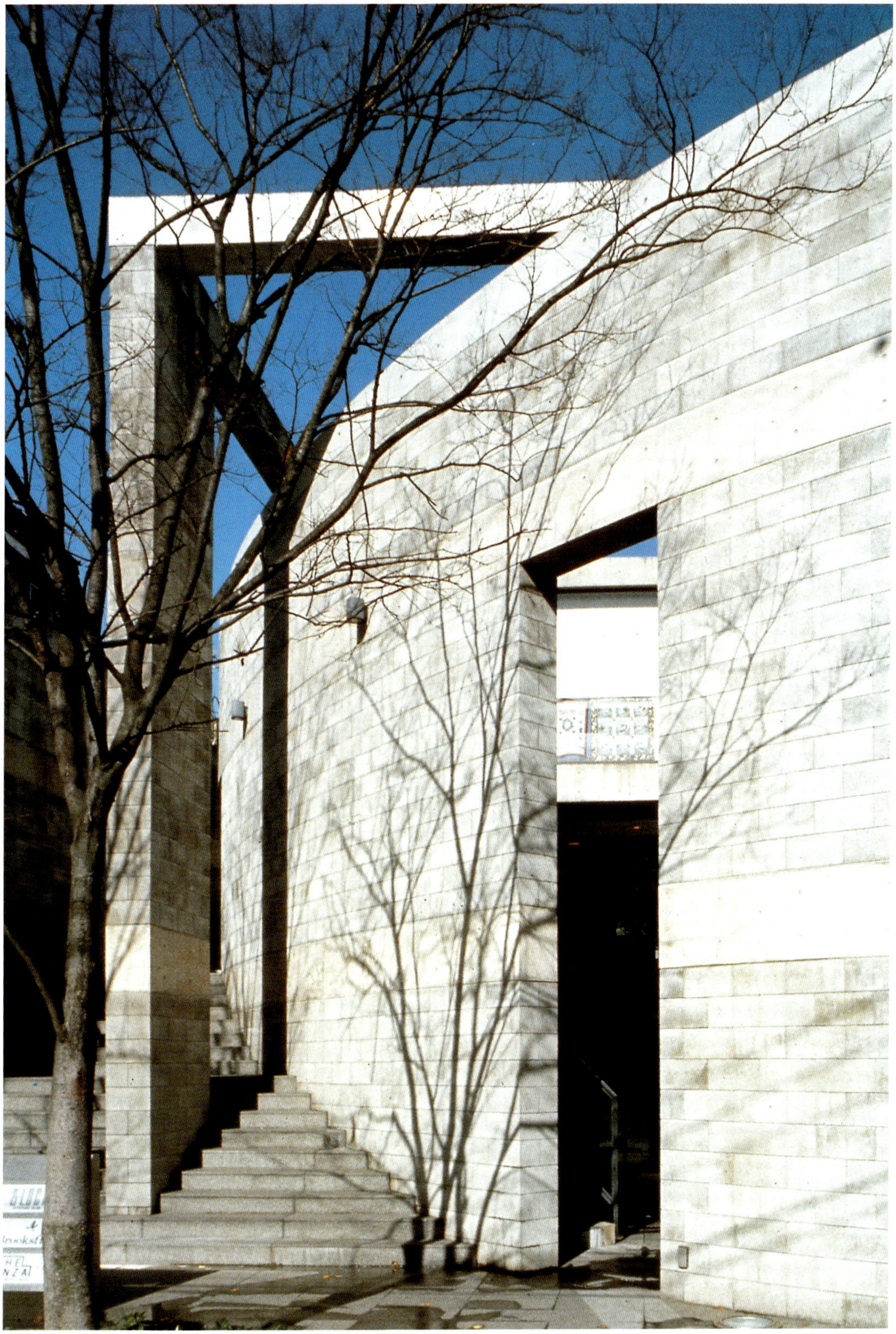

Kara-za Mobile Theatre

Conceptual sketches, elevation with plan and elevation.

This is a mobile theatre structure, with a capacity of 600, for the avant-garde theatre group led by Kara Joro. The project began with an idea to build a playhouse in Asakusa; then it was later used as an exposition pavilion. At first, it was a wooden watchtower-like structure. The plan is dodecagonal, 40 metres wide and 27 metres high. The exterior wall consists of black boards and the roof is a red tent.

The approach is by an arched bridge symbolizing the passage from the world of reality to the world of illusion, from this world to *higan*, the Buddhist term referring to the world after death. The playhouse is surrounded by a traditional fence of woven bamboo, known as *takeyarai,* which emphasizes the other-worldly nature of the theatrical space.

When the idea that it should be movable was added to the brief, the main structure was changed from wood to an assemblage of scaffolding poles like those used on construction sites. This way, the construction period has been shortened to around fifteen days and transportation of building materials is unnecessary. With the exception of certain special parts, everything is locally available. If the drawings and instructions are sent ahead, construction is possible anywhere in the world.

Location Sendai and Tokyo
Design 1985–7
Construction 1988 (Sendai), 1987 (Tokyo)
Structure Scaffolding steel pipe
Building area 1,145 m^2
Total floor area 601.4 m^2

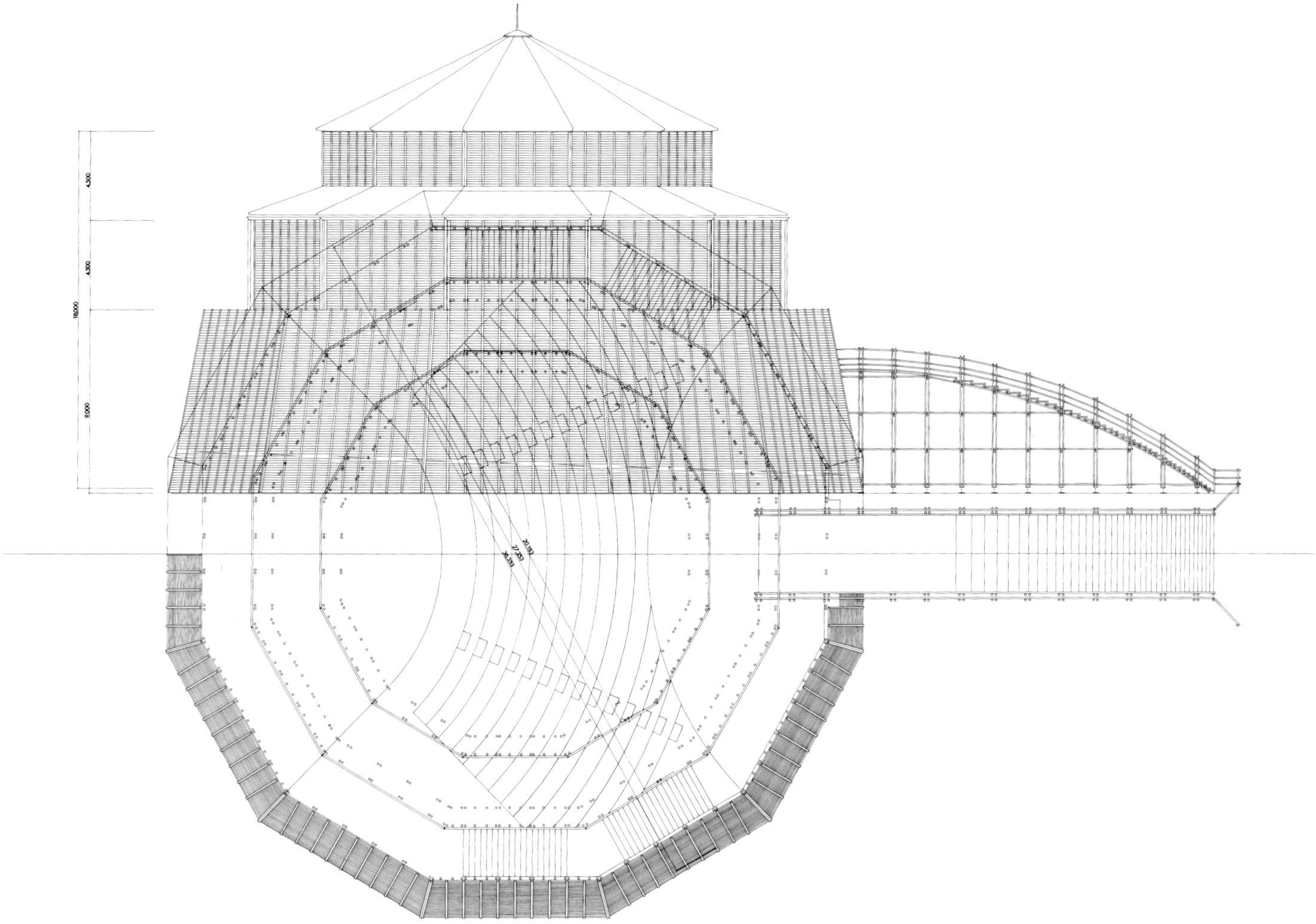

4,500
4,500
18,000
9,000

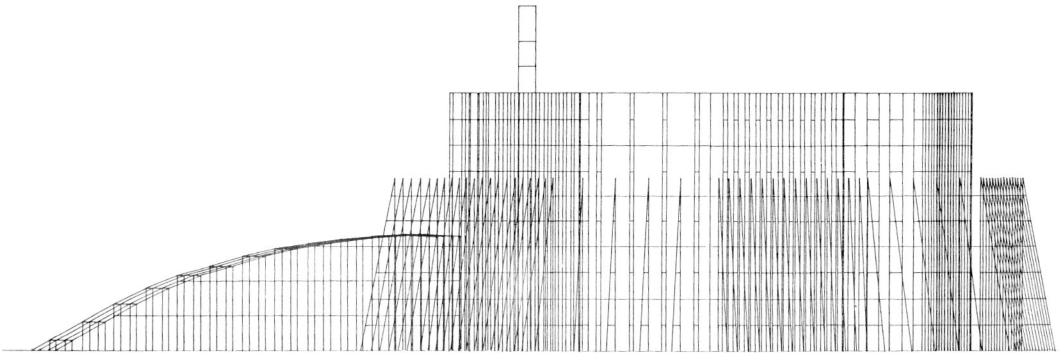

Elevations.

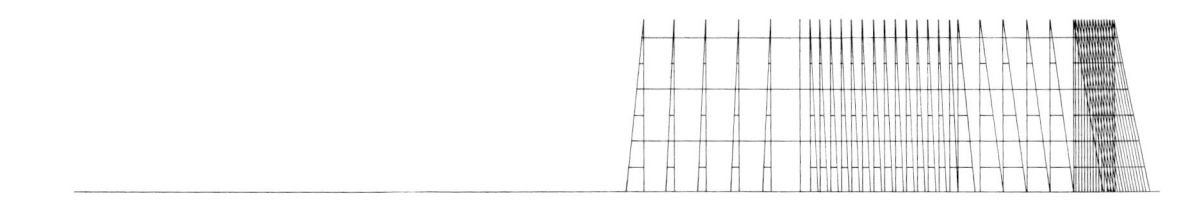

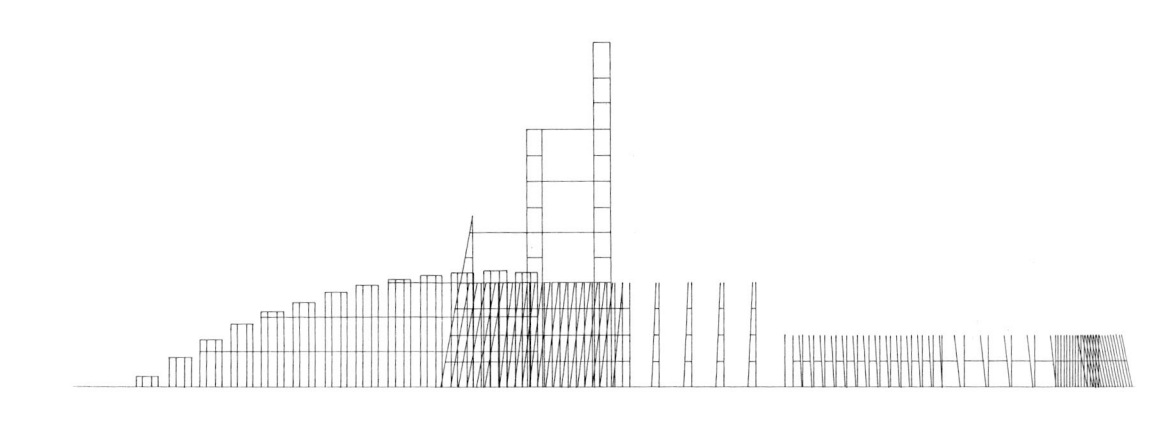

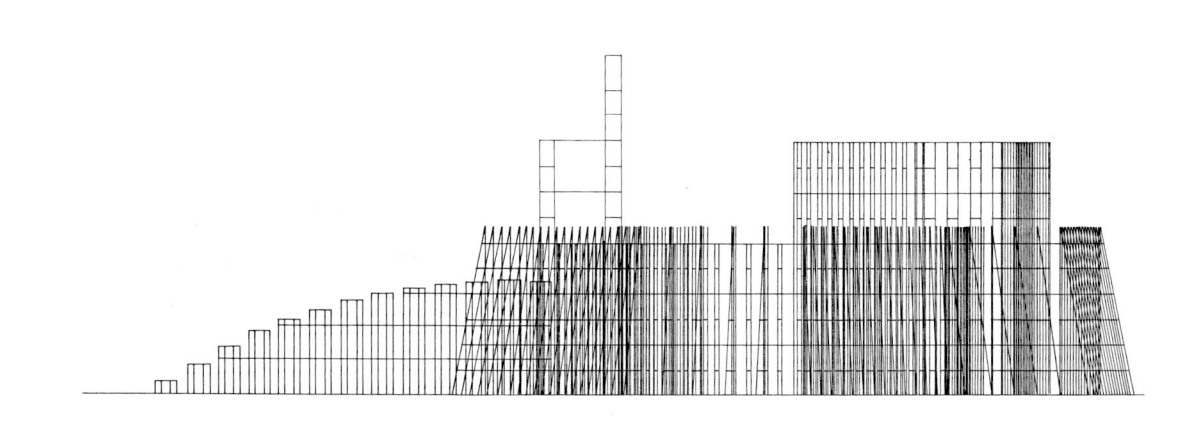

272

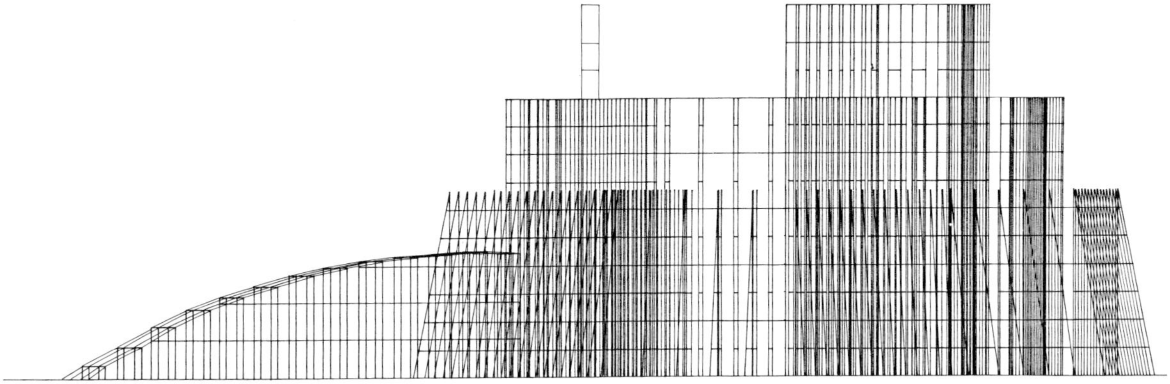

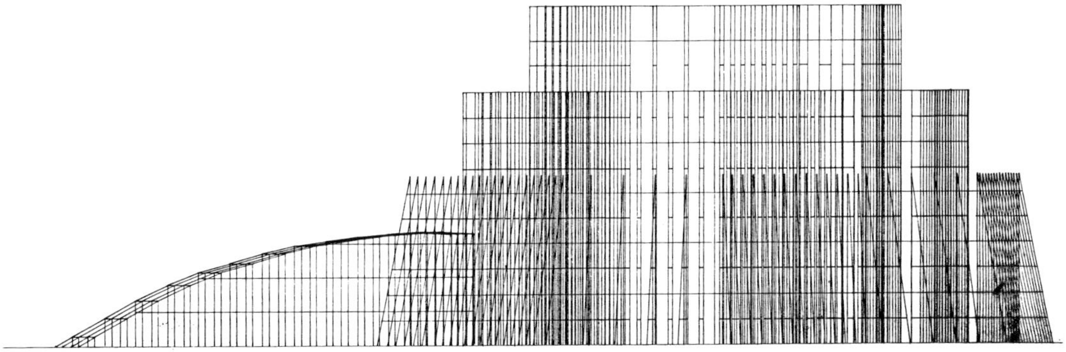

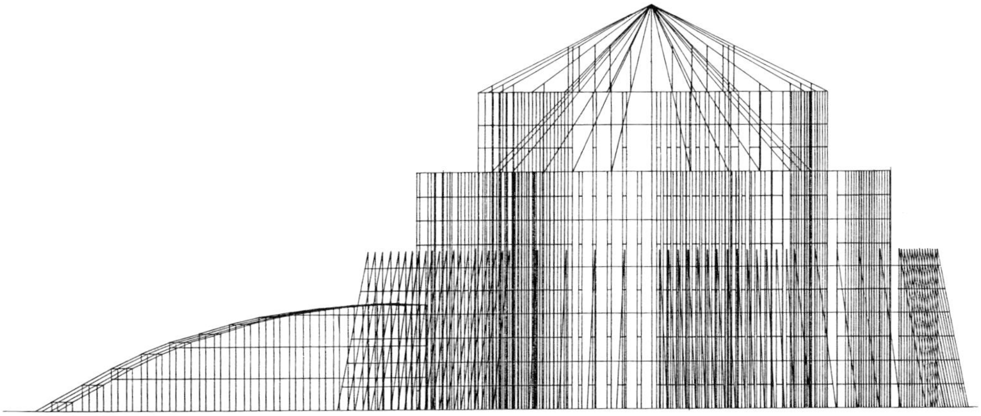

I House

Axonometric and floor plans.

This house was planned as a guest house. The building has a cylindrical core, with a 7.5-metre radius, forming an atrium. An L-shaped volume interlocks with the cylinder, and a protective perimeter wall encloses the site. The building is on the north side of the site, with a garden to the south. The upper level – a rectangular volume, 6.5 x 29.1 metres – has a vaulted roof that is one-sixth of a circle. The triple volume atrium, while enclosed by the curving wall of the cylinder, opens towards the outside through large glazed apertures, affording views of seasonal changes in the garden.

The building has three levels – two above ground and one below. The ground level contains the hall and a guest room and the upper level has a bedroom and living room. The sloped garden of the court is visible from rooms on the underground and second levels. This court, which receives a blanket of white flowers in the spring, changes completely with each season. The ground-level terrace is surfaced with phanerite, which lends it an inorganic mood, in sharp contrast with the natural green of the garden.

Location Ashiya
Design 1985–6
Construction 1986–8
Structure Reinforced concrete and steel
Site area 987 m^2
Building area 263 m^2
Total floor area 907.9 m^2

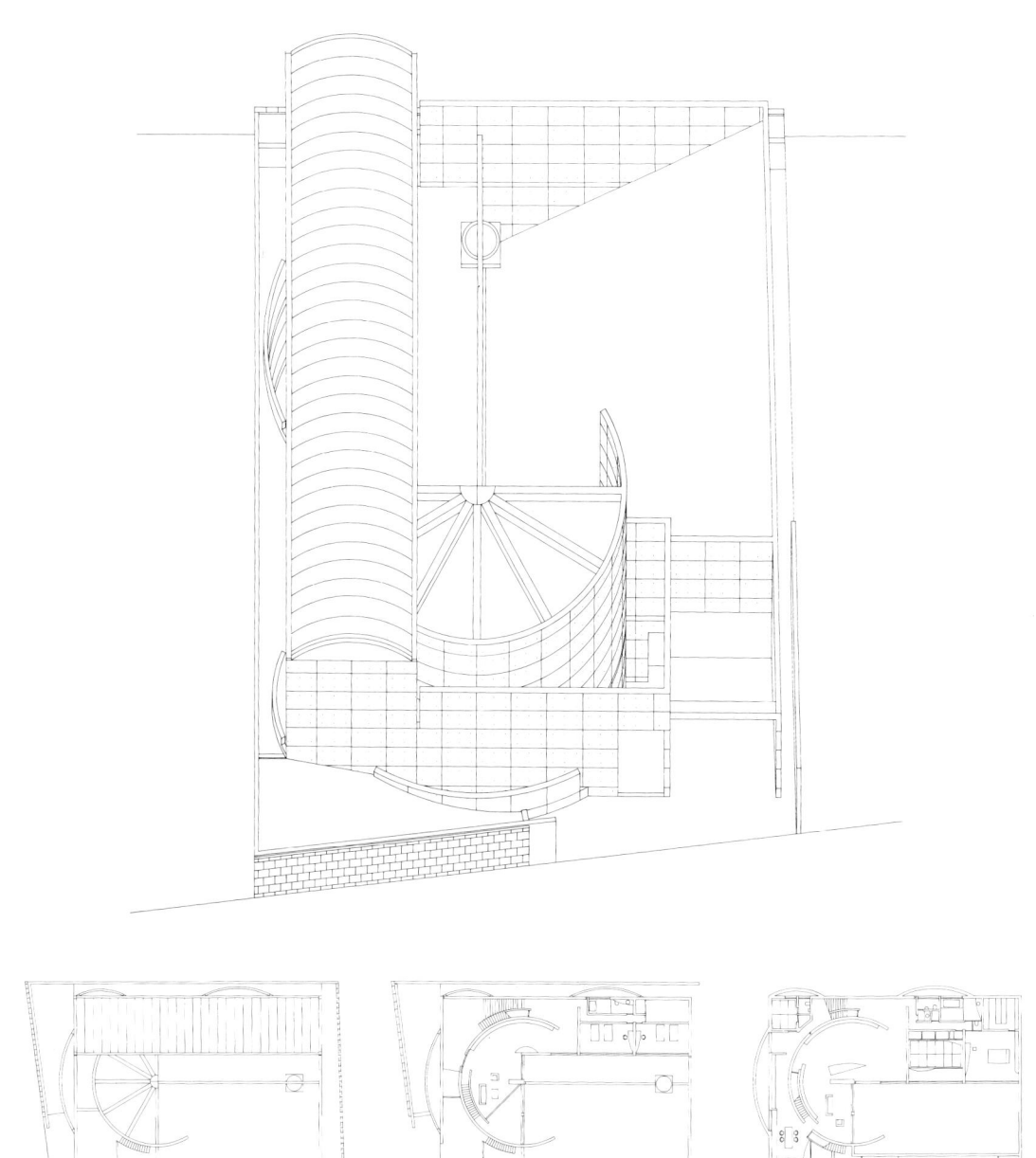

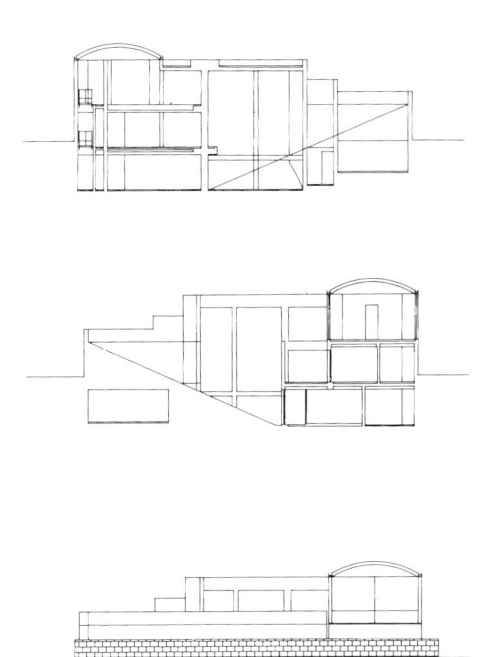

Views of the vaulted roof, oblique view of the building, sections and elevation.

View to the garden from the bedroom.

Exterior views and conceptual sketch.

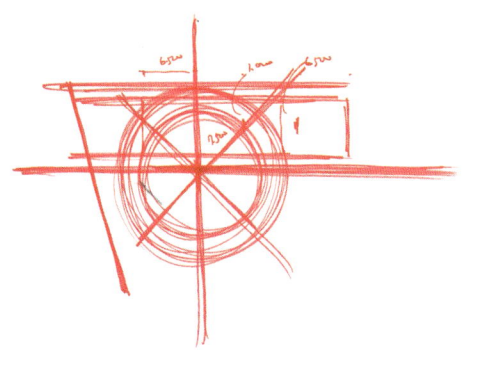

Rokko Housing II

Conceptual sketch and aerial view of the building.

Adjacent to Rokko Housing I, this housing complex shares the same 60-degree slope but has an area nearly four times as large. The building is founded on a uniform grid of 5.2 x 5.2 metres, and has three connected, but distinct, clusters of dwellings, each five-units square. Adapting the grid to the steepness of the slope generates asymmetry in plan and section – introducing complexity into the consistency of the geometry and producing a dynamic architectural order. The resulting symmetry also allows the entire complex to benefit from eastern light.

The building is composed axially around the line of a central staircase, which shifts at the intermediate level where it links with approaches to each cluster. A north–south gap separates the clusters, providing communal space and satisfying lighting and ventilation requirements. Indoor pool facilities are provided on the rooftop plaza of the intermediate level, where the ocean view is spectacular. Within the overall geometric uniformity of the complex, each of the 50 dwellings is unique in size and format.

Location Kobe
Design 1985–9
Construction 1989–93
Structure Reinforced concrete and steel
Site area 5,998.1 m^2
Building area 2,964.7 m^2
Total floor area 9,043.6 m^2

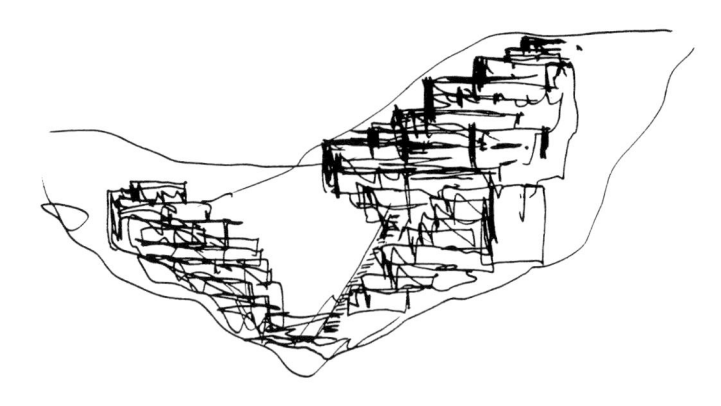

Perspective and section with plan.

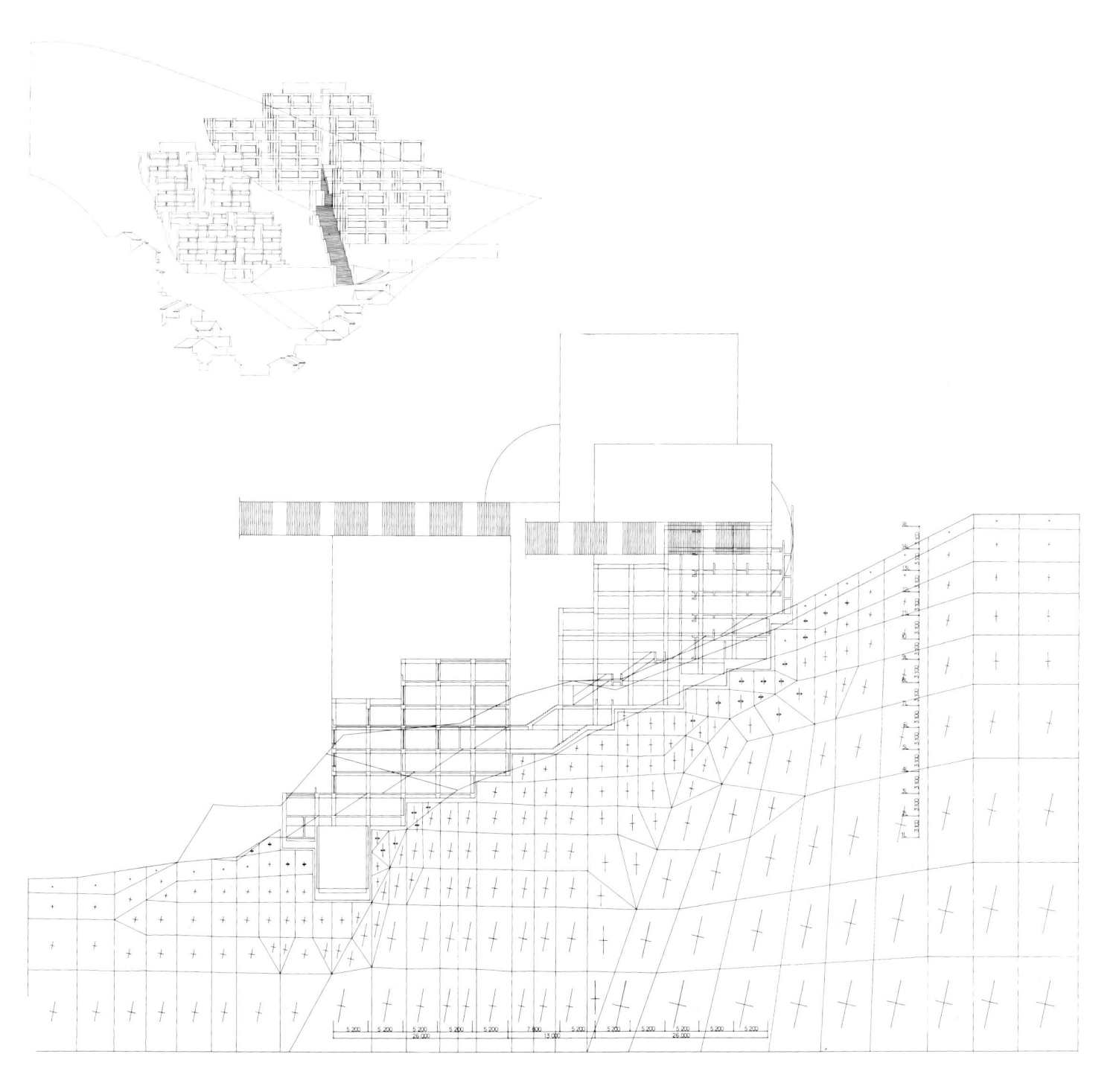

Exterior and interior views.

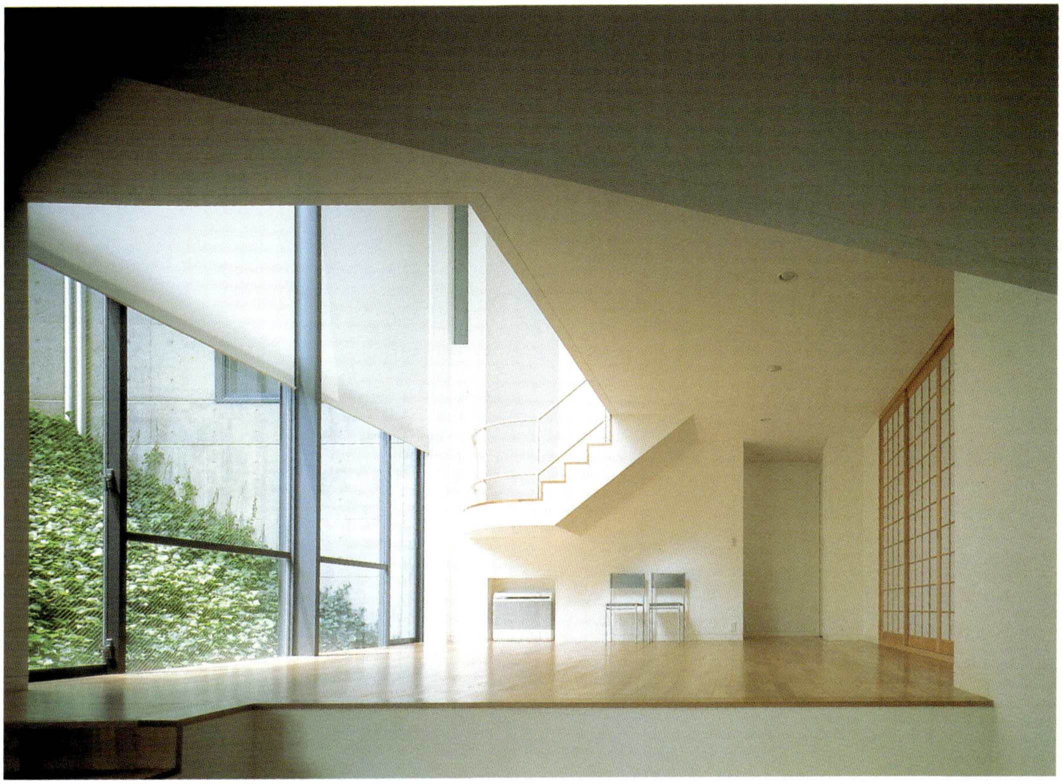

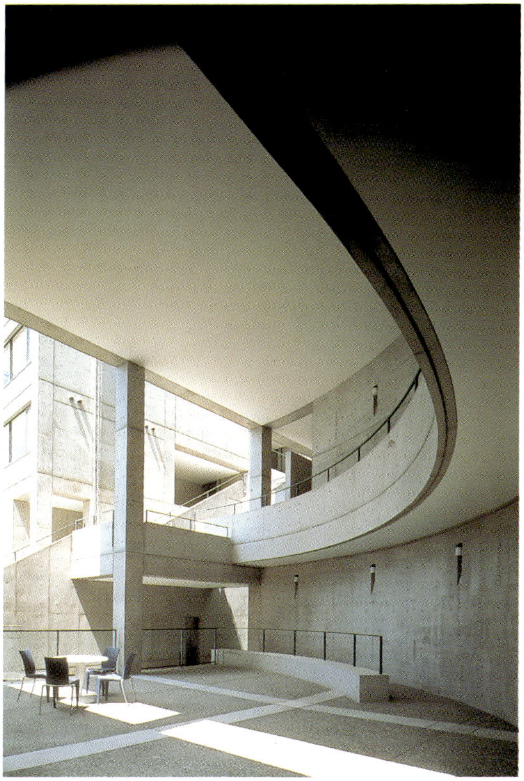

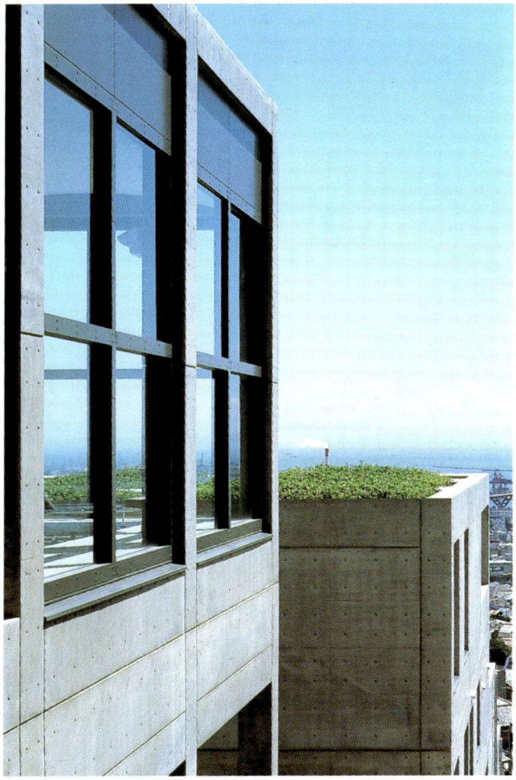

Church on the Water

Conceptual sketches, section with plan and overall view.

On a plain in the depths of the province of Hokkaido, this church has a plan of two overlapping squares of different sizes. It overlooks a shallow artificial lake which has been created by the diversion of a nearby stream. A freestanding, L-shaped wall hugs one side of the lake and the back of the church. A gentle slope, facing the lake, ascends alongside the wall, leading to the top of the smaller volume where, within a glass-enclosed space open to the sky, there are four large crosses in a square formation, their transverse arms almost touching. From this point, the visitor descends a darkened stairway to emerge in the rest of the chapel. The wall behind the altar is fully glazed, providing a panorama of the lake, in which the large crucifix is seen rising from the surface of the water. This wall can be slid aside, directly opening the interior of the church up to the natural surroundings.

Location Tomamu, Hokkaido
Design 1985–8
Construction 1988
Structure Reinforced concrete
Site area 6,730 m^2
Building area 344.9 m^2
Total floor area 520 m^2

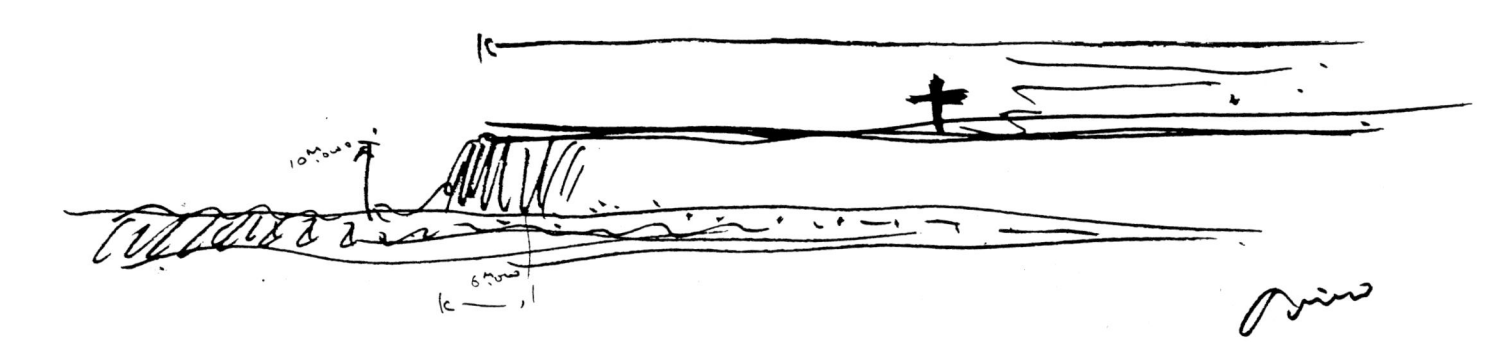

283

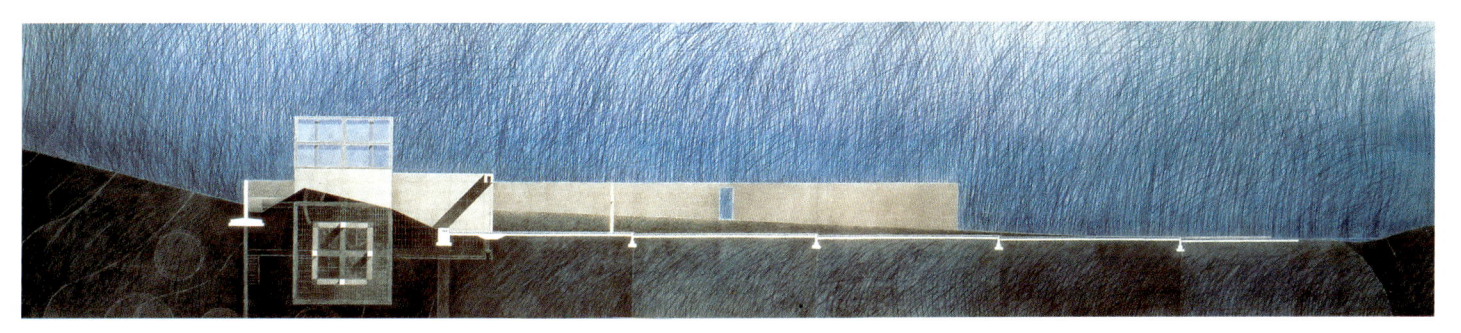

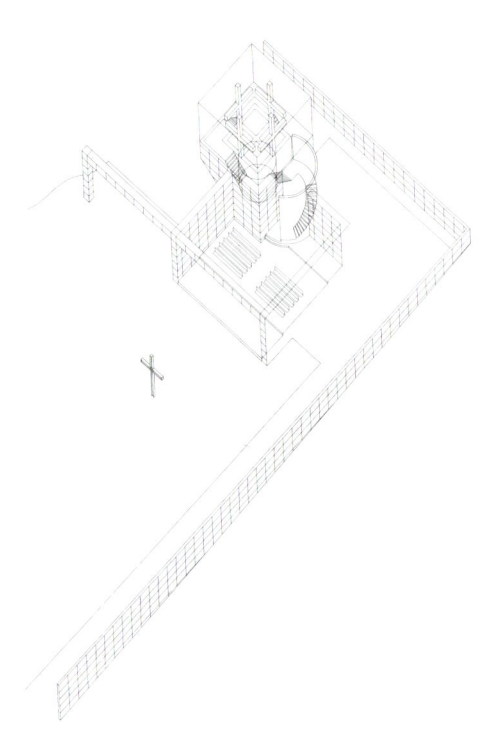

Axonometric and views of the lake and the church grounds.

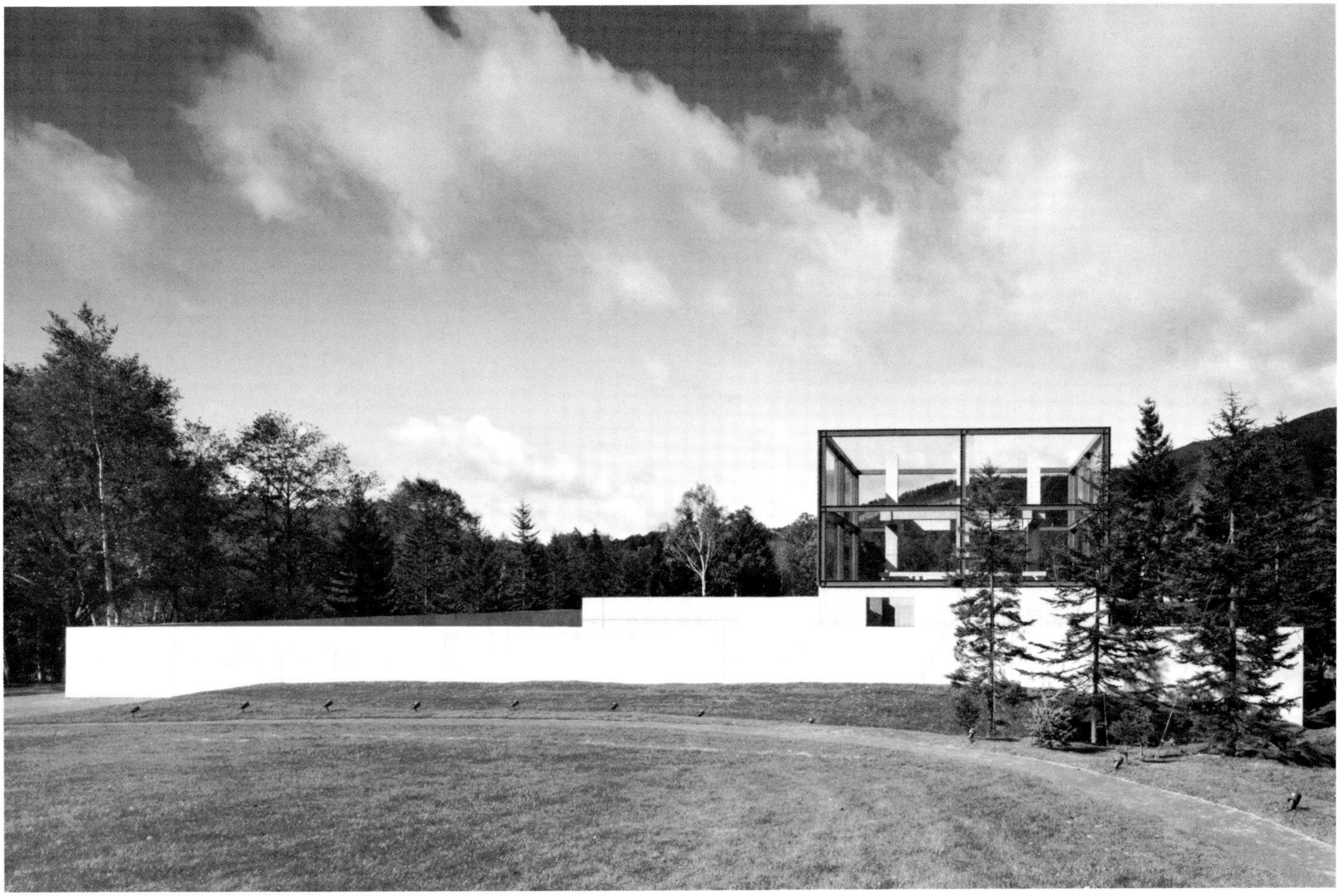

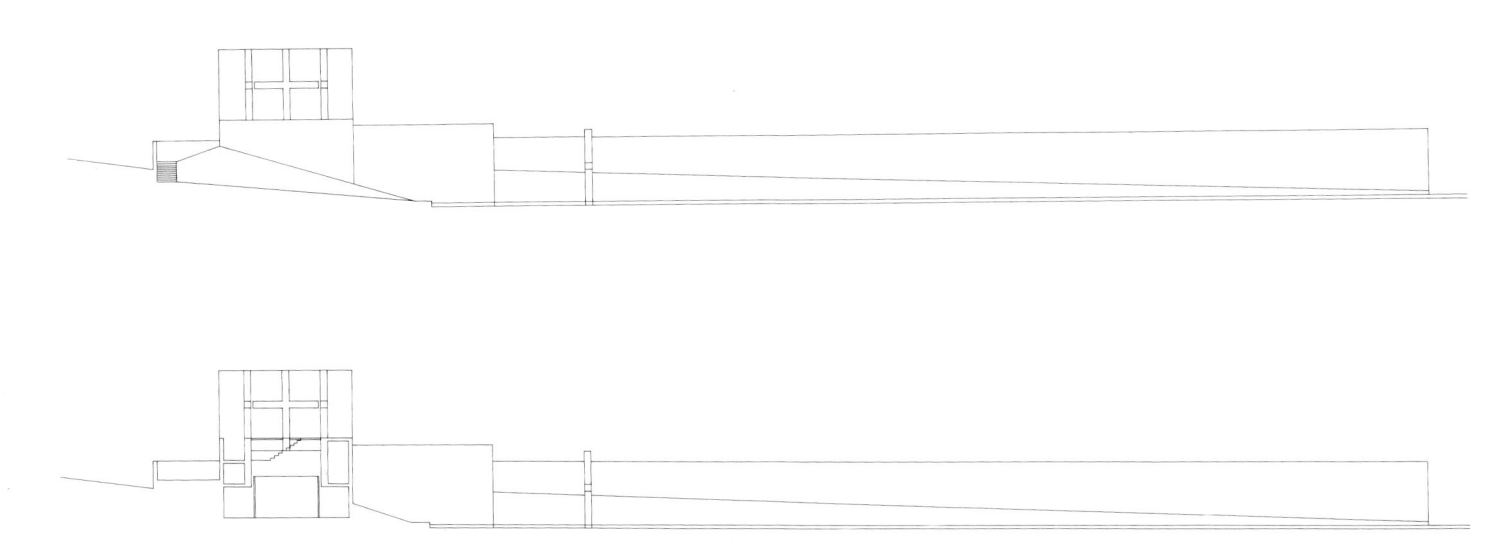

Exterior and interior details, sections and view looking out onto the lake.

286

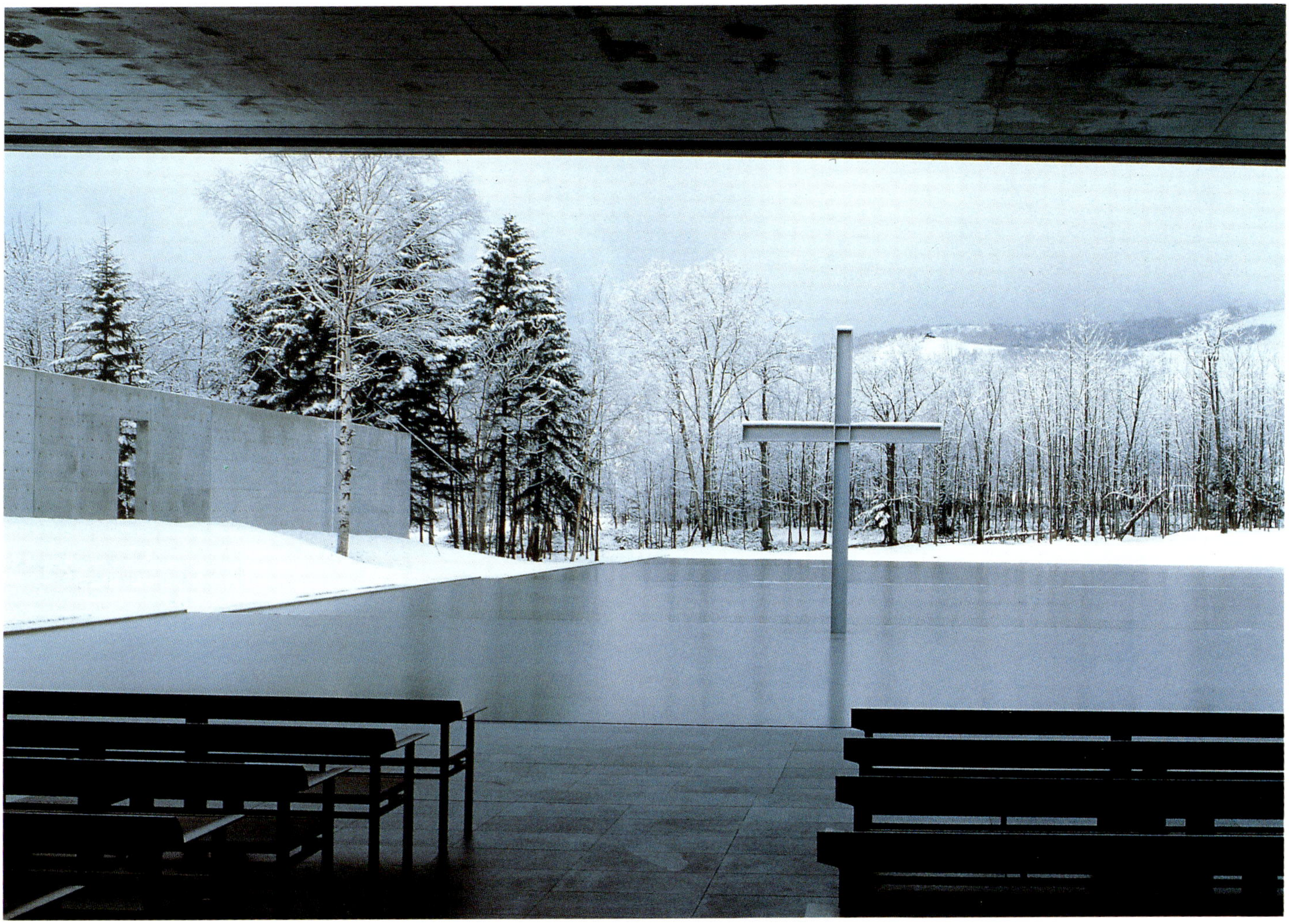

Theatre on the Water

Site plan and conceptual sketch.

This theatre was proposed for a site 400 metres away from the Church on the Water, yet connected to the church by the water. The two structures form a geometrically-linked pair, on a flat plain in Hokkaido.

The theatre was conceived to accentuate the excitement of its events – so it is in the form of an arena, surrounded by the drama of nature. It provides an open-air setting for concerts and fashion shows during the warmer weather of spring, summer and autumn and functions as, among other things, a skating rink during the winter.

The structure is a 6,000-seat semi-circular theatre, set in a fan-shaped artificial lake created on the course of the stream. A long, 13 x 200 metre bridge-like stage intersects the theatre, while a freestanding colonnade penetrates the entire configuration of theatre, stage and lake.

Location Hokkaido
Design 1987

Views of the model showing both the church and the theatre, the site and detail of the theatre.

Galleria Akka

Floor plans and section.

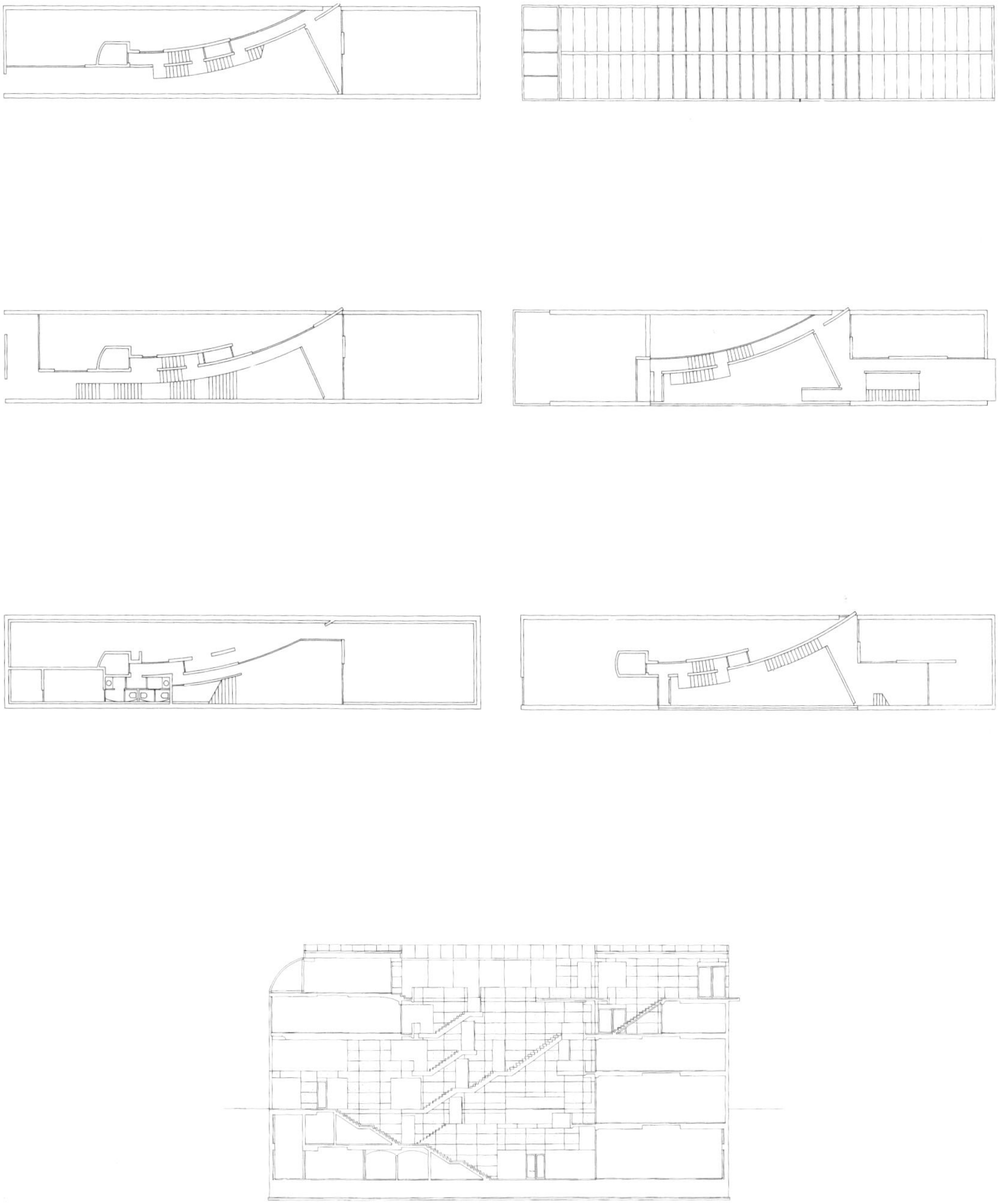

This retail/gallery structure in a shopping district of central Osaka, is a rectilinear volume inserted among a chaotic array of low-rise commercial buildings, on a rectangular lot with a frontage of 8 metres and a depth of 40 metres. The tranquility of the building's exterior belies the drama within. There you are confronted with a central atrium – a vertically oriented space whose unconventional presence is overwhelming. Rising up through five floors from the basement, the atrium accounts for half of the building's volume. Facing it is a curved wall with a 28-metre radius, and ascending and descending flights of steps pass each other on opposite sides of the wall. The unifying character of the curved, frosted-glass roof at the top of the atrium gives the building a strong architectural identity.

Location Osaka
Design 1985–7
Construction 1987–8
Structure Reinforced concrete
Site area 324.2 m²
Building area 226 m²
Total floor area 1,027 m²

View of the atrium and axonometric.

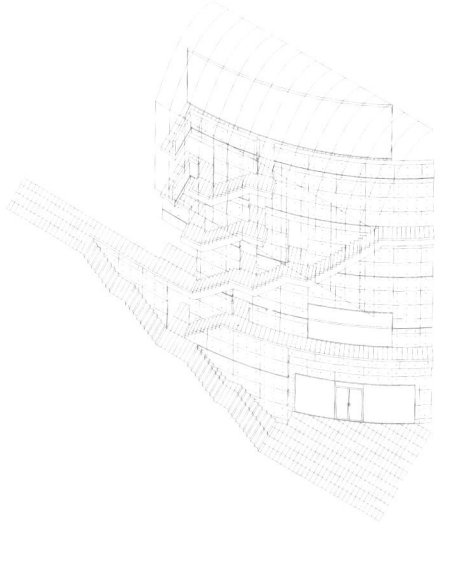

Conceptual sketch and interior views.

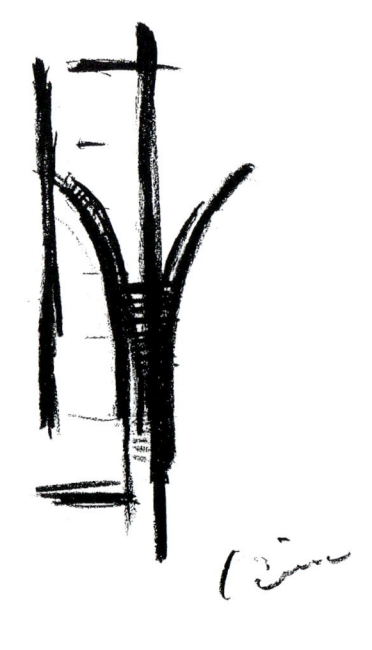

293

Bigi 3rd

Plan, elevation and sections and view of the entrance.

Bigi 3rd is in the centre of Osaka. The site is only 3.6 metres wide but 15 metres deep, and adjacent structures have been constructed right up to the property line. The building itself is 3 metres wide, 14.5 metres deep and 7.5 metres high. It had to be as spacious as possible, despite its narrow frontage, and there were two ways this could be done: by reducing the dimensions of the structural system to a minimum, and by pushing the wall up to the property line. In order to increase the inner dimensions of the building, it was cantilevered from the columns on one side. Only those on one side of the prime are structural, and the opposite side is a curtain wall suspended from beams. The columns and beams are regularly spaced at 2.3 metre intervals and articulate space in the longitudinal direction. Furthermore, in order to increase the inner dimensions of the building, the exposed mechanical system was adapted, which then needed to be arranged in order. The interior is a single space. By making the ceiling height (7.5 metres) three times the normal dimension, the space was allowed greater verticality.

Location Osaka
Design 1986
Construction 1986
Structure Steel
Site area 55.2 m²
Building area 43.5 m²
Total floor area 43.5 m²

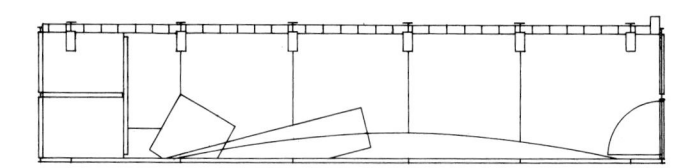

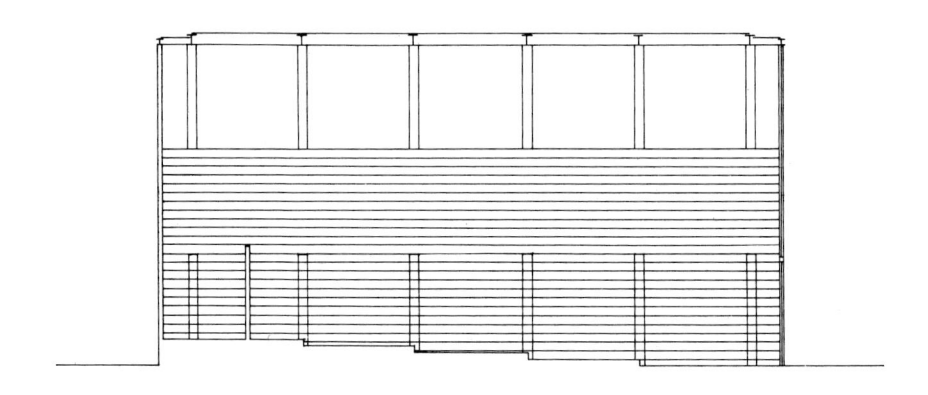

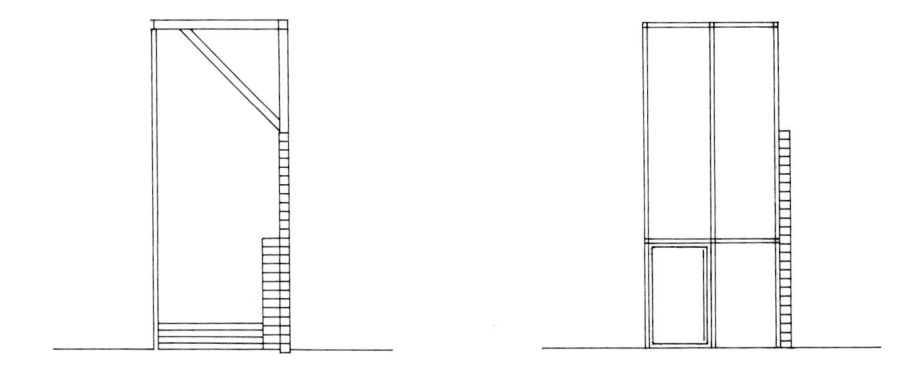

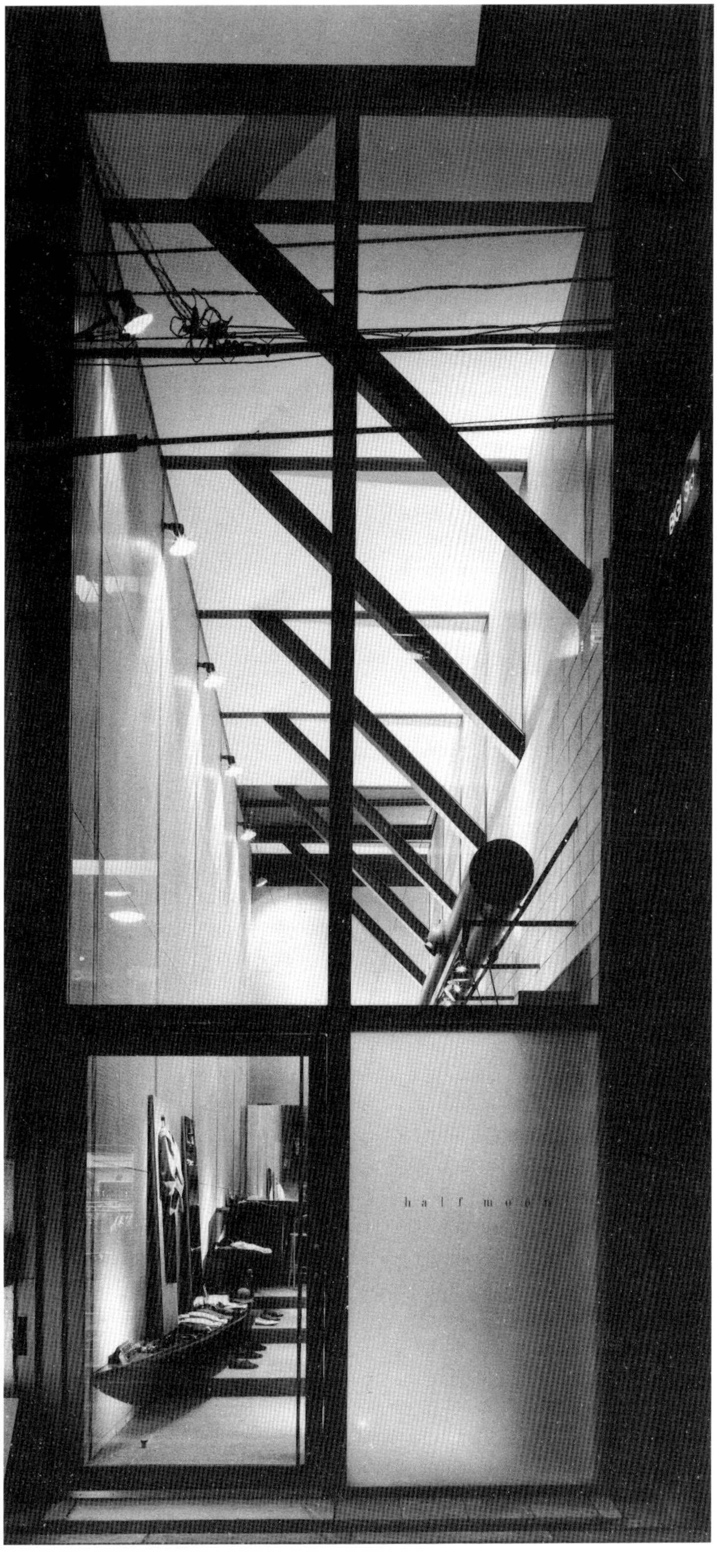
half moon

Collezione

Conceptual sketch, view of the entrance and floor plans.

Collezione is a commercial complex in a fashionable district of Tokyo. It consists of two rectangular volumes spanned by a cube, an interlocking cylindrical volume and a protective perimeter wall, which inscribes an arc. To harmonize the building with those surrounding it, half of its volume is below ground level. Car parking is on the lower basement floor, while the upper two basement floors house an exercise club and a swimming pool. Boutiques occupy the ground and first floors, and the upper two floors accommodate showrooms, galleries and, independent of the other functions, the owner's three-apartment residence. A stepped plaza and a staircase, which spirals around the outer wall of the cylindrical volume, are at the centre of the building's composition. The plaza forms a spatial void which rises from the depths of the building, inviting light and wind into the lower floors.

Location Tokyo
Design 1986–7
Construction 1987–9
Structure Reinforced concrete and steel
Site area 1,683.5 m^2
Building area 1,175.3 m^2
Total floor area 5,709.7 m^2

297

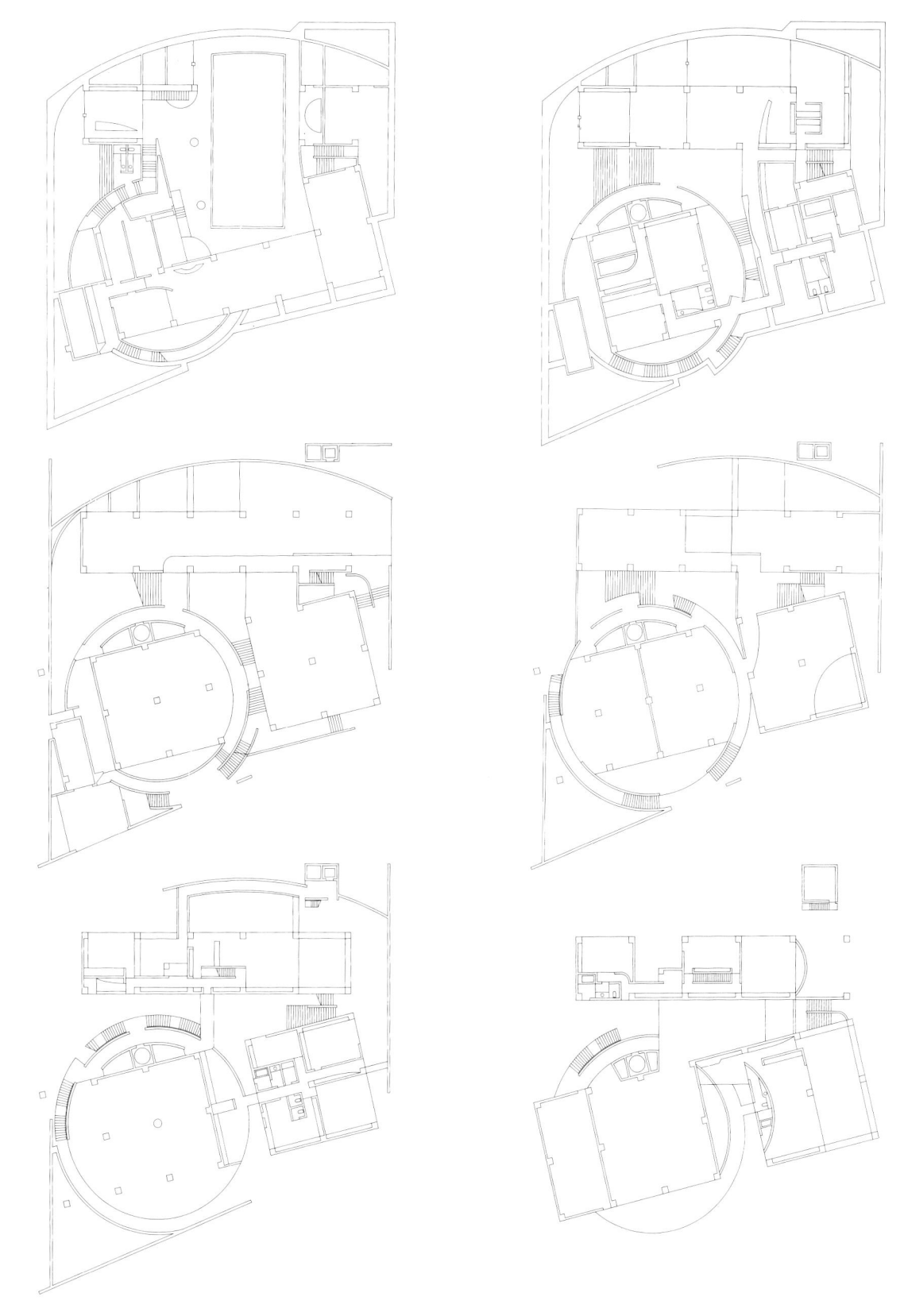

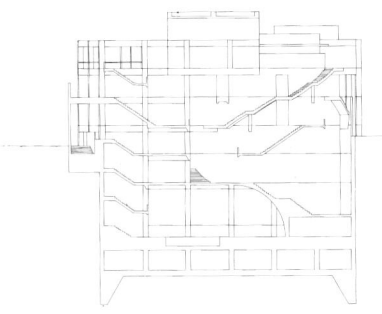

View of the perimeter wall stairway and section.

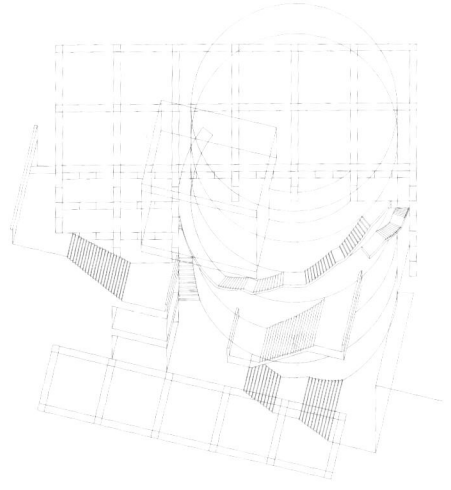

View showing the interlocking semi-circular and cubic volumes, and axonometric.

Views of the spiral stairs and the swimming pool.

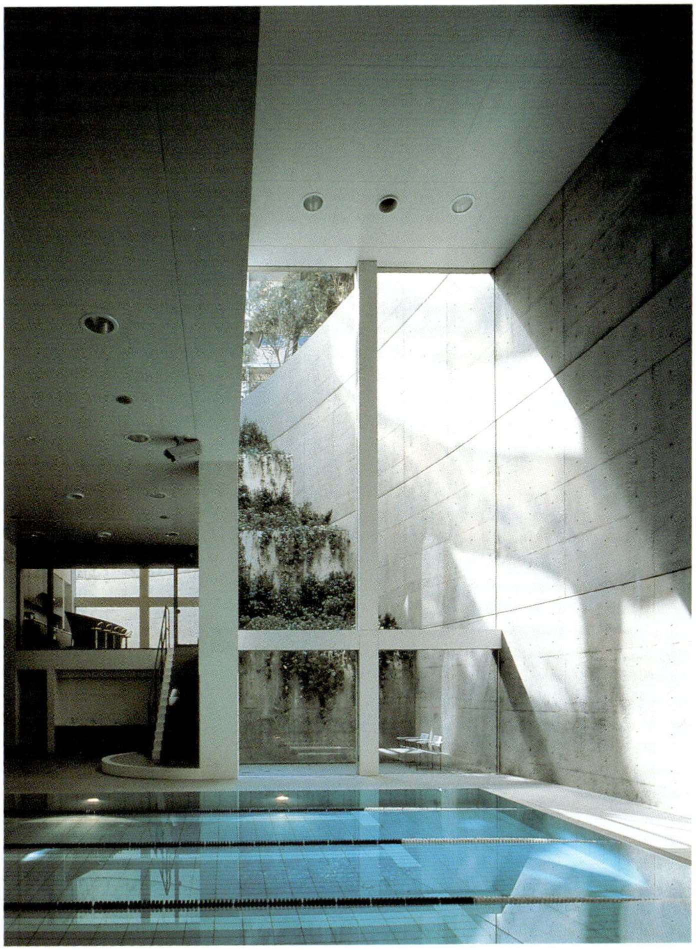

Kaguraoka Apartment Block

Floor plans and view showing the curved wall.

The building is at the foot of a hill in Kyoto. It is a small-sized condominium of seven one-room apartments and a maisonette, constructed of moulded concrete blocks with 3 mm joints. Rooms are arranged in the south–north direction, and there is an arched wall on the west side. This wall defines the border of the irregular site and emphasizes the form of the building; it has also created a passageway. There is a courtyard to the east and a service yard to the north. The ground of the site was lowered from the level of the surrounding lots and the first floor is made a sub-basement so as not to disturb the environment.

Seven one-room apartments face east overlooking the courtyard. The maisonette near the southern boundary of the site has a south-facing opening on the second floor to fully take in the greenery on the hill.

Location Kyoto
Design 1986–7
Construction 1987–8
Structure Reinforced concrete
Site area 244 m^2
Building area 118 m^2
Total floor area 211 m^2

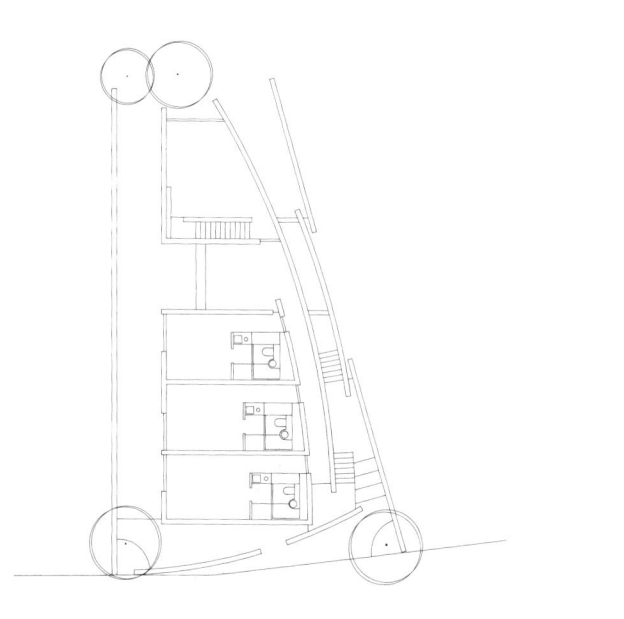

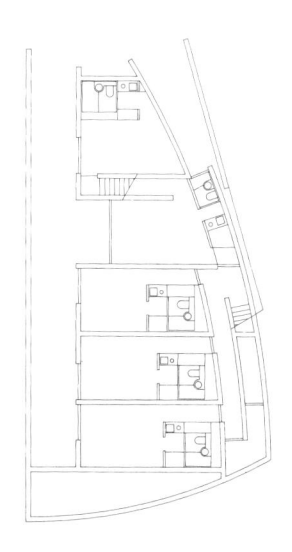

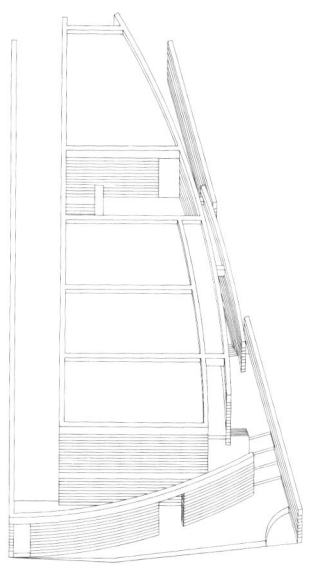

Detail of the entrance stairway and axonometric.

Morozoff Studio

Perspective and view of the entrance.

This building is located on a square lot, and divided into four sections by large walkways which, at their intersection, form an eight-sided plaza. The studio is split into two separate buildings – one of which, located in the smaller part of the lot, consists of two adjacent rectangular volumes. The other section, in the larger part of the lot, is composed of a square-gridded form and a lower linear volume; together, these form an L-shaped building.

Location Kobe
Design 1986–8
Construction 1988–9
Structure Reinforced concrete
Site area 985.5 m^2
Building area 530.2 m^2
Total floor area 1,620.6 m^2

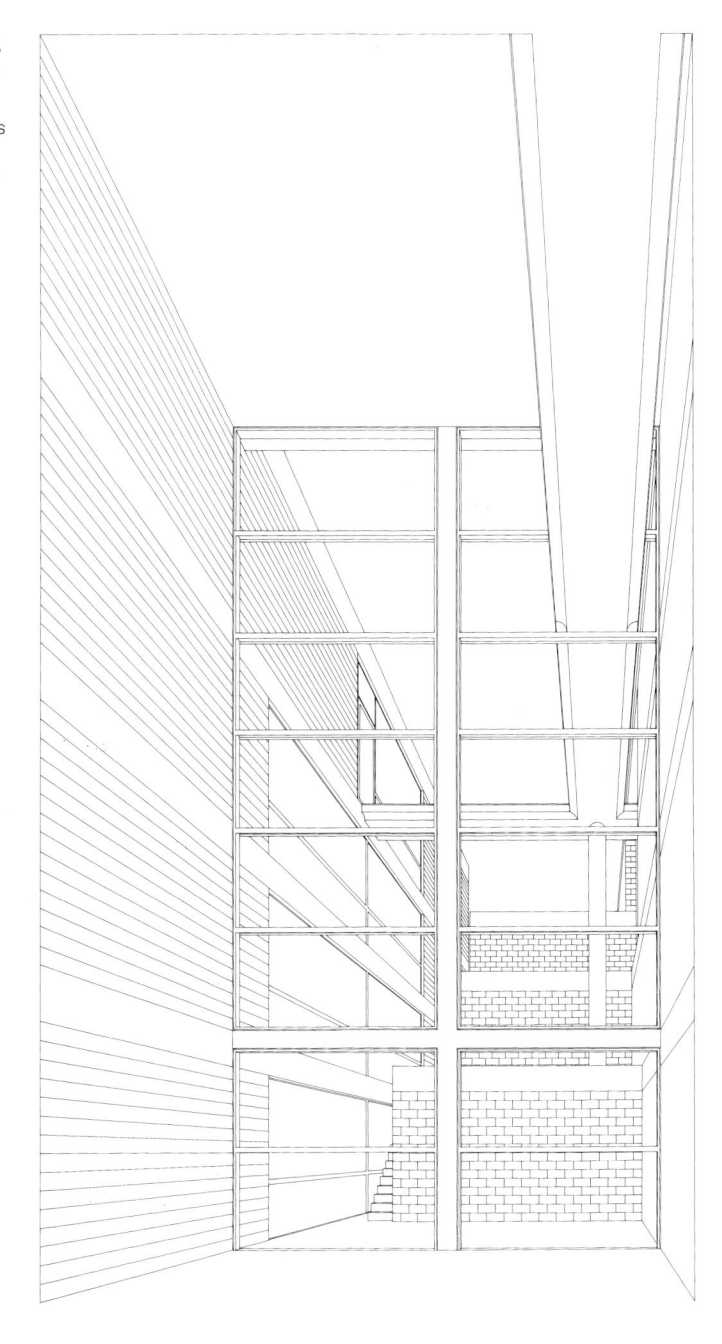

View of the garden and axonometric.

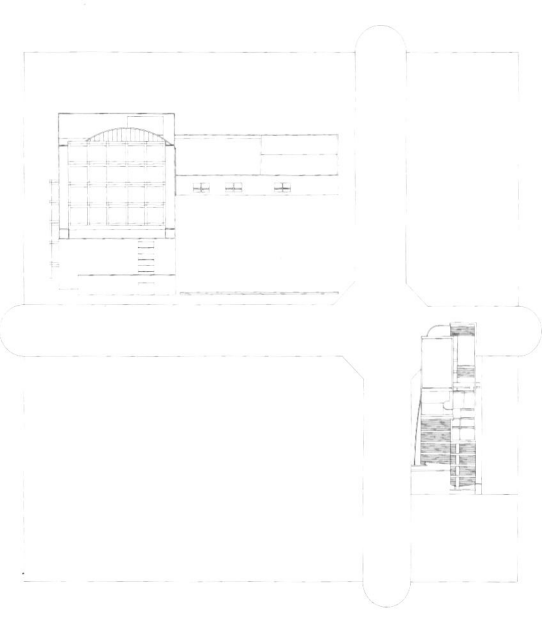

Yoshida House *Floor plans, elevation and sections.*

This house is in a city south of Osaka. It combines a shop and a residence for a woman, her younger brother and his family; thus it was important to respect the residents' mutual privacy.

Overall, the site is a small rectangle of property quartered roughly into 3.8-metre sections. There is a sunken court to the south-east where natural elements, such as light and wind, are called into play. Along the north of this court is the shop with its small atelier. The residential part of the building occupies the western half of the property. The sister's bedroom sits on a level with the sunken court, while above it are the dining room, living room and the tatami-floored room that serves as the family gathering area. This area opens out onto a terrace above the store, where greenery corresponds with the plants in the court below. On the uppermost floor is the brother's master bedroom and his children's rooms, each of which has its own terrace.

Location Tondabayashi
Design 1986–7
Construction 1987–8
Structure Reinforced concrete
Site area 252 m^2
Building area 124 m^2
Total floor area 211 m^2

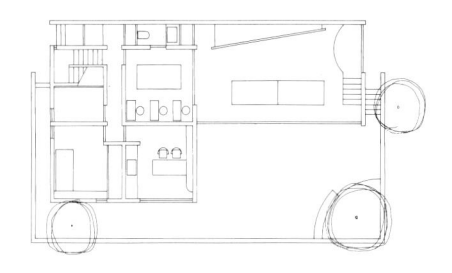

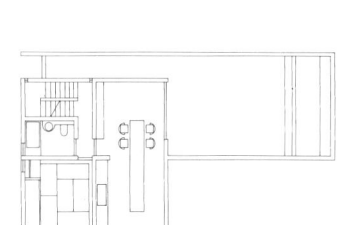

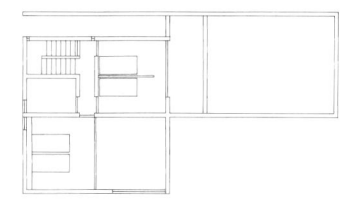

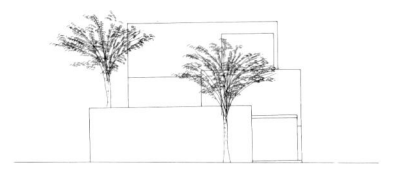

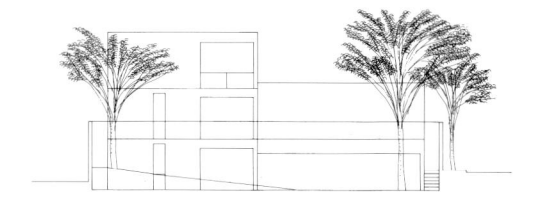

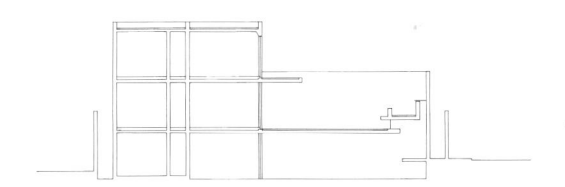

View of the courtyard and conceptual sketch.

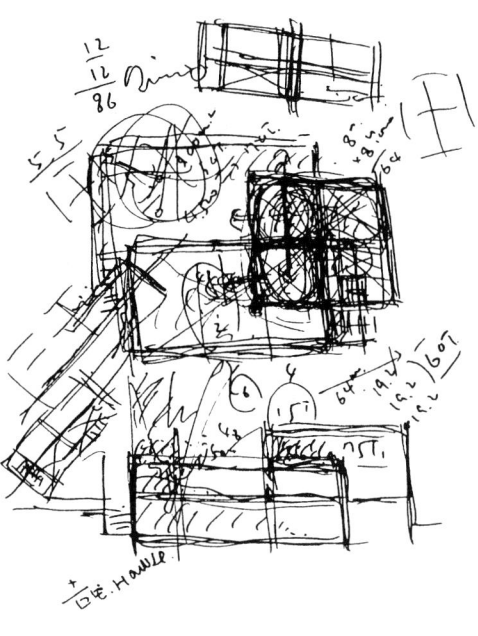

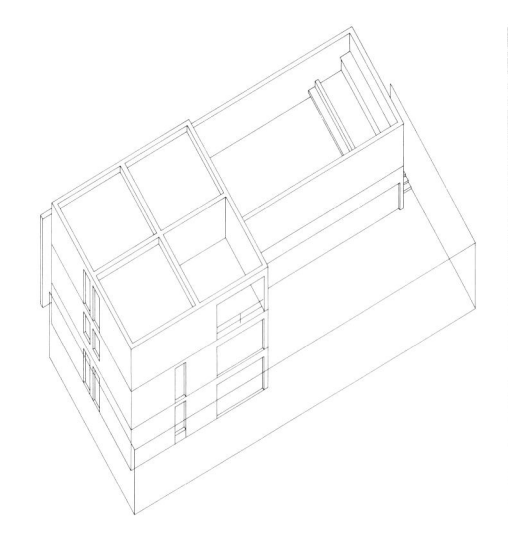

Axonometric and views of the courtyard and the terrace garden.

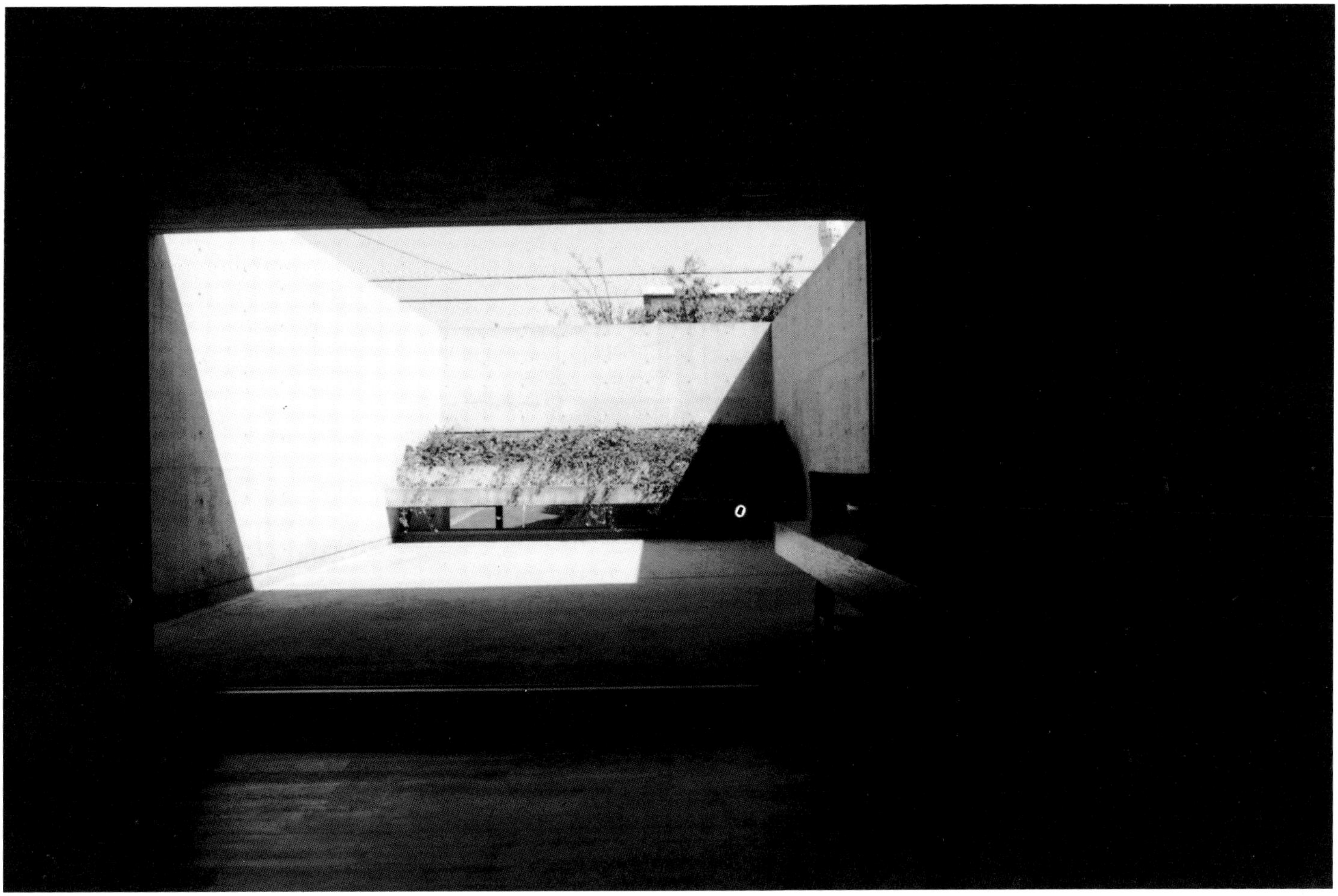

Raika Headquarters

Aerial view and fourth- and seventh-floor plans.

These offices, designed for a clothes manufacturer, are on reclaimed land that is being developed in Osaka Bay. The lobby, the spacious atrium and the rooftop garden, are all conceived as functional yet relaxed and comfortable spaces. The building is composed of several rectangular volumes arranged around a cylindrical form 40 metres in diameter. There are three connected but distinct units, of moderate height, which step back from the frontal thoroughfare. Trees, planted in double rows along the perimeter of the site, partially screen the building and play down its presence in the immediate environment.

A public plaza has been created at the south-west corner of the site, adjacent to a building containing shops, an exhibition hall and training facilities, with galleries on the upper levels and parking in the basement. Within the seven-storey cylindrical atrium of the main building, there is a ramp, dramatically silhouetted against the arc of the glass-block curtain wall.

Location Osaka
Design 1986–7
Construction 1987–9
Structure Reinforced concrete and steel
Site area 23,487.8 m^2
Building area 9,771.4 m^2
Total floor area 42,791.8 m^2

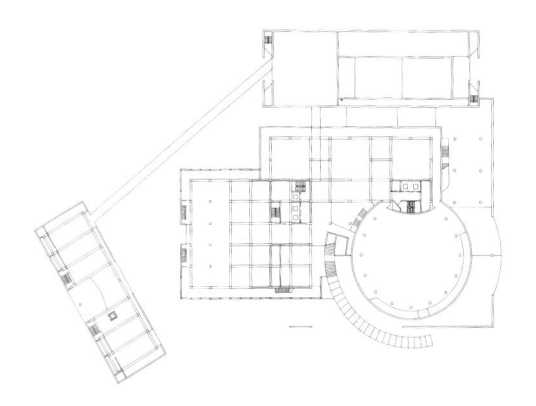

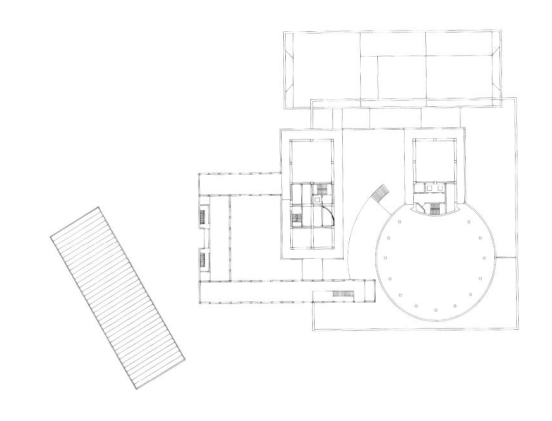

View of the entrance and conceptual sketch.

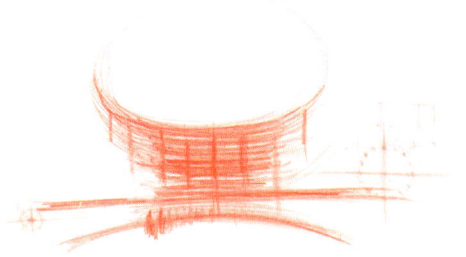

Exterior views and section.

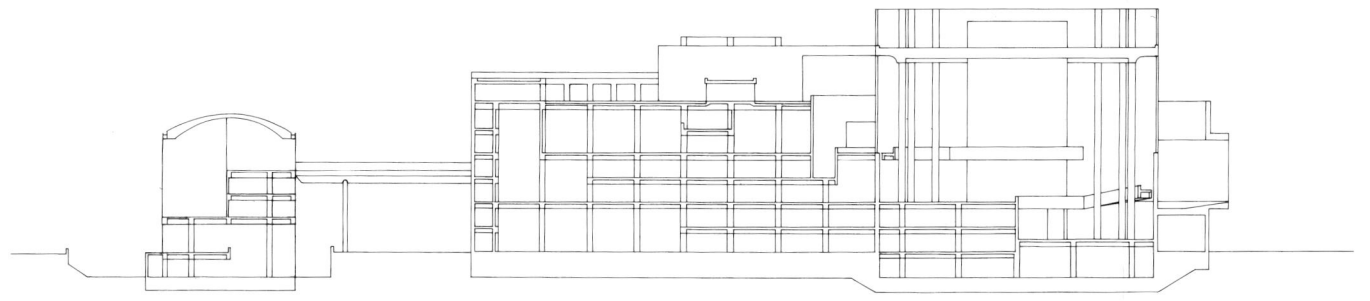

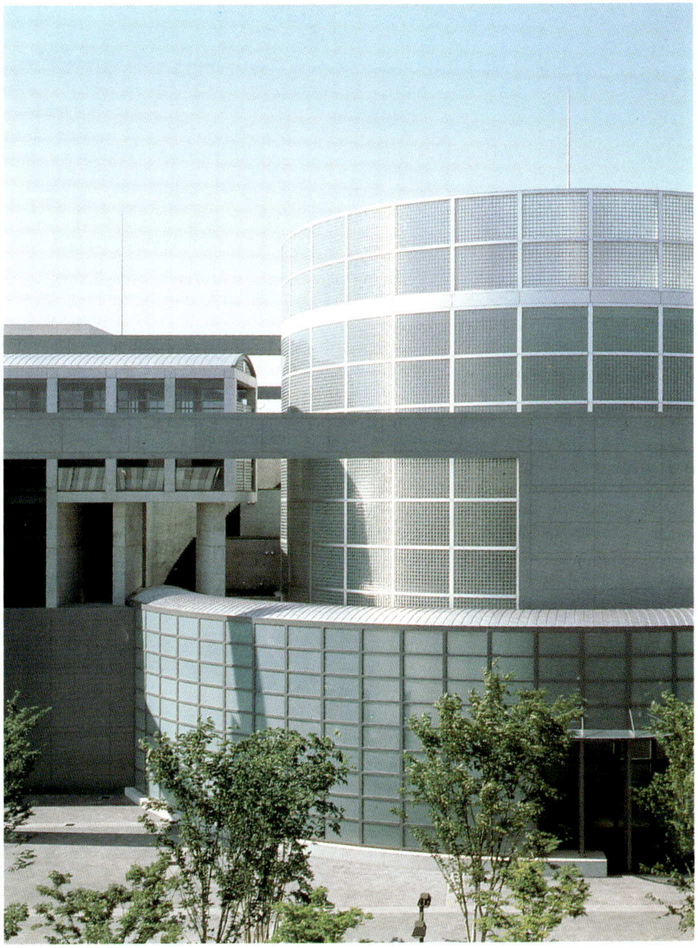

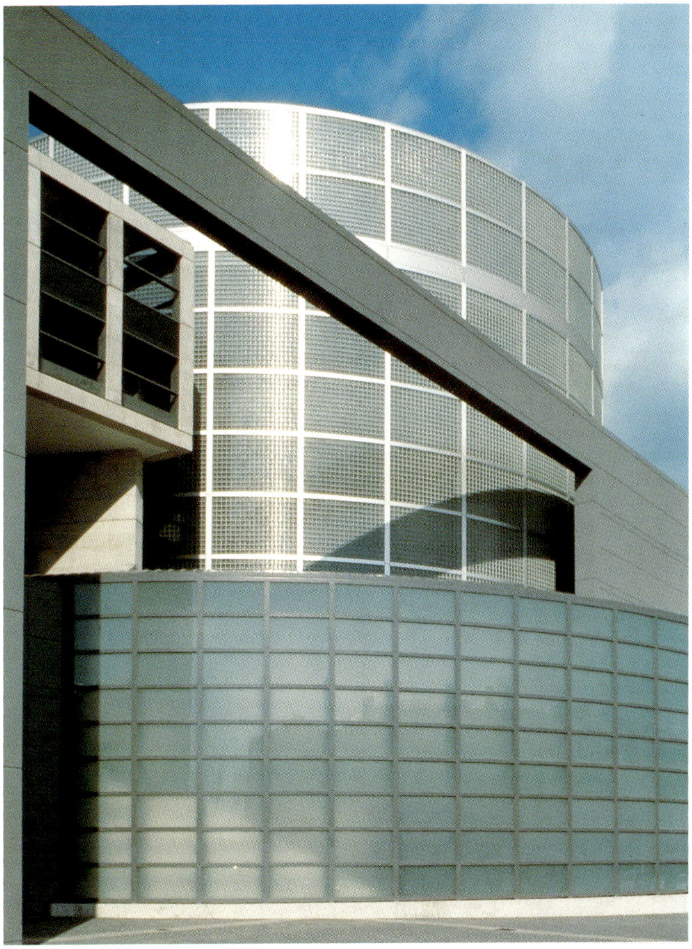

Interior views.

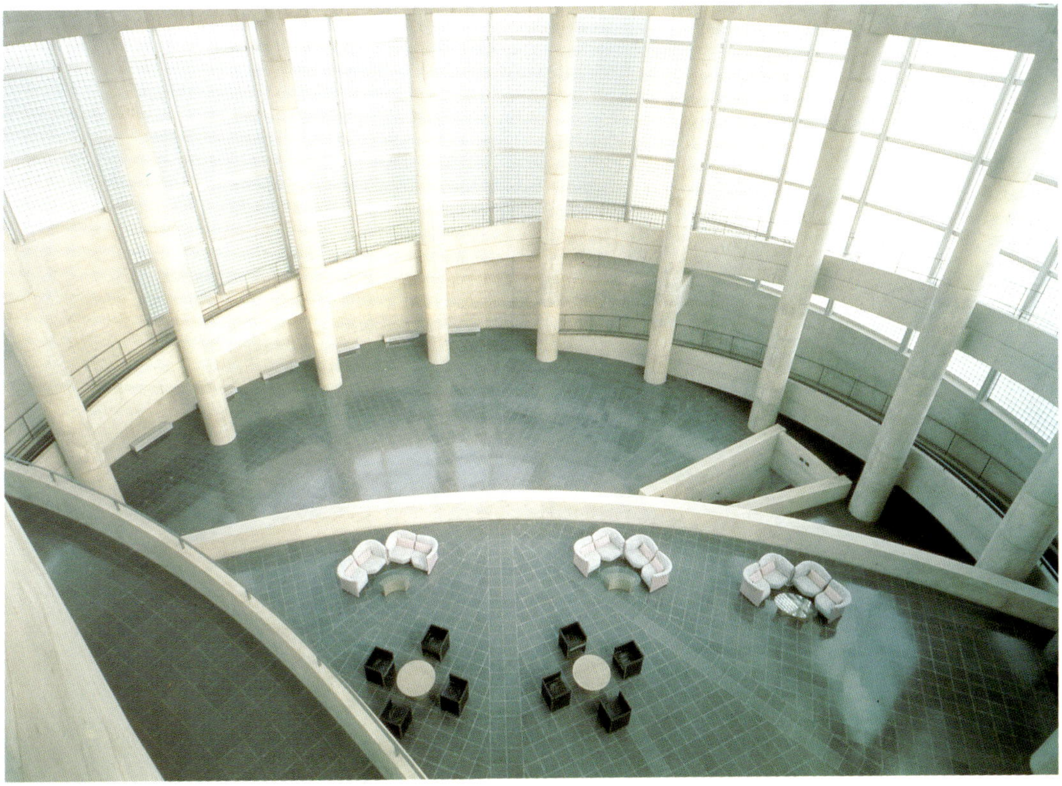

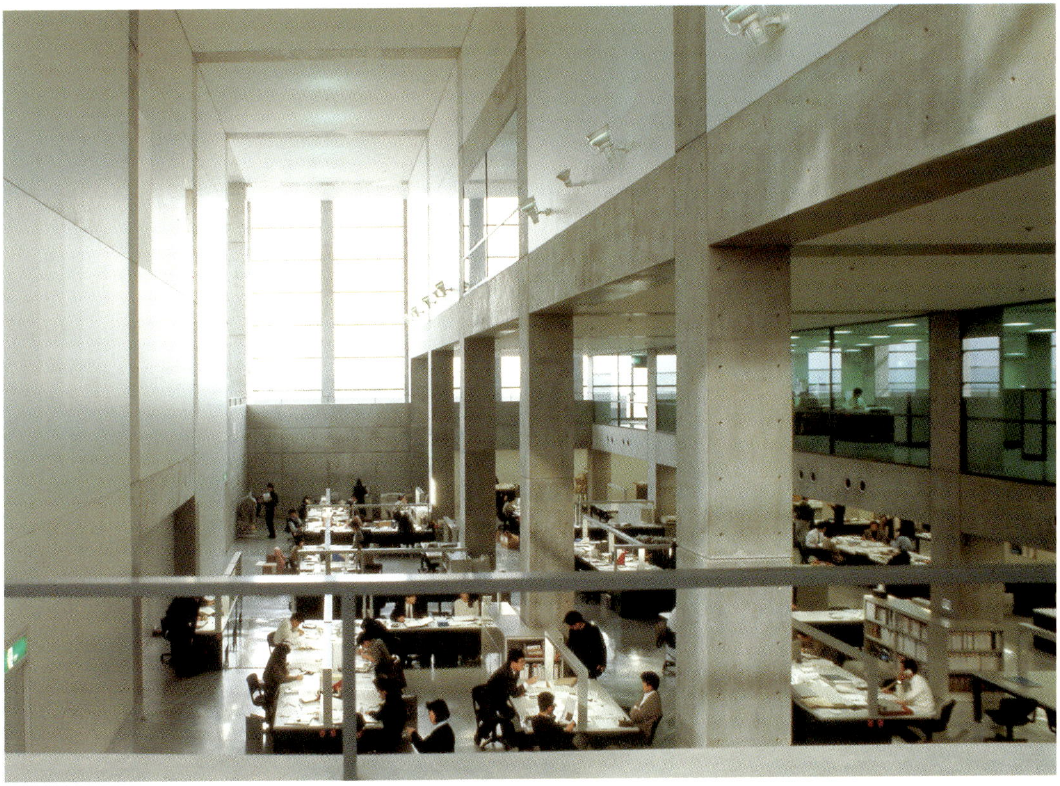

Shinto Shrine Project

Section with plan of the auditorium and site plan.

If the square is regarded as the centre of the European city, then the Shinto shrine and Buddhist temple represent equivalent spaces at the heart of Japanese cities. The existence of these buildings is under threat due to the exorbitant land prices; their survival is therefore dependent on the possibility of transforming them into economically independent bodies by diversifying and rationalizing their function.

This project aims at such a transformation for a shrine located at the centre of Tokyo, not far from the downtown area of Shibuya. The temple itself is to be found on the top floor of the building, while at its intermediate level there is a commercial area and, on the ground floor, a theatre and a gallery. A cubic volume and a lower, rectangular volume in line with the entrance constitute the main compositional elements of the project. The majority of the service areas are located below ground.

Location Shibuya, Tokyo
Design 1986

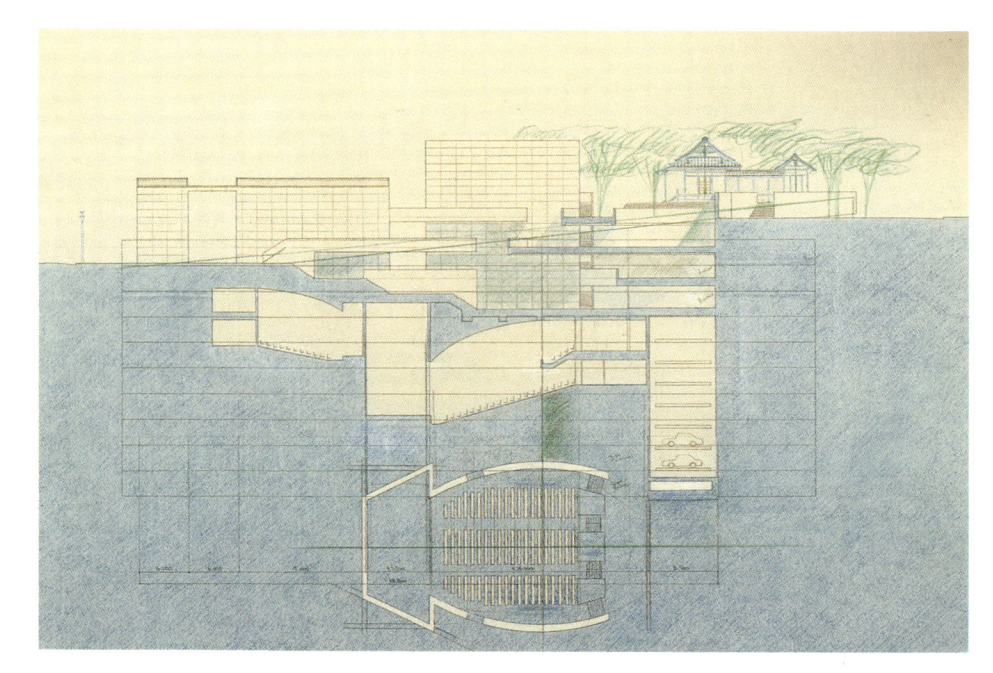

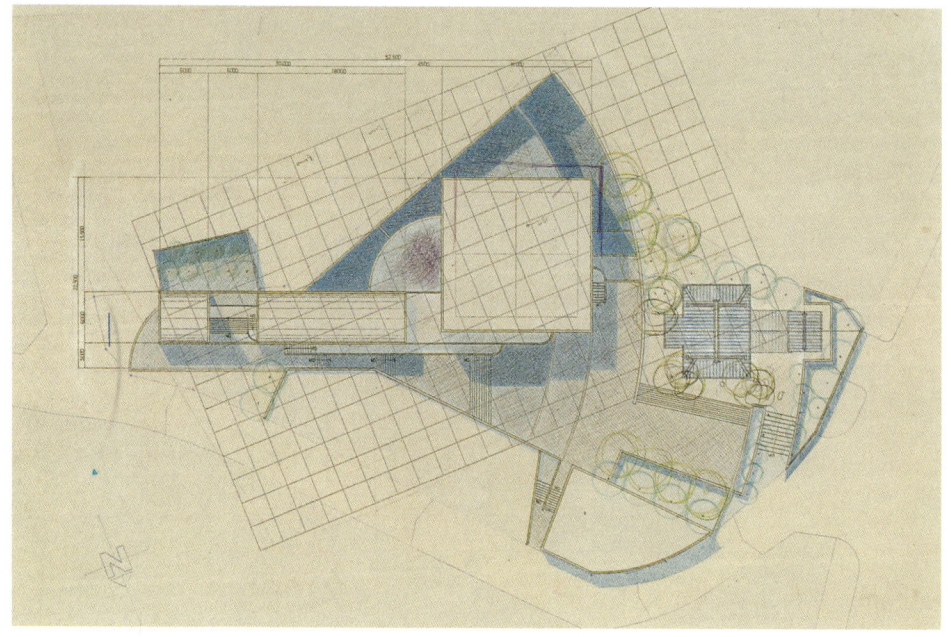

Mount Rokko Banqueting Hall Project

Aerial view of the model.

At 923 metres high, Mount Rokko is the highest mountain in the area of Hanshin and dominates the bay of Osaka. This project is a design for a banqueting room to be located near the summit of the mountain, next to a hotel and close to the Church on Mount Rokko. The plan of the building continues the axis running from the hotel to the church. Although not realized, this project has served as a reference for the Naoshima project.

Location Kobe, Hyogo
Design 1987

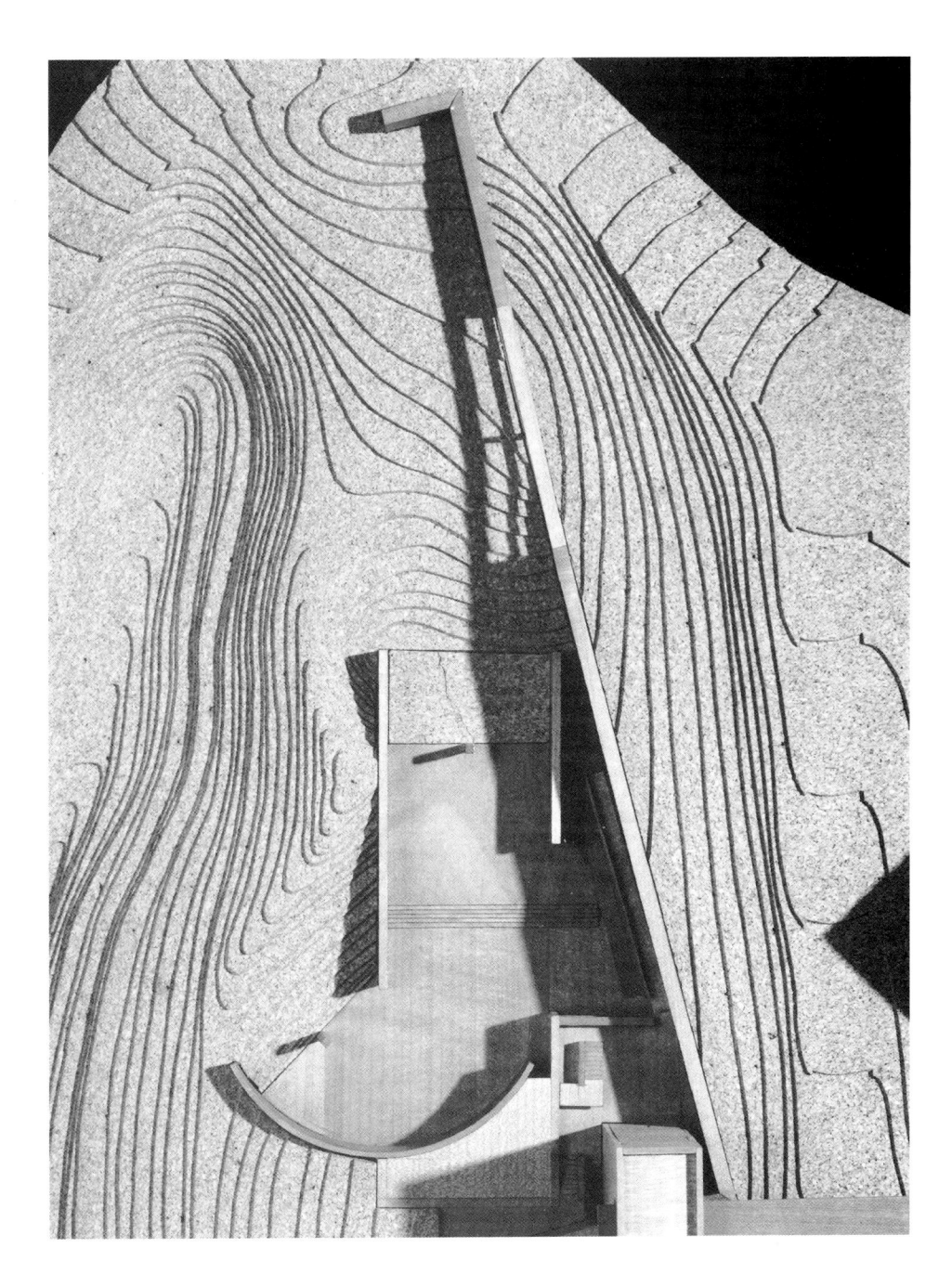

Church of the Light

View showing the cross cut into the concrete wall, section and view of the roof.

In a quiet residential suburb of Osaka, this chapel is positioned in accordance with the direction of the sun and the location of an adjacent church building. The church consists of a rectangular volume (a triple cube) bisected at a 15-degree angle by a freestanding wall, which defines the chapel and its triangular entrance space. Entering through an opening in the angled wall, you have to turn 180 degrees to be aligned with the chapel. The floor descends in stages towards the altar, behind which is a wall penetrated by horizontal and vertical openings forming a crucifix. Light radiates through these openings into the stillness of the chapel. Both the floor and pews are made of scaffolding planks which, with their rough-textured surface, emphasize the simple and honest character of the space.

Location Ibaraki
Design 1987–8
Construction 1988–9
Structure Reinforced concrete
Site area 838.6 m^2
Building area 113 m^2
Total floor area 113 m^2

319

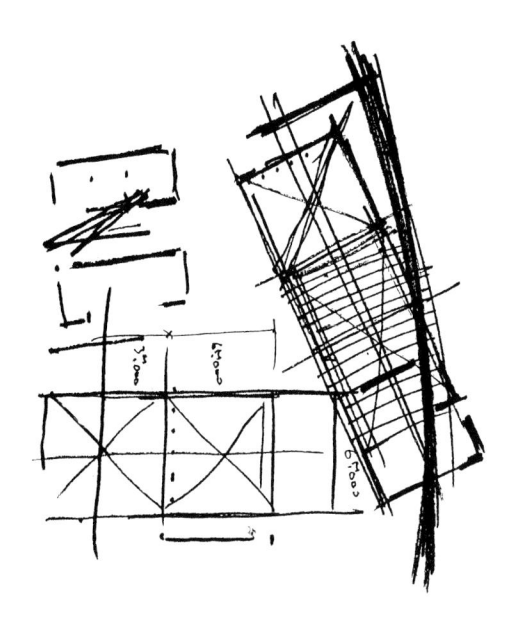

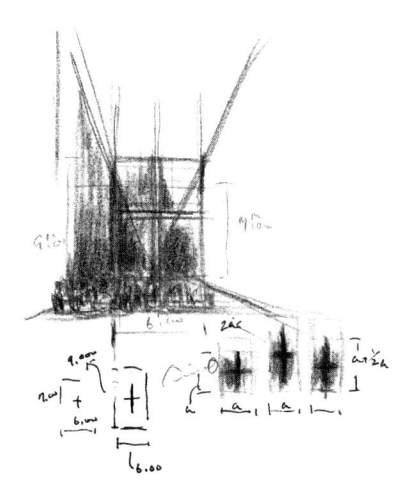

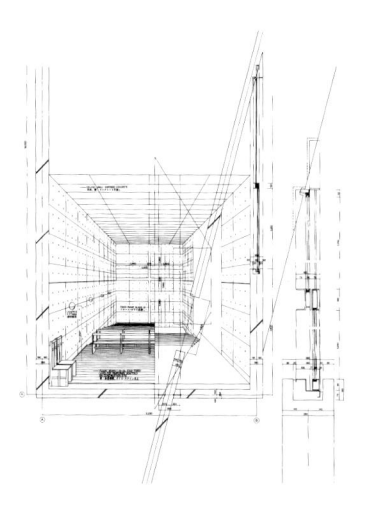

Conceptual sketch, perspective and interior views.

320

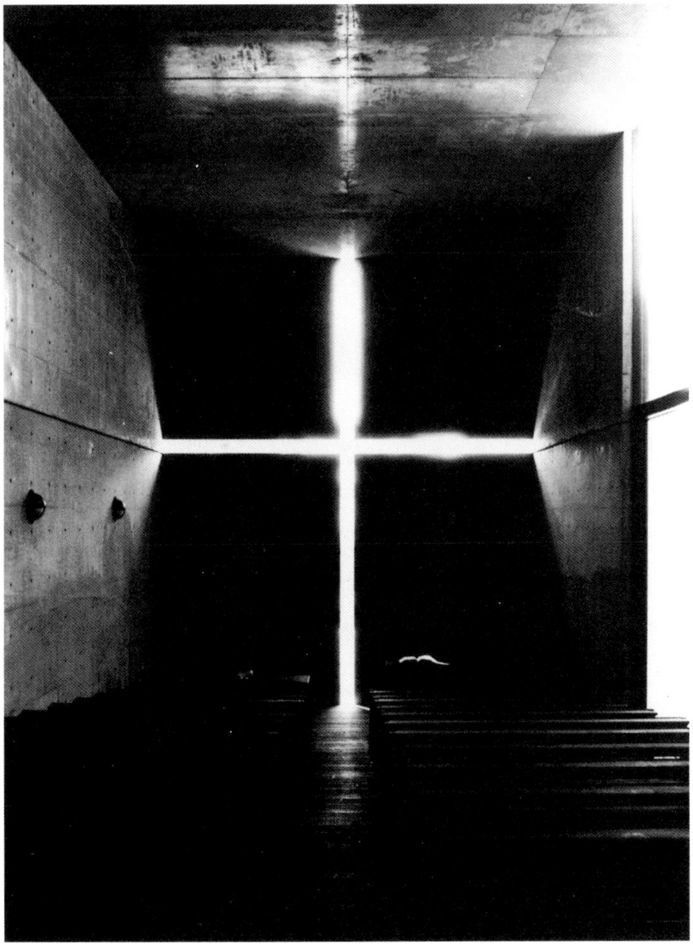

Children's Museum

Site plan, conceptual sketch, overall view and section.

On a hill overlooking a large lake, this museum is a cultural facility for the artistic education of children. It is made up of three units – the main museum, an intermediate plaza and a workshop complex – all linked by a long pathway punctuated by a series of walls, which dramatically slice through the hillside. The main unit is a multi-functional complex, containing a library, indoor and outdoor theatres, exhibition gallery, multi-purpose hall and restaurant. It is composed of two staggered volumes, one of which connects with a fan-shaped building housing the theatres. The outdoor theatre is on the roof and benefits from the verdant setting. A series of pools built around the centre serve to unify the architecture with the scenery of the lake. The intermediate plaza is a walled external space, containing a grid of sixteen 9-metre-high columns. The workshop complex consists of a two-storey workshop building, square in plan, and set within a plaza.

Location Himeji
Design 1987–8
Construction 1988–9
Structure Reinforced concrete and steel
Site area 87,222 m^2
Building area 3,575.6 m^2
Total floor area 7,488.4 m^2

323

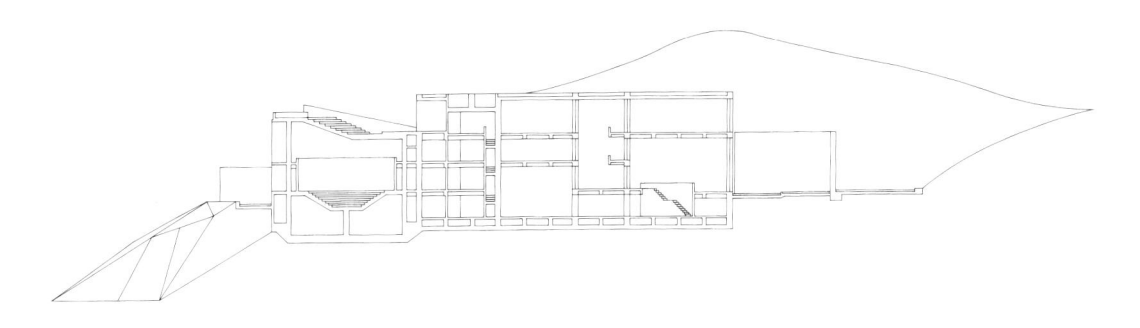

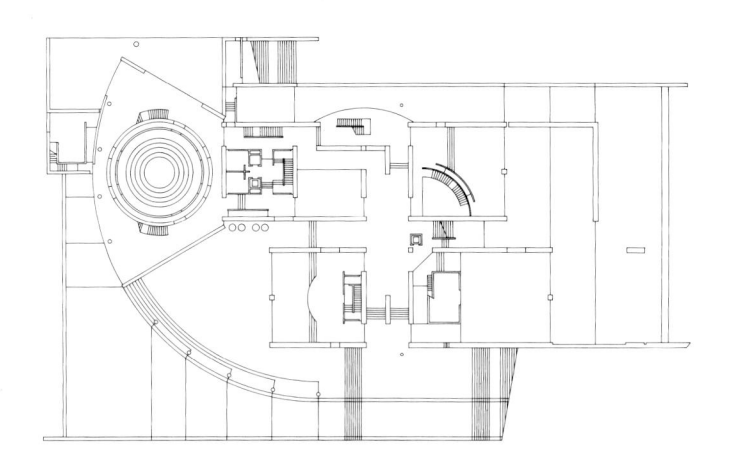

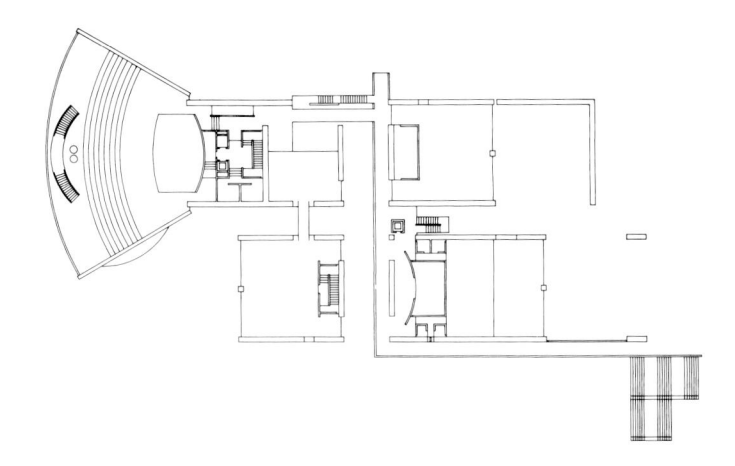

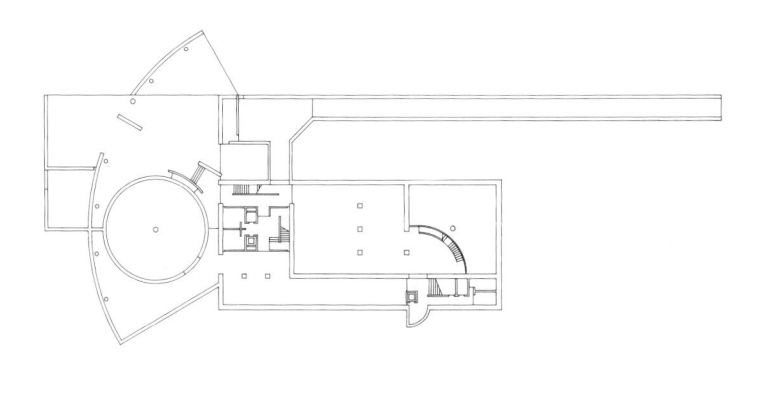

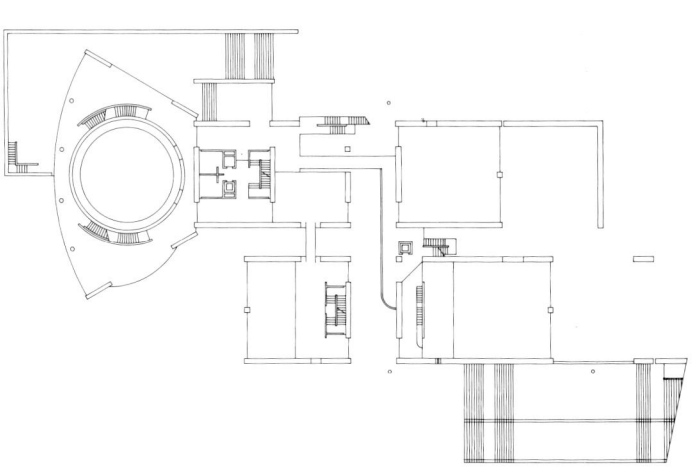

Floor plans and view showing the intersecting walls.

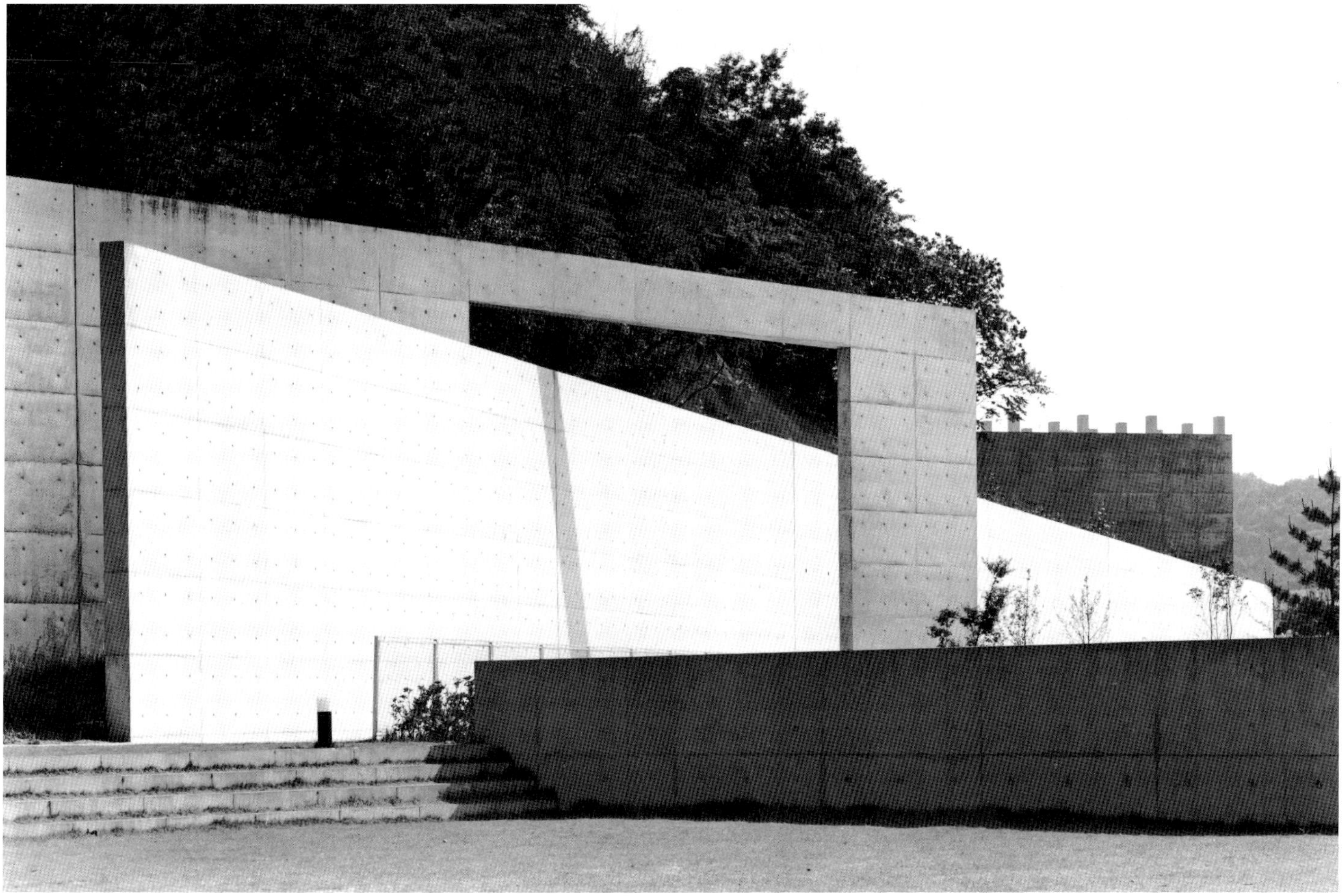

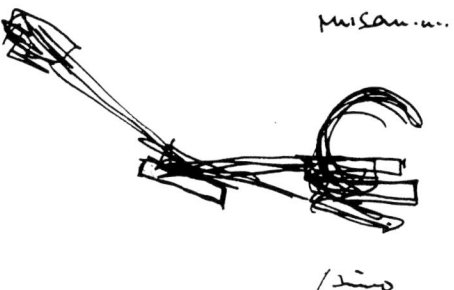

Views of the plaza and pools, and conceptual sketch.

326

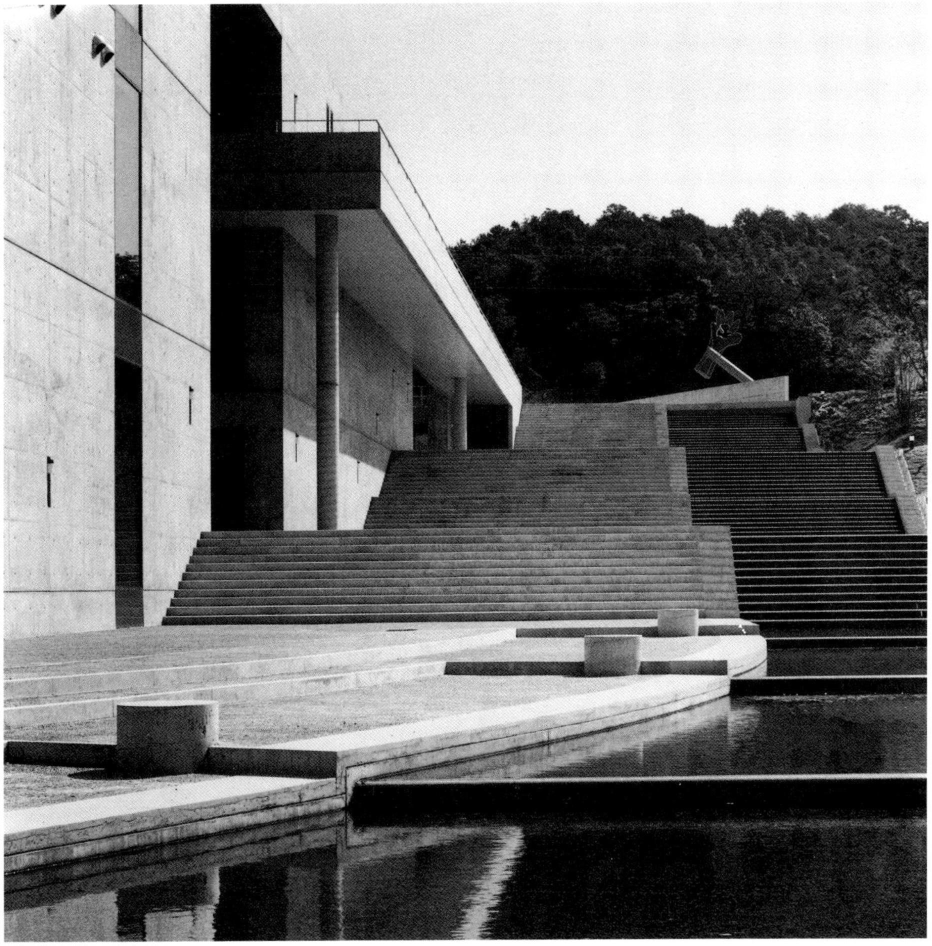

Natsukawa Memorial Hall

View of the building showing roof garden and floor plans.

This off-campus facility for a private high school is in the traditional commercial quarter of an ancient fortified town.

While focusing on drama, painting, music and cinema, the facility offers an environment conducive to communication among the students. The building consists of a rectangular concrete box, with a 24 x 19.2 metre plan. In order to harmonize with its quiet surroundings, the building has a simple external appearance and one-third of its volume is below ground. The basement contains a small conference room and a 150-capacity multi-purpose hall. The upper levels accommodate the entrance hall, a roof garden and conference rooms.

A ramp and a spiral staircase connect spaces on all floors – from the basement foyer to the third-level roof garden – and lead people through various spatial voids, including the foyer and the entrance hall, giving the interior a labyrinthine complexity.

Location Hikone
Design 1987–8
Construction 1988–9
Structure Reinforced concrete
Site area 768.2 m^2
Building area 521.1 m^2
Total floor area 1,205 m^2

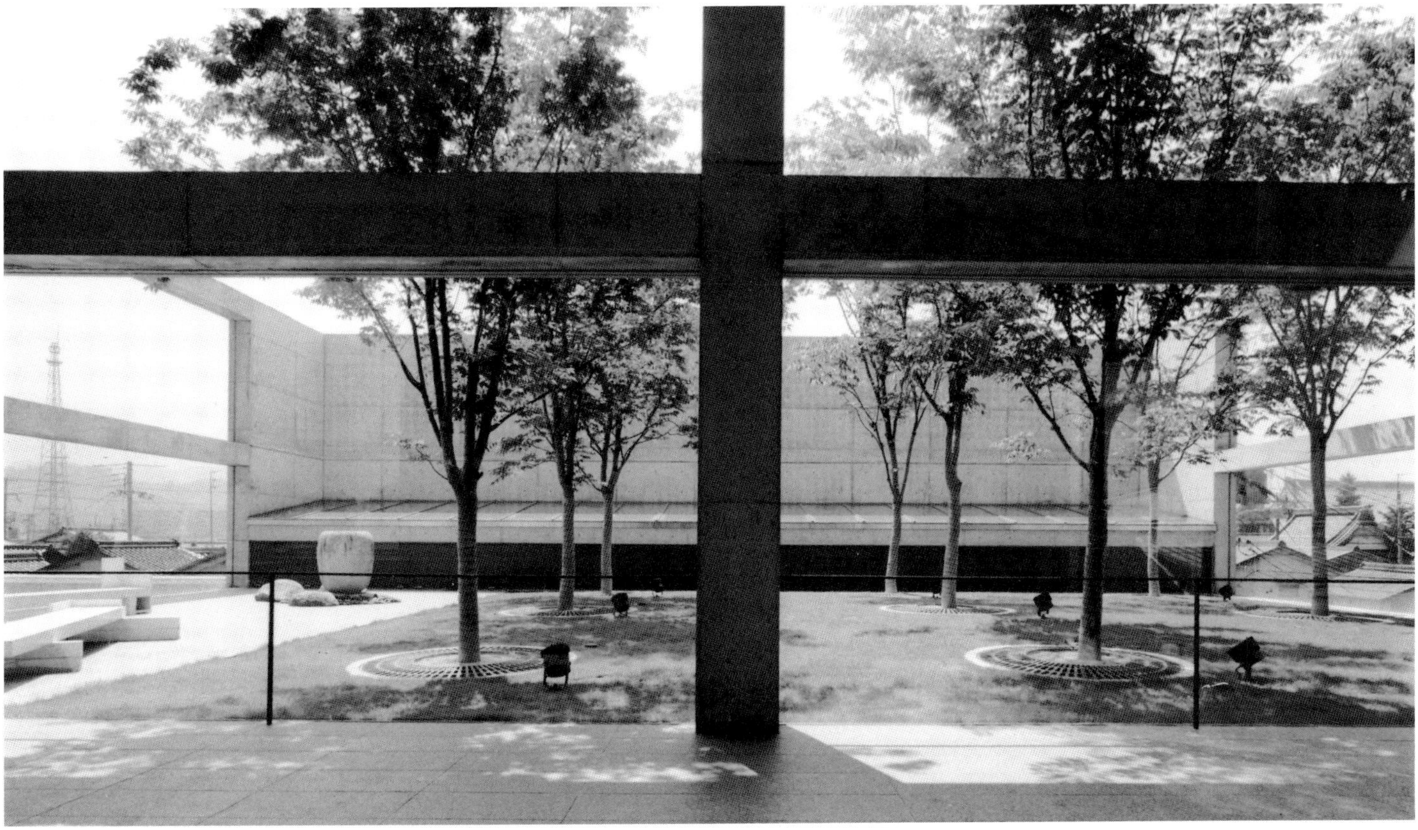

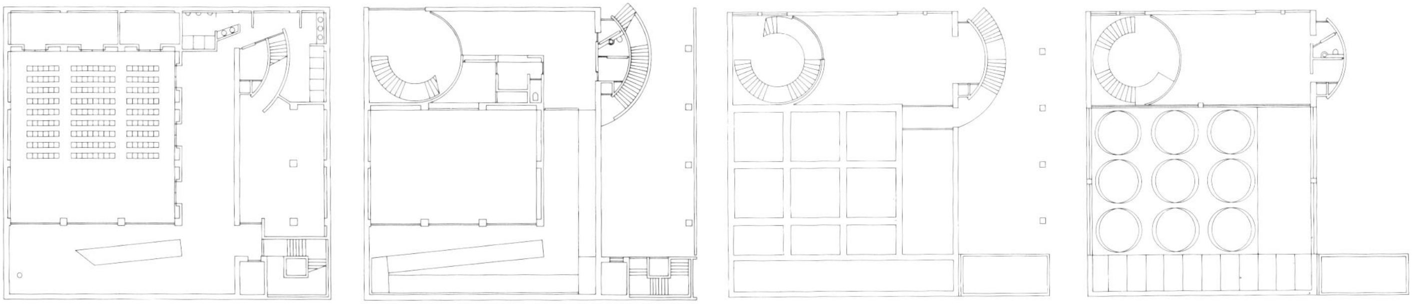

Views of the ramp and section.

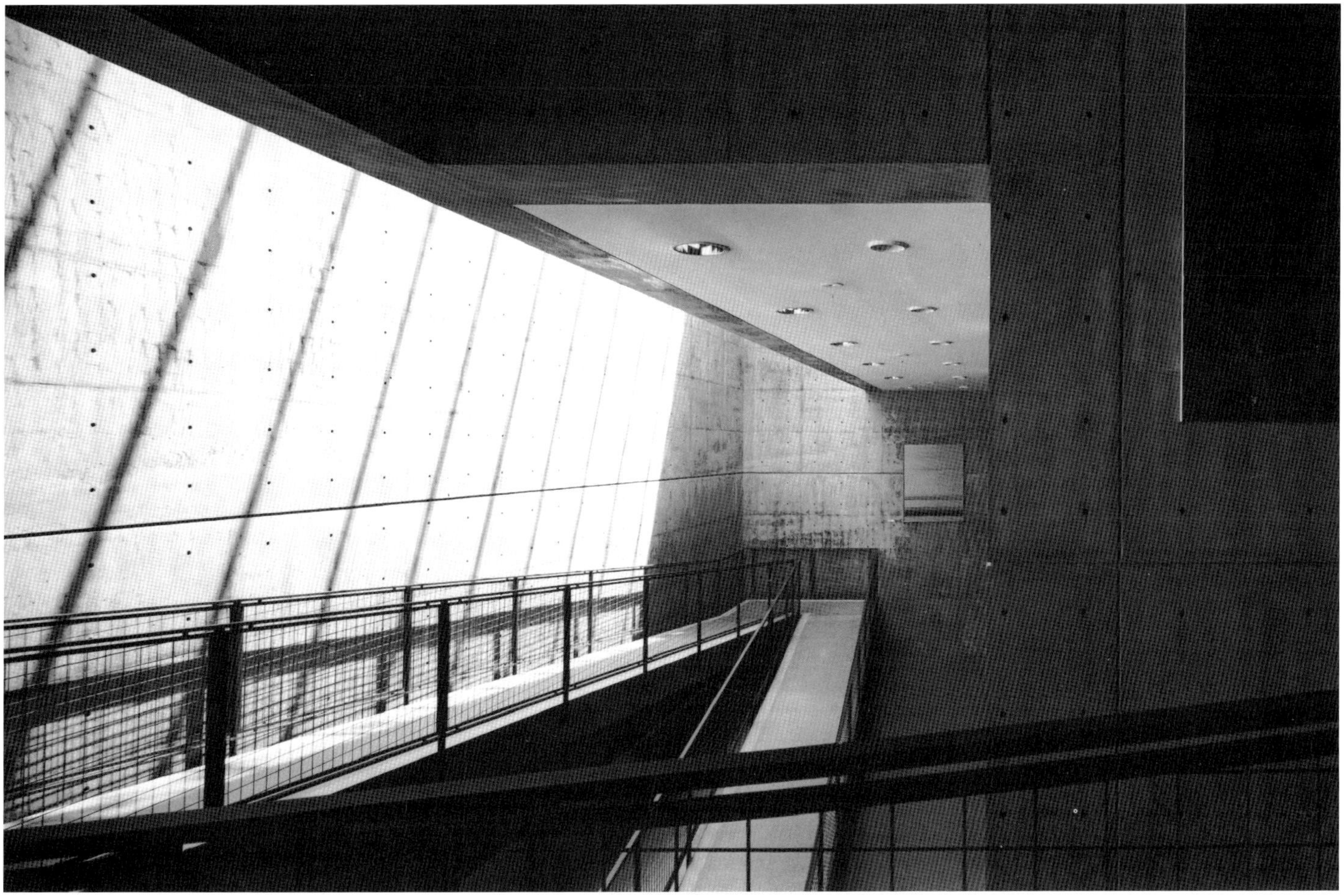

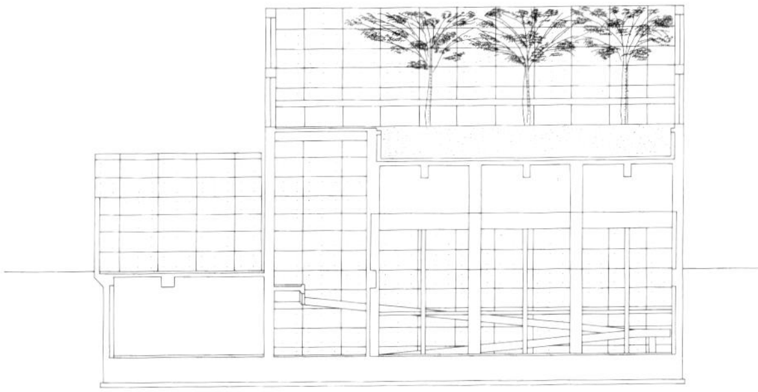

Izu Project

Views of the model.

This project was proposed for a seaside resort in a national park, in the southern part of the Izu Peninsula. The site is encircled by sheer cliffs, on a low promontory which projects straight out into the ocean.

Viewing the entire cape as an extension of the site, the aim was to include its unique natural characteristics in the design, and to 'architecturalize' them. The hotel is in a central position on the cape, with various elements arranged around it – a restaurant, observation platforms and an art gallery – in an attempt to make life on the cape self-contained.

The building is a cluster of rectangular volumes, each founded on four units of a uniform 5.6 x 5.6 metre grid. Within the total composition, each volume is adapted to the topography of the site, generating asymmetries in section.

After passing through a central gate at the neck of the cape, visitors follow a long wall to arrive at a café. Proceeding on, they are led by a curved wall into the hotel lobby, which offers the panorama of an artificial lake through glazed openings. Water from the lake weaves around the buildings and flows over a series of cascades in the direction of the sea. There are views of Mount Fuji or the ocean from every room in the guest maisonettes.

Location Shizuoka
Design 1987–9

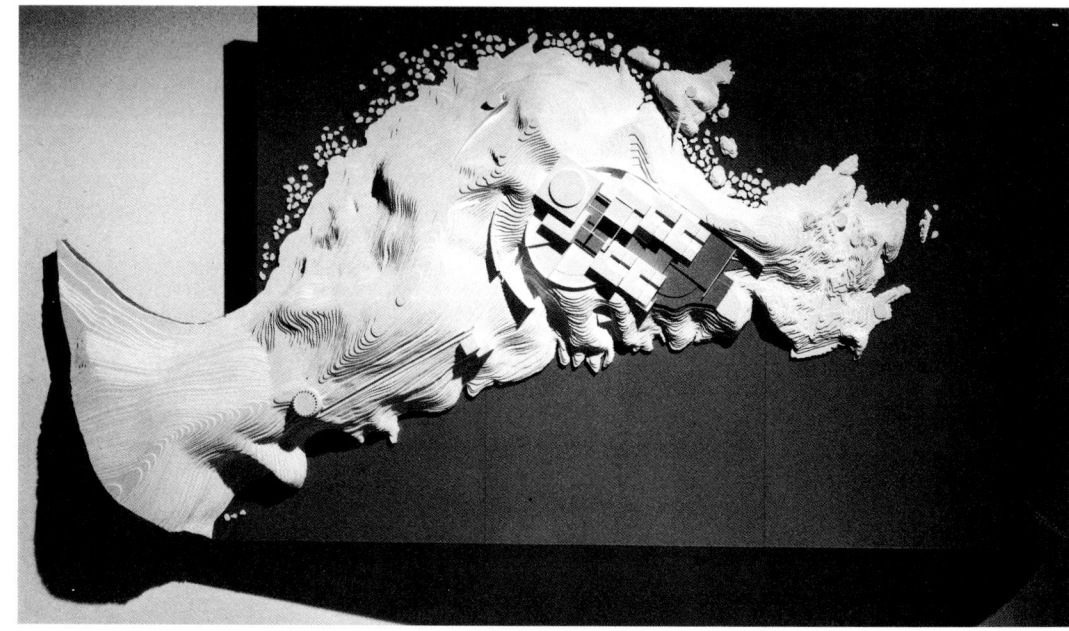

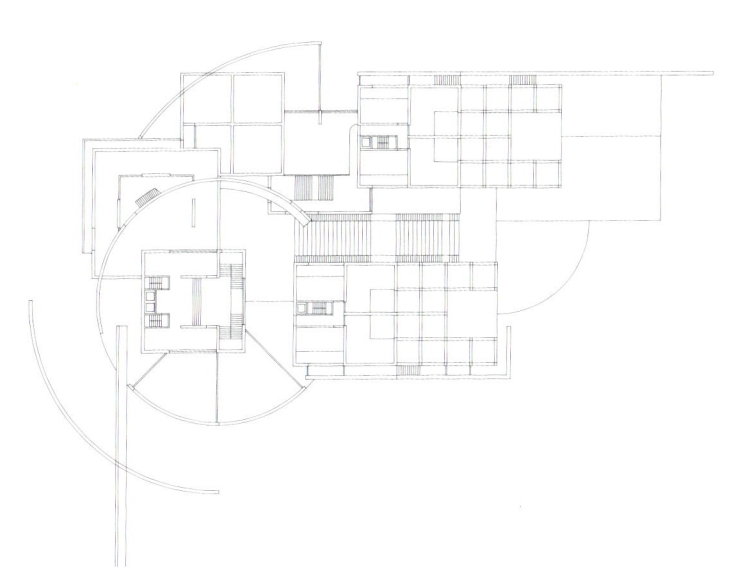

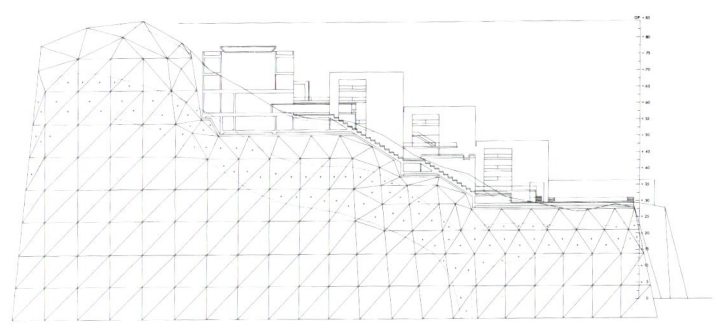

Elevational drawing showing the building and the adjacent lake, plan and section.

Nakanoshima Project II – Space Strata and Urban Egg

Conceptual sketches, plan and section through the Assembly Hall, longitudinal section and site plan.

Nakanoshima is an island 920 metres in length and 150 metres in maximum breadth, intersected by Midosuji Boulevard, running north–south through Osaka. This proposal for an urban park seeks to retain the historical character and natural beauty of the island while making it into a multi-use facility for the twenty-first century.

Lying between two rivers, the island is a rare green belt in the metropolis, and contains numerous historical buildings. The proposal would integrate the city's cultural facilities into a multi-level composition that articulates the site into three distinct plazas: a water plaza, a plaza for plants, and an underground plaza. The principal facilities of art museum, historical museum, conference hall and concert hall, are contained underground, leaving the ground level open as a park. Water is brought into play by placing a guest house and a restaurant on the river.

The part of this proposal known as the 'Urban Egg' calls for the restoration of the exterior of the decrepit Public Assembly Hall, a four-storey building built in 1918, and the installation in its interior of an ovoid structure derived from recent technology. This would renew the building's status in the city, while the surrounding interior spaces would be revitalized in the form of gallery space. The building thus pursues intersections of past and present through its dichotomy of old/new spaces which, nestled together, open towards the future.

Location Osaka
Design 1988

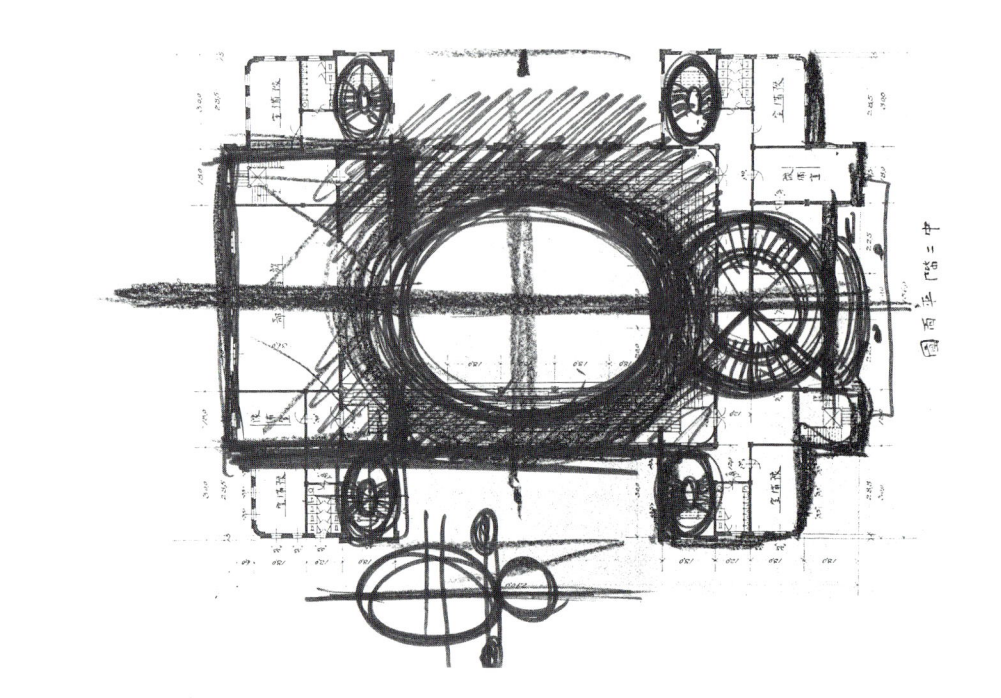

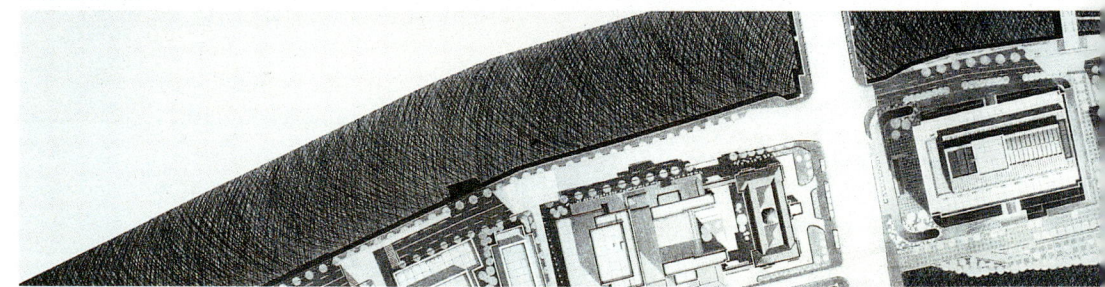

335

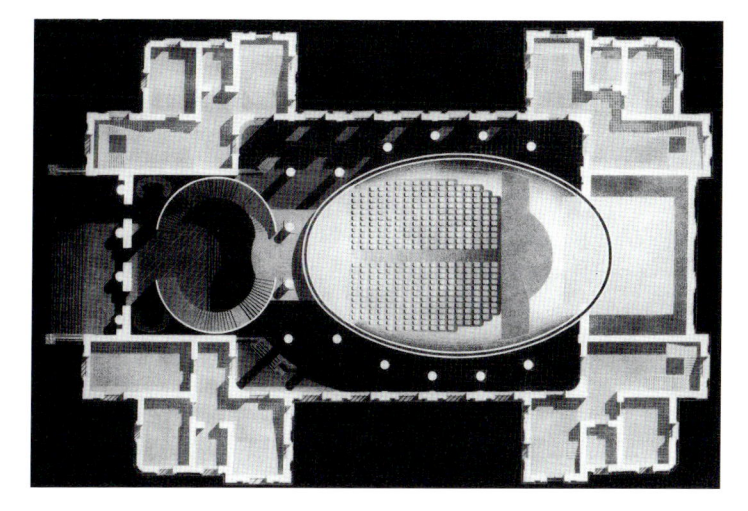

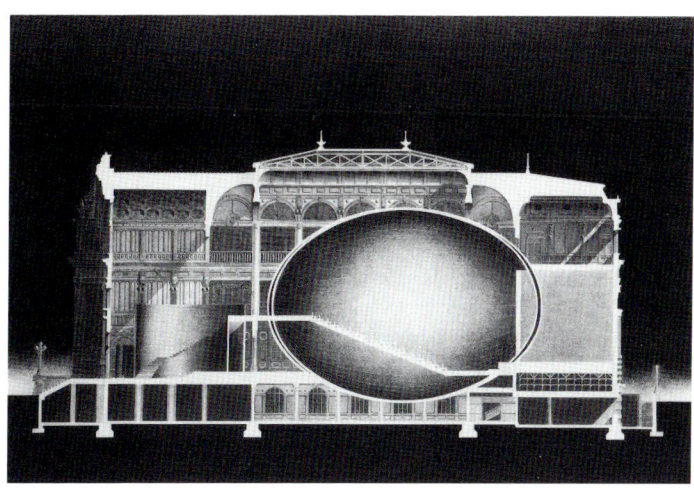

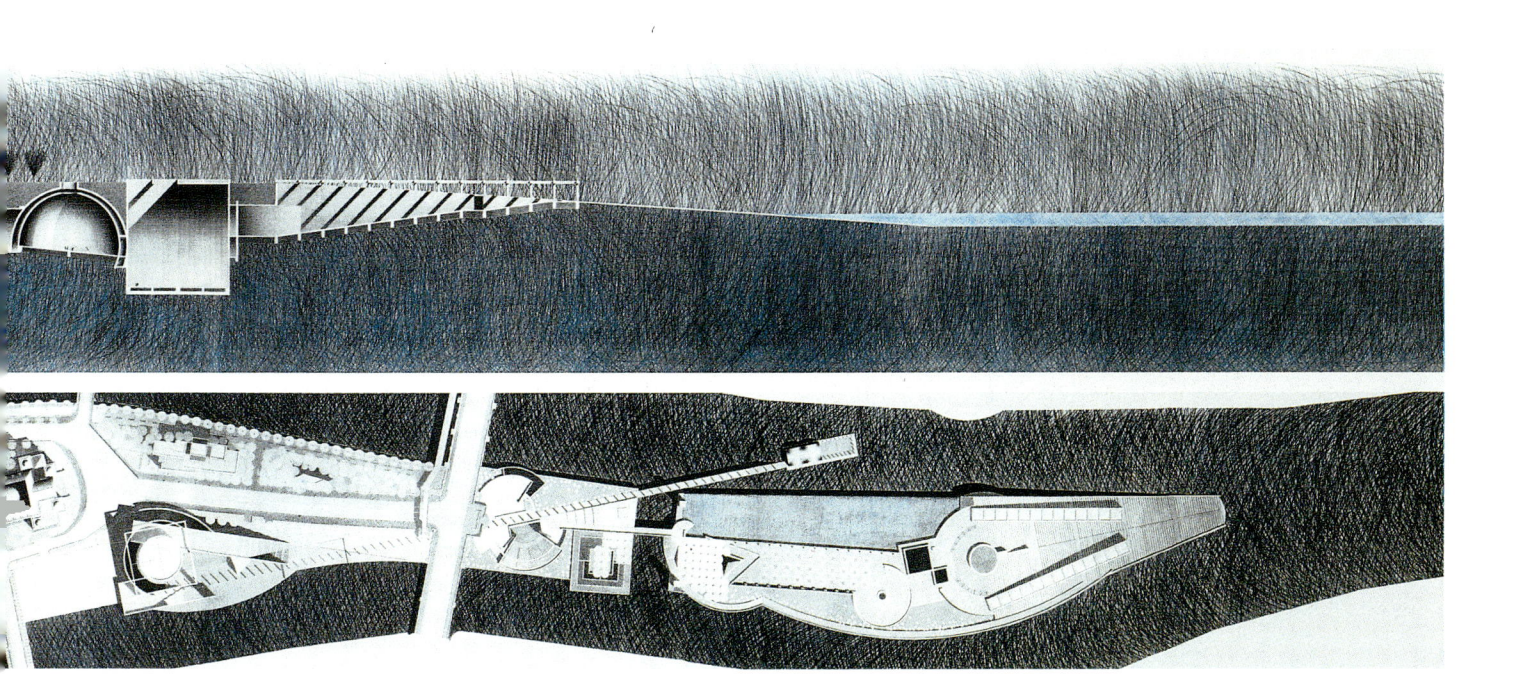

View of the model and perspectives.

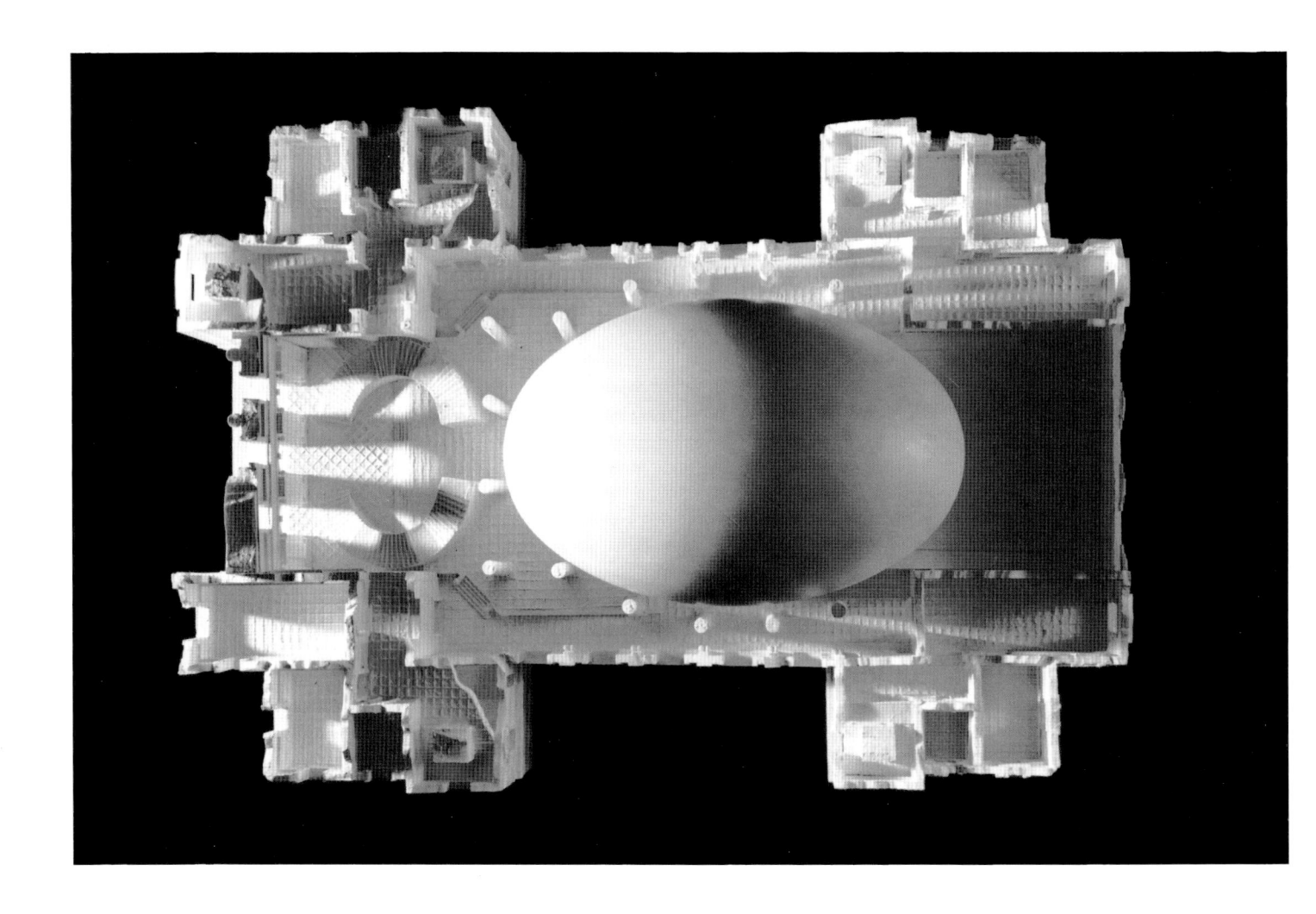

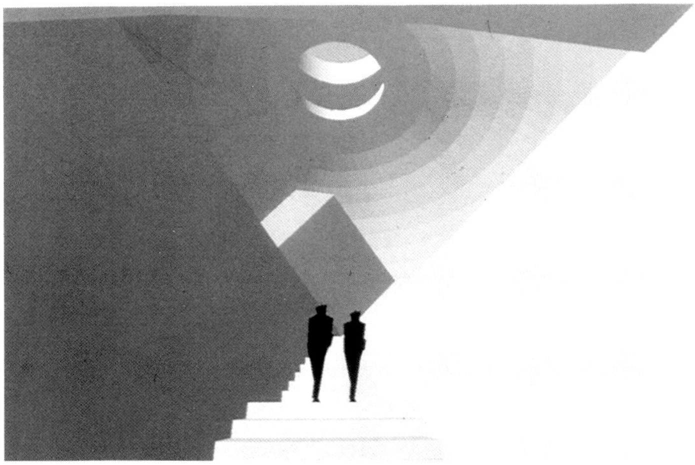

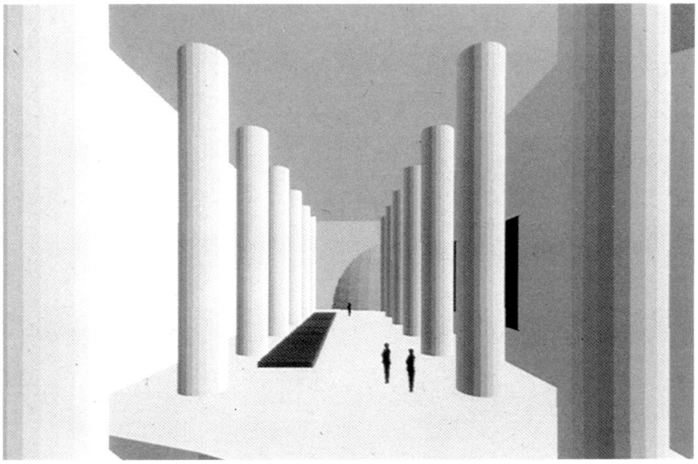

I Gallery Project

Conceptual sketches, ground-floor plan and views of the model.

The project is for a building located in a residential area not far from the city centre. Designed to respect the existing surrounding trees, it is a rectangular form, 11 x 16 metres, and consists of a gallery, atelier and two residential units at four levels which includes one below ground. The owner's residence is located on the top floor; his mother's is on the lower level; and on the ground floor and basement are the gallery and atelier. Between the building itself and the surrounding wall lies a courtyard onto which the gallery opens. The gallery and atelier are accessed from a bridge at a 45-degree incline which runs above the garden.

Location Setagaya, Tokyo
Design 1988

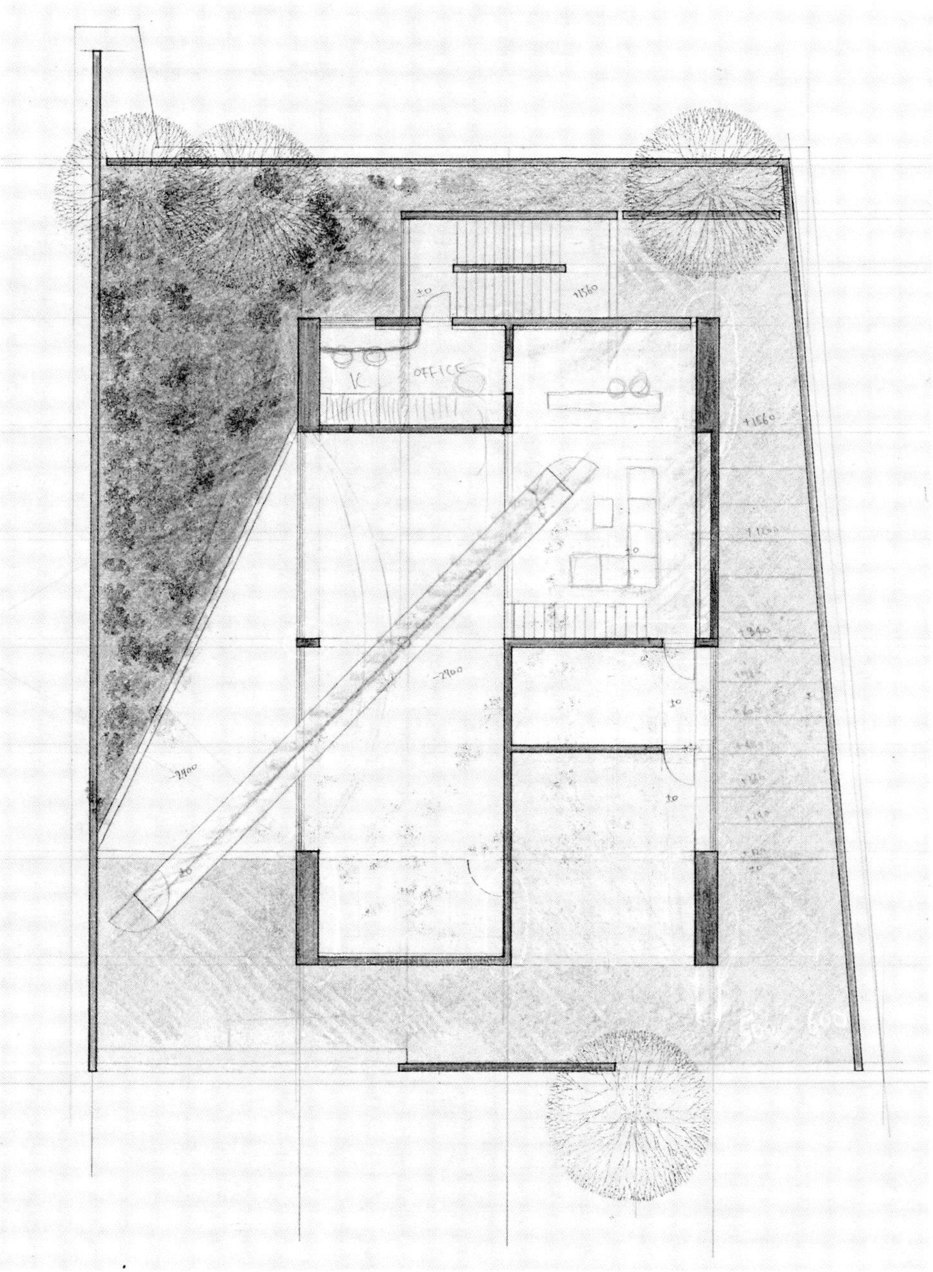
K
OFFICE

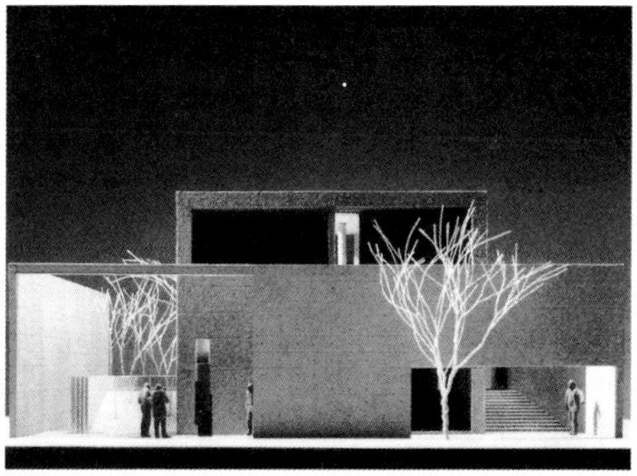

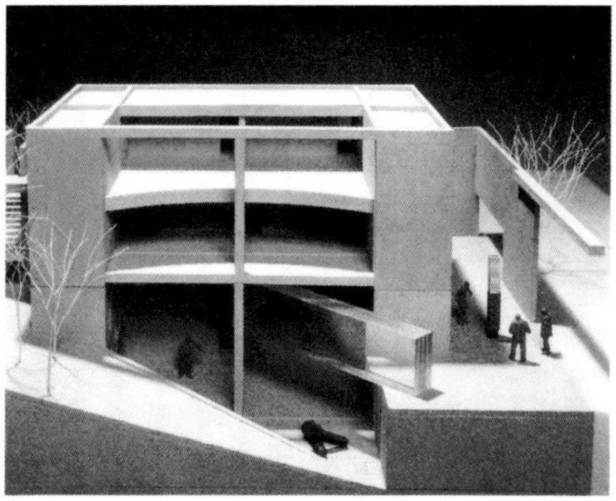

Ito House

Axonometric, first- and third-floor plans and view showing the entrance stairs.

This three-family house is located in a prestigious residential district in Tokyo. The site presented several unique features – dogwood trees, an aged cherry tree, and a distinctive old concrete wall – which were preserved by 'inserting' the building into the space between them.

The building has a rectangular core, founded on a 5,600 mm x 5,600 mm grid, and a protecting wall. The rectangular volume is offset at a 6-degree angle from the north–south axis of the front road. The protecting wall penetrates the main volume of the building in the form of a half-circle arc, defining the entry space of the house. Two freestanding pillars, on a line with the intersection of the adjacent street, indicate the axis of approach, and echo the 5,600 mm span of the grid.

The functions of the building – separate apartments for the parents and the families of their son and elder daughter, and a boutique/atelier operated by the son and his wife – are independent and with individual character, and have been organized in a complex three-dimensional manner within the total composition.

Location Tokyo
Design 1988–9
Construction 1989–90
Structure Reinforced concrete
Site area 567.7 m^2
Building area 279.7 m^2
Total floor area 504.8 m^2

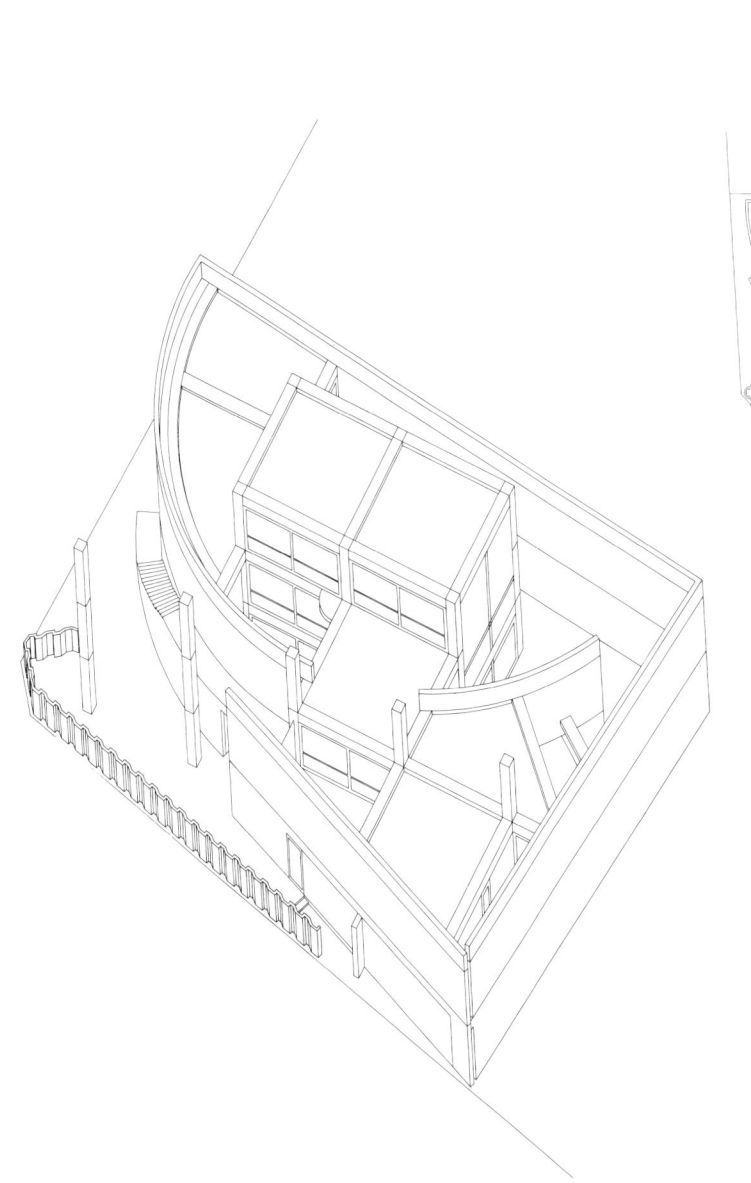

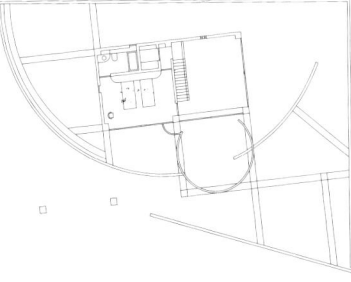

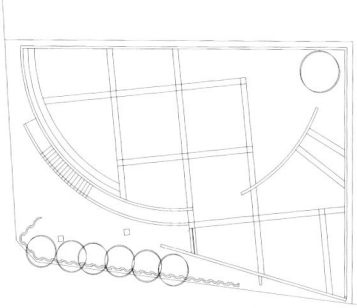

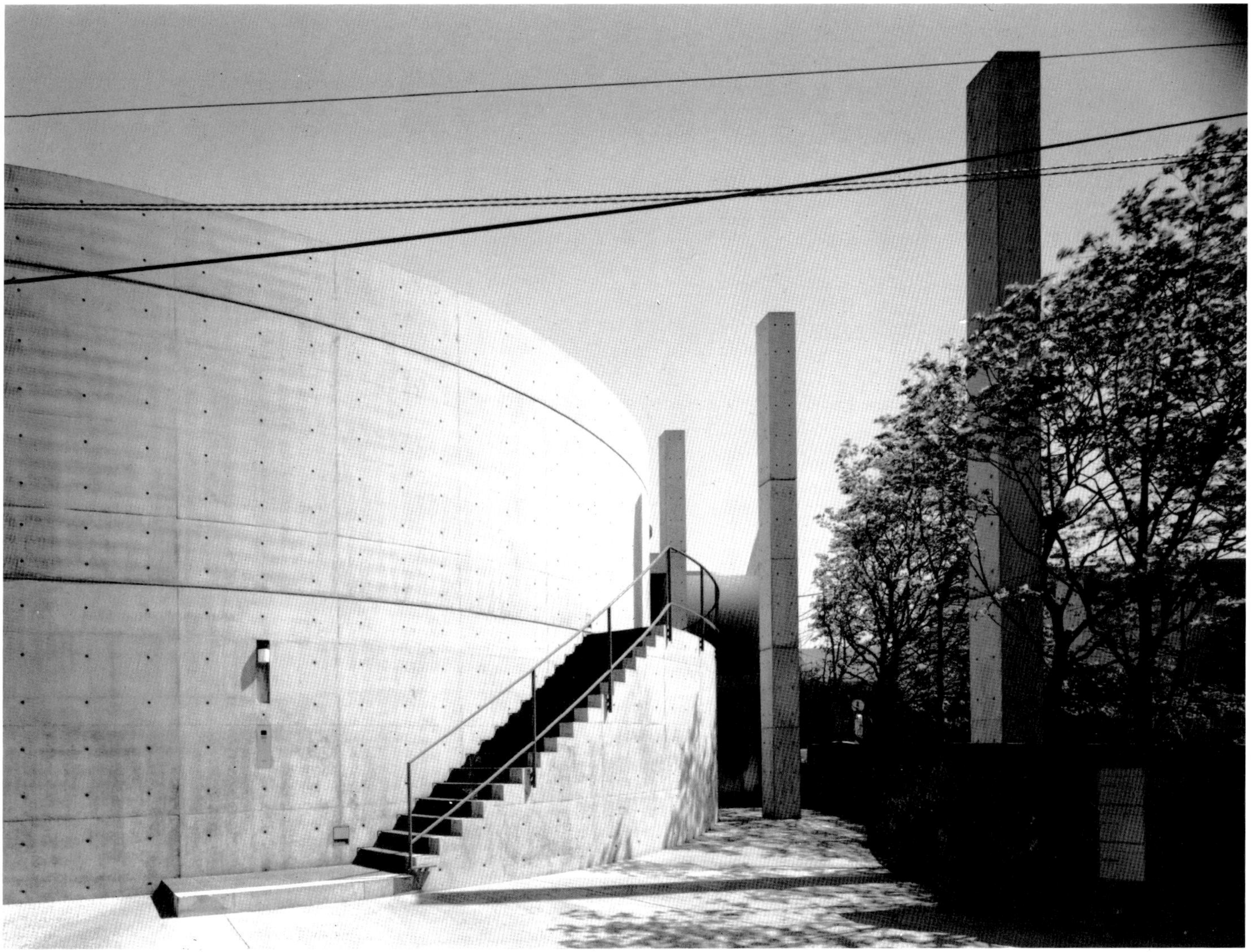

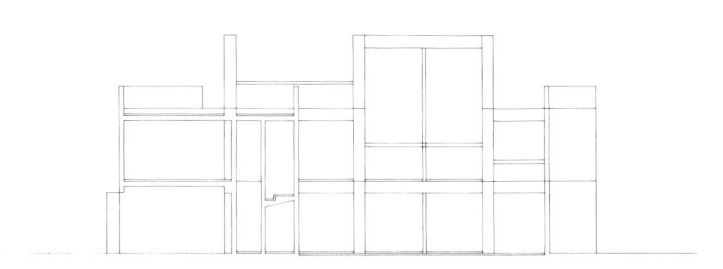

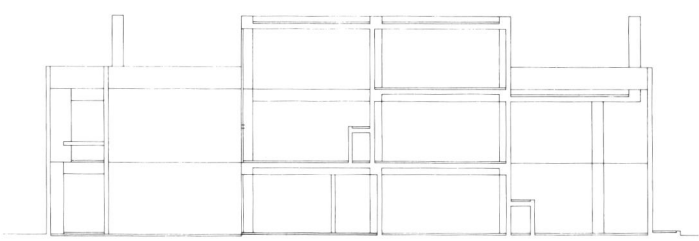

Side view of the building, sections and view of the courtyard.

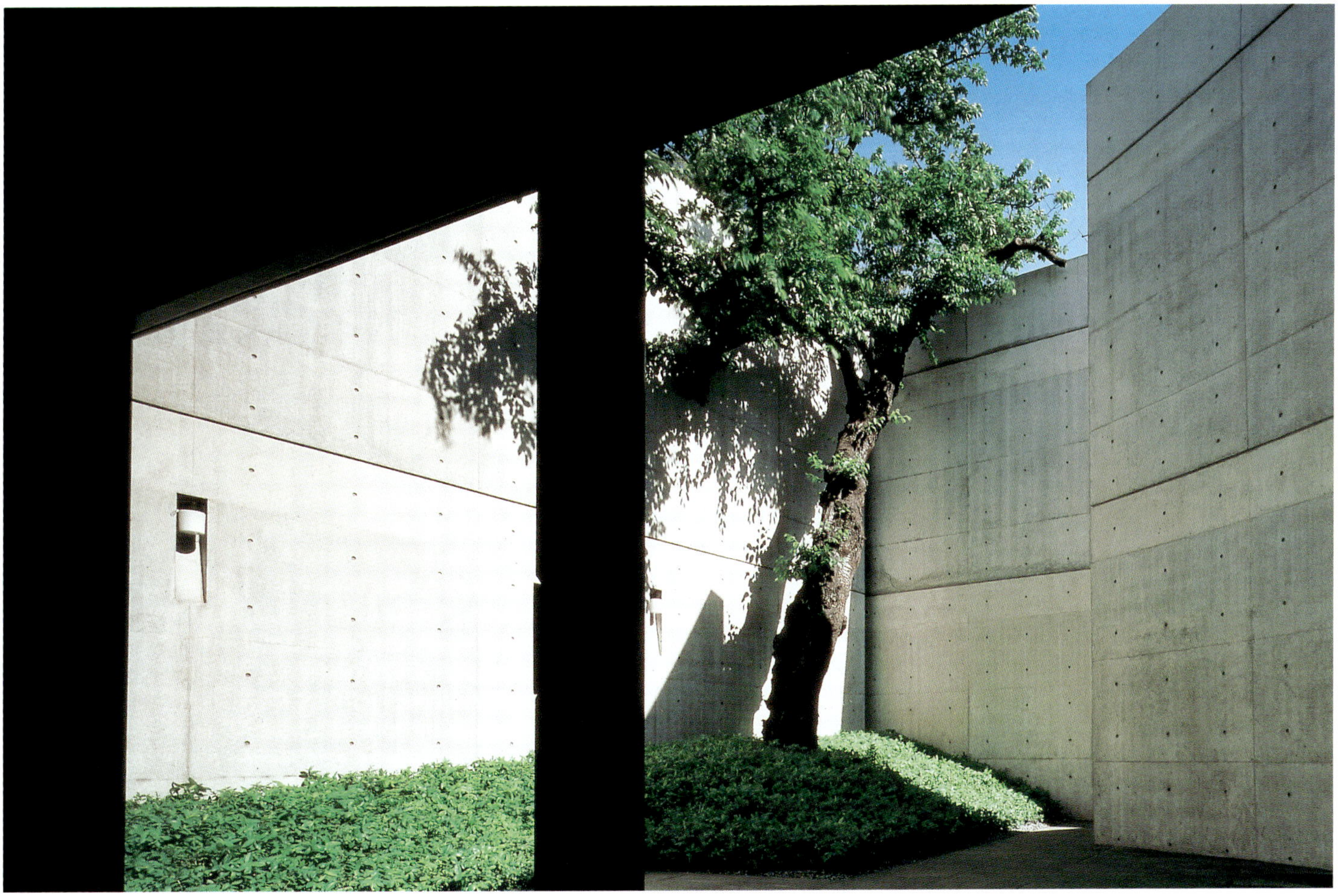

Naoshima Contemporary Art Museum

Site plan and conceptual sketches.

The museum is on the bluff of a slender cape on Naoshima Island's southern tip, overlooking the gentle waves lapping on the beach below. It was designed to receive visitors arriving by boat. Disembarking at a landing-stage, they are greeted by a stepped plaza that acts as the museum entrance, but also houses a museum annexe underground and doubles as a stage for outdoor performances. Only after climbing the plaza steps do the stone-rubble walls of the main museum come into view. More than half of the building's volume sits underground so as not to intrude on the national park which surrounds the museum. Visitors ascend the slope, enter the main building and are then led into the gallery – a large underground volume two levels high, 50 metres long, and 8 metres wide. The hotel building, gallery and stepped terrace all face the ocean, and the interior spaces of each absorb the tranquil ocean scenery of commuting boats and setting sun.

Location Naoshima
Design 1988–90
Construction 1990–92
Structure Reinforced concrete
Site area 44,700 m^2
Building area 1,775.5 m^2
Total floor area 3,643.4 m^2

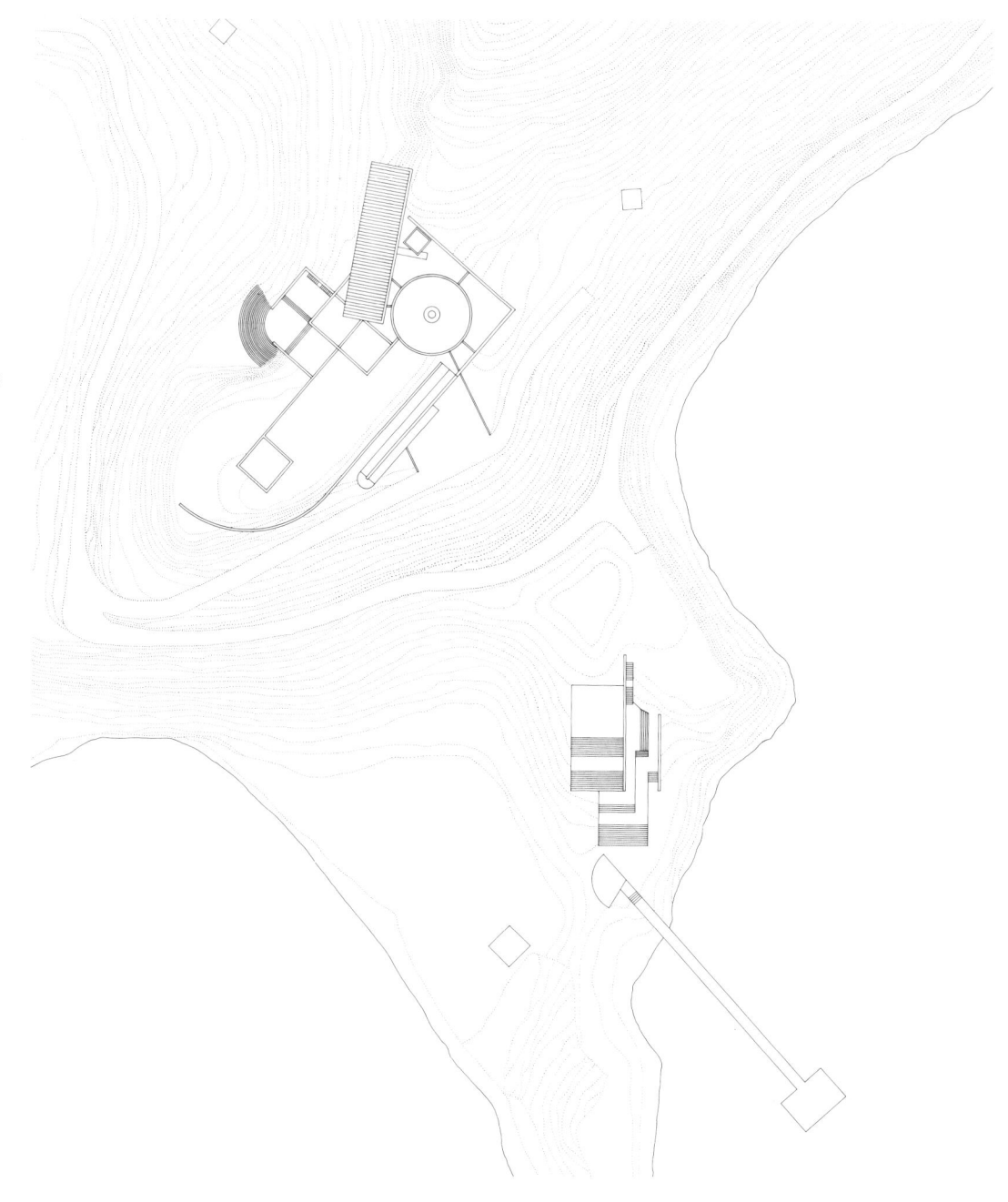

345

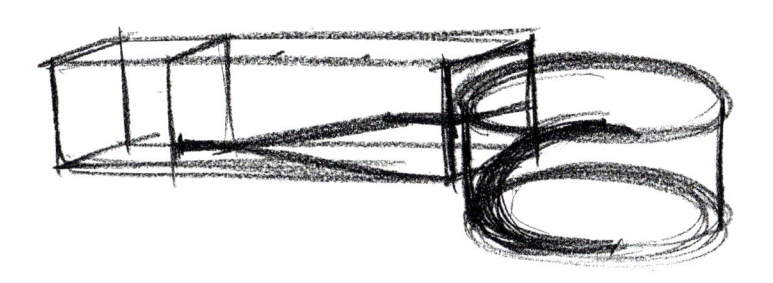

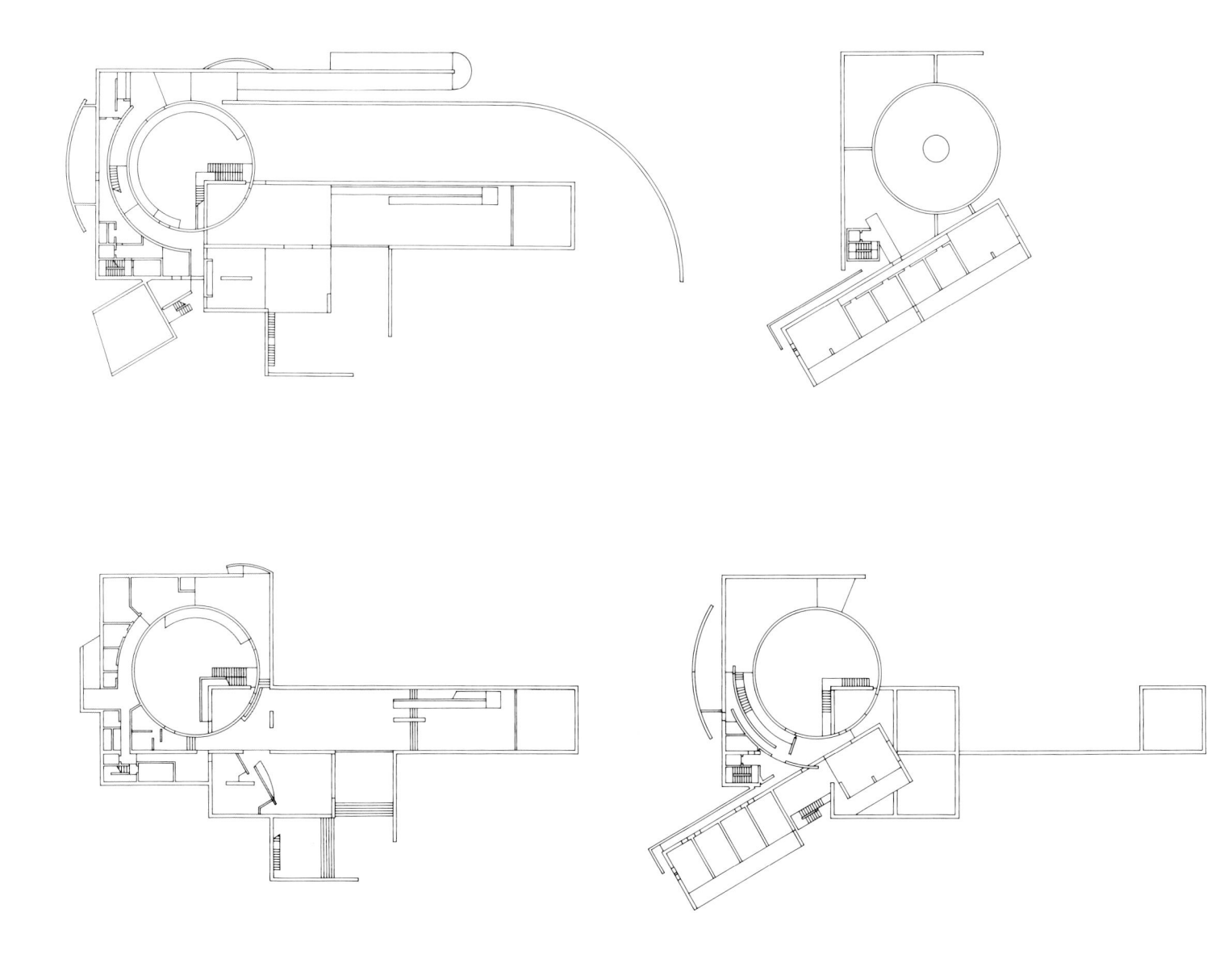

Floor plans and view of the building's stepped terraces.

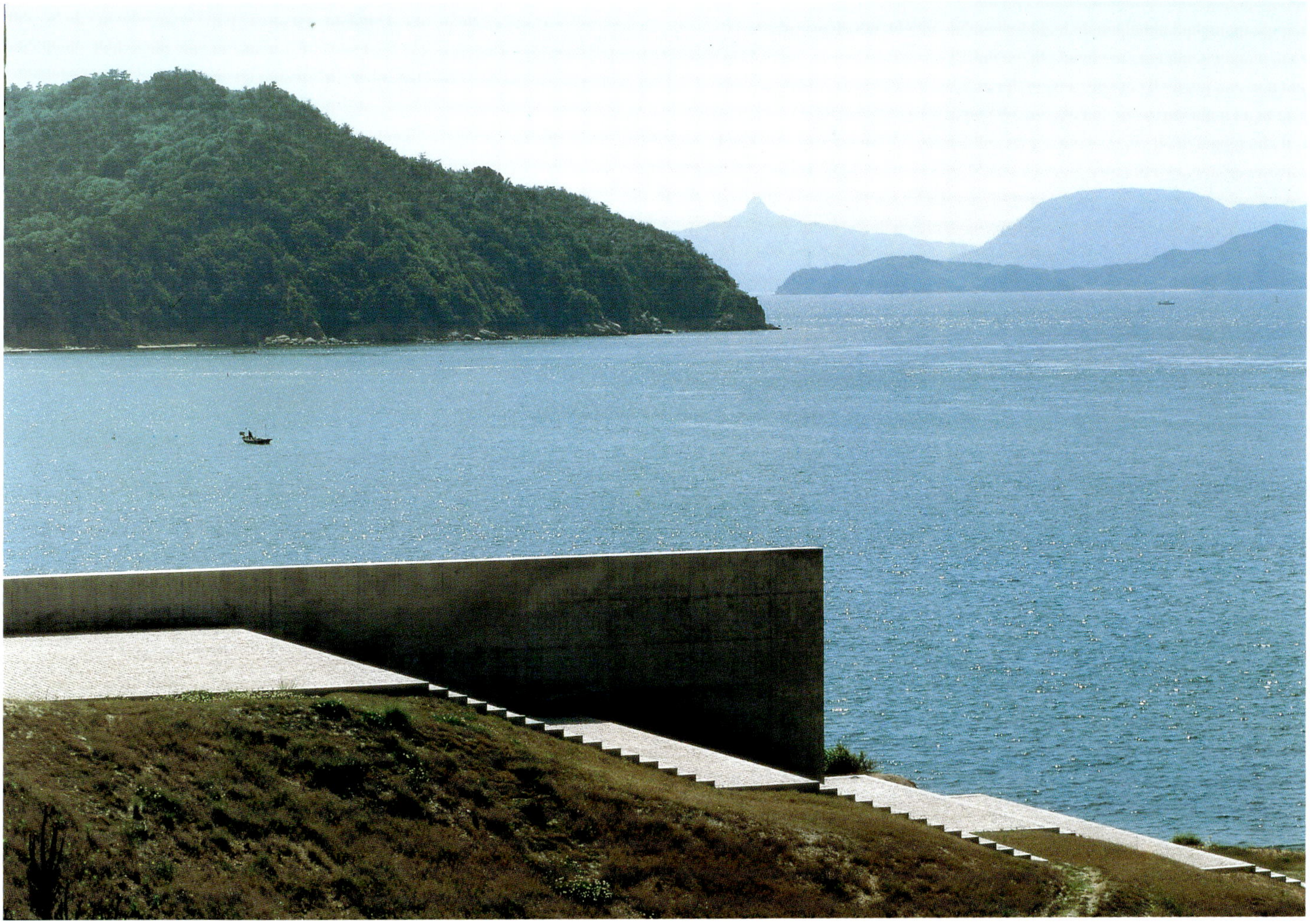

Axonometric, view of the stepped terrace, interior view of the entrance hall and view of the museum roof.

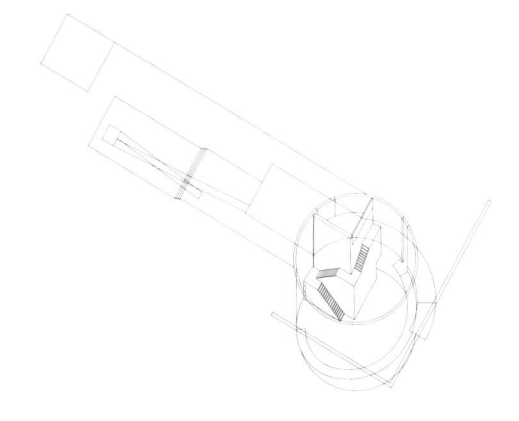

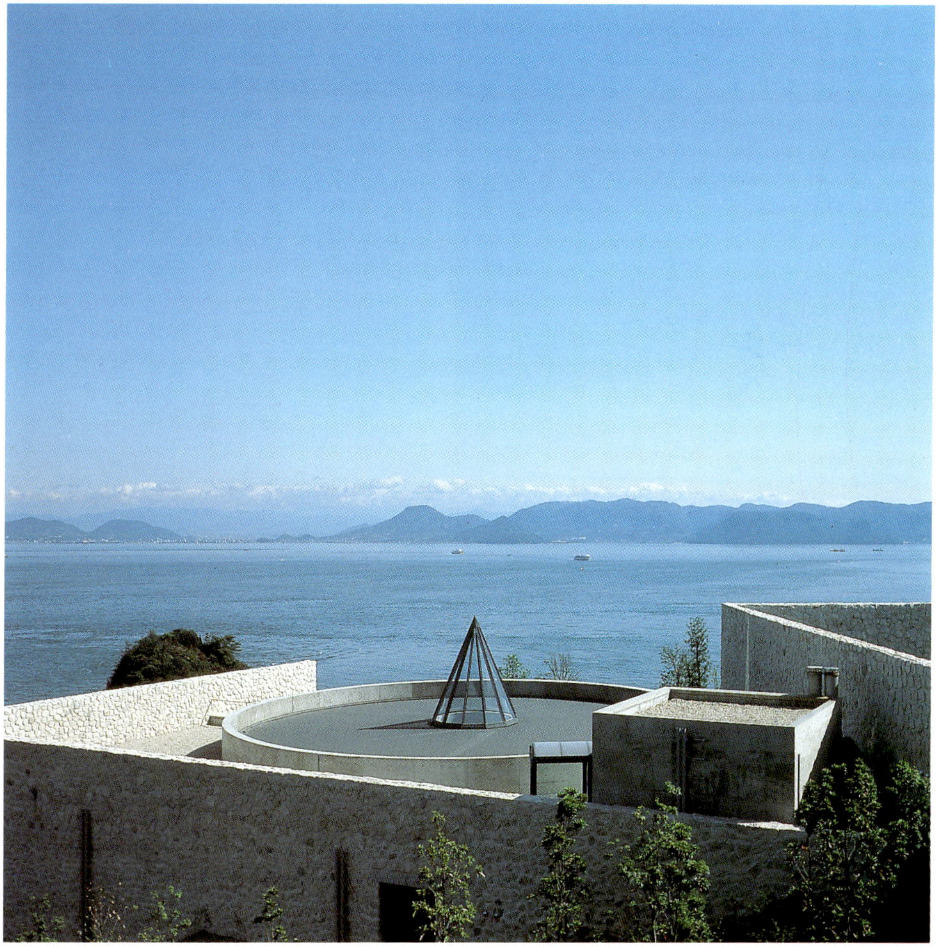

Garden of Fine Arts, Expo 90, Osaka

Conceptual sketch and view of the garden.

The theme of Asia's first international horticultural exposition – the International Garden and Greenery Exposition, held in Osaka in 1990 – was the exploration of new concepts in horticulture and gardening, with a view to the twenty-first century. As one of the pavilions created for the Exposition, the Garden of Fine Arts featured open-air displays of fine art masterpieces, reproduced full-size on weatherproof ceramic tiles by means of the most advanced ceramics technology.

The design stemmed from an inquiry into the essential nature of gardens – the composition of which should include not only plants, but all the elements of nature. Taking water, wind and light as its motifs, the Garden came to embody a proposal for a new form of *kaiyu-shiki* – or 'tour-style' – garden.

Forty-five pillars, 12.6 metres high, were arranged on an even grid in a pond. Ramps, taking the form of glass-walled roofless corridors, ascended in opposite directions, suspended above the pond. In the entrance space, Michelangelo's *The Last Judgment* and Leonardo Da Vinci's *The Last Supper* were presented as large murals, overlooking a sunken garden. A format of display producing optimal viewing conditions was adopted for each picture, which, rather than being viewed from one level in the conventional manner, could be viewed from all angles.

Location Osaka
Design 1988–9
Construction 1989–90
Structure Reinforced concrete
Site area 3,003 m^2
Building area 441.5 m^2
Total floor area 692.3 m^2

Perspective and section.

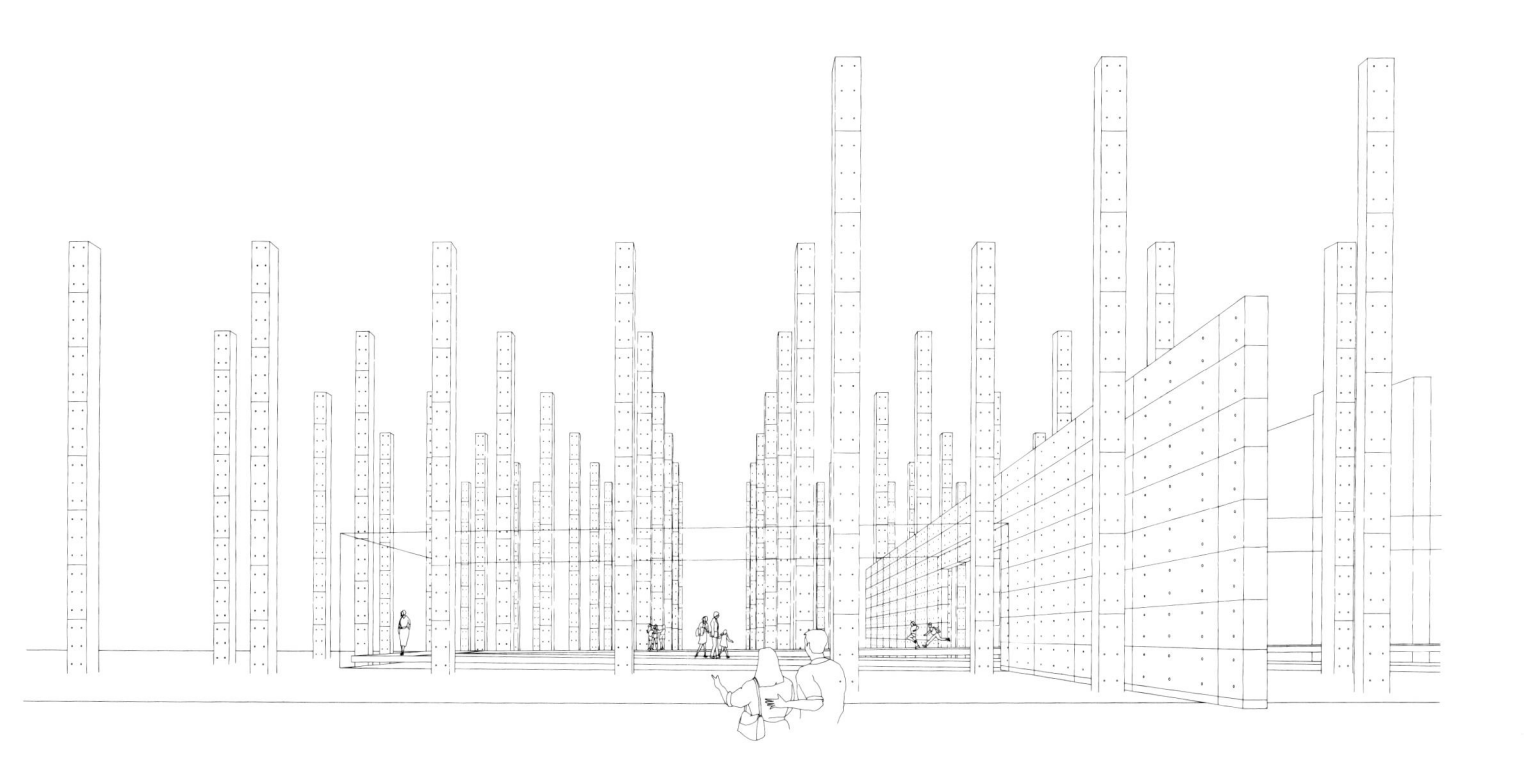

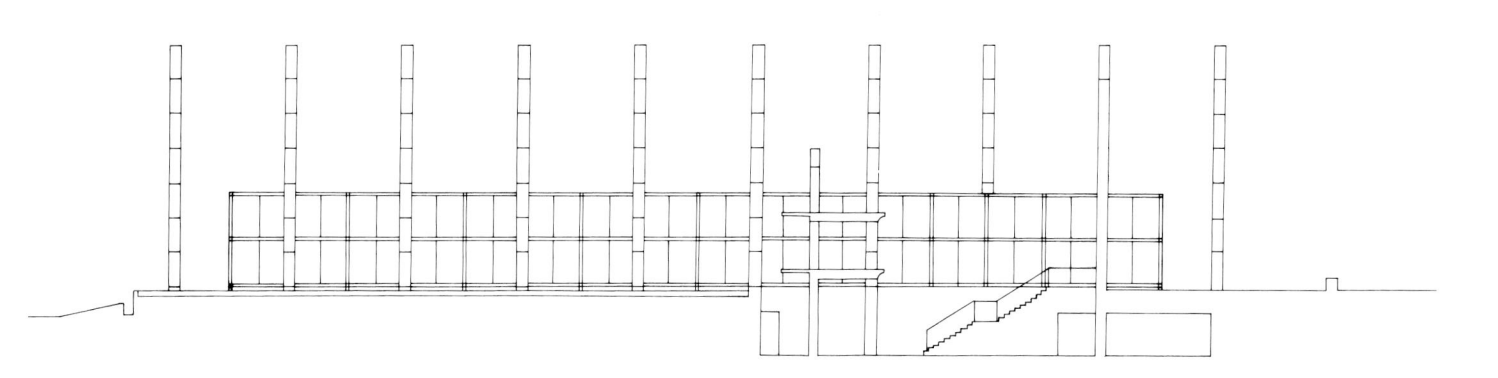

Museum of Literature

Site plan, conceptual sketch and overall view of the museum.

The Museum of Literature sits on a verdant hill about 500 metres from Himeji Castle, which is a national and historic landmark. The design of the building consciously reflects its proximity to the castle. Principally devoted to the philosopher Tetsurou Watsuji (1889–1960), the museum also exhibits material related to eight other writers and philosophers from Himeji. There are three floors above ground level and a basement which houses exhibition space and a lecture hall. The building consists of two cubic volumes, with ground plans of 22.5 metres square overlapping at a 30-degree angle. A cylinder with a 20-metre radius, housing the exhibition space, encompasses one of the cubes, forming a three-level atrium. Water cascades and ramps wrap around the exterior of the building, and on approaching the museum, Himeji Castle can be viewed in the distance.

Location Himeji
Design 1988–9
Construction 1989–91
Structure Reinforced concrete and steel
Site area 15,600.9 m^2
Building area 1,324.1 m^2
Total floor area 3,814.5 m^2

353

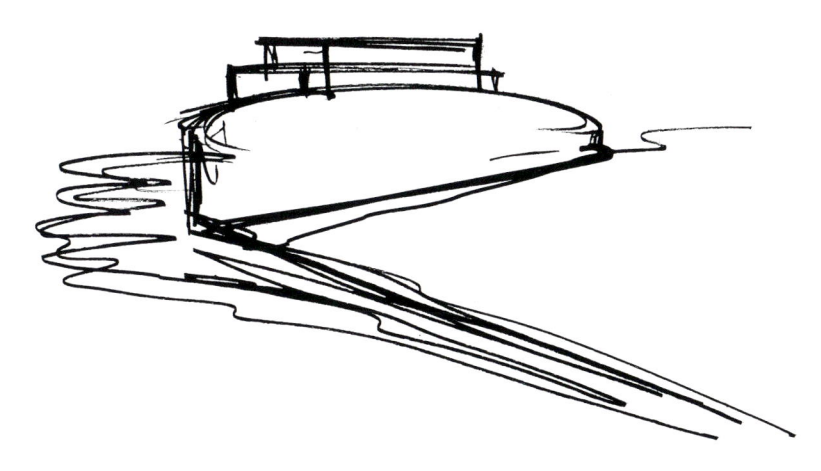

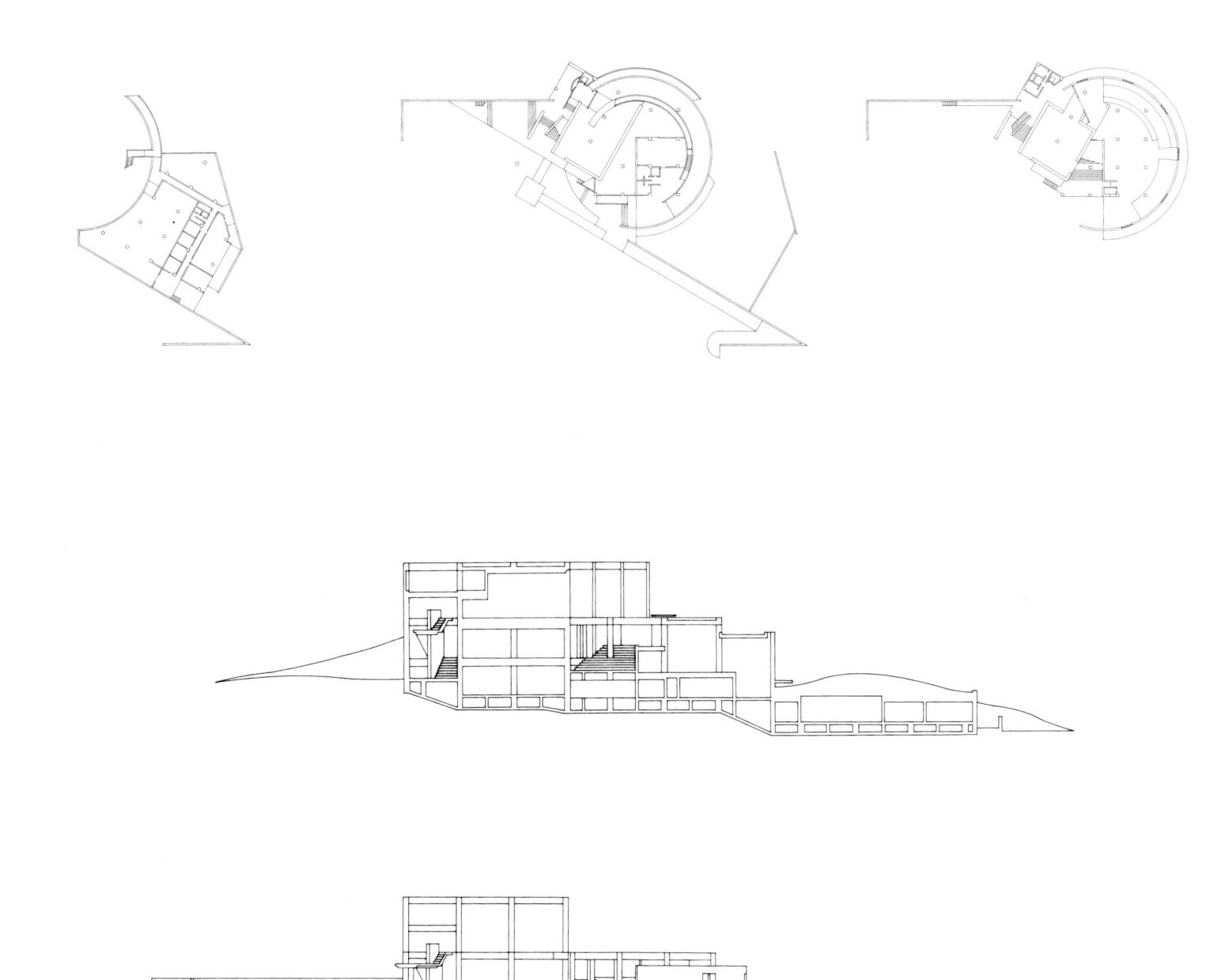

Floor plans, sections and view of the ramp showing Himeji Castle in the background.

354

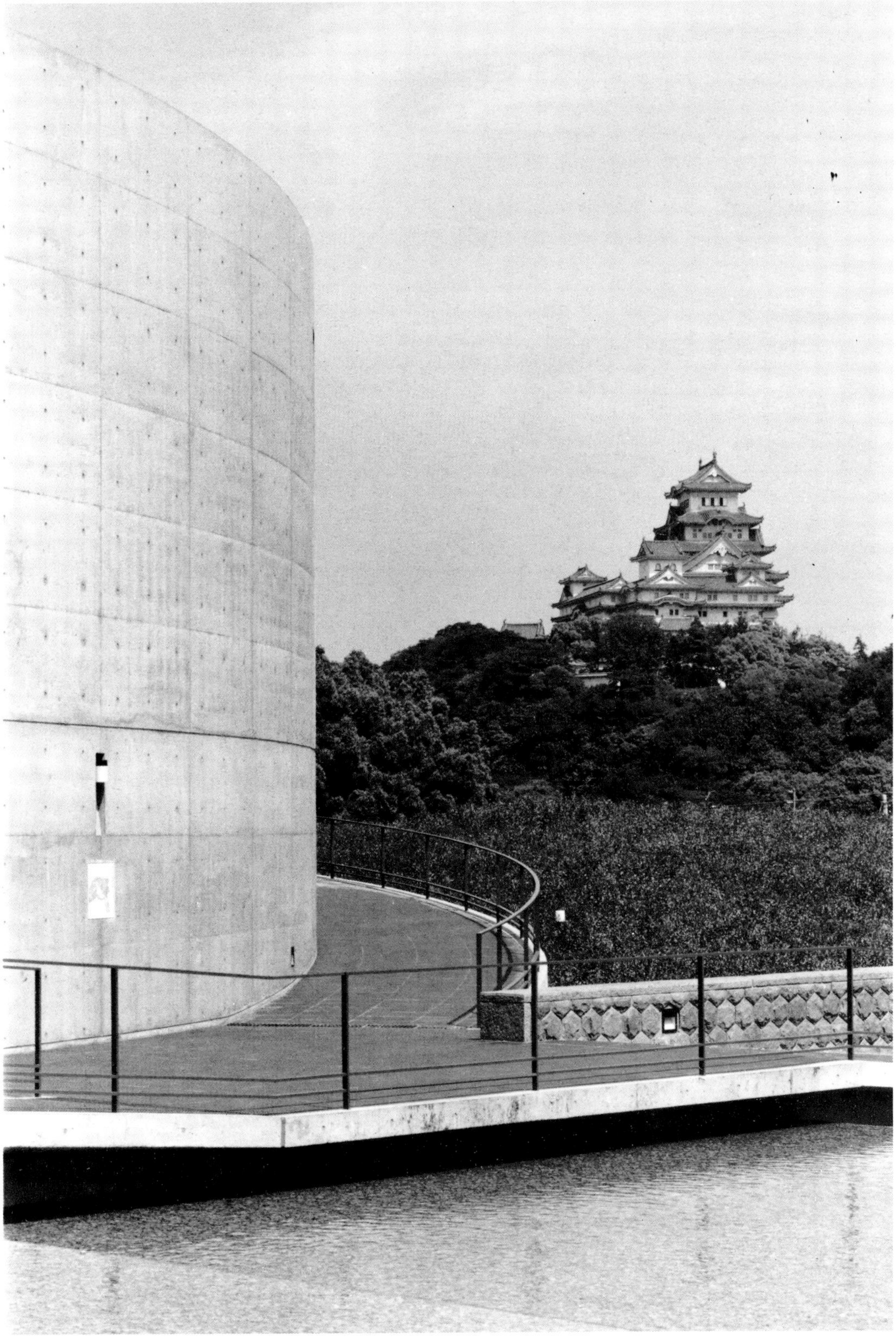

Ishiko House

Interior and exterior views and floor plans.

This building addresses the problem of its corner site with extreme rigour. The primary form of this one-family house is a portion of a cylinder. Facing the street is a curvilinear wall which follows round the corner of the street. At the same time, this wall forms a screen to the house beyond, which itself is a cubic volume on three floors.

Location Takatsuki
Design 1989–90
Construction 1990–91
Structure Reinforced concrete
Site area 179.3 m^2
Building area 107 m^2
Total floor area 239.8 m^2

357

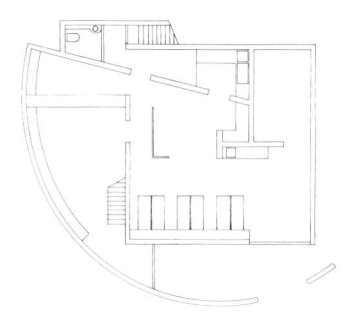

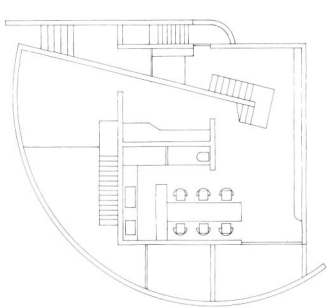

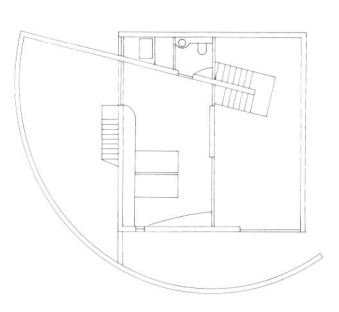

Vitra Seminar House

Conceptual sketch, section, axonometric and aerial view of the model.

This guest house was designed for use by the executive personnel of a furniture company, and is located near the company's production base in southern Germany. As it is on a flat woodland site, the height of the building is minimized by situating part of the volume underground. Simple geometric forms, squares and circles, are used to create a rich interior space. The building has three elements: a rectangular volume running parallel to the walls of the square sunken court; another rectangular volume penetrating the court at a 60-degree angle; and a cylindrical volume that forms a spatial void and interlocks with two rectilinear volumes. The building's two levels accommodate conference rooms, a library, private rooms and a lobby, and all of these open onto the sunken courtyard. The enclosed courtyard reinforces the austere silence of the architecture and draws the elements of nature – light and wind – within.

Location Weil-am-Rhein, Germany
Design 1989–92
Construction 1992–3
Structure Reinforced concrete
Site area 19,408 m²
Building area 360.9 m²
Total floor area 508.3 m²

359

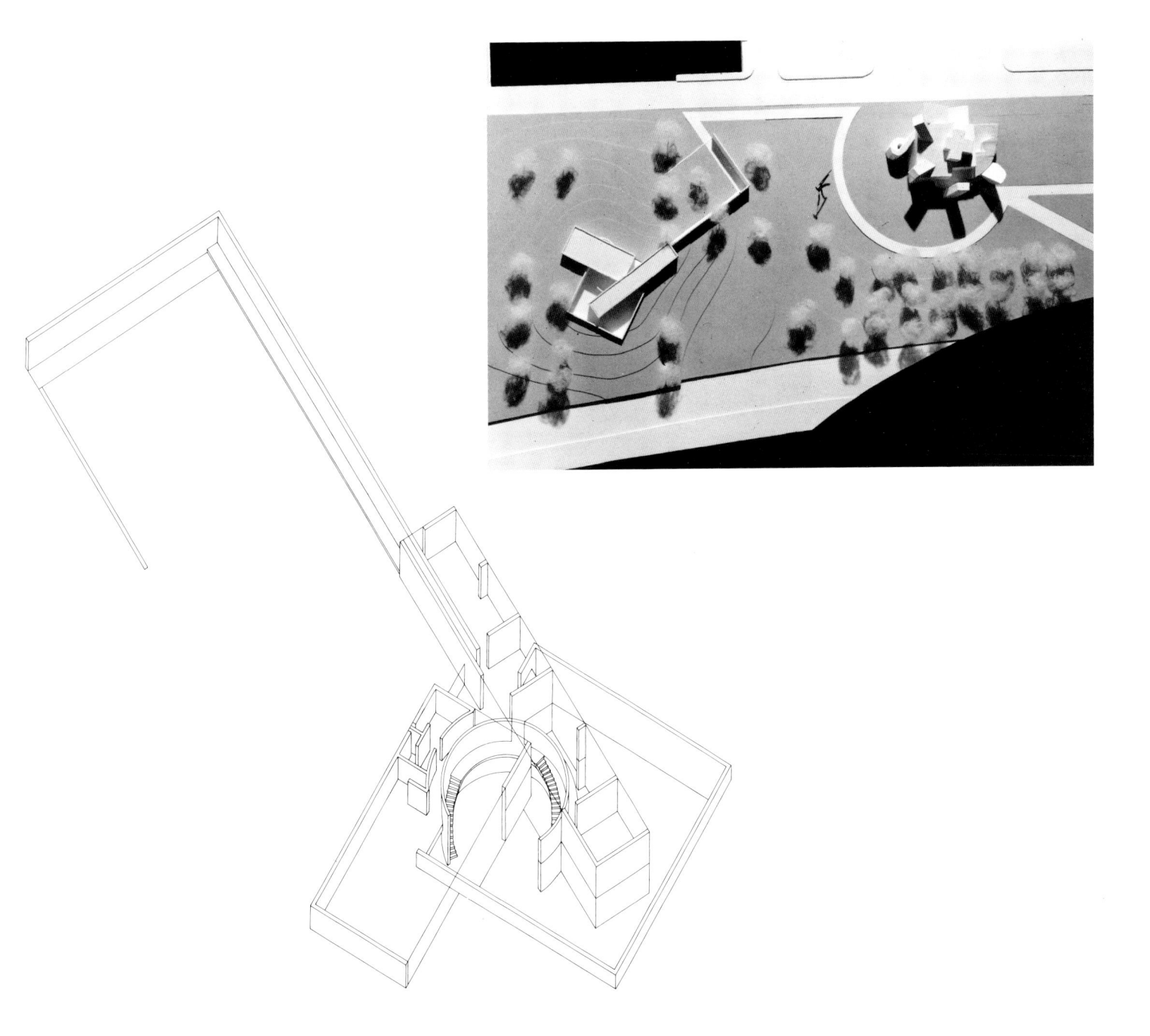

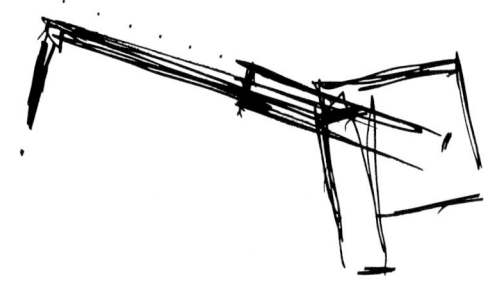

Views of the perimeter wall, conceptual sketch and night time view through the glazed wall.

361

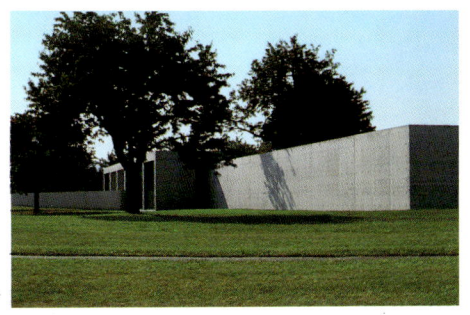

Gallery for Japanese Screens, Art Institute of Chicago

Views through the gallery, perspective and floor plan.

In the front half of the gallery stand sixteen pillars, a foot square and ten feet high. These obstruct the gaze yet help suggest the depth and resonance of the space. As the visitor moves in this space, the static pillars change their relationships, at times overlapping and uniting.

Byobu, the temporary dividing panels that allowed privacy in the traditional multi-purpose Japanese room, functioned visually to suggest spatial depth. Here, they are displayed not only as objects, but also as a means to make observers experience Japanese spatial aesthetics by placing them in a contemporary setting reflecting the spirit of the original Japanese space. Thus, the *byobu*, seen through the pillars, embody the profound love of nature by the Japanese forefathers and evoke the image of their way of life.

Location Chicago, USA
Design 1989–91
Construction 1991–2
Total floor area 160 m^2

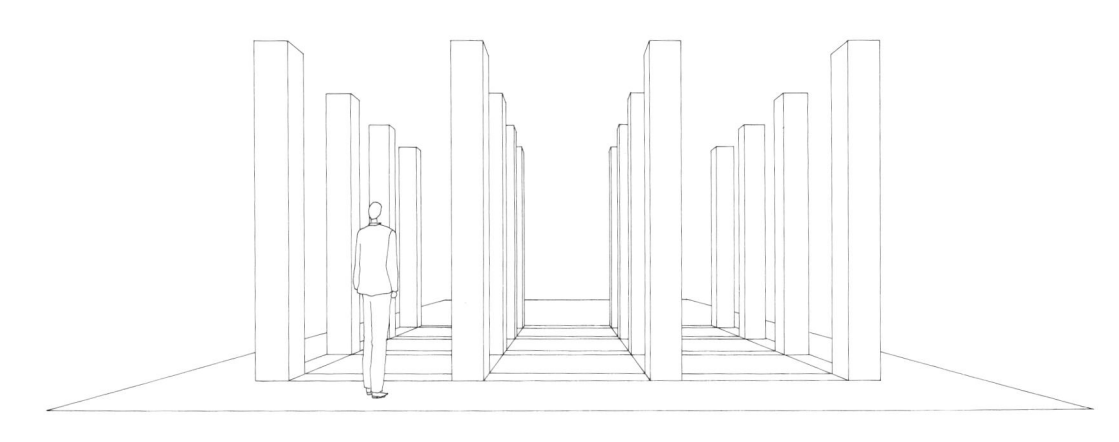

363

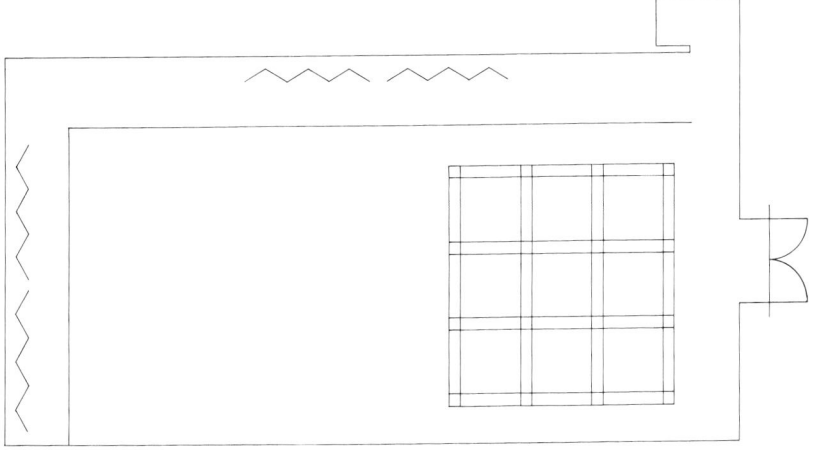

Rokko Island

View of the upper level terrace and overall view, plans and elevation.

This highly articulated building is a collection of interpenetrating forms and dimensions. It thus introduces visual and volumetric diversity into a long and narrow lot.

Location Kobe
Design 1989–91
Construction 1991–3
Structure Reinforced concrete and steel
Site area 3,740 m²
Building area 1,798.63 m²
Total floor area 2,570.17 m²

365

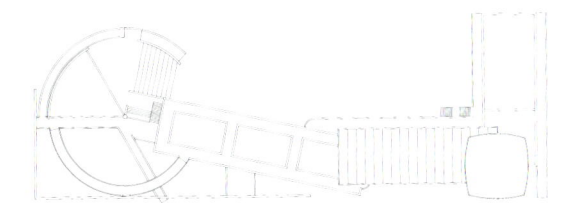

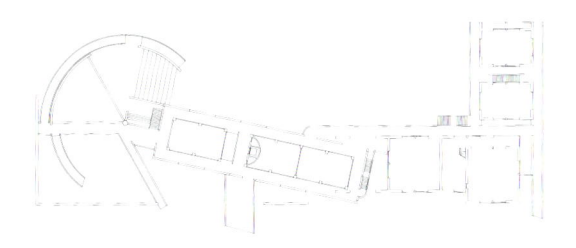

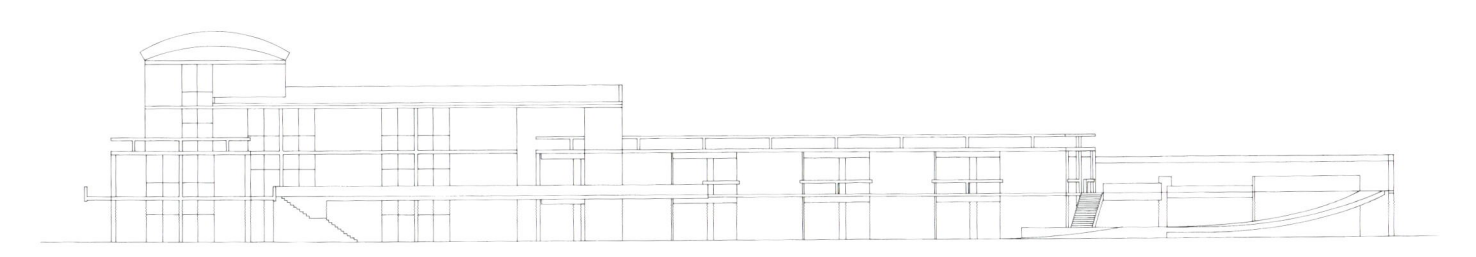

Sayoh Housing

Elevation, section, site and floor plans.

This resort apartment complex is on the border of the Okayama and Hyogo prefectures, in a forested area interspersed with spas and ski slopes.

The building is composed of three tall elements with square plans, and a low rectilinear volume. The low volume is positioned at a 60-degree angle to two of the tall elements. A roof garden on the low element offers a visual feast to people using the building's ramps and stairs. A four-metre wide staircase extending east–west shares a plaza at the foremost part of the site. The third tall element, to the north of the site, is joined to the circular plaza by a ramp, positioned at a right angle to the low element. Instead of the linear horizontal arrangement of dwellings characteristic of the orthodox housing complex, the apartments have been overlaid vertically, with one or two occupying each floor, allowing each dwelling unimpeded views of the lush surrounding countryside.

Location Hyogo
Design 1989–90
Construction 1990–91
Structure Reinforced concrete
Site area 6,989.0 m^2
Building area 1,270 m^2
Total floor area 3,854.2 m^2

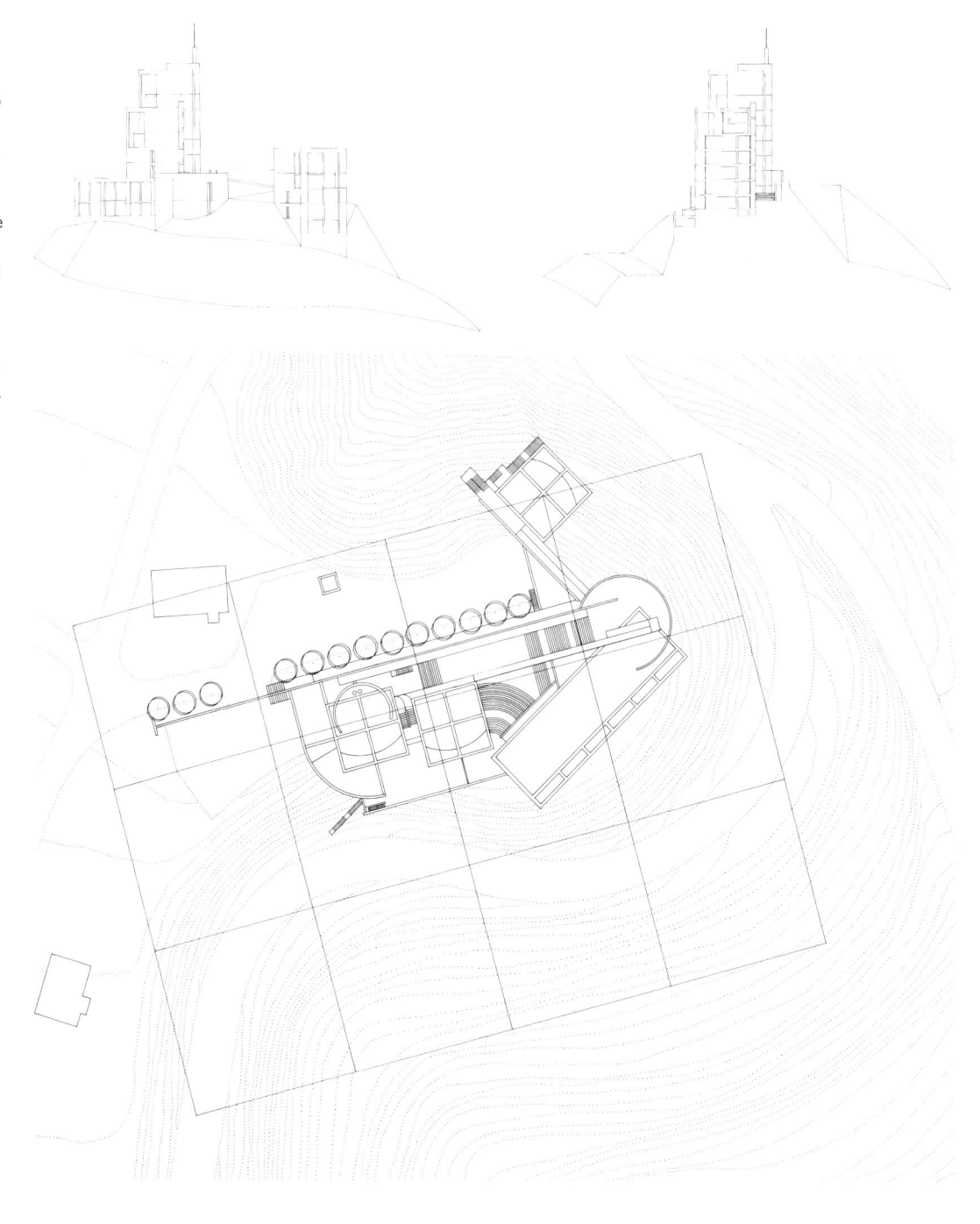

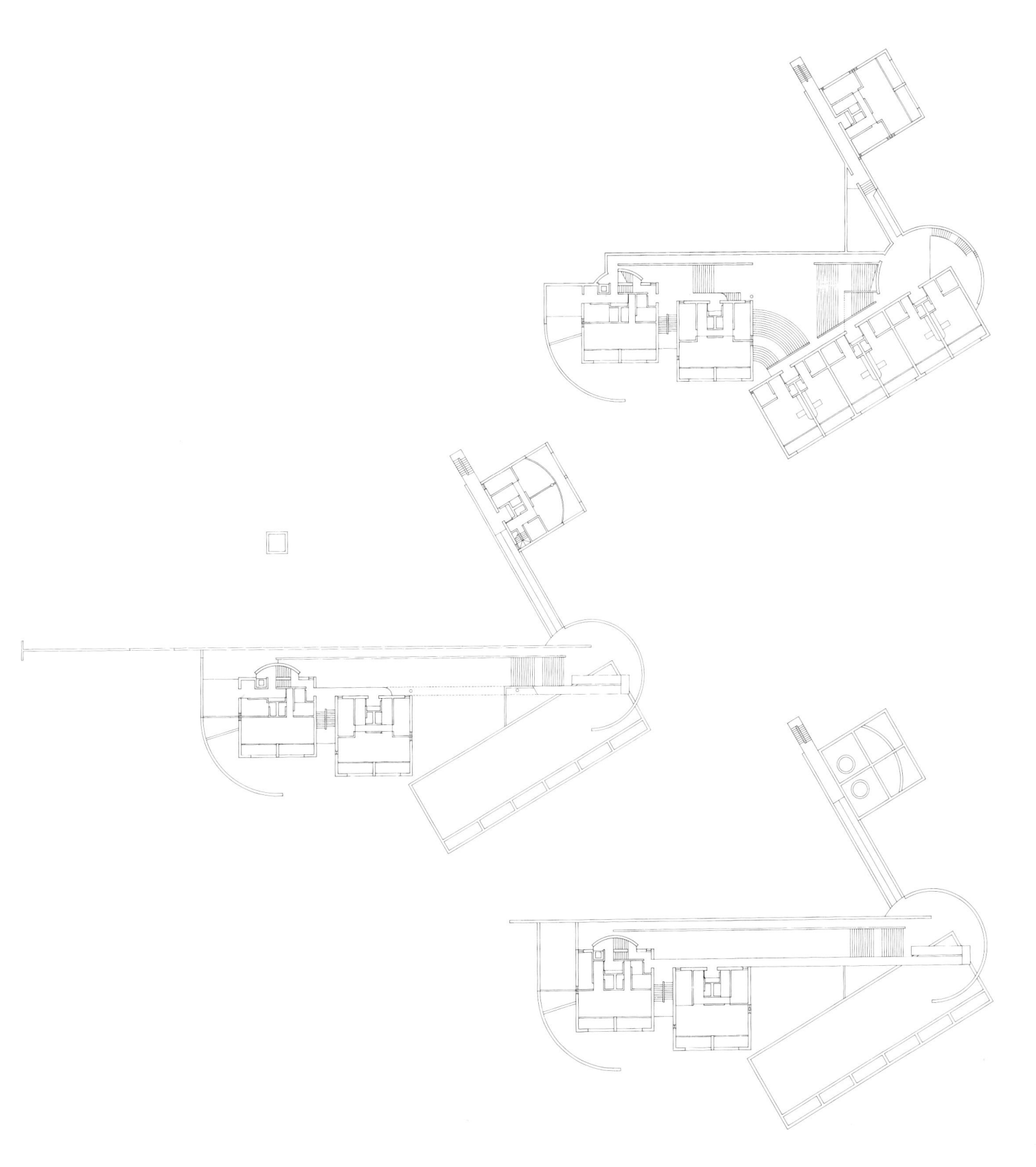

Views of the plaza, and overall view of the building.

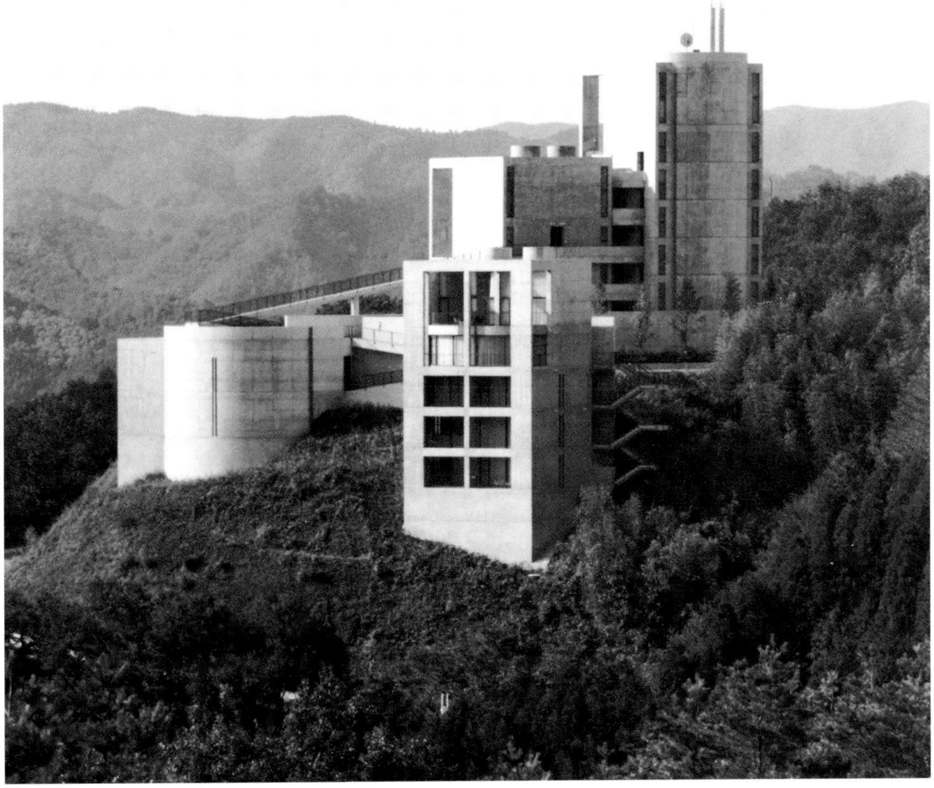

Minolta Seminar Building

Site plan, views of the courtyard and axonometric.

The two volumes that make up this work intersect and interpenetrate to form one building overall, yet whilst maintaining their individual autonomy, as can be seen from the outside and experienced from within. The volumes are five floors and six floors high respectively, and both contain spacious verdant courtyards that draw nature into the building.

Location Kobe
Design 1989–90
Construction 1990–91
Structure Reinforced concrete
Site area 4,132.9 m²
Building area 1,859.26 m²
Total floor area 4,556.35 m²

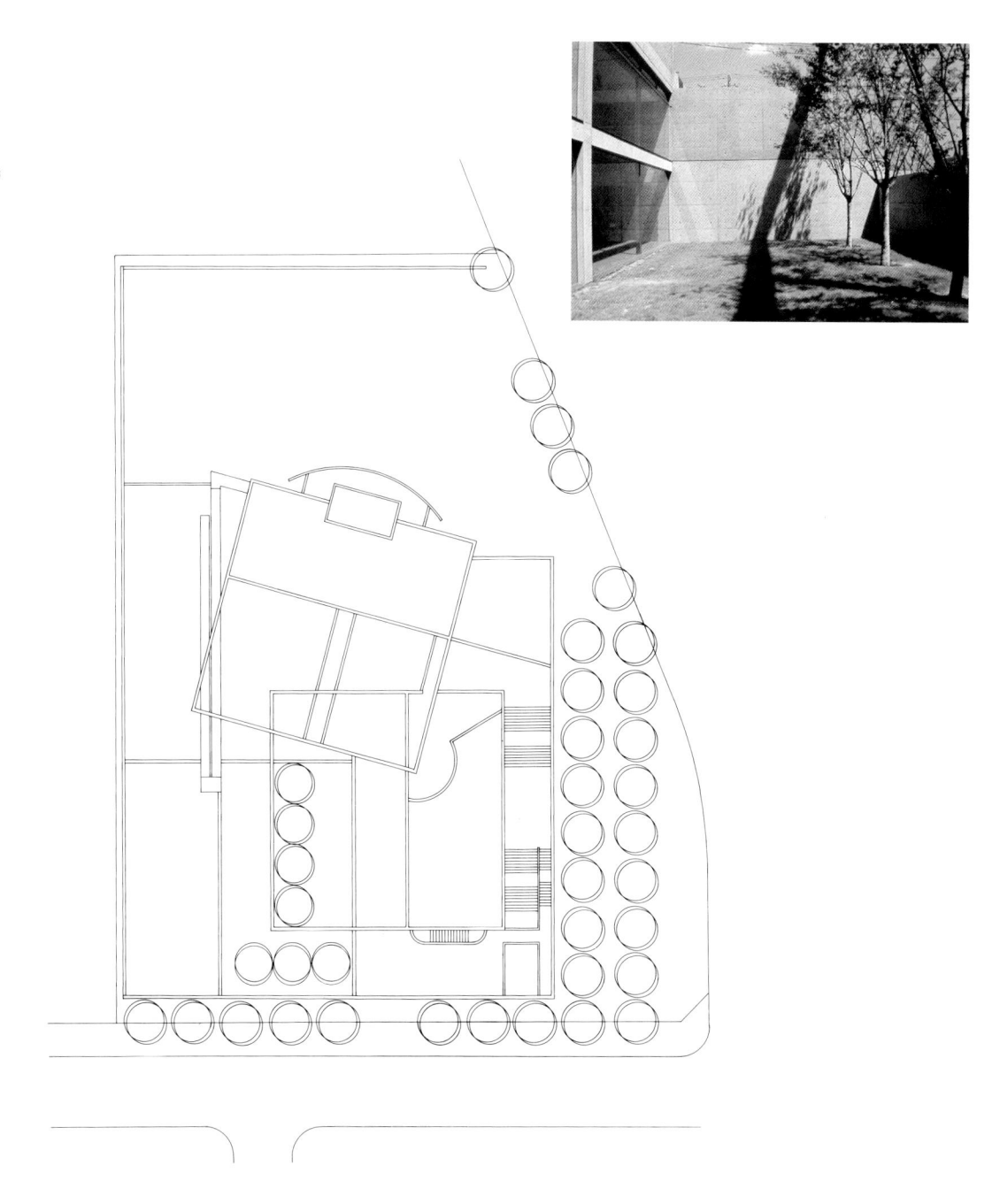

371

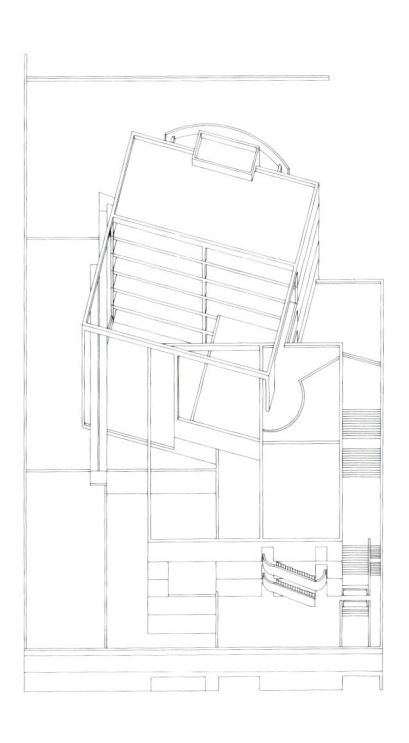

Otemae Art Center

View of the lobby and conceptual sketch.

This university art faculty, located in a residential district near the Osaka/Kobe border, comprises studio space and a gallery used both for temporary exhibitions and for the permanent display of art. Located directly across the road from the university, the centre is surrounded by greenery.

One-third of the building's volume is set below ground, and the perimeter of the site is lined with trees, thus ensuring that the building does not overpower its surroundings. The lobby, on the first level, takes the form of a large atrium – intersected by ramps – with nature penetrating its space through large apertures in its walls and roof. All rooms enjoy some form of connection with the lobby space, which functions as a stage for the comings and goings of the students.

The underground level accommodates an art gallery and a 200-capacity multi-purpose hall. On the second and third levels are a roof garden and a café. The presence of nature is felt within the facility in a central court and a walled pond that opens to the basement level, and the building – though circumscribed by walls – is enveloped in greenery, both within and without. The large apertures in its walls, furthermore, reveal it to the surrounding community.

Location Nishinomiya
Design 1989–90
Construction 1990–92
Structure Reinforced concrete
Site area 2,267.9 m^2
Building area 1,122.5 m^2
Total floor area 1,999.6 m^2

Oblique view of the entrance and floor plans.

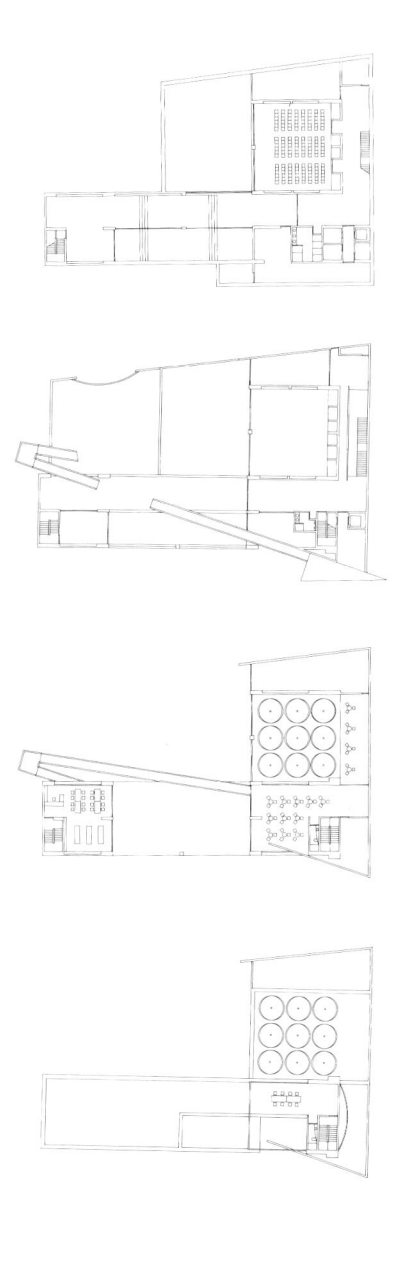

Atelier in Oyodo II

View looking up from the courtyard, plans, section and view of the building from the street.

This building consists of seven floors, two of which are below ground level. An atrium soars through the full height of the building, its width increasing at each successive level. The stepped recessing of upper floors around the atrium lends a dynamic complexity to the interior space, and sunlight admitted through a skylight reaches deep into the building. Occasionally the atrium doubles as a lecture hall with the speaker using the staircase as a podium. This introduction of an area with an irregular function makes the workplace a more stimulating space, even when it is organized around day-to-day routine.

Location Osaka
Design 1989–90
Construction 1990–91
Structure Reinforced concrete
Site area 115.6 m^2
Building area 91.7 m^2
Total floor area 451.7 m^2

375

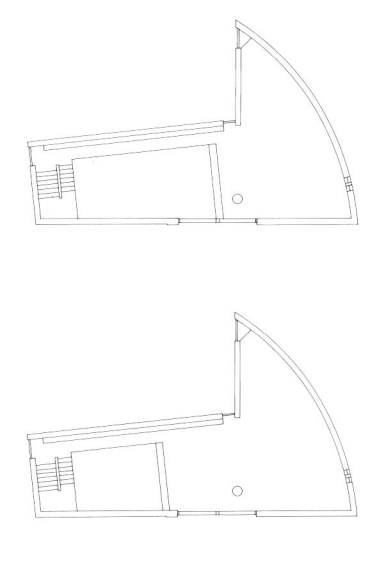

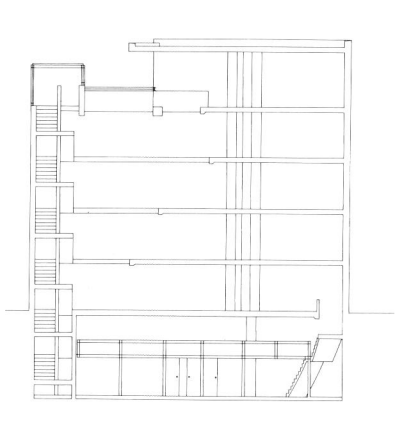

Interior views.

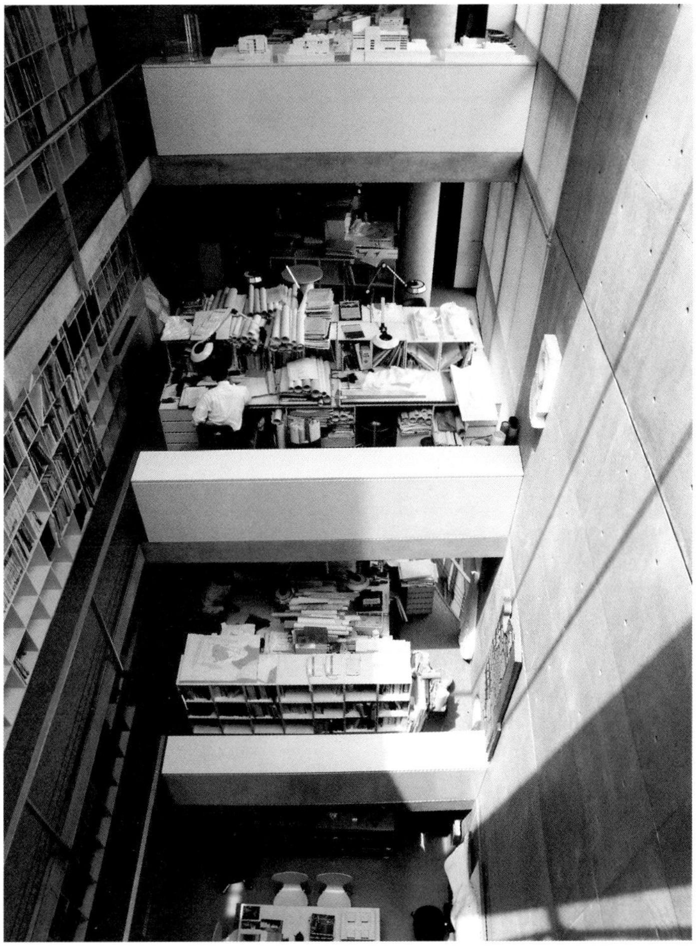

Rockfield Factory

Longitudinal section, main elevation, view of the tower and floor plans.

The building is in an industrial park on a natural land elevation overlooking the Tenryu River to the west. It is a production facility for a food-processing company. To dispel the oppressive darkness found in the work environment of conventional factories, and to alleviate stressful working conditions as much as possible, external spaces such as roof terraces and gardens have been created throughout the building.

The building consists of a rectilinear volume with an 84 x 42 metre plan. This has vaulted sections along both ends, and a colonnade curved on an arc of 36-metre radius, enclosing a stepped garden. The successive stages of the production line are established on the ground level of the rectilinear volume, so that production materials are introduced at one end and completed products distributed from the other. Offices occupy the second level, and the vaulted sections on the third level house a cafeteria/foyer and main lobby, with a garden on the roof between them. Within the colonnade is a ramp leading to the factory, while services are housed beneath the stepped garden.

This building, now completed, constitutes the initial phase of a two-phase project – the second phase calling for another production facility and a museum related to the company's products on the same site.

Location Shizuoka
Design 1989–90
Construction 1990–91
Structure Reinforced concrete and steel
Site area 75,474 m^2
Building area 8,150.2 m^2
Total floor area 5,157.5 m^2

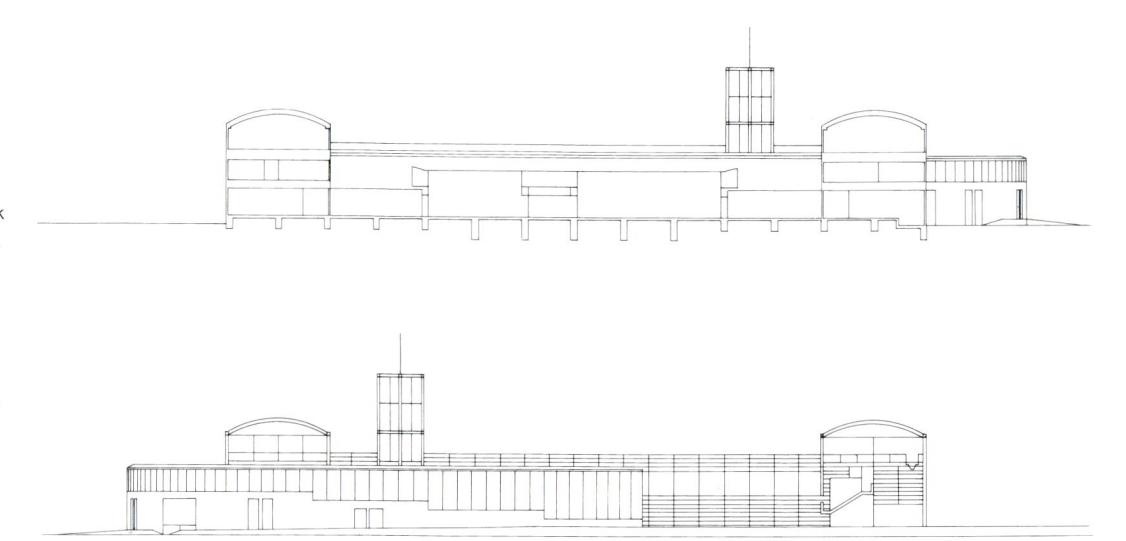

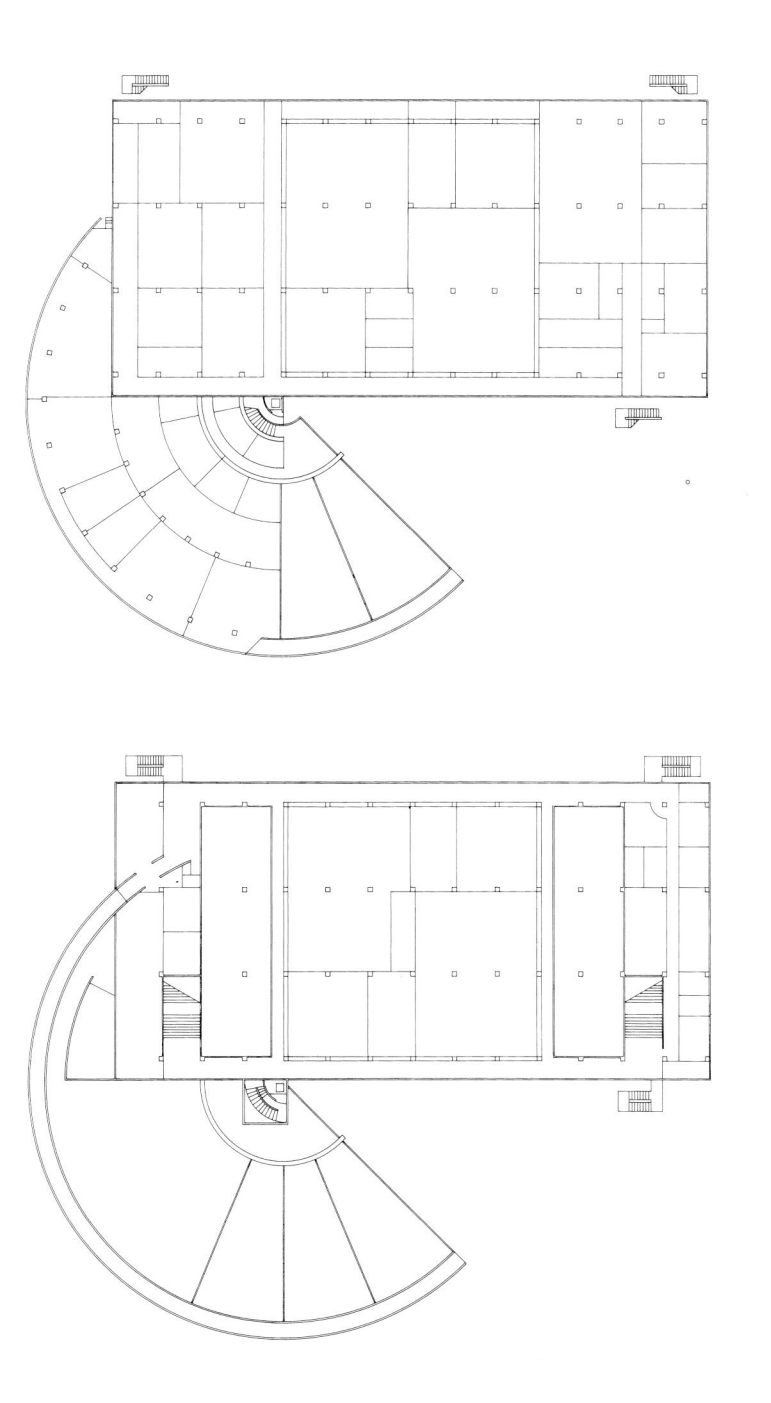

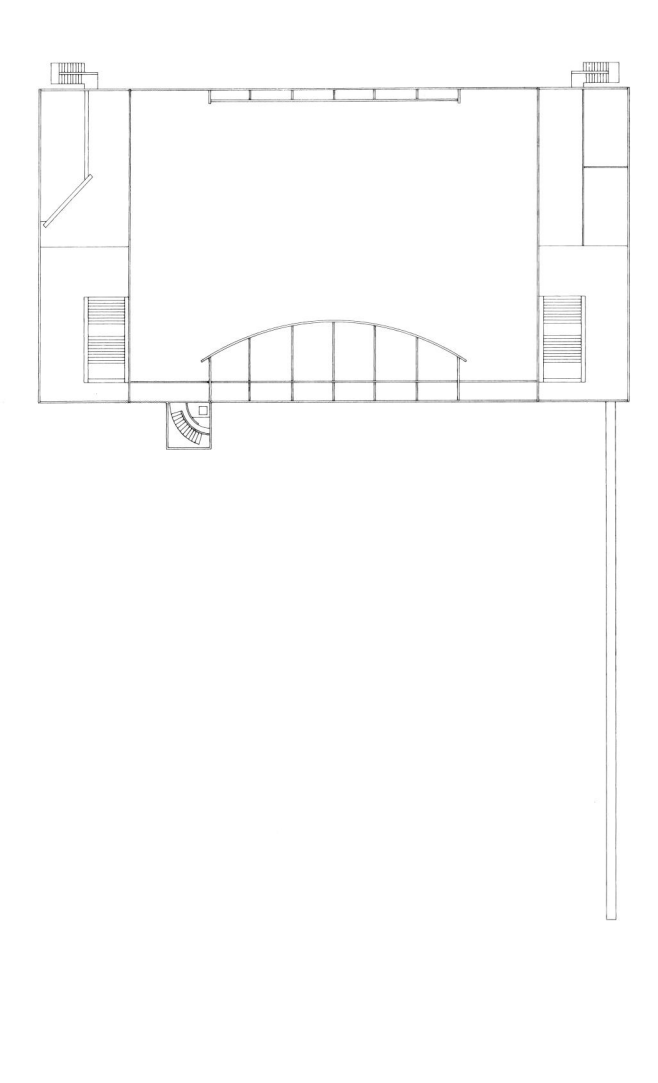

Japanese Pavilion, Expo 92, Seville

Overall view, conceptual sketch and floor plans.

This Pavilion for Expo 92 in Seville was intended to acquaint people with the traditional aesthetic of Japan, one of unadorned simplicity, as manifested in unpainted wood construction and white mortar walls. The creation of this wooden building relied on recent technology to reconstruct and give full play to the philosophy behind traditional Japanese structural assembly methods.

With a 60-metre-long frontage, depth of 40 metres, and greatest height of 25 metres, it is the world's largest wooden structure. Outside, the building demonstrates such characteristics as *sori* – the curvature of its large walls – and unpainted wooden high lap boards. To enter the building, visitors ascend to the top of a *taikobashi*, or drum-shaped bridge. The bridge offers the visitor entry to the realm of illusion awaiting within and a link between East and West. The large gallery space has a ceiling height of over 17 metres and contains an assembly of two columns and numerous beams that stand symbolically, illuminated by sunlight permeating the building's translucent Teflon covering. Varying the sizes of the display rooms heightens the viewers' tension and relates their movements to the unfolding narrative of Japanese history. Thus the building serves to introduce people of all nationalities to Japan's culture and history, and to promote international exchange.

Location Seville, Spain
Design 1989–90
Construction 1990–92
Structure Wood
Site area 5,660.3 m^2
Building area 2,629.8 m^2
Total floor area 5,660.3 m^2

381

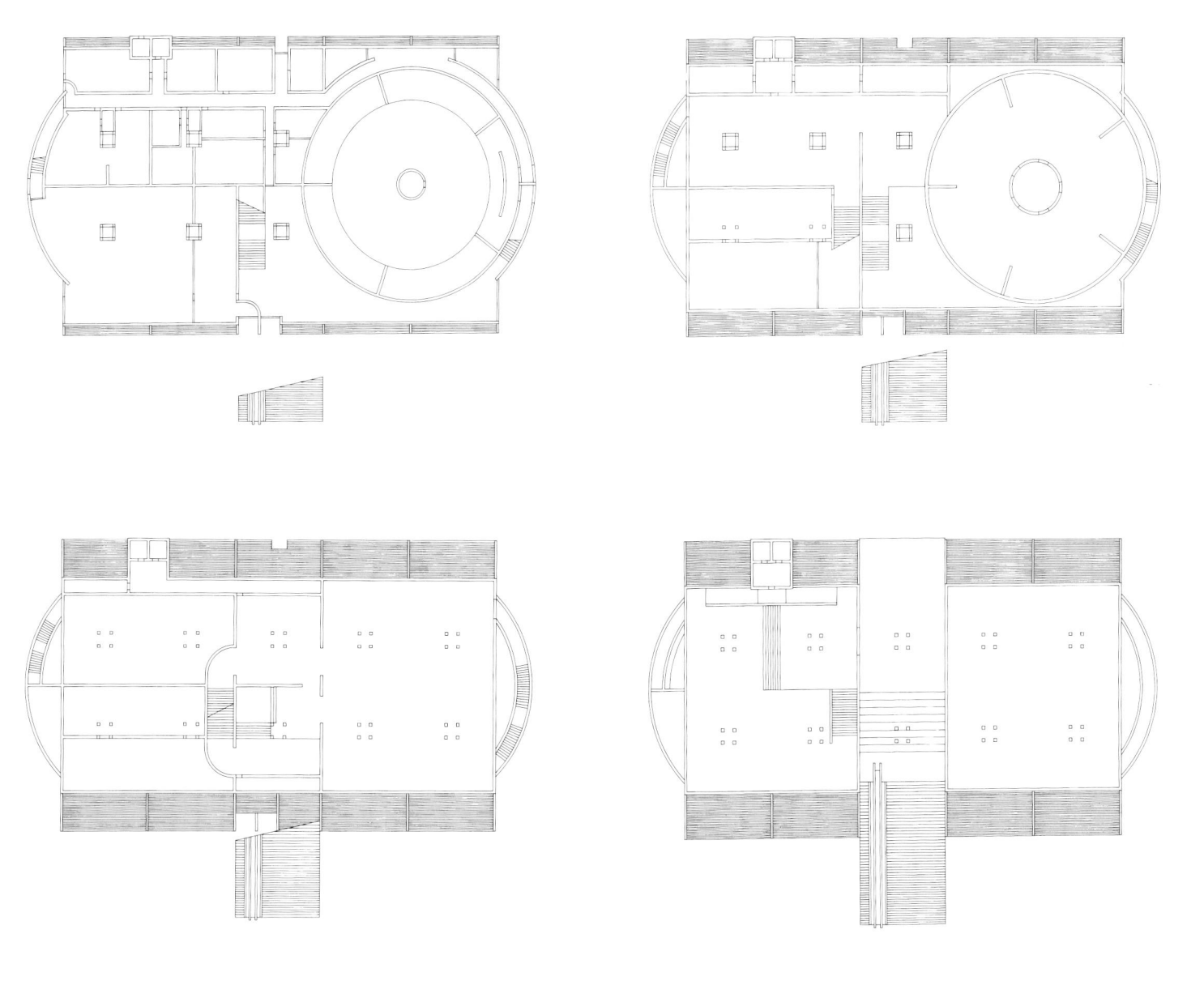

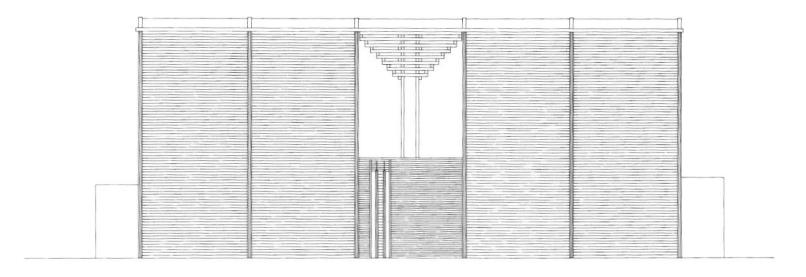

Overall and detailed views and elevation of the entrance.

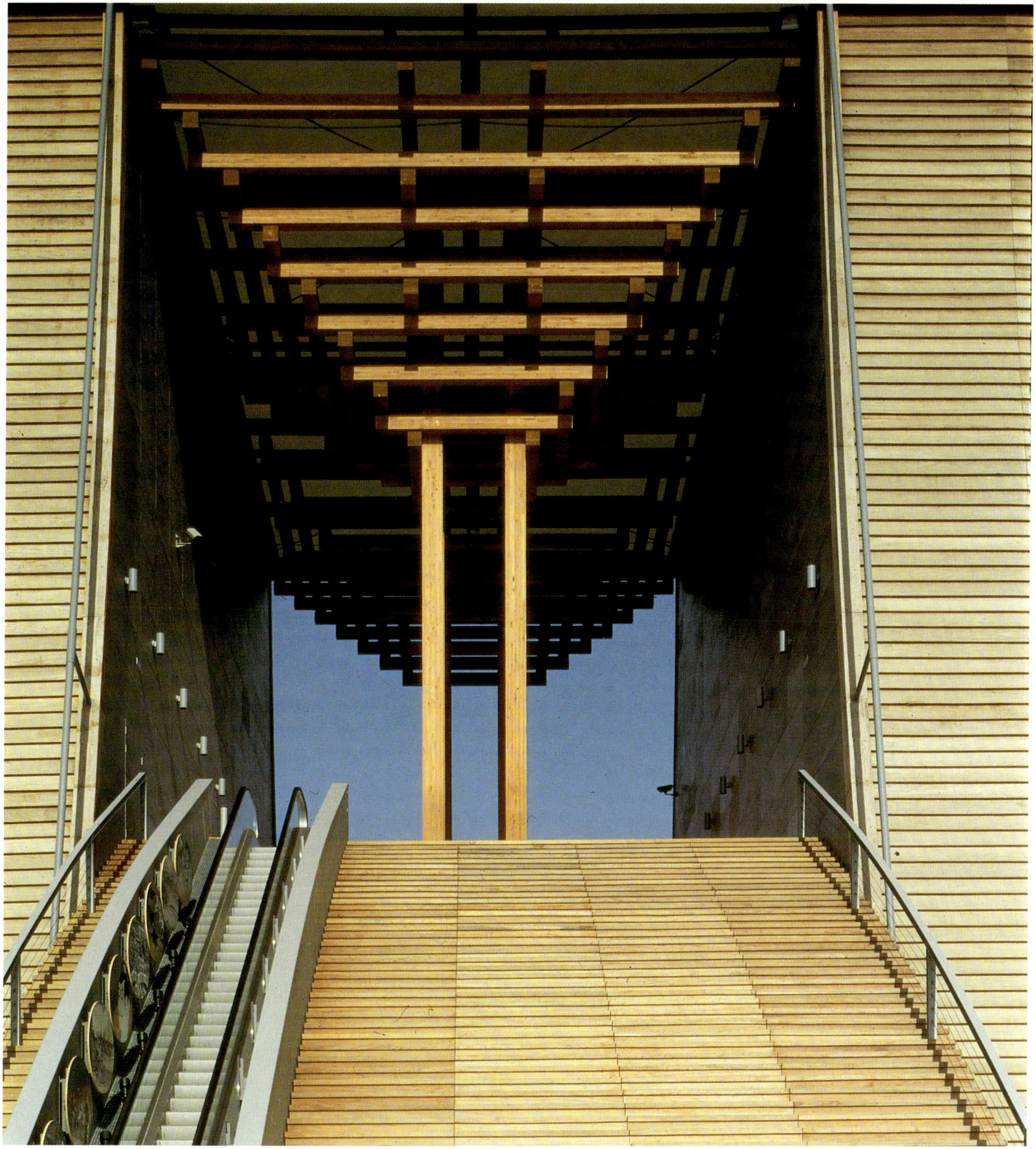

Water Temple

Conceptual sketch and view of the lake.

The water temple of Hompukuji is a new main temple for the Shingon Buddhist sect. It nestles on a hill on Awaji Island, and has sweeping views of Osaka Bay. The temple hall is below ground, beneath a large oval pond filled with lotus plants. It is reached by means of a descending stair which divides the pond, and appears to draw visitors under water. The hall is composed of a square space, gridded with timber pillars, contained within a round room. The interior of the hall and its pillars are stained vermilion; this traditional Buddhist colour intensifies when the reddish glow of sunset floods the space, casting long shadows from the pillars deep into the interior.

Location Awajishima
Design 1989–90
Construction 1990–91
Structure Reinforced concrete
Site area 2,990.8 m²
Building area 859.5 m²
Total floor area 417.2 m²

Site plan and view of the model.

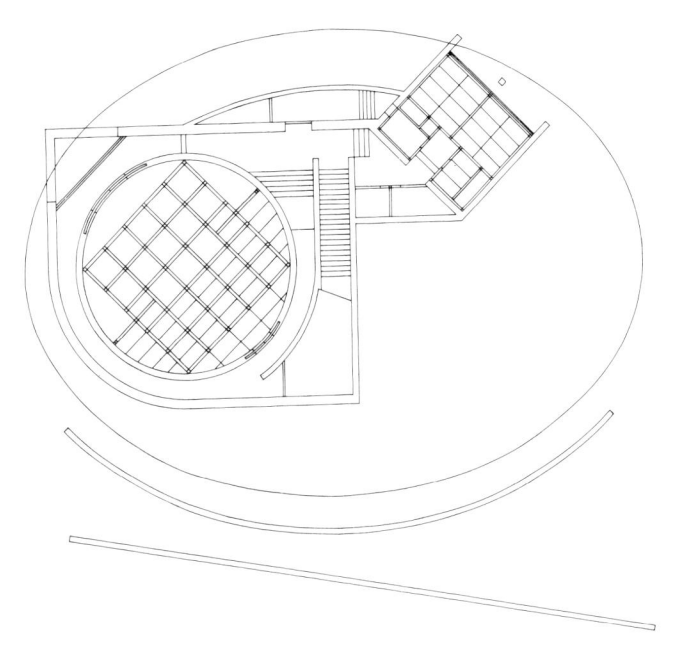

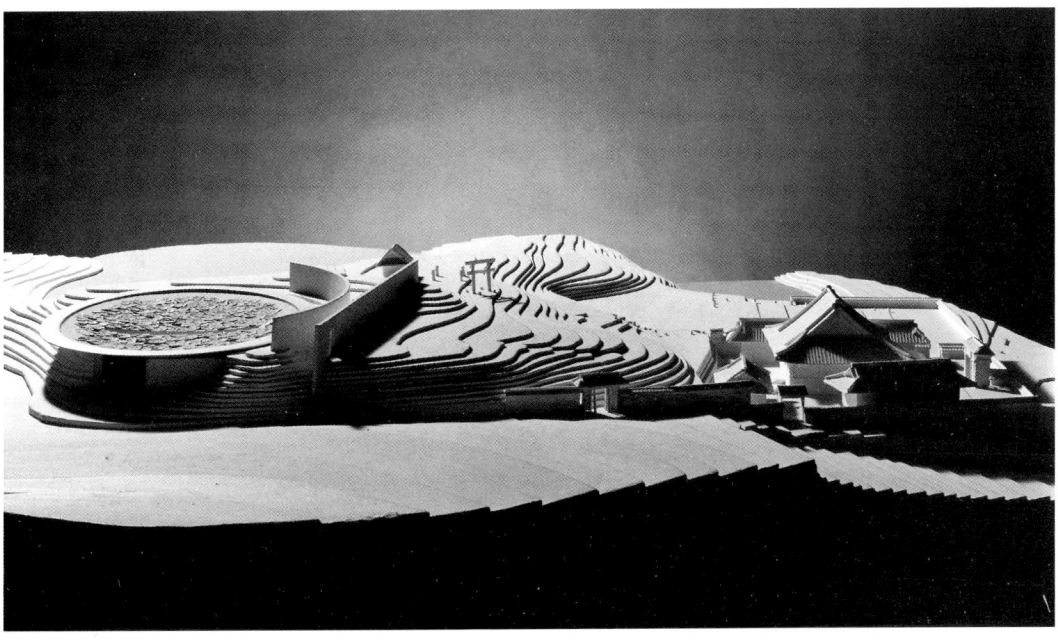

Views of the temple entrance, the pond and looking into the temple.

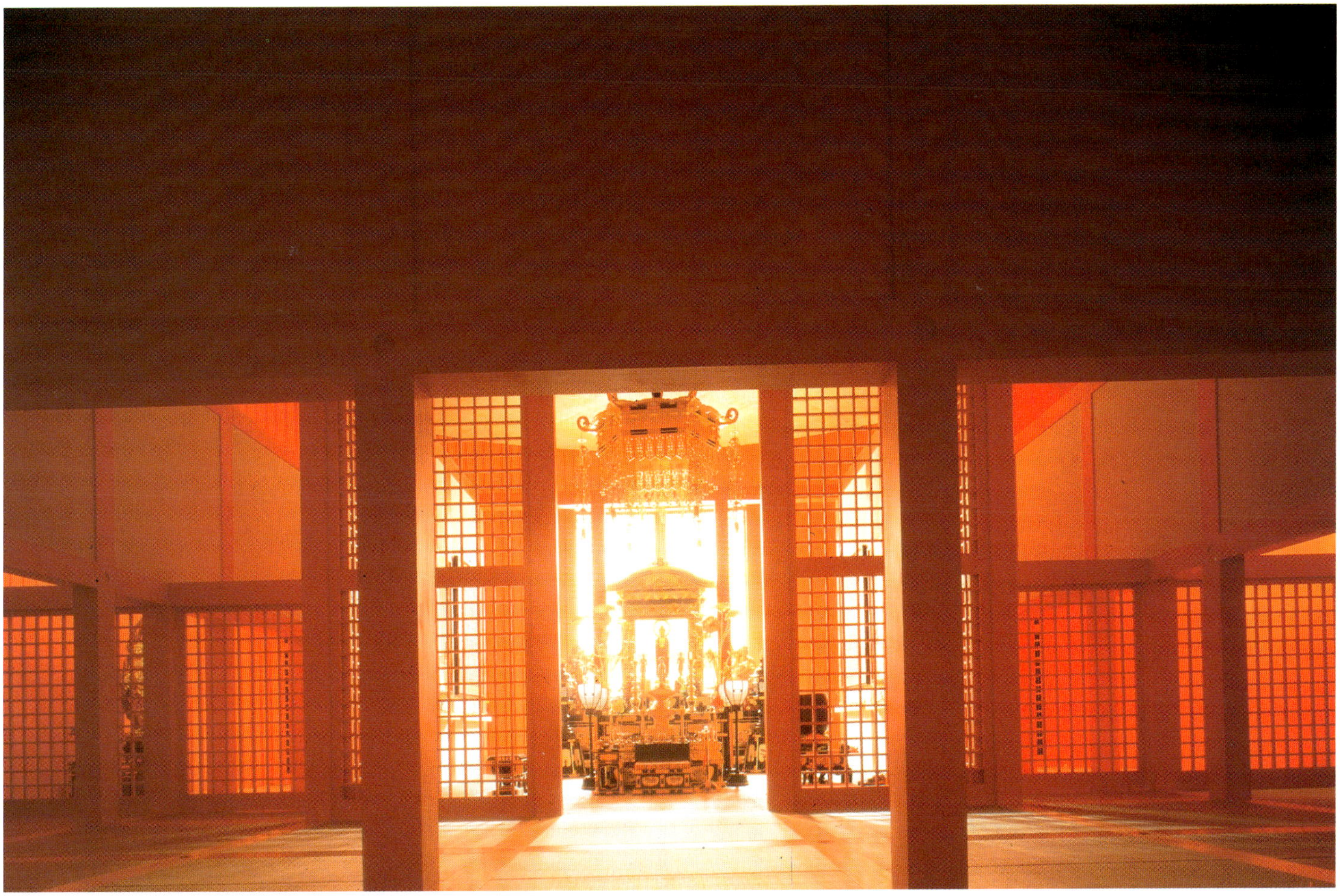

Forest of Tombs Museum

Floor plans and conceptual sketch.

This museum is dedicated to the historic Iwabari burial mounds in Northern Kumamoto Prefecture. To be as unobtrusive as possible, the museum is designed as a raised platform from which the tombs can be viewed in their surroundings, and half of its volume is buried below ground. Visitors approach on foot, through a lush green forest. Though 250 metres away from the famed Futago-zuka, a large keyhole-shaped tumulus, the museum is positioned symmetrically to it. This encourages the image of the museum as a contemporary burial mound.

The building is composed of a rectangular volume that is 26 x 79.2 metres; a circular courtyard, which is 15.8 metres in radius; and an L-shaped wall that penetrates to the centre of the circular courtyard. The excavation grounds lie just beyond the wall of the circular courtyard, while a ramp winds around the inside of the wall, guiding visitors through displays of artefacts.

Location Kumamoto
Design 1989–90
Construction 1990–92
Structure Reinforced concrete and steel
Site area 6,338 m²
Building area 1,448.8 m²
Total floor area 2,099 m²

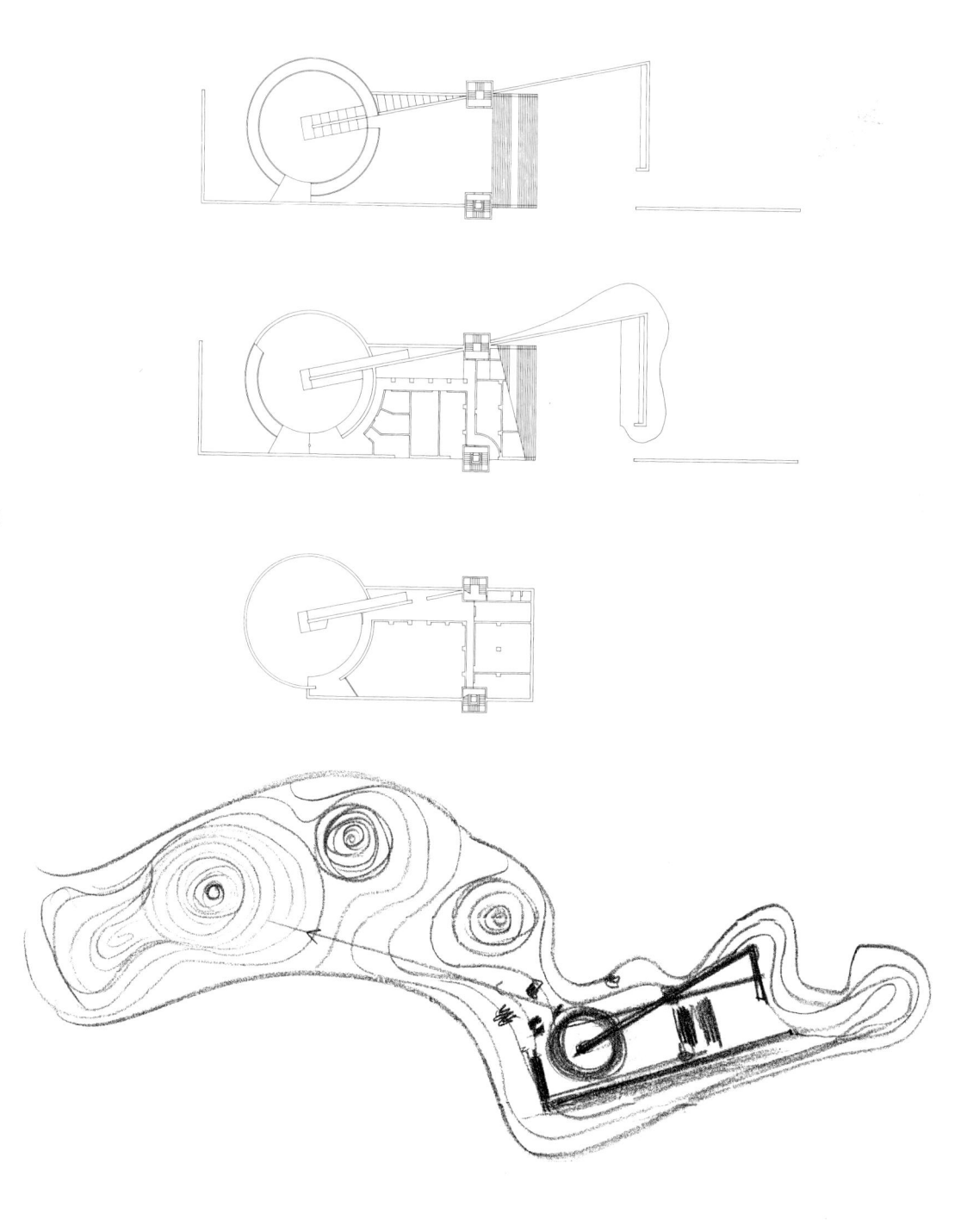

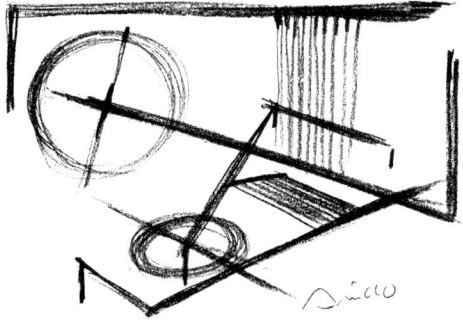

View of the circular courtyard and conceptual sketch.

Overall view and section.

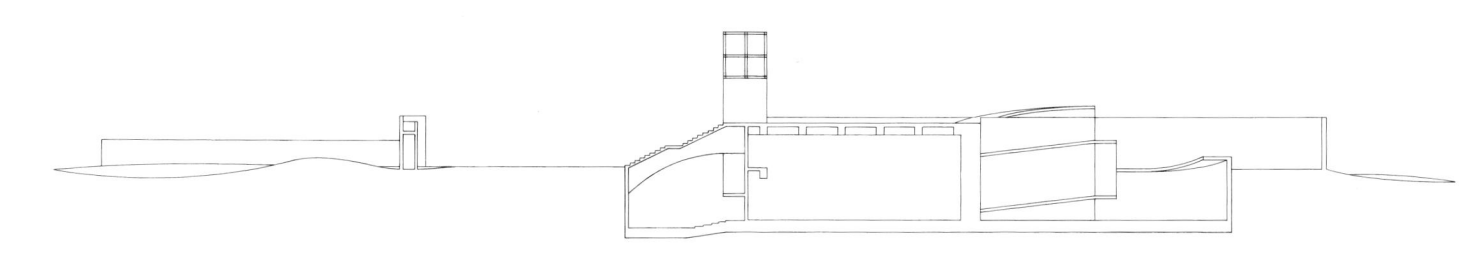

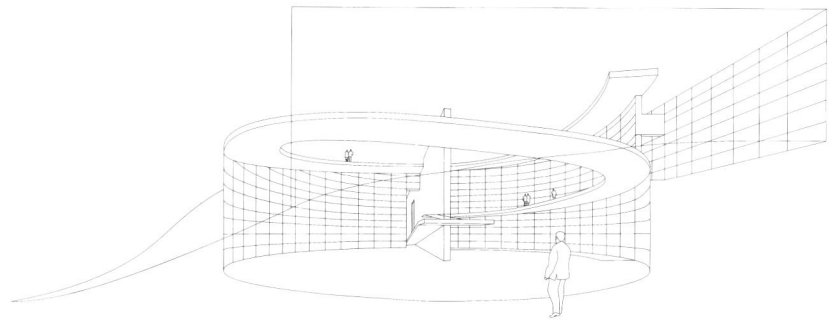

Perspective view and drawing of the cylinder and ramp.

391

Miyashita House

Detail of the exterior wall and observatory, and sections.

This house and studio, designed for an artist, is on a small hill overlooking western Kobe and the Inland Sea of Japan. A rectilinear volume with an 8 x 14 metre plan, positioned north–south, forms the core. The site is significantly lower in elevation than the front road – a factor that has influenced the design of the building, which is entered by bridge at the second, or middle, level. With plants below the bridge, the occupants enter the house amid greenery.

The studio and master bedroom occupy the ground floor, with the living room and dining room on the middle level. These rooms interconnect with the external spaces – a court and a terrace – provided on both levels. On the top level, two rooms face each other across an open terrace, one of them capped by an observatory. A spiral staircase leads to the observatory from the middle level. As vertical spaces, the spiral staircase and the external triple-volume court introduce fluidity into the building.

Location Kobe
Design 1989–90
Construction 1991–2
Structure Reinforced concrete
Site area 332 m^2
Building area 148.7 m^2
Total floor area 250.9 m^2

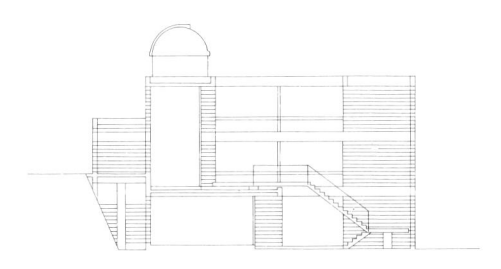

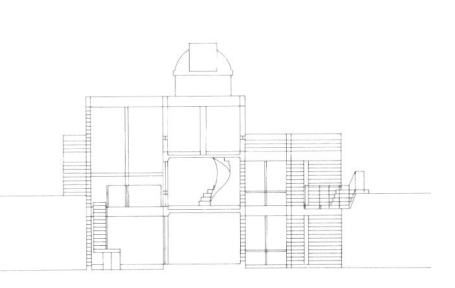

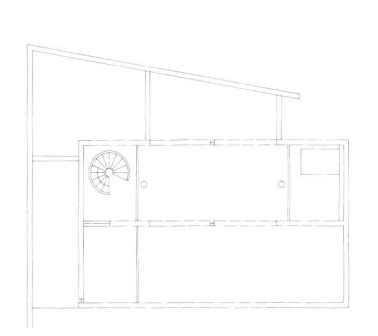

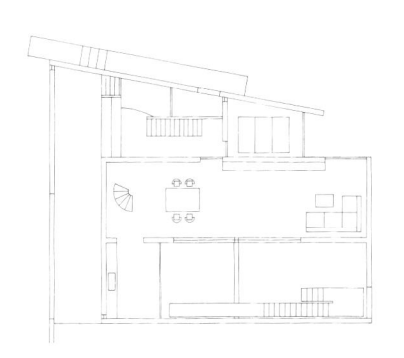

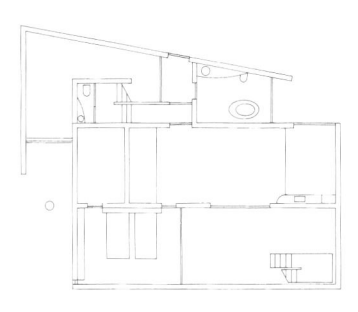

Views showing the circulation areas and floor plans.

Temporary Theatre for Photography

Axonometric, plan and view of the theatre.

In a setting rich in three-dimensional contrasts, this temporary high-definition TV theatre presented the work of the photographer Bishin Jumonji, for the brief period of four days. Erected inside an exhibition hall, the installation consisted of a roofless rectangular box 7.2 x 10.8 metres and 4 metres high, containing a roofless oval thirty-person capacity theatre, constructed of overlapping wooden scaffolding planks with a dark oil-stained finish. The floor surrounding the theatre was covered with white cotton canvas to accentuate the massive visual weight of the black construction.

Location Tokyo
Design 1990
Construction 1990–92
Structure Wood
Total floor area 80 m^2

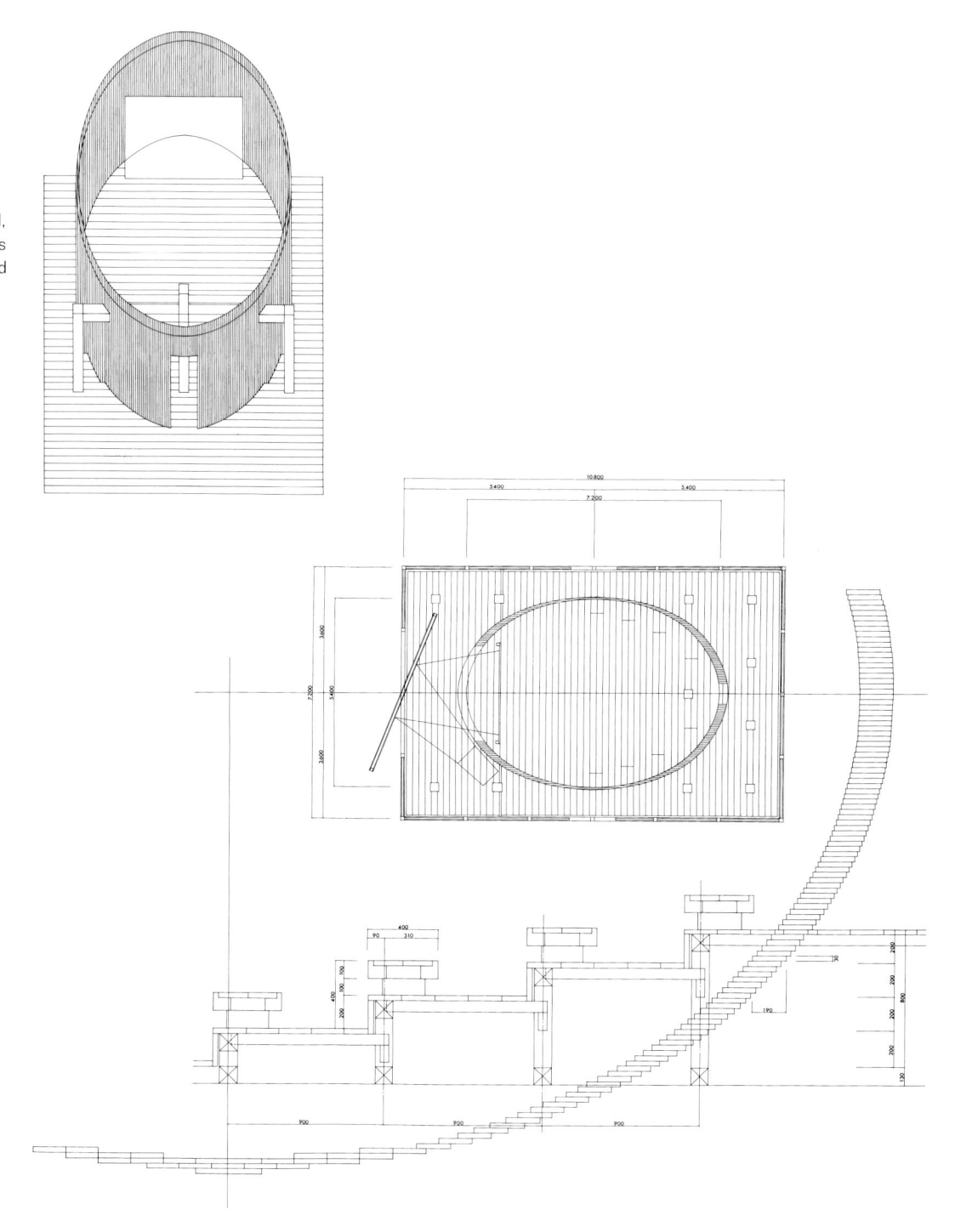

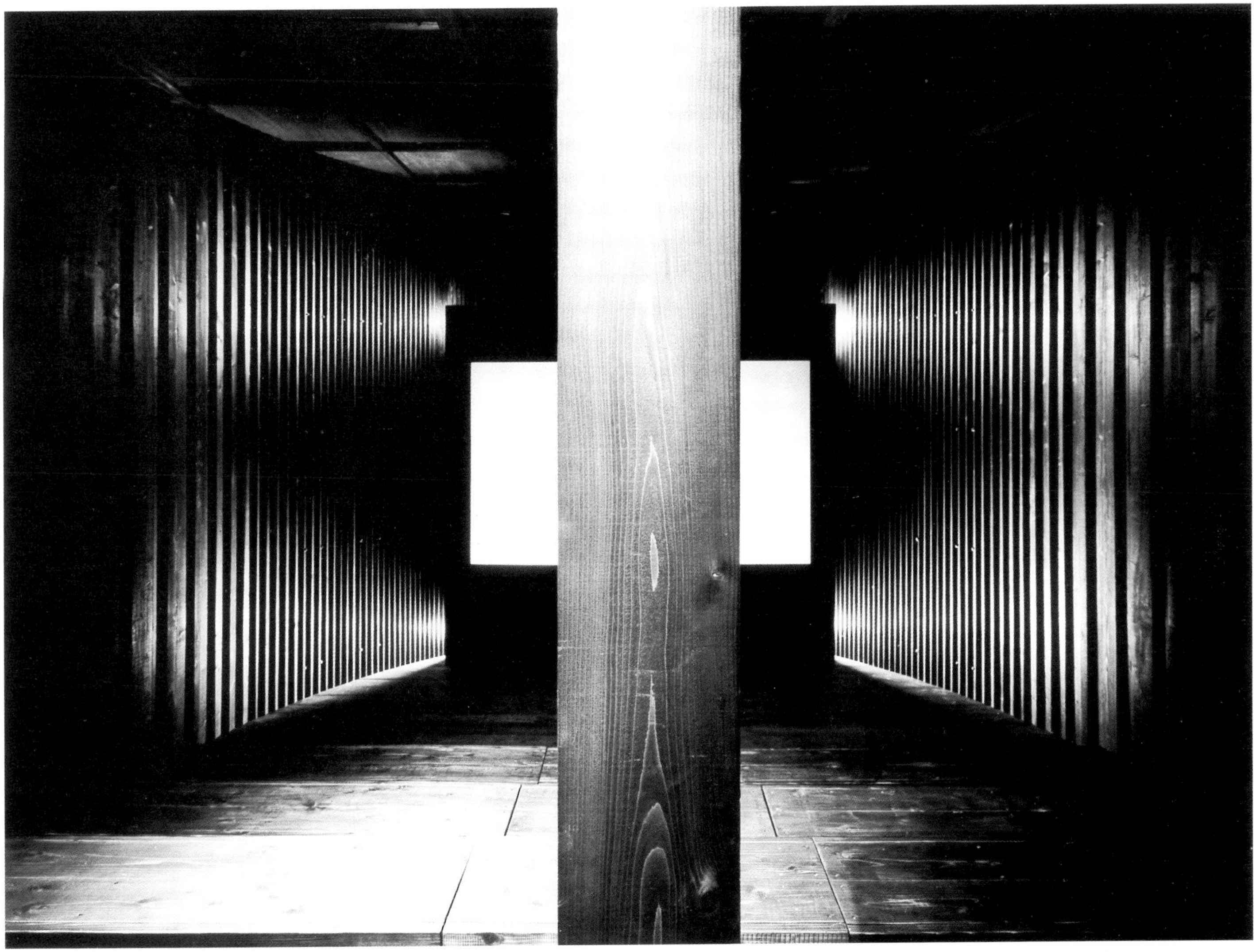

College of Nursing

View showing the entrance ramp, site plan, elevation and section.

This project is for Japan's first state nursing college. The building is composed of a high-rise element with a square plan, an interlocking low rectilinear volume, and an annexe offset at a 15-degree angle.

The low rectilinear element – fronted by a continuous longitudinal concrete colonnade – houses lecture rooms and laboratories on either side of a central three-level atrium. The tall element comprises study rooms. Positioned around the tall element are a library and a cafeteria with a double-height atrium, within two cylinders of 18.9 and 50 metre radius. The annexe, with a vault in the form of one-sixth of a cylinder, houses a gymnasium and lecture hall.

The building as a whole is embraced between two large ponds and enclosed by trees on its perimeter. The approach – extending 500 metres along a stream and lined with zelkova trees – introduces a tranquil mood suitable for a place of education. With a park proposed for a neighbouring site, the college will operate within a lush natural environment.

All college areas, those of its natural environment included, are intended as places for learning. Here, the students, the teachers, the patients of the neighbouring hospital, and the residents of the surrounding community will feel inspired to communicate regardless of generational differences.

Location Akashi
Design 1990–91
Construction 1991–3
Structure Reinforced concrete and steel
Site area 36,000 m^2
Building area 5,128 m^2
Total floor area 13,872.8 m^2

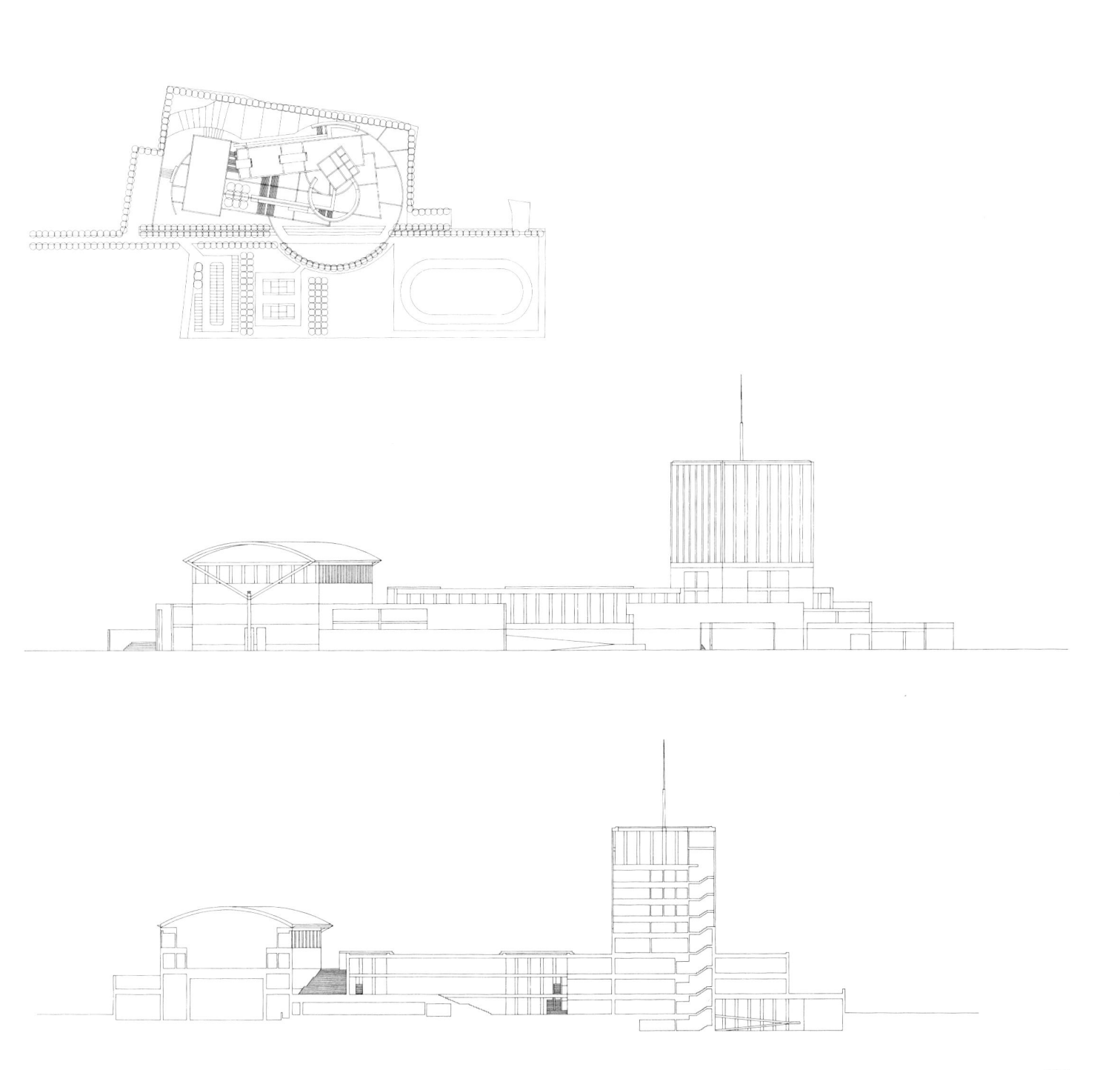

Exterior and interior views.

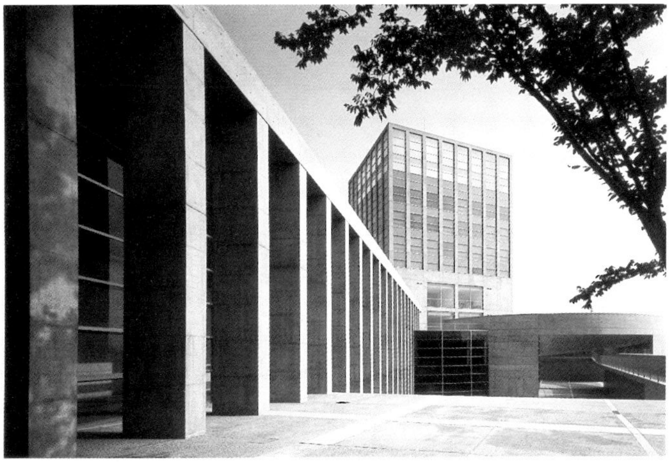

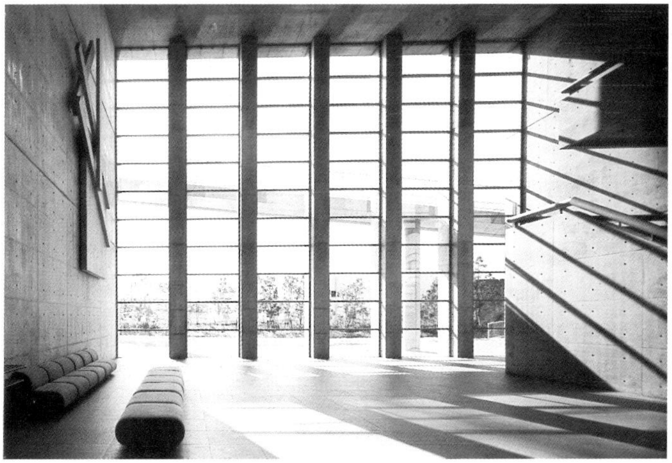

Modern Art Museum and Architecture Museum, Stockholm, Design Competition

View of the model, site plan, axonometric and plans.

Stockholm held an open design competition for a modern art museum and designated five foreign architects as entrants. The theme of this entry was the city's inheritance and a strengthening of its longstanding commitment to richness in more than just the economic sense. Positioning the building on the axis of an old church, it was brought forward in the form of a cascading stepped plaza. The landward unit of the structure houses a contemporary art museum, and there is an architecture museum across the plaza by the water.

By connecting the new art museum with the old church, dialogue is opened between past and present. Considering the changing attitudes of contemporary art, an environment going beyond the orthodox gallery was necessary for its display. Hence the structure was conceived as an art museum integrated with its surroundings. Seen from the interior, the building's outer stepped plaza is also a gallery space. Expression of the gallery space can then be seen to continue on in the artificial pond, and ultimately, the ocean. The stepped plaza connecting the two museums becomes a place for dialogue among people, the environment, and art. Nearby, water from the artificial pond flows into the ocean, with which it has visual continuity.

Location Stockholm, Sweden
Design 1990
Structure Reinforced concrete and steel
Site area 153,000 m^2
Building area 10,070 m^2
Total floor area 17,350 m^2

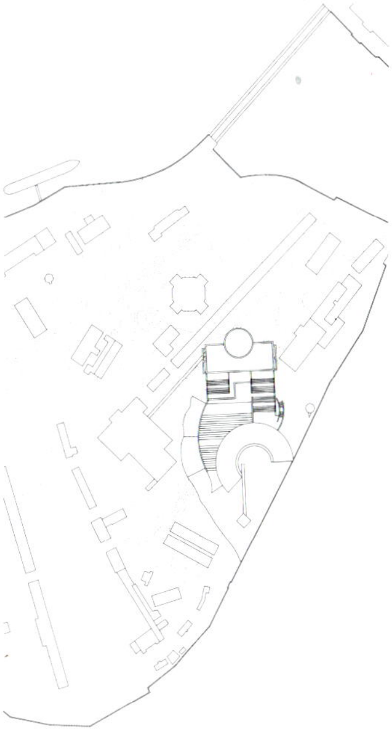

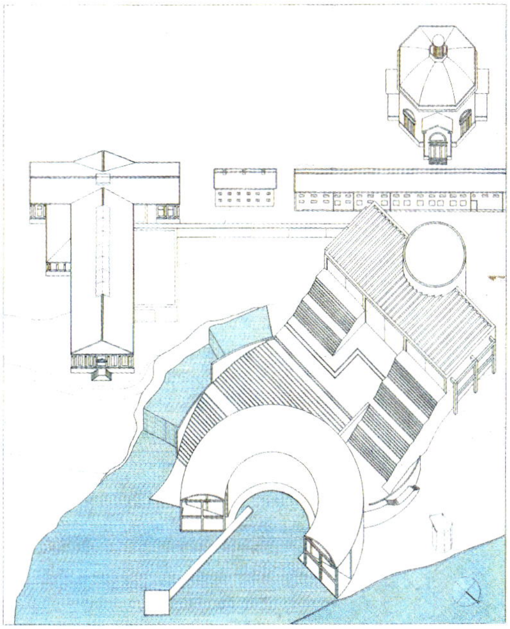

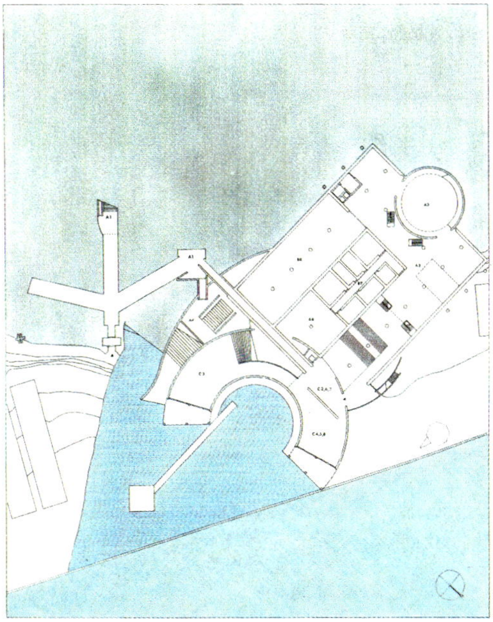

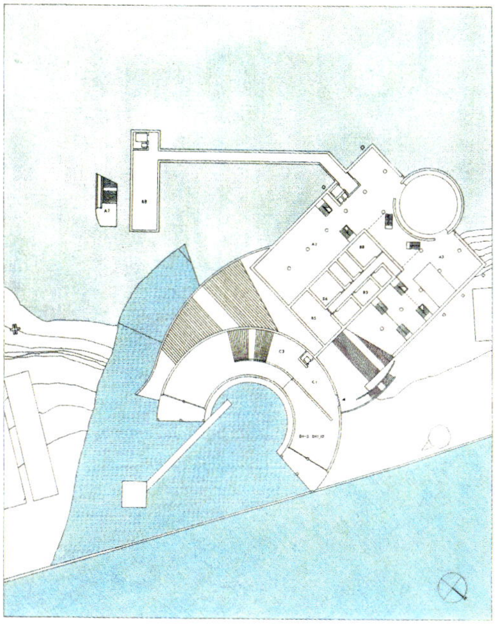

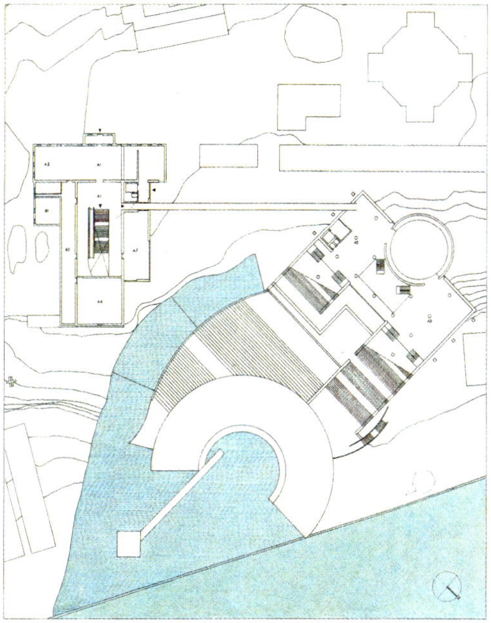

Chikatsu-Asuka Historical Museum

View of the model, conceptual sketch and site plan.

Chikatsu-Asuka, in the south of Osaka prefecture, was centre-stage to the earliest period of Japanese history, and has one of the best collections of burial mounds (*kofun*) in Japan, with over 200 examples, including four imperial tombs. The Chikatsu-Asuka Historical Museum is dedicated to the exhibition and research of *kofun* culture.

To produce a museum integrated with the burial mounds, it was conceived as a stepped hill lifted tectonically from the natural terrain, from where the visitor could view the entire burial mound group. Nearby, plum trees, a pond, and paths among the surrounding hills envelop the museum in an environment conducive to outdoor activity and allow it to function as a regional hub. Its roof, which is really a large stepped plaza, will be used for drama and music festivals as well as lectures and other performances.

Inside the building, the display areas are dark and the objects are exhibited as they were found in the tombs. Visitors experience the sensation of entering an actual tomb and feel drawn, in mood, back to ancient times.

Location Osaka
Design 1990–91
Construction 1991–4
Structure Reinforced concrete and steel
Site area 14,318.3 m^2
Building area 3,407.8 m^2
Total floor area 5,925.2 m^2

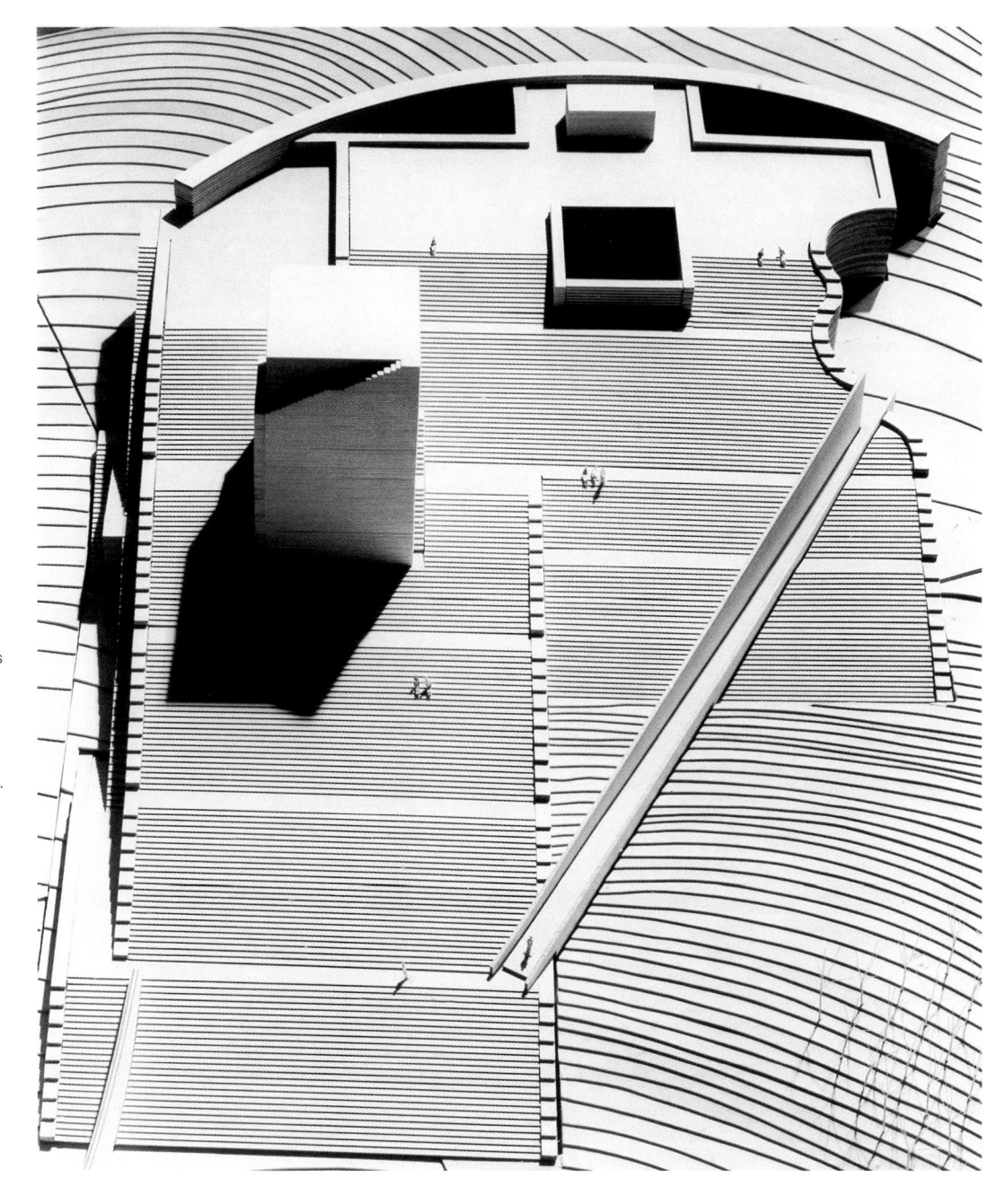

403

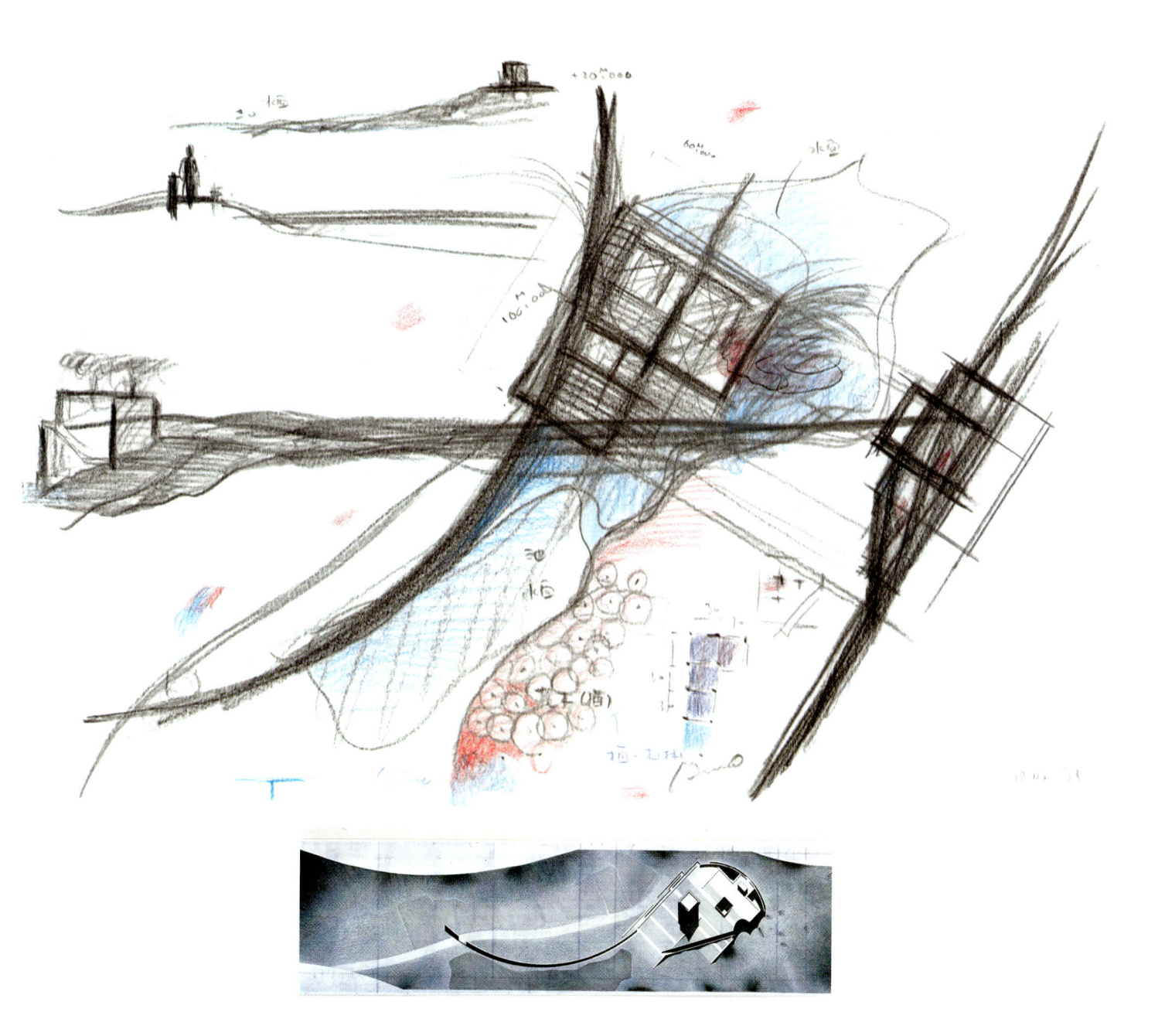

Overall view and conceptual sketch.

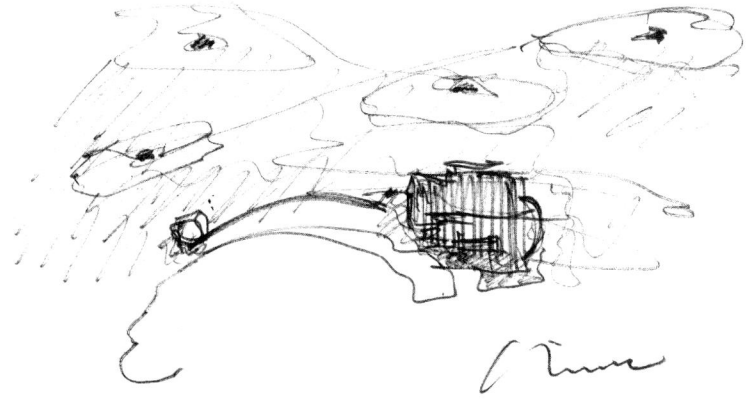

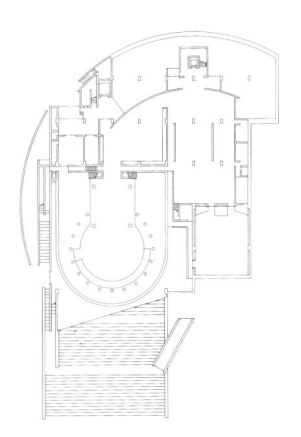

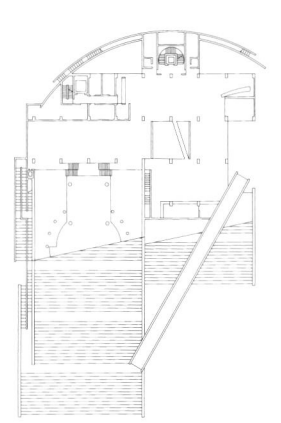

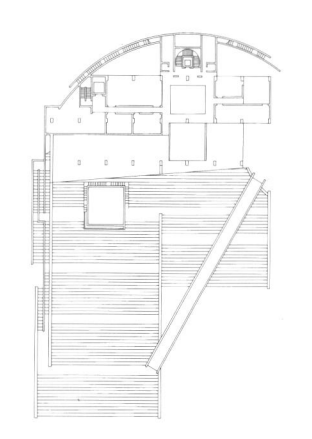

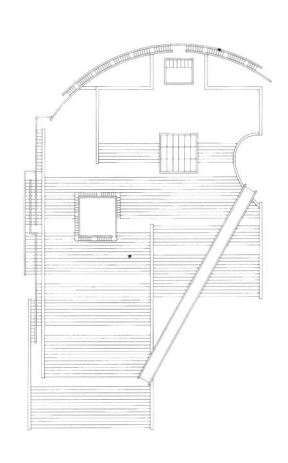

View of the roof, detail of a burial mound and floor plans.

YKK Seminar House

Views of the courtyard and the ramp.

This is a seminar house for the young employees of a corporation whose headquarters are in an urban centre. The building, which has six floors above ground and one below, comprises 93 rooms arranged inside a two-level-high perimeter wall enclosing the square site. Each room connects with courtyard space. They are accommodated in two elements to the east and west of the site and are separated by courtyards, yet connected by a bridge.

The western element is a low, two-storey volume, while the eastern element is a low, three-storey volume from which project two six-storey high-rise volumes with square 8.7 x 8.7 metre plans. Such public facilities as cafeteria, lounge and hall are contained in the underground level, which fronts onto a courtyard.

Each floor of both elements is simple in plan – regular rows of rooms with a 2.9-metre frontage. Variation is introduced into the spaces of the rooms by orienting their openings towards courtyards of distinct, individual character. The central court area of the building obtains three-dimensional character through its articulation into two underground and ground-level courts. A connecting ramp, however, gives them continuity as a spatial experience, and unity as the unclear space of the building.

Location Narashino
Design 1990–91
Construction 1991–3
Structure Reinforced concrete
Site area 2,067.8 m^2
Building area 870.5 m^2
Total floor area 4,199.8 m^2

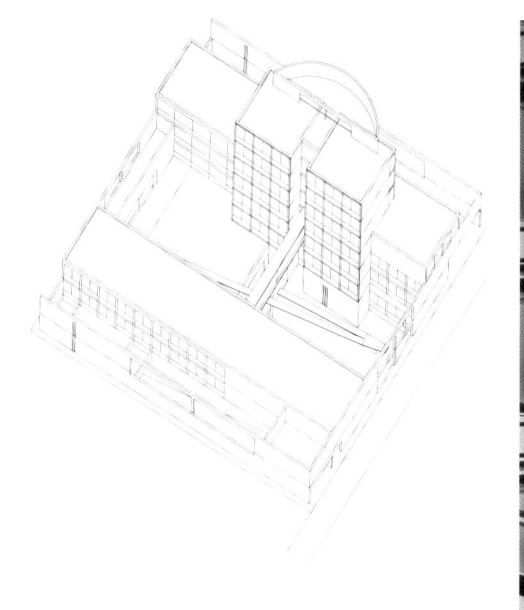

Axonometric and views of the courtyard and the ramp.

Children's Seminar House

Location plan, axonometric, overall views of the building and conceptual sketch.

This building is a residence for schoolchildren on vacation in the rich, natural environment not far from the Hyogo Children's Museum, completed in the summer of 1989, which the Seminar House is intended to complement. Full advantage is taken of the excellent surroundings in the creation of a place where children can look forward to spontaneous encounters with nature in unsupervised play.

A series of stairs runs up to the facilities by following the natural contour of the land, and an artificial pond has been established at the base of the building. The highest volume is capped with an observatory so that children staying here can experience the thrill of star-gazing. A waterfall – formed by water running off the pond in front of the bath house – helps to accentuate their experience of oneness with nature. The ascent to the facilities is by footpath to increase the excitement in arriving children and to encourage their appreciation of nature's splendour.

Location Himeji
Design 1990
Construction 1991–2
Structure Reinforced concrete
Site area 26,078 m²
Building area 817.9 m²
Total floor area 2,810.5 m²

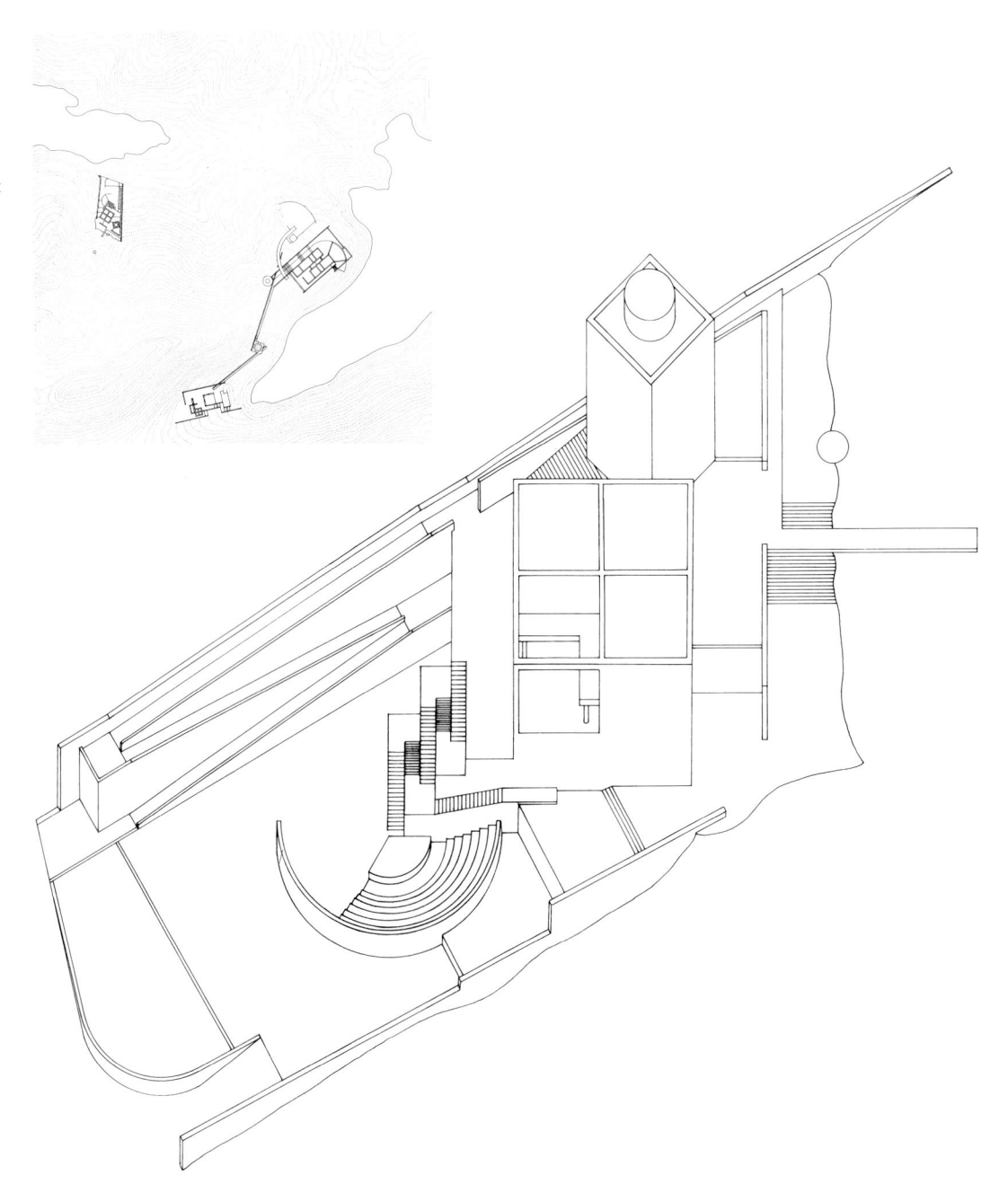

409

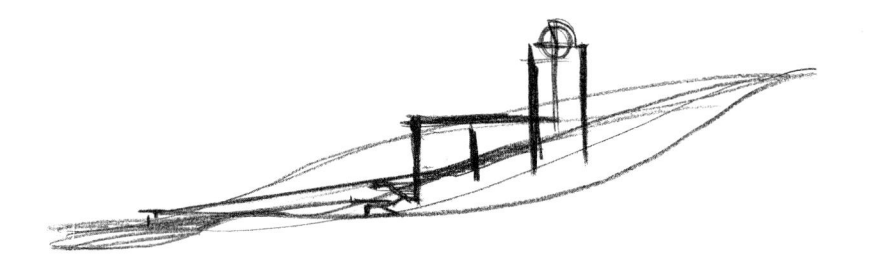

Kyoto Garden of Fine Arts

Views showing the circulation areas and the ramp, plan and section.

The Garden of Fine Arts is located next to a botanical garden on Kitayama Boulevard in Kyoto and is an open-air museum for the enjoyment of masterpieces of Western and Japanese art while in contact with natural phenomena such as light, wind and water. The museum itself is a conceptual extension of the Garden of Fine Arts in Osaka designed for the 1990 Garden and Greenery Exposition, and reflects a recurring interest in developing processional spaces along the approaches to such projects as the Water Temple (1989–91) and Church on the Water (1985–8). Here, such outdoor spatial sequences constitute the entire project.

There is an enclosed area below ground level within which three walls and a circulation area consisting of bridges and ramps create a rich variety of spaces on three levels. Water is introduced into the experience through three waterfalls and pools at each level. The project was conceived as a contemporary, volumetric version of a stroll garden.

Location Kyoto
Design 1990–92
Construction 1993–4
Structure Reinforced concrete
Site area 2,824.4 m^2
Building area 28 m^2
Total floor area 212.2 m^2

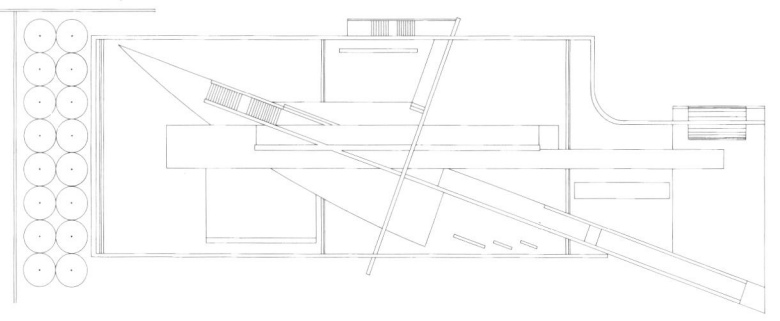

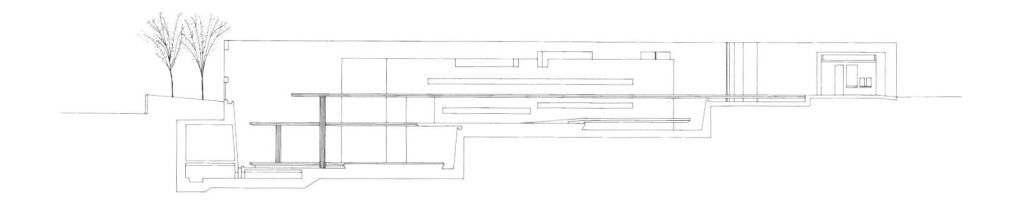

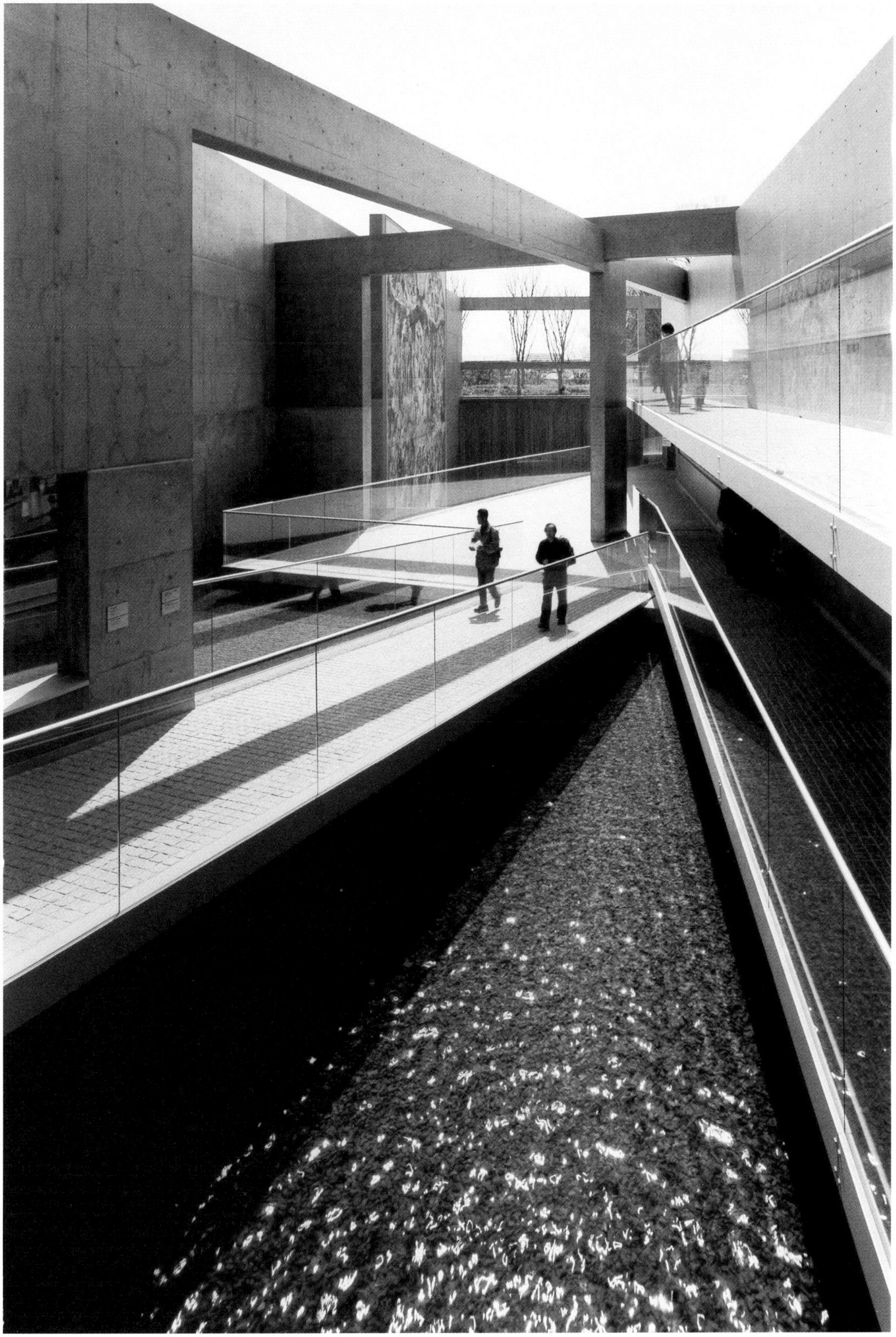

Kyoto Station Reconstruction Project

Perspective, conceptual sketch, views of the model and plan.

This proposal is a response to the critical issue of how a new station building should be handled in Kyoto, a city of immense historical value. It therefore transcends the functional conditions assigned to the programme for the competition. A city does not grow from utilitarian or economic reasons alone; as a collective body of historical legacies, it has a multiplicity of values. To create architecture in the city therefore means bringing to conscious life all that the vastness of time has concealed. And, the station, as public facility, must offer some kind of structure for the city's public face.

This building consists of two parallel gate-like structures (the Twin Gates), a vast elevated ground-level area, running north–south, that functions as a plaza, and an immense sunken mall (the Yellow Circus), conceived as a 'well of light'. The station facilities are in a central location beneath the Twin Gates. These identical gates simultaneously hold a dialogue with the past, the present and the future, and reunite Kyoto's landscape, which was fractured into north and south by the introduction of a railway line. As a whole, the building is a public area of three-dimensional character that invites nature within and endeavours to generate a new environment.

Location Kyoto
Design 1990–91
Structure Steel
Site area 38,000 m^2
Building area 34,340 m^2
Total floor area 201,000 m^2

413

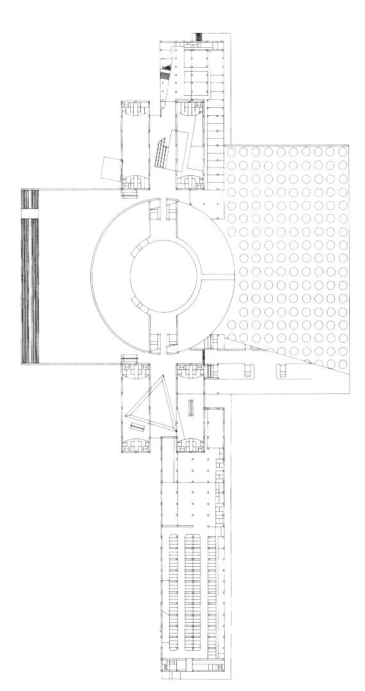

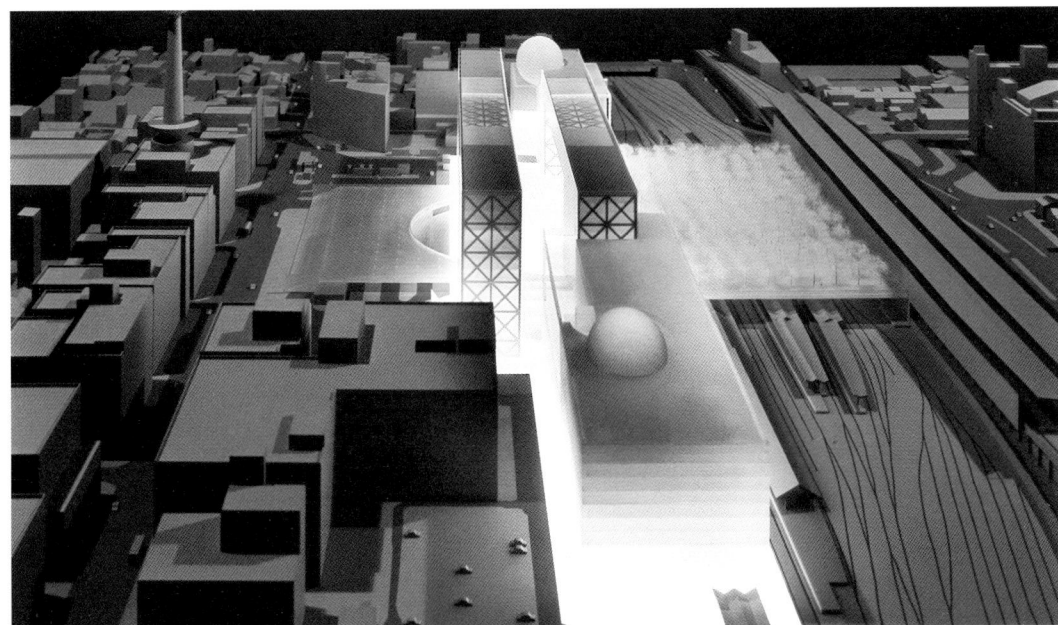

Oyamazaki Museum

Site plan, section and perspective.

This project is an attempt to give an old villa, built in the suburbs of Kyoto in the 1920s, new life as an art museum. The existing building was constructed at a time when western-style architecture was still rare in Japan. Its original owner based its design on the Tudor architecture he had studied in England.

A cylindrical gallery of 6.25 metres diameter has been set below ground in close proximity to the existing building. Plants are grown on the roof and in the periphery of the gallery, to meld it with the garden. The gallery is connected with the old building by a linear staircase, placed at the approach to the existing building, so that visitors are required to pass through the old building to reach the new. The new structure has been placed underground out of respect for the old building, and to avoid disturbing its continuity with past memory. Ceramic works are displayed in the old building, while the new art gallery exhibits Impressionist works.

The two spaces allow visitors contrasting spatial experiences. Embraced by the natural environment, visitors can enjoy art within an ambience of coexisting past and present eras.

Location Kyoto
Design 1991–4
Construction 1994–5
Structure Reinforced concrete
Site area 5,481 m^2
Building area 699 m^2
Total floor area 1,006.3 m^2

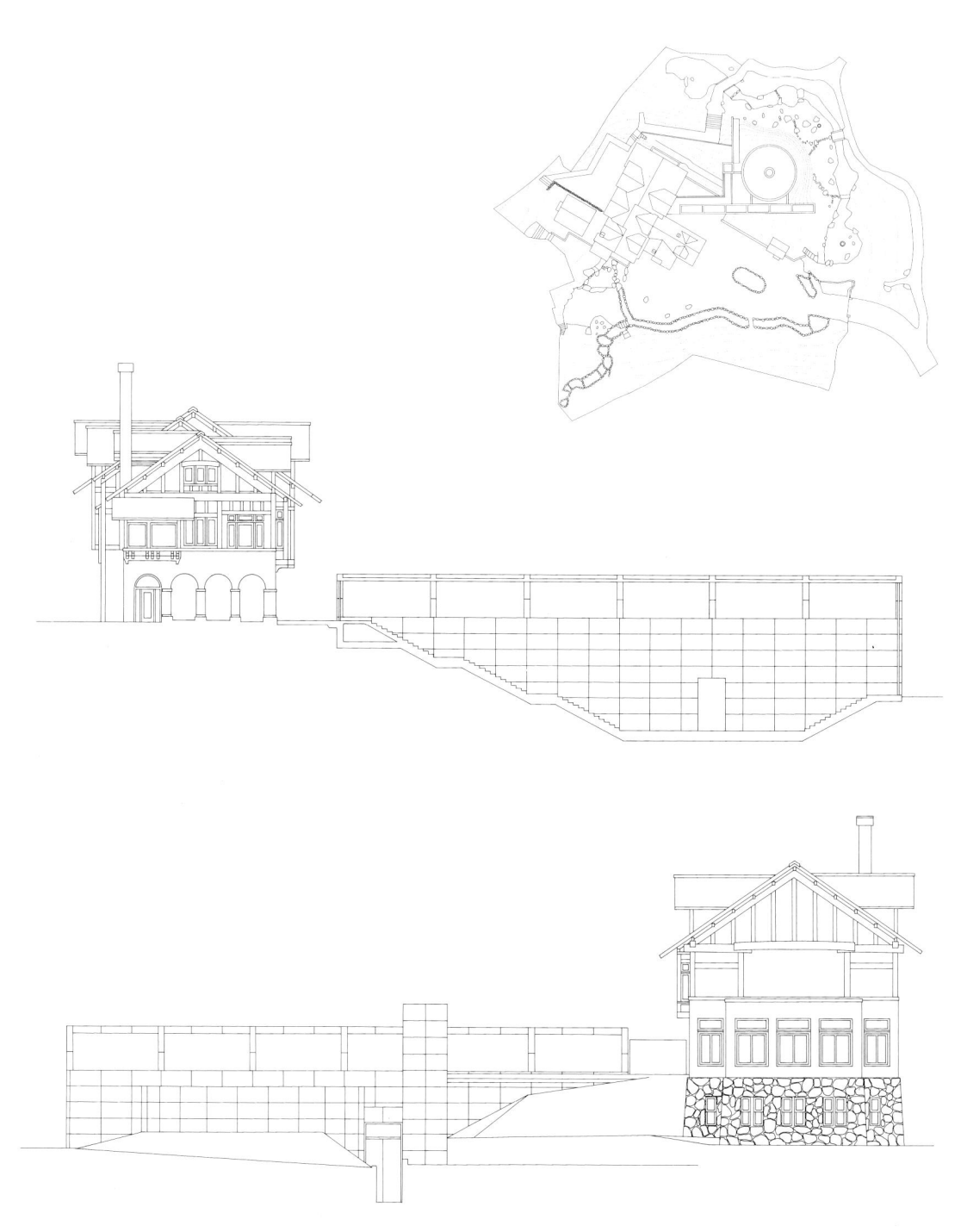

View of the model and plans.

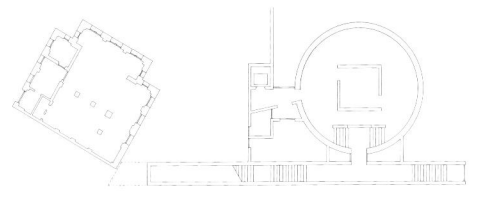

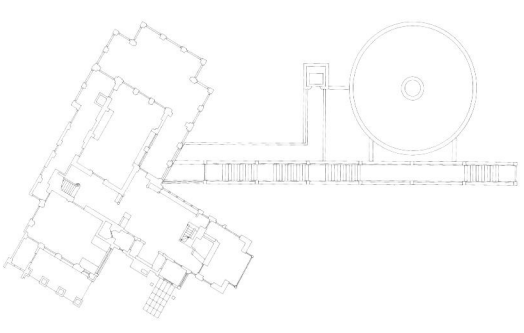

Konan University Student Centre

Floor plans, views of the model and site plan.

Konan University is near the Osaka/Kobe border, in a hilly district overlooked, from the north, by Mount Rokko. This proposal for an on-campus building – comprising an open-air theatre, a multi-purpose hall, restaurants and cafés – attempts to provide students with stimulating arenas for college life outside the lecture theatre. The building has a large outdoor space at its core, around which there are complexly interwoven interior and exterior spaces.

The building contains two cylindrical volumes, expressing contrary rotational movement. The western cylinder is an outdoor amphitheatre – ringed with restaurants and cafés on three levels, and offering rich opportunity for contact with nature. Interlocking with this is a three-storey rectangular volume with a 9 metre span double-vault roof, containing space for student shops. The eastern cylinder is an indoor multi-purpose hall with triple-volume atrium. This cylinder is concealed by the rooftop plaza at the second level, next to the stepped plaza that serves as the approach to the building.

The plazas provide vibrant external spaces and contrast distinctly with the existing campus buildings that surround them.

Location Kobe
Design 1991
Structure Reinforced concrete
Site area 7,885 m^2
Building area 3,031 m^2
Total floor area 7,315 m^2

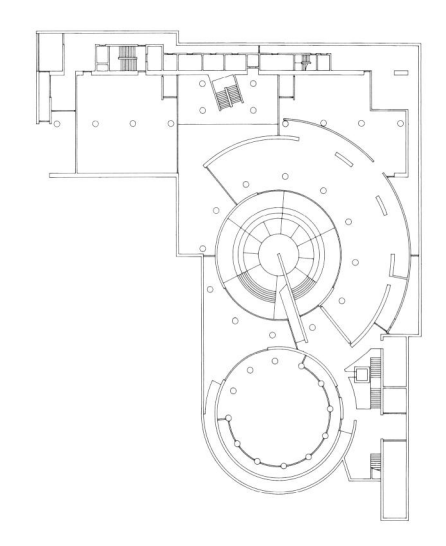

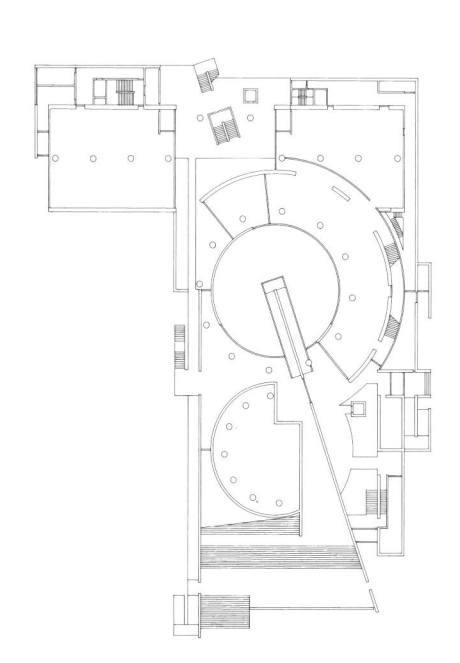

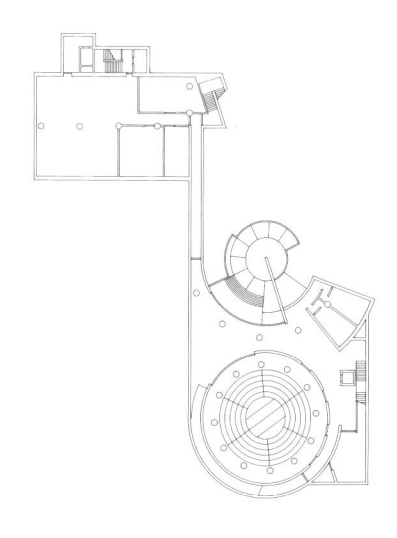

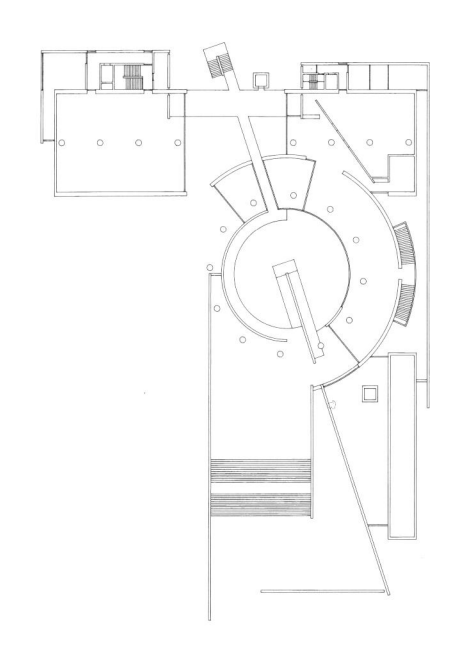

417

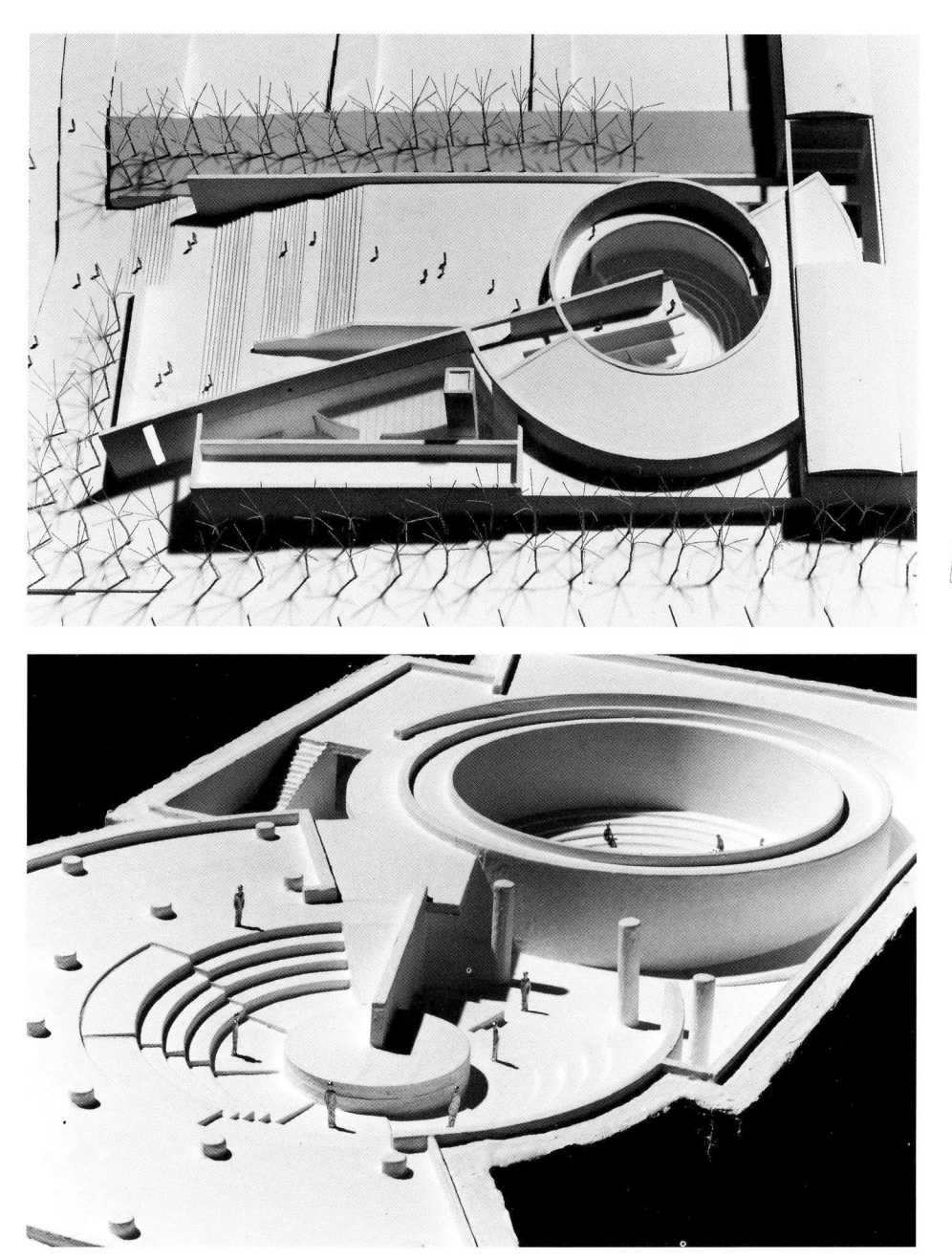

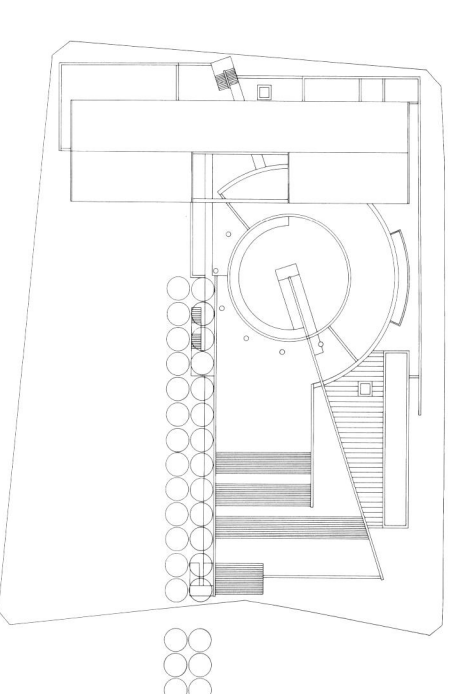

Nara Convention Hall Project

Site plan, view of the model and section.

The proposal endeavours to promote the past by evoking a strong future-oriented image, thereby giving Nara, an ancient city with 1,400 years of history, a direction to the future and a return to vitality. The building consists of two plazas with distinct directional movement, one descendant and one ascendant, a shelter that articulates their territories at ground level, and three interior theatres. As in older cities, the downtown environment of Nara has become monotonous, its individual character now faded. Inserting this public place into the environment will help to generate a city core with a strong identity.

The shelter's shape is an entirely original one that borrows from recent technology. The articulation of the 'Twin Forums', as the plazas have been named, has bestowed an innovative characteristic to the space that is simultaneously an interior and exterior. In its function as a public stage, this space stimulates varied movement among people, and produces new energy for the city.

The design layers and interconnects spaces of contrasting character and function, each stimulating the others. As a city core, the building connects past, present and future, and radiates a vibrant message to the city around it.

Location Nara
Design 1991–2
Structure Reinforced concrete
Site area 16,390 m^2
Building area 5,282 m^2
Total floor area 16,037 m^2

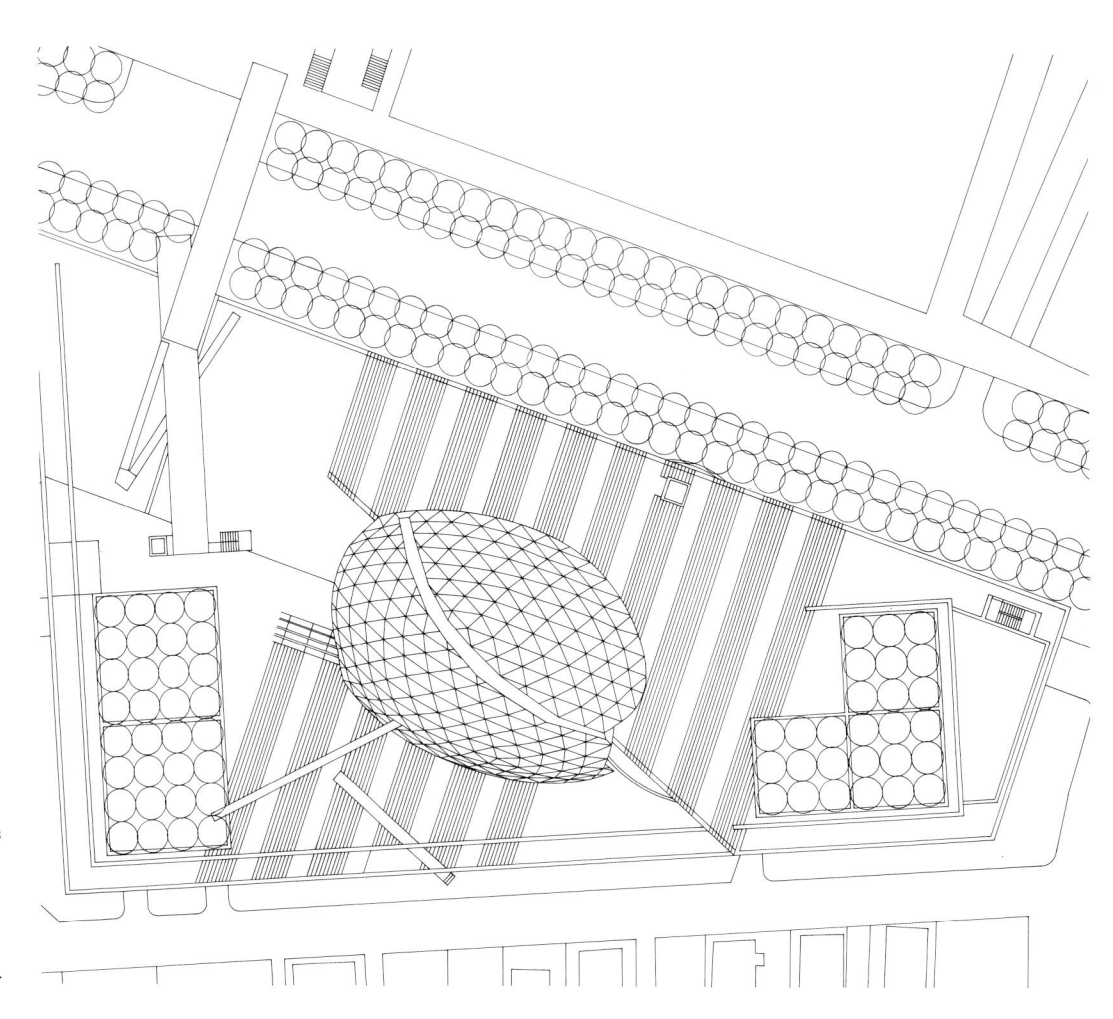

419

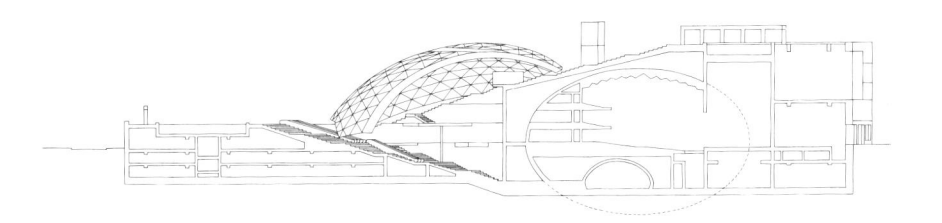

Church in Tarumi

Floor plans and view showing the cross in the concrete wall.

This church, on a low hill, combines the functions of a chapel and a parsonage. A large zelkova tree has been planted in its approach, as if to welcome visitors. Ascending a ramp along a curved wall on the property line, they arrive at the central court, and finally the chapel. The purpose of this approach is to mediate between the mundane space of day-to-day life and the sacred space for worship in its chapel.

The building is composed of a 5.4 x 33.8 metre rectangular volume and a penetrating diagonal wall. The chapel and the parsonage are on the same axis, facing each other across the central court, so that the mass of the rectangular volume is divided in two.

The chapel is a double-volume space. The wall behind the altar is articulated from the box space in the chapel by slits between it and the side walls and ceiling. This produces, in the deeply recessed chapel, a quality of spatial depth that transcends physical space. Light, piercing the slits, illuminates the surface of the walls and envelops the freestanding cross from behind, giving it definition.

The upper level of the parsonage accommodates the minister's quarters while the ground level contains a meeting room for the daily activities of the congregation. Each level has an independent court, to give it openness and closeness to nature.

Location Kobe
Design 1991–2
Construction 1992–3
Structure Reinforced concrete
Site area 622.1 m²
Building area 187.5 m²
Total floor area 304.5 m²

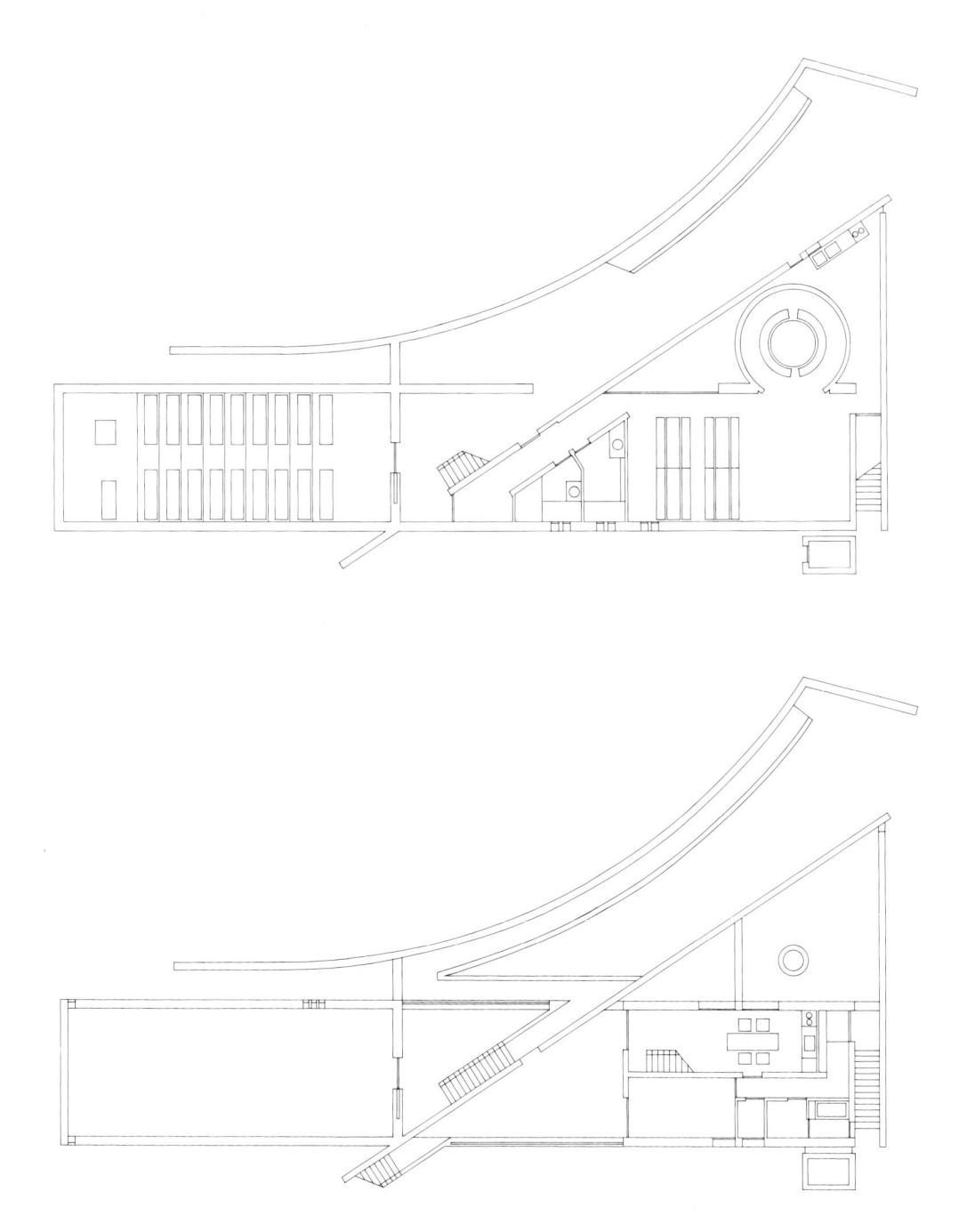

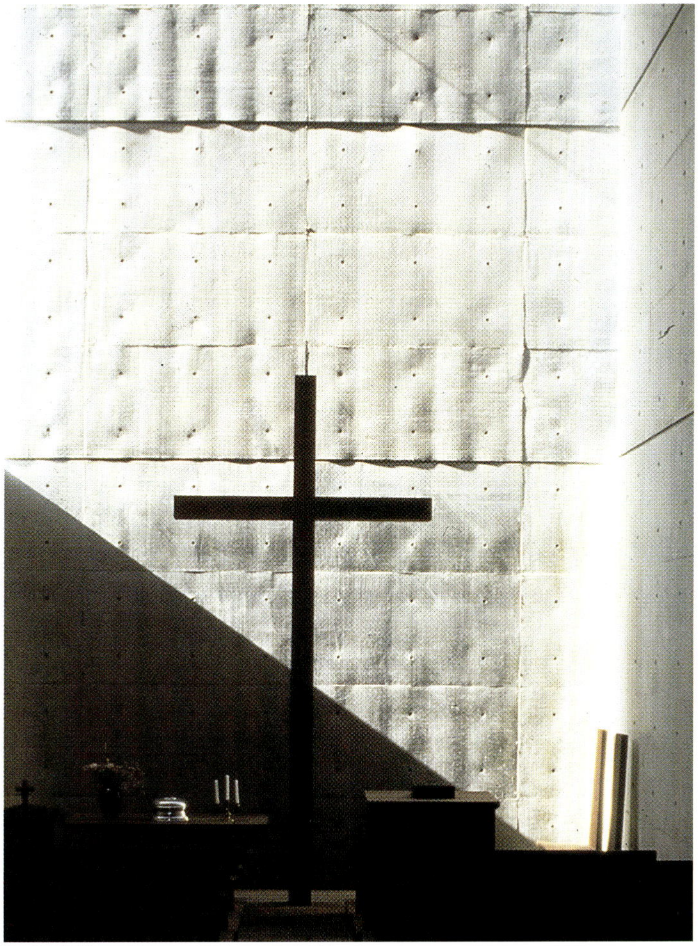

Suntory Museum

Views of the model, plans and section.

This project seeks to explore the richness water bestows on our lives when we can enjoy a vital relationship with it, and to bring a familiarity with water into daily life. The aim was to unify the seaside plaza of a museum with a descending plaza fronting the water. The descending plaza is large – 100 metres long and 40 metres across – and runs down to the water in slopes and stairs.

An art museum should act as a forum for encounters between people and art; so it was just a matter of extending this idea to a forum for exchange between people and the ocean. Here you can enjoy the sea breeze, the motion of the tides, the sun setting in the ocean, the people who have gathered – all of these things intermingle. The steps can be seen as seating for the audience and there are any number of stages that you can turn to for entertainment. Five monumental pillars are arranged at the water's edge and are repeated on the breakwater 70 metres from the shore as evidence of the architect's intention to reinforce the sense of contiguity of plaza and ocean. The building consists of a massive drum-shaped volume, or inverted cone (48 metres across the top) penetrated by two rectangular volumes. The drum-shaped volume contains a 32-metre-diameter sphere that houses an IMAX theatre.

Location Osaka
Design 1991–2
Construction 1992–4
Structure Reinforced concrete and steel
Site area 13,429.4 m^2
Building area 3,983.8 m^2
Total floor area 13,804.1 m^2

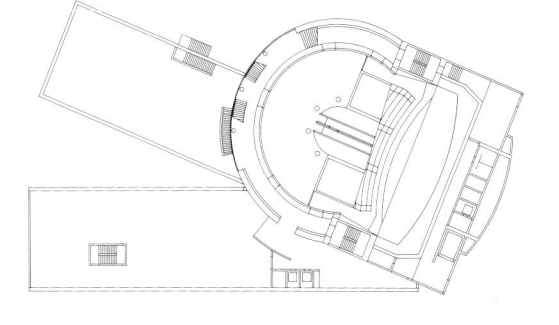

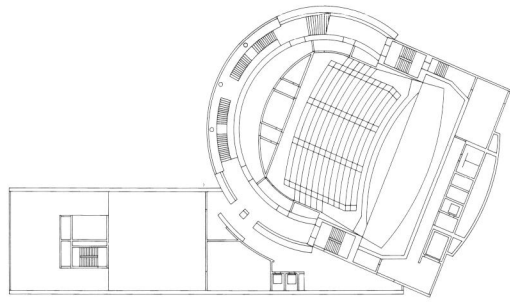

423

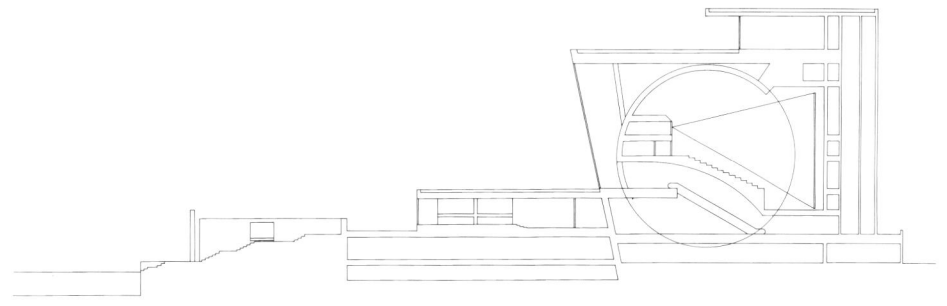

Lee House

Oblique view of the entrance, axonometric and view of the courtyard.

This private house is built on a hill in the suburbs of Tokyo. Small garden courts of varying character are stacked on different levels within the building to grant each court its own distinct character.

Overall, the house has a three-level rectangular core with a 5 x 21 metre plan. An internal court is positioned in the mid-section of this rectangular structure, with rooms at either end. The rooms face each other across the court at staggered half-floor intervals, and are connected by ramps running parallel to the court.

The ground floor houses the living room and dining room where the family gathers, while individual bedrooms are arranged on the upper floors. The dining room faces the gentle, green slope of the garden. This garden brings nature into the lives of the residents, while ensuring privacy by obstructing visibility from outside.

Location Funabashi
Design 1991–2
Construction 1992–3
Structure Reinforced concrete
Site area 484.1 m^2
Building area 174.8 m^2
Total floor area 264.8 m^2

425

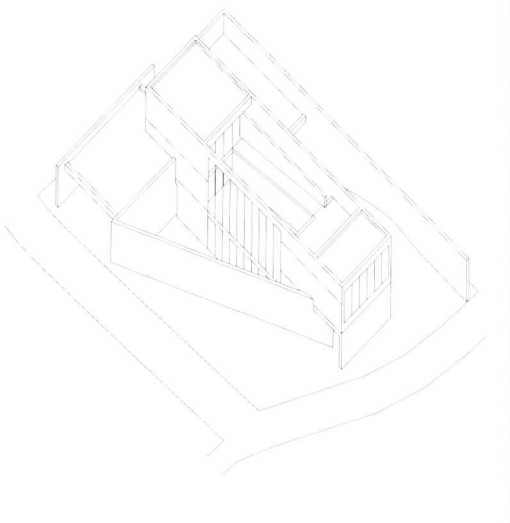

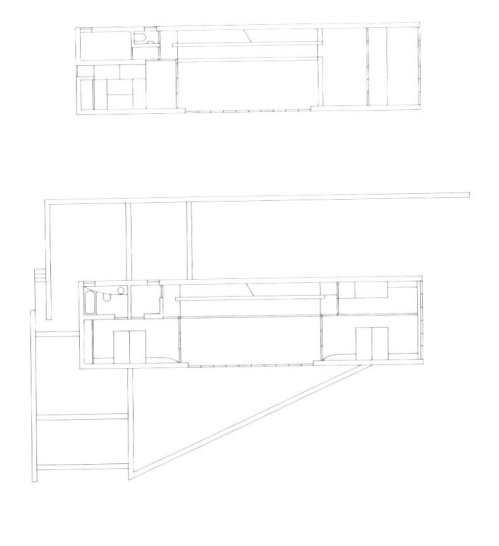

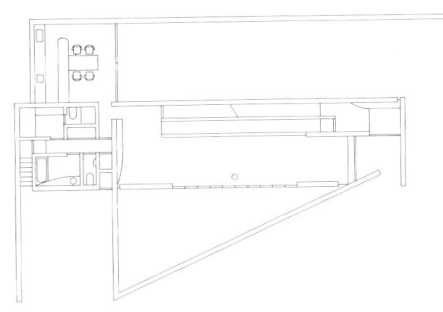

Floor plans, views of the garden and the courtyard, and interior view.

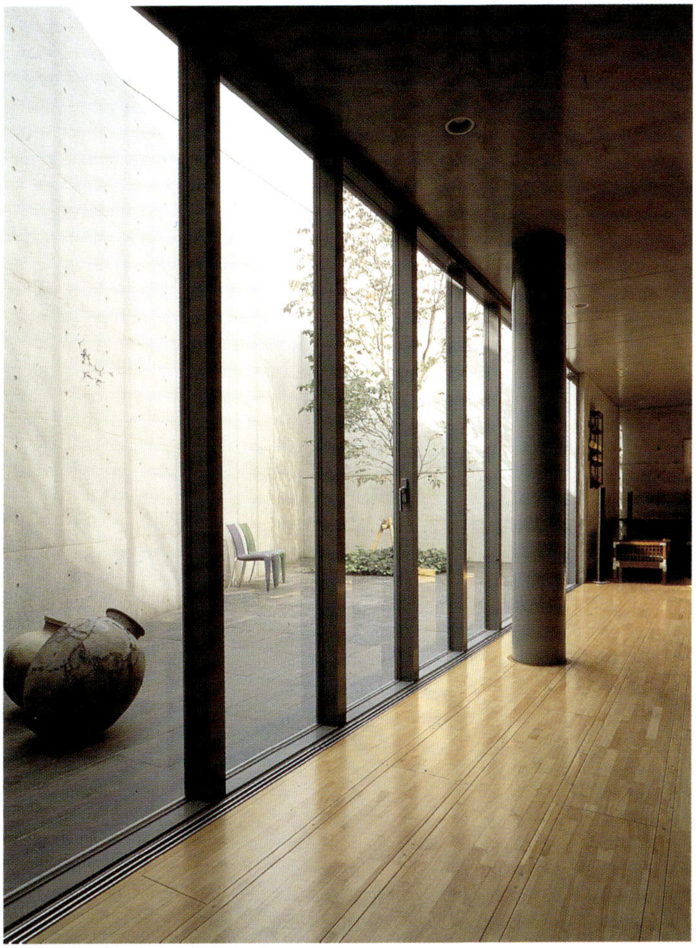

Museum of Wood

Elevation and plan with section.

The Museum of Wood was built for the celebration of the 45th National Arbor Day. It is in a region which enjoys rich stands of forest, a region blessed with a unique natural environment in its location between the Pacific Ocean and the culture that environment has produced.

The first consideration of the project was to avoid cutting the existing forest, where possible. The museum, it was felt, should come naturally to its site within the enclosing trees. The building has a ring-shaped plan, 46 metres in diameter, and contains a one-room, ring-shaped space, 18 metres high. Pillars stand aligned on a circular arc within this space, which displays the characteristic power of space formed by wooden pillar and beam construction. Here, items related to cultures of forest and wood are exhibited, along a curvilinear ramp winding through the interior. The space in the centre of the building – which is devoted to a pond – facilitates a dramatic encounter between sky and water. An inclined bridge penetrates the building, crossing the pond and leading to the annexe, which offers views of rich enclosure of forest.

Museum visitors can thus experience both the profound wealth of the forest and, in the powerful space produced by the building, a recreation of the human culture nourished by that wealth.

Location Hyogo
Design 1991–3
Construction 1993–4
Structure Wood
Site area 168,310 m^2
Building area 1,951.3 m^2
Total floor area 2,694.6 m^2

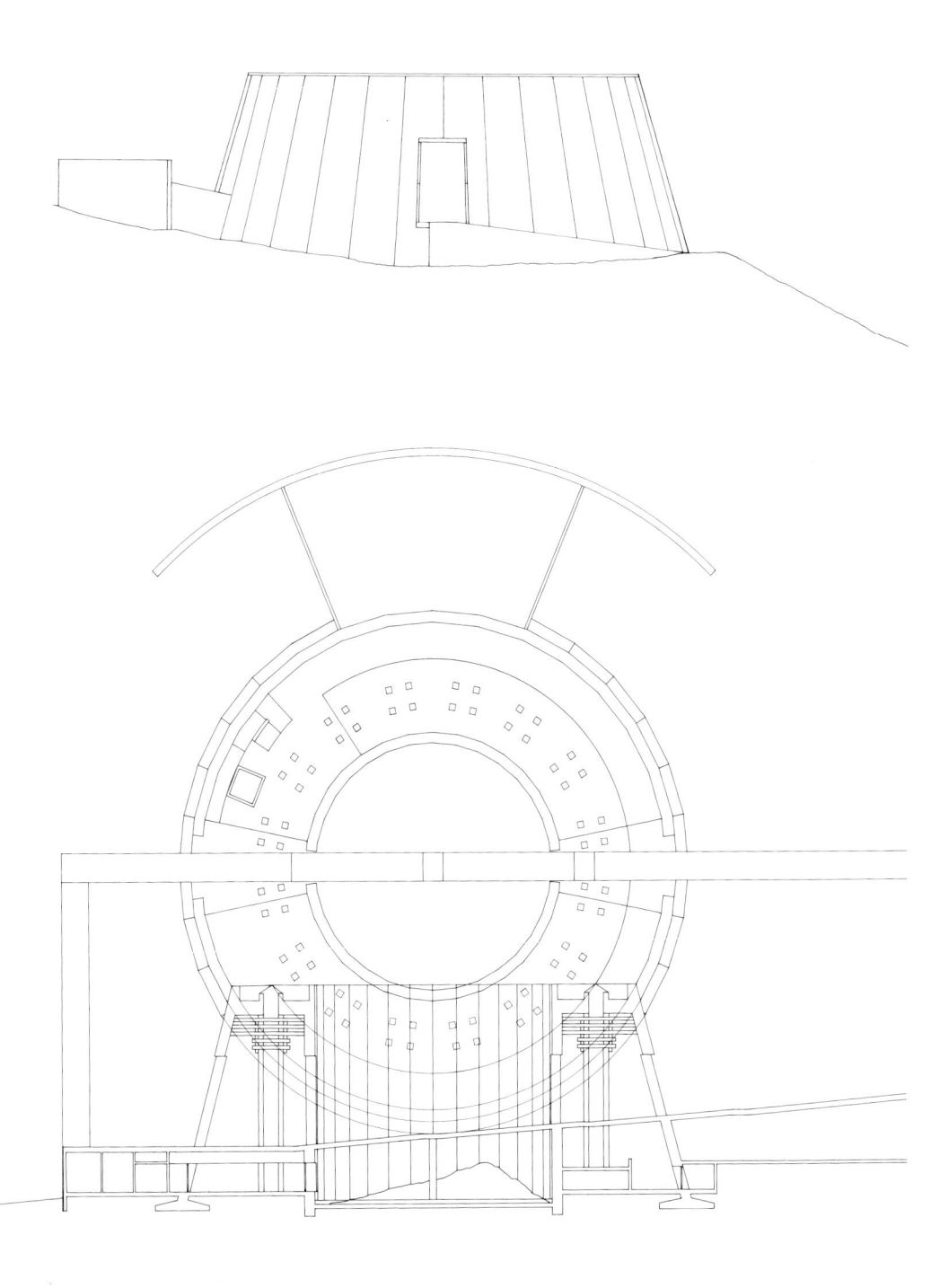

Overall view and plans.

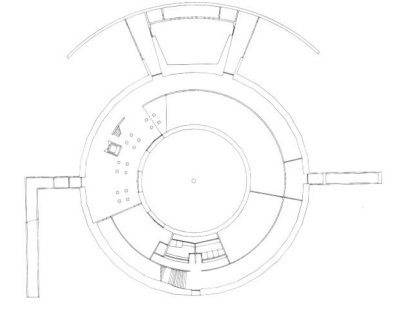

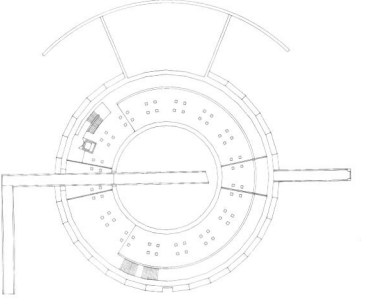

Interior views of the museum.

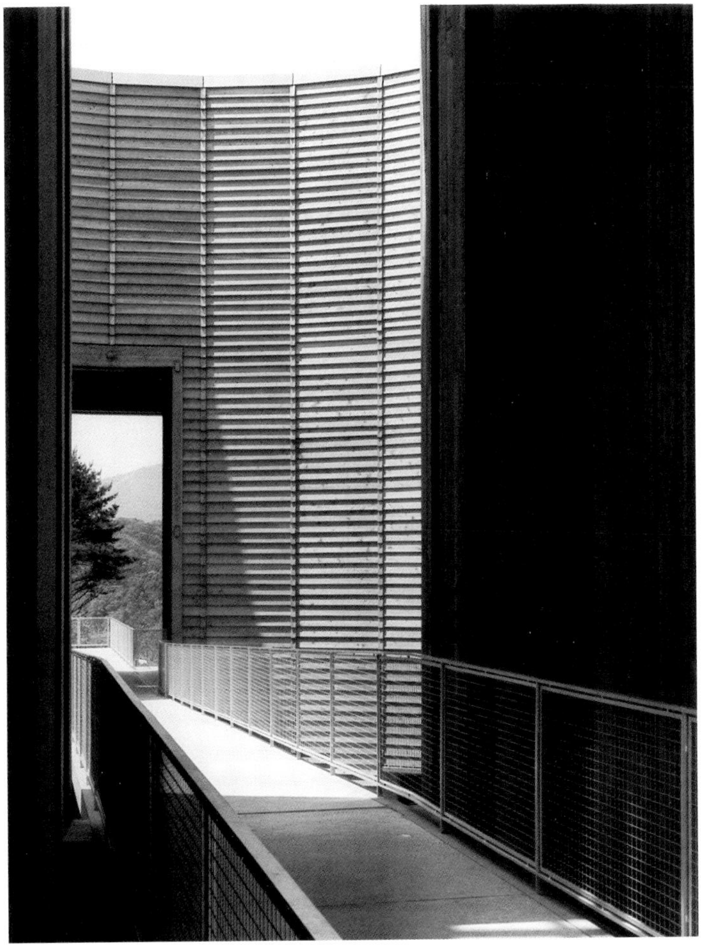

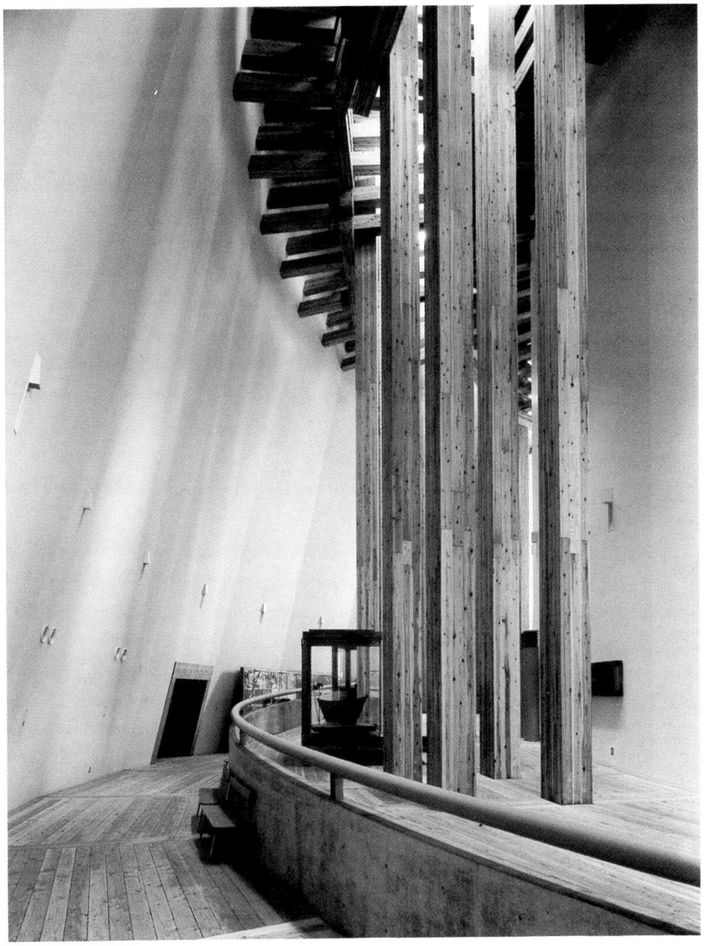

Gallery Noda

Detailed views of the stairs, axonometric and view from the street.

The site is near a railway station in central Kobe, on a corner lot facing the railway tracks across the road. It is exceedingly small and irregular in plan. The client requested a complex package of disparate functions: a bar, an art gallery, an atelier and a residence. These difficult requirements were resolved by overlaying the four functions around a 10-metre-high atrium that penetrates all four levels of the building.

A staircase rises around the atrium, and doubles as the sole path of movement and the art gallery. The art gallery originates at the ground-floor entrance as a balcony overlooking the bar, which is at a semi-basement level. The atelier occupies the second level, with the residence on the top floor. A skylight at the top of the atrium allows natural light to suffuse the darkness of the interior space, which is otherwise sealed within concrete walls. The residence has a large window through which the presence of the railway tracks below and the chaotic urban surroundings are felt in the room.

The size of the project site and restriction of budget seemed to conspire to reject all architectural possibilities. However, the extensive study concluded with the successful production of a rich microcosm within the buildings.

Location Kobe
Design 1991–2
Construction 1992–3
Structure Reinforced concrete
Site area 39.8 m^2
Building area 27 m^2
Total floor area 79 m^2

433

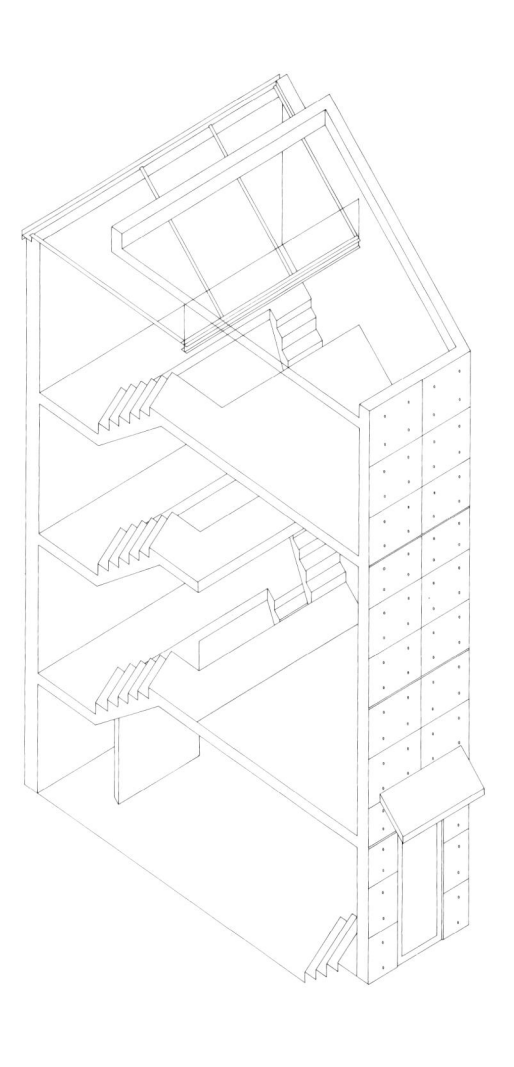

Rokko Housing III

Axonometric of the residential complexes, view of the model and conceptual sketch.

When designing, the site in question is not viewed in isolation – the neighbouring sites and even areas that lie beyond are also taken into consideration. Rokko Housing III can be placed within such a conceptual scheme. It also introduced new facilities such as a kindergarten and a housing complex for the elderly.

Though in line with the axis of projects I and II, project III used L-shaped blocks, which served to make it both an open and closed space. This design does not merely continue on a greater scale the aims of projects I and II, but strives to make the lives of the residents richer through the introduction of new facilities for public use and through the use of mutually connected and continuous space.

In challenging the theory of development which sees from beginning to end only a quantitative expansion of surface, the Rokko Housing series has instead contributed a critical character and a qualitative stimulus to the area.

Location Kobe
Design 1992

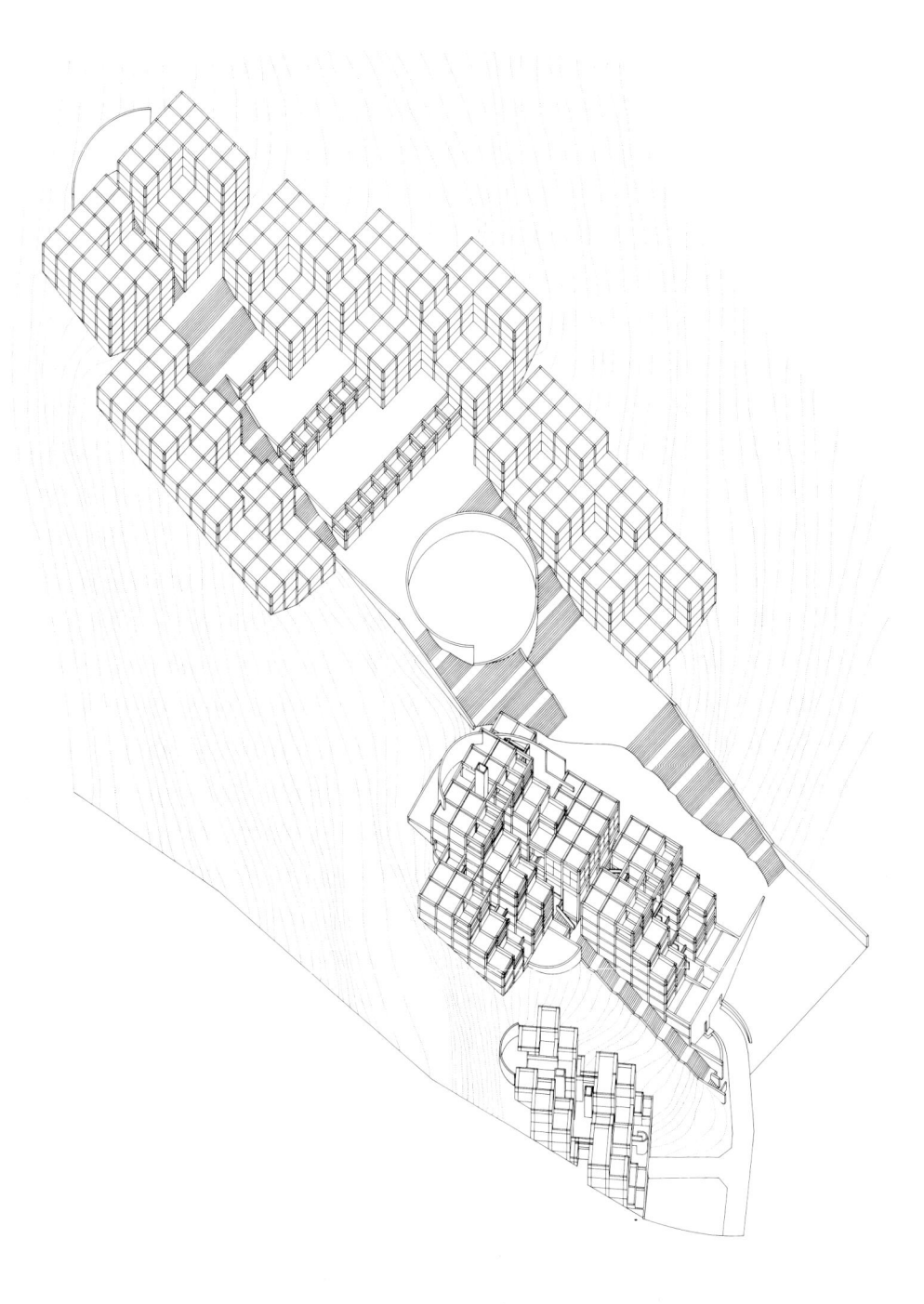

435

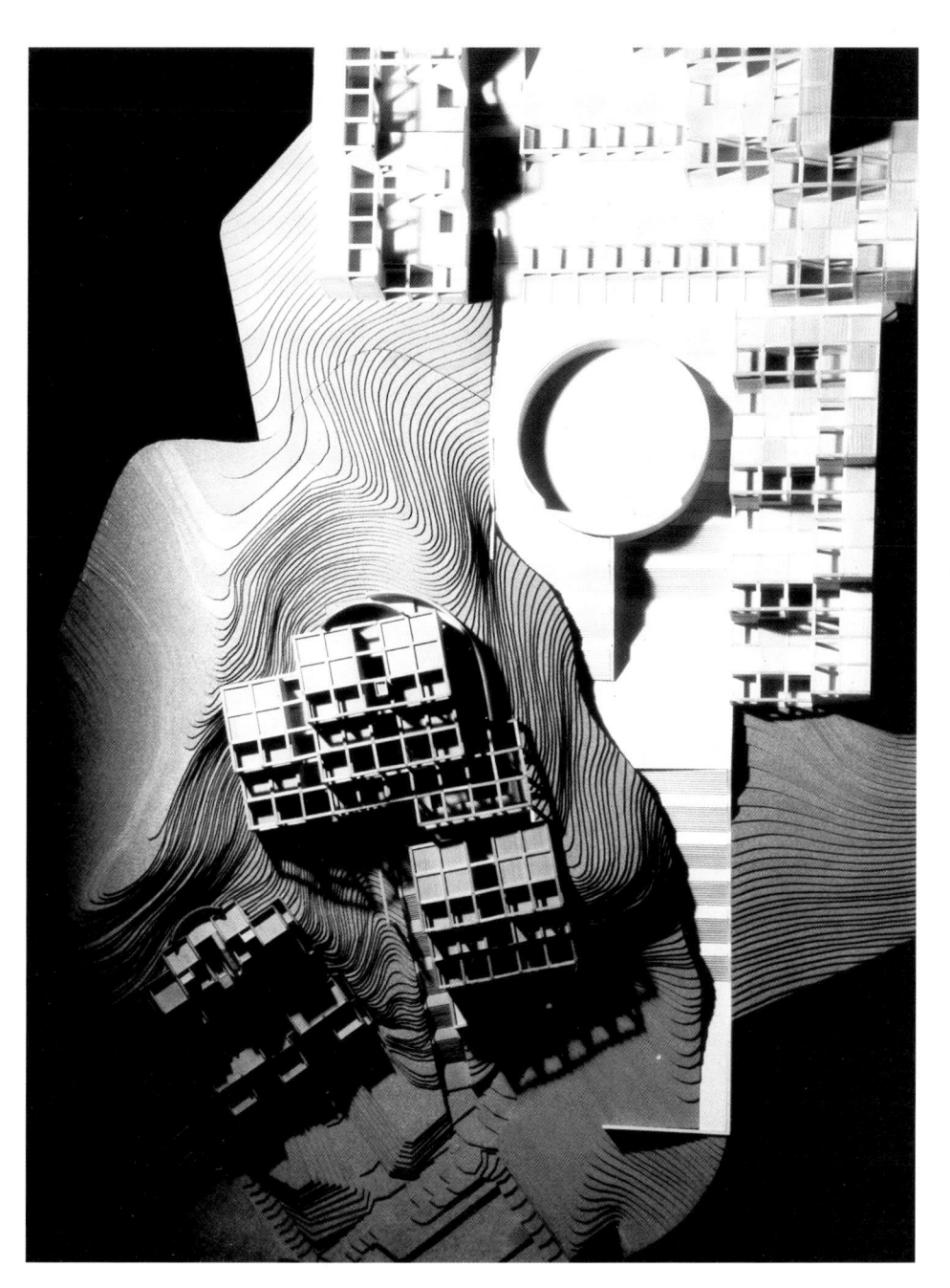

'Fabrica', Benetton Research Centre

Overall and detail views of the model, site plan and sections.

A seventeenth-century Palladian villa stands on the site in a suburb of Treviso, a city 30 kilometres from Venice in northern Italy. Restoring this villa was the point of departure for the design, which is for a research centre for students from around the world in the fields of architectural design, photography, graphic art, image media, and textiles. The facilities include a restaurant and library. All rooms front onto, and find interconnection through, the plaza, which becomes a place for varied exchange. A new colonnaded gallery 7 metres wide penetrates the old villa, and its colonnade extends across a pond in front. The colonnade combines with the villa's reflection in the pond to create a new landscape.

The intention was, by adding new architecture, to bring out the old villa's charm and vitality, and produce – within an overall harmony – a mutually catalytic relationship between the old and the new that would transcend time. Through this research centre, students coming together from various international backgrounds exchange their cultures. The aim was to express the spirit of the new engaging in dialogue with the old, and the subsequent emergence of new creativity.

Location Villorba, Treviso, Italy
Design 1992–5
Construction 1993–6
Structure Reinforced concrete
Site area 51,000 m^2
Total floor area 11,000 m^2 (first phase, 5,000 m^2)

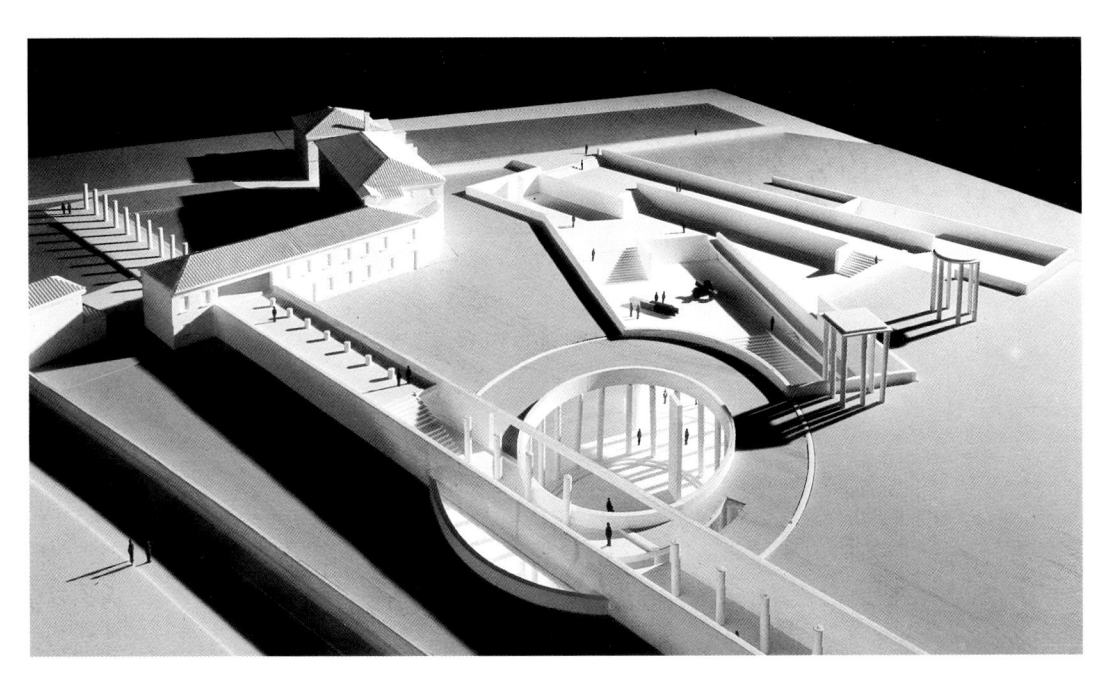

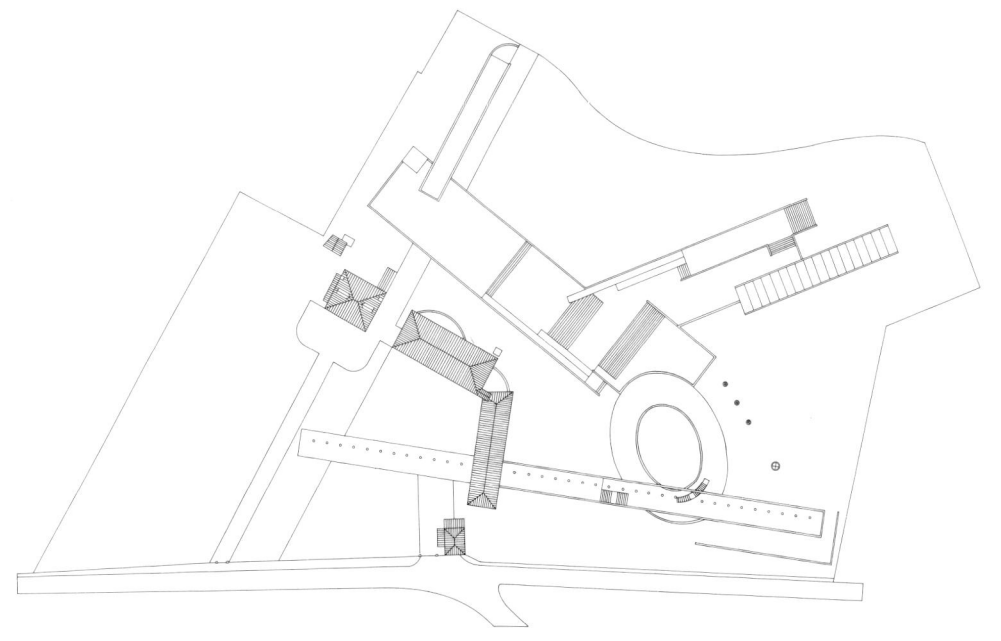

436

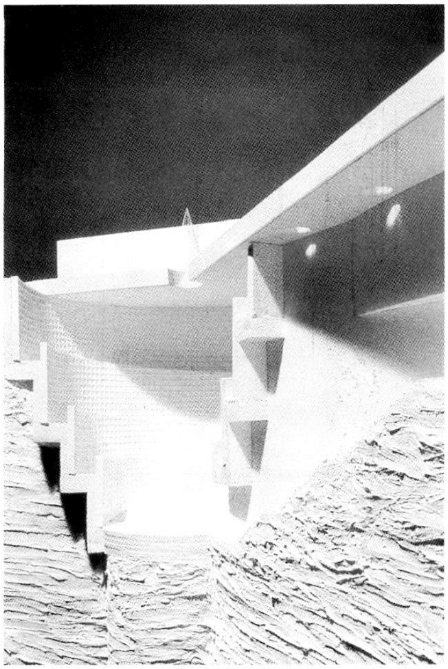

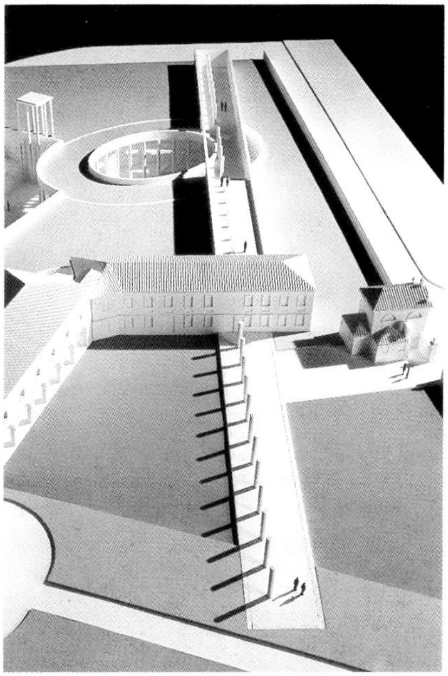

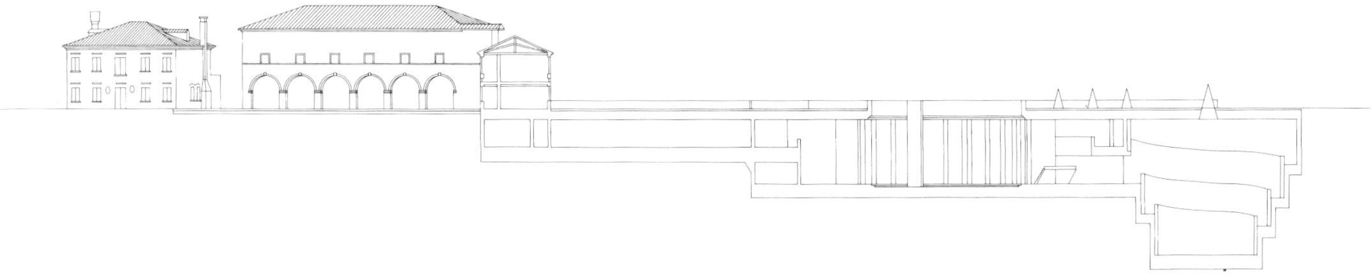

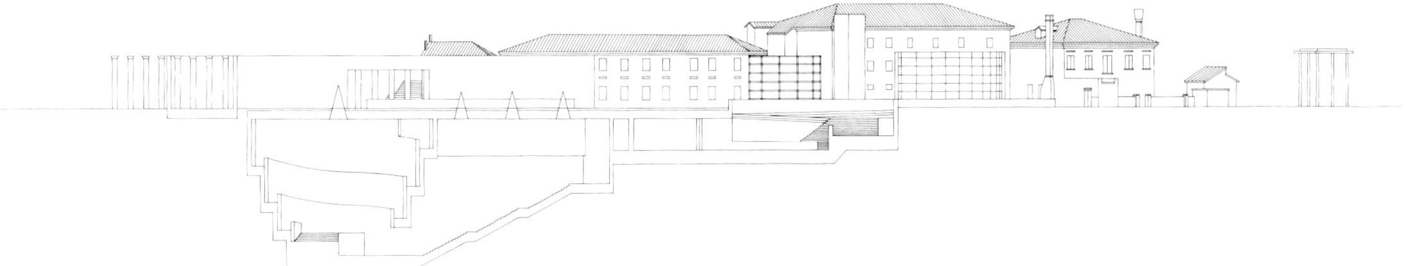

Site plan and section of the underground areas.

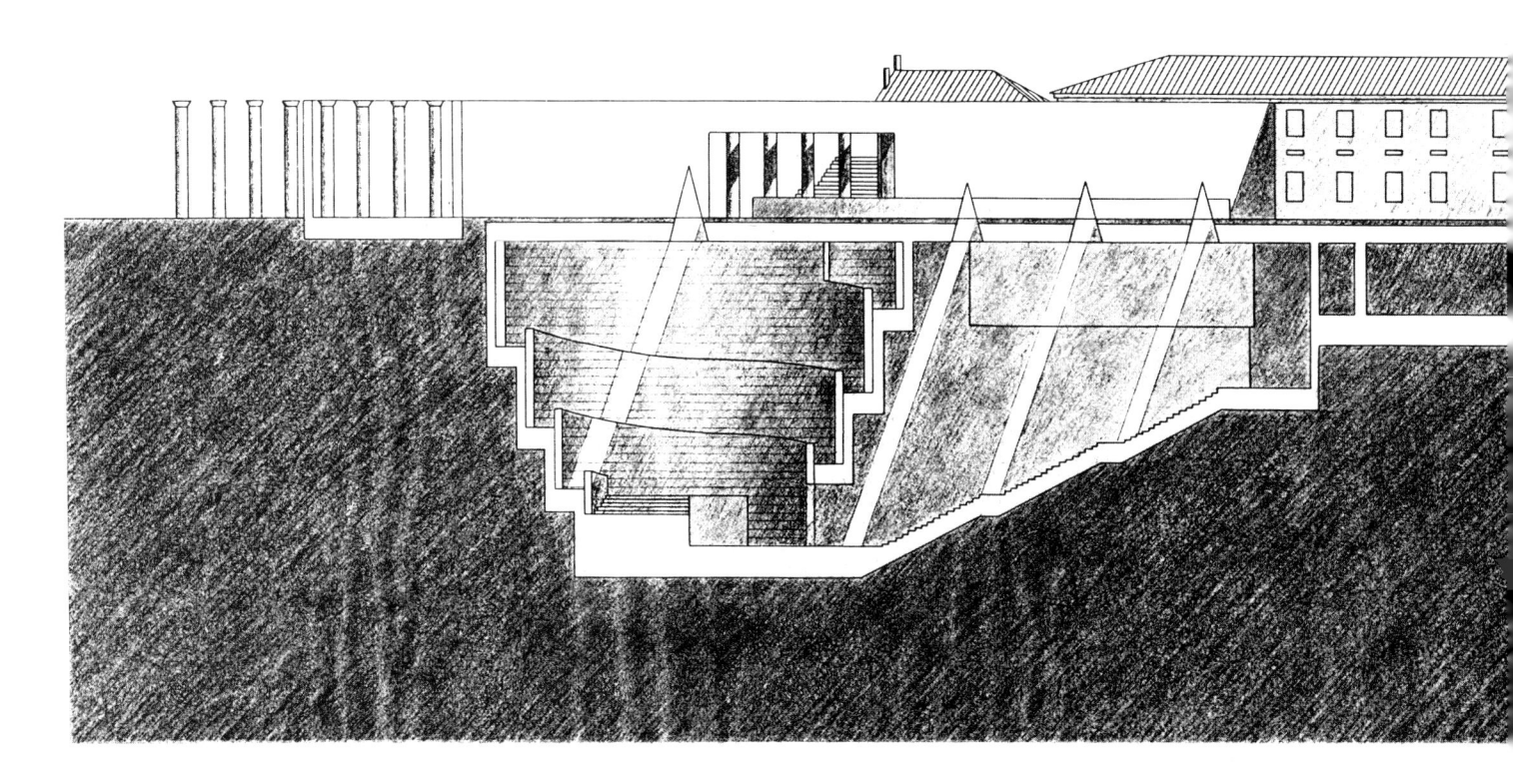

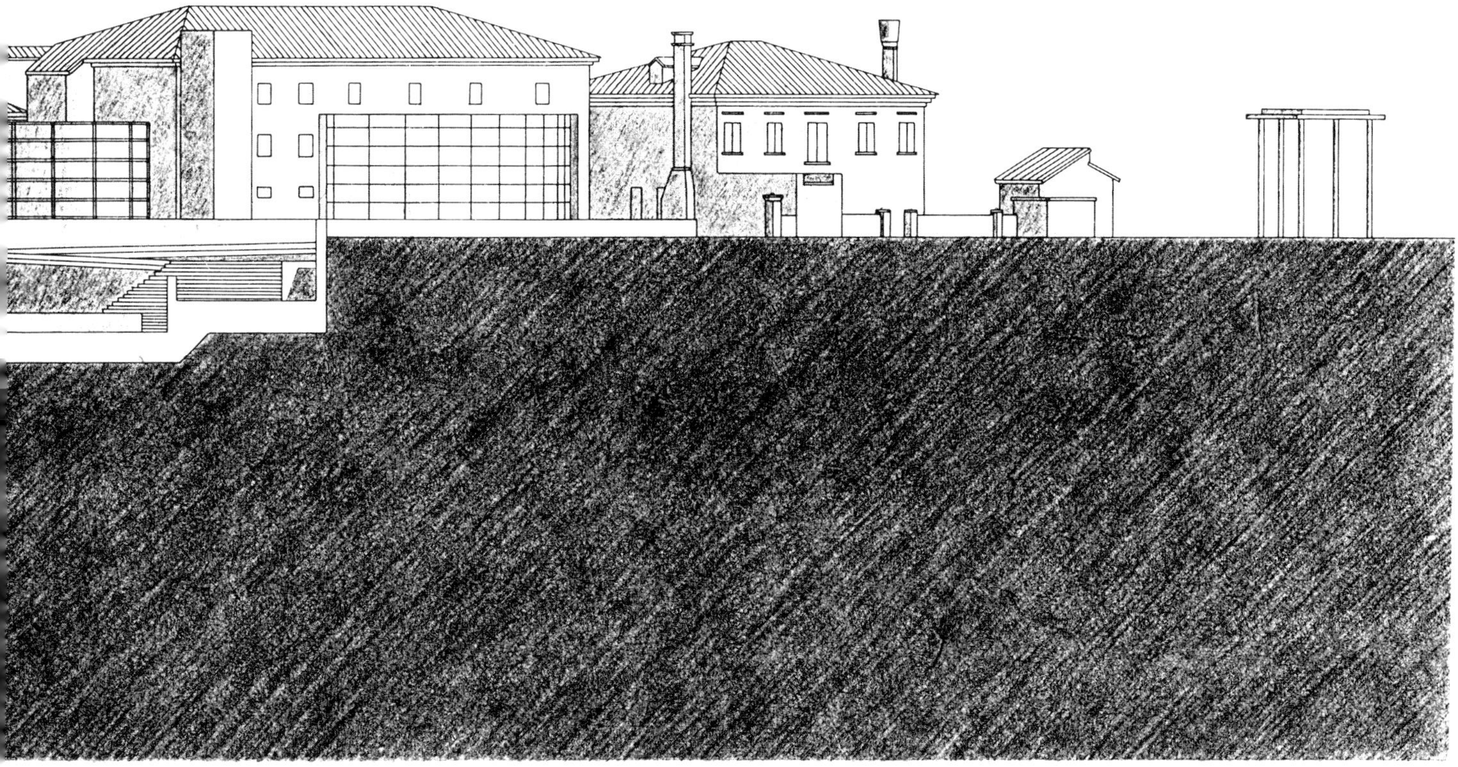

Installation for 'Tadao Ando Architectural Works' Exhibition

View of the model and perspective of the basilica.

Into the large hall of a Palladian basilica several elements have been introduced to create varied routes through the exhibition. Four voided cubes, located at the centre of the hall, emphasize the two axes of the exhibition space; these also contain the exhibition itself. A long wall, parallel to the main elevation of the basilica, separates the exhibition from the circulation spaces. Finally, two wide stairways between the cubes and the hall's perimeter wall enclose while at the same time lead the visitor to and from the exhibition.

Location Vicenza, Italy
Design 1994
Construction 1994

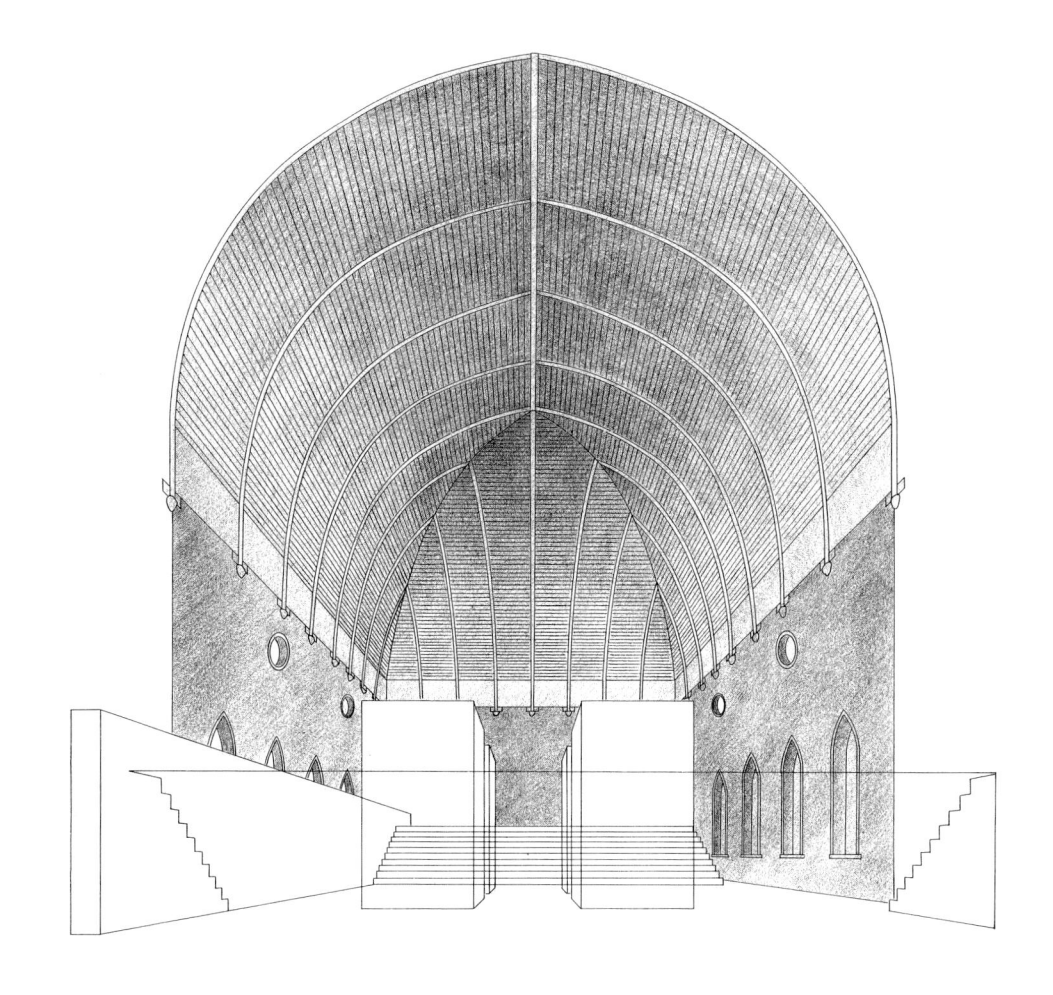

Conceptual sketch, plan and section.

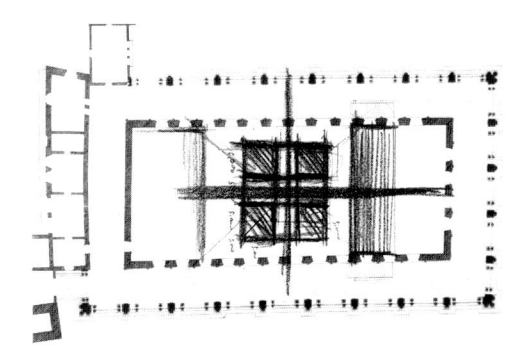

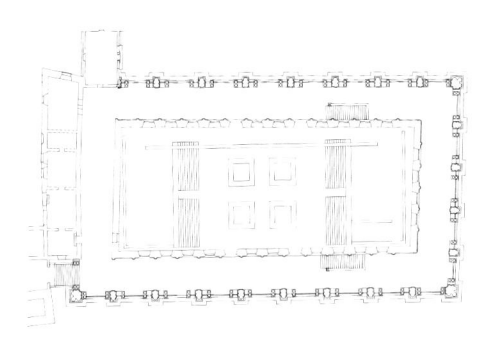

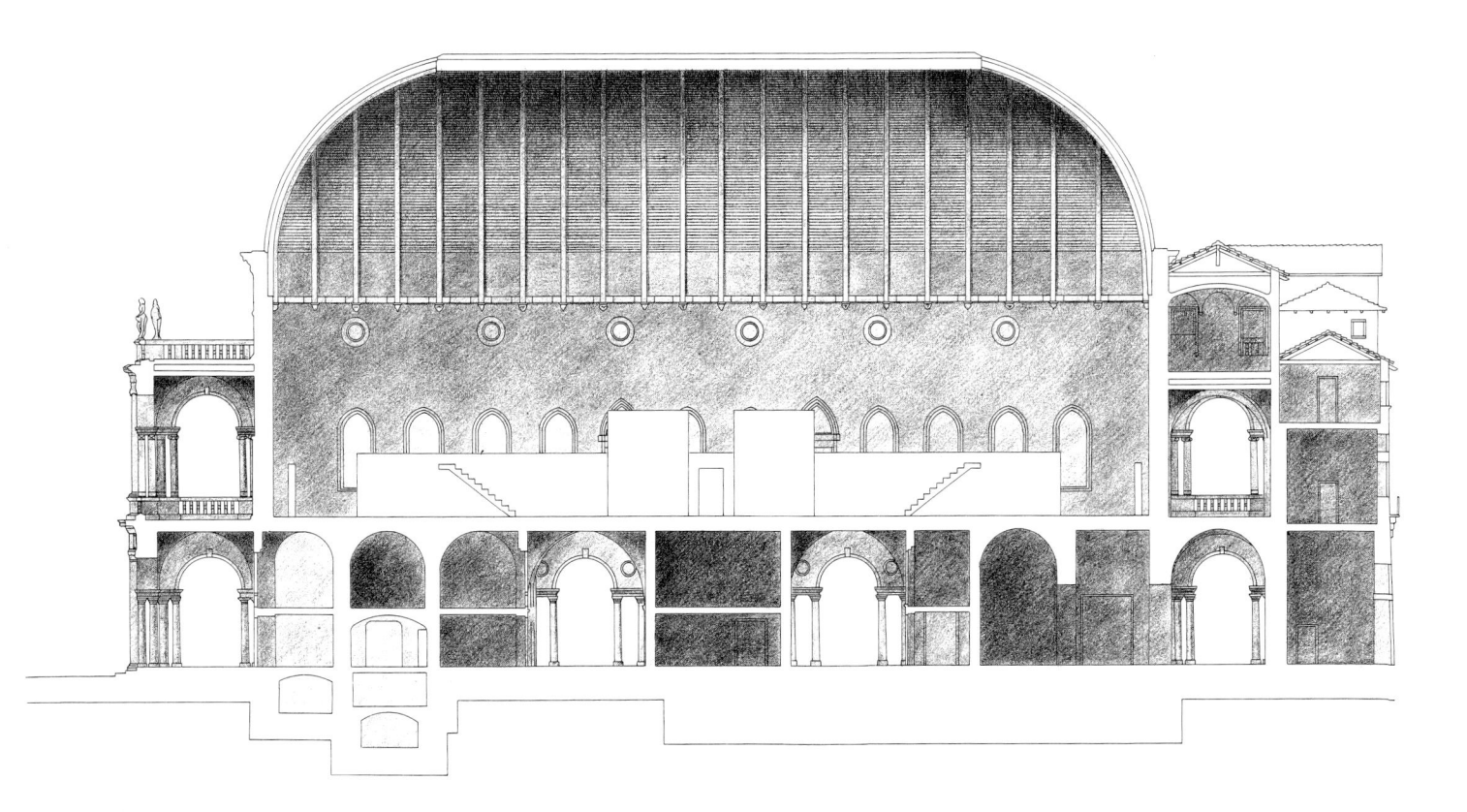

Writings by Tadao Ando

Editorial note: The majority of the following texts are edited versions of previously published writings. Sources for the texts are given at the end of each piece.

A Wedge in Circumstances

On the surface, my architecture may look like abstract space trimmed of all humanity and function, and any other aspect of daily life. This is because the spaces in my work are naked. I am not attempting to produce spatial abstractions, but spatial prototypes. My spaces are the emotional expression of various people rather than an intellectual operation. I wish to create prototypes because I wish to make my work into a long investigation, which is continuously developing. This attempt justifies the life of someone who builds buildings. My approach to the person who will be using these spaces amounts to that of an intermediary in an in-depth dialogue between the user and the architecture; my spaces transcend theory and appeal to the deepest spiritual levels. In other words, my spaces relate to fundamental aspects of humanity.

It may be true – as Gaston Bachelard says – that all architecture has a basically poetic structure and that the fundamental structure of spaces cannot be given a physical manifestation. But since the circumstances of the environment in which we work are absurd and since we can only vaguely understand our own existence, we hope to infuse architecture with a sense of the actual by coming into contact with the deepest aspects of human nature.

Two features are characteristic of my work: a use of limited materials, which have their textures exposed, and an ambiguous articulation of the function of space. I believe that these attributes enable me to produce effective spatial prototypes. The strong nuances of simple materials and their textures emphasize simple spatial compositions, and thus provoke an awareness of a dialogue with natural elements such as light and wind. In all of my works, light is decisive in forming space.

The lack of clear functional articulation does not arise from connections with the exterior, since the spaces are almost completely enclosed. My reason for adopting this method is always related to the desire to inspire internal vistas within the individual which correspond to spaces that the individual harbours within himself. For this reason, I emphasize the indefinite parts related to human emotion and to the interstitial zones between functionally established spaces. I call this spatial prototype the *emotionally fundamental space*. Once it has been created, I follow this procedure to sublimate it into a symbolic space. I do not submit to this process for the sake of creating spaces. Instead, I am aiming for architecture that symbolizes and includes spaces for modern daily life. By doing this, I hope to create social meaning and mutual feelings with the user of the space on a fundamental level; the acquisition of social meaning by a work of architecture does not signify the participation of the architect in social movements, nor does it relate to the general understanding of architecture. Architecture is a one-time thing. Only through architecture is it possible for the architect to create social relations. In other words, the only way an architect can endorse his own independence is to drive one wedge in after another into any given situation.

No matter how dramatic the space is in itself, I believe that it must not be cut off from the daily life of the occupants. Examples of the way in which I think the emotional space and the symbolic everyday-life space ought to fuse include the so-called alleyway in the Kyoto-style townhouse and the earthen-floored entranceway in the traditional Japanese farmhouse. Though the dimly lit alleyway is spatially wonderful, it also serves as a link to the shop at the front of the townhouse with the residential zone in the rear. The earthen-floored zone in the farmhouse is simultaneously symbolic and functional, since it is the place in which cooking is done and where farm-related work is carried out at night when daytime labour in the fields has ended.

Although I consider any emotionally fundamental space extraordinary, I feel that it must have meaning for everyday ordinary affairs. The meaning may be functional. It may be related to such technical matters as lighting and ventilation, or it may be important from the standpoint of the distinctive lifestyle of the occupant. But, if the meaning is related to function and techniques, it must not be fixed in any way, but must vary from case to case according to the requirements of the case in hand. The emotionally fundamental space, which is connected with deep spiritual levels, is unique. For that reason, it offers something fresh to the ordinary spaces, to which it is opposed. It both enlivens these spaces and speaks to the heart of the viewers. However, only when it has meaning on the level of daily life does it result in a structure that includes both space and life. It it only then that the emotionally fundamental space becomes symbolic of daily life.

I create enclosed spaces mainly by means of thick concrete walls. The primary significance of enclosure is the creation of a place for oneself, an individual zone, within society. Society today, like the high-level bureaucracy that represents it, stresses overall structures; the individual is subordinate to society. The same can be said of problems of architecture and the environment. The dullness of our environment reveals how senseless it is to abandon and submerge the self in its surroundings. It seems to me that the only way to produce a living and vibrant environment is for strongly individual entities to aggregate. I first create the wall that will establish the place for the individual and that can express the will to set up relations with society.

From the outset, because of the cruel urban surroundings, we determined to create an individual zone by means of thick walls without openings. When it is impossible to leave a house unprotected from external factors and one has to employ an enclosure of this type, the interior must be especially full and satisfying. It must be the place where the individual can develop even when isolated from the world outside. Special considerations must be taken of livability in urban residences since cities are now attempting to force out residential spaces.

If, as I believe, architecture ought to contain living spaces conducive to the physical and psychological development of the individual human being, I want to create buildings that reveal indications of human life. For this purpose, I must produce things that become supports for the life of the self and that create a sense of existence. In the circumstances under which we live – circumstances in which the things surrounding us fail to speak to us in a convincing fashion – I feel that my attempts in this direction are important. Though it may seem to be arbitrary or prejudiced on the part of the architect, I am convinced that a creative approach that drives wedges into this situation is of great significance. The friction generated in the act of driving these wedges helps the architect become more intensely aware of his circumstances and provides hints for his next development.

T Ando, 'A Wedge in Circumstances', in *The Japan Architect*, 243, June 1977.

The Wall as Territorial Delineation

Tadao Ando, Matsumoto House.

The erection of a single post has the effect of interrupting a scene. Similarly, a single wall severs, interrupts, opposes and violently alters the site on which it is placed; it begins to show signs of evolution into architecture. At the same time, shadows cast on the wall by the leaves of nearby trees can cause the wall to blend with its landscape. Generally, various elements coexist in a series of mutual rhetorical relationships. But in the urban environment surrounding us in Japan today, in spite of an over-abundance of material things, it is difficult to establish such relationships. I believe that the first step to take in revitalizing such an environment is that of reconsidering the basic, primitive significance of the post and the wall.

The post's verticality gives it a symbolic quality which has been traditionally acknowledged in Japanese architecture. For instance, the sacred, non-structural posts that form an important part of the great Ise and Izumo shrines represent a simple kind of religious faith. The massive post called the *daikokubashira* in the vernacular Japanese farmhouse dominates the surrounding spaces. It symbolizes the authority of the head of the house, and the strength involved in supporting the roof over the family. One of the most significant uses of the post is as a definer of space. Another is its establishment of rhythm by means of colonnades, or rows of posts. [...] The colonnade suggests a partition, and its movement is horizontal instead of soaring. The development of the modern rigid-frame structure undeniably liberated architectural spaces, but in giving precedence to function it underplayed the significance of the post.

The rigid-frame system is based on modernization and economic balance. It has robbed the post of its myths and the colonnade of its rhythm. Under such circumstances, the wall emerges as a major theme. I am not attempting to make relative comparisons between the post and the wall or to claim that the wall is in any way superior to the post. Instead I have in mind an operation in which the wall and the post are rhetorically interrelated.

The cheap scrawl and crowded conditions of the modern Japanese city reduce the liberation of space by modern architectural means, and the resulting close connection between interior and exterior, to a mere dream. Today, the major task is building walls that cut the interior off entirely from the exterior. In this process, the ambiguity of the wall, which is simultaneously interior and exterior is of the greatest significance. I employ the wall to delineate a space that is physically and psychologically isolated from the outside world.

As is suggested by their application in the house, I am implying that walls can be used to help break the unlimited monotony and random irrelevance of walls as they appear in the modern urban environment. In other words, I think walls can be used to control walls. In the Matsumoto House, for example, walls which stand independently in the world of nature delineate a territory for human habitation. Inexpressive in themselves, the two major bounding walls are protective devices for the interior. At the same time they reflect the changes taking place in the natural world and help to introduce it into the daily lives of the inhabitants. The limiting operation of the walls directly reveals the boldness of the house itself. [...]

T Ando, 'The Wall as Territorial Delineation', in *The Japan Architect*, 254, June 1978.

From Self-Enclosed Modern Architecture towards Universality

The kinds of houses, apartments and commercial buildings that I have worked on over the past ten years pose problems that take a long time to solve, in proportion to the effort they demand, and are unprepossessing, stimulating little public reaction. Although they undeniably lack the glamour and flair of large architectural projects like theatres, libraries and art museums, buildings of this kind, from the point of view of everyday relations with human beings, represent the basic points around which architecture develops.
Architecture still depends, at a fundamental level, on the forms and methods created by the Modernists. This is especially true in Japan for many reasons. First is the immense gap between life in Japan before and after World War II. I suspect that no Westerner could comprehend the distance between the old-fashioned Japanese way of life and the changes introduced into this country in the postwar period. [...] The result has been that, whereas in the broader current of architectural culture Modernism is a thing of the past, it remains unassimilated in Japan. Still, the Japanese display a strong dichotomy even in this regard. For instance, although they continue to unhesitatingly use the standardized, uniform materials that are souvenirs of Modernism, they vigorously pursue conceptual novelty and as a result ostentatiously display an eccentricity of formal expression that is isolated from both outer and inner human life. [...]
Born and bred in Japan, I carry out my architectural work here. I suppose it could be said that my approach applies the vocabulary and techniques developed by an open, universal Modernism within the enclosed realm of individual lifestyles and regional conventions. It seems impossible to me to try to attempt to explain the sensibilities, customs, aesthetic awareness, distinctive culture and social traditions of a given race by means of the open internationalist vocabulary of Modernism.
Between 1955 and 1960, many attempts were made to link this open vocabulary with the indigenous Japanese tradition of aesthetics and forms. [...] But trying to reproduce in modern materials (concrete and steel) with compatible techniques forms that came into being in relation to Japan's traditional building material (wood) amounted to ignoring the inevitable and fundamental connections between material and form. For this reason buildings making this attempt encountered many difficulties, and before long, ceased to emerge. The contradiction between the unaltered forms of the past and today's lifestyle, which differs so sharply from that of the past, is too great.
After World War II, when Japan launched on a course of rapid economic growth, people's values changed. The old, fundamentally feudal family system collapsed. [...] Overly dense urban and suburban populations made it impossible to preserve the most characteristic feature of Japanese residential architecture: an intimate connection with nature and openness to the natural world. What I refer to as enclosed modern architecture is a restoration of the unity between house and nature, which Japanese houses have lost in the process of modernization.
In my buildings, relations with nature are expressed as a theory of parts. I emphasize the background against which a building comes into being. My architecture is definitely modern. And it demands both an overall compositional theory of a kind that traditional Japanese architecture was unable to generate and a theory providing for the life of the individual parts.
I create architectural order on the basis of a geometry, the basic axis of which is simple forms – subdivisions of the square; the rectangle and the circle. In addition, I attempt to choose from the forces latent in a particular region where I am working, and in this way to develop a theory of parts that is founded on the sensibilities of the Japanese people. [...]
In front of the house where I grew up was a wood workshop, in which I spent a lot of time as a child, where I became interested in trying to make shapes out of wood. [...] With young eyes and a child's sensibility I observed the effects of a tree's environment, and how sunlight could alter the thickness of a tree's growth rings and thus change the tactile qualities of the lumber produced from it. I gained a direct physical knowledge of the personalities of woods, their fragrances and their textures. I came to understand the absolute balance between a form and the material it is made of. My very body came to know how extremely important that balance is. I experienced the inner struggle inherent in the human act of applying will to give birth to a form. In addition, my flesh came to know that creating something – that is, expressing meaning through a physical object – is not easy. Later my interest came to concentrate on architecture, which rendered possible the consideration of intimate relations between material and form, and between volume and human life.
Through experiences instilled in me during my youth, I came to understand these relationships in actual architecture, not only with my mind, but with my entire physical being. From about the age of twenty I began wandering in pursuit of the things that I found present in Japanese farmhouses (*minka*) and townhouses, and in western architecture. For instance, the light filtering through high windows into farmhouses in the snowy north or sharp contrasts of light and shade in the streets of medieval Italian city states, when projected into modern spaces, reveal to me richly real, unadorned relations between architectural space and people.
The aim of my design is, while embodying my own architectural theories, to impart rich meaning into spaces through such things as natural elements and the many aspects of daily life. Such things as light and wind only have meaning when they are introduced inside a house in a form cut off from the outside world. The isolated fragment of light and air suggests the entire natural world. The forms I have created have altered and acquired meaning through elements of nature (light and air), which give indications of the passing of time and the changing of the seasons, and through connections with human life. Although many possibilities for different kinds of development are inherent in space, I prefer to manifest these possibilities in simple ways. Furthermore, I like to relate the fixed form and compositional method to the kind of life that will be lived in the given space and to local regional society. In other words, I select solutions to problems in reaction to the prevailing circumstances. [...]
As I mentioned before, in the late sixties, it was popular to talk about the so-called Japanese style and to use it – in the form of the traditional post-and-beam structure – in buildings constructed of modern materials. Most of these buildings, however, did no more than copy old-fashioned elements like roof forms, deep eaves, lattices and verandas. I prefer not to deal in the actual forms themselves,

Shoji panels at the Katsura Palace and drawing by Tadao Ando of a tea house.

but in their spirits and emotional contents. The spirit of the Sukiya style has stimulated the most varied developments in traditional Japanese architecture. Verbal explanations of the whole nature of sukiya architecture, which evolved to provide places for the tea ceremony (not only a purely Japanese complex of art and performance, but also in itself a concentration of Japanese conduct), are virtually impossible.

On a small scale, Sukiya can refer to a single isolated tea-ceremony house; on a large scale, it can stand for a whole series of fairly elaborate quarters like those of the Katsura Detached Palace. The tea ceremony that resulted in buildings of this kind was popular in the past among people of a high social position. No matter what their sizes, no Sukiya buildings were related to ordinary daily life. In more modern times, the Japanese have developed the tea ceremony into an extremely simple and brief art form, characterized by a highly rational order of execution. And this art form has given rise to a group of extraordinary buildings based on the uncategorizable concept of Sukiya.

Although Sukiya itself is not the property of ordinary people, the aesthetic awareness and emotion evident in it is fundamental to the Japanese people as a whole. Some of the aspects of that aesthetic in architectural terms are low eaves, extended verandas and the delicate combination of the two. The Sukiya tradition takes the loose natural scene and recreates it artificially in a tense composition. It uses shoji panels to contain light, and simultaneously separates and connects the inner and outer garden walls by means of fences.

Both the shoji panels and the fences stand for an interval, separating and connecting at the same time. Intervals of this kind, which demarcate and interrelate elements and scenes, are a characteristic feature, not only of Japanese architecture, but also of all Japanese art, and might be called a symbol of Japanese aesthetics. Their major role is to stimulate anticipation of the scene to come. Parts made independent by intervals interweave and overlap to develop a new scene within the overall setting. This image is deeply rooted in the relationship between the Japanese house and the world of nature. In the past, the house in Japan was at one with nature. Articulation directed the thoughts of the inhabitant outward. This relation with nature is especially deliberately pursued in buildings of the Sukiya style. [...]

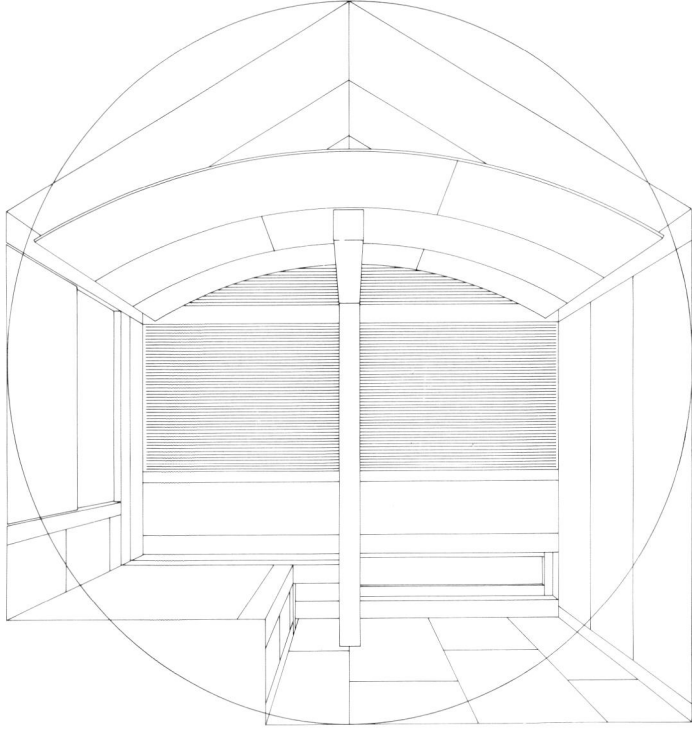

In the traditional Japanese house, the wall does not actually exist. Of course walls were used. But their main aim was not to express the simplicity of the wood, paper, earth and straw of which they were made. According to the traditional Japanese interpretation, architecture is always at one with nature and attempts to isolate and freeze at a point in time nature as it exists in its organic metamorphoses. In other words, it is an architecture reduced to the extremes of simplicity and an aesthetic so devoid of actuality and attributes that it approaches theories of *Ma*, or nothingness. Further connections with nature are effected by the subtle transformations caused in part by delicate contrasts of light and shade. In all these connections it is the wall, made as light and thin as possible, that permits – or perhaps more accurately evokes – space. Openings can be made in the walls of Sukiya buildings, anywhere in accordance with the demands for views from within. Such openings make possible two kinds of time-related alterations of the scene: alterations depending on the time of day, the changing climate, and the seasons of the year and alterations depending on the movement of the human observer. Ironically, however, these alterations isolate individual scenes from time as a current, and brand them as static worlds or isolated moments of time to generate what might be regarded as a peculiarly Japanese form of eternity. The true value of the Sukiya style is to be found in the ways it permits these isolated world to overlap and interweave.

Interiors of Sukiya-style spaces are smaller and lower than spaces in western-style houses. The dimensions depend on the placement of the human body. In sukiya buildings people sit on tatami mats on the floor. This very position transcends the smallness of the spaces. In short, because they are static and enclosed, sukiya spaces make it possible for people in them to exist in limitless mental spaces. Enclosed in small places, people can allow their thoughts to range into infinity. When they do so, at the extreme limit of contemplation, they can hear the voices of nature and travel to cosmic distances. The Japanese interpretation of time and aesthetic awareness is essential to the generation of spaces as condensed as those of Sukiya buildings. Nevertheless, while dealing subtly with parts and their relationships, Sukiya buildings lack a strong orientation towards overall unity. […]

Another traditional Japanese architectural style that attracts me strongly is that of the old-fashioned farmhouse (*minka*). […] These farmhouses have a simplicity of composition evolved through years of struggle and amity with nature, and which reflects a settled and tranquil way of life that is distinctive of people who till the soil. The notion of controlling the composition of the whole building determined the spatial structure and the lifestyle of the large family living together as a group under one roof.

Unlike Sukiya-style buildings, farmhouses had frameworks assembled as spatial totalities that determined everyday life. The simplicity of the inhabitants' way of life accounts for the power of the simple farmhouse's framework. The Japanese view of life embraced a simple aesthetic that grew stronger as inessentials were eliminated and trimmed away.

I attempt to use a modern material – concrete and, specifically, concrete walls – in simplified forms to realize a kind of space that is possible because I am Japanese. This rests on a simple aesthetic awareness cultivated in me as a Japanese person. It seems to me that, at present, concrete is the most suitable material for realizing spaces created by rays of sunlight. But the concrete I employ does not have plastic rigidity or weight. Instead, it must be homogeneous and light and must create surfaces. When they agree with my aesthetic image, walls become abstract, are negated, and approach the ultimate limit of space. Their actuality is lost, and only the space they enclose gives a sense of really existing. Under these conditions, volume and projected light alone float into prominence as hints of the spatial composition.

And this is what gives meaning to a geometric composition. Universal geometric forms clearly determine spaces and elevate an entire piece of architecture in a single direction. People living in spaces formed on the basis of this principle gradually lose superficial awareness of them. The forms transcend their nature as forms and become invisible except in certain instances. The space is the only thing with the power to stimulate emotions. The field of vision in daily life, without taking into consideration the total image of the buildings, expands only through a continuity of parts. Compositional theories are at work as invisible, latent forces. The architectural totality supports the order of daily life; the parts enrich the scenes of daily life and deepen its texture. Space attains a sense of transparency when the current moving from the level of abstraction to the level of concrete, and the current moving from the level of the whole to the level of individual parts flow together and become replete from end to end with a single creative intention.

Spaces of this kind are overlooked in the utilitarian affairs of the everyday and rarely make themselves known. Still, they are capable of stimulating the recollection of their own innermost forms and of stimulating new discoveries. This is the aim of what I call 'enclosed modern architecture'. Architecture of this kind is likely to alter with its locality, in which it sends out roots and grows in various distinctive, individual ways. Still, though enclosed, I feel convinced that, as a methodology, it opens up towards universality.

T Ando, 'From Self-Enclosed Modern Architecture Towards Universality', in *The Japan Architect*, 301, May 1982.

Interior, Exterior

At times walls manifest a power that borders on the violent. They have the power to divide space, transfigure place and create new domains. Walls are the most basic elements of architecture, but they can also be the most enriching.

Historically, walls have had negative associations for many people. The enclosing boundary of a prison immediately comes to mind when one thinks of walls, and they are often perceived as devices that physically and psychologically separate the inside from the outside. Walls are heedless of the inmate's longing to be outside, forcibly keeping him in. To the outside world, the walls of the prison proclaim that the place is for those who are to be shunned. Walls are symbols of separation and have been regarded as a means of closure. Having been relegated to such roles, they have quite naturally been used only to cut off space.

To reject what is to be abhorred and to accept only that which is desirable is very much a part of man's most basic behaviour, that of habitation. It is a central concern of habitation to keep out the external world and to protect the world inside, to accept and assimilate only those aspects of the outside world that promote the maintenance of the inner realm. In other words, habitation depends on the skilful manipulation of rejection and acceptance.

There is generally less tension in the act of acceptance than there is in rejection. To accept is to affirm and with this one tends to put down one's guard. However, if everything is allowed to penetrate into the interior, the internal world disintegrates and its centrality collapses. This results when there is an absence of tension in the act of acceptance. I believe therefore that tension should be as present in acceptance as it is in rejection. In architecture this tension signifies an intense confrontation between the inside and the outside. Thus, those places where the internal order meets the external order, that is, the areas of fenestration in a building, are of extreme importance.

In my buildings, walls play a dual role, serving both to reject and affirm. By positioning a number of walls at certain intervals, I create openings. Walls are freed from the simple role of closure and are given a new objective. They are calculated to accept even as they reject. The amorphous and immaterial elements of wind, sunlight, sky and landscape are cut out and appropriated by walls which serve as agents of the internal world. These elements are assimilated as aspects of the architectural space. This tense relationship between inside and outside is based on the act of cutting (as with a sword), which to the Japanese is not cruel and destructive but is instead sacred; it is a ceremonial act symbolizing a new disclosure. To the Japanese this act has become an end in itself. It provides a spiritual focus both in space and time. In that tense moment, an object loses its definition and its individual and basic character becomes manifest. Walls 'cut' into sky, sunlight, wind and landscape at every instant, and the architecture reverberates to this continual demonstration of power.

The more austere the wall is, even to the point of being cold, the more it speaks to us. At times it is a sharp weapon menacing us. At times it is a mirror in which landscape and sunlight are dimly reflected. Light that diffuses around a corner and gathers in the general darkness contrasts strongly with direct light. With the passage of time these two 'lights' blend and enrich the space. Man and nature, mediated by architecture, meet. Contemporary culture is based on the energy produced by the liberation of the species, originating from the restraint placed on its desires. Once a desire approaches satisfaction, it grows larger and stimulates other ambitions. Man enters a never-ending cycle and becomes dominated by his own excessive desires. What really enriches an individual's life in an age such as ours? It is important to discover what is essential to human life and to consider what abundance truly means. An architectural space stripped of all excess and composed simply from bare necessities is true and convincing because it is appropriate and satisfying. Simplification through the elimination of all surface decorations, the employment of minimal, symmetrical compositions and limited materials constitutes a challenge to contemporary civilization.

Introducing nature into a building has been an important theme in my work since the design of the Azuma House in 1976. A courtyard may draw one's attention to its blank, interstitial quality, but rarely does it have a presence as strong as that of the building itself. I believe that such interstices should have as much significance as the buildings themselves. If a building is to have presence and individuality, its interstices must also be given their intrinsic logic. A building is enriched if these interstices are structured according to a clear design and made meaningful as architectural spaces.

The courtyard in the Azuma House occupies one third of the site and links the inside with the outside. It is a device for appropriating a fragment of nature. By nature I mean not an artificial and domesticated nature, but a true nature that is capable of confronting the individual. Of course, bringing nature into the house tends to make life more severe. However, it was precisely in this way that traditional Japanese townhouses were enriched despite their physically cramped form and spatial impoverishment. Today's residential spaces may be quite comfortable and functional, but a house into which nature has been introduced is more suitable for man and is more true to the basic character of the house. The courtyard is an important place where seasonal changes can be directly perceived through the senses. The expression of nature changes constantly. Sunlight, wind and rain affect the senses and give variety to life. Architecture in this way becomes a medium by which man comes into contact with nature.

I do not believe architecture should speak too much. It should remain silent and let nature in the guise of sunlight and wind speak. Sunlight changes in quality with the passage of time. It may gently pervade space at one moment, and stab through it like a blade at the next. At times it is almost as if one could reach out and touch the light. Wind and rain are equally transformed by seasonal change. They can be chilling or gentle and pleasant. They activate space, make us aware of the season, and nurture within us a finer sensitivity.

T Ando, 'Introduction', in *Tadao Ando. Buildings, Projects, Writings*, New York, 1984.

Facing up to the Crisis in Architecture

Universalization is today a worldwide phenomenon. The dissemination and advancement of civilization has undoubtedly been made possible by making the particular universal, yet universalization is another word for generalization and standardization. It is advantageous to civilization but is antagonistic to culture, since culture comes into being only in opposition to generalization and standardization. Therefore, progressive universalization endangers culture and may even force it into a state of crisis.

I believe that architecture belongs not to civilization but to culture. Architecture comes into existence only against a background of history, tradition, climate and other natural factors. Universalization is threatening to destroy this foundation. Behind the promotion of the universalization of architecture is the idea that functionality equals economic rationality. The principle of simple economic rationality does away with the rich, cultural aspect of architecture. Similar buildings are being constructed throughout the world, and cities are losing their individuality to become ominously monotonous.

Today, strict functionalism is being questioned in architecture, and there are various movements complicating the situation in terms of expression. Post-modernism, which is particularly notable among these movements, sees only one side of Modernism – which is after all the most important legacy of architectural culture of the twentieth century – and capriciously rejects it. It serves no purpose to introduce ornament just because ornament was eliminated by Modernism. If Modernism had an anti-human aspect, it must have been rooted in its fundamental approach to architecture and not in the forms of Modernist architecture. To my mind, post-modernism appears to be just old wine in new bottles, with nostalgic ornamentation applied. I don't believe it provides a fundamental solution. Nevertheless, I acknowledge that the best post-modernist architects are resisting the trend toward universalization.

Universalization does not allow individuality. People, with their diverse emotions and wills, are lumped together and labelled 'the masses' and are deprived of their individual character. They are reduced to units that ease analysis and manipulation. Architectural creation is particularly individualistic work, but the trend today is to divorce production from individuals and to leave the making of things to organizations. Individualistic dreams and emotions that were once such important elements in architecture are being replaced with mediocrity and common sense. Mediocre buildings are going up in cities all over the world.

I believe that, however anachronistic it may sound, it is important to ask the fundamental question, 'What is architecture?' The creation of architecture must surely be a criticism of today's problems. It must resist existing conditions. And it is only when one squarely faces up to today's problems that one can really begin to deal with architecture.

In architecture there are certain social, economic, legal and political constraints. In today's Japan in particular, it is impossible to consider architecture in isolation from construction as an economic activity. However, it is also true that architecture is not solely a matter of dealing with such external conditions. I believe in the autonomy of the ideas of architecture. Architecture as an autonomous set of ideas has in fact nothing to do with the tackling of such constraints. Today, architects no longer tend to think seriously about architecture and are simply kept busy at everyday tasks, treating architecture as just an economic activity, resolving problems posed by external conditions. The organization of society leaves architects with no time to consider an 'architecture of discovery'; at best they can only create 'mistake-free architecture'. This gives rise to an undistinguished architecture.

I believe that architecture must be individualized once more if the standardized and monotonous cityscape is to be transformed into a place of discovery and surprise. We must give flight once again to an architectural imagination based truly on the individual.

T Ando, London, 1986.

Mutual Independence, Mutual Interpenetration   *Tadao Ando, Noguchi House.*

1 There are both aggressive walls and defensive walls. In other words, they can express both violence and rejection. In the series of urban houses I have designed up to now the walls have certainly been aggressive in their appearance and have had an element of violence even in their silence. The walls were intended to question the nature of contemporary society.
2 In my urban houses, multi-storey spaces and courtyards are provided inside closed buildings. The exterior environment is invariably cut off, and a new, separate world is created inside.
3 Walls in urban spaces are fundamentally different from walls of violence and rejection and must seem to flatter the observer at the start. In other words, they must reject while inviting and invite while rejecting. They represent an architecture of betrayal.
4 Passageways must not be closed corridors if intimacy is to be restored between the street and the house. They are invigorated by the mutual interpenetration of the public and private realms. This allows one to sense the life within each unit.
5 A building site is a pool on the river that is the street and the city. It is a room with the sky for a ceiling.

Light and Wind
1 Light adds drama to beauty, and wind and rain through their action on the human body give colour to life. Architecture is a medium that enables man to sense the presence of nature.
2 In my works light is always an important factor in dramatizing space.
3 In the courtyard, nature presents a different aspect of itself each day. The courtyard is the nucleus of life that unfolds within the house and is a device to introduce natural phenomena such as light, wind and rain that are being forgotten in the city.
4 By introducing nature and changing light into simple geometric forms that are closed off from their urban contexts, I create complex spaces. I inject the extraordinary into what is the most ordinary and familiar of environments – the house – and thereby encourage people to reconsider what is ordinary.
5 In the West, there is a kind of sky that is integrated with architectural space; such a sky can be seen when closed places suddenly meet open spaces.

Stamp of the Individual Will
1 The primary landscape is a consciousness concealed in the darkness, a light that gradually fades with depth, a cold tactile sensation, an awesome colonnade in a faintly lit space, and laughter that emanates from among the columns in response to the dim, wavering light.
2 What I can do is to push Modernism a little further and to explore its possibilities – to make use of what it has neglected. Architecture must relate in very specific ways to the city and society and avoid indulging in intellectual manipulations such as historicism or semiotics.
3 In design, it is important for me to balance what is logical with what is illogical.
4 I want my buildings to transcend physical limitations of size. I want people to

ask themselves what dwelling really is about and to awaken in people's bodies a feeling of life.
5 My buildings are characterized by a limited range of materials and the direct expression of textures. As for spatial composition, my spaces are not necessarily clearly articulated according to function.

Field of Force
1 There are many approaches to architecture. However, to the extent that architecture is an important component of the city, architects must fulfil their responsibility to the city.
2 A hillside demands a comprehensive, inclusive approach to sitework, directed toward the creation of a three-dimensional 'emptiness' (*yohaku*).
3 The framed sky generates light and shadow, inspires one to question the meaning of nature, and helps one understand the compositional elements of space. Site-craft becomes the three-dimensional design of land.
4 Japanese architecture developed from the fusion of the man-made and the natural, out of a reading of topography and an awareness of nature. Rapid urbanization prevents architecture from seeking help in nature, and architecture alone cannot create a favourable environment.
5 Within a site, architecture tries to dominate emptiness, but at the same time emptiness dominates the architecture. If a building is to be autonomous and have its own character, not only the building but emptiness itself must have its own logic.

The Will of the Wall
1 Like a fortress built in the desert, a wall is not only a protective barrier but a spiritual bridgehead, clearly asserting its presence in the changing flow of the city and rejecting any preconceived notion of community.
2 A wall tempts one to draw on it, perhaps because it is flat. However, this temptation must be resisted. A wall that has been drawn on is robbed of its material significance. In becoming a sign, it loses its presence.
3 The frame structure of equal span was the basis of Modernism. It robbed columns of their meaning, sacred character and rhythm. That is why walls have come to replace columns as an architectural theme.
4 An enclosing wall is not simply defensive. It is an aggressive wall expressing the strong will of the occupant to dwell in the city. At the same time, it provides a place for the private life that unfolds inside.
5 A wall is the point where the logic of the city meets the logic of the site. It is the smallest and most basic regulator of the urban structure.

Homogeneous and Multi-Layered Landscape
1 Landscape gradually begins to take on a higher, architectural character when columns, walls and individual building elements are arranged so as to be mutually related.
2 My objective may seem to be the creation of abstract spaces from which humanity, functionality and life styles have been stripped because my buildings enclose what appear at first to be naked spaces. What I am searching for, however, is not abstract space but prototypical space.
3 The discrepancy between a highly ordered geometry and man's everyday life gives rise to collisions that help generate new spaces. That is how a building comes to have a clear identity.
4 A homogeneous space created through a structural frame of equal span is the first principle of modern architecture, but my intention is to create spaces that may appear simple at first but are actually far from that – that is, complex spaces that are the result of simplification.
5 Individual spaces, protected yet open, are combined to create a whole. It is not simply a combining of parts, nor are the parts controlled from outside. The individual element is the basis of the design, and the relationship between the individual element and the whole is always considered as the design develops from the inside to the outside.

T Ando, 'Mutual Independence, Mutual Interpenetration', in *Nihon no Kenchikuka*, 6, 1986.

Shintai and Space

Architecture is the art of articulating the world through geometry. However, the world is not articulated as isotropic, homogeneous spaces. It is articulated, not abstractly or homogeneously, but as concrete spaces (topoi) that are each related to a totality of history, culture, climate, topography and urbanity. A 'place' is not the absolute space of Newtonian physics, that is, a universal space, but a space with meaningful directionality and a heterogeneous density that is born of a relationship to what I choose to call *shintai*. (Shintai is ordinarily translated as 'body', but in my use of the word I do not intend to make a clear distinction between mind and body; by shintai I mean a union of spirit and flesh. It acknowledges the world and at the same time acknowledges the self.)

Man articulates the world through his body. Since he has an asymmetrical physical structure with a top and a bottom, a left and a right, and a front and a back, the articulated world in turn naturally becomes a heterogeneous space. The articulation of the world by architecture is in reality the articulation of the world by the workings of mankind.

Man is not a dualistic being in whom spirit and flesh are essentially distinct but a living, corporeal being active in the world. The 'here and now' in which this distinct body is placed is the point of departure, and subsequently a 'there' appears. Through a perception of that distance, or rather the living of that distance, the surrounding space becomes manifest as a thing endowed with various meanings and values. The world that appears to man's senses and the state of man's body become in this way interdependent. The world articulated by the body is a vivid, lived-in space.

The body articulates the world. At the same time, the body is articulated by the world. When 'I' perceive the concrete to be something cold and hard, 'I' recognize the body as something warm and soft. In this way the body in its dynamic relationship with the world becomes the shintai. It is only the shintai in this sense that builds or understands architecture. The shintai is a sentient being that responds to the world. When one stands on an empty site, one can sometimes hear the land voice a need for a building. The old, anthropomorphic idea of the *genius loci* was a recognition of that phenomenon. The point is that what this voice is saying is actually 'understandable' only to the shintai. (By 'understandable', I obviously do not mean comprehensible only through reasoning. Architecture must also be understood through the senses of the shintai.)

In order to perceive an object in all its diversity, the distance between the self and the object must be changed in some way. This change is brought about through the movement of the shintai. Spatiality is the result, not of a single, absolute direction of vision, but of a multiplicity of directions of vision from a multiplicity of viewpoints made possible by the movement of the shintai. Not only the movement of the shintai but natural movement such as that of light, wind, or rain can change the (phenomenal, as opposed to physical) distance between the self and the object. By introducing nature and human movement into simple geometrical forms, I have been trying to create complex spaces. What had been self-sufficient and still, is transformed by the addition of natural or human movement into what is motion, and diverse views are superimposed in the eyes of the peripatetic observer. Order is reconstructed within the shintai through the recognition of differences between the total image inscribed on the shintai by that superimposition and what is immediately and visually apprehended. What I care about is precisely the way in which each person relates to architecture.

The problem with modern architecture lay in the abstract and homogeneous character of its spaces. Such spaces and the shintai simply did not blend. Architecture is given order through abstract geometry and thereby becomes an autonomous existence. However, that order is something essentially different from everyday order. Architecture, though a material presence, is a medium that can take into account factors without palpable form such as climate and history; this is what gives architectural forms their order.

Today, the functionalist approach is being questioned in the architectural world, and various contending approaches to architectural expression are making the situation complex. Post-modernism, which is prominent among these approaches, chooses to interpret Modernism, the greatest architectural heritage of the twentieth century, in a one-dimensional fashion and capriciously rejects it. There is nothing to be gained by simply introducing ornament, just because Modernism rejected it. If Modernism has an inhuman aspect, then the problem lies in its basic ideas about architecture and not in its architectural forms. The problem is to be corrected by the expressive character of architecture and the individual who is the expresser, while at the same time the need for rationality and functionality is satisfied. The distinctive national character and sensibility of each individual are being rejected and everything is becoming homogeneous. Cultural factors that make architecture possible such as history and tradition, and even natural conditions, are being turned into abstractions, and the simplicity (ie uniformity) and mediocrity that are the by-products of a pursuit of economic rationality are dominant qualities of our era. I care not for interesting forms but for the spatiality of forms. Through the medium of simple geometrical forms, I seek to introduce a diversity of intentions and emotions and to take into account intangible factors. My ultimate objective is not expression but instead the creation of symbolic spaces founded on substantiality.

It is as someone whose sensibility has been shaped by a distinctive culture and history that I have in the past concerned myself with architecture, and it is as such a person that I hope to continue to concern myself with architecture in the future. I hope to continue to resist the homogenization of the world. In this the shintai will no doubt provide a key.

T Ando, 'Shintai and Space', in *Architecture and the Body*, New York, 1988.

Representation and Abstraction

Josef Albers, Homage to the Square, *1964*.

I find it difficult to answer the question whether architecture is abstract or representational, for I believe architecture is both.

The word 'abstract' calls to mind the triumphant abstract paintings of twentieth-century art, and I am drawn particularly to the work of the Bauhaus artist Josef Albers whose position with regard to the concept of 'perception' was diametrically opposed to that of the Suprematist Kazimir Malevich. The series by Albers called *Homage to the Square* represents for me the height of modern painting. Albers took up the challenge of depicting the square in a most thorough manner, but it was not just a matter of systematically working out all possible compositional variations. Whereas Malevich had as his objective the absolute purification of the human senses, Albers' method permitted ambiguities of perception. The artist, working within the self-imposed constraints of the square, used distinctive, transparent colours. The observer notes a gentle vibration and expansion in the works and experiences diverse modes of freedom. [...]

What then does representation mean in terms of architecture? For me it is architecture's physical or carnal quality, or, rather, the labyrinthine quality of the body. I am reminded of Piranesi's *Carceri d'invenzione*. Their overwhelming power and extraordinary sense of space have long remained vivid in my memory. These oneiric prisons, so like the trick pictures of Escher, are precisely what I imagine the maze of the body to be.

I choose simple circles and squares for my architectural forms. Just as Albers manipulated squares by means of distinctive colours, I manipulate or make manifest architectural spaces. The result is architecture that has been transformed from something extremely abstract, and constructed according to a rigorous geometry, to something representational and bearing the imprint of the human body. I believe what makes this transformation possible is a labyrinthine quality in the work. A major objective for me is to create an architecture that is simultaneously both abstract and representational by giving simple geometrical forms a maze-like articulation; ie by concealing an imaginary Piranesian maze in a framework like Albers'. I have at the same time another objective, concerning nature as opposed to human reason. Like the maze, nature is an important element endowing architecture with a representational quality. I want to see whether or not these two elements can co-exist, separately yet simultaneously, in a single work. I seek to locate in the midst of nature a building that conceals within it a maze, and to introduce nature into architecture, thereby creating a man-made nature. Like a *basso ostinato*, this theme appears in all my past works, though I may not always have been aware of its presence. [...]

T Ando, 'Représentation et abstraction', in *L'Architecture d'aujourd'hui*, 255, February 1988.

From the Church on the Water to the Church of the Light

Tadao Ando, Church on the Water and Church of the Light.

The Church on the Water is on a plain in the middle of mountains north-east of the Yubari Range in Hokkaido. Covered with snow from December to April, the area becomes a beautiful white expanse of land. Water has been diverted from a nearby river, and a man-made pond 90 x 45 metres has been created. The depth of the pond was carefully set so that the surface of the water would be subtly affected by the wind, and even a slight breeze would cause ripples.

Two squares, one 10 metres to a side and the other 15 metres, overlap in plan and face the pond. Wrapped around them is a freestanding L-shaped wall in concrete. Walking along the outside of this long wall, one cannot see the pond. It is only on turning 180 degrees at an opening cut out at the end of the wall that the pond is seen for the first time. With this in view, one climbs a gentle slope and reaches an approach area surrounded on four sides by glass. This is a box of light, and under the sky stand four separate crosses. The glass frames the blue sky and allows one to look up the zenith. Natural light pervades the space, impressing on the visitor the solemnity of the occasion. From there one descends a curving, darkened stairway leading to the chapel. The pond is spread before one's eyes, and on the water is a cross. A single line divides earth and heaven, the profane and the sacred. The glazed side of the chapel facing the pond can be entirely opened, and one can come into direct contact with nature. Rustling leaves, the sound of water, and the songs of birds can be heard. These natural sounds emphasize the general silence. Becoming integrated with nature, one confronts oneself. The framed landscape changes in appearance from moment to moment. […]

In designing a number of chapels I have thought about sacred space. The question I asked myself was what is sacred space to me. In the West, a sacred space is transcendental. However, I believe that a sacred space must be related in some way to nature. Of course this has nothing to do with Japanese animism or pantheism. I also believe that my idea of nature is different from that of nature-as-is. For me, the nature that a sacred space must relate to is a man-made nature, or rather an architecturalized nature. I believe that when greenery, water, light or wind is abstracted from nature-as-is according to man's will, it approaches the sacred. The Church of the Light, now under construction, represents an effort to architecturalize or abstract in the above sense the natural element of light. Space is nearly completely surrounded by substantial concrete walls. Inside is true darkness. In that darkness floats a cross of light itself. That is all there is. Outdoor light that has been architecturalized and rendered abstract by the opening in the wall imparts tension to the space and makes it sacred.

T Ando, 'From the Chapel on the Water to the Chapel with the Light', in *The Japan Architect*, 386, June 1989.

Materials, Geometry and Nature

Piranesi, Interior View of the Pantheon *and* Carceri d'invenzione, (fig XVI).

I first experienced space in architecture inside the Pantheon in Rome. It is often said that Roman architecture generally has a more spatial character than Greek architecture, but what I experienced was not space in a conceptual sense. It was truly space made manifest. The Pantheon of course is composed of a semi-spherical dome of a 43.2 metre diameter, placed on top of a cylinder with the same diameter. The height of the building is also 43.2 metres, so that the structure may be said to be composed around a huge spherical volume. It is when this structure is illuminated from an oculus nine metres in diameter at the top of the dome that architectural space truly becomes manifest. A condition such as this of matter and light cannot be experienced in nature. It is only in architecture that such a vision is encountered. It was this power of architecture that moved me.

There is another western space vivid in my memory: the space in the imaginary structures of Piranesi, found in the elaborate maps of the Roman empire and the famous engravings of imaginary prisons in which he must have expressed his own sense of alienation from reality. In particular, his interiors of prisons, which embody that quality we have come to call Piranesian, made a powerful impression on me. The space of traditional Japanese architecture is extended in a horizontal direction. However, the three-dimensional, maze-like prison of Piranesi has the verticality of a rising spiral stairway.

The geometrical order of the Pantheon and the verticality of Piranesian space are in marvellous contrast to traditional Japanese architecture. Japanese architecture is markedly horizontal and non-geometrical, and hence characterized by irregular spaces. It is, in a sense, an architecture without form. Architecture is integrated with nature, and space is seemingly adrift. The Pantheon and Piranesian interiors, because they are in complete contrast to Japanese architecture, represent for me western architectural space. It seems to me that my work has long had as its objective the integration of these two contrasting spatial concepts.

I believe three elements are necessary for the crystallization of architecture. The first is authentic materials, that is, materials of substance such as exposed concrete or unpainted wood. The second is pure geometry, as in the Pantheon. This is the base or framework that endows architecture with presence. It might be a volume such as a Platonic solid, but it is often a three-dimensional frame because I feel the latter to be a purer geometry. The last element is nature. I do not mean raw nature but instead domesticated nature – nature that has been given order by man and is in contrast to chaotic nature. Perhaps one can call it order abstracted from nature: light, sky and water that have been rendered abstract. When such a nature is introduced into a work of architecture composed, as I have said, of materials and geometry, architecture itself is made abstract by nature. Architecture comes to possess power and becomes radiant only when these three elements come together. Man is then moved by a vision that is possible, as in the Pantheon, only with architecture.

T Ando, 'Materials, Geometry and Nature', in *Tadao Ando*, London, 1990.

Spatial Composition and Nature

A site always has a distinct field of force that affects man. The field is a language, yet not a language. The logic of nature affects one subjectively, and becomes clear only to those who seriously attempt to perceive it. Architecture is ultimately a question of how one responds to these demands made by the land. In other words, the logic of architecture must be adapted to the logic of nature. The aim of architecture is always the creation of an environment where the logic of nature and the logic of architecture are in fierce conflict yet co-exist.

Architecture is not simply the manipulation of forms. I believe it is also the construction of space and, above all, the construction of a 'place' that serves as the foundation for space. My aim is to struggle first with the site and thereby get a vision of the architecture as a distinct place. The inside and the outside of architecture are not separate things but instead form one continuous place. Architecture ought to be seen as a closed, articulated domain that nevertheless maintains a distinct relationship with its surroundings.

In order to bring out and make apparent the invisible logic of nature, one must oppose it with the logic of architecture. It is at this point that geometry comes in. Geometry is a kind of game of axioms and deductive reasoning. However, it is also a symbol – one possessed of autonomy and a pre-established harmony – of human reason, which transcends nature. Ever since Vitruvius, the use of the figural attributes of geometry – for example, simplicity, regularity, repetition and symmetry – has stamped architecture as a product of human reason, in other words, the opposite of nature.

Geometry, despite its non-arbitrary character, or even because of it, serves to concentrate diverse meanings and takes on a distinct significance. Geometry forms not only the framework for the whole but fragments of scenes. It can be simultaneously a frame for a view of the surroundings and a screen. It can be a passageway that makes people walk, stop, ascend or descend. Moreover, it can be closely related to the articulation of light. It can appropriate light, concentrate shadows behind an object, and determine the distribution of spatial density. The site, having undergone this process, becomes something that stands in opposition to yet co-exists with the architecture. I believe architecture becomes oriented only when this happens, not only in its parts but as a whole.

T Ando, 'Composición Espacial y Naturaleza', in *El Croquis*, 44, 1990.

Light, Shadow and Form

Light gives objects existence as objects and connects space and form. A beam of light isolated within architectural space lingers on the surfaces of objects and evokes shadows from the background. As light varies in intensity with the shifting of time and changes of season, the appearances of objects are altered. But light does not become objectified and is not itself given form until it is isolated and accepted by physical objects.

Light attains significance within the relations among objects. In the instant when one of those fluid relations is fixed, all relations are determined. An instant of light is simultaneously the instant of that light's own extinguishing. At this boundary between light and dark, the individual object is articulated and given shape.

When objects are articulated in this fashion, mutual relations are established among them, and a chain of elements comes into being. Nonetheless, since the tendency towards generalizations is always concentrated within the individual element, this chain is the realization of a whole, permeated with the aesthetic awareness existing in the inner world of a single human being.

My interpretation of all relations as determined by the interaction of light and dark is based on my own spatial experiences. One very important experience was a visit I once made to a medieval monastery. The building was of rough stone masonry, and the treatment of the openings was totally devoid of ornament. But the interior was imbued with a feeling of great power. In the deep silence of the place, I was aware of something penetrating, something transcending the severity of religious precepts. And, in spite of differences between West and East, I sensed a connection between that something and the mood pervading a Japanese tea ceremony room.

Light patterns and overlapping relations between them and various parts of the design were very important to traditional Japanese architecture, which actually can come into being only through the establishment of mutual relations among parts made possible by light changing with the passage of time. In Zen Buddhist thought, space is said to come into being at the boundary where material things vanish. In this Zen context, space is non-existence. In size and expression, the traditional tea ceremony room is a microcosm revealing this boundary on the edge of vanishing. A person sitting silent and contemplative in such a space has the feeling of experiencing limitless size within the interplay of light and dark.

The combination of East and West within me is an accurate illustration of the Japanese cultural structure. Japan has created a distinctive culture by importing and assimilating elements from other countries. Today, however, there is a tendency to submerge our distinctiveness so that much that is particular to the Japanese is being lost. I believe that the time has come for us, while continuing cultural overlapping with the West, to re-evaluate our own indigenous tradition. In my opinion, one important thing being lost from modern Japanese culture is a sense of the depth and richness of darkness. As we grow less aware of darkness, we forget spatial reverberations and the subtle patterns created by light and shade. When this happens, everything is uniformly illuminated; and object and form are limited to simple relations. The remedy to this situation is a restoration of richness to space. To give expression to my own spatial experience and thus to make something distinctive of it, I employ a geometry of simple, inorganic shapes.

In this process, I attempt to go beyond purely intellectual operations and discover an important drive for relations with human nature as a whole.

Some time ago, while in the United States, I was astounded by the freshness of wooden furniture made by the Shakers. It inspired in me an awareness of the significance of 'form-mode.' Based on symmetry, the proportions of the shapes were good. The mood of the pieces was simple and reserved and exerted a restraining and ordering effect on the surroundings. Technically, the furniture was rationally made with no waste of any kind. Part led inevitably to whole, generating the kind of strength of will characteristic of the lifestyle of the manufacturers. In the great diversity of modern times, to experience objects representing an extreme simplification of life and form was very refreshing.

Although they are essentially very different from the normal regularity of daily life, geometric principles both give order to architectural form and serve as a mediator in making architecture a material representation of an intangible theory of life. Introducing the processes of nature and human movement brings dynamism to architecture that has acquired self-control and tranquility as a result of the imposition of geometric order. The eye of the person walking through spaces ordered in this way encounters various overlapping scenes. The discrepancy between the overall image resulting from the accumulation of these scenes and the things that can be comprehended visually reassembles the spatial order within the mind of the beholder. With this assimilation of the spatial order, geometry as such gradually recedes from awareness, and the space alone provides emotional stimulus. The whole supports the order, and the parts have an enriching effect on each individual scene within the whole.

Dialogue with materials is the main support of attempts to fix in actuality the spaces I wish to create. I hope to imbue each material with the intent of the whole and then to select details. The way I employ it, concrete lacks sculpturesque solidity and weight. It serves to produce light, homogeneous surfaces. The traces of regularly attached shuttering and separators are finished to produce smooth surfaces and sharp edges. I treat concrete as a cool, inorganic material with a concealed background of strength. My intent is not to express the nature of the material itself but to employ it to establish the single intent of the space. When light is drawn into it, cool, tranquil space surrounded by a clearly finished architectural element is liberated to become a soft, transparent area transcending materials. It becomes a living space that is one with the people inhabiting it. The actual walls cease to exist, and the body of the beholder is aware only of the surrounding space.

My aim is to limit materials, simplify expression to the maximum, eliminate all non-essentials, and in the process interweave in my spaces the totality of the human being. By reducing style to the utmost, I hope to produce a maximum effect of equilibrium. In the course of natural change, within simplified forms, a multilevel accumulation of complex scenes unfolds. To achieve this effect, it is necessary to return to the point where the interplay of light and dark reveals forms, and in this way to bring richness back into architectural space.

T Ando, 'Light, Shadow and Form: the Koshino House', in *Via*, 11, 1990.

Tadao Ando, interior views of the Koshino House.

Nature and Architecture

Society today is becoming increasingly information-oriented, and architecture too is becoming a piece of information. The value of architecture as information cannot be ignored. However, the worrying tendency is to emphasize only that aspect of architecture and to concentrate on how to attract people's attention. As a result, the value of architecture as a material object is given little weight, and much is made of flashy buildings designed to look good in photographs. Architecture is closely related to the economy and society, and is affected by rapid social changes. In Japan in particular, the tendency is to regard a building as something that can be demolished in a few years, partly because of the high land prices.

Modernism, which reached its peak in the late 1950s, began to be questioned, because of its functionalism and economic rationalism, as post-industrial society gave way to information-oriented society. Various movements such as a narrowly-defined post-modernism appeared. However, post-modernism has remained superficial in its objectives, using, in a nostalgic way, simplistic allusions to historical forms and the ornamentation that had once been rejected by Modernism. It has only dealt with architectural forms and has not offered a true solution to the problem that confronted Modernism. Post-modernism is today moribund, appropriated as it has been by the mechanism of consumption. [...] The time has come to re-examine the Modernism that was once rejected because of its monotonous homogeneity and to reconsider its basic approach to architecture. To generalize is to treat people as quantities. It is to call individuals with emotions and wills the 'masses' and to ignore their separate identities; they become nothing more than units to be measured. To generalize in architecture once meant to espouse functionality and economic rationalism. Unlimited generalization endangers culture because one aspect of generalization is standardization. If the principle of economic rationalism is allowed to supersede the cultural value of architecture, cities worldwide will be full of uniform buildings. If culture is not to be sacrificed for the sake of advances in civilization, basic questions such as 'what is architecture' must be asked, even if they seem somewhat anachronistic. The creation of architecture is the work of individuals and takes place in a context of history, tradition, and climate. It belongs to culture rather than to civilization. The making of architecture is being increasingly entrusted to organizations rather than individuals. Computers are being introduced and everything is being quantified. The dreams and passions of individuals that are so important to architecture are being replaced by mediocrity and convention.

Architecture not only mirrors the times; it must also offer criticism of the times. It represents an autonomous system of thought. To think architecturally is not merely to deal with external conditions or to solve functional problems. I am convinced that architects must train themselves to ask fundamental questions, to give free rein to their individual architectural imaginations, and to consider people, life, history, tradition and climate. We must create architectural spaces in which man can experience – as he does with poetry or music – surprise, discovery, intellectual stimulation, peace and the joy of life.

T Ando, 'Natur und Architektur', in *Tadao Ando. Sketches*, Zeichnungen, Basel-Berlin-Boston, 1990.

The Traces of Architectural Intentions

Tadao Ando, conceptual sketch for the Church of the Light.

During the process by which an architectural idea is realized as a building, the whole and the parts enter into a tense relationship which persists until all work is completed. This relationship of tension provides the context for architectural details; details are the traces left by an architectural idea as it bridges the gap between the whole and the parts. It is out of the complications encountered in this process that the most appropriate details for a building emerge. The intention is to create details that activate one another and take on life.

All materials in this world have already been given recognized meaning. However, the design of architecture is not simply a matter of projecting that meaning onto a building. It is only when one has perceived the essential nature of the subject to hand that one is able to shape and refine the form that matter will take. The more profound one's idea, the more thoroughly will form be crystallized. Only this approach will make the process of creation apparent. However, there is considerable distance between logic and substance, or between form and material in architecture. In my case, what closes that gap is my own aesthetic sense. It is that sensibility which brings architecture into existence, making subtle adjustments in the building's relationship to function and maintaining the autonomous character of material and form.

Architectural details are not just matters of technical treatment or arrangement. In designing, the point of departure is a search for an architectural logic that will permeate the whole, and eventually one always returns to that starting point. Within that cycle, the relationship between the whole and the parts, and between materials and forms must be considered. I believe it is important to be sensitive to the weight, hardness and texture of materials and to have an intuitive grasp of the technical limits in their fabrication. Above all, the architect must define his own vision with respect to technology. Without precise individual aims, the architecture will become subject to the economic logic and banal conventions that dominate technology. Technology is nothing more than knowledge. The architect's intentions and ideas control knowledge; these are more essential.

Drawings are a means of communication among people concerned with architecture. At the same time, they represent a system of signs that breathe life into matter. The intentions of the designer therefore ought to be stamped on the drawings, without which architecture would be impossible. [...]

The orthodox method of architectural drawing is the projection of three-dimensional architectural space onto two dimensions. This is a time-tested method but it is by no means ideal since architectural spaces, which involve the relationship between planes, cannot be understood completely from two-dimensional descriptions. I like having the sum of my intentions condensed into and expressed in one drawing; I overlap plans, sections, perspectives and axonometrics; and occasionally insert into a plan a drawing at a different scale in order to indicate a detail. The interrelationship of parts that makes up an architectural space can be understood only when such drawing methods that have a three-dimensional quality are combined, ultimately leading to an understanding of the whole.

T Ando, 'The Traces of Architectural Intentions', in *Tadao Ando: Details*, Tokyo, 1990.

From the Periphery of Architecture

A stream called the Isuzu River flows through the compound of the Ise Shrine. I find the sight of its pure current very moving and beautiful. Revisiting the river brings back memories I had almost forgotten in the intervening years. Gazing at the long continuous wall that rises from the surface of the water to the level of the eye is strangely relaxing. Perhaps it is because that wall by the water endures even as nature undergoes change and time passes in a never-ending flow.
Water has the strange power to stimulate the imagination and to make us aware of life's possibilities. Water is a monochromatic material, seemingly coloured yet colourless. In fact, in that monochromatic world there are infinite shades of colour. Then, too, water is a mirror. I believe there is a profound relationship between water and human spirit.
The plans of my early buildings were all symmetrical, as if they had been reflected on water. With time, the symmetry of the plans was gradually relaxed, and thinking about it now, I feel that may have been caused by the profound influence traditional Japanese architecture has had on me. When I was young, I often went to Kyoto and Nara and visited old Japanese buildings such as works of Sukiya architecture and *machiya* (townhouses). However, when I began my practice, I looked to the West for my architectural models and believed that to create works of architecture was to design western buildings. I rejected traditional, Japanese-style architecture. Nevertheless, I have always remained conscious of it. Wherever I steep myself in foreign, particularly western, architecture, the sight of traditional Japanese architecture for some reason is deeply moving to me. I am made aware once more that there are many wonderful buildings in Japan. Traditional Japanese architecture offers many answers with respect to man's relationship to nature – a relationship that is very troubled today. Consequently I have been thinking recently of studying traditional Japanese architecture once more. Such thoughts first come to me on journeys. It is more important that I learn things through my own body and spirit than through books. I can better see the circumstances and the Japanese cultural context in which I live when I am in a far-off foreign country, and at the same time I am exposed to the culture of that country. In effect by going abroad I become closer to both Japan and that foreign country, and the things inside and outside me intermingle and stimulate each other. Ever since I was young, my approach has been to try to understand things through my own body and spirit and to make that understanding my starting point. My wish is to create buildings that I myself would find interesting to experience. By an 'interesting' building I mean a stimulating work that in some way is contrary to, that is, *betrays* one's expectations.
I have tried to create works that betray the expectations of the people who experience my spaces. For example, a work that seems symbolic or symmetrical on the outside will turn out inside to be asymmetrical, or what appears simple on the outside will be spatially complex inside. I feel that the greater the complexity of an apparently simple spatial arrangement, the more effective and interesting it becomes. The greater the divergence between the space as experienced and the rigorous geometry of the architecture, the more stimulating the work is to people. I want to create, through the drama of betrayal, unforgettable spatial experiences that affect in a profound way the human spirit.

For me, architecture continually swings between extremes and takes definite shape only when I will it to do so. It oscillates between inside and outside, West and East, abstraction and representation, part and whole, history and the present, past and future, and simplicity and complexity. It never occupies one fixed position. Perhaps that is because I am afraid to seal inside something singular that which is a complete whole. It is a fear that I experience even when designing individual buildings. Even when I am confident in my decisions, I find myself beset subsequently with second thoughts. I am subject to a tension in which confidence and insecurity are blended. In creating works of architecture I continually waver between such extremes. The greater the amplitude of these swings during the process of design, the greater the dynamism apparent in the finished product.
Cultural conditions today are in a sense closed. In architecture in particular, the historical and regional aspects of culture have been rendered abstract and in their place those qualities founded on economic rationalism, namely simplicity and mediocrity, have become dominant. Everything is made on the basis of functionality and rationality, and homogeneous spaces lacking in individuality are taking over. The homogeneous spaces of the modern era are a product of the single-minded pursuit of functionalism. Space is being extended indefinitely, people are being drawn to huge structures, and the distinguishing features of space are being erased. Places are being made abstract and diffuse in character. They are being robbed of humanity, and the result is the condition that has been described as 'the loss of the centre'. Architecture is becoming a product. On the other hand, a powerful economy is enabling many architects to realize wilful designs, particularly in this country. When architects don't curb expressions of their individuality, the human and urban contexts are forgotten, and architecture becomes merely acts of self-indulgence. My architecture has as its premise the idea that we must somehow get out of this predicament.
I hope always to be sensitive to social movements and trends in architecture, but I am not swept along by them. Instead, I only assimilate what is truly useful to me from the great mass of available information. In the last twenty years, various architectural movements have come and gone. What have they left us with? Post-modernism and deconstruction were critical of Modernism which had pursued uniformity and homogeneity. However, post-modernism looked at only one aspect of Modernism, and in reaction evoked the styles of the past. It ended up being a superficial debate about which forms were more interesting. And the deconstruction movement, which aimed at dismantling the language-centred culture of the West, must be discussed within the context of western culture, and its relevance for the Japanese must be carefully re-examined. Over the last twenty years, as various architectural movements rose to prominence, I continually asked myself the question, what is it about certain works of architecture that is so deeply moving? I have come to the conclusion that I must understand architectural issues not through abstractions but through my body and spirit if I am to attempt to open new architectural horizons.
My architecture is based on the compositional methods and forms of Modernism, but I place importance on place, climate, weather, and the historical and cultural background to each situation. I want to rediscover in each given set of

Tadao Ando, Rokko Housing and Time's Commercial Centre.

circumstances the starting point of architecture. In other words, I want to integrate dynamically two opposites, abstraction and representation. Abstraction is an aesthetic based on clarity of logic and transparency of concept, and representation is concerned with all historical, cultural, climatic, topographical, urban, and living conditions. I want to integrate these two in a fundamental way. What appears on the surface may be geometrical abstraction. However, inside there must be much that is representational, and specific problems must be resolved. As abstraction enters into a relationship with representation, the compositional method and forms also become unique. Architecture exists in conflict between abstraction and representation. Into the relationship another element, nature, is introduced, which occupies a different plane from that of abstraction and representation. Architecture is not just the manipulation of forms but the establishment by man of place. Geometry condenses the various meanings that attach themselves to architecture. Nature in the guise of light, water, and sky – introduced into the basic architectural form ordered through geometry – oscillates between abstraction and representation and produces an architecture that is something of both. The greater the distance between abstraction and representation, the more forcefully is nature introduced and the more dynamic is the overall work of architecture.

Much was discarded in postwar houses in the name of rationalism: contact with nature, a real sense of life, the rays of the sun, the flow of the wind, and the sound of the rain. I do not want to discard these things that speak directly to the body and spirit. I want to create living spaces that are simple shells on the outside and labyrinthine inside, into which nature is introduced and in which people can really feel that they are living. For example, the Azuma House, a row house in Sumiyoshi, is divided into three parts, with the middle portion occupied by a courtyard. I wanted to create a microcosm centred on that courtyard. One enters the house and feels secure, but then one notices beyond that space an open courtyard. To enclose an outdoor space inside a building is contrary to common sense. To have an outdoor space where one would expect the indoors is to reverse space and to make space discontinuous. By the tenets of modern architecture this is preposterous and quite inconvenient. However, the discontinuity allows nature into the house. The building remains a simple box, but nature and human movement alter the architecture in complex ways. To harbour spaces of great complexity in compositions that are geometrical and simple is to provide the unexpected and to stimulate a person's consciousness. In the end, the simple box proposed by Modernism is by itself nothing but a simple box. I want to enrich architecture by introducing complexity into that simple box. I did not coolly analyze what I was doing at the time, however, and it was only later that I realized what I wanted to do. At the time I was absorbed in my work. I learned many other things in the process of creating the truly minimalist Azuma House. For example, I found that nature, that is, sunlight and the sky, gave to the inorganic concrete a much richer appearance. The house became the starting point for my subsequent work in everything from space to materials. It is a small building but many things have been put into it. I want to create intense yet quiet buildings where the voice of their creator can be heard.

In Japan it is common practice in developing land to destroy nature and to create

Tadao Ando, Children's Museum and Raika Headquarters.

terraces, thereby eliminating undulations. As a result, the site becomes characterless. I believe that to make the site homogeneous is to discard something that is valuable for architecture. The commission for Rokko Housing I came just when I was crystallizing such thoughts. I decided to use that opportunity to reconsider once more the relationship between building and nature. On my first visit to the site, I found that the 60-degree slope afforded a wonderful view of Osaka Bay. I wanted to make full use of the special character of that place. That was when the concept for Rokko Housing emerged. I decided to keep the building height low, to have the structure hug the slope, and to integrate the architecture with the lush surrounding greenery. In that way, each unit was given a terrace on the roof of an adjoining unit, and the ocean was visible from each unit.

Here too I wanted to restore what had been rejected by Modernism. At first I wanted to create a simple gridded frame. People often think mistakenly that the gridded frame is the orthodox expression of a homogeneous space, but in reality it is not central to the ideas of Modernism. To achieve a homogeneous space in which boundaries are removed and there is infinite horizontal extension, Modernism sought to erase the meaning that attached itself to columns by converting them into an abstract, homogeneous grid of points. My treatment of the gridded frame is different in that I attempt to give meaning to the frame. What I learned then made me more aware of the whole issue of Modernism and provided the key to the subsequent Rokko Housing II. I was also considering, at a time when uniform apartments were being mass produced in Japan, what non-uniform housing might be like. A major issue for me is whether or not architecture can be made to be both abstract and representational. Rokko Housing II is my most completely developed solution to date in that regard. The overall composition is nothing more than simple volumes made up of square, gridded frames, but in fact various types of units are arranged in complex fashion. To abide by only one logic makes architecture monotonous and uninteresting; this is a major fault to which Modernism is susceptible. I want to create buildings that seem simple in composition but have in fact a rich, labyrinthine quality. The paintings of two different artists, Albers and Piranesi, come to mind. In the series called *Homage to the Square*, Albers, who continued the ideas of the Bauhaus, limited himself to the square and in the single-minded pursuit of that figure achieved the freedom to express that which is universal, eternal and essential. And the *Carceri* of Piranesi are for me truly complex images of the labyrinths of the flesh, and I can still vividly recall their overwhelming power and sense of space.

I worked on the design of Time's after Rokko Housing. The issue of contextualism was then attracting interest. A concern for context leads to an interest in linking architecture to the site in a fundamental way. The traditional culture of Japan cannot be discussed apart from the natural beauty of the four seasons in Japan or the geographic and topographic characteristics of the country. Architecture is the introduction of an autonomous object into the site, but at the same time it is the designing of the site itself. It is the discovery of the building that the site desires. The structure of the city within which the site is located is also important. The ways of life and customs of people from the distant past to the future lie concealed there. Architecture is the act of discovering these things and bringing them to the surface. I want to capture, not the things that appear as forms, but the invisible, formless things, namely the ways of thinking and feeling that lie hidden beneath those forms, and to employ them in a new context and to give them life. In a traditional tour garden of Japan, such as that of Katsura Detached Palace, the rooms of pavilions are situated around natural features, particularly water. At Time's, I wanted to achieve a three-dimensional circularity with the Takase River as the centre. I arranged the building so close to the river that visitors can dip their hands in the water. The building is intended to make visitors more aware of the city's history and cultural tradition so that they will look on Kyoto not just as a sort of museum. I was also interested in seeing how forms that were thoroughly geometric and simple might be related to elements that were representational or traditional, and how the strength and beauty of concrete blocks might be expressed.

Even rational architecture, when closely examined, is revealed to be irrational. Not everything can be accounted for reasonably. I feel that the things that cannot be completely explained or described in fact are valuable to architecture. In the case of the recently completed Children's Museum, I put a great deal of effort into the design of a special outdoor space (which I call 'landscape'). Up to now society has not allowed the building of things that cannot be explained in terms of functionality. However, I want to show that there are things in society that cannot be explained just in functional terms. I wanted to create a place where children, who today tend to play very little, could contend with nature. There is practically no play equipment as such. The children are exposed to nature, that is, released into the landscape, as much as possible, because I feel that children ought to discover games by themselves. There is a long wall that cuts across the greenery, but it is roofless. I have provided functionless columns and walls because I wanted the architecture to allow people to live animatedly in nature. I feel this irrational quality is important. The Modernism of the past became insipid because it rejected such irrationalism.

I was designing the Raika Headquarters Building at the same time as the Children's Museum, and given this opportunity to design office spaces, I thought about what it meant for people to work. Offices tend to be designed on the basis of functionality and rationality. Moreover, the current trend towards intelligent office buildings is reinforcing this tendency. If one goes beyond the beautiful surface finishes and the convenience of these buildings, one finds office spaces that are still based on functionality and economic rationalism and aimed at making people work efficiently and increasing productivity. However, people are not just components to be plugged into functional spaces but creative, active beings. I believe that from now on the idea that work is a part of life will be important in offices. There ought to be buildings in which function is produced or surrounded by excess. I want to create places that encourage creativity and increase human energy. This may be difficult to explain rationally. The headquarters building is centred on a cylinder with a huge atrium inside it, and there are various multi-storey spaces in the office areas. On top there is a roof garden. These features may seem wasteful, yet such spaces represent the extra margin of space that will encourage communication between people. I also wanted to try to embody in my own work the ideals, that is, the five 'points', of Le Corbusier in the 1920s: *pilotis*, roof garden, continuous horizontal windows, free plan, and free facade. [...]

Too much contemporary architecture is designed in direct response to the demands of society. Instead of responding directly to such demands, I want to learn what the fundamental issues are and to consider their essential character. Then, after getting functional feedback, I want to design what is really needed. That is because the creation of architecture must be simultaneously an act of criticism. One then begins to clearly understand the framework of the conceptual basis of architecture. The strength of one's concepts determines, I think, the longevity of one's architecture. Perhaps it does not matter how pretty the details are or how beautiful the finish is. What is important is the clarity of one's logic – that is, the clarity of the logic behind a composition and the consistency with which that logic is applied. One can call it spatial order or the quality that one recognizes through reason, not perception. What is important is transparency – not the transparency one associates with superficial beauty or a simple geometrical quality but the transparency of a consistent logic.

Then I introduce nature into a building based on such a transparent logic. Nature in the form of water, light, and sky restores architecture from a metaphysical to an earthly plane and gives life to architecture. A concern for the relationship between architecture and nature inevitably leads to a concern for the temporal context of architecture. I want to emphasize the sense of time and to create compositions in which a feeling of transience or the passing of time is a part of the spatial experience. They must appeal to the sensitivity of the person who undergoes that experience. The best Japanese gardens are not static but dynamic. One clearly sees subtle changes taking place from moment to moment, from season to season, and from year to year in such things as the moss, the trees, or the birds that come to the garden. There is life in the parts, and these parts together breathe new life in the whole. When I look at a garden that like an organism is never complete but instead exists in time, I wonder if I cannot create buildings that live – that is, buildings that are adrift in time. In a sense, real buildings require the creator to halt his process of thought at some point and to complete them. It is difficult to introduce the concept of time. However, I want to try depicting the parts while suggesting the whole, and capturing the moment while giving glimpses of eternity.

A number of facilities for children are currently being built around the Children's Museum. I would like to see the facilities scattered throughout the rich natural environment with its verdant hills and beautiful waters. Nature in the form of wind, water and sun animates an architecture ordered by geometry. Elements that are all different overlap and integrate and strike a sympathetic chord in visitors. I would like to continue to create buildings that can enter into such a dialogue with people.

T Ando, 'From the Periphery of Architecture', in *The Japan Architect*, 1, January, 1991.

The Power of Unrealized Vision

Tadao Ando, Shibuya Project and the Naoshima Contemporary Art Museum.

Once the norms of an era collapse, there emerges the illusion that everything has become possible. And then all things abruptly decline into endless barrenness. The creators of architecture today are like travellers roaming a boundless desert. Once they enjoyed the luxury of simply following the beaten track; now they find themselves in an uncharted, desolate land with no guideposts in sight. Perhaps it should be said that in any era and in any field of endeavour, this is the sort of realm a creative person inevitably works in. Anyone who hopes to navigate its expanse and eventually re-enter charted territory has to constantly place imaginary markers before him as he goes. Only with an intense commitment to architecture can an architect sustain the vision of the track that propels him forward.

For an architect, creator in a barren land, building structures is the projection of his strong commitment to the future. What matters most is the intensity of that commitment as reflected in the architecture. Only when a building opens up a new world does it provide truly fresh stimulation. Indeed, a fundamental requirement of architecture is its enduring capacity to stimulate the human spirit. Still, the stronger the architect's zeal the more likely he may be to deviate from the framework of realistic conditions. Or rather, the more likely society may be reluctant to accept a truly stimulating plan. If that plan is not realized, or even *because* it is not realized, the architect's thought moves even deeper and further towards some new projection of his commitment.

The Okamoto Housing project of 1976 was a plan that held such a meaning for me. In that building I tried to materialize through a simple grid a complex, labyrinthine space. I was determined to reincarnate the complex, ambiguous human being within the ideal of Modernist architecture with its simple, orderly forms; to achieve a somewhat abstract, geometric responsiveness within organic nature. Unfortunately, due to technological difficulties, legal problems, and economic constraints, the plan had to be abandoned. The architectural ideas forged at that time were realized several years later in the Rokko Housing project, and then developed further in multi-storied form in Rokko Housing II.

The Shibuya Project of 1985, too, represented my strong desire to insert into the context of an exhausted modern city a lively culture-oriented space. That desire was realized in the Nakanoshima Project, which consisted of a museum, conference hall, music hall and other facilities to transform the island of Nakanoshima in Osaka Bay into a zone of culture and the arts. Without a specific client, there was no possibility of the Shibuya Project materializing; it all started simply because of the intensity of my yearning.

Even if an architectural plan is not translated into reality, the architect's idea projected at the future should endure. It is certain to surface at some later time or some different place. Looking back on unfulfilled plans, I know that all the ideas were a source of energy that kept me continually moving forward. It is probably into such unmaterialized 'architecture' that I myself, who conceived it, am most sharply etched.

T Ando, 'The Power of Unrealized Vision', in *SD-Space Design*, 333, June 1992.

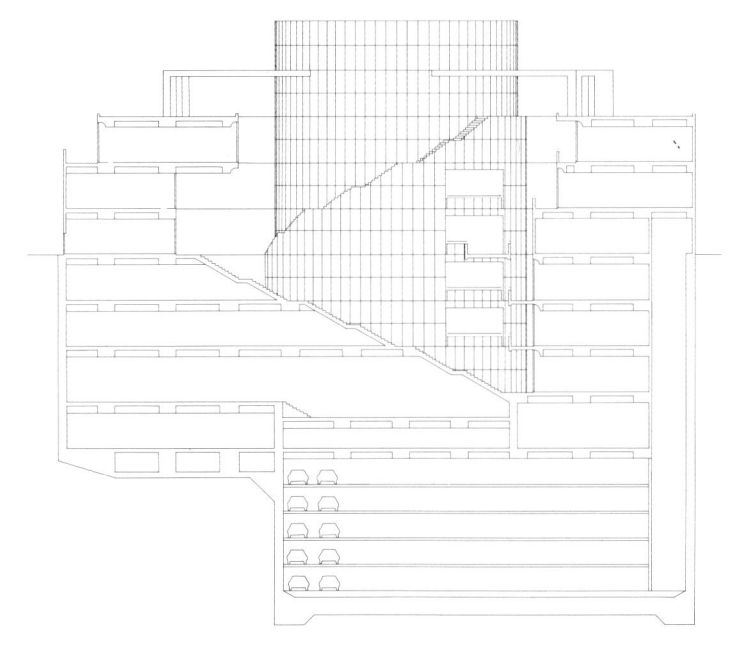

Sensibility and Abstraction

Mies van der Rohe, Friedrichstrasse office building project, Berlin.

Every expressive act is a refinement of what is sensed to its essential nature: opening, through the power of reason, new horizons and manifesting as-yet-unknown time and space. […]
The innovative character of Marcel Duchamp's *Fountain*, for example, could only derive from solid logical thought, replete with intuitive discovery and caustic irony. Or, there are Josef Albers' squares, which, in a contrary manner, speak through their intensity the plenitude of tremulous sensibility in the depths of Albers' logic.
In architecture, then, this strength of logic that carries forth what is sensed might be characterized as geometric power, or the activity of geometrization. And this is none other than abstraction. By abstraction, of course, I mean to signify no mere eliminative simplification of the concreteness embraced by the real world; for this would only result in diminishing the richness of the real. Indeed, by taking abstraction for a process of popularization, Modernist architecture succumbed to deterioration. It is my intention instead to meditate on the essence of the real, in order to organize, purify and universalize this essence, and deliver it to manifestation as a lucid, crystallized order. This is the true character of abstraction; and it was the subjection of this essential abstraction to relentless experimentation that marked the radical spirit of the early Modernists. The fact that even today Mies van der Rohe's glass skyscrapers, drawn in the 1920s, still retain their gleam testifies to their having taken abstraction and geometrization not as an ultimate goal – not as style, in other words – but as an experiment in thought aimed at abstracting an essential spirit transcending the times.
I subject to abstraction the elements of nature – water, wind, light, and sound. In bringing nature's vital energy to a crystallization within an austerely composed architectural order, I confront people with its presence. Out of this confrontation startling encounters between people and nature are born, and a tension is evoked that can awaken the spiritual sensibilities, still covetous of sleep, in contemporary humanity. Through architecture that transcends being a mere product of conceptual thought, I want to give nature's power a presence in contemporary society and thereby provide the kind of stimulating places that speak directly to man's every sense as a living, corporeal being. Moreover, retrieving from history's strata not form or style but the essential view of nature and life that runs through its depths – the spirit of a culture, in other words – I want to put this into dialogue with the present and even project it as far as possible into the future. In this way layers of depth can be added to the society of the future. When this happens, architecture, rather than withdrawing into form, will emerge to resonate sympathetically with its environment and times, and revitalize the natural and city landscape.

T Ando, 'Probing, Through Sensibility, Every Manner of Phenomenon', in *Tadao Ando: Beyond Horizons in Architecture*, Tokyo, 1992.

In the Japanese Pavilion at Expo 92, Seville

Tadao Ando, Japanese Pavilion, Expo 92, Seville

When I built this wood structure, people asked somewhat surprised, 'why did you build it in wood?' This was an honest reaction to my use of a material other than concrete after having designed concrete architecture for so many years.

Although building material is an element which creates space, I believe that material alone cannot be an architect's theme. Concrete is not my theme; rather, I am concerned with spaces enveloped in concrete. Similarly, when I make wooden architecture, the main issue is not the material wood, but the space that wood carves out, as well as an aesthetic sensibility about wood.

In the belief that at international expositions the architecture of the pavilion itself introduces one's culture more than the exhibits inside, I attempted to express Japanese culture, Japanese people's aesthetic sense, or consciousness, in wooden architecture. I felt I wanted to show the culture of wood and the beauty of the post in Europe, a culture of stone and walls. I find one source of Japanese culture in the Ise Shrine, which was first built in the seventh century. In this simple and severe architecture, set in thick forest, surrounded by giant cryptomeria trees, the powerful will of human beings to create is expressed in a primitive form. In this shrine is an austere and forceful aesthetic, distinct from the delicate beauty that the Japanese have pursued for the past several centuries. At the Ise Shrine, two identical sites are prepared next to each other, and the buildings are reconstructed every twenty years. If there is a quest for immortality here, it is the eternal longing of the Japanese for purity, symbolized in the ritual of reconstruction (*shikinen sengu*) which gives birth to completely new buildings every twenty years – an immortality distinct from that of the stone architecture of the West. Twenty years is said to be the span over which the special techniques for the shrine's construction can be effectively transmitted, at the same time that it is the span of time that white wood can be maintained untreated. There is a solemn strength, brevity and abstraction in the use of wood at Ise, entirely different from the vocabulary of tea houses.

I wished to adopt this kind of thinking in the context of new ways of expression in the Japanese Pavilion at Seville. I wanted to pursue free expression in a space enclosed by materials restricted basically to wood both inside and out, and build a rich environment in which the strength of the pillar would come forth. For this, the texture and colour of materials could not be ignored. Traditionally, the living space of the Japanese has been built with many natural materials, and the colours of the materials themselves have been admired. I believe that the colours of nature – of wood, earth and stone – can be reduced to monochrome. Building consistently with concrete over the years I came to think in terms of finding richness and recognizing depth in this seemingly dull world of monochrome. The same is true in building wooden architecture. I am seeking my own roots in the monochrome world of Japanese living space and in the Ise Shrine's strength of abstraction.

The aesthetics of Japanese architecture are frequently described through the contrast of the seventeenth-century architecture of the Nikko Toshogu Shrine and Katsura Detached Palace, but I believe it is also possible to interpret Japanese architecture in terms of the two poles of pre- and post-Sukiya style. While Sukiya architecture expresses its richness in the artifice scattered throughout its details, architecture prior to the Shoin (sixteenth-century) style in which Sukiya architecture has its roots, seeks rather the elegance of freedom within essentially one composition method, or one form – that is, within limited bounds. There is an appeal to a powerful spirit in the spatial volumes, for instance, or in the control of light, and in changes and contrasts of light and dark. The essence of Sukiya architecture, on the other hand, might be said to rest on subtle control of nature, concentrating its modes of expression more on surfaces. The architecture of the tea house is the archetypal example. The tea house is a dense space, in which the thoughts of the designer are reflected everywhere and the life of the designer dwells in every detail. This aspect of craftsmanship in the architecture of Sukiya has exercised enormous influence on contemporary Japanese architecture and is of great significance. Looking at it in another way, I think one could say that although the forms are completely different, there was a Sukiya character to the flood of different post-modern styles that appeared in the 1980s, particularly in post-modernism as it developed in Japan. Perhaps more significant still is to recognize what resulted from the tendency in this period to formal game-playing, devoid of the original spirit of Sukiya.

In the consciousness of contemporary Japanese, wood architecture is definitely represented by Sukiya and the tea house. Against this background, for me, the issue of building wood architecture and the point of greatest interest, is continually how to combat this orientation of awareness toward surfaces and details that is a characteristic of our internalized Sukiya sensibility, in order to return to the origins of wood construction, and draw from them a leaner, more forceful contemporary expression.

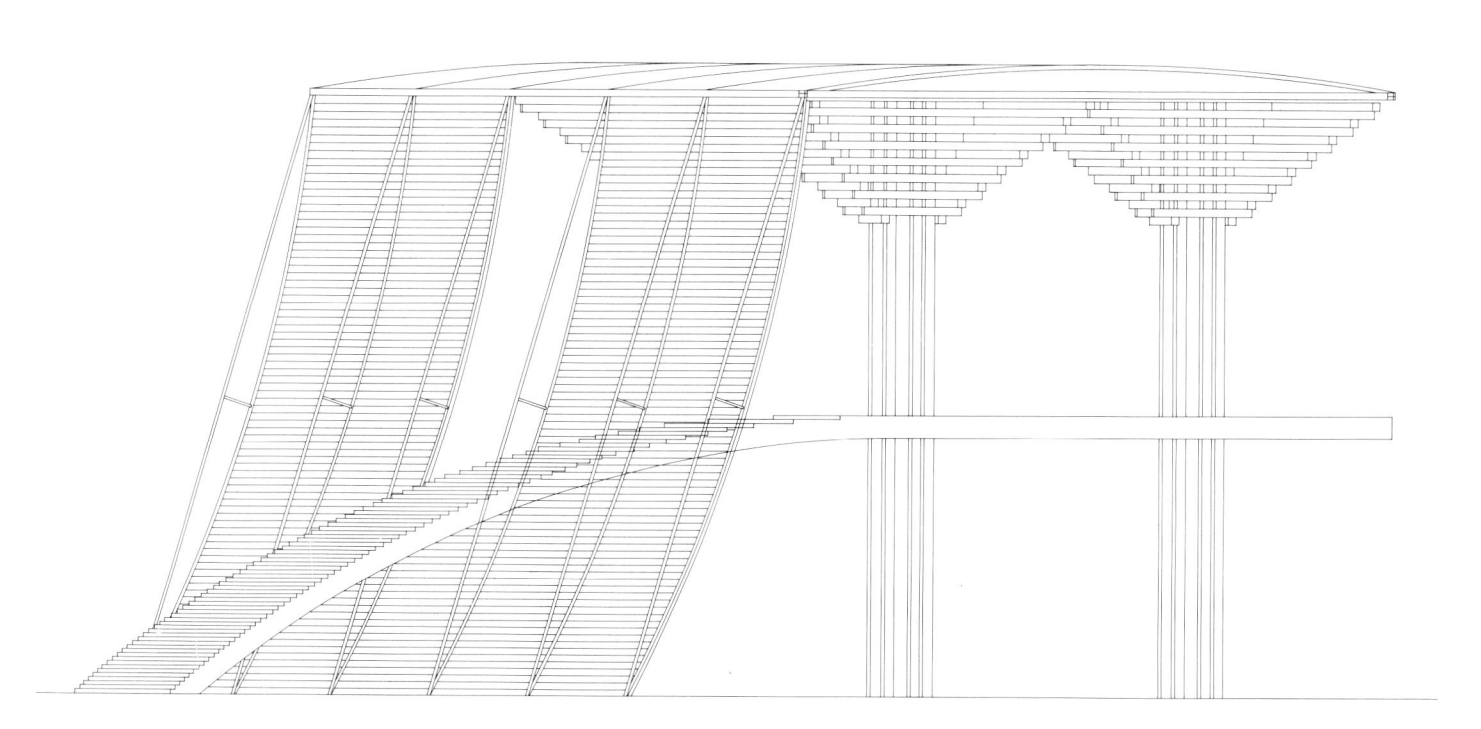

Light

Tadao Ando, Church of the Light.

Light is the origin of all being. Striking the surface of things, light grants them an outline; gathering shadows behind things, it gives them depth. Things are articulated along borders of light and darkness, and obtain their individual form, discovering interrelationships, and become infinitely linked. Light grants autonomy to things and, at the same time, prescribes their relationships. We might even say that light elevates the individual to distinction in the context of its relationships. Light: the creator of relationships that constitute the world; yet although the origin of all being, it is by no means an immobile source. Light is, rather, tremulous motion – out of its ceaseless transformation, light continually re-invents the world.

Architecture – which endeavours to slice off some of this omnipresent light, and sustain its presence in a fixed place; which has sought, through the ages, to carefully ensnare this light with all of its vitality intact – is it not that which purifies the capabilities of light, bringing light to our consciousness? Light gives, with each moment, new form to being and new interrelationships to things, and architecture condenses light to its most concise being. The creation of space in architecture is simply the condensation and purification of the power of light.

Such perceptions as these of the relationship of architecture and light are not so much constructed from ideas, perhaps, as they are drawn from the layers of spatial experience that have been etched into my physical being. Experiences, say, of Japanese architecture – the tea house, for example, where space is partitioned simply by means of paper, stretched over a delicate wood frame. Passing through such a partition, light quietly diffuses into the interior, to mingle with darkness, producing a space informed by monochromatic gradation. Japanese architecture has traditionally endeavoured, by means of its sensitive technology, to break light down to its individual particles. The subtle changes it achieves at the level of tremulous energy bring space almost imperceptibly into being.

Western architecture once used massive stone walls to partition the interior from the exterior. Windows, let into walls so thick as to seem a rejection of the outside world, were small and severely constructed. Such windows, almost more than they allowed light to enter, shone with intense brilliance, as if they were the very embodiment of light. They expressed, perhaps, the fundamental desire of man, inhabiting the darkness, for light. The brilliance of a shaft of light, penetrating the profound silence of that darkness, amounted to an evocation of the sublime. Windows were made, not for visual entertainment, but purely for the unmediated penetration of *light*. And light that pierced the interior of architecture produced a space of solid, resolute construction. The severely built openings caught the movement of light with precision. Space was carved – like a sculpture in the making – by a line of light that pierced the darkness, its appearance altered with each successive moment.

In modern times, architecture has liberated windows from structural limitation, allowing them to be freely constructed in any size. But instead of resulting in the liberation of light in architecture, the vitality of light has now been allowed to scatter ineffectually, and be lost. Modern architecture has produced a world of exceeding transparency – a world of homogeneous light, bright to the exclusion of all else, and devoid of darkness. This world of light, halation-like in its diffusion, has meant the death of space as surely as absolute darkness.

For ancient man, light performed as a measure of time. Powerful rays of light, projected onto the land by the vastly distant sun – light that varied in direction, angle and intensity, depending on the place, the season and the time of day – gave fundamental form to man's sense of space. This light, drawn through openings into the interior of his built structures, enabled man, who dwelt inside, to understand his own being, relative to his surroundings.

From medieval to pre-modern times – in both Japanese and western architecture – light required cautious handling in response to a considerable variety of constraints. As a result, one was readily made aware, in the interior of architecture, of the relationship that bound man and nature. Today, the expanse of technological potential has rendered architectural lighting effortless and devoid of sensitivity, with the result that one is no longer made to feel the individual character of places. Indeed, with artificial lighting, one is not even conscious of one's relationship with nature.

For such reasons, I view as profound the role of natural light, which can speak to us – at any point in our built environment – with remarkable immediacy of 'place' and 'time'. Through precise inquiry and detailed attention, I seek to lead light into the interior of architecture in a manner that will inform space with depth, and produce richly stimulating places.

Light, alone, does not make light. There must be darkness for light to become *light* – resplendent with dignity and power. Darkness, which kindles the brilliance of light and reveals light's power, is innately a part of light. Yet, the richness and depth of darkness has disappeared from our consciousness, and the subtle nuances that light and darkness engender, their spatial resonances – these are almost forgotten. Today, when all is cast in homogeneous light, I am committed to pursuing the interrelationship of light and darkness. Light, whose beauty within darkness is as of jewels that one might cup in one's hands; light that, hollowing out darkness and piercing our bodies, blows life into 'place'. It was space constructed of such light as this that I sought, for example, in Church of the Light. Here, I prepared a box with thick enclosing walls of concrete – a 'construction of darkness'. I then cut a slot in one wall, allowing the penetration of light – under conditions of severe constraint. At that moment, a shaft of light sharply fractures the darkness. Wall, floor and ceiling each intercept the light, and their existence is revealed, as they simultaneously bounce back and forth among them reflected light, initiating complex interrelationships. Space is born. Yet, with each increment of change in the angle of light's penetration, the being of things, and their relationships, are recreated. Space, in other words, never begins to mature, but is continually made new. In this place of ceaseless birth, people will thus be able to evoke the resonant implications of life.

Architecture must set forth places whose vitality of spirit can liberate man in the context of daily life. Light is that which awakens architecture to life; and which informs it with power.

T Ando, 'Licht', in *Jahrbuch für Licht und Architektur 1993*, Berlin, 1993.

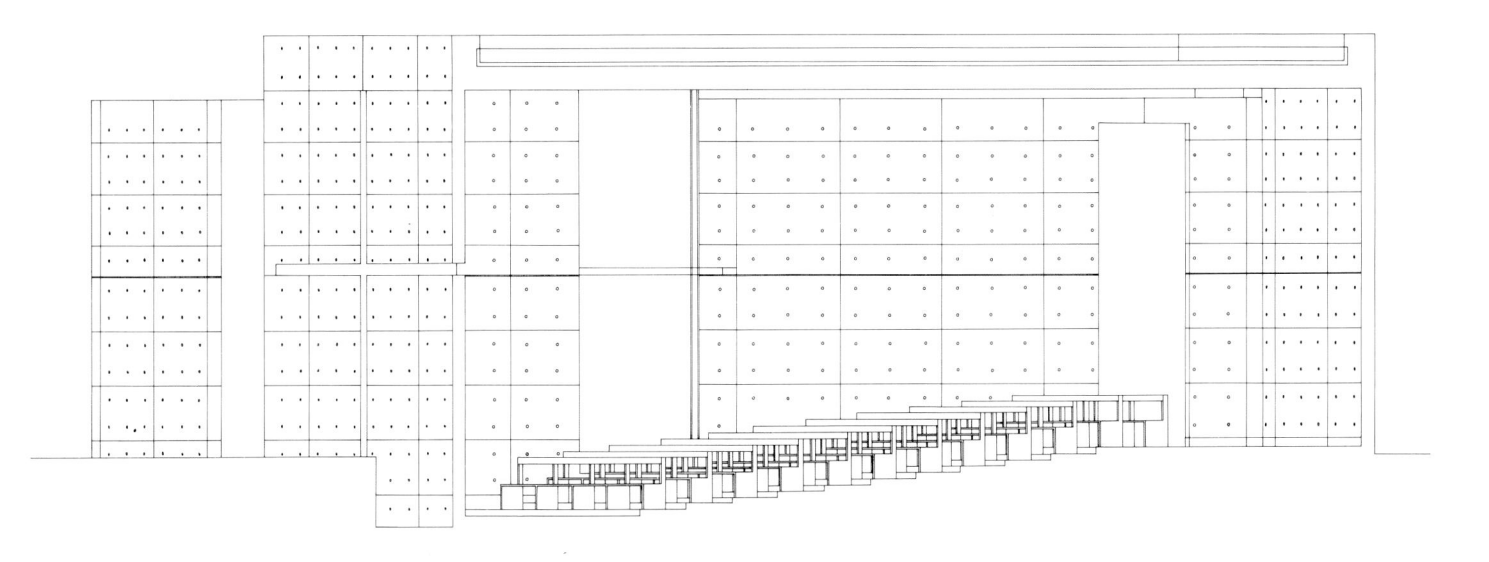

The Agony of Sustained Thought: The Difficulty of Persevering

Mies van der Rohe, Farnsworth House.

Function separates architecture from all the other arts. By function, I do not mean how easy or difficult a building is to use. The question is whether or not man can put himself into the space of a building. It does not matter if it is an actually constructed building, an unrealized project, or even a proposal in which the architect has given free rein to his imagination. Architecture cannot exist without relating to human beings. The programme from which architecture is generated and an interpretation of the programme are indispensable to architecture.

Being engaged in architecture is for me the same thing as thinking. However, that does not mean I develop a cogent logic with respect to a project. It is my nature to always want to discover the essence of a thing. In every case I go back to the starting point. Thinking is for me a physicalized process, performed through sketches. A given programme may take devious paths inside me and undergo profound changes. I will not sacrifice freedom of thought merely to satisfy requirements in a precise way. A historical perspective on a project, an understanding of nature, climate and ethnic traditions, an understanding of the times, a vision of the future, and most of all, a will to bring all these things to bear on the problem to hand – the absence of any of these things weakens the work of architecture, yet none of these things ought to be apparent in the final work. They need to be fully assimilated by me, so that even a single line expresses my will. I want all these things to be sublimated in the space that is created.

Recently, projects in Venice, Basel and Chicago have given me opportunities to revisit buildings that to me have always been refreshing and stimulating. In 1967, there were practically no skyscrapers in Japan, and the vertically extended structures of steel and glass in Chicago had for me then a strange fascination. However, when I visited the city for the first time, I felt let down. The skyscrapers did not have the power or tension I had come to expect of modern architecture. There was an emphasis only on practicality and rationality, and a beauty that was only skin deep. They celebrated the products of an industrialized society and gave no hint of the individuals who had made them. There was nothing that conveyed what those individuals had felt or thought.

What saved that trip from being a complete disappointment was the Lake Shore Drive apartments by Mies van der Rohe. Although they were made of steel and glass just like other apartments nearby, I could sense in them the presence of an individual, that is, Mies himself. I also felt his presence at the Farnsworth House. Its appearance was perfect. Of course the materials – steel, glass, precast concrete and travertine for the floor – were skilfully combined to show off their qualities and there was a clarity of detailing made by possibly the highest craftsmanship available then in the United States. However, to someone who was himself engaged in architecture, the amount of effort obviously expended by Mies to achieve his spatial concept was intimidating, despite, or rather precisely because of, the decorousness of the house. Much skill and effort had gone into a rigorous architecturalization of geometry intended to create a model of space.

In the pursuit of his architectural ideal, Mies sought a degree of precision that was seemingly impossible in architecture, and his efforts crystallized into an aesthetic. That aesthetic, however, was so thoroughgoing as to be intimidating; it harboured a kind of violence. It is difficult to believe that this building could have been

Le Corbusier, Ronchamp Pilgrimage Church.

intended to serve as an actual dwelling. The powerful design owes its existence of course to a very understanding client, but it is also the product of a painful intellectual journey by Mies van der Rohe, one in which he thought through the problems of steel-and-glass architecture and developed radical solutions.

Another building I recently revisited is the chapel of Ronchamp, although I have been there a number of times since my first visit in 1965. This highly plastic work, with bold forms of rough concrete, dates of course from the final years of Le Corbusier's life. Inside Ronchamp, the visitor is assaulted by phantasmal lights entering through windows of diverse sizes fitted with coloured glass. This chapel, unlike earlier works by Le Corbusier, which were controlled by reason and expressed rationality, seems to have been created directly and intuitively, almost in the manner of a painting. Its brutal physical strength remains undiminished and continues to shock us.

How did Le Corbusier, who had always remained true to modern architecture, come to create such a building? One factor may have been the hoarding of ideas forced on him by the Second World War. Thinking was the only thing permitted an architect in wartime since nothing could be built. I believe his thoughts turned inward and he attained a deep level of understanding so that he was eventually able to transcend reason and create Ronchamp with an almost intuitive speed and energy.

The act of creation can produce joy, a sense of achievement, satisfaction and pleasure, but to reach that point requires an intellectual journey full of anguish, in which ideas are accumulated. A work is based on a subtle equilibrium, one in which anguish is balanced against the pleasure of liberation from that anguish. The creator's ideas, however, are often not compatible with the attributes of architecture – that is, its economic, social and functional character, or the ideas of the client and the contractor. Architecture as a form of expression can succeed when efforts are made on both sides to bridge those gaps.

I am now working on a project for the third stage of Rokko Housing. The site for this is four times the size of that for the second stage, and the number of units will be 300, compared to the twenty units in the first stage and fifty units in the second. Completion will probably take another ten years. My dream, which is to contrast housing on an urban scale to nature on a 60-degree slope, may not be acceptable to present-day society, which places greater value on practicality and economy. Yet that dream is an extension of the idea to provide an enclosure for traditional Japanese life in a simple geometrical form that was the basis for the 1976 Azuma House. [...]

Sustaining the process of thought is agonizing and difficult. However, the Farnsworth House and Ronchamp provide me with inspiration. I want to retain freedom of thought and to create buildings that continue to be thought-provoking to those who experience them. The fact that these two works still stand like signposts before me gives me hope.

T Ando, 'The Agony of Sustained Thought: The Difficulty of Persevering', in *GA Document*, 39, May 1994.

The Eternal within the Moment

Born and raised in Japan's richly historical Kansai region, I have been blessed with plentiful opportunities to examine traditional Japanese architecture in ancient cities like Kyoto, Nara and Osaka. Few of the innumerable and often obscure shrines, temples, and residences that I have visited, however, have had as much power to impress and influence me as the Ise Shrine. Bound since time immemorial in intimate association with the *Tenno* system, Japan's form of monarchical government, the Ise Shrine has taken hold as a spiritual cornerstone in the unconscious of the Japanese. Even today with the *Tenno* system still a deeply rooted presence in the psychological make-up of each individual Japanese, the shrine retains profound meaning as an abode of Japan's traditional aesthetic consciousness.

The visitor crosses the Isuzu River at its approach to the shrine compound, falling naturally into a solemn mood as he trudges up the entrance path into growing darkness of forest, feet pulled at by gravel. The Ise Shrine, enveloped in silence and evincing a forceful beauty of primordial simplicity, seems an apt symbol of the aesthetics and life style of the agrarian Japanese of antiquity.

The shrine is completely rebuilt every twenty years in accordance with the practice of *shikinen-sengu*, a custom, unparalleled elsewhere in the world, of regular removal of a shrine according to a fixed cycle of years. This custom, believed to have been established in the Nara period (around AD 750), has been nearly faithfully observed until the present. In the shrine compound are two alternate sites, and while one shrine is still intact, another, identical down to the smallest measure, is built on the adjacent site, the old shrine then being demolished after the ritual of *sengu*, or transferral of the god-body to the new shrine. A religion preoccupied with ritual beauty, Shinto here attains its most beautiful expression. There could be, moreover, no surer means of passing down through the generations a manner of construction founded on materials and methods as temporal as miscanthus-thatch roofing and columns set into bare earth. In this way, through the shrine's rebirth every twenty years for over a millennium, an ancient mode of architecture has reached us today virtually unchanged.

What has been transmitted through the Ise Shrine is not a building in physical substance, but 'style' itself and spiritual tradition. In it we find that a sensibility which pursues a beauty of simplicity, fresh vitality and grace in its most pristine expression has been successfully handed down among the Japanese from generation to generation.

Whereas western thought is hinged on individual consciousness, the Japanese have traditionally held a pantheistic view of nature and entrusted consciousness to god, who is seen to dwell in all things. Accordingly, within an architecture's form a spiritual and invisible something inherited from previous ages is felt to lie concealed, though ever refined and transforming in character. The Japanese, moreover, have been inclined since ancient times to discover eternal character in that which fades and dies, feeling the eternal to be intuitable, contradictorily, in what has only fleeting existence. A flower is an ideal metaphor for this, for it withers, scattering its petals, just when we find it to have attained its optimum beauty. Though we would pray for that beauty to endure, nothing in this world is immortal, and there is, finally, no more apt symbol of our yearning for the eternal than that which fades in an instant.

Rather than choose an inheritance of Japanese tradition and its unique conception of beauty in form or materials, terms that are physical and apparent to the eye, I have opted for an inheritance in spirit and sensibility, and tried to project these qualities into my work. While partly deliberate, this endeavour stems more fully from an unconscious inheritance in my physical being. I have sought to give expression to this traditional sensibility in the Japanese Pavilion at Expo 92 in Seville. My theme for this project was expressing through architecture the culture produced by the Japanese in uniting custom to climate. An exposition building is destined to be dismantled after a short life. I therefore wanted to create an architecture that, though losing its physical presence, would have impressed itself deeply upon the spirit of those who came in contact with it, achieving an eternal character as an image in their memory.

I chose to create a wood structure of great size for its capacity to speak directly of Japan's culture and aesthetic consciousness to people from a cultural sphere characterized by stone and walls. This means of expression was feasible owing to the high technology developed in this age using artificial intelligence. Japan is home to what is said to be the world's largest wood structure, the temple Todaiji in Nara, yet that building's structural methods elude contemporary analysis and, hence, cannot be applied today. To realize my conception of this work, sophisticated computer technology capable of minute analysis of complex structure was indispensable. [...]

The sensibility that informs *shakkei*, the borrowed landscape method of gardening, in which one attempts to read and give form to the character inherent in a site or place is a uniquely Japanese view of nature; indeed, such qualities are what have produced Japan's traditional building culture. I have tried to grasp and bring to architecture not so much the real and readily apparent as the abstract and formless logic or image that lies invisibly behind it, a logic or image that, by transforming its character, lends itself to a new context. [...]

I introduce nature – light, wind, and water – within a geometric and ordered architecture, thereby awakening it to life. Climatic changes in turn transform the condition of architecture from moment to moment. Contrasting elements meet with startling results, and in these results, architectural expression is born that is capable of moving the human spirit and allows us to glimpse the eternal within the moment. The abode of the eternal is thus within he who perceives it.

Ise Shrine.

Interview with Tadao Ando
Hiroshi Maruyama

Hiroshi Maruyama You first went to Europe in 1968 to study the architecture of the old world and at that time the student movement was no less vociferous there than it was here in Japan. Young people thinking of becoming architects were a lot less interested in Japanese tradition than they were in making critiques of society. Compared to then how do you think it has turned out?

Tadao Ando We find ourselves in a twentieth-century *fin-de-siècle*. The world changed enormously between the nineteenth and twentieth centuries and, as I see it, the transition into the next century will be just as traumatic. If you'd asked me this question in the 1980s I'd have said we would probably slip lazily from one century into another without noticing, but now – and I say it with some anxiety – we seem to be about to enter an epoch in which history will take a completely new direction once again.

The last big change was the Industrial Revolution in the eighteenth century. Europe became the centre of the world and society reorganized itself into new hierarchies which then led to new forms of exploitation. The rise of Spain, England and France to imperial power caused those societies to redefine themselves in terms of class distinctions which did not come to an end until the French Revolution of 1789. This in turn determined the course of the ensuing hundred years until, at the end of the nineteenth century, cultural and artistic movements emerged simultaneously in the industrialized countries. Art Nouveau, *Jugendstil* and the Vienna Secession brought about far-reaching changes in architecture and the arts and (leaving aside the well-known names) it is important to see these movements as the products of vast social and historical transformations going on around them. These early stirrings of Modernism spawned an affluent bourgeoisie with aesthetic pretensions and a consequent demand for expressive freedom which gave rise to new philosophical problems.

In our own century, wars and technology have transformed values and suggest there will be further change. I didn't understand this clearly in the eighties but now I think the next changes will go beyond anything that went before and the prime factor will be computer technology. Think of those early IBM mainframes: even though we already called them 'computers' we were still trapped in the Industrial Revolution mentality and thought of them as just a new kind of machine. Then Apple set new standards for personal computers which modified attitudes so drastically that in twenty years computers have completely changed our lives. So it seems inevitable that, as science fiction predicted, humans are going to be replaced by a technology which will control the whole system. Industrial society will make humans irrelevant by eliminating jobs and computers will prove far more productive than people. They are already transforming our natural consciousness and it's too late to turn back now; an information net is enveloping the planet and beginning to eliminate all differentiation between one culture or lifestyle and another. In Asian countries, particularly Japan, traditional values and ways of life have disappeared in only five years.

When this computer technology combines with the manipulative power of the mass media, artificial intelligence will change the lives of individuals and take over the natural functions of the brain. In our field what we used to call 'architecture' was the result of intellectual creative processes which are probably going to disappear.

HM Your anxiety may be that as an architect whose search for integrity depends on staying true to modernist ideals, you fear the imminent collapse of a world and a society which are ideologically still rooted in the Industrial Revolution. You worry about a world in which technology will render all human activity meaningless. This was already a problem when Modernism was beginning – has it not always been the big question about modernity?

TA When modern architecture was first developing people like Mies worked out uniform systems for organizing space. Crude attempts were made to humanize these by introducing informal events into repeating grids. With Mies, uniform space always left this margin for freedom and difference, but now we have to work with technologies totally controlled by computers and which only understand whatever is normal and leave no margin for diversity; indeed, human intervention is only a nuisance. Our intellect doesn't work only by using rational processes and functional logic grasping at homogeneous blocks of data, but intuitively and emotionally, at deeper levels beyond thought, extending beyond rational comprehension and nourished by a spiritual component which cannot be measured. If heterogeneity can be said to reside in these inaccessible mechanisms of the spirit, then in a world taken over by computers, we will have no more reason to live and will have to ask if all our long struggles have been worth the effort. For myself, as an architect concerned with problems of existence and context, I think my task is to create places which express regional and cultural particularities which bring out man's relationship to nature and other people.

I seek to create places which embrace the diversity there is in the world and to give expression to whatever ideas and ideals reject uniformity. But if we do ever get to a point where computers control everything then there will be no need for this any more and architects will simply disappear. Despite this, architects still seem confident about their status as 'creative people' and many only use computers to do mundane tasks; as technology marches on far too few understand how precarious their position is.

HM Mies van der Rohe's architecture is not only about physical transparency but is also philosophically transparent. Don't you think you're looking at him from an excessively negative viewpoint?

TA But Mies' architecture belongs to everywhere and nowhere – New York, Chicago, anywhere in the world. After seeing photographs of his skyscrapers I visited some of them during the sixties when I went to America for the first time, and all I remember is the coldness of those endless uniform spaces. I realized that in Mies there was something tragic and cruel which wanted to push everything to a totally logical conclusion completely ignoring all human considerations. I told myself this was just the time, that if he hadn't done it someone else would, as I suppose Einstein's ideas would have come through even if Einstein hadn't existed or just as telephones would have been invented even without Bell. If Mies had never been born, I said to myself, somebody else would have made those dreary buildings, spurred on by the need to create a homogenized space capable of absorbing all difference.

When I first went to Chicago and felt this uniformity at first hand I was amazed at how little difference there was between being outside or inside. In fact if you have a building 'A' which is identical to building 'C' and you are in one of them, the complete lack of any difference between the two takes away all chance of perceiving any space at all. After that I went on being astonished at how those projects set out to annihilate all relationships between people and things. I have no way of knowing what may have been going through Mies' mind when he was designing spaces like that and no doubt he didn't realize people would hate them so much. The fact is that if you force people to live in uniform spaces from birth you'll make them completely unable to perceive spatial difference.

We perceive difference by thinking in terms of different spaces and to me diversity means history, tradition and humanity – rooms which are not all the same. Mies is dead now and hopefully the desire to design whatever is most monotonous has come to an end. Nevertheless a generation has grown up in that scenario – the computer generation. These people have no inkling of the kind of spatial difference that interests me. They're only able to think of space as the place where men talk to machines, where life and sensibility have disappeared. These are the people who actually admire Mies and don't feel right unless they're sitting staring at their computer screen. We do have to live with computers now but the standardizing process has accelerated more and more, there doesn't seem to be any way out for those who, like me, want to go on asking questions about architectural conceptions of space.

HM People do usually say that uniform space kills off multiplicity of experience, but Peter Eisenman uses shifted grids to create heterogeneous situations so that he can work on the differences that he thus creates. When you talk about grids you seem to be saying that the only opportunity to create difference in this way is at the beginning when you set up the grid for the first time. Can you explain this more fully?

TA Some people say if you use grids the result will only be uniform space of one sort or another, but I disagree. When two homogeneous spaces, represented as grids, interfere with each other there is a slippage between them which creates the estrangement you get when identical entities collide. That's what I mean by 'difference' and it's what I look for. However unless you're able to feel these tensions and small differences within the infinite space of the universe itself, you will not be able to design anything spatially meaningful. Slippage will only work for you if you already understand the differences between one space and another and ultimately, the universal homogeneity of all space. By seeking diversity in my work I look for opportunities to create the slippages which thus happen in universal space. Grids can be useful as a way to make buildings and don't necessarily have to be boring. However if you follow Eisenman through his methodical design process and his dictum that 'the grid is right' you may indeed come up with spaces that look diversified and certainly different from Mies, but I find his approach very ambiguous. His drawings are always based clearly on shifting grids but if you visit his buildings you find spaces which, although not uniform, are actually unable to be truly heterogeneous.

HM Eisenman seems to have realized this and has announced his abandonment of the grid…

TA In his way of working with grids, Eisenman was looking for a new approach – but not many architects went as far as he did in trying to elevate this to the level of a doctrine.

HM According to Eisenman the irregular spaces you can create by shifting one grid across another are the spaces of life itself.

TA Yes, people do look for a crevice in which to exist, some small corner of their own outside uniform space – an interstice in which to work – but not many are as sophisticated as that. In my own way I still believe in modern society and I have faith in man. I think Modernism and Humanism are values which must somehow be able to coexist even if, during our century, they have more often been in conflict. Now, however, I think we're entering a time in which the ideals which dominated the modern age will probably no longer have any validity.

HM In your way of using the intervals and interstices caused by shifting grids some see an affinity with traditional Japanese conceptions of space and others see an attentiveness to nature which is characteristic of Japanese culture. No doubt both are right but I'd like you to say more about how you approach the process of design.

TA To me, all buildings contain interstices of space imbued with aesthetic value – a sense of place, the character of the people who live there, local tradition, history, and so on. No matter what they are or what shape they have – walls, ceilings, roofs, even floors – these spaces hold life and spirit. However this is not the same as the Japanese tradition of *Ma* ('space-in-between'); *ma* spaces are consciously designed and do not come about by the coincidental interaction of grids, and *Ma* or *Oku* ('hidden potential') spaces have to be designed according to fixed rules. Nevertheless, I often wonder if despite its individualistic vocation, the process of architectural design does acquire universal meaning by mixing modern conceptions of space with these traditions.

HM Would you say that using shifting grids to make irregular spaces shows how rational decision-making can make spaces in which the imagination can begin to take flight?

TA You could, but it's always misleading to carry forward creative work by forcing it to conform to such conventional descriptions. It's true that I look for spatial configurations by working imaginatively in the interstices whilst making use of the rationality offered by grids. But before this begins there has to be desire – the desire to make spaces in which something can be experienced. Imagination and fantasy – not grids – are the means by which I bring my aspirations into reality, and it's a battle you have to fight in a world dominated by information technology, in a society which doesn't care about the little differences between one thing and another or the relationships between human beings – rather like Don Quixote's battle with the windmills. And I can tell you it sometimes feels like torture. Nevertheless for as long as men continue to live on earth and carry on discourse with one another it will be my job to break through into the imaginary and the intuitive – where the computer can never go.

HM So you believe technology endangers life and creativity…?

TA Computers can only reproduce whatever already exists within the logic of technology. All the relational systems which computers generate are worth nothing compared to the physical presence of a single human body. True creativity encompasses the whole of life and is expressed with the instruments of intuition, beyond logic and what any language is capable of expressing. The architect, operating from within this world, thinks about society in profound ways which have nothing to do with social, economic, political analysis and suchlike.

HM What may be missing then, is a context in which to place these questions. We know they're important but we lack a common background against which to discuss them. This causes social and political disorder and also affects architecture. Is that why you feel anxious?

TA Just like clients or politicians, architects can sometimes lack enthusiasm for life; but anyone incapable of feeling and dreaming will not survive into the twenty-first century. How could an ice-cold human race with no more great ideas to inspire it continue any sort of existence? If we do finally stop seeking each other out, animated by some great idea, looking for the possibilities life offers, then we really will be lost. This is already happening and there's a question-mark hanging over the future of architecture. The situation has now become critical as architects have begun turning out projects designed by computers and only based on the logical patterns computers understand. The outcome will be a loss of all differentiation and everything reduced to the kind of calculations computers can do. What will be left for architecture? In the eighties and nineties architects thought they could have a dialogue with computers and explore the possibilities and for another two or three years it will still seem amusing. But then all differentiation will be lost and the kind of architecture I believe in will no longer be required in a world where everything will have become the same, everywhere. I won't be surprised if the curtain then finally comes down on architecture as we have known it.

HM You talk about differentiation. Let's take examples. In economic science there is no profit unless there is a difference in the value of something. Thus the Deconstructivists would say diversity is more valuable than uniformity…

TA Deconstructivism made a splash by deliberately emphasizing the value of being different in what is essentially a homogenized society, but I don't work that way. Since I began as an architect thirty years ago my projects got bigger and bigger and the only buildings I was really able to control were houses. But I can't do only houses, so for medium-sized projects I take a twin-track approach. On the one hand I do use computers and follow their logic to lay out all the repetitive, homogeneous spaces these buildings need to have. Simultaneously I use my own sensibility to introduce changes into these spaces and make them sensual. Thus I find it's still possible to get the kind of result I'm looking for, even with large buildings, so when I talk about differentiation I mean the difference between uniform spaces and other spaces where the repetition breaks down and local particularities become apparent. The architect must make it possible for those differences to be experienced.

HM Because you're more comfortable working on small buildings I imagine the larger size of your current projects has brought about changes in your thinking. When you were designing the Suntory Museum I'm sure computers played a bigger role. Doesn't this put you into a confrontational situation in which your personal creativity is fighting against your use of advanced technologies?

TA But the concept of the Suntory Museum derives from very humanistic considerations about man and architecture. I started from this premise and only used computers during working drawings to solve particular problems. While this was going on I was still using my own imagination in ways the computers could never have understood, but without computers I wouldn't have finished the job at all. This is the age of computers, everything has to be reduced down to manageable bits of information, and the only escape from this tyranny is to try to clearly define whatever parts of the project might benefit from this approach. Even so I'm deeply unhappy about being compelled to do it.

HM Compared with your earlier work the Suntory Museum exhibits a very evident divergence between structure and space.

TA In one sense the Suntory project is an evolution from my earlier projects but at the same time I wanted it to exhibit a greater self-assurance. It might seem I always use the same sorts of grids and range of materials but I think my forms do change and that on the whole my work is varied. In the case of Suntory I wasn't happy about having to make spaces which would all be the same, so I took an experimental approach and tried to take advantage of whatever unexpected possibilities I came across. The question was whether I could design a building whose repetitive parts would be fresh and not banal. As the project developed and crystallized I found this approach opened up new horizons for me to explore.

HM So computers did help you to find a dynamic and differentiated concept rather than something static?

TA These days it's fashionable to think of computers as an extension of the brain but for me they're really just giant calculators. I have to use this technology to make my conceptual explorations of space in which I want human relationships to come about, and when I visit the Suntory Museum I do feel it's possible to experience something of this sort. Hopefully others can also feel that the place is neither ingratiating nor familiar, but unusual and cliché-free.

The fundamental thing about Suntory isn't its external form but the spatial experience of the interior. Some people are very struck by the intensity of the architecture and ask me if I'm not worried that it might be too hard and barbaric. I myself am not so much concerned about the building's formal eccentricity as the way in which the continuous differentiation of the interior spaces makes it possible to rediscover them over and over again. The Chikatsu-Asuka Museum, which has just been finished, will probably be judged either a disaster or a scandal and for this reason already attracts many visitors. In future I want to find ways of using computers to transform the things I have been learning and accumulating by intuition, into something I can express through my own body and physicality.

HM But the virtual space created by computers doesn't call for physical involvement. Your Suntory Museum and the grand staircase in your Chikatsu-Asuka Museum both give a strong physical sensation of space, and your Museum of Wood in Kumamoto consists of walls which impose powerful changes in perspective and have their own strongly-felt physical presence. Could it be said that your biggest interest is in the physical impact such buildings can have?

TA Well, if it is true to say that the world is becoming more and more computerized every day and the physical aspect of things is getting weaker and weaker, then architects have to create places which will intensify the sense of the body and give respite from this progressive loss of opportunity to really feel space in a physical sense. If the body is deprived of this opportunity, no other experience will be possible and the feeling of being alive will actually disappear if physical relationships are lost. Architecture has to create spaces which enable people to renew awareness of their physical existence so yes, this is central to all my recent work.

To approach the Chikatsu-Asuka Museum you have to walk around the outside, following the line of a wall and then another which leads in a different direction. This movement together with the grand staircase itself is intended to make visitors feel a physical reaction in their own bodies. In the Suntory Museum you move round the central space and your senses feel this movement – that's what I'm trying to achieve. Something similar happens in the Rokko housing project where the stairs are intended to heighten the relationship between man and his body. So the stairs at Rokko and in the Chikatsu-Asuka Museum are not intended to be purely functional and in the Chikatsu-Asuka Museum the staircase doesn't even lead anywhere at all. It's a strange sensation to walk up a staircase that doesn't take you anywhere!

At Rokko, which is fifteen floors high, the occupants are encouraged to walk down the stairs instead of using the elevator because if you walk down a building this high you get an excellent sense of your own body. Walls and floors with which the body comes into contact have always had great importance for me in redefining these relationships between the body and architectural space and, more and more, I'm coming to a conception of space which (unlike Miesian uniformity) is all based on the physicality of the human body.

HM This care you take to design stairs which heighten relationships between the body and space is rather unusual; you want people to understand your building by climbing eight or nine flights just to feel it themselves. Is this not just a pointless and unnecessary way of tiring them out?

TA Physical existence can't be separated from other aspects of existence and I don't think it's pointless to use your whole body to experience a space. We Japanese have a particular sense of our bodies which isn't the same as that of Europeans or even other Asiatic peoples. Traditional Japanese poses and gestures have a delicacy which relates us to our particular civilization and even though Japanese habits have been changing recently you can still put an American in a crowd of Japanese and he will soon notice how different our behaviour is from his. The term 'regionalism' is often used to describe material differences of local architectures but in reality it's the body which expresses particular relationships to place. People differ according to history, tradition, regional situation, and the types of space to which they're accustomed. A person's body language will tell you where they come from so regional differences exist in the body itself. I think this is very important for architects.

HM You work mainly in Osaka but travel a good deal elsewhere. We live in a system of cities where it can be hard to keep a sense of human scale and where our perception of our bodies tends to be falsified.

TA Cosmopolites will tell you they can live anywhere but I can't think of the world as a big uniform space. Personally I prefer Japan because my architecture is about specifically Japanese regional and cultural history and tradition, and I always try to relate materials and proportions to the human body. However I do travel a lot and have work in Spain, Italy, France and the United States. This does create problems because although I remain attached to Japan I also have to be cosmopolitan. Nevertheless although my buildings in Italy or France are used by Italians or Frenchmen I maintain my own Japanese sensibility and the spaces still reflect my essentially Japanese ideas about the body. So working in those other places leaves me very unsure as to how these projects will turn out, how the spaces will be perceived, and what this might mean for an architect like me. The fact is I continually have to find new hypotheses on which to base my work and go on trying to express whatever seems universal and particular at the same time. It's a common dilemma for many architects today and if you ignore it I think your work loses meaning. For instance I find Frank Gehry's buildings in Los Angeles far more vigorous than the work he's done in Japan and no doubt the same applies to my work outside Japan. I don't know what the answer is in these days of global information networks.

HM So in this changing world is it your ambition to make an architecture which can somehow address a deeper truth?

TA I've been wondering if there's an architecture that can express the end of our century. Steel, glass and reinforced concrete architecture was typical of the twentieth century and is associated with Modernist ideas about universality. I'm working on some projects which start from there and perhaps I'll come up with something that could be called 'the logical conclusion of twentieth century architecture'. I've always tried to imbue my buildings with some particular historical, physical or spatial attribute but many of them are just concrete boxes designed on grids. Now I'm working on a museum made of glass with a concrete box inside and set out on a grid. The building will be like a nest with the outside made of glass containing the lobby and circulation and enclosing the exhibition rooms inside the concrete box.

HM You've always preferred concrete so why use glass for this building?

TA The modern tradition went for uniformity but I've always tried to accentuate the differentiation between one thing and another. Concrete is a monolithic material and the transparency of glass is even more typical of modern architecture. Paradoxically, though, I am finding ways of making uniform spaces, using concrete and glass, which have varied meaning and the building I'm talking about could turn out to be part of the closing chapter of the twentieth century. Although the transparency of glass is a quintessentially modern concept and relates to an idea of uniformity, there are relations between human beings that are far more archaic and which involve bodies and physicality in ways which pre-date modernity. I think it will be possible to make a new world in which contemporary concerns mix with pre-modern attitudes. Before modernity there were stronger, clearer relationships and people were more aware of their bodies. That was lost when modernity subordinated human considerations to the dictates of rationality and utilitarianism, so at present I'm working on three museum projects in which I want to create spaces with different meanings but contained inside deliberately opaque, monotonous shells. I have another project going up in Awajishima which you will only be able to understand by using your legs and feet and walking through it.

HM Your early projects were typified by concrete walls inviting contact. Now you seem interested in the human body standing erect.

TA Since there has been life on earth it is our feet which remind us we are alive. We know we exist when we feel it in the soles of our feet and all of us from infancy begin by learning to walk. No matter how computerized the world may become we will probably keep on walking and that will probably be the last thing we feel. If we finally lose all perception of reality our psychological disintegration will follow and in the midst of environmental catastrophe, famine and natural calamities, being alive will mean nothing any more. If the world is determined to destroy itself the only thing architects can do is make sure we don't lose our sense of touch.

HM Donald Judd said his work was accessible to all and anyone could understand what it was about, despite the mystery that lies behind its apparent simplicity. But only Judd actually understood what he was doing and no-one made any effort to help him; his only point of reference was himself. In architecture surely this solipsistic approach would not be tenable?

TA Absolutely. I start from the assertion that we can't exist without company, that nothing in life can survive unless we make relationships. Judd thought the relationships between human beings and works of art could be manifested by mere objects but for me humanity has to express itself by relationships and questioning what life is about. Judd is about death and he is totally focused on his own mortality, eliminating any need for any dialogue at all. I'm the opposite and I think life matters. So far as architecture is concerned I don't think it would exist at all unless we thought it was worth something to be alive in the first place.

HM Carlo Scarpa is obsessed with detail but his work has a kind of humour not dissimilar to that of, say, Rem Koolhaas, and even in Judd there's always a kind of irony. There's nothing like that in your work.

TA There's no irony in my work because I'm very serious about architecture and the dedication it takes. All the same it would please me if someone could find some element of humour, even though as I say, I work with a concentration which doesn't leave any room for such nuances. The hand-made quality of Scarpa's architecture makes it playful and gives eccentric effects which suggest he was enjoying himself. I work to my own scrupulous rules and don't think I could do as he did. Sense of humour has something to do with the warmth you get in relationships between people and things; humour should be part of a sincerely affectionate attitude and never too brash or obvious. The architecture of Koolhaas is based on sophisticated concepts which translate into a richly ironic architecture very much in tune with contemporary sensibility and easy on the eye, but I care about saving connections and relationships we risk losing, so it's only logical that my work doesn't set out to ingratiate itself in that way.

HM Peter Eisenman's work is also devoid of irony even though as a person he can be very amusing…

TA Eisenman's work is indeed extremely severe although you can perhaps see something ironic in the use of colour in his systems of grids. This righteousness is what he is, it's in his genes, it's there before he starts and is so deeply a part of him that he's just not capable of putting anything funny into his work – even though his version of so-called 'Deconstructivism' could be seen as the end product of a dialogue involving rigour on the one hand and wit on the other. Gehry, too, is not just a comedian. His Temporary Contemporary Museum of Art in Los Angeles and his museum for Vitra are witty but his American Center in Paris – a magnificent piece of work – is something else; it's still humorous but the very rich marble finish is so elaborate that it works against the wittiness. In general I don't think it's possible to deliberately design irony into a building any more than you could strategically predetermine some particular reaction you want people to experience.

HM As in Aldo Rossi's childlike architecture nostalgia is another thing that seems to fascinate architects. Is that also true of your work?

TA I don't think so. It's true I'm a pessimist but that doesn't have to mean I look back instead of forward. In going forward I continuously question my own motives but I'm not longing for bygone days. In one way I consider myself a humanist but at the same time I'd like to think I'm very much a realist. My work comes from the contradiction between these two positions.

HM You stand for freedom of expression and the right to criticize contemporary society, but you've said that this aspect of your work is not understood in Japan. Why not?

TA My architecture deals in powerful images which attract attention but even before the Azuma House I wanted my designs for spaces and forms to be much more a way of directing criticism against society. That's what matters to me but other people seem more interested in my use of concrete, the way I work with grids, and so on. For me the important thing is freedom – not freedom to express yourself but freedom to exist at all, in the midst of all sorts of constrictions and conventions: the freedom to get right down to the bottom of things as and when you need or want to. Architecture, too, is held back by conventional notions of construction so I keep up to date with new developments that might help me express my ideas more effectively. I try to state what I believe in by expressing it through the medium of architecture but I'm afraid people still don't understand that this is what I'm trying to do. The social implications of what I do just haven't been comprehended as much as the formal aspects. I say we have to go out and fight against anything that tries to restrict our freedom – whoever we are and whatever we do and I happen to do it with architecture.

HM Yet the critics have only talked about your architecture as though it were all a matter of aesthetics and nothing else. Maybe this will change as your buildings become more important and more of an aesthetic challenge. Are you influenced by critics?

TA Critics are like a lubricating oil; they can make it easier for dialogue to take place between architecture and the rest of society but some of them only know how to sling mud at this or that architect. That sort of controversialism only trivializes what should be serious and for the sake of architecture it's essential we do have proper criticism which knows how to be even-handed, has a clear understanding of history and a clearly stated point of view about where we are now. Regrettably, not many Japanese critics are good enough – which is a shame because if they were able to exacerbate the confrontation between architecture and society in a more serious way, I'm sure this would gain a greater public respect for what architects do.

HM The young people in your office all belong to the computer generation. Do you get on with them?

TA Well, I'm diffident. I find computer freaks have no emotion or sentimentality and only react if you feed them hard information. They don't know how to feel things in their bodies and minds. But the young people who work with me, even the ones who use computers, first of all have to know how to draw by hand using their brains and reacting emotionally to what they're doing, showing me they have feelings about it. If you depend totally on using computers you risk wiping out human relationships and a whole way of doing architecture. Imagine if you could set up all the equipment you need at home and do a project without leaving the house. You could modem your computer drawings directly, have them checked, and put up the building without intervening at all and in the complete absence of any architect working on site. How could a computerized person like that know anything about what building means? How could such a person produce humane buildings capable of creating effective physical relationships between real people? An architecture that is only concerned with handling quantities of information would be dangerous and it worries me even more to think about where we're going.

The future? Sometimes I think the developed world with its continual bombardment of information that makes it impossible for us to cultivate the spirit and respect the needs of our bodies, is in fact paving the way for its own extinction. Maybe it's outsiders who live on the edge of our civilization, or the primitive societies which still survive despite the immense threats they face – maybe these are the people who will turn out to be the saviours of humanity. At the moment, people don't seem remotely worried about what the ever-increasing presence of computers is doing; they just see them as friendly slaves and no-one notices the profound effect they're having on the way we live with one other. Computers are spreading a net round the world which will make space absolutely uniform wherever you go. The only thing left is to find a residual space in which architecture can still happen and to ask what it will mean to work as an architect in a world like that.

(May 1994)

Critical Anthology

Editorial note: The majority of the following texts are edited versions of previously published writings. Sources for the articles are given at the end of each piece.

Tadao Ando
Vittorio Gregotti

I believe it is very difficult to get to the bottom of Ando's architecture if one only thinks about it as a form of minimalism or if one attempts to find out his technique, his culinary secrets, by creeping up from behind hoping to understand where it all belongs emotionally. He himself always gives the most laconic of summaries and perhaps every further attempt at analytical dissection only reduces any hope of understanding what he is about.

Undoubtedly, when we go to Japanese restaurants and look at the *Cangi* characters painted on canvas, their very incomprehensibility makes their meaning all the more mysterious to us. I am not saying our European predilection for exotic things and our taste for incomprehensible texts is the only way we know how to classify and understand the manifestations we see of foreign cultures; nevertheless the arbitrariness of every attempt we make at translating them, and even any attempt we might make to transcribe such signs into written words, does give an air of mysteriousness to our efforts to understand the creativity which comes out of that most contradictory of cultures, in its current phase of violent transformation.

So I am convinced that before doing anything else it is necessary that we understand how to stand respectfully on the threshold of those most mysterious spaces which, without doubt, are the most fascinating aspect of Ando's work.

Naturally, anyone who knows even a little about Japan cannot avoid remembering a series of historical facts about the Japanese concept of place as measurement of nature and about the processes of formalization which, in Japanese culture, affected and characterize interpersonal relationships at this particular time, and of which spatial clarity and the measurement thereof is but one aspect. Often, these reference points we use are too generic and useless in that they depend on analogy. It is no less probable that even our notion of what an image is, is ineffective to describe the process by which a building by Ando is to be understood just as, in my view, all attempts at explanation which depend only on an analysis of the syntax (referring to combinations and variations of systems of linguistic signs) would be equally inapplicable.

We know that the Japanese language is highly situational, in other words that both the reciprocal collocation of its parts and the condition in which action takes place, alter not only the overall meaning but often require the use of quite different words to indicate what for us would be exactly the same thing.

That seems as good a way as any to describe something of the oscillation that takes place between a very visible and universally comprehensible tension in Ando's architecture (its extremely simple geometry of direct type, the absolute unity of its use of material, the abstract handling of matter which is nevertheless careful about weight, the radical reduction of the adjectives, the tension towards a total detachment so far as the ideas of historical process and time are concerned) and, on the other hand, the absolute specificity of the way in which it responds to its own Japanese environment in terms of orientation, size, scale and form.

I have visited a few of Ando's buildings (and despite the strongly abstract way in which they tend to be presented I also know them from magazines) and I see in them a real instrument for measuring the surrounding circumstances, a finishing line through which it is possible to measure oneself against them with respect to which the very context solidifies and shows its own constructional logic. […] The weight and thickness of columns and beams, even when reduced to the level of mere spatial indicators to complete and enclose the geometric rule of support, are an indispensable adjectivization of Ando's architecture. […]

Certainly in Ando's work the most authentically architectonic soul of Arata Isozaki seems to solidify and chase after itself. Ando is undoubtedly indebted to Isozaki for some linguistic elements of his earliest projects; and it is an obvious thing to say that in the ways in which he employs geometry he was not wasting his time when he looked at the experience of Carl Andre or Richard Serra or, from even closer, to the architecture of the great Louis Kahn and even some of Kahn's offspring like Mario Botta or Gino Valle. Still, when Ando talks about 'the light from the window high above the beaten earth floor of the traditional house', he is looking for a totally personal point of equilibrium in the primordial condition, that 'logic of the part', which is the very symbol of his relationship with nature. This extremely widespread relationship is obtained just by facing up to the case of the specific place, paying maximum attention for the smallest difference. Only in this way is it possible to reach the great simplicity which is the entrance door to the elementary and eternal gestures: to nature.

Only then, 'the light and wind which move within time, their transformation according to the seasons, the daily life which comes into contact with them, assign meaning to created form; it changes its appearance only when they have intervened'.

V Gregotti, *Casabella*, 484, October 1982.

Tadao Ando: Heir to a Tradition
Kiyoshi Takeyama

The custom of drinking tea was introduced to Japan by Zen priests in the thirteenth century, and gained wide popularity among members of the ruling warrior class, the court aristocrats and later the rich merchants. As time went by, the preparation and imbibing of the beverage were worked into an elaborately formalized system demanding a certain number of utensils and architectural appurtenances. Several tea masters concentrated on codifying the hospitality associated with tea, and the result was the *Way of Tea*, or the tea ceremony.
Sen no Rikyu (1522–92), one of Japan's greatest tea ceremony masters, introduced fresh vigour into the tea ceremony by designing rooms and small pavilions for it that departed from former architectural traditions. In contrast to all of the major architectural styles of the past – the Shinto shrines represented by the splendid buildings at Ise and Izumo, the aristocratic residences of the *shinden-zukuri* style, the warrior homes of the *shoin* style, and the temple buildings – Rikyu gave refined expression to the aesthetic value he found in the humble houses of the common people and strove to create spaces that, though small, could bring peace and calm, even for a short while, to members of the warrior class plagued by strife and conflict. In the rooms he designed, guests could become so absorbed in the affairs of the tea ceremony that they forgot the troubles of daily life. The methods he used to produce the kind of microcosm he wanted were enclosure and the adaptation of vernacular elements from folk dwellings. Through Rikyu's tea ceremony buildings (built in a style that came to be called *so-an*, or grass-thatched retreat), these elements became fashionable with the wealthy. Thus, the domestic architectural traditions of the common people exerted an influence on the design of the homes of the aristocracy and the military ruling class.
An outcome of the nature of the tea ceremony pavilion was the evolution of it as an element of social criticism. As I have said, warriors hoped to find relief from the tumult of their everyday lives in the microcosm of the tea house. In other words, by fleeing to its peace and seclusion, they were, at least tacitly, criticizing the existing social condition. The same can be said of the aristocracy, who found in the tea ceremony a respite from a world where, in spite of their ancient nobility, they were subordinate to military rulers who were often of much less dignified lineage than themselves. In short, examples of tea ceremony architecture can be interpreted as statements of criticism of the status quo.
The spirit of the tea ceremony, and of everything associated with it as it was developed by and after Sen no Rikyu, is often expressed by the Japanese word *wabi*, which means a deliberate striving for simplicity. But the word carries a connotation of dissatisfaction and is used to point out the failing of things or persons deemed worthy of criticism. For instance, the refined, quiet, calm *wabi* style is sometimes mentioned as an antonym for the gaudy, ostentatious taste associated with the great military leader Toyotomi Hideyoshi (who was a patron of Rikyu). The idea of *wabi* can stand for dissatisfaction with authority.
In addition to its anti-establishment qualities, the tea ceremony and its architecture are the results of the art and thought of one person. Conceived and created by individual human beings exerting their utmost physically and spiritually, tea ceremony rooms are places for human discipline and refinement and never symbols of social or religious status.

Although there is no resemblance in terms of style or actual forms, there is much in common between the tea ceremony designs of Sen no Rikyu and the residential designs of Tadao Ando in the nature of their spaces. Both are enclosed and concentrated. Both have a deliberately created simple appearance. Both are calm, quiet and pure. Both are gentle, austere and clear in mood. Both are dimly lit but have light within their darkness. Both give a feeling of expansiveness in spite of their small size. Though set in cities, both are rural in nature. Though artificial, both are natural. They are neither commonplace nor monumental.
The most decisive of the many ideas and devices Rikyu used to cut the tea ceremony room off from the noisy world and make of it a calm, quiet, inner-reflective microcosm was spatial enclosure. For instance, in the tea ceremony room called the Tai-an of the Myoki-an, in the outskirts of Kyoto, Rikyu created a space which, although only two tatami mats in area, is a broad world of spiritual abundance. In rooms of this kind no one ever feels cramped; the smaller the space, the more intensely fulfilled it is. Ando employs the same spatial concept. In addition, he shares with Rikyu an interest in manipulating light, in overlapping spaces, and in introducing the world of nature.
For enclosed spaces, natural lighting, and therefore the placement and sizes of openings in the walls delineating the spaces, deserves maximum care. Since the kinds of spaces I am discussing are typified by light within darkness, they are to be calm and settled and their dimness is not to generate a sense of smallness, rendering the question of openings all the more important. If the enclosed world is a microcosm, the shaft of sunlight penetrating it is a ray of hope rendered vivid by the enclosure and the surrounding darkness.
The location of openings has a determining effect on the mood of a space. In most traditional Japanese residential architecture, the major openings are on the south, where they receive full sun in winter. For their purposes, however, both Rikyu and Ando avoid southern openings because the bright illumination pouring through them has an unsettling effect on the space. For instance, the south wall at the Tai-an has no windows. Similarly, in keeping with a desire for refracting instead of directly admitting light, in some of Ando's houses, such as the Yamaguchi House (1975), the Ueda House (1979), and the Koshino House (1981), there are no southern windows.
Other natural illumination devices of which Ando is fond can be traced, if not directly to Rikyu, at least to his influence and to other tea masters who built on the foundation he laid. Though there is no example of it at the Tai-an, the small skylight window called the *tsukiage-mado* found in other tea ceremony pavilions, is thought to have been originated by Rikyu. It may be propped open from within and admits both light and air without allowing the interior to be otherwise greatly influenced by the exterior environment. Ando's own predilection for skylights is traceable to a desire similar to the one that inspired the invention of this kind of window.
Another notable tea ceremony master, Kobori Enshu (1579–1647), employed a lighting device resembling those that Ando uses. At a tea ceremony room called the Koho-an Bosen, at the Kyoto temple Daitoku-ji, Enshu devised an unusual set of shoji that are completely open in the bottom zone to permit views of the

garden and admit reflected light, but are filled with translucent white paper in the top to admit only diffused light. In many of his houses, Ando uses walls of glass blocks to admit only diffused light into interior spaces. [...] In saying this, however, I do not intend to give the impression that Ando is quoting traditional vocabulary. It is only that his thoughts on the treatment of light have led to a conclusion similar to the traditional one.

In an enclosed world, shut off from the exterior environment, spaces which overlap and figuratively fold in on each other add depth and richness to the composition and stimulate excitement and expectation in the person experiencing the space. The approach is one place where such an effect can be achieved. For example, the approach to a tea ceremony pavilion often leads through a garden space called a *roji*. In the course of traversing this garden, the visitor must pass through several gates, usually delicately and exquisitely designed, before finally reaching the pavilion where the tea ceremony will be performed. [...]

The *roji* garden at Ando's Okusu House varies the spatial experience between the entrance gate and the tea ceremony room and stimulates anticipation of new things lying ahead. To achieve these aims it employs a number of different features to complicate that space: gates, stepping stones, ritual water basins, small garden plots, waiting pavilions, and so on. Having passed through the *roji*, the visitor must crouch to enter the tea ceremony room through a small, low door called the *nijiriguchi*, which is about 79 centimetres high and 72 centimetres wide. The psychological effect of crouching through this low doorway is to make the small, dimly lit space inside seem much deeper and more complex. The carefully placed windows controlling the natural light in the low-ceilinged room and the difficulty of entering it, intensify the impression of enclosure.

In tea ceremony architecture and in the devices – architectural and other – used in the spaces around it, a certain hint of the labyrinth pervades the atmosphere. Ando's architecture is characterized by a similar mood of the maze. Though his plans and compositions are usually simple and lucid, movement lines within them develop in a complicated way. One of his major concerns is discovering the degree of complexity possible in simple plans. [...]

At the Koshino House, a staircase leads downwards from the entrance to a spacious living room. From this space, one turns 180 degrees and descends along a dark, narrow corridor, at the end of which one must turn again to reach the wing housing the private quarters, all opening onto another corridor with one wall pierced by narrow slit windows admitting light into the dimness and enriching the spatial experience. In all of these houses, there is a series of spaces in which light and shade are contrasted in dynamic sequences to inject complexity and depth into fundamentally static plans with highly surprising results.

Architecture for the tea ceremony is based on an aesthetic of action inherent in the static state; and the architecture of Sen no Rikyu, where static elements are arranged to create active tension, is the ultimate expression of this aesthetic. Transcending the expression of mere action, and subtly revealing the active inherent in the static – a fundamental goal for all Japanese art – are aims shared by Rikyu and Ando.

The symbolic representation of nature is a major current in all Japanese art, as is readily seen in such outstanding examples as the garden of the temple Ryoanji, where stones and white sand are used to depict islands and the sea. Other gardens of this style – called *kare-san-sui* – are found in Zen temples in various parts of the nation. Their symbolic effect is heightened by their lack of moisture. In a climate like that of Japan, where humidity is generally high, they might be described as dryness in wetness.

The same mood of a dry element placed in a generally moist atmosphere pervades the courtyard gardens that are always a part of Ando's residential designs. In them, without directly introducing nature by planting trees, Ando symbolically includes invisible natural elements: light, wind and sound. The courtyards, open to the exterior only from the top, are generally composed of dry elements such as concrete walls and flooring, which is sometimes covered in stone. Into this space, light, sound, wind and rain fall to caress, illuminate and moisten the dry materials and in this way give the people living in the house an association with nature. All of the rooms of the house open onto this courtyard, from which they derive their only natural lighting and ventilation, since the entire building is usually closed on the periphery.

Taking the humble houses of the common people as its model, tea house architecture often employs unfinished logs, simply split bamboo, and walls made of clay with an admixture of chopped straw. Coarse materials were deliberately used for the sake of creating an aesthetically pure, ideal world of sobriety, calm and refined rusticity. For example, miscanthus-thatch roofing in tea ceremony pavilions is selected, not out of economic or functional considerations, but solely for aesthetic effect. Designers of tea ceremony architecture carefully selected only those materials conducive to the production of a microcosm compatible with the aesthetics of *wabi*.

Ando is most deeply concerned with creating his own ideal kind of space and, like the designers of tea ceremony buildings, carefully chooses the materials his ideal requires. In the case of the modern urban environment, the most natural of all materials is concrete. [...] In light of the conditions prevailing in Japanese cities today, Ando's preference for unfinished concrete can be interpreted as the spirit of the *wabi* aesthetic expressed in modern terms. [...]

The desire for simplicity is related to the tenets of Zen Buddhism, with which tea ceremony masters such as Rikyu maintained close spiritual connections. The exclusion of all superfluous things – a fundamental Zen attitude – pervades all good tea ceremony architecture.

As I have pointed out, designers of such architecture like to use natural materials, to have them look as natural as possible, and to employ muted – almost monochrome – colour schemes. Ando also severely limits the range of interior colours. His buildings are almost entirely unfinished concrete with the exception of floors and furnishings, which are of natural materials, and window sashes, which, although steel, are always painted grey, never bright assertive colours. [...] In addition, Ando is a direct heir of tea ceremony disdain for ostentatious decoration. When tea ceremony architecture was in the process of evolution, monochrome ink paintings imported from China became popular in Japan and exerted great aesthetic influence. Their use in tea ceremony rooms and buildings gave added impetus to the preference for severely limited colours and to the reduction of interior ornament to no more than a vase containing a very small number of simple flowers.

Since it prizes the value of abbreviation, Zen philosophy tends to prefer a perfectly empty space to a space that is perfectly complete. The same preference is to be seen in both tea ceremony architecture and in Ando's work. For example, not only are Ando's courtyard gardens empty, but their walls seem to have been deliberately stripped of expression. He strives to create space by means of invisible, apparently non-existent things. In short, his kind of space can be called a void, but, ironically, a void in which all things are inherent. The idea underlying such a space is common to much oriental philosophy.

Rikyu aimed for regular forms and balanced proportions but included an element of distortion in his designs. Similarly, Ando employs almost exclusively straight lines and geometric forms. When curves occur in his work, they are in the form of circles or parts of circles. His designs stress floor plan pattern, in which balance between symmetry and asymmetry is important.

At a glance, Ando's buildings, especially his early ones, seem highly symmetrical. This is partly because of his fascination with the number 2 and relations between pairs of things. A perfect relation evokes symmetry, and a basic image in his design is that of two things turned towards each other. When two things face each other, the intercession of a third is unnecessary to the creation of a world. This is why Ando designs houses that are open on the inside (where pairs of things face each other) and closed to the outside (on which the same pairs of things turn their backs). But, instead of insisting on symmetry, Ando creates a subtle distortion by means of lines of human motion, light or sight. Symmetry is the premise governing the total composition. But, within the whole, asymmetry in individual parts infuses the dynamic into the static totality. [...]

Behind the methods and intentions employed by Sen no Rikyu was a spirit of reaction against the authority of his time, against the military ruler of the nation, Toyotomi Hideyoshi, and against the opulence and extravagance of the culture of the age (the so-called Momoyama culture). This spirit of rejection evoked the culture of unostentatious refinement described as *wabi*. In rejecting the gilt and glory of decoration of the Momoyama period, the spirit of *wabi* sought beauty in coarse, plain materials.

Ando too is dissatisfied with the culture of his time and with what goes under the classification 'modern living'. He speaks out in favour of a simple way of life and against the trends prevailing in a consumer society. His void spaces are a criticism of the insipidness of the overly materialistic modern way of life. Rikyu detested the insipid as lacking tension. Because Ando too is unable to tolerate the insipid, he produces houses with hard, stone cold surfaces that resound on being tapped and that result in spaces taut with tension. The chill of Ando's concrete void spaces is symbolically similar to the ideal world Rikyu wanted to create in tea ceremony architecture.

It is by no means coincidental, then, that Tadao Ando is the man who produced what is undoubtedly the first tea ceremony room in concrete erected in Japan. The room is a physical manifestation of Ando's spiritual fellowship with tea ceremony architecture in general and especially with that of Sen no Rikyu. As if it were a resurrection of Rikyu's world of *wabi*, the room is filled with the tension of the dynamic contained within the static, and it exemplifies the act of inheriting a tradition on its spiritual plane.

K Takeyama, 'Tadao Ando: Heir to a Tradition', in *Perspecta*, 20, 1983.

Tadao Ando's Critical Modernism
Kenneth Frampton

Tadao Ando belongs to that small circle of Japanese architects whose practice may be identified as critical on the grounds that it has assumed a culturally oppositional stance to the instrumentality of megalopolitan development. […] In Ando's case, this resistance is predicated on emphasizing the boundary, thereby creating an introspective domain within which the homeowner may be granted sufficient private 'ground' with which to withstand the alienating no-man's-land of the contemporary city.

At the same time, Ando remains aware that this pervasive modern predicament cannot be resolved by any kind of fictitious 'homecoming'; that is to say, by the mere simulation of traditional Japanese timber construction or the use of evocative domestic components, such as the shoji screen or the tatami mat. And while such elements are still available, despite the industrialization of Japanese society, Ando has stoically refused the nostalgic ethos which such vernacular elements imply. He has, in fact, consistently rejected the current vogue for evoking another, more benign period of history, remote from the harsh facts of industrial and post-industrial society. Thus, the material conditions of modern society are always indirectly present in Ando's architecture, as implicit in its reinforced concrete walls as in the flood tide of development, which is only momentarily checked by these same massive boundaries. These walls reflect, through their surprising weight, not only the seismic conditions of the country, but also the 'storm of progress' which rages throughout the Tokaido megalopolis.

Ando uses walls not only to establish 'a human zone where the individual will can develop in the midst of the standardization of the surrounding society,' but also as a means of countering the ubiquitous monotony of commercial architecture; 'the use of the walls', as Ando puts it, 'is 'to control walls.' And yet, while the wall on the exterior acts to delimit and reflect the surrounding urban chaos, on the interior it serves to encapsulate a 'primitive' space which, in Ando's own words, 'is able to symbolize relations between human beings and things', as these are mediated by the interaction of material with light, wind and water.

Ando's dichotomous attitude towards the wall reflects the two primary themes which underlie the entire body of his work: on the one hand, there is a preoccupation with an *oppositional* perception of modern reality, on the other, there is a pronounced stress on the *ontological* experience of the sensate being rather than on the abstract processes demanded by the imperatives of industrialized society. This joint concern for what might be termed the 'dialectic of being' had perhaps never been more comprehensively formulated by Ando than in his essay 'From Self-Enclosed Modern Architecture Towards Universality' of 1982, wherein modern architecture (now seen as a potential paradigm of place creation rather than space-endlessness) is posited as a counterthesis to the universal domination of history and technology. Indeed, throughout this essay Modernism appears as an ambiguous indication. It is perceived in its universal mode as leaving no room for autochthonous culture; but it is also recognized for its capacity to be inflected with regard to the attributes of a specific place. In a world overrun by media Ando values the 'silence' of modern form for its resistance to consumption. […]

It is possible to claim that Ando's work is critical on two interrelated counts. It criticizes universal modernity from within by establishing new goals and limits for modern architectural practice without at the same time denying its continuing validity as a vital cultural force. Yet it also evokes as a precedent for a more autochthonous critique, the enduring significance of the Sukiya tea-house style invented in the second half of the sixteenth century by Sen no Rikyu.

With regard to the first aspect, Ando has evidenced his breadth of critical understanding by remarking on the comparable devaluations suffered by the post and the colonnade as a consequence of the invention of the reinforced concrete frame. Ando has argued that the fundamental tropes of architecture in both the East and the West have been effectively nullified by the advent of the universal rigid frame. He has also cited the salient role played by the symbolic, non-structural post in traditional Japanese architecture, pointing out how the rhythm of the western colonnade has been rendered technically obsolete and hence culturally inaccessible by the infinitely greater spanning capacity of the reinforced concrete frame. […]

Ando aspires to a form of cross-cultural criticism which attempts to compensate for the generic devaluations which architecture has suffered at the hands of technique. In this respect, his criticism is as valid for the West as for the East. But it is equally clear that Ando's work is at its most subversive in a Japanese context, where the deeper significance of its Sukiya references can be readily appreciated. For evidently the original Sukiya style comprised certain fundamental characteristics which are consciously reinterpreted in Ando's work. Of the basic (non-stylistic) features which Ando's work and the Sukiya style have in common, Kiyoshi Takeyama cites calmness and purity, gentleness and clarity of mood. Ando follows the Sukiya manner in his preference for dim lighting broken by shafts of light unexpectedly entering the darkness. Likewise, he attempts to create a feeling of spiritual expansiveness within a small domain. And while both expressions are patently artificial they succeed nonetheless in evoking a feeling for nature as an ineffable, all-pervasive presence. Thus, even in the midst of a highly congested urban fabric the tonal reference of the Sukiya style is ultimately rural. […]

For Ando, architecture must always embody a double movement, it must accommodate daily life while remaining open to the symbolic. To this end his work has always been structured through absolutes: wall versus column, square versus circle, concrete versus glass, dark versus light, materiality versus immateriality. The essential character of his work resides finally in the *interaction* between these last four terms, in the way that light transforms both volume and mass; in the way in which it effects changes according to the hour, transforming dark into light and ponderous mass into scintillating surface. It is for this reason that Ando, unlike his peers, insists upon the paradoxical rendering of concrete as though it were a light material, like a paper screen, where all the energy is concentrated on the surface. […]

For Ando concrete, as for the Shakers, whose culture he has long admired, the abstract, purified form is merely an agent for the realization of being.

K Frampton, 'Tadao Ando's Critical Modernism', in *Tadao Ando, Buildings, Projects, Writings*, New York, 1984.

The Story AND O
Peter Eisenman

Much as the primary concern of science is no longer the conquest of the natural through reason, so too can Tadao Ando's architecture be said to have suspended its dependency upon reason. That Japan should be the first country to have an architecture in a condition of suspended reason is not surprising. Like no other country, Japan has constructed a post-industrial world. Its cities have already become the fantastic futuristic vision seen in a film like *Blade Runner*. Japan is the first icon of the electronic age – an atopia in terms of western classical space. This liberation from the classical topos/atopia, whether western or Japanese, produces in an architecture a corollary breakdown of figure/frame, and, ultimately, the unframing of the human figure. No longer is the architecture between man and nature, but between man and knowledge.

This new relationship is more easily understood by Japanese culture because the Japanese language itself has always acknowledged the condition. In the structure of western languages the human subject is automatically understood when the idea of 'natural' is introduced. In Japan, this is not the case. The structure of Japanese grammar is uncentered, it already contains this absence of man.

Thus Japan has constructed this post-industrial world not as a stage set of nostalgia (although pockets of sentimentality remain), but as a documentation of its ever-expanding achievements. This lack of pretense is not surprising. There was never any theatricality in the architecture of Katsura, or Shokintei, or Ryoan-ji. Rather, the fusion of signs in a Ryoan-ji, the metaphor as traces of its making, produces a condition of between meaning; a silence between metaphor and mask. The architecture of Tadao Ando obviously has its cultural roots in this work. So, equally, it is not surprising that his work should be without nostalgia. Ando penetrates the mask of Japanese culture, placing us like Edgar Allan Poe and *Blade Runner* within the horrors of a mundus ex-nihilo. Something in his work is shivering, beyond the cool, the rational, the poetic or the sublime. Something which in its emptiness has a sense of both the terror and awe of the *other*. Space is no longer either the western topos – the condition of place, nor the Japanese *Ma* – literally the condition of between place, but rather now between place and no place, between topos and atopia. What had seemed *other* to the western observer of Japanese space, was merely within a Japanese lexicon of space such as *Ma*. [...] But this space of Ando's is now outside of, or other in the Japanese sense as well; it is, as it were, a between of the between. [...] Ando's space is not the other of either the West or the East, nor is it the other of a formal dialectic – old or new, inside or outside. Rather it has an eerie sensibility that neither transcends nor is metaphysical, neither banal nor sublime, reeking rather of an estranged locution of the ordinary and the hyperreal, or, in Roland Barthes' terms, 'the phantasm of the commonplace'.

Ando's is an absence which is not the space of the void of the West, nor the space of emptiness of Japan. Rather it is borne of this hybrid fusion, one which is a trace of the absence of known signs. Ando's spaces are also seemingly inert; they contain no physical metaphors of shear, compression or tension. Equally they are in the inert state of something which was formerly live and now is in a state of shock. His space is outside of these concerns. If western space is animate, and eastern space is silent, then Ando's space is other, without speaking to a theatricality of silence. In Ando, space is not measured from light to dark, from thin to deep, as it is in the paper-panelled shoji and the hewn alcoves of Shokintei. Rather, his light is between; neither dense nor sparse, opaque nor translucent.

In most other architecture these oppositions, western or eastern, rest in a statement or presentation and then a resolution of visual tension or hierarchy. In Ando's work visual resolution is not at issue. For Ando there may be a mathematical and thus visual or geometric order, but these signs are mute; they explain nothing. Ando's work, instead, deals with a suspension of signs, a suspension of the visual screen that keeps us one step from chaos. This suspension, this emptiness of the sign, is not a formal suspension; it is that which Ando calls 'natural'. This is not the natural of nature, but rather, as Barthes says, 'a brief event which immediately finds its proper form'. This is the essence of what might be called the not formal or the textual in Ando's work.

P Eisenman, 'The Story AND O', in T Ando, *The Yale Studio & Current Works*, New York, 1989.

Tadao Ando and the Cult of Shintai
Kenneth Frampton

In many respects Ando is a builder rather than an architect in the liberal bourgeois sense. An autodidact from his unofficial craft training to his first uncertain projects as an independent designer (he has never worked for anyone), Ando secured for himself an autochthonous upbringing in its endemic closeness to nature and craft. This formation was almost medieval in its underlying character, and he still retains today an envy for the way in which craftsmen create directly with their hands.

Struggle is the condition of life as far as Ando is concerned, and he brings to the drawing board and his studio the same physical stamina, tactical concentration and agility that was to stand him in such good stead in his somewhat anomalous early career as a professional boxer. He is, to adapt the boxing metaphor, always on his feet, and in almost fifteen years of practice, his architecture has been brought forth as the product of an unflagging energy and intensity of spirit. Achieving over forty buildings in not much more than a decade, Ando's output can be compared to that of A W N Pugin who was to build over a hundred churches and other structures in barely seventeen years. This somewhat outlandish comparison may be taken further, for while they could hardly be culturally more removed from each other, and while they are separated by 150 years, they, nonetheless, share a similar, virtually religious conviction about the spiritual calling and capacity of architecture and about its critical potential for the revitalization of society and life. In addition to this, they have certain things in common in tectonic terms, in as much as they are both (like Auguste Perret) antithetical to plaster or to scenographic revetment of any kind, and it is to this ethical line of modernity that Ando belongs. Removed from Pugin in his strong grasp of reality, Ando remains convinced about the responsibility of the architect for the creation of fragmentary places, to stand, like enclaves, against the ubiquitous placelessness of the late modern city. In this way Ando sees architecture as an act of creative volition, informed, as always, by critical intelligence.

Typical of Ando's realistic/symbolic creativity is his 600-seat, demountable Kara-Za Theatre (1985–7) which he first projected as a wood-framed, tapering tower construction with black siding and a red-fabric roof. Although he sensed that the chance of realizing such an unusual proposal was somewhat slight, he nonetheless pursued this architectonic image, which derived from an experience he had once had of the traditional timber Kanamaru Theatre in Shikoku. He had felt then that, as in the typical Shinto shrine, the structure possessed an uncanny capacity to resonate with the actors' voices and their emotive movements. This experience fed into Ando's intuition about the role of the body in architectural space – his feeling for the *élan vital*, without which architecture remains unconsummated. Ando explored this notion at length in his essay 'Shintai' (1986). Rather than the standard translation of *shintai* as body, Ando intends, by his use of the word, the inseparable union of body and spirit. [...]

Ando strove to establish the realm of the *shintai* in his Kara-Za Theatre in part by assuring its theatrical otherworldliness. That is to say, he designed it in such a way that both audience and actor would be able to realize their own respective *shintai* in the same theatrical space; the former transforming itself through crossing an asymmetrical arched bridge, symbolizing the passage from the realms of reality to illusion, the latter coming into being through the resonant octagonal volume of the auditorium/stage. This transition to the thereafter of the drama is reinforced by Ando's enclosure of the playhouse in a traditional compound surrounded by a woven bamboo fence known as *takeyarai*.

The theatre director Juro Kara had initially intended to build a permanent playhouse, but due to a change in patronage the programme was changed to require a demountable theatre, a building that would be first built at the Tohoku Exposition in Sendai. Ando met this new programme with characteristic simple, single-minded brilliance and wilfulness. He decided to assemble the structure entirely out of standard tubular scaffolding poles, thereby working in a partially dematerialized element comparable to his equally ineffable use of fair-faced concrete as the single constituent material in almost all of his other permanent works.

Made out of 1,500, two-inch diameter tubular steel poles (a material that can be found almost anywhere) and braced by a structural steel octagon, this theatre took fifteen days to erect, and while a suspended cable structure may well have been erected more rapidly, it would hardly have been an appropriate cradle for Ando's reinterpretation of the traditional Japanese stage. Aside from the red canvas roof and the stained timber siding, it is typical of Ando to exploit a single material to its utmost and to push both his design staff and the semi-skilled construction workers to the limits of their respective metiers, in order to achieve an imaginative and precise result. [...]

Traditional craft production and modern technology have always found an unlikely but necessary unity in reinforced concrete construction and never more so than in Ando's precision-cast concrete structures. Here, highly crafted traditional formwork in wood is absolutely essential to the accuracy and tolerance of the final result, so that equally precise, prefabricated timber door frames can be popped into concrete openings with no more than $3/32$ inch tolerance on either side of the frame. Concrete of this quality depends upon the exercise of strict discipline involving, among other 'mysteries': first, the use of an engineering grade concrete mix, having a slump-test reading of $6 3/8$ inches as opposed to the standard 8 inches; second, the maintenance of reinforcing bars at no closer than $1 1/2$ inches apart; third, the thorough vibration of the pour; and last but not least, the creation of a perfectly watertight mould, without which the surface of the concrete is weakened and subject to fracture. This last, needless to say, returns us to the quality and strength of the timber formwork and to the fact that Ando has the capacity to sustain a number of highly trained carpenters, who, working in teams, are always engaged in the production of his formwork. Ando sustains a certain fraternal competition between these teams as though they were rival, medieval guilds competing with each other for their prowess in the production of quality concrete.

Looking back over Ando's work of the last decade, one is constantly struck by the way in which certain themes are returned to, above all, the dialogical relationship between the building and the site, together with the subsequent articulation of the structure through the changing impact of light. The Rokko Housing in Kobe (1978–83) and the Festival centre in Naha, Okinawa (1980–84), are both quite typical in this regard; the last exemplifying, in an assertive way, Ando's critical contextualism. By this last term I wish to refer to the way in which he both respects and challenges the attributes of the site. Thus the vast, cubic, introspective concrete box that constitutes the Festival building more or less repudiates its immediate downtown context, although it aligns itself with an existing arcade and a main shopping street. [...]

To an even greater degree than in the work of Louis Kahn, by whom he is evidently influenced, Ando depends upon light for the registration of the poetic interaction of his work with the necessary, ever-changing passage of climate and time. While in the Koshino House (1981) a single shaft of sunlight functions as an introverted sundial, in the Festival, '...rays of light, striking against the coarse surface, are absorbed and crystallized by each of the block units, forming an infinite sparkling of brilliance.' In addition to all this, the Festival serves as an introspective city in miniature, wherein the open escalator, full-height atrium and gallery present themselves jointly as a compensatory public realm, a realm that continues on the inside, the 'street-sitebuilding' continuum of the surrounding downtown area.

To the degree that it is a totally commercial structure, the Festival building is typical of Ando's capacity for symbolic realism. There can be few, if any, contemporary architects who have been so consistently successful in rendering everyday production and/or marketing facilities as 'places of public appearance' or into an occasion for a spiritual *temenos* in the form of an enclosed court. [...]

It is a remarkable fact that many of Ando's commissions have indeed emerged from a dream, and that in many instances, he has imagined the project first and found a client for it later. And while he fully recognizes that 'architecture, unlike art, cannot end in mere expression', he nonetheless insists on the creative priority of the initial, bold vision that begins to search for the means or for the agent of its realization, as in all the various Mount Rokko projects, in the Time's building, and in the most recent Church on the Water under construction in Hokkaido.

Like many of the finest architects of this century, Ando renders his religious works ambiguously so that they are, at one and the same time, both liturgically viable and spiritually archaic. Thus all of Ando's churches are as much Shinto shrines in their attitude towards the paramount divinity of nature as they are places of Christian worship. Thus he writes of his Church on the Water, 'unlike in traditional Christian churches, the symbol of the cross stands at the exterior chapel'. (cf The underlying paganism of Gunnar Asplund's placement of the cross and meditation mound in his Woodland Cemetery.) Ando continues: 'On a typically cold, snowy day on the plains of Hokkaido, one will notice a cross lit by the setting sun, in a field of pure white snow. To experience God in this natural setting, perhaps, is to experience an encounter with one's own spirit.' [...]

K Frampton, 'Tadao Ando and the Cult of Shintai', in T Ando, *The Yale Studio & Current Works*, New York, 1989.

Infinitesimally Small and as Palpable as Silence
Giordano Tironi

Since the sixth century, the Shinto shrine of Naiku in Ise has been demolished every twenty years and rebuilt on a neighbouring site. Of the two sites, the one which 'waits' is fenced off with ropes and there are only a few tell-tale marks on the ground; at the centre is a sacred column covered by a little roof. Between these two sites virtuality and presence, void and solid, inaccessibility and usability seem so inextricably linked that somehow the empty one has a stronger presence than the one on which the shrine actually stands.

In Tadao Ando's work we also find something of this atmosphere of duality, like the perennial condition of something which will never be finished where form – not ready to show its face – occupies the space of its own absence. Each of Ando's buildings seems to reiterate (but not repeat) all the projects which went before: imprints left behind by architectural forms which have since moved on but which sometimes turn back on themselves, retrace their steps, and then proceed. Sometimes, out of the background of this introspective itinerary something condenses, some theme in his work which becomes manifest. It might be circulation, as the experience of time and space directly felt in the body; horizontality as something which is scooped out of the ground; or a certain solemnity conferred on commonplace things or the action of fencing things off and making enclosures which form a series of layers, one inside the other. If such themes are not in themselves a coherent way of understanding every aspect of Ando's work they at least give us some idea of what the territory is. In this territory there are sometimes moments of architecture which inaugurate new themes for exploration or which act as prototypes for moving forward his painstaking explorations of the flimsiness of immaterial things, the particular sacred moment which presents itself to us out of the infinity of time and brings us close to the still, silent nothingness whence all life comes.

Each project is an almost imperceptible moment in which there is a flicker in the continuum and, as on a photographic plate, some shadow of this is captured. It is only an instant, but one in which things come together in a particular way: the crucifix shape in his recent work (not only in his chapels); dramatization of water as a vast gesture; exploration of the difference between absolute emptiness and another kind of space which is also empty, but because the form which belongs there has vacated it.

That is how I see the three Ando projects I would like to look at here. They emerge indistinctly, as a group: the Church on the Water on the island of Hokkaido (and an open-air theatre which has now been added to it); the Church of the Light, in Osaka; and a Children's Museum in Hyogo which consists of two buildings linked by a long open-air pathway – these pieces are widely spread out, almost like a liturgical manual of how to perform the ritual of creating place by marking out the stations of an itinerary through it. Although the two chapels are not large they imply that their territory of operation is vast; they remind us as architects that to become the protagonists of a place or at least to be allowed to ask questions about what it is, the architecture we make does not have to be gargantuan in size. A notion (or a confirmation of something) comes out of these realizations. Each new project, instead of clarifying Ando's ideas for him, adds an extra level of complexity to his way of perceiving things, complicating whatever can be said about their many shades of meaning. As one project evolves out of another it seems that his 'forms' try to attain a place of absoluteness somewhere outside, beyond the process in which we try to manipulate forms to make architecture out of them or, as he says himself, 'rather than stick to architectural forms as such I find it more worthwhile to think about their spiritual and emotional content'.

Architecture like this does nothing to make our outlook any clearer or more intelligible. As it leads us into its own landscape, this very landscape becomes evanescent, as though seen through a clouded crystal or peering into a great depth. When we try to look into the compositional procedures used by Ando, apparently so absolutely clear, we realize we have moved into a very subtle zone of 'transparent opacity', variable densities of nothing, evanescent solids and voids, as in Junichiro Tanizaki's description of the *toko no ma* (a particular excavated space found in traditional Japanese houses): 'We seem to feel that the air itself contains its own layer of silence, in a darkness of eternal serenity.'

Moving closer to investigate Ando's architecture more deeply requires that we decide what to do about the various possible kinds of architectural silence we encounter – form being only one stage along the various paths we might take and which consist of nothing at all except sensibility, where our very presence is the only animating agent and where we have to be careful, as we talk, not to miss what his projects themselves are quietly saying; it would be so easy to get carried away by some concept of one's own. Can we just say they are beautiful, these works of suspended profound architecture? Would it not be better to leave them alone?

Other Japanese architects (Isozaki, Maki, Shinoara, Kurokawa are the star names, but there are others) seem intent on saying something about the tremendous contradictions of contemporary Japan by deliberately introducing as much *angst* as possible using irony or what one could call 'fragmentationalism' – all sorts of implied or allusive ideas about order as some sort of metaphor or symbol; but in the case of Ando, the response to the barely-controlled chaos that is the Japanese city is an icy silence of pure sound untouched by their *urban panic* and which makes only a few tightly controlled gestures as brief as *haiku*: clear, decisive, definitive, responding to the desperate rushing of everyday life with a calibrated slowness in which there is time to feel and to see something.

Ando has gone out of the city into the calm of the sky, leaving architecture far behind, to a place where he has found his own vision of a possible city. This comes back down out of that sky and penetrates as light into openings he controls or as the winds that blow in courtyards, or just a single threads of light which, for an instant, shows that they have come from the most incredible depths of a space which is somewhere else. In the middle of the deafening racket of the city, here we have Ando's far more ancient order: just a few austere moves.

But the recent projects I mention are also concerned with something else. When Ando makes buildings which are not in cities there is still the same feeling that his architecture is urban – even in the most remote places there is still some sense that he is working against that far-off noise – even on the top of a mountain. I recently talked to him about this and asked him if there is any change or variability in the 'critical distance' he puts into his work when working on urban sites or in the country. He says that, 'one's reaction to that kind of chaos can just as well work itself out in a totally natural setting as much as when you are actually in it. If you intend to make a stand against it, it doesn't matter where you do it but how.' I suppose that means that if this is a kind of city which is to be resisted, the alternative city can only be conceived by going away somewhere else.

This distance/resistance enables us to get back to the selves we had forgotten, where our submerged emotions come out again. In cities where there are incredible numbers of houses, heaped on top of one another, signs and messages screaming at us, where anything and everything just happens all the time, it may be that there is no way of having any influence. When that is the situation, Ando limits himself to setting out a few lines and points to make enclosed buildings which only look inward, stealing a few square feet of sky from the totally controlling straitjacket of planning restrictions; this is done by using walls. In Ando's hands light (or rather, the shadows light makes) become a way of switching the context on or off, controlling the way it penetrates the farthest crevices of the building. Walls control other walls, making houses which put distance between themselves and the other useless buildings nearby with which no interaction would be possible or relevant. Empty spaces fit inside each other, concrete or glass-block screens create lost corners, left-over fragments of space/time in houses where every spatial element is powerfully present, but remote.

The Church of the Light exemplifies this perfectly. Transcending matter, Ando presents a fragile wall, suspended in the air like an eternal question at the finest point of an equilibrium, where 'the spatiality makes it impossible to ask any more questions' (as he had written many years earlier).

Just as in *Fragments d'éternité* (1978) Bretagnolle, writing about Ando's abstract geometry, observed that 'like the etymology of the word itself, something abstract is torn from the substance to which it belongs, thus bringing it back to its own essence all the more effectively'. We come back again to think again about this crucifix. The changing seasons of eternity pass one after the other through the arms of the cross itself, into a delicate, precisely-machined, inward-looking space where every other sensation is eliminated: 'a state in which one feels that everything exists, as if nothing exists' (Ando). An articulated wall brings us into a rectangular space which is then sectioned off for its whole length. Here, the screen-walls do not exist for what they are but for what they create: a depth, which urges us to imagine what there is beyond, behind the appearance of things, exploiting the sense of premonition *(kehai)* which is innate in us. This gives us the impression of going through the wall and thus relating the usual notions of inside and outside.

The same theme returns in the Church on the Water where another cross, just outside, stand as a final element interposed between us and the landscape. Like the *torii* which stand in front of Shinto temples, this reconfirms nature as the storehouse of 'sacrality'. The Church itself seems to slide towards the water; its interior is in the form of three steps descending towards 'slabs' of water which flows into the stream. The limits of this progressive slipping of the construction towards what existed there before, are clearly defined by the construction details, which are free of confusions and superimpositions. It is left to us to decide what we feel.

The route of the existing stream was not deviated to form the new stretches of water, as it may seem, but was taken as a suggestion from which to draw inspiration for the project. The building thus constructs the real origin, in the temple, of this specific place. If we imagine the site as it was before, we can understand how important the presence of water was in those woods. We might also remember that at Time's I there was earlier evidence of how important water was for Ando (and the Rokko houses already suggested it). The gradual steps of this building upward from the water were thought out in terms of the Tekase which flows alongside. Jean Herbert writes of water and the *hongu* (sanctuary): 'water is a powerful purifying agent; even a modest stream puts up an effective barrier against everything bad or sacrilegious'.

Through the side door of the Church on the Water the exact repetition of the facade (though it is not easy to talk about facades when the real facade is nature itself repeated by its own reflection in the water) allows air to pervade the construction, filling its voids with the space of preceding projects. It also clearly establishes the limits of the intervention as nearby walls, thrust into the ground, cause the organized space to be protracted towards infinity. At the same time they define a virtual enclosure fed by the tensions created in its intervals, and reaching as far as the open-air theatre nearby. By sending back reflections of themselves, they thus create a territorial triangulation marked by a slight, but very long incision on the ground like a scratch left in a wall, making imaginary shiftings which go far beyond the chapel itself. This tends to remove weight from these enormous freestanding concrete walls (one thinks of the works of Richard Serra) giving the impression of begin able to slide them through the landscape like thin dividing screens (shoji). The portal frame also reads as a potential screen or a potential structure standing in the landscape. It is designed to act as the guide on which the large glazed screen-wall slides across the surface of the water. When the chapel is left open overlooking the water, the glass wall is shifted to one side, introducing as it goes yet another crucifix, movable this time, into nature.

Another role which the wall plays is that of defining the interstitial route which envelops the project, subtly invading it from one level through to the next. This theme was particularly present in the Time's I project and was also suggested in the spiral arrangement of the Kidosaki House. In all these projects from being simply a way of getting from A to B the pedestrian route transforms itself into an experience operating both in physical and mental territory. At Hyogo the pathway connecting the two buildings penetrates them and then continues through, involving the context at the bigger scale. The seemingly endless wall which runs alongside this route seems to sustain the whole thrust of the hill above the lake and to open towards the water. Without any doubt, the piazza with its twenty-five columns like a house with the roof taken off, is a mechanism which intensifies our relationship with nature. It introduces an element of discontinuousness, whilst articulating the two levels of the route between the entrance pavilion and the main building. 'It is important to know that the avenue *(sando)* leading to the sanctuary must not be straight. It would be considered a mark of disrespect to walk in a straight line towards the sanctuary' (Herbert). The unusual theme of the isolated columns perhaps has affinities with *minka* houses in which a central pole symbolizes the act of foundation and is thought to offer protection from evil spirits. This theme has been elaborated by Ando only once before: outside his recent pavilion for the Tennoij exhibition we find five columns aligned on the main elevation almost as though they wanted to bring the very structure of the building outside; an 'incomplete' architecture which leaves space for the imagination to envisage infinite completions.

In Ando's earlier public buildings the symbolic meeting places between man and nature (for example in the form of a courtyard) were physically inaccessible, as in the Rokko Chapel, at Jun Port Island, or in the Old/New restaurant complex. Here at Hyogo, however, the theme of inaccessibility is suggested by the water which surrounds the buildings. But because of the pervasiveness of green space in these three projects the concrete, whether internal or lateral, is always open to the sky and radicalizes itself in the complexity and essentialness of the pathway, making the strong relation with the context less restrictive than on earlier occasions.

Without introducing any hierarchy of time and space there is a succession of voids in which there is no 'wasted time'. The way they are made suggests a kind of immobility, perhaps analogous to that noticed by Gilles Deleuze in the early films of Ozu: 'Movements become more and more rare; the dolly makes slow, low "blocks of movement"; the camera angle is always from below and usually fixed frontally or always at the same angle; dissolves are abandoned in favour of the simple clean cut.'

Absence of verticality and, therefore, exaltation of the horizontal pedestrian pathway, is a specific aspect of traditional Japanese architecture. Here it is strongly emphasized almost as though to correct the outline of the hill of Hyogo itself. Both the pathway and the buildings seem to want to join *oki* (horizontality of the sea) and *oku* (height, mountain) and, in Ando's own words, 'permit us to communicate with the place'.

Like Hokusai's bridges which lead us away into the mist and the unknown, Ando's architecture leads us on interior journeys which we find in the writings of Yasunari Kawabata: 'he walked, contemplating the lake; it seemed that the reflected images would continue forever, and never separate'.

G Tironi, *Casabella*, 558, June 1989.

Dormant Lines
Darell Wayne Fields

The drawings of an architect can be used either to perpetuate a seductive mysticism or to clarify precise intentions – Ando chooses to be precise. This acute precision conveys an inherent relationship between Ando's sketches, construction documents and architecture. To perceive and understand that relationship is to rediscover the lines that are the essence of Ando's work – the lines that are not seen. To watch Ando sketch is to become aware of his intensity and his intentions. His manner, manifested in the physical exertion that takes place during this initial act of making, is more attuned to carving than to drawing. Although filled with emotion, the sketches are imbued with a technical knowing that directs the construct of an architectural space. His sketches embody a myriad of lines, fluctuating between ideas of materiality and 'voidedness'. Lines depicting either eminent walls or reverent spaces are treated at the same level of substance. These lines and their interrelationships are quite transparent. Suddenly, an architectural composition exists whose primary components – form and space – are absolutely inseparable.

In the initial sketches and in the more final construction documents, one finds circles – volumetric spheres – and orthogonal lines inscribed into plans and sections; these are consistent throughout the process. Their measurements are predetermined by Ando, and rarely does their initial impetus conform to the external constraints of programme or site; they are pure and remain so. Clearly, these are lines that embody Ando's conception of proportions. In the hierarchy of the built environment, however, they are never seen. It could be said that this reflects Ando's personal preoccupation with geometry. To think this, however, would be to understand his work only at the level of mere drawing. The meaning of these lines is truly engaged by placing your body in that presumably abstract space: it is the phenomenon of feeling that the space is correct and could be no other way. It is the presence of the thing not seen and the revelation of existential qualities found in apparently formal constructs. These lines are constructed and drawn not for the sake of the drawing, but for the sake of the body.

At the construction document phase, one finds that these intrinsic lines are also the most dormant. They are reduced to lines of measurement and become mere markings for the placement of now apparently more important concrete walls. Their wilful intensity has been subdued by the pragmatics of building, and it appears that their initial meaning could be lost at any moment. It is in this possibility of *loss*, however, that the presence of Ando's spatial intentions are found and preserved. These lines must be lost for them to merge with the construct of architectural space – they must be sacrificed. It is in this unseen world of sacrifice that Ando's architectural endeavour is given its conviction and spatial integrity.

Essentially, there is the need for drawing, but drawing is not essential. There is the need for intentions, but intentions without guidance are of little use. Finally, there is the need for construction, but simple construction rarely conveys architectural passion or conviction. If this ensemble of events is brought into equilibrium, however, then there is meaning – there is the *whole of architecture*.

D W Fields, 'Dormant Lines', in *Tadao Ando: Dormant Lines*, New York, 1991.

Indicencies: in the Drawing Lines of Tadao Ando
Peter Eisenman

This title has no meaning in English, therefore, this title cannot be literally translated into Japanese. It is a combination of sound and spelling which plays with the linguistic sign in English to give to it an indexical quality. As sound it refers to a word which is spelled with an E, instead of an I, *indecencies*, which means the qualities or states of being which are offensive to manners or morals. On the other hand, the word *indices* is a plural noun of the word index, its strange spelling and sound in the plural making it closer to the word *indece* than to index, hence the play between the two creates an index of its own.

In his work on the problem of signification the American philosopher Charles Sanders Peirce set up the difference between three conditions of the sign. These he termed *icon*, *index* and *symbol*. For our purposes here we will be concerned with only the first two terms, icon and index, since they bear directly on the problem of architectural drawing, and in particular they provide an insight into the condition of drawing in the work of Tadao Ando.

Traditionally, in Peirce's terms, architectural drawing is iconic. For Peirce an icon is a sign which has a primary and direct relationship to an object. The number one or the number two are iconic signs in that they relate directly to one or two of something. Architectural drawing is in this sense iconic since a building is developed directly from a set of measured line relationships in a two dimensional plan. But Ando's drawings are not merely iconic; they are also indexical. For Peirce an index is the sign of a set of relationships such as a syntax or a mathematical equation which describe the complex interactions in an object that may be known but are not necessarily seen. These are relationships of secondarity in that they do not reveal themselves upon initial viewing. Traditional architecture tends to repress possible issues of secondarity in favour of such primary relationships as form to function, form to shelter, site to building. Now while all of these iconic relationships are present in the work of Tadao Ando, his drawings indicate the presence of some other relationship, which may also be hidden even in the primary forms of his buildings. The drawings then can be seen as a way to probe within the seemingly rational abstraction of the raw concrete lines, planes and volumes, the primary icons of his architecture. But like much that is Japanese, Ando's drawings are like a hieroglyphic map that if read properly does not lead one to the buried treasure but becomes the treasure itself. There are three conditions of these mappings, these indices of the *other* in his work. The first can be likened to the structure of *haiku*.

Haiku is a compact evocative verse form; it deals with the capacity of a structure of written lines to be a poetic experience. In the written line of a haiku the poet attempts to present a spoken object – through the devices of assonance, alliteration, rhyme and rhythm – in the time and space of a single breath. Meaning is evoked in a haiku by a simple unadorned relationship of words in each line. These relationships always deal with the conditions of where, what and when, necessary to the structure of an experience of the object of haiku. For haiku the when, its time of experience, does not lie outside the object but rather is internal to it; the where also represents a condition of interiority. Thus to understand the what of haiku, its objectness, one must be inside the time and space of the lines. For objects in haiku are presented not described. Haiku presents its objectness alone without comment. While haiku seems to be nothing other than what it is, it is this seeming to be 'what it is' which is other, for its object is not represented completely as it is. It is this strange difference between what the object is and what it seems to be, that leads us from haiku to the architecture of Tadao Ando. The objectness of Tadao Ando's work are the lines of haiku. Like haiku, Ando's lines do not present themselves completely.

Like haiku, the understanding of Ando's forms comes immediately and instinctively rather than through logic and reason. We physically sense the minimalism of the spare, articulated, raw concrete skeletons yet their unseen complexity seeps into our intuition. Like haiku there is no blurring; these lines seem to speak for themselves. And yet there is always something else, something elusive which is sustained not necessarily in the drawing or the photograph but in the real space.

Like haiku, Ando does not give us spaces which allude to meaning, he gives us the real/concrete objects which are meaning. Ando's lines contain the when of the four seasons of haiku: the movement in Ando's drawing is like a moment between an early winter haiku and a deep summer Kanji. The cool tones of the hard edge drawings of, say, the chapel on Mount Rokko or the Church on the Water, where the lines appear as some palimpsest scratched from beneath a thin film of graphite to reveal their condition of body. Compare their stillness and opacity with another kind of drawing seen in the intense fire of the sketches for the Raika Headquarters, and what is one to make of the almost inscrutable sketches for the Children's Museum in Hyogo or for the Theatre on the Water? And, finally, how does one read the supposed autonomy of the computer drawings for the Urban Egg Project? These do not represent a transition over time, the narrative record of an architect's development, but instead the fragile, translucent layers of a single moment in time. These different types of drawing do not stand for the evolution of an architect's style, but rather the gradual revelation of the many layers of the work itself. What is being argued here is that any of these many types of drawing lie within each project. Rather than marking a transition from project to project they represent the many different realms that drawings occupy in Ando's work; and, in this sense some of the drawings are decidedly iconic while others are more indexical. Thus the graphite hard-edged drawings are iconic, they are the building itself. While the seemingly quick sketch-like strokes are indexical; they describe this other, this secondarity of Ando's space. This difference is like that between Japanese Kanji and haiku. The one cannot explain the other alone.

The movement from haiku to Kanji is in reality only a movement from the structure of relationships at one scale to another – in this case from the many to the many. In this sense Ando's drawings are very much like Japanese Kanji which are both iconic and indexical. This is because Kanji, like hieroglyphics, are essentially pictures – iconic representations – which over time have become so stylized that they are no longer recognizable as such; they have lost much of their overt iconicity. Hiragana is derived from Kanji; it is Japanese cursive writing. Hiragana and Katakana are like alphabets; they only express sounds. In this sense they are primary or iconic structures. Kanji also can be used only for their sound value (ie a character which gives a sound which is also related to some other sign) as opposed to any inherent sign value. When the inherency (ie its iconicity) of Kanji is reduced its indexicality intrudes. All plays on words, whether in English or Japanese, rely on this idea of the potential indexicality of the sound to obtrude the iconicity of the sign.

Ando's drawings are like Kanji in that they contain this doubling of both index and icon; both the literal reference to the built object of architecture and the abstract reference to the poetic and philosophic object. His drawing is tied to this difference between architectural presence and nothingness, but the nothingness of Ando's Kanji describes space as void, a void which is not empty but full; full to overflowing with an excess – a negative which is not negative, a nothing which is more than nothing.

Kanji themselves are also used to investigate the quality of a line, and it is here that one moves from Kanji to calligraphy. Japanese calligraphy takes simple lines without variation, but in combinations, and produces a dense variety of iconic and indexical signs. But calligraphy also has another quality other than structure and meaning, and that is its form. Good calligraphy can be instantly seen from bad. But what is interesting since beauty is not necessarily its object, is that calligraphy problematizes the sign. Calligraphy is involved in a simple paradox in that it is both icon and index at the same time. In one sense it involves a primary co-ordination between hand, mind and eye. Nothing can be rewritten or over-written – yet legibility or neatness is not a factor. At the same time, however, calligraphy is in a sense always a rewriting. In that sense it is an index. It is an attempt to endow words which have already been written, with a character or the quality of object. Ando's recent drawing is in many senses a form of calligraphic haiku. The colour of the ink, the pulse and quality of the lines are not merely the rhythm of classical drawing. Rather, they seem to defy the purpose and meaning of traditional architectural drawing. To understand this one must go back to the nature of architectural drawing.

In architecture when one draws the crossing of two lines, it produces a cross which is an obvious icon of point, centre, focus, etc. The repetition of this crossing produces a grid, which is no longer concerned with centre and focus but rather with surface, texture, etc. The grid is no longer primarily iconic but rather is also an index. As an index the grid is used in many conditions of mapping as well as in making certain reference tables where the horizontal columns are used for one kind of information and the vertical columns are used as a cross reference for other information. But in architecture when the grid becomes the plan of a city or a real building, its abstract co-ordinates become literal intersections for the simple extrusion of three-dimensional space. When this happens the secondary or relational aspects of the grid as an index becomes transformed into a primary, direct one-to-one relationship between abstraction and reality, space and three-dimensional volume, form and function. So most grid-drawn lines in architecture become iconic because of the priority of extruded three-dimensional space.

The thrust of this apparent iconicity can be seen in the modern movement invocations of Mies and Le Corbusier. Both used the grid as an icon of modernist architecture. It represented the new conceptions of space as abstract, unlimited and tectonic in a mechanism or machine-like imagery.

In Ando's built work the three dimensional grid seems to assume a priority – that is, to have upon initial viewing an iconic value. However, upon reflection, it is possible to see Ando's grids as neither the ground nor the figure, the dialectical propositions inherent in Le Corbusier and Mies. Ando's lines elude dialectics, just as Ando himself defies the western categorizations of rationalist or humanist. He is neither, but nor is he anti-rationalist or anti-humanist; he is involved in another kind of drawing and another kind of object, with the intersection of drawing as index, with the three-dimensional grid as index.

Here the grid is no longer an icon. The grid has secondarity – a quality of an index without adjectival or hierarchical complexity, yet not a primary form. As such Ando's lines are no longer just a grid; they contain this *other* which is both index and icon, which stubbornly refuses mediation into a symbolic or referential sign. They stand mute and soundful at the same time. As such they become unique in current architectural practice.

Like the simple trigrams of the I Ching which in their play of complete and interrupted lines map out a complete psychology, so too do the furious strokes of Ando's pen, the hot and cold lines, map out an architectural universe whose stillness speaks in the manifold presences of an unseen being.

P Eisenman, 'Indicencies: in the Drawing Lines of Tadao Ando', in *Tadao Ando. Details*, Tokyo, 1991.

'Brutalizing' History and the Earth
François Chaslin

There is something fickle about the architectural system in Japan; although it continually produces international stars, and on occasion great architects who seem as if they will last forever, they often disappear without notice after only a few years. Tadao Ando is on the way to becoming the official Japanese architect, having built the national pavilion for Expo 92 in Seville. Yet this is precisely the moment at which he is most at risk; and this risk is reflected in the unease felt by visitors to the Ando exhibition at the Pompidou Centre in Paris (3 March to 24 May 1993). 'How can he make a laughing stock of his own work?', complained one of France's own rising stars as he left Ando's lecture. 'Why have you forsaken us?' seemed to ask those who had considered Ando as a kind of demi-god. To some others, Ando emerged, rather, as a minor Japanese master suffering from an inflated ego.

It would truly be a pity if Tadao Ando's architecture were but a brief, although perfect, moment in architectural thinking and aesthetics only to be ruined by stardom and politics. Now that Ando's work has world-wide renown, he can no longer be protected by his former provincial isolation, which had for a long time kept him apart from the Mafia-like, social, economical and political architectural network operating in Tokyo.

Ando's life has a mysterious quality; we know only that he was born in 1941 in Osaka, was separated abruptly from his twin brother, grew up with his grandmother who ran a store, became a professional boxer, and went travelling. When in his home town, he frequented the 'Guntai' – 'concrete art' – group, begun by a group of Osaka artists. More or less self-taught in architecture, he has learned how to sense space intuitively with his body rather than having spatial rules and notions inflicted on him by academia. Ando set up practice in 1969 and in 1973 designed a small house in Oyodo which later became his own office, and which has since been redesigned and expanded.

Ando's first outstanding work was the Azuma House in the Sumiyoshi area of Osaka, completed in 1976. Just under three metres wide, it consists of two floors either side of a small courtyard. Seen from above, the house is squeezed between the varnished tiled roofs of the neighbouring houses; its facade a rectangle of rough concrete, a dark hole for an entrance cut into its centre. Like many of his Japanese contemporaries, Ando's work develops certain themes or rather pretexts with spatial variations – namely pairing and symmetry. Critics have sometimes read these as manifestations of Ando's own anxieties about the loss of a twin brother – closed spaces, spaces protected by translucent screens of glass tile, all evoking a sense of stillness. After a number of built projects, all of which were visually striking although occasionally somewhat theoretical and over-demonstrative, Ando achieved a sort of state of grace at the beginning of the eighties, most notably in his house at Ashiya for the fashion designer Koshino. Critics have already dissected the work of this period, commenting on its quietude, its calmness, its rich abstraction, and, to quote at random, its 'fragments of eternity, its shadows and quasi-celestial light'.

In today's chaotic, sign-saturated city, in our world of momentary pleasure, of commodities and impermanence, Ando has been able to express his rejection of all of this, and has instead withdrawn almost monastically into a world of simple concrete walls onto which fall shadows and light, and which are touched by the wind and the rain. His architecture offers a universe of contemplation, bathed in a kind of mysticism and asceticism. The buildings themselves have always been striking because of their pared-down quality and their untreated smoothness. His early works are as powerful as those of Mario Botta built on the slopes of Ticino at about the same time. Over the years, however, they have become calmer and more delicately polished. They seem to renew the link between moments of universal architecture and moments of peace and spirituality arising from the innermost depths of Japanese or western memory, from a Zen garden or a Cistercian Abbey. And all of this is captured in a geometric abstraction and sculptural simplicity, and articulated in a language whose sobriety, almost naive pedantry, and refusal of the modern, reads like a statement for a new renaissance: 'I wanted to recapture the spirit of Modernism in all its purity.'

The modern spirit that Ando wished to reclaim was essentially of a sculptural nature, combining the Purism of early Corbusier, the feeling of presence of Louis Kahn's work and the shifting in plan of the Mexican architect Luis Barragán; but it has some characteristics of the work of minimalist artists such as Donald Judd, Richard Serra and Sol LeWitt. Each of Ando's works is fascinating both as an object in itself and because it manages to emanate a radiance, a sobriety and a clarity that has universal value. His architecture has an air of calm assurance and is free of any kind of post-modern confusion. For many critics, Ando's work is exemplary, a true revelation in a theoretical landscape still caught up in historicism, that can be evinced internationally from Tokyo to Portland, Oregon, or the gardens of the Venice Biennale to those of Les Halles in Paris, in which the Neo-Classicism of Ricardo Bofill holds sway.

Thus, by virtue of geometry, a subtle balance of natural light and the sensual quality of his plans, this pared down yet contemporary architecture is able to be perfectly coherent using a simple and general philosophical message. And, when one remembers how we had lost all hope in this kind of simplicity after the crisis of the 1970s with its excess of quotation, its frippery and its fake ornamentation, this is an achievement indeed.

Some of Ando's buildings are pure masterpiece: for example, his houses. The most beautiful of these is without doubt the house designed for the Kidosaki family in 1986, located in the Setagaya area of Tokyo. Other work is equally polished: the rigorous and highly articulated housing complex dug into the cliffs of Mount Rokko facing the bay of Kobe; or the churches: one at Ibaraki, the Church of the Light, which consists of a simple rectangle in play with an end wall pierced by a window in the form of a cross, and another church at Tomamu, near Hokkaido, the Church on the Water, whose cross is reflected in the adjacent lake; or restaurants such as Old/New at Rokko, shops and shopping precincts such as Time's in Kyoto, which is delicately poised on the river, or another building dug into the ground in Tokyo's Shibuya district. These works encompass Ando's 'concrete period', characterized by smooth and shiny masonry surfaces which capture the slightest nuance and change in the light. Gradually, however, there has begun to appear in Ando's work clearly defined steel frames, along with curved, reflecting or translucent glass, immaculate blockwork and rough stone. Finally, last year saw the design of the splendid pavilion at Expo 92 in Seville – a noble cenotaph built in wood, a grand, aloof, archaic structure, its silence dominating the chaos of the international exposition. Ando thus majesterially demonstrated that his architecture was not merely of reinforced concrete, nor was he confined to the formal repertoire which had made his reputation, but rather that his work was able to follow a course of its own.

Ando has shown a rare sensitivity to the tactile quality of things and to the physical effect of spaces. He has traced labyrinthine and ritualized routes within and around his spaces, inspired by Le Corbusier's notion of the 'promenade architecturale'. His compositions have a perfect sense of contact with nature, and the way in which one can place oneself in and respond to the landscape, unite with or constrain a topography. Moreover, by testifying to an innate sense of the poetics of space, or a kind of phenomenological intuition, Ando's work reflects a deeper imagination made of light and darkness, and manifests a desire to sublimate everyday life, to make the ordinary sacred, which is itself a very Japanese way of viewing the world.

Ando's larger-scale work, however, has given cause for anxiety. Plummeting stairways and high curved walls, cylindrical forms and towers and spiral ditches – all of these have contributed to a general monumentalization which has led him to experiment on a large scale with spatial arrangements which, hitherto, we have been used to seeing treated at a 'human' level. At the same time that Ando achieved international renown, he began dealing with other design problems, experimenting (a little too often perhaps, but we must first wait and see if they are built) with oval forms with over-explicit and literal foetal connotations and ellipses which 'carry movement within themselves', thus confronting issues which leave the viewer rather perplexed.

Ando's project for the reconstruction of the narrow island of Nakanoshima at the heart of Osaka is a case in point. Here, a buried pyramid, sphere and cube, huge amphitheatres and porticoes are spread over a site of over 900 square metres. This is no longer the vocabulary of Le Corbusier but the borrowed armoury of Etienne-Louis Boullée – the epic visionary and sublime draughtsman whose large drawings and *Essai sur l'art* from the Reign of Terror exactly two hundred years ago, expressed the contemporary taste for the colossal, the funerary, for 'absolutely naked' walls, buried architecture and 'shadowy pictures drawn by even darker shadows'.

Thus if one feels an unease on visiting Ando's spectacular exhibition it might be attributed to certain flaws in the organization of the exhibition (very few photographs of the built work are on display for example; instead we are offered a plethora of models depicting contour lines and with layers of opaque glass signifying stretches of water, as well as charcoal drawings and highly sophisticated working drawings). The unease also has to do with the difficulty one has of understanding the way in which Ando's work is developing, especially given that it seemed to have reached an immutable serenity. How is one to accept this sudden change in the work of an architect who seemed to have chosen soul's peace as a guide, yet who now writes that we have to 'brutalize history and the earth' in order to reactivate a sense of place, and who states that the force that builds is 'anger'? While it is easy to see the philosophical project that linked Boullée's art to the end of the Age of Enlightenment and its terrible upheavals, it is difficult to discern in our own end of century, its own upheavals notwithstanding, what exactly it is that is leading Ando to where he seems to want to go, or which collective project (even though the social idea is not the same in Japan as in Europe), is at the root of his desire to do battle with the world.

F Chaslin, 'Brutaliser l'histoire et la terre', in *L'Architecture d'aujourd'hui*, 287, June 1993.

The Architecture of Tadao Ando – Predicated on Participation
Tom Heneghan

Throughout the twenty-one-year course of his career to date, while architectural discussions have ricocheted between any number of stylistic *isms*, Ando's architectural language, thoughts, and approach have remained resiliently consistent. The formal and conceptual 'oscillations' to which he is subject take place within a theoretical framework established at his Azuma House (1975–6), the project with which he can be said to have 'discovered' himself, and his philosophy of design. Perhaps, materials aside, his early works would appear to have little in common with his recent Chikatsu-Asuka Museum, or, particularly, with his Suntory Museum. Yet, the originating philosophies remain the same.

Ando's extraordinary facility for the exquisite sculpting of form is, in some ways, misleading, since 'form' is rarely his primary concern. In communicating his ideas to his Japanese and international following, most of whom will never have the opportunity to visit the actual buildings, his words are overpowered by the potency of the photographic images. What can never be expressed through this medium is the 'experience' of the actual buildings, an intangible quality which can be analysed, but never adequately described, except perhaps, through Ando's words: 'I want to make space in which people are so quietly moved that they don't talk about it to others'. [...] Indeed, Ando's 'creative intent' is centered on *dialogue* with human sensibilities, with the 'sentient being' he described in his essay 'Shintai and Space'. Sometimes he conceives of this 'being' as 'audience', usually as 'participant', but never merely as 'occupant' or 'user'. He conceives his houses more as sensitizing devices than as functional shelters. [...]

In his search to re-establish an architecture centered on the individual, he has looked inside his own culture, to traditional Japanese architecture, a source which, ironically, exerted a similarly profound influence on early European Modernism. [...] In the lessons he has drawn from traditional architecture, Ando has found neither form nor style. He makes no reference to traditional architectural elements, but draws on his own cultural background to evoke the feeling of traditional space, a space which resonates through the common cultural heritage of a Japanese society in which past and present remain tenuously entwined. [...]

In the sense that Ando's architecture is linguistically descended from European Modernism, which was itself influenced by traditional Japanese architecture, we can see Ando's work as consistent with both legacies. But his works cannot be considered in any way derivative. Nor can his works be considered a synthesis of these two cultural legacies. In architectural terms, his body of work is reminiscent only of itself. [...] The apparent simplicity of Ando's architecture makes it both easy to understand – and to misunderstand. Generally, it must be said, he is perceived as an architect of light and of concrete walls. Ando has said: 'I believe that "architectural materials" are not limited to wood or concrete that have tangible forms, but go beyond to include light and wind – which appeal to our senses'. However, we must, inevitably, discuss his use of the more palpable material.

For many architects throughout the world, there is *concrete*, and there is *Ando concrete*, which are considered to be almost two different materials. Ando has, on many occasions, made public the 'formula' for his concrete. It is, in fact, a surprisingly standard specification, but with emphasis placed on supervision, and the craft of the construction team. The resultant concrete is perceived, principally through magazine illustrations, to achieve flawless perfection. In reality, while his walls are of the highest standard of finish, they are not without blemish – bearing the traces of successive concrete pours and the patching of imperfections. While Ando defines space by the abstract and immaterial surfaces of his concrete planes, he views the material itself not as an abstract substance, but as an everyday material which shows the skill of the craftsmen who form it. It is Ando's architecture – the simplicity of his geometric proportioning, and the 'presence' of the spaces which the walls define – that endows the material with its apparently transcendent qualities. [...]

Ando has spoken of his walls 'as agents of the internal world'. In other words, their role is not passive. Their role, in harsh surroundings, is to stand in opposition, protecting the individuality of the occupant, while remaining permeable to the elements of nature. Ando writes: 'Such things as light and wind only have meaning when they are introduced inside [a building] in a form cut off from the outside world. The isolated fragments of light and air suggest the entire natural world.'

This complicated concept might be understood through Ando's repeated references to the Pantheon in Rome, a building which had a considerable influence on him during his early visits to Europe. In this ancient building, geometrically formed around a conceptual sphere, rain and shafts of sunlight penetrate through the open roof oculus into the stillness and geometrical purity of the darkened central void, confronting the unchanging datum of the architecture, and giving an emphasis and reality to these natural elements which are lost in the expanse of the external world. Ando's repeated use of apertures between walls and ceilings is not primarily for the architectural purpose of identifying the independence of the two planes, nor is it to allow falling patterns of light to beautify the wall as a backdrop to human life; the essential purpose is to render the perfectly-proportioned space fluid. By measuring time and nature through the movement of shadows, or the sound of rain on the rooflights above, these apertures forge a union – or *dialogue* – between the 'life' of the space itself, and the lives of its human inhabitants. It is through differing methods of *dialogue* with the external world that each of Ando's buildings can be clearly distinguished. [...]

It can be noticed that, in discussing his own work, Ando's use of the words *dialogue* and *confrontation* are virtually interchangeable. The subtle nuances of these words can be judged by the manner in which he states that – while his buildings may be *in dialogue* or *in confrontation* with nature – they are never *in opposition to* nature. Certainly, *dialogue*, albeit a sometimes *robust dialogue*, is the essential theme of his architecture. Ando has described how his architecture constantly oscillates between the polar extremes of inside and outside; West and East; abstraction and representation; part and whole; history and the present; past and future; and simplicity and complexity – all of which imply additional protagonists, including light/shade; natural/artificial; wall/column; logic/illogic; materiality/immateriality. While Ando clearly has no interest in the formulation of a systematic design method, each of his projects can be seen to participate in this *dialogue of extremes*.

T Heneghan, 'The Architecture of Tadao Ando', in Y Futagawa (ed), *Tadao Ando, 1988–1993*, Tokyo, 1993.

Tadao Ando and the Enclosure of Modernism
Fredric Jameson

Those who scan the streets of Tokyo or Osaka, let alone the Japanese countryside, for the buildings of Tadao Ando know those telltale slabs of poured concrete, marked at regular intervals by round indentations (like the tracings left by fabric on your skin during a brief nap), that unerringly spell your approach and peremptorily demand your attention. 'Brutalism' may not be the most exact technical or historical term for these massive surfaces; they have nothing of the exquisite polish of Louis Kahn's Yale Center for British Art (where concrete is transformed into a type of precious metal), and they certainly shoulder aside the characteristically formless agglomeration of Japanese urban structures with a decisive ruthlessness.

Infallible signatures – recognizable at a glance anywhere in the world – such walls are also pre-eminently misleading. We will wish to retain their gesture of radical disjunction, a significant index in the light of that primal modern or Modernist act whereby the space of the new building is wrenched free of its fallen context and isolated, sculpture-like, on *pilotis* that reject the formlessness of the former streets and sites from which they rise. […]

Indeed, if, as Adolf Loos noted, 'wall plaster is a skin; stone is structural', then the ambiguous significance of concrete can be traced out, its capacity to pass from surface to solid, and from the most extraordinary polish to the very signifier of weight and mass without refinement. Concrete is a kind of plaster that has become stone: engaged in a kind of Bachelardian 'psychoanalysis of the elements', it is a non-natural substance that, unlike its nearest competitor, plastic, has succeeded in naturalizing itself, passing for some traditional element in its own right. Whence the mediatory uses to which Ando is able to put this material, as an outside radically different from its interior function. […]

To pass from the outside, the street or context ('as lifeless buildings fill our cities, I have become acutely conscious of the deadly, oppressive nature of the environment in which I live'), to an interior in which a very different kind of experience is vouchsafed, is therefore a moment of ambivalence in which the very categories we deploy to grasp Ando's work become modified. It is necessary to discuss those categories themselves for a moment. Not only do I not think that 'modern' and 'post-modern' constitute general concepts with properties and attributes of the precision required to organize and reorder empirical perceptions and observable features; I also think that it is fruitless to attempt to make them over into such general concepts (and/or to fight about these definitions in the first place, to invest one's energies in struggling to secure some correct or proper description of the modern or the post-modern that secures for the one or the other those qualities to which you happen to be personally attached). If one likes the terminology, then it must be admitted that these are very much supplementary concepts, and indeed, in the case of the post-modern, doubly so: for if the modern (like the sublime) comes as a supplement to a poorly identified first term, which it ends up marginalizing in its triumphant progress, then the post-modern is the supplement of a supplement, open to waves of confusion or gestalt alternation in which it now looks like more of the same, like a fundamental break and turn in some radically new direction. […]

Thus the particular mental operation which consists in sorting out the attributes of a given phenomenon, with a view towards classifying it once and for all in this or that category – an operation that depends on the pre-existence of typologies and classification schemes, permutational mechanisms and *combinatoires*, and which in literary criticism, having exhausted itself in genre criticism, knew a miraculous renewal with the various structuralisms – is surely never very interesting in its own right; nor is it generally deployed 'in its own right' but for other, less well-identified or covert purposes which it is always crucial to unmask and identify and which sometimes amount to little more than the attempt to validate this or that pre-existent academic aesthetic ('what is tragedy? tragedy is …'). Only if the exercise in definition and classification bears on 'the current situation', on trends in the present and stakes for the future, does the decision to classify Ando's buildings as modern rather than post-modern take on concrete content and become interesting. To be more precise, it is in the context of a more general ideological return to certain aesthetic values often associated with Modernism that the discussion about Ando acquires cultural-political significance.

It is a discussion that must begin with what I think of as Ando's quintessential spaces, in the Church of the Light (in Ibaraki, outside Osaka) and the Water Temple at Hyogo (Tsuna-gun), where, to be sure, the other-worldly function of both buildings already authorizes a certain aesthetic regression. Both, however, allow us to articulate and specify the precise value and significance of Ando's gesture of disjunction, and thereby to compare it more accurately with the classic high Modernist one. What one observes, then, is that it is an incomplete disjunction; or rather that the act of separation and the sealing off of the interior from the exterior is a structurally complex or even dialectical one, since it systematically includes the filtering and transmission of certain features from the outside world.

Light is the primordial form of all such features in which externality has been extraordinarily concentrated and purified so as to be admitted in the form of an element in its own right, rather than as what allows other objects to be visible. In the Church of the Light itself, indeed, the symbolic cross is displayed before the worshippers in the form of two transversal slits in the concrete wall through which light passes; while light seeps down into the Water Temple through the immense lotus pool under this sacred space – a traditional wooden construction within the concrete substructure, to which one descends by a narrow concrete stairway that leads down through the middle of the pool itself.

Both are, in addition, miniature spaces; yet it must also be said that the shock one would expect to feel in such a reversal, as we pass from the massive concrete exterior, is quickly dissipated and forgotten. This is indeed, surely, like the sleep cure in Shakespearean tragedy, the desired therapeutic effect of these extraordinary spaces, which allow withdrawal from the outside world in some other mode than repression: and the nature of that mode is clearly another occasion for the issue of cultural difference to reimpose itself, here in the strong form of religion as such, always the most inaccessible version of sheer otherness. Is it indeed Japanese Buddhism – or Japanese Christianity for that matter – that, utterly alien to anything we can imagine under the category of religion in the West, enables so thoroughgoing a withdrawal from the worldly spaces of an overcrowded sociality and a tendentially overpowering commodification? The question contains within itself the coiled yet unavoidable issue of the ascription of Ando's unique spaces to some putatively unique Japanese culture, to a Japanese exceptionalism apparently far more difficult to dispel than any equivalents elsewhere (from the well-known American kind to that of the 'Russian soul', from the sempiternal Chinese negotiation of the historical millennia to Indian 'spirituality', or even simply from the eccentricities of the English to Gallic reason and 'civilization'). I have bought into this ideological ambush by choosing the religious buildings as the most characteristic forms of Ando's production; but attention to the private dwellings (I was privileged to visit the Ito House in Setagaya-ku, Tokyo) would end up having the same effect, in the form of questions about the unique cultural status of Japanese daily life as such. The cultural issues are then slowly dispelled or dispersed as one moves to Ando's larger public buildings (among which I include the monumental Rokko Housing project in Kobe and the enormous Children's Museum in Hyogo). On the other hand, I must also register my feeling that with them are also slowly dispersed the intensity of one's perception of Ando's unique style and space; and that may be too great a price to pay.

What is lost in the larger public spaces is essentially the aesthetic *experience* of the smaller ones; and it is this above all that marks Ando's relationship to the Modernist tradition, for the very conception of experience as such, as a closed and intelligible phenomenon that can be abstracted from the random stream of life, is itself very much a modern development, from Georg Simmel to Raymond Williams, or even from Wordsworth's 'spots of time' to Marcel Proust. [...]

What, then, of the classification of Ando's work? Do any of the current categories – Modernist, late modern, or post-modern – seem appropriate for this unique construction of space? One is certainly tempted to think of his work as a belated Modernism, reinvented under adverse conditions and sheltered against a degraded urban environment (one of whose degradations is clearly, in his own opinion, a cheap and omnipresent post-modernism itself): this characterization would serve perhaps as one kind of gloss on Ando's own expression, 'an enclosed modern architecture', a 'self-enclosed' Modernism. And it is certain that if the Moebius strip, always external to itself and infinite in its very finitude, is the emblem of the post-modern generally, the monad, always interior to itself and finite in its very boundlessness, is that of Modernism proper. Ando's inner spaces are clearly monadic rather than Moebian, and reinvent categories of inside and outside that we thought were tabooed and abolished by a post-structural and post-modern age. [...]

Ando cannot be considered a late modern, even though the emphasis in his work on the production of a unique aesthetic space may certainly be considered Modernist. But we have not yet raised the other insistent question about this work which has to do with its relationship to Japanese culture as such – which is generally ideologized in terms of its radical difference from modernity insofar as this last is identified with the West. In a key article on the subject, Harry Harootunian has described the famous Kyoto 1942 symposium on 'overcoming the modern' in precisely this way, as an attempt to imagine a radically different culture from that of western modernity or modernization; while later reprises of the debate change the valences on the subject – Takeuchi's postwar discussion calling for an alternate to western modernization based on the mobilization of popular masses, while the later governmental programme of 1980 proclaims the 'conquest of the modern' – that is, the definitive identification of modernization with Japanese exceptionalism as such. [...]

Thus, the classical Japanese way of life is today available only by way of image and pastiche, historicist allusion. But so, today, is Modernism itself, whose aesthetic and conceptuality have been driven into obsolescence by changes in the infrastructure fully as much as by new fashions and intellectual and cultural fads and doxa. This homology between the Japanese and the modern – two things hitherto radically opposed in the polemics that reached their climax in the 'overcoming the modern' debate – now puts us in a position to grasp the originality of Ando's work, for in effect his spaces operate a profound identification between the two antithetical terms and offer to recapture the lost secret of the Japanese aesthetic by reinventing the lost spaces of the modern. [...]

F Jameson, 'Tadao Ando and the Enclosure of Modernism', in *ANY*, 6, May–June 1994.

Three Houses by Tadao Ando
Vittorio Magnago Lampugnani

Ando's architecture is truly the architecture of silence. Bare, reduced to very few essentials and apparently made of almost nothing, it is not easily discovered amid the hubbub of boisterous multicoloured shapes when passing through burgeoning Japanese cities. But its presence has weight. Rather like small surviving historical monuments, Ando's buildings form a fine but easily recognized and undoubtedly comforting fabric in the stupefying labyrinths of the immense urban areas of Tokyo, Osaka, Kyoto and Hyogo.

It is not only through obsessively strict formalism, elementary geometry and the use of very few materials that Ando achieves silence. His simplicity is not a front. It is the product of the true solution of a problem, the conquest of a state of disorder which is transformed into discipline. In fact on his own terms and in those well-defined cases where he himself has made a specific statement, Ando resolves the contradictions between the two cultures, of the East and of the West, translating both to a very high level of abstraction. Thus the pure spaces of Euclidean geometry are combined with those equally pure spaces which nevertheless incorporate the asymmetrical stresses of ancient Japanese architecture. The identity between a structure and the boundaries of space, between the bones and the skin of a building, which is present in Greek temples as it is in Buddhist temples and Shinto shrines, is offered again (despite the enormous problems of heat insulation) by the very carefully worked exposed concrete which, unlike Le Corbusier's *béton brut*, emphasizes not its own bulk but the empty space which it bounds and defines. Fluid space, which Frank Lloyd Wright and Mies van der Rohe had already 'imported' from Japan and made an integral part of the Modern Movement, reappears not as a novelty and a break with the past, but, drawn with the brush of a Japanese architect, as continuity. A symphony of light ably orchestrated without succumbing to theatrical temptations, perhaps the most prominent feature of Ando's work, is common to both the Pantheon in Rome and the Ryoanji temple. Finally, simplicity, the emblem of all the modern West and the most exquisitely and exclusively Japanese tradition, links Ando's probing with the best examples of European and American architectural culture. [...]

The Azuma House lies in the very centre of Osaka, in the Sumiyoshi district. It is a very small row house in a row of other equally small houses which, despite being built of wood, survived World War II. It in fact replaces one of these small traditional residential buildings, adopting its surface area and boundaries, but not its type.

From the street it is almost unnoticed. Or, rather, it is noticed only because of the almost irritating simplicity of its facade. The house fronts the public roadway with an incredible rectangular wall of reinforced concrete which is pierced only by a narrow, again rectangular, entrance slot, which is gained by climbing a single step. Nothing more. No window, no balcony, no cornice, no base. Not even a door. The slot is left bare and invites entrance into a minuscule hall which even a skylight barely draws from darkness. It is only from this that the entrance door finally opens. But we must not get ahead of ourselves. Let's for the moment remain on the street and observe the facade. This, as we have noted, is made of virtually nothing. But this almost nothing is skillfully orchestrated and includes a number of architectural features which only gradually reveal themselves to the attentive eye.

The bare wall of exposed reinforced concrete is constructed with great mastery, and the marks left on the surface by the formwork trace an unobtrusive geometrical design which provides a key to the subtle rules of its composition. The slender rectangle of the facade is seen to be two almost square elements placed vertically one above the other, each consisting of three layers of concrete picked out by fine horizontal lines, as if they were rows of paper and wood panels or courses of facing stone. A more pronounced line at the point where the two 'squares' join acts as a story marker, the other, at the top of the second 'square', distinguishes a half layer of cement added by way of a cornice. The central axis of symmetry is marked by a double vertical line which starting from the centre of the 'cornice' runs to the middle of the entrance slot, rather like a keystone of exaggerated height. The entrance slot, the only true architectural feature in the facade, is elegantly proportioned and roughly cut into the concrete wall.

The front of the house, although complexly subdivided in this way, reveals nothing or almost nothing of its internal organization. To discover this we must cross the threshold – an action which is invited not only by the entrance slot with its bare edges and its symbolic solitary step. Passing through the extremely small hall we gain access to the side of the living room, where we face a french window opening onto an inner courtyard. On the same level, across and thus separate from the living room, a kitchen/dining room also opens onto the courtyard.

From the inner courtyard a stairway to one side gives access to the upper level. Here two bedrooms, one for adults (with a skylight similar to that which gives light to the entrance) and one for children, face each other as the kitchen and living room do on the ground floor. Both open onto the courtyard with wide windows and are connected (and separated at the same time) by a central concrete bridge which spans the full length of the courtyard. The reinforced concrete, with its smooth grey-blue surface and austere texture with traces from the formwork, determines the nature of all the internal spaces, from which all forms of rendering are strictly banished. The concrete is flanked by the glass of the large doors and windows, the steel of the frames, the slate of the ground-floor paving and the wood of the upper floor.

The tripartite plan has an absolutely strict geometry. The three main elements are identical, and only almost imperceptible variations in the implacable precision of the basic plan mark a reluctant compromise with the imperatives of life. This, however, is somewhat unpleasant. Access to the individual spaces is in fact provided via an inner courtyard, which is not in any way protected from weather, and one is therefore always obliged to go outside, regardless of cold, rain or snow. The only exception merely confirms the rule of inconvenience; the bathroom is only accessible from the kitchen/dining room. Measured by western (now international) standards of comfort the Azuma House is inhospitable, not very practical, and thus not very easy to live in. This is of course a hasty and superficial verdict. It takes no account of the eminently contentious purpose of the little building. Neither does it consider that its purpose essentially concentrates on precisely this question of living.

There is no doubt, at least on reasonably thorough investigation, that the Azuma House is, as far as Tadao Ando is concerned, a show house, like the Maison Dom-

Ino for Le Corbusier, like the 'brick house' for Mies van der Rohe, like the house which Konstantin Melnikov built for himself in Moscow. It embodies and gives expression to the philosophical principles and design themes fundamental to the work of its architect and it does so in a manner which is extreme, radical, and perhaps exaggerated, but effective.

The first theme, which can be felt as soon as one sets foot in the house, is that of shadow, or better, the modulation of natural light. In 1933, writer Junichiro Tanizaki published the book *In Praise of Shadows*, as a sort of poetic manual which encouraged a return to the traditional use of soft gradations of light, which was once very dear to eastern culture. Ando has treasured the lucid admonishments of this renowned poet. At the most symbolic points in the house (the entrance, the bedroom), he has provided skylights which hark back to the old *tsukiage-mado* and emphasize the change in light from day to night by letting it in, in filtered form, to the living space. The rooms too do not open onto the street or onto the rear of the house, but onto an inner courtyard, where natural light is already softened and domesticated by the walled perimeter.

The inner courtyard however has a much greater and more important task than that of acting as a first filter for the light of the sun or the moon. It is that of bringing a fragment of nature within the walls of the house in a highly artificial way. This is the second great theme in Tadao Ando's architecture. For him architecture is a means through which nature can be seen and felt. But nature cannot be incorporated into architecture as it is (and this explains the Japanese architect's profound aversion for any type of domestic greenery); it must be appropriately mediated. A courtyard is one of the best ways of effecting this mediation. In the courtyard, nature presents a different aspect of itself each day. The courtyard is the nucleus of life that unfolds within the house and is a device to introduce natural phenomena such as light, wind and rain that are being forgotten in the city.

Is this task of subordinating functionality and habitability, as in the Azuma House, to a kind of artificial obstacle in the flow of spatial connections between one room and another so important to Ando? Probably. The problem does not arise however, and misrepresentation is not necessary. Because the third great theme of Ando's architectural exploration is living itself, and, more specifically, questioning the concept (and the necessity and desirability) of functional comfort in a house.

'I am interested in discovering what new life patterns can be extracted and developed from living under severe conditions. Furthermore, I felt that order is necessary to give life dignity. Establishing order imposes restrictions, but I believe it cultivates extraordinary things in people. I believe in removing architecture from function after ensuring the observation of functional basis. In other words, I like to see how far architecture can pursue function and then, after the pursuit has been made, to see how far architecture can be removed from function. The significance of architecture is found in the distance between it and function.' This was his creed, and Ando wrote it down in 1980, five years after he had drawn the plans for the Azuma House, to some extent summarizing his experience there. The key sentence is still the first: 'I am interested in discovering what new life patterns can be extracted and developed from living under severe conditions.' Ando sets an asceticism derived from his own cultural tradition, which is not thereby obscured by any nationalism, against the rampant consumerism clearly derived from the West. In an increasingly uniform world where anything can be had at any time, for payment of course, although only as a surrogate, Ando offers the extreme luxury of a new self-imposed discipline which enforces reflection about real values and the experience of many realities: heat, cold, sun, rain, wind, snow, light, dark, and the infinite gradations and nuances which life creates between such extremes. Conditions of strict simplicity (which westerners might refer to as being Franciscan) bring forth maximum refinement, and the most sublime richness.

All this might appear plausible for a simple and 'poor' building as the Azuma House undoubtedly is, with only 63 square metres of useful area obtained from a plot only 57 square metres. The argument would appear however to be different for the Koshino House, another architectural work by Ando which we will now set about observing more closely. This is no longer an urban residence, but a house in the mountains, a second home whose size, especially in the cramped context of Japan, must be regarded as being decisively and exceptionally luxurious – some 285 square metres of useful space in a small park of 1,000 square metres. Is it still possible to speak of asceticism when faced with such opulence? Before attempting to answer this question we will describe the architecture to which it refers. The Koshino House consists of three separate units, arranged in parallel to each other and rotated through approximately 45 degrees with respect to the boundaries of the site to obtain better exposure to the sun and preserve the ancient trees of the park. The site, located in the middle of a splendid nature reserve on Mount Rokko near the city of Ashiya, is quite steep. Because of this, and so as not to spoil its profile, the three parts of the building are partly buried. Access is gained to the house from the top, a little like Mies van der Rohe's Tugendhat House. A short drive bounded by metal railings on the right and a concrete bench on the left leads asymmetrically to the body of the main fabric. This, a reinforced concrete rectangle, contains on its upper level, in addition to the entrance, the main bedroom, a bathroom and a small study. A straight stairway leads down to the more extensive lower level, occupied by the vast double-height living room, the dining area and the kitchen. The living room is lit by two large rectangular windows with steel frames of different size as well as long narrow skylights which pierce the flat ceiling along the perimeter walls, through which surges of changing light skim across the gigantic surfaces of the bare concrete walls. The furnishings are extremely spare. One emblematic detail is the long narrow dining table which in the dining area has the standard western height and can therefore be used conventionally (from the western point of view, of course), while in the living area, by comparison, it is only slightly raised, to the traditional Japanese height, and can therefore be used kneeling on the floor. The whole forms a grandiose composition where space and objects assisted by the clever play of light and shadow follow the subtle rules of an inexpressible harmony distilled from the traditional architecture of the sixteenth-century Japanese tea house (Sukiya) revisited with the knowledge of the near plastic poetry of a Piet Mondrian or Theo van Doesburg. To the south of the first part of the building there lies the second, a rectangle of the same width, but longer and lower. This contains eight small bedrooms (for children and guests) in an orderly line along a corridor, and, at the western end, a bathroom. The corridor is lit by eight tall narrow slits in its central portion and by a large window at the east-facing end. The rooms are traditional Japanese four-and-a-half tatami rooms. They all open to the south, screened on the outside by a kind of portico and partly by a retaining wall which runs parallel to the building.

The two parts of the building are connected together by an underground passageway which begins behind the kitchen and runs perpendicularly into the corridor serving the bedroom wing. Between the two buildings there is a sort of inner courtyard open on its two narrower sides. To the east its slightly ambiguous space merges with the slope. To the west a stairway which occupies the full width of the courtyard provides geometrical access to the flat parapeted roof of the second building. The reference to the outside staircase conceived and constructed by Adalberto Libera for the Casa Malaparte in Capri is immediate. Likewise, Ando's stairway is not only a staircase but also a roof. Likewise, it is an architectural metaphor and at the same time a grand gesture organizing a spectacular nature which is otherwise left intact. Likewise, it alludes to a social monument and invites one to ascend towards an altar which is only there to consummate a non-existent rite. Likewise, it in fact leads nowhere, to an empty space, to a terrace exposed to the weather, an unreal setting for adoration not of the sun, as in the legendary Mediterranean island, but of the moon.

The third part of the building is on the left of the central rectangle on entering. Laid out on an approximately semi-circular plan, its circular wall contrasts with the nearby straight boundary of the site, thus formally shutting off the architectural composition from the outside. Although a later addition and not part of the original design, it seems to be a logical conclusion and organic extension of the house. It contains the workroom of the mistress of the house, a designer, and a small bathroom. The enclosed area is almost wholly buried and is therefore shut off by stark concrete walls. Only in the east where the slope exposes the architecture as a sand dune exposes archaeological remains, is the semi-circular shape brusquely interrupted and the wall rent by a large window. Along the curved wall a narrow skylight allows a disturbing shaft of ever-changing light to filter into the bare and abstract space.

In this great structure of the Koshino House it is not difficult to find again the three architectural themes stated (and developed) by Ando in the minuscule Azuma House: the modulation of natural light, here made to achieve effects of rare mastery and suggestion; the inclusion of 'artificialized' nature into the architecture in the form of the inner courtyard, here much more skillfully incorporated than it was possible to do in the small row house in Osaka; and finally the search for a new lifestyle which the constructed form suggests and in fact imposes on the inhabitants, perhaps less implacably but certainly with no less determination than a few years previously at Sumiyoshi.

It could in fact be maintained that the Koshino House merely reproduces the refined inconvenience of the Azuma House on a larger scale. This is less of an exaggeration than its witty tone might suggest. Is not the dark underground corridor which connects the two main parts of the building perhaps a functional obstacle similar to the inner courtyard of the row house? Are not too perhaps the eight identical minuscule and spartan rooms, which occupy almost all the southern wing of the house, isolated from the heat of summer, but above all from the cold of winter, with the same deliberate moderation as the small plain rooms of the Azuma House? Do not perhaps the large spaces of the opulent weekend house in the mountains also harbour the same qualities of essentiality, simplicity and starkness as the infinitely smaller spaces in the little house in the centre of the great city? The greater architectural potential of the Koshino House has, when viewed closely, been pressed into service of the same ascetic ideal which inspired the more lowly (but thereby no less effective) Azuma House.

The same comments apply to the Kidosaki House. This again can certainly not be said to be either small or poor – 556 square metres of useful surface on a 610-square-metre site at Setagaya, one of the most desirable residential areas in Tokyo. Is it still possible to talk again of simplicity, discipline and asceticism?

Let us visit this third house which bears Ando's stamp. We will have to enter a quiet and gently hilly part of the city where a rather close-set mesh of surprisingly narrow streets bounds regular groups of plots occupied almost exclusively by single family houses set in small, extremely well-tended gardens. The plot which is our goal is a slightly irregular square completely enclosed by a bare reinforced concrete wall which protects the interior from any indiscreet gaze. The wall only curves inward at one point, inviting access to a kind of funnel which gives way to a wide staircase leading to an inner garden onto which the entrances to the two apartments located on the ground floor open. Immediately alongside the curvature of the wall there is also a kind of narrow passage divided from the access funnel by a solid breast wall, also of concrete. Scaling the steps of a second stairway, which is parallel to the first but offset with respect to it, this passage leads to the apartment located on the first floor.

This is in fact a house consisting of three residential units: one for a couple, another for his father and yet another for her mother. The couple occupy the larger apartment on the first floor. The two elders occupy the two apartments on the ground floor. The garage, the basement and the open spaces are used communally.

The functional theme consisted of bringing all the members of the family to live under the same roof, but offering each the necessary privacy. Ando has achieved this by spatially fusing together three independent apartments. The father's apartment, which consists of a living and dining room, bedroom, bath and kitchen, is all on the ground floor and opens onto both a small light well made on the street side and an extensive carefully planted courtyard on the southern side of the site. The mother's apartment, which has the same elements as the father's apartment, is organized around a space of double height which also faces the southern courtyard through a large window. This space provides direct communication to the couple's apartment in its upper level. The couple's apartment, which also has a dining area separate from the living room, and a study, in addition to the rooms in the other apartments, extends over two levels on the first and second floor. On the first floor it faces a terrace which suggests a sort of extension of the open space of the dining area to the east. On the second floor it faces another very large terrace which is completely enclosed by concrete walls and therefore absolutely private. The living room, bounded by a curved wall (the one which forms the entrance) onto which a skylight throws a glancing shaft of light, opens onto the same small courtyard which illuminates the bedroom in the father's flat.

To achieve such a complex functional programme Ando has designed a formal plan of disarming simplicity – a 12 x 12 metre cube place almost exactly in the centre of the plot in such a way as to create a sequence of carefully modulated protective spaces around it. The cube is, as usual, all constructed of bare reinforced concrete, both externally and internally (the only exception being the mother's apartment, which is surfaced with white plaster). The frames are of metal painted dark grey. The flooring is of dark slate or elegant wood laid in such a way as to allow immediate access to the underlying surfaces. Even the sober wooden wall cupboards have been designed by the architect.

A building, one might say, of disarming simplicity, but this simplicity incorporates an extremely sophisticated positioning of a room within another, a courtyard within another, an apartment within another. To take advantage of the clear geometry of his design, Ando has had to invent a spatial machinery which, as revealed by the plans and section, proves to have Piranesian characteristics. These are heightened by the necessity of concealing all the services beneath the floors and behind the bare walls, and therefore the need to create invisible spaces, ducts and double ceilings. All of this, by the way, in reinforced concrete, and therefore without any possibility of correction on site. It is not surprising that the design of the Kidosaki House took all of four years from 1982 to 1985.

A simplicity, in fact, which is achieved with great effort. An unflagging, strongly desired simplicity. A simplicity, even in this other wealthy house, artificially created and deliberately displayed so as not to show off its wealth. And also not to cause that wealth to overwhelm its inhabitants. Here again, as already at Sumiyoshi and Ashiya, Ando constrains his architecture to an abstemious life. No softly finished walls, no windows 'clothed' with blinds, shutters and curtains, no disturbing or intrusive fittings. There is even nothing to be seen outside. The courtyards and the terraces are introverted worlds, complete in themselves, and neither can anything be seen from the large upper terrace which could overlook a large part of the city because of the slight incline between them. This is prevented by high solid walls, cast in bare grey concrete. It is only possible, and with difficulty, to squint at the view through the three enigmatic slots with which Ando pierces the two eastern and western walls, in the same way as one can look onto the street through the narrow gaps left against all the rules of construction and laws of statics at the corners of the perimeter wall enclosing the southern courtyard, as if to emphasize its relegation to the wings. The ascetic does not enjoy a view of the city, even the selected view through the periscope which Le Corbusier allowed Charles de Buistegui; instead he observes, with greater profit, an ever-changing sky set in its metaphysical concrete frame.

In the sixteenth century in the Japanese province of Kansai (which includes Osaka, Ando's birthplace), the great warlord Toyotomi Hideyoshi and his protégé, the tea master Sen no Rikyu, created the discipline of *wabi* and promoted it vigorously, soon to be followed by numerous disciples. The term implies adherence to the virtues of simplicity, poverty and modesty which are opposed to the vulgar ostentation of wealth. It also has the connotation of dissatisfaction with institutional power, and resistance to tyranny. Within the bounds of *wabi* the artist-intellectual, rejected and vexed by the unresponsive world of merchants and politicians, can create his own universe, openly challenging that from which he longs to dissociate himself, where self-discipline and rigour become moral strength and ascetic refinement.

Through his birth and inclination Tadao Ando belongs to this still living tradition, as do many of the protagonists of the new Japanese fashion who are his clients, above all Hiroko Koshino. It is not by chance that he has chosen the poorest and most commonplace material in existence, concrete, for his architecture. It is not by chance that he fashions this into the most simple and elementary shapes. It is not by chance that he leaves it bare, open, devoid of all decoration or covering. At the same time however Ando lays vigorous claim to his own role as an artist. His houses are of value not because of the materials of which they are made, but because of the ideas to which they give material form. Their ascetic qualities are not something extra, they are their essence and their very substance. Behind their design must lie the professionalism of the poet. [...]

The architecture of Tadao Ando in general and the Azuma, Koshino, and Kidosaki Houses in particular, are to be included among those physical elements of which some kind of future might conceivably be built. They have thus silently become the architecture of hope.

V Magnago Lampugnani, 'Three Houses by Tadao Ando', in *GA*, 71, March 1994.

Minimalism and Architecture
Vittorio Gregotti

Even though minimalist art will shortly have been with us for thirty years, its oppositional attraction so far as architecture is concerned does not seem to have diminished. The contrast between the intransitive character of the 'minimal' work of art, even with respect to its own constructionality, and the way that architecture unfolds in space immersed in its own dialectic with the conventions of the social; between the mythology of the 'one' which dominates minimalism and the multiplicity of connections and adaptations typical of the work of architecture, has not yet ceased to produce a positive tension within the idea which unites them: the procedure of the project.

Some years ago Harold Rosenberg wrote of minimalism: 'every modern work is a participant in the conception from which its style drew its origin' that is, as we architects would say, it is the result of a theoretically-based project; and further on, Rosenberg added, 'instead of deriving principles from what it sees it teaches the eye to see the principles'.

Minimalism for us is a form of this way of relating, of this mode of thinking about the created work; but above all it is, in our case, a suggestion of meaning which I want to interpret freely here from the point of view of architecture.

It is therefore pertinent and important to try to describe the nature of the thrusts in the architectural project which minimalist ambiguity has engendered during the past twenty years. These are thrusts which come out of what are often misrepresentations, deformations, even betrayals of the ideas that the 'minimal' movements in their diverse articulations actually proposed and developed. All the same, I find such movements active today, particularly in the variegated but recognizable area of architecture which gives pride of place, in the practice of its art, to escaping from evocativeness.

First and foremost I have to admit that when I think today about minimalism, reference to the rupture between it and some protagonists of the conceptual movements of the 1960s, from earthwork to Arte Povera, a few years later, becomes obligatory. Some works by Louis Morris seem thus to rekindle new family relationships with some by Robert Morris. The story of this visual adventure finds a possible paternity in the work of Ellsworth Kelly, Kenneth Noland and even in Frank Stella and Barnett Newman, the latter a great artist who worked with emptiness as a material to be profiled and subdivided. But the various family relationships converge at least at one point: they consciously run the risk, almost inevitably, of not seeming to be works of art at all, of abandoning the world of representation. Some run this risk within the traditional fields of painting and sculpture, while others move outside those realms. A very considerable group of these artists has taken its stance around the themes of refoundation of the environment, even making of it a special material with which their work is concerned. Or rather, it is possible to read many works of this tradition (and indeed perhaps all the contemporary traditions of the visual arts) from the point of view of the surrounding environment. What unites these endeavours is the prospect of liberation from object-based (and mercantile) overcrowding, a lifting of the veil from elementary gestures: an archetypal response – in the face of a reconstituted or experimentally rediscovered relationship between things, places, spaces – towards the principle of original one-ness.

And then one must recognize that the work of many of these artists seems to be underlined by a more marked interest in environmental construction even though by very different means. On one side, the work of some is characterised by a concern for relating to the specific space as a determinate place. Many works of those years require a specific spatial context and are deliberately designed for one place, or one locality; they seem to want to take over a field, define it, or defend as if it were a threatened territory. But they also propose themselves as elements of interrogation and revelation, more than as orderer, of the systems of meaning of that field. There is no expectation of being able to exert global control via design, but the introduction into the environment of disturbing elements, of small shifts, can lift the veil from and change the meaning of a contextual system. The fundamental characteristic of this work seems to be the construction of a double way of relating the object to the surrounding space in so far as, by its very existence it recognises, and yet simultaneously alters, the context.

From this extremely general convergence there remain two divergent directions of experience which run through a wide part of this tradition. The first of these proposes facing up in the open, at full-scale, to these questions, assessing their value by means of the modifications measured on the larger territorial scale. That may entail new ways of using traditional instruments, or in the conceptual type of operation, the exploration by way of material action of accumulation and shifting, and in that, of mimicking scientific or ecological thought. The other route allows these operations to be conducted in the laboratory as it were, interposing an ideal or real barrier between the field of work and the totality of the physical world: the box compared with which every experiment acts either by difference or separation.

Artists like Donald Judd, Sol LeWitt, to say nothing of those who work at the large environmental scale, seem, further, to want to propose the instrument of the project as the postulate of the work, at times attributing all the creative value to this. On the other hand, some others, even though via the idea of the project, assign a particular value to the labour involved in carrying it out. In them there is a sort of changeover between the necessary materiality of the artisanal tradition towards a direct clash with the resistance of objects and geometries, even if the very encounter with material reality is an essentially conceptual operation of de-aestheticization. Here I would like to underline the reference to the minimalist world of the dominating presence of physical material, to its weight, to its specific and contrasting perceptible presence. It is frequently via the presence of such heterogeneous material and its being outside the natural picture (and, therefore, the spatial structure of the room as environment for experimentation) that action is also carried out at the level of the large environmental scale. Someone has written that minimalism, especially American minimalism which involves large movements of matter, is essentially a representation of an opposite and symmetrical type, with respect to the spiritualist tension of the 'abstractism' of the period from 1910 to the 1930s.

It is not simply a matter of restoring the realm of geometry as the representation of the absolute (a problem, even when developed in different ways, which is common to numerous artists and architects of the first avant-garde), but of giving back meaning to the primal and elementary gesture of setting down, laying out, surveying, spreading around, accumulating, dividing up.

Here no resolving power at all is attributed to technology (if not to science). For the minimalists (but also for some architects of these past years) technology exists without any particular sense of marvel, it is not something either to be fought against nor to be excited by, it is the natural territory of action, but absolutely not an instrument of liberation or model to which to refer formally and methodologically.

It is probable that in this description of the various forms of minimalism some will recognize a necessary connection with architecture. There is no doubt that the 'minimal' principles of the visual arts have a vast methodological and theoretical debt so far as the tradition of modern architecture is concerned. But this is a model in which minimalism offers a reversed interpretation. This has come about somehow in the architecture of the last fifteen years. There is a vast faction among architects which recognizes a connective system with minimalism, a faction at least as vast as the one which likes to trace its family relationships, in my opinion a very great deal more improperly, in the *transavanguardia* experiences of the last ten years.

An exemplary case is that of Tadao Ando, in whose work it is possible to recognize a meeting between the principles of minimalism and a rigorous and highly religious interpretation of the Japanese tradition of making buildings and of constructing large complexes on the land.

Of course I believe it is very difficult fully to understand Ando's architecture with only the instruments of minimalism to hand; to try, that is, to discern the mechanisms of its formation, the secrets of his process, or to understand its emotional place on the horizon. Of all that he only ever gives a laconic summary. Perhaps an attempt at compositional analysis would, then, also become an operation of reduction. Rather, I am convinced that it is necessary before going further, to understand, to respect the profoundly mysterious and symbolic tradition which in Japan has imbued all desire to construct anything which without doubt constitutes one of the most fascinating aspects of Ando's work.

This is as good a way as any to construct the oscillation between the clearly visible universal tension of Ando's architecture (its extremely simple geometry, the absolute unity of the material used, his abstract handling of matter which is nonetheless well balanced, the tension towards a total detachment so far as the ideas of historical process and time are concerned) and the absolute specificity of the way in which it responds to the surrounding physical environment: for location, size, scale and form. His way of dealing, for example, with concrete walls, differs from the Corbusian tradition, and tends towards a regard for the sharp, defined, continuous surface rather than an expression of a material and therefore its weight. It is only the presence of the human figure, with its movements and gestures, which animate the otherwise motionless scenario of geometry and space. Yet, while waiting for the arrival of the human figure, the space can engage privately with the landscape.

When I met Ando in 1980 in Osaka, even before showing me his extraordinary pencil drawings, or his architecture, he took me to visit parts of his city. Each one had its own special, pitiless disorder, its own typical aggressiveness, to which the only logical reply could be the construction of new realms of silence, the various pauses of time – a radical reduction of the elements by way of which to start off again to give meaning to the human gesture, a new possible rhythm to behaviour. Even so, in the context of the urban chaos of Osaka, Ando's buildings themselves also have some of this urban chaos; in fact they seem to entrap something of this inside their cages of dense and simple geometries, making their elements thicker, their material heavier. This leads us to the question of how the buildings sit on the ground – the time-old question of how architecture should make contact with the earth and listen to its geology.

In understanding and representing in his own work the principles of minimalism, Ando has certainly found a methodology and the instruments with which to implement it. But a possible continuity with minimalism cannot really be taken further than that since Ando's work is exemplary in terms which distinguish architecture from the visual arts. To interpret Ando's work only in relation to minimalism is, therefore, insufficient.

Reflections on the Architecture of Tadao Ando
Yuzuru Tominaga

I

The Koshino House, set in the wooded mountains of Okuike outside Ashiya City, is one of Ando's most beautiful projects and possesses a highly artistic quality that prefigures his later architectural developments. Two concrete boxes of nearly equal width are carefully placed, side by side, half sunk into a deep green mountainside. [...] Ando has designed a number of houses in these woods, but the Koshino House stands out for its superb adaptation to the site. The site is a sloping, rectangular piece of property, 28 metres wide and 40 metres deep, sandwiched between two roads, to the north and south, that follow the mountain's contour and are about 10 metres apart in height. A diagonal axis is established, and three concrete volumes are arranged in parallel, slightly shifted one from the next. In early projects, like the Azuma House, Ando's walls rise up defiantly, as if wrestling space from the densely built central urban area. [...] Here, the diagonal rhythm determines every exterior scene, and it is where human gesture is embedded. The axis guarantees southern exposure for interior rooms, and maximizes the lengths of wall within the rectangular site, drawing the eye in a diagonal direction, and emphasizing the horizontality of the composition. More importantly, this axis determines how scenes unfold as one approaches the three concrete volumes along the edge of the site from the road to the south. While maintaining a dialogue with the irregular undulations of the topography, the zig-zagging series of volumes strikes a responsive chord in someone climbing the hill, luring the visitor closer and closer and deeper and deeper. The walls and roof line of the southernmost block – which houses the bedrooms – cross one's line of vision horizontally, and the wall in front of it, that bends at a right angle, defines the topography and then disappears into the lawn as one proceeds further. Next, the taller living and dining room block appears, shifted to one side. A semi-circular platform extends from it at the western corner of the site at the top of the hill, facing the road to the north. This is the entrance to the house. When one stands at the entrance, one finally notices the atelier block that is practically buried in the ground; its walls are repeating curves that seem to absorb the full force of the shifts that the building volumes have undergone. This sequence of scenes unfolds as one climbs the fairly steep hillside of the site. The diagonal axis makes possible a panorama in which the three blocks successively appear and disappear. As one climbs the hillside, the temporal rhythm of these appearances and disappearances, which a number of other bodies have experienced before, is continually reborn.

The plan of the Koshino House is simple. However, one's experience of the interior of the building is extremely diverse and complex. It begins when, keeping in view the simple exterior, one is led to the entrance, passes through the foyer, and then descends the stairway leading to the two-storey living room. In fact, it is not in the least easy to reconstruct the plan of this building by joining the partial views that unfold in the course of one's movement. Subtle perceptual illusions have been planted here and there. One descends from the entrance and, passing through an underground corridor, arrives on the other side of the courtyard at the corridor off the bedrooms. A series of slits introduces light from the courtyard that illuminates the ceiling and floor of the corridor. It takes only a passage through this underground corridor to completely upset one's sense of orientation. [...]

It is light above all that determines 'the way a thing appears'. The contrast between light entering a room as a square plan, and light that is crafted into lines. The contrast, furthermore, of their configurations. For example, the vivid contrast between the curved strip of light in the ceiling of the atelier and the straight strip of light in the living room. Ando painstakingly stages the way the expression of the light, ever-shifting like the hands of a clock, projects itself onto the walls. He consistently demands a sameness from the exposed concrete (the way a thing is) precisely so that this strip of light may record the passing of time and animate the surrounding matter. Compared to the rough concrete of his early work, which displayed a raw physicality, the concrete in the Koshino House turns more delicate. Its smooth texture succeeds the memory of the pleasurable, tactile world of living in a traditional Japanese house. [...]

From the start of his career, Ando has chosen to work in the densely-built city of Osaka; he has forced dwellings onto this inhospitable environment, rejecting the surroundings and creating microcosms within walls of exposed concrete. As he gradually made bare, exposed concrete a material all his own – and at the same time began extending his field of activity to suburban subdivisions – Ando began to dismantle the closed box, to cup open its ends, to treat walls as planes and to induce the nature outside to enter into the house. The wall was no longer something that enclosed and defined the box as it did in the Azuma House in Sumiyoshi; in this phase, care was taken to dismantle that wall into planes that simply happened to meet at four corners, it no longer imparted a solid presence. Ando's treatment of the exposed concrete wall seems to have changed around the time the Matsutani and Ueda residences were finished in 1979, about a year before the Koshino House. This can be seen even in the way he shifted the openings from the centre to the side, while maintaining a dialogue with the irregular undulations of the topography. It represented a process of moving away from the massiveness and static solidity that one associates with masonry construction towards a more immaterial and weightless architectural enclosure; here there is more of an effect of planes wrapping an interior, and a sensation of open volumes. More accurately, however, the effect of this change is a richness in the ambiguity that results from two possible interpretations; the outer shell of the box can be read either as an enclosure or as separate planes that have been erected on four sides. One is torn between interpreting the box as something closed and something open. [...] The walls partitioning the rooms in the bedroom block are separated into autonomous planes – this kind of treatment is extended to all the walls composing the Koshino House. What is wonderful about this new deployment of the concrete 'wall', beginning with the Matsutani and Ueda residences, is the way in which the closed box has been dismantled into planes, the way the light falls among the planes, illuminating their dismantled nature and, after all this, that they can be substantial and partition space yet at the same time seem to float weightlessly. [...]

In experiencing this building, one becomes aware of the fact that square planes of different scales are repeated here and there throughout. The same proportions are used in a large space (the living room) and a small space (the bedroom), and those who experience the interior sense the expansion and contraction of scale as a punctuating spatial rhythm. One does not find the manipulation of overlapping figures – the visual oscillations experienced by an observer – that one finds in Le Corbusier's architecture, but one understands that from the start the intention has been to build an order through the addition of squares, which themselves are complete figures. This formal principle is applied throughout the house, down to the small details, with squares of smaller dimensions being used in furniture and fixtures. As this transparent order is spread over the whole house, the sense of weight that matter originally has is gradually dispersed into the autonomous composition of geometry.

The integral gesture of accumulating geometric shapes as seen in the bedroom block, gives rise to a repetitive, regular rhythm. The colonnade supporting the overhang accelerates that rhythm. Together with the horizontality that is emphasized in this long, low mass, this rhythm is made more pronounced by its contrast with the irregular undulations of the topography. In this way bodily gestures, memories and sensations are inscribed throughout the Koshino Residence through the use of a restricted range of materials and restrained forms. Our bodies and spirits are shaken by this combination of what is still and what is living, what can be expected and what is unforeseen. On the surface, the Koshino Residence appears to be simply three concrete volumes. However, as it is experienced, it transmits diverse wave vibrations to the human spirit. But the persistent sensation experienced in the interior space is some sort of feeling of unfulfillment or lack; human drama or the figure is not latent in the space but only discovered as one walks; the space is always awaiting the entrance of the human. The artistic character of this work of architecture is built on paradox: the diagonal disposition of the building on a rectangular site; the incorporation of complex human experience into simple forms; substantiality and spatiality; closedness and openness; still proportions and active rhythm; the unexpected reversals of content happening with the contours of two boxes; the power of nature exposed within man-made regularity. These paradoxical qualities characterize Ando's buildings as surely as the qualities more often cited – the craftsmanlike beauty of the texture of concrete, the rigorous order permeating every detail, the clarity and simplicity of form – and suggest an understanding of human complexity, a requisite for any great work. It is precisely because there is a restrained, geometrical order in the 'way things are' that a richness of detail is assured in the 'way things appear'. To look at the architecture that Ando presents in vivid relief, despite its simple repetitiveness, is to experience once again the conflict within our bodies between these two basically different modes coexisting in one and the same form. Although architecture is inevitably bound to institutional, economic, functional and technical constraints, on the occasion of this coincidence individual hopes, memories and cries can be released as a one and only moment.

II

The Japanese word 'fukei', derived from the Chinese, means 'landscape', a compound of 'fu' meaning wind and 'kei' meaning sunlight. (It is also called 'fuko' – wind and light.) 'Fukei'/landscape implies natural things filled with wind and light; furthermore landscape (as fukei) is a humanized natural scenery, staged through wind and light, and not nature as matter itself.

Ando's recent work is characterized by his attempt to create a new 'landscape'. By transforming the existing geography, he attempts to reconstruct a nature that is more natural than nature, an ideal nature, a human nature – that is, landscape. The Naoshima Contemporary Art Museum (1988–92) is located on the small island of Naoshima in the Setonaikai, the Inland Sea. Leaving Takamatsu Bay and passing through a landscape of small mountains visible now and then above the horizon of the glistening ocean, a ferry approaches and a small geometric mass with a single wall in front comes into view on a hilltop on the southern tip of the island. It is said that this area was originally a salt farm, a field of exposed, textured white rocks, with no green. Landing at the pier one encounters a stepped plaza made of bare concrete which houses the museum annexe; this plaza is designed to function as the reception hall. The building conveys a distinct sense of urbanism in a natural environment: it has only a huge sliding door as an entrance and resembles either a warehouse or a church – it almost seems like a minimalist work of art. Approaching the plaza, the main lobby, a cylindrical volume and a rectangular hotel come into view, yet the main part of the complex is still hidden in its entirety. A slab wall, running all the way across the site, and the slope signal an entry into the interior space. The rooftop of the architecture – the majority of the building is buried underground – is planted; the overall effect is of a new geography. [...]

Visitors are attracted to 'singular points' of scenes which have been cropped and refined through the interaction of the architecture with nature rather than to the geometrical clarity of the architectural composition. As one wanders around the site, the constant backdrop, and that which integrates the various visual images of the site, is a commanding view of the glimmering ocean of Setonaikai. Ando has written that 'it is the domain of the liminal, where mountain, sea, and sky encounter each other. The geometric lines are drawn to accentuate this limen, and then projected into a rectangular orthogonal form and a cylinder, the former protruding from the slope and the latter buried below ground. The rectangle connects mountain and sea, while the cylinder connects sky and ground; they become a crossroads through which natural elements interact with each other'.

Just as Time's I and II use architectural form to present an ideal state of the city by interacting with the city of Kyoto and establishing a new urban network, Naoshima Contemporary Art Museum attempts to unfold a topos for a new network for human/nature relationships by burying the geometry underground. The design is no more nor less than an artificial mechanism which distributes a network of attractive destinations by digging into the surface of white rocks and planting a new nature. Light and wind come into the gallery space through an underground court. To conceal geometries with nature; to orchestrate the views of nature, light, and wind that are formed by these geometric hermitages and spaces between them – such an archetypal image of an ideal space for living is a recurring theme in Ando's recent work. Blurring the silhouettes of the geometry into the land, the architect attempts to extend the network of human topoi beyond architecture and 'environmentalize' further, for instance to include the entire southern extremity of the island.

If the Naoshima Museum implies the creation of a landscape for humans fused with the ocean, the Water Temple at Honpukuji (1989–91) might be said to establish a completely new form of place for prayer by invoking the landscape of the lotus pond latent in human memory. [...]

The new main hall of Honpukuji is located under a shallow, oval-shaped pond that is raised above the ground, and it is a striking new style of temple. The artificial lotus pond is installed in a naturalistic way, as it might have been placed had it been an essential element of the traditional landscaping in the old area of the temple. The promenade that leads the visitor to the lotus pond was meticulously planned. Passing along a gently undulating stone pavement surrounded by flowering plants, one comes to a single stretch of wall rising up against an expanse of sky from a surface filled entirely with white sand. The path leads to an opening cut into the wall, and looking through it, one sees another wall, solid and curved, almost at a tangent to the first. Both are about three metres high. To reach the pond, visitors are led along a passage staged with a strong sense of formality: face the wall, pass the wall, walk along the narrow passage between two walls, and turn back around at the end; this is precisely an abstraction of the compositional technique used in traditional Japanese gardens. A 'symbolical eye stop' (*sawari*) is placed at the vanishing point of the approaching visitors' gaze; this device disrupts one's sightline in order to enhance attention. Furthermore, rear walls that have a 'forced line' (*yugami*) continually break open to reveal new views one after another as one approaches, always surprising the visitor. The two walls erected on the white sand vividly entrap the blue sky in the traditional manner of 'borrowing space' (*ikedori*). This use of the technique of 'alternating turns' (*oremagari*) to connect totally different spaces is also seen in the traditional composition of Japanese fortresses. Ando's memories of pilgrimages to traditional gardens are enfolded within the arrangement of these two plain walls that lead to the lotus pond.

The lotus pond, of contoured concrete, is surrounded by the natural landscape and reflects trees as well as the ever-changing features of the sky. As one descends the stairs that run into the centre of the pond, the oval form of the structure becomes invisible and the outline of the pond is seen only as a horizontal line of concrete that cuts across the edge of the water. Here the geometry that is often seen as an alienating element looks extremely natural from a human point of view. While many of the Amitabha Halls built during the Fujiwara Period (such as Joruriji and Byoudouin) 'face the pond', here the traditional placement is shifted to 'under the pond'. By resurfacing this common arrangement of architectural history – the main hall in front of pond – and restaging the elements in a more multi-dimensional and dynamic relationship, the architecture defamiliarizes one's consciousness and experience. The highly developed architectural engineering of the end of the twentieth century is employed for the sole purpose of recalling the architectural history in man's memory and awakening one's perception; it does not show itself off. But on the other hand, it is this same technology that is being used to construct the extension of the new Honshu-Shikoku bridge which pierces through the whole island by cutting a narrow slit into a mountain and modifying the natural topography to the extreme.

At the end of the descent into the centre of the pond, the round-shaped, vermilion-coloured main hall comes into view. Sunlight is cast into the interior of the hall from the rear garden to the west and one soon realizes that the main hall, seemingly located underground, is actually on the ground level at this particular point, adjacent to the rear 'garden of light' of the west. The placement was skilfully contrived by careful observation and use of the undulating topography. The colour and composition of the main hall are reminiscent of the Jodo Hall at Jodoji Temple, designed by Jugen; however, the architectural style of this hall for the Shingon sect has been freely reinterpreted by Ando and thus creates a uniquely individual architectural space. This hall marks Ando's maturity in solving architectonic problematics: at the same time as pursuing the idiosyncrasy of his style, he has shown his potential to carry out a symbolic programme of architecture burdened with historicity and also responded to specific topographical requirements.

The theme of the Chikatsu-Asuka Historical Museum (1990–94) focuses exclusively on the creation of landscape; here stages have been set from which to view human history as well as nature. In this landscape visitors are led to climb up a man-made hill only to encounter the vast emptiness of the sky. Hidden behind the stepped hill is an exhibition space of darkness reminiscent of a tomb. Ando has said that the space was 'built as an "ancient tomb of the Heisei Period", a repository for the Japanese sensibility to enjoy and glorify nature'. The building is a museum which is used mainly for the research and exhibition of tomb culture, but it was also conceived as a platform from which to observe the ancient tombs that are scattered throughout the surrounding area. Although the architectural site is completely nestled in a valley, by installing the stepped viewing stage this project attempts to manipulate the space beyond the building and territorialize the surrounding landscape – a 'hill' of *Fudoki*. This recalls an aspect of Japanese garden design that tends physically to divide and territorialize nature and consists of *tsukijibei* and *engawa*. In combination they become a stage from which to see 'space articulated by the wall'. The wide stone stairway and the sloping platform cut into the stairway, along with the geometry of the tower, are a sign of a topos territorialized by human beings, just as a territory surrounded by *tsukijibei* used to be a sign that distinguished the tranquility of inner space from the outer world. To view the changing nature of the outside from a separate quiet room behind is a prototypical image of man's living space and a particular attribute of Japanese living space. In this project it seems that Ando attempts to establish what would be the original features of a topos for human living and its typical expression; however, the relationship between the place for viewing scenery and the place to retreat, as well as the planar seriality of traditional Japanese architecture, gave way to a more multi-dimensional and dynamic sequence of events than at the Water Temple. Two different spaces, with different conditions, are virtually separated (although they are adjacent to each other in section); they are connected only by people moving between them: only in one's consciousness do these spaces exist together. Herein lies the reason why humans walk. And indeed, it is the reason why the organization of the passage is deemed one of the most important aspects in Ando's architecture. The closed space, the open space with a view: these are the two kinds of places essential for the human being; and how to segue from one to another in a skilful manner becomes a major architectural theme, whether it be the composition of the succession from room to garden or from wall to window. [...]

The entrance is placed, nonchalantly, at a corner where a part of the building has been partially gouged out. The strong sense of formality is never given a definitive conclusion, but rather is thrown into the field of negotiation between man and nature. This procedure is not common in Ando's earlier work; it is said that he determined the position of the entrance by taking as an omen the fact that a number of tombs had been excavated around that spot during construction. Crossing the bridge, right in front of the entrance of the building, one notices a man-made, stepped stream of water on one side. The glistening and murmuring of the water are intended to be natural, without showing the deliberate artifice – although this was made by transforming the topography and making an artificial waterfall, it was designed as if it were 'one of the natural scenes one might encounter in the mountain'. Along the passage that cuts across towards the pond, the attraction of the changing perspectives created by the two walls – that 'borrow the landscape' in the direction of the sunset – reminds one of the ritual of following the passage next to the two walls at the Water Temple. This offers a fresh contrast between nature and artifice. As one ascends the slope, wondering where the passage leads, the field of sky grows larger and larger, conveying more and more of a sense of openness. Arriving at the stepped plaza one overlooks a pond surrounded by trees; however, one's impression is more of a huge empty space being offered to the sky. After reaching the summit of the stairway, there is nothing except a blue sky contoured by the shapes of distant mountains, spread out all over and accentuated with white clouds.

A state-of-the-art exhibition space, equipped with the latest technologies, is hidden behind the stepped hill. In the middle of the complex is the gallery for permanent installations which is designed in such a way that the entire space is taken in with one sweeping glance: the interiors of the space are stepped and echo the exterior structure. At the bottom of this gallery, a 1:150 miniature model of the Tomb of Emperor Nintoku is exhibited. The interior space consists of a wooden floor, concrete walls, and plaster-board ceiling, yet it is dominated by a magnificent sense of balance; the space has the serene quality of imperial comfort which is enhanced by the addition of a sofa in celadon green.

What is common to these three projects is the lack of intention to make a statement of the entire skyline; rather, all three are to be seen as a part of the topography. There is an intention to nullify form. This is because the architect feels strongly that modern cities and architecture already have an excess of styles on the skyline that opposes the essence of human nature, and furthermore, that these styles of form reflect only the consumerist nature of our society.

The same holds true of the interior space of the architecture. Ando's space is concerned instead with a sense of insufficiency or lack that is a requisite for an architecture-as-receptacle of a human body. It is this feeling of lack or a formal void that Ando presents to modern society and it is precisely this lack and void that are most lacking in our society with its overabundance of things and forms. Likewise, freedom of action or interpretation is allowed to happen to a man only so long as architecture secures these voids and gaps. The individual place, suffused with ambivalent meaning, ought to be secured in the public place, where the relationship between human beings is accommodated. It is thus essential that cultural memory and the topography of a particular locality, nurtured by the history of human community, should be attracted to this void or gap, for it is at this very moment that the essence of both human relations and the relationship between man and nature will be reflected within the context of architecture.

It may be that the architectural programmes demanded by modern society tend to be trite and decadent, and therefore it is necessary to reinvoke the point at which architecture came into being – it is there that human/human and human/nature relations must reside in their original forms. It is not accidental that some of Ando's recent work is reminiscent of the architecture of primitive societies, where human history, human communication, and natural heterogeneity are sheltered in the void or chasm; in this way, architecture, instead of being only functional, becomes a locus onto which ambiguous meanings are incessantly thrown.

I would like to briefly point out as a final observation the fact that Japanese traditions have been coming to the forefront in Ando's recent works. First, he has shifted his concerns from the inner garden to the outer garden. By contrast to the courtyard developed in the West – an enclosed space where humans confront and interact with one another – Ando's gaze is focused on the outer court, where humans release their visual attentions to the exterior, to nature, to find relief and comfort. Secondly, it is evident in his creation of human nature or 'landscape' that Ando is concerned more with situation than matter, with relation more than object; there is an emphasis on the establishment of an atmosphere of the topos as a whole much more than on designing an interior space for architecture. His environmental concern is supported by his organization of passageways – the route from place to place – each with a different sensuality; and this is becoming an underlying principle for his architectonics.

Concerning the Japanese garden, Ando has said that 'a superb form of Japanese garden is never still; it is a space where things are constantly moving. Through the subtle transformations of everything – moss, plants, trees, migrating birds – the way time subtly changes, year by year or season by season, is clearly experienced. The lives of the parts speak up and tirelessly form a new life of the whole. By seeing a garden as a metaphor for the process of time interminable, like a life of some sort, there might be a chance that I can express a living architecture, an architecture floating amidst time. This sensation motivates my work every day.' This statement embodies a world without hierarchy, a world where various spaces conjoin – each place with different hues – to participate in a whole by playing different roles. This is the cosmology presented by the Mandala, and it is perhaps the very essence of the Japanese view of nature.

Appendices

Biography

Tadao Ando was born in Osaka in 1941. A self-taught architect, he travelled as a young man to the United States, Europe and Africa. In 1969 Ando set up the practice Tadao Ando Architect & Associates in Osaka. In 1972 Ando built the Tomishima House in Osaka which was the first in a series of one-family houses by the architect, while 1976 saw the realization of the internationally acclaimed Azuma House, also in Osaka.

Tadao Ando Architect & Associates have participated in a number of international competitions, including the Modern Art and Architecture Museums in Stockholm (1990–91), the reconstruction of Kyoto Station (1990–91), and the Nara Convention Hall (1992).

Tadao Ando has also taught at various American universities, including Yale, Columbia and Harvard.

Since 1979 the work of Tadao Ando has been exhibited internationally at such museums as the Museum of Modern Art, New York and the Centre Georges Pompidou, Paris.

Awards
1979: Architectural Institute of Japan Prize for the Azuma House.
1983: Japanese Cultural Design Prize for Rokko Housing.
1985: Alvar Aalto Medal.
1986: Japanese Ministry of Education Prize.
1987: Mainichi Art Prize for the Church on Mount Rokko.
1988: Isoya Yoshida Award.
1989: *Medaille d'or* from the French Architecture Academy.
1991: Nominated Honorary Fellow by the American Institute of Architects; awarded the W Brunner Memorial Prize.
1993: Nominated Honorary Fellow by the Royal Institute of British Architects.
1994: Japan Art Grand Prix for the Chikatsu - Asuka Historical Museum.

Bibliography
in chronological order

Writings by Tadao Ando

Periodicals

'Jyokyo-ni-kusabisu', in *Shinkenchiku*, February 1977.
'Conforming to the Environment', in *Schinkenchiku*, May 1977.
'A Wedge in Circumstances', in *The Japan Architect*, 243, June 1977; also in *Tadao Ando: Buildings, Projects, Writings*, Rizzoli, New York, 1984; Spanish edition, Gili, Barcelona, 1985.
'Kankyo-ni-kotaeru', in *The Japan Architect*, 245, August 1977.
'New Relations Between the Space and the Person', in *The Japan Architect*, 247, October–November 1977.
'Ryouheki', in *Shinkenchiku*, February 1978.
'Shikichi no Yohaku', in *Shinkenchiku*, March 1978.
'Blank Space on the Site', in *The Japan Architect*, 253, May 1978.
'The Wall as Territorial Delineation', in *The Japan Architect*, 254, June 1978; also in *Tadao Ando: Buildings, Projects, Writings*, op cit; Spanish edition, op cit.
'Who and How', in *The Japan Architect*, 254, June 1978.
'Katarikakeru', in *A+U*, February 1979.
'Seikatsukukan-to Concrete-Geijutsu-no Yugo-o', in *Shinkenchiku*, February 1980.
'The Emotionally-Made Architectural Spaces of Tadao Ando', in *The Japan Architect*, 276, April 1980.
'Steps Upward Through Light', in *The Japan Architect*, 279, July 1980.
'Sekkei-process Q&A', in *Shinkenchiku*, December 1980.
'Ryoheki House', in *Parametro*, 99, August–September 1981.
'Kitano-cho no 4-tsu-no shigoto o Toushite', in *Shinkenchiku*, September 1981.
'From Self-Enclosed Modern Architecture Towards Universality', in *The Japan Architect*, 301, May 1982; also in *Tadao Ando: Buildings, Projects, Writings*, op cit; Spanish edition, op cit.
'Gairo no Rittai-teki-kakucho', in *Shinkenchiku*, June 1982.
'Sumiyoshi-no-Nagaya kara Kujo-no-machiya e', in *Shinkenchiku*, July 1983.

'Kenchiku-ka-sareta Yohaku', in *Shinkenchiku*, October 1983; also in *Tadao Ando: Buildings, Projects, Writings*, op cit.
'Space Determined by Concrete Blocks', in *The Japan Architect*, 318, October 1983.
'Town House at Kujo', in *The Japan Architect*, 319–320, November–December 1983.
'Kenchikukatsudo-o Toushite', in *Shinkenchiku*, November 1984.
'Bulwark of Resistance, Shinkenchiku Residential Design Competition. Judge: Tadao Ando', in *The Japan Architect*, 325, May 1985.
'Wombless Insemination – On the Age of Mediocrity. Judge's Comment on Shinkenchiku Residential Design Competition 1985', in *Shinkenchiku-Jutaku Tokushu*, winter 1986; also in *The Japan Architect*, 347, March 1986.
'Gendai Chashitsu Kou', in *Shinkenchiku-Jutaku Tokushu*, August 1986.
'A Concrete Teahouse and a Veneer Teahouse', in *The Japan Architect*, 354, October 1986.
'Chapel on Mt Rokko', ibid.
'The Culture of Fragments – Poetic Architecture', in *Precis*, 8, 1987.
'Ba o Yomu', in *Shinkenchiku*, May 1987.
'Chusyo-to Gusyo-no Kasaneawase', in *Shinkenchiku-Jutaku Tokushu*, October 1987.
'Représentation et abstraction', in *L'Architecture d'aujourd'hui*, 255, February 1988; also in *The Japan Architect*, 372, April 1988.
'Kenchiku ni Omoi o komeru', in *Shinkenchiku*, June 1988.
'Ika-suru', in *Shinkenchiku*, October 1988.
'Kenchiku-Watashi-tono-Deai 107', in *Kenchiku Bunka*, December 1988.
'Basho-no Ronri', in *Shinkenchiku*, February 1989.
'From the Chapel on the Water to the Chapel with the Light', in *The Japan Architect*, 386, June 1989.
'Chiso-e', in *Shinkenchiku*, December 1989.
'Wall: The Time's Building, 1984', in *Perspecta*, 25, 1989.
'Building Essay', in *The Harvard Architecture Review*, 7, 1989.

'Composición Espacial y Naturaleza', in *El Croquis*, 44, 1990 and 44+58, 1994.
'Kenchiku no shuhen kara', in *Shinkenchiku*, August 1990.
'Light, Shadow and Form: The Koshino House', in *Via*, 11, 1990.
'From the Periphery of Architecture', in *The Japan Architect*, 1, January 1991.
'Tousou-no Katei', in *Shinkenchiku*, July 1991.
'Shinkenchiku Residential Competition 1991: Another Glass House', in *The Japan Architect*, January 1992.
'Nihonkan-ni-yosete', in *Shinkenchiku*, May 1992.
'Arataneru chihei-ni mukete', in *Shinkenchiku*, June 1992.
'The Power of the Unrealized Vision', in *SD-Space Design*, 333, June 1992.
'Museum of Literature, Himeji', and 'Chikatsu-Asuka Historic Museum, Osaka', in *Architectural Design*, 9–10, September–October 1992.
'Sul progetto di Architettura', in *Domus*, 738, June 1992.
'Sukiya-mind o koete', in *Shinkenchiku-Ki no Kukan*, December 1992.
'Thinking in Ma, Opening Ma', in *El Croquis*, 58, January 1993 and 44+58, 1994.
'In Dialogue with Geometry: The Creation of "Landscape"', in Y Futagawa (ed), *Tadao Ando, 1988–1993*, ADA Edita, Tokyo, 1993.
'From Landscape', in *JA Library 3*, autumn 1993.
'Kenchiku-Toshi e mukete', in *GA Japan*, 5, October 1993.
'Venice-de kangaetakoto', in *Shinkenchiku*, February 1994.
'The Agony of Sustained Thought: The Difficulty of Persevering', in *GA Document*, 39, May 1994.
'Natura e architettura', in *Materia*, 16, 1994.

Books and Catalogues

'The Genealogy of Memories and the Revelation of Another Space', in *A New Wave of Japanese Architecture*, The Institute for Architecture and Urban Studies, New York, 1978.
'Mon architecture moderne: du moi à l'universel', in *Tadao Ando: Minimalisme*, Electa Moniteur, Paris, 1982.
'Kenchiku o Tsukuru Hitsuzen toushite Detail o Toraeru', in *Ando Tadao no Detail Genzu-shu-Rokko Housing, Sumiyoshi-no-Nagaya*, Shokokusha Publishing, Tokyo, 1983.
'Introduction', in *Tadao Ando: Buildings, Projects, Writings*, New York, 1984.
'Lichtbrunnen', in *Prolegomena 50 Tadao Ando*, Technische Universität, Vienna, 1985.
'Alvar Aalto Medal Address by Recipient', in *Modernity and Popular Culture*, Alvar Aalto Museum, Museum of Finnish Architecture, Helsinki, 1985.
'Light and Dark, Transparent Area', in *Hip-Hop Design Series a-1*, Rikuyo-sha Publishing, Tokyo, 1985.
'Mutual Independence, Mutual Interpenetration', in *Nihon no Kenchikuka*, 6, 1986.
'Facing up to the Crisis in Architecture', in *Tadao Ando: Breathing Geometry*, 9H Gallery, London, 1986.
'Teehaus in Oyodo, Café Mon Petit Chou, Fluß der Zeit', in *Jahrbuch für Architektur 1987–1988*, Vieweg, Braunschweig-Wiesbaden, 1987.
'Geometria e natura', in *Tadao Ando: Rokko Housing*, M Zardini (ed), Electa, Milan, 1986.
'Profondeur et obscurité', in G Tironi, *Tadao Ando: Ombres Portées*, Halle Sud, Geneva, 1988.
'Man and Nature', in *Architecture Contemporaine*, 10, Presses Polytechniques, Lausanne, 1988.
'Shintai and Space', in *Architecture and the Body*, New York, 1988.
T Ando, *The Yale Studio & Current Works*, Rizzoli, New York, 1989.

Writings on Tadao Ando

'Place-Geometry-Nature', in *Gendai no Kenchikuka – Tadao Ando 1981–1989*, Kajima Institute Publishing, Tokyo, 1989, and in *SD-Space Design*, 300, September 1989.
'Natur und Architektur', in *Tadao Ando: Sketches, Zeichnungen*, Birkhäuser Verlag, Basel-Berlin-Boston, 1990.
'Materials, Geometry and Nature', in *Tadao Ando*, Academy Editions, London, 1990.
'The Traces of Architectural Intentions', in *Tadao Ando. Details*, ADA Edita, Tokyo, 1990.
'Beyond Horizons in Architecture', in *Tadao Ando*, Museum of Modern Art, New York, 1991.
'Akka Gallery', in *Museo d'arte e architettura*, Charta, Milan, 1992.
'The Power of Unrealized Vision', in *Gendai no Kenchikuka. Tadao Ando Unbuilt Projects*, Kajima Institute Publishing, Tokyo, 1992; also in *SD-Space Design*, 333, June 1992.
'Probing, through Sensibility, Every Manner of Phenomenon', in *Tadao Ando: Beyond Horizons in Architecture*, catalogue, Tokyo, 1992.
'Light and Darkness', in *Lichtfest/Licht und Architektur*, catalogue, Ingolstadt, 1992.
'Licht', in *Jahrbuch für Licht und Architektur*, Ernst & Sohn, Berlin, 1993.
'Ando par lui-même', in *Tadao Ando*, Editions du Centre Georges Pompidou, Paris, 1994; also in *Tadao Ando/Mas allá de los horizontes en arquitectura*, Ministerio de Obras Publicas, Transportes y Medio Ambiente, Fundación 'La Caixa', Fundación Mies van der Rohe, Madrid-Barcelona, 1994.

Periodicals

T Ito, 'Suso-Hirogari no biru no Katarumono Seshu mo Kenchikuka mo Shisou Hinkon', in *Asahi Shinbun*, October 1976.
F Nishizawa, 'Chikagoro no Ando-san', in *Shinkenchiku*, May 1977.
M Miyawaki, 'Up to now', in *The Japan Architect*, 254, June 1978.
P Peters, 'Zeichenhaftigkeit und Schwelle', in *Baumeister*, December 1978.
AA VV, 'Anthology of Houses of Residential Architecture of the 1970s in Japan', in *GA Houses*, 4, 1978.
K Oshinomi, 'Jyutaku Binbo-Monogatari to Gen-ei Toshi no Topology no aida o', in *Shinkenchiku*, May 1979.
H Watanabe, 'Nine Neo "Wrinkles on the Water"', in *AIA Journal*, November 1979.
D Morton, 'Japanese Minimalism', in *Progressive Architecture*, May 1980.
T Azuma, 'Simplicity or Elegance. 1980 Winners of the Japan Institute of Architects Award', in *The Japan Architect*, September 1980.
B Bognar, 'Redefinition of Space, Time and Existence', in *Architectural Design*, 51, May 1981.
Y Futagawa, 'From a Crack in Time', in *SD-Space Design*, 201, June 1981; also in *Gendai no Kenchikuka – Tadao Ando*, Kajima Institute Publishing, 1981.
F Nishizawa, F Maki, 'Touch of Raw Freshness and Abstract Sense', *ibid*.
K Takeyama, 'The World of the Gentlehearted Nestled in Austerity', *ibid*.
T Takahashi, 'Ando-san no Koto', in *Shinkenchiku*, September 1981.
H Yatsuka, 'Architecture in the Urban Desert. A Critical Introduction to Japanese Architecture After Modernism', in *Oppositions*, 23, winter 1981.
V Gregotti, 'Tadao Ando', in *Casabella*, 484, October 1982.
P Peters, 'Tadao Ando: Ein Japanischer Architekt der Neuen Welle', in *Baumeister*, January 1982.
H Watanabe, 'From Utopia to the Corner Drugstore', in *Art News*, February 1982.
T Azuma, 'The Osaka Influence', in *The Japan Architect*, 301, May 1982.
H Watanabe, 'Tadao Ando: The Architecture of Denial', in *The Japan Architect*, 301, May 1982.
B Bognar, 'Latest Works of Tadao Ando', in *The Architectural Review*, 1029, November 1982.
T Okumura, 'Interview with Tadao Ando', in *Ritual*, 1, 1983.
T Ito, 'Conference', in *Shinkenchiku*, January 1983.
K Taki, 'The Work of Fumihiko Maki and Tadao Ando by Koji Taki', in *Shinkenchiku*, July 1983; also in *The Japan Architect*, 319–320, November–December 1983.
K Matsuba, 'Self-Renewal from Minimalism', in *Kenchiku Bunka*, October 1983.
F Nishizawa, 'Detail of Tadao Ando', in *Detail*, November 1983.
K Takeyama, 'Tadao Ando: Heir to a Tradition', in *Perspecta*, 20, 1983.
W Arets, 'Tadao Ando's Architectuur van contradicties', *Der Architect*, March 1983.
R Miyake, 'Kabe-ha', in *Shinkenchiku*, August 1984.
R Miyake, 'Tohmei Fukei', in *Shinkenchiku*, September 1984.
J Kestenbaum, 'A Series of Planes Cupped in the Palm of a Mountainside', in *Architecture*, September 1984.
M Speidel, 'Tadao Ando – Ein neuer Purismus', in *Baumeister*, November 1984.
H Watanabe, 'Kahn and Japan', in *Progressive Architecture*, December 1984.
A Campo Baeza, 'De boda es de ormigon', in *On*, 48, 1984.
Y Yoshimura, 'Ima Dento wa Soshoku o Osaeta Biishiki o Tsuikyu', in *Asahi Shinbun*, October 1984.
M Yoshida, 'Kankyo eno Subarashii Isseki', in *Shinkenchiku*, February 1985.
C Fawcett, 'A Cube Descending A Staircase – On Tadao Ando', in *The Japan Architect*, 336, April 1985.
Y Akasaka, 'Taiji kara Kaihoh' and 'From Confrontation to Liberation: Metamorphosis of Spaces Seen in the Works of Tadao Ando', in *Shinkenchiku Jyutaku Tokusyu*, summer 1985; also in *The Japan Architect*, 342, October 1985.
D Brenner, 'Shopping with Ando', in *Architectural Record*, November 1985.
M Furuyama, 'Geometry and Landscape', in *The Architecture Show*, December 1985.
K Matsuba, 'Box of Light – The Residential Architecture of Tadao Ando', in *Kurashi no Interior*, February 1986.
K Frampton, 'Ando e Oku', in *Casabella*, 522, March 1986.
A Maes, 'Raggi di luce', in *Abitare*, 244, May 1986.
K Negishi, 'Cubic Nature', in *The Japan Architect*, 354, October 1986.
Y Iijima, 'Kuukan no Hibiki (Chapel on Mt Rokko)', in *Bijutsu Techo*, January 1987.
S Salat, F Labbé, 'Ce que le Terrain nous raconte', in *L'Architecture d'aujourd'hui*, 250, April 1987.
D Brenner, 'Chapel on Mt Rokko', in *Architectural Record*, February 1987.
K Nishi, 'Ando Tadao no Hito to Sakuhin Tsuyoi Ishi, soshite Shinayakana Kansei', in *Shinkenchiku*, February 1987.
AA VV, 'Ando Tadao', in *FP*, 12, May 1987.
K Matsuba, 'Ando Tadao no Kako, Genzai, Mirai', in *FP*, 12, May 1987.
A P Leers, 'Two Ando Buildings', in *Architecture*, September 1987.
M Zardini, 'Tadao Ando – Due opere recenti', in *Casabella*, 539, October 1987.
AA VV, 'Japan', in *The Architectural Review*, 1089, November 1987.
R Miyake, 'Kikagaku no Yorobi', in *Shinkenchiku Jyutaku Tokusyu*, January 1988.
F Chaslin, 'Les temps modernes, le temps perdu et le temps retrouvé', in *L'Architecture d'aujourd'hui*, 255, February 1988.
H Ciriani, 'Volonté d'architecture, architecture de volonté', *ibid*.
J Iijima, 'Théâtre du secret', *ibid*.
A Bretagnolle, 'Parcours vers la connaissance', *ibid*.
R Miyake, 'The Path from Minimalism', in *The Japan Architect*, 372, April 1988.
G Feldmeyer, 'Die großen Architekten – Tadao Ando', in *Häuser*, April 1988.
Y Iijima, 'Idou to Hauten', in *Icon*, May 1988.
P Adam, '1985 Mit Beton, Kraft und Witz Ansporn für die Phantasie', in *Geo*, 5, May 1988.
G Vorreiter, 'Arthritis Clinic, Tokyo. Criticism', in *The Architectural Review*, June 1988.

K Matsuba, 'Ando Tadao no Futatsume Shukusai no Bigaku to Zoukei', in *FP*, 19, July 1988.

M Ueda, 'Ando Tadao Shogyo Kenchiku no Kiseki', in *FP*, 1, September 1988.

J Ishida, 'Osaka Minami ni-okeru Ando Kenchiku', ibid.

M Bellini, 'Una tecnica sovversiva', in *Domus*, 700, December 1988.

G Auer, 'Vom Nutzen des Nichts', in *Daidalos*, 30, December 1988.

R Knafo, 'The Last Angry Architect', in *The Connoisseur*, 924, January 1989.

H Suzuki, Toshi Jyutaku Fu-iyu Fu-se Ha, in *Shinkenchiku Jyutaku Tokusyu*, January 1989.

R Miyake, 'Kataki no Kioku-Setsudan suru Hikari', in *Taiyo*, February 1989.

D Gomez-Valcarol, 'Espacio Puro', in *Casa Vogue España*, 2, March 1989.

K D Stein, 'Travelling Show', in *Architectural Record*, March 1989.

G Tironi, 'Architetture sacrali di Tadao Ando', in *Casabella*, 558, June 1989.

G G Feldmeyer, 'In Japan ist nicht mehr japanisch', in *Schönes Wohnen*, August 1989.

Y Iijima, 'Kenchiku to Zoukei-Geijyutsu tono Setten', in *Shinkenchiku*, August 1989.

G Nitschke, 'Ein Raum für Interaktionen', in *Daidalos*, 33, September 1989.

Y Iijima, 'Ando Tadao no Mittu no Kyohkai "en 'jyuji' seihoukei"', in *Kenchiku Bunka*, September 1989.

R Miyake, 'Kenchiku to Gaibu Kukan no Aida o Samayou', in *Taiyo*, September 1989.

J Ishida, 'Tradizione come metodo', in *Phalaris*, 4, September–October 1989.

C Magnani, 'La descrizione del limite', ibid.

Y Iijima, 'Chika-kukan eno Manazashi', in *Bijutsu Techo*, November 1989.

P M Bode, 'Bausteine der Zukunft', in *Vogue*, November 1989.

V Panton, 'Tadao Ando y el teatro de Karaza', in *Arquitectura Viva*, November 1989.

F Ruiz de la Puerta, 'El Espacio del Silencio: la Capilla del agua de Tadao Ando', in *Arquitectura*, 281, November–December 1989.

M Ueda, 'Nakanoshima 2001 – no Zentai-zo', in *Design no Genba*, December 1989.

T Yamamoto, 'Bir Japan Mimar: Tadao Ando', in *Yapi*, 97, December 1989.

V Magnago Lampugnani, 'Tadao Ando: due recenti architetture giapponesi', in *Domus*, 712, January.

J Korhonen, 'Tadao Ando: luo unelmia betonista', in *Betonituote*, 1, January 1990.

J Pallasmaa, 'Askeesin rikkaus', in *Betonituote*, 1, January 1990.

J M Dixon, 'Tadao Ando: Abstraction Serving Reality', in *Progressive Architecture*, February 1990.

J M Dixon, 'Urban Inlay', ibid.

T J Ward, 'Beyond Shelter. Ando: The Bridge', in *Metropolitan Home*, March 1990.

H Watanabe, 'Monastic to Fantastic', in *Art in America*, 4, April 1990.

G G Feldmeyer, 'Tadao Ando: Beton-Monch', in *Ambiente*, April 1990.

C Kreiser, 'Über den Verlust des (dunklen) Innenraums', in *Daidalos*, 36, June 1990.

J Kestenbaum, 'Tadao Ando and Contemporary Ruin', in *Kenchiku Bunka*, July 1990.

T Nibuya, 'Indo o Sumawaseru Kenchiku', in *Icon*, July 1990.

R Piano, 'Kenchiku to Poetry', in *Shinkenchiku*, August 1990.

P Adreu, 'Space o Tsukuru Jiyuna Seishin', ibid.

K Matsuba, 'Kenchiku no Landscape 10 – Hikari no Chokyo Gendai Kenchiku 50-sen', in *Taiya*, August 1990.

J L Gonzalez Cobelo, 'La Arquitectura Sin Velos', in *El Croquis*, 44, August 1990 and 44+58, 1994.

A Bretagnolle, 'El Mensaja Intemporal de la Naturaleza', ibid.

F Schoeller, 'Luz Cursiva', ibid.

M Furuyama, 'Haikyo-sei o Kanjyusuru Kanseido no Takai Kukan', in *Asahi Shinbun*, 22 September 1990.

K Kodo, 'Kumo Nagareru Hateni', in *Shinkenchiku*, October 1990.

H Watanabe, 'A Tale of Two Churches', in *Mainichi Daily News*, November 1990.

K Matsuba, 'Modernism no Koshitsu to Senren kara Landscape no Sozo', in *Box*, December 1990.

Y Iijima, 'Hyoso-teki Postmodern o Utsu Jikoinpei, Hi- Jikoshucho no Keitai', in *Asahi Graph*, 28 December 1990.

K Kudo, 'New Horizons in Architecture', in *News Line*, 1991.

E Mix, 'I seek to revive the meaning and spirit of each place', in *Archidea*, spring 1991.

H Watanabe, 'Tadao Ando', in *L'Information Immobilière*, 45, summer 1991.

R Piano, 'Architecture and Poetry', in *The Japan Architect*, 1, January 1991.

P Andreu, 'Freedom and Determination to Create Space', ibid.

K Kobayashi, 'Tadao Ando and His Architectural World-Fertile Abstraction', in *The Japan Architect*, 1, January 1991.

H Okabayashi, 'Kukan o Umetsukusu Kyodaina Kukan', in *FP*, 34, January 1991.

A Richert, 'Karaza: A Movable Theatre', in *Perspecta*, 26, 1991.

M Treib, 'Silence may be the most significant gift an architect can give a noisy society', in *Metropolis*, January–February 1991.

P Bertrand, 'Parcours de la méthode', in *L'Architecture d'aujourd'hui*, 273, February 1991.

P Popham, 'The Architect as Fundamentalist: Tadao Ando', in *Blueprint*, 74, February 1991.

L Basso Peressut, 'Edificio per uffici Raika, Osaka', in *Domus*, 726, April 1991.

M Uno, 'Extension of Tadao Ando', in *Shinkenchiku Jutaku Tokusyu*, April 1991.

AA VV, 'Immeuble Collezione', in *L'Architecture d'aujourd'hui*, 274, April 1991.

K Usami, 'Mikitekuru Koe no Sazameki', in *Musashino Bijyutsu*, 1991.

K Matsuba, 'Gendai to Dento no Iwakan naki Renzoku', in *Asahi Shinbun*, 8 June 1991.

P Jodido, 'Tadao Ando: Le Géant d'Osaka', in *Connaissance des Arts*, June 1991.

M Ueda, 'Sokuryo surukoto no Doujidaisei ni tuite', in *Kenchiku Bunka*, July 1990.

S Heck, 'East in the West', in *The Architecture Review*, 1134, August 1991.

T Mayne, 'Master of Light', in *Graphis*, 275, September–October 1991.

B Fooggy, 'The Ando Dynasty. Japan's Great Architect in Moma's Retrospective', in *Washington Post*, 5 October 1991.

K Kudo, 'Utsukushii Nippon no Ando', in *Asahi Shinbun*, 5 October 1991.

K Frampton, 'Ando and Kahn play with the moods of light', in *Elle Décoration*, 18, October 1991.

P Goldberger, 'A Cult Figure Survives Overkill at the Moma', in *New York Times*, 10 November 1991.

M Suzuki, 'Chikyu Tanken "Ma" ni Yadoru Nippon no Biishiki', in *Nihon Keizai Shinbun*, November 1991.

P Bertrand, 'Ruimtelijke Strategie', in *Archis*, November 1991.

J Giovannini, 'Tadao Ando, Museum of Modern Art Exhibition', in *Atelier*, 54, November 1991.

K Frampton, 'Tadao Ando', in *Forum International*, 10, November–December 1991.

P Johnson, 'Beyond Horizons. Tadao Ando Architecture Exhibition', in *Shinkenchiku*, December 1991.

J M Dixon, 'Ando Exhibit at Moma', in *Progressive Architecture*, December 1991.

I Cases, 'Tadao Ando, Invitation au silence', in *Marie-Claire Maison*, January 1992.

B Kojoer, 'Ceremoniel Geometri', in *Arkiyekten*, February 1992.

K Nishi, 'Details-shu mo mata Hitotsu no Sakuhin', in *SD-Space Design*, February 1992.

A Barrionuevo, J C Theilacker, 'Tadao Ando y el Pabellón de Japón', in *Tecnologia y Arquitectura*, 17, February 1992.

R Hollenstein, 'Karge Spiritualität', in *NZZ Folio*, 3, March 1992.

B Bognar, 'Critical Intentions', in *Architectural Design*, March–April 1992.

B Dyer Szabo, 'Humanism in Abstraction', in *Habitat Ufficio*, 55, March–April 1992.

M Goozner, 'Tadao Ando, a Designer of Dreams', in *Chicago Tribune*, May 1992.

A Debartolo, 'Art in All Its Majesty', in *Chicago Tribune*, June 1992.

M Monninger, 'Zauberer in Beton und Licht', in *Frankfurter Allgemeine Magazine*, June 1992.

D Lewis, 'The Power of Culture', in *Newsweek*, June 1992.
V Patón, 'Abrir los Sentidos', in *Arquitectura Viva*, 24, May–June 1992.
K Matsuba, 'Ando Tadao no Shinsaku-Honpukuji Mizumido', in *Taiyo*, June 1992.
T Sugimoto, 'Mizu no Seitai to Kikagaku Kenchiku', in *Shinkenchiku*, July 1992.
R Miyake, 'Hasuike no Higan ni', in *Kenchiku Bunka*, July 1992.
K Nishi, 'Kaijyo ni Minagiru Kinchokan – Tadao Ando Kenchiku-ten o mite', in *Kenchiku Bunka*, August 1992.
M Zardini, 'Legno grezzo e gesso bianco', in *Lotus*, 73, August 1992.
M Uno, 'Kenchiku no Chihei o Koete', in *Shinkenchiku Jutaku Tokushu*, August 1992.
M Yonekura, 'Yamaraka Fuhen-Ando Tadao', in *Art Top*, August–September 1992.
N R Pollock, 'Japanese Screen Gallery, The Art Institute of Chicago – In the Japanese Spirit', in *Architectural Record*, September 1992.
B Bognar, 'Between Reality and Fiction', in *Architectural Design*, September–October 1992.
T Heneghan, 'Place, Time, Architecture', in *Shinkenchiku*, October 1992.
R Miyake, 'Water Temple', in *Domus*, 742, October 1992.
G Auer, 'Gartenminiaturen', in *Daidalos*, 42, December 1992.
C Slessor, 'Pearl of the Orient', in *The Architectural Review*, 1144, 1992.
H Yatsuka, 'The Spirit of Hospitality. Tadao Ando's Evolution', in *El Croquis*, 58, January 1993 and 44+58, 1994.
J Kestenbaum, 'Tadao Ando: Modernism and Its Discontents', *ibid*.
V Magnago Lampugnani, 'Haus Azuma in Osaka Ordung und Wurde', in *Baumeister*, February 1993.
O Mandeline, 'La Lumière de Tadao Ando', in *Le Spectacle du Monde*, 372, March 1993.
J L Pradel, 'Tadao Ando, L'esthète du béton', in *L'Evénement du Jeudi*, March 1993.

F Robichon, 'Ando par Ando', in *D'Architectures*, 33, March 1993.
D M Baude, 'Tadao Ando', in *View on Colour*, 2, March 1993.
G Davoine, 'Tadao Ando au Beaubourg', in *Le Moniteur*, March 1993.
I Flagge, 'Vom Bau der Zukunft', in *Lufthansa Bordbuch*, March 1993.
T Heneghan, 'Museo della Foresta delle Tombe, Kumamoto', in *Domus*, 749, March 1993.
C Grau, 'Profesión de fe: Tadao Ando en el Pompidou', in *Arquitectura Viva*, 29, March–April 1993.
F Jonquet, 'Tadao Ando, le Zen et l'architecte', in *Globe Hebdo*, 9, April 1993.
T Muramatsu, 'Ando Tadao: (Kosei) ga Sakebu le o Tsukuritai', in *President*, April 1993.
P Cuvelier, 'Tadao Ando, un temperament de béton', in *Libération*, 16 April 1993.
F Edelmann, 'Tadao Ando, du minimalisme au baroque', in *Le Monde*, 19 April 1993.
F Rambert, 'Choc, Modération, Liberté. Ando en trois mots', in *D'Architectures*, 34, April 1993.
F Lamarre, 'Tadao Ando, Plein les yeux', *ibid*.
A Colonna-Césari, 'Ando, L'Archi Ecolo', in *L'Express*, April 1993.
M Ritzenhofen, 'Tadao Ando in Paris – Eine Ausstellung', in *Der Architekt*, 4/93, April 1993.
H Binder, 'Beton und Licht', in *Ideales Heim*, April 1993 and in *Atrium*, 4–5, September–October 1993.
P Barriere, 'Tadao Ando-L'Architecture du moi', in *Créer*, April–May 1993.
H Nakao, 'Nijyu-ten Aruiwa chushin no Nijyu', in *SD-Space Design*, May 1993.
G Auer, 'Bauen als Versenken', in *Daidalos*, 48, June 1993.
D Sudjic, 'The Concrete Peacemaker', in the *Guardian*, 28 June 1993.
C Kent, 'Enlightenment Below', in *Progressive Architecture*, June 1993.
I Windhofel, 'Konferenz Pavillion in Weil am Rhein', in *Bauwelt*, 28–29, June 1993.
F Chaslin, 'Brutaliser l'histoire et la terre', in *L'Architecture d'aujourd'hui*, 287, June 1993.
M Binney, 'Windmiller of the Mind', in *The Times*, 1 January 1993.

D Danner, 'Zen im Markgraferland', in *Architektur*, July–August 1993.
G Pirazzoli, 'Il Simbolico', in *Materia*, 13, August 1993.
S Milesi, 'La logica di Ando', in *Casabella*, 603, July–August 1993.
R Piano, 'Kenchiku o Meguru Oufuku Syokan n 1', in *Brutus*, 299, July 1993.
R Piano, 'Kenchiku o Meguru Oufuku Syokan n 2', in *Brutus*, 300, August 1993.
R Piano, 'Kenchiku o Meguru Oufuku Syokan n 3', in *Brutus*, 301, August 1993.
S Brandolini, 'Una recente opera di Tadao Ando', in *Casa Vogue*, 253, July–August 1993.
H Binder, 'Sinnliche Geometrie', in *Werk, Bauen + Wohnen*, September 1993.
U Daus, 'Konferenz Pavillon in Weil am Rhein', in *Baumeister*, September 1993.
H Watanabe, 'Paisaje arqueologico', in *Arquitectura Viva*, 32, September–October, 1993.
R Miyake, 'Rokko no Syugo-jyutaku II o mite', in *Shinkenchiku*, October 1993.
D Libeskind, 'Beauty is not Dead', in *JA Library*, 10, autumn 1993.
H Yatsuka, 'Architecture as Social Reality', *ibid*.
M Furuyama, 'Sekai no Chitsuiyo to Kenchiku no Yashin', in *Mainichi Shinbun*, 13 January 1994.
A Muschg, 'Two Stories and a Factor for Tadao Ando', in *Archis*, January 1994.
G Nitschke, 'Tadao Ando. The Lotus Pond Hall of Honpukuji', in *Architectural Design*, 1–2, January–February 1994.
M Furuyama, 'Tadao Ando. Museo d'Arte Contemporanea nell'isola di Naoshima', in *Domus*, 758, April 1994.
K Oshinomi, 'Kincho to Renkei – Ando Tadao', in *Detail*, 120, spring 1994.
V Magnago Lampugnani, 'Three Houses by Tadao Ando', in *GA*, 71, March 1994.
L Breslin, 'Architect of the Dunes', in *ANY*, 6, May–June 1994.
F Jameson, 'Tadao Ando and the Enclosure of Modernism', *ibid*.
F Levrat, 'Addition by Subtraction', *ibid*.
F O Gehry, 'Wing and Wing', *ibid*.
C C Davidson, 'Dear Reader', *ibid*.
H Maruyama, 'Interview with Tadao Ando', *ibid*.

Books and Catalogues

C Fawcett, 'Disinterested Space – Encapsulated Man', in *The New Japanese House*, Granada, London ,1980.
AA VV, *Tadao Ando. Minimalisme*, Electa Moniteur, Paris, 1982 (with texts by: F Chaslin, A Isozaki, V Gregotti, H Watanabe, B Bognar, K Takeyama, J L Dumesnil).
AA VV, *Tadao Ando. Obras y proyectos*, Museo Español de Arte Contemporaneo, Madrid, 1982 (with texts by: A. Campo Baeza, K Frampton, Y Futagawa, F Maki).
K Pike, 'The Poetry of Light and Shade', in *The Architecture Show*, New South Wales, 1984.
Tadao Ando: Buildings, Projects, Writings, Rizzoli, New York, 1984; Spanish edition, Gili, Barcelona, 1985 (with texts by: K Frampton, T Okumura, K Taki).
R Miyake, 'The Transparent Landscape', in *Prolegomena*, Technische Universität, Vienna, 1985.
H Suzuki, R Banhan, K Kobayashi, *Contemporary Architecture of Japan*, Rizzoli, New York, 1985.
Nihon no Kenchikuka. Ando Tadao chohatsu-suru Hako, Maruzen, Tokyo, 1986 (with texts by: G Yoshimasu, S Fujiwara, J Kara, Y Tominaga).
Tadao Ando: Breathing Geometry, 9H Gallery, London, 1986 (with texts by: K Frampton, R Weston).
S Salat, F Labbé, 'La Grille et les signes. La memoire de l'ombre', in *Créateurs du Japon*, Hermann, Paris, 1986.
M Zardini (ed), *Tadao Ando. Rokko Housing*, Electa, Milan, 1986 (with texts by: V Gregotti, R Miyake).
K Frampton, 'The Work of Tadao Ando', in Y Futagawa (ed), *Tadao Ando*, ADA Edita, Tokyo, 1987.
S Slesin, S Cliff, D Rozensztroch, *Japanese Style*, Potter, New York, 1987.
Ando par Ando, Arc en rêve, Bordeaux, 1987 (with texts by: E Ambasz, M Botta, F Fort, S Salat).
H Klotz, 'Japanische Architektur zwischen Tokio und Kioto', in *Jahrbuch für Architektur 1987–1988*, Vieweg, Braunschweig-Wiesbaden, 1987.

Bibliography of Works

G Tironi, *Tadao Ando, ombres portées*, Halle Sud, Geneva, 1988 (with texts by: V Gregotti, L Snozzi).
A Unami, 'Do-jidai no Kenchiku', Sheido-sha, Tokyo, 1988.
L Dru, C Aslan, *Cafés*, Moniteur, Paris, 1988.
M Ueda, *Japan Houses in Ferroconcrete*, Grafic-sha, Tokyo, 1988.
Y Ijima, 'Mizu no Shisoh', in *Tabi -India, Turky, Okinawa*, Sumai-no-Tosyokan, Tokyo, 1989.
A Asada, 'A bolt out of the blue', in *Raika Headquarters Building*, Osaka, 1989.
H Klotz, 'Tadao Ando: Bauten und Projekte', in *Jahrbuch für Architektur*, Vieweg Verlag, Brauschweig-Wiesbaden, 1989.
H P Schwarz, 'Das Architektenhaus der Gegenwart', Deutsches Architekturmuseum, Frankfurt, 1989.
K Frampton, 'Tadao Ando and the Cult of Shintai', in T Ando, *The Yale Studio & Current Works*, Rizzoli, New York, 1989.
P Eisenman, 'The Story AND O', *ibid*; also in *Shinkenchiku*, April 1989.
G T Kunihiro, 'The Ando Studio at Yale', *ibid*.
P Eisenman, 'Correspondence', in *Gendai no Kenchikua – Tadao Ando 1981–1989*, Kajima Institute Publishing, Tokyo, 1989, and in *SD-Space Design*, 300, September 1989.
J Kestembaum, 'How to Fit a Square Peg in a Round Hole: the Artistry of the K House', *ibid*.
M Furuyama, 'A Study in Walls', *ibid*.
K Kobayashi, 'The Compelling Basics of Architecture Design', *ibid*.
K Sei Takeyama, 'The World of Tadao Ando Built Under the Super-1941ers Wave', *ibid*.
N Dan, 'The Dialectic of Tadao Ando's Architecture', *ibid*.
M Panizza, 'Figure. Cinque novelle di architettura contemporanea', Edizioni Associate, Rome, 1989.
M Botta, 'The "measure" of the place, the "transparency" of the wall, the "depth" of the light', in *Tadao Ando. Sketches Zeichnungen*, Birkhäuser, Basel, 1990.
W Blaser, 'Einleitung', *ibid*.
M Kawamukai, 'Tadao Ando: A Dialogue Between Architecture and Nature', in *Tadao Ando*, Academy Editions, London, 1990.

M Zardini, 'A Note on Tadao Ando', *ibid*.
A Berque, 'Preface', in *Tadao Ando: La Maison Koshino*, Mardaga, Liège, 1990.
D Treiber, 'Situation de Tadao Ando', *ibid*.
P Bertrand, 'La Maison Koshino', *ibid*.
B Bognar, *The New Japanese Architecture*, Rizzoli, New York, 1990 (with texts by: J M Dixon, H Yatsuka, L Breslin).
A Kraft, 'Architecture Contemporaine', Presses Polytechniques, Lausanne, 1990.
Y Ijima, *37-non no Kenchikuka*, Fukutake shi-ten, Tokyo, 1990.
B Lacy, *100 Contemporary Architects Drawings & Sketches*, Abrams, New York, 1991.
P Mauger, *Centres Commerciau*, Moniteur, Paris, 1991.
D W Fields (ed), 'Dormant Lines', in *Tadao Ando: Dormant Lines*, Rizzoli, New York, 1991 (with texts by: R Moneo, K Negishi, K Kobayashi, D W Fields).
P Eisenman, 'Indicencies: in the Drawing Lines of Tadao Ando', in *Tadao Ando. Details*, A D A Edita, Tokyo, 1991.
G G Feldmeyer, 'Erneuerung einer Japanischer Aesthetik', in *Architektur Licht Architektur*, Kramer, Stuttgart, 1991.
K Matsuba, '(Ji) no Kenchiku e – Tenkan suru Nihon Gendai Kenchiku', in *Gendai Kenchiku – Post Modern Igo*, Kajima Institute Publishing, Tokyo, 1991.
E Ambasz, 'Unbuilt Projects: Unforgettable Images', in *Gendai no Kenchikuka – Tadao Ando Unbuilt Projects*, Kajima Institute Publishing, Tokyo, 1992; also in *SD-Space Design*, 333, June 1992.
K Matsuba, 'The Enduring Concept of "Public"', *ibid*.
A Katagawara, 'Intention in Architecture', *ibid*.
Y Tominaga, 'Kikagaku ni yoru Ba no Kiritori', *ibid*.
T Ito, 'Eien narumono Utsoroi yukumono', *ibid*.
A Lederer, J Ragnarsdotter, *Wohnen Heute, Housing Today*, Kramer, Stuttgart, 1992.
S Roché-Soulié, 'Piscines', Moniteur, Paris, 1992.
K Usami, 'A Will that Manifests Voids', in *Tadao Ando: Beyond Horizons in Architecture*, Osaka-Tokyo, 1992.

I Miyake, 'A Personal View of Tadao Ando', *ibid*.
M Ueda, 'The Unearthing of "Place"', *ibid*.
F O Gehry, 'East East Meets West West', *ibid*.
B Bognar, 'The Japanese Architecture', in *Contemporary Japanese Architecture*, Van Nostrand, New York, 1992.
G Nitschke, *From Shinto to Ando*, Academy Editions, London, 1993.
A Guiheux, 'Avant-Propos', in *Tadao Ando*, Editions Centre Georges Pompidou, Paris, 1993.
Y Ijima, 'Regard à partir de la fin', *ibid*.
Y Ijima, 'Ando Tadao, Owarikarano Shisen', in *50 Contemporary Architects*, Tosho Suppan-sha, Tokyo, 1993.
T Heneghan, 'The Architecture of Tadao Ando', in Y Futagawa (ed), *Tadao Ando, 1988–1993*, A D A Edita, Tokyo, 1993.
I de Solá-Morales, 'El "caso" Ando', in *Tadao Ando*, MOPT, Madrid, 1994, Fundación "La Caixa", Barcelona, 1994.

Osaka Station Area Reconstruction Project
SD-Space Design Tadao Ando Unbuilt Projects, 333 (Special Issue), June 1992; *Gendai no Kenchikuka/Tadao Ando Unbuilt Projects*, Kajima Institute Publishing, Tokyo, 1993.

Tomishima House
Modern Living, 86, May 1972; *Toshi Jutaku*, July 1973; *GA Houses*, 6, October 1979; *De Architect*, 10, October 1982.

Hiraoka House
Kenchiku Bunka, 330, April 1974; *Toshi Jutaku*, May 1974; *Modern Living*, 92, November 1974, Tokyo.

Tatsumi House
Kenchiku Bunka, 330, April 1974; *Japan Interior*, April 1974; *Toshi Jutaku*, May 1974, *GA Houses*, 6, October 1979, Tokyo.

Port Island Project
Previously unpublished.

Shibata House
Kenchiku Bunka, 332, June 1974; *Japan Interior*, July 1974; *GA Houses*, 6, October 1979, Tokyo.

Soseikan – Yamaguchi House and Extension
Kenchiku Bunka, 347, September 1975; *The Japan Architect*, 243, June 1977; *Ontology of Houses 4, Residential Architecture of 1970's in Japan*, A D A Edita, October 1978, Tokyo; *Baumeister*, November 1984, Munich.

Extension *Contemporary Japanese Architecture*, Van Nostrand Reinhold Company, October 1985, New York; *The Japan Architect*, 354, October 1986, Tokyo; *L'Architecture d'aujourd'hui*, 255, February 1988, Paris; *Tadao Ando: Buildings, Projects, Writings*, Rizzoli, April 1983, New York.

Twin Wall Project
Kenchiku Bunka, 347, September 1975, Tokyo.

Azuma House
Shinkenchiku, February 1977, Tokyo; *The Japan Architect*, 243, June 1977; *Catalogue 10, A New Wave of Japanese Architecture*, The Institute for Architecture and Urban Studies, September 1978, New York; *The Japan Architect*, 281, September 1980, Tokyo; *Baumeister*, February 1993, Munich, *GA-Global Architecture*, 71, A D A Edita, March 1994, Tokyo.

Hirabayashi House
Kenshiku Bunka, November 1976, Tokyo; *Catalogue 10, A New Wave of Japanese Architecture*, The Institute for Architecture and Urban Studies, September 1978, New York; *Oppositions*, 23, MIT Press, winter 1981, Cambridge; *GA Houses*, 6, October 1979, Tokyo; *Contemporary Japanese Architecture*, Van Nostrand Reinhold Company, October 1985, New York.

Bansho House and Extension
The Japan Architect, 243, June 1977; *GA Houses*, 6, October 1979, Tokyo, *The Japan Architect*, 301, May, 1982; *Shinkenchiku*, June 1981.

Tezukayama Tower Plaza
L'Architecture d'aujourd'hui, 196, April 1978, Paris; *GA Houses*, 6, October 1979, Tokyo; *The Japan Architect*, 301, May 1982, Tokyo.

Rose Garden
The Japan Architect, August 1977, Tokyo; *Kenchiku Bunka*, 377, March 1978, Tokyo; *Baumeister*, February 1979, Munich.

Manabe House
Kenchiku Bunka, 385, November 1978, Tokyo; *The Japan Architect*, 270, October 1979, Tokyo; *GA Houses*, 6, October 1979, Tokyo; *Architectural Design*, 51, May 1981, London; *Baumesiter*, January 1982, Munich.

Koto Alley
Previously unpublished.

Okamoto Housing
L'Architecture d'aujourd'hui, 196, April 1978, Paris; *The Japan Architect*, 301, May 1982, Tokyo; *Tadao Ando Architectural Monographs 14*, May 1990, Academy Editions, London, St Martin's Press, New York.

Matsumoto House
The Japan Architect, 254, June 1978, Tokyo; *L'Architecture d'aujourd'hui*, 211, October 1980, Paris; *Parametro*, 99, August–September 1981, Bologna; *The Architectural Review*, 1029, November 1982, London; *Industria Italiana del Cemento*, 606, December 1986, Rome; *Oppositions*, 23, MIT Press, winter 1981, Cambridge.

Kitano Alley
Kenchiku Bunka, 377, March 1978; *The Japan Architect*, 253, May 1978, Tokyo; *Baumeister*, February 1979, Munich.

Art Gallery Complex
The Japan Architect, 301, May 1982, Tokyo; *Tadao Ando Architectural Monographs 14*, May 1990, London-New York.

Step
The Japan Architect, 279, July 1980, Tokyo; *L'Architecture d'aujourd'hui*, 210, September 1980, Paris; *Domus*, 618, 1981, Milan; *Wiederhall*, 1, 1986, Amsterdam.

Ishihara House
The Japan Architect, 270, October 1979, Tokyo; *L'Architecture d'aujourd'hui*, 206, December 1979, Paris; *Domus*, 603, February 1980, Milan; *Progressive Architecture*, May 1980, Stamford; *La Casa Unifamiliar*, 1984, Barcelona; *Forum International*, 10, November–December 1991, Antwerp.

Okusu House
GA Houses, 6, October 1979, Tokyo; *The Japan Architect*, 301, May 1982, Tokyo; *Contemporary Japanese Architecture*, October 1985, New York.

Horiuchi House
The Japan Architect, 270, October 1979, Tokyo; *GA Houses*, 6, October 1979, Tokyo; *L'Architecture d'aujourd'hui*, 206, December 1979, Paris; *Progressive Architecture*, May 1980, Stamford; *Key Buildings of the 20th Century Vol 2: Houses 1945–1989*, December 1990, London; *Daidalos*, 33, January–February 1994, Berlin.

Matsumoto House
The Japan Architect, 301, May 1982, Tokyo; *The Architectural Review*, 1029, November 1982, London; *SD-Space Design*, 201 (Special Issue), 1981, Tokyo; *Gendai no Kenchikuka Tadao Ando*, 1982, Tokyo.

Onishi House
The Japan Architect, 301, May 1982, Tokyo; *L'Architecture d'aujourd'hui*, 226, April 1983, Paris.

Kitano Ivy Court
Shinkenchiku, September 1981, Tokyo.

Matsutani House and Extension
The Japan Architect, 274, April, 1980, Tokyo; *The Japan Architect*, 301, May 1982, Tokyo.

Extension *The Japan Architect*, 1, January 1991, Tokyo; *Shinkenchiku Jutaku Tokushi*, April 1991, Tokyo; *Abitare*, 305, March 1992, Milan.

Ueda House and Extension
The Japan Architect, 276, April 1980, Tokyo; *The Japan Architect*, 301, May 1982, Tokyo; *GA Houses*, 14, July 1983, Tokyo.

Fuku House
Baumeister, January 1982, Munich; *The Japan Architect*, 301, May 1982, Tokyo; *La Mia Casa*, 153, December 1982, Milan.

Rokko Housing I
Casabella, 484, October 1982, Milan; *GA Document*, 7, April 1983, Tokyo; *Kenchiku Bunka*, 444, October 1983, Tokyo; *The Japan Architect*, 322, February 1984, Tokyo; *Architecture intérieure-crée*, 199, March–April 1984, Paris; *L'Architecture d'aujourd'hui*, 232, April 1984, Paris; *Architecture*, September 1984, Washington DC, *Quaderni di Casabella*, 1986, Milan; *Créateurs du Japon*, 1986, Paris; *Forum International*, 10, November–December 1991, Antwerp; *JA Library 3 Tadao Ando Rokko Housing I II III*, October 1993, Tokyo.

Rin's Gallery
Shinkenchiku, September 1981, Tokyo.

Koshino House and Extension
L'Architecture d'aujourd'hui, 220, April 1982, Paris; *Progressive Architecture*, December 1984, Stamford; *Abitare Annual 2*, November–December 1987; *Tadao Ando et la Maison Koshino*, July 1990, Liège; *Atrium*, 04/05, September–October 1993, Zurich; *GA-Global Architecture*, 71, March 1994, Tokyo.

Sun Place
Kenchiku Bunka, 428, June 1982, Tokyo; *The Japan Architect*, 305, September 1982, Tokyo; *Tadao Ando: Buildings, Projects, Writings*, April 1983, New York.

Atelier in Oyodo I
The Japan Architect, 301, May 1982, Tokyo; *Grosse Architekten*, February 1992, Hamburg.

Nakanoshima Project I – Osaka City Hall
Wonen Tabk, December 1984, Amsterdam; *SD-Space Design, Tadao Ando Unbuilt Projects*, 333 (Special Issue), June 1992, Tokyo; *Gendai no Kenchikuka, Tadao Ando Unbuilt Projects*, November 1993, Tokyo.

Festival
Casabella, 495, October 1983, Milan; *L'Architecture d'aujourd'hui*, 235, October 1984, Paris; *Kenchiku Bunka*, 457, November 1984, Tokyo; *The Japan Architect*, 336, April 1985, Tokyo; *Precis*, 6, September 1987, New York; *The Harvard Architecture Review 7*, August 1989, New York.

Kojima Housing
L'Architecture d'aujourd'hui, 219, February 1982, Paris; *The Japan Architect*, 301, May 1982, Tokyo; *Progressive Architecture*, November 1982, Stamford.

Ishii House
Techniques & Architecture, 345, December 1982, Paris; *GA Houses*, 14, July 1983, Tokyo; *De Architect*, 3, March 1984, Den Haag; *Villas Decoratie*, 1986, Brussels.

Bigi Atelier
GA Document, 7, April 1983, Tokyo; *The Japan Architect*, 329, September 1984, Tokyo.

Akabane House
Kenchiku Bunka, 444, October 1983, Tokyo.

Umemiya House
The Japan Architect, 318, October 1983, Tokyo; *Baumeister*, November 1984, Munich.

Fukuhara Clinic
GA Document, 17, April 1987, Tokyo; *The Architectural Review*, June 1988, London.

Izutsu House
Le Moniteur, January 1983, Paris; *The Japan Architect*, 319/320, November–December 1983, Tokyo; *De Architect*, 3, March 1984, The Hague.

Doll's House Project
Previously unpublished.

Festival 0
Previously unpublished.

Iwasa House
Casa Vogue, 184, April 1987, Milan.

Melrose
Previously unpublished.

Kidosaki House
Kenchiku Bunka, 492, October 1987, Tokyo; *Shinkenchiku Jutaku Tokushu*, October 1987, Tokyo; *The Japan Architect*, 372, April 1988, Tokyo; *Casa Vogue España*, No 2, March 1989, Madrid; *Casa Vogue*, February 1990, Milan; *Ambiente*, April 1990, Munich; *Villas Decoratie*, September 1991, Brussels; *Domus*, 738, March 1992, Milan, *GA Global Architecture*, 71, March 1994, Tokyo.

Kaneko House
Previously unpublished.

Ogura House
Shinkenchiku Jutaku Tokushu, November 1988, Tokyo; *GA Houses*, 25, March 1989, Tokyo; *Abitare*, 278, October 1989, Milan.

Time's I
Shinkenchiku, February 1985, Tokyo; *The Japan Architect*, 336, April 1985, Tokyo; *Architectural Record*, November 1985, New York; *Casabella*, 522, March 1986, Milan; *Detail*, April 1987, Munich; *Perspecta*, 25, December 1989, New York; *The New Japanese Architecture '91*, 1991, New York.

Time's II
Kenchiku Bunka, 479, September 1986, Tokyo; *Shinkenchiku*, July 1992, Tokyo.

Jun Port Island Building
Kenchiku Bunka, 476, June 1986, Tokyo; *The Japan Architect*, 354, October 1986, Tokyo; *GA Document*, 15, December 1986, Tokyo; *Casabella*, 539, October 1987, Milan; *Architecture intérieure-crée*, April–May 1993, Paris.

Yoshie Inaba Atelier
El Croquis, 44, July 1990, Madrid; *The Japan Architect*, 346, February 1986, Tokyo.

Nakayama House
The Japan Architect, 342, October 1985; *Casa Vogue*, 184, April 1987; *L'Architecture d'aujourd'hui*, 255, February 1988; *Baumeister*, May 1988.

Mon Petit Chou
Architecture, September 1986; *Jahrbuch für Architektur 1987–88*, Braunschweig 1988; *Abitare*, 262, March 1988, Milan.

Hata House
GA Houses, 20, September 1986, Tokyo; *Kenchiku Bunka*, 479, September 1986, Tokyo; *Architecture Contemporaine*, 1986, Lausanne; *Casa Vogue*, 184, April 1987, Milan.

Sasaki House
Kenchiku Bunka, 492, October 1987, Tokyo; *GA Architect*, 8, 1987, Tokyo.

Guest House for Hattori House
Kenchiku Bunka, 492, October 1987; *GA Architect*, 8, Tokyo 1987.

Taiyo Cement Headquarters
Architecture Contemporaine, 1986, Lausanne; *The Japan Architect*, 361, May 1987, Tokyo.

TS Building
The Japan Architect, 361, May 1987, Tokyo; *Casabella*, 545, April 1988, Milan.

Church on Mount Rokko
Kenchiku Bunka, 479, September 1986; *Architecture*, September 1986; *Architectural Design*, December 1986; *Casabella*, 530, December 1986; *GA Document*, 15, December 1986; *Architectural Record*, February 1987; *L'Architecture d'aujourd'hui*, 250, April 1987; *Abitare*, 262, March 1988; *Schonen Wohnen*, August 1989; *Arquitectura*, 281 November 1990; G Nitschke, *From Shinto to Ando*, London, 1993.

Old/New Restaurant
GA Document, 17, April 1987; *Kenchiku Bunka*, 487, May 1987; *The Japan Architect*, 363, July 1987; *Architecture intérieure-crée*, 226, October–November 1988.

Tanaka Atelier
Metropolitan Home, March 1990; *Graphis*, September–October, 1991.

Shibuya Project
GA Document, 17, April 1987, Tokyo; *Casabella*, 539, October 1987, Milan; *The Japan Architect*, 367/368, November–December 1987, Tokyo; *L'Architecture d'aujourd'hui*, 255, February 1988, Paris; *El Croquis*, 44, July 1990, Madrid.

Noguchi House
Japan Houses in Ferroconcrete, November 1988, Tokyo.

Oyodo Tea Houses
Veneer tea house *Kenchiku Bunka*, 479, September 1986, Tokyo; *Abitare*, 253, April 1987, Milan; *The Japan Architect*, 354, October 1986, Tokyo; *The Architectural Review*, 1089, November 1987, London; *Shinkenchiku Jutaku Tokushu*, January 1989, Tokyo; *Kenchiku Bunka*, 479, September 1986, Tokyo.

Block tea house *Shinkenchiku*, January 1989, Tokyo; *SD-Space Design Tadao Ando Unbuilt Projects*, 333 (Special Issue), June 1992, Tokyo; *Gendai no Kenchikuka, Tadao Ando Unbuilt Projects*, November 1993, Tokyo.

Tent tea house *Shinkenchiku*, January 1989, Tokyo; *SD-Space Design Tadao Ando Unbuilt Projects*, 333 (Special Issue), June 1992, Tokyo; *Gendai no Kenchikuka, Tadao Ando Unbuilt Projects*, November 1993, Tokyo.

Kitayama Apartment Block
Previously unpublished.

Kara-za Mobile Theatre
The Japan Architect, 374, June 1988, Tokyo; *L'Architecture d'aujourd'hui*, 259, October 1988, Paris; *Domus*, 701, January 1989, Milan; *Casabella*, 555, March 1989, Milan; *Architectural Record*, 2, March 1989, New York; *Arquitectura Viva*, 9, November 1989, Madrid; *Perspecta*, 26, 1991, New York; *Kenchiku Bunka*, 501, July 1988, Tokyo.

I House
Domus, 712, January 1990, Milan; *Progressive Architecture*, February 1990, Stamford; *Casa Vogue España*, 20, December 1990, Madrid; *Architectural Design*, June 1991, London.

Rokko Housing II
L'Architecture d'aujourd'hui, 250, April 1987, Paris; *JA Library 3 Tadao Ando Rokko Housing I II III*, October 1993, Tokyo; *GA Japan*, 5, October 1993, Tokyo; *Shinkenchiku*, October 1993, Tokyo; *GA Houses*, 39, November 1993, Tokyo.

Church on the Water
GA Document, 22, January 1989; *Kenchiku Bunka*, 510, April 1989, Tokyo; *L'Architecture d'aujourd'hui*, 262, April 1989, Paris; *The Japan Architect*, 386, June 1989, Tokyo; *Casabella*, 558, June 1989, Milan; *Art in America*, April 1990, USA; *Arquitectura*, 281, November 1990, Madrid; *Architectural Record*, CLXXIX, 10, October 1991, USA; *Techniques et Architecture*, December 1992; *Architecture Crée*, 253, April–May 1993, Paris.

Theatre on the Water
The Japan Architect, 372, April 1988, Tokyo; *GA Document*, 20, June 1988, Tokyo; *Casabella*, 558, June 1989, Milan.

Galleria Akka
The Japan Architect, 367/368, November–December, 1987, Tokyo; *Detail*, 2, April–May, 1990, Munich; *The New Japanese Architecture*, 1991, New York; *L'Information Immobilière*, No.45, 1991, Geneva; *A&V*, 28, 1991, Madrid; *Domus*, 707, August 1989, Milan.

Bigi 3rd
The Japan Architect, 346, February 1986, Tokyo; *Architecture Contemporaine*, 1987–88, Lausanne; *Architecture intérieure-crée*, 226, October–November 1988, Paris.

Collezione
Kenchiku Bunka, 518, December 1989, Tokyo; *The Japan Architect*, 395, March 1990, Tokyo; *Casabella*, 573, November 1990, Milan; *Progressive Architecture*, February 1991, Stamford; *L'Architecture d'aujourd'hui*, 274, April 1991, Paris.

Kaguraoka Apartment Block
Previously unpublished.

Morozoff Studio
Previously unpublished.

Yoshida House
Previously unpublished.

Raika Headquarters
GA Document, 25, April 1990, Tokyo; *Kenchiku Bunka*, 525, July 1990, Tokyo; *The Japan Architect*, 1, January 1991, Tokyo; *Domus*, 726, April 1991, Milan; *Connaissance des Arts*, June 1991, Paris; *Habitat Ufficio*, March–April 1992, Milan; *El Croquis*, 58, January 1993, Madrid.

Shinto Shrine Project
Previously unpublished.
Mount Rokko Banqueting Hall
Previously unpublished.
Church of the Light
GA Document, 22, January 1989, Tokyo; *Kenchiku Bunka*, 515, September 1989, Tokyo; *The Japan Architect*, 391/392, November–December 1989, Tokyo; *Domus*, 712, January 1990, Milan; *L'Architecture d'aujourd'hui*, 273, February 1991, Paris; *Detail*, 3, July 1991, Munich; *Festival of Light*, 1992, Ingolstadt.
Children's Museum
Kenchiku Bunka, 526, August 1990, Tokyo; *GA Document*, 27, September 1990, Tokyo; *The Japan Architect*, 1, January 1991, Tokyo; *Casabella*, 582, September 1991, Milan; *L'Architecture d'aujourd'hui*, 279, February 1992, Paris; *Arquitectura Viva*, 24, May–June 1992, Madrid; *Architectural Design*, 62, September–October 1992, London.
Natsukawa Memorial Hall
The Japan Architect, 1, January 1991, Tokyo; *Casabella*, 582, September 1991, Milan; *El Croquis*, 58, January 1993, Madrid.
Izu Project
GA Document, 23, April 1989, Tokyo.
Nakanoshima Project II – Space Strata and Urban Egg
L'Architecture d'aujourd'hui, 268, April 1990, Paris; *Architectural Design*, July–August 1992, London; *The Japan Architect*, 391/392, November–December 1989, Tokyo.
I Gallery
Previously unpublished.
Ito House
Kenchiku Bunka, 537, July 1991, Tokyo; *GA Houses*, 35, August 1992, Tokyo; *Daidalos*, 46, December 1992, Berlin; *Heim*, June 1993, Zurich; *Atrium*, 4/5, September–October 1993, Zurich.
Naoshima Contemporary Art Museum
Connaissance des Arts, 493, March 1993, Paris; *GA Japan*, 4, July 1993, Tokyo; *Kenchiku Bunka*, 561, July 1993, Tokyo; *Shinkenchiku*, July 1993, Tokyo; *Domus*, 758, March 1994.

Garden of Fine Arts, Expo 90, Osaka
Shinkenchiku, May 1990, Tokyo; *Casa Vogue*, 224, November 1990, Milan.
Museum of Literature
Kenchiku Bunka, 537, July 1991, Tokyo; *GA Document*, 30, September 1991, Tokyo; *Architectural Design*, 62, March/April 1992; *Casabella*, 599, March 1993.
Ishiko House
Previously unpublished.
Vitra Seminar House
The Japan Architect, 1, January 1991, Tokyo; *Atrium*, 4/5, September–October 1993, Zurich; *L'Architecture d'aujourd'hui*, 288, September 1993, Paris; *Archis*, Vol 94, January 1994, Amsterdam.
Gallery for Japanese Screens, Art Institute of Chicago
Architecture, Vol 81 No 9, September 1992, Washington DC; *Architectural Record*, Vol 180 No 9, September 1992, New York; *Shinkenchiku*, January 1993, Tokyo.
Rokko Island
Previously unpublished.
Sayoh Housing
GA Architect 12: Tadao Ando 1988–1993, 1993, Tokyo.
Minolta Seminar House
Previously unpublished.
Otemae Art Center
GA Document, 35, August 1992, Tokyo; *Shinkenchiku*, February 1993, Tokyo; *RIBA Journal*, Vol 100 No 6, June 1993, London.
Atelier in Oyodo II
Previously unpublished.
Rockfield Factory
Previously unpublished.
Japan Pavilion, Expo 92, Seville
L'Architecture d'aujourd'hui, 277, October 1991, Paris; *Connaissance des Arts*, December 1991, Paris; *A&V*, 34/35, March 1992, Madrid; *GA Document*, 33, April 1992, Tokyo; *Casabella*, 591, May–June 1992, Milan; *Domus*, 739, June 1992, Milan; *The Architectural Review*, 1144, June 1992, London.

Water Temple
Shinkenchiku, July 1992, Tokyo; *GA Document*, 35, August 1992, Tokyo; *Domus*, 742, October 1992, Milan; *Daidalos*, 46, December 1992, Berlin; *Arquitectura Viva*, 29, March–April 1993, Madrid; *Progressive Architecture*, June 1993, Stamford; *Casa Vogue*, 253, July–August 1993, Milano; *Materia*, 13, August 1993, Parma.
Forest of Tombs Museum
Shinkenchiku, October 1992, Tokyo; *Kenchiku Bunka*, 552, October 1992, Tokyo; *Domus*, 749, March 1993, Milan; *Arquitectura Viva*, 32, September–October, Madrid; *Architectural Design*, 64, January–February 1994.
Miyashita House
GA Houses, 36, November 1992, Tokyo.
Temporary Theatre for Photography
Shinkenchiku, June 1990, Tokyo; *SD-Space Design Tadao Ando Unbuilt Projects*, June 1992, Tokyo; *Gendai no Kenchikuka: Tadao Ando Unbuilt Projects*, November 1993, Tokyo.
College of Nursing
Previously unpublished.
The Modern Art Museum and Architecture Museum, Stockholm, Design Competition
SD-Space Design: Tadao Ando Unbuilt Projects, 333 (Special Issue), June 1992, Tokyo; *Gendai no Kenchikuka, Tadao Ando Unbuilt Projects*, November 1993, Tokyo.
Chikatsu-Asuka Historical Museum, Osaka
Arquitectura Viva, 29, March–April 1993, Madrid; *GA Document*, 39, May 1994, Tokyo.
YKK Seminar House
Previously unpublished.
Children's Seminar House
Kenchiku Bunka, 537, July 1991, Tokyo; *L'Architecture d'aujourd'hui*, 279, February 1992, Paris; *GA Document*, 35, August 1992, Tokyo.
Garden of Fine Arts, Kyoto
GA Japan, 8, May 1994, Tokyo; *Shinkenchiku*, May 1994, Tokyo.

Kyoto Station Reconstruction Project
SD-Space Design: Tadao Ando Unbuilt Projects, 333 (Special Issue), June 1992, Tokyo; *Gendai no Kenchikuka Tadao Ando Unbuilt Projects*, November 1993, Tokyo.
Oyamazaki Museum
SD-Space Design Tadao Ando Unbuilt Projects, June 1992, Tokyo; *Gendai no Kenchikuka, Tadao Ando Unbuilt Projects*, November 1993.
Konan University Student Centre
GA Document, 33, April 1992, Tokyo; *Shinkenchiku*, June 1992, Tokyo.
Nara Convention Hall, Project
SD-Space Design: Tadao Ando Unbuilt Projects, 333 (Special Issue), June 1992, Tokyo; *Gendai no Kenchikuka: Tadao Ando Unbuilt Projects*, November 1993, Tokyo; *Tadao Ando: Beyond Horizons in Architecture*, June 1992, Tokyo; *El Croquis*, 58, January 1993, Madrid.
Church in Tarumi
Previously unpublished.
Suntory Museum
Shinkenchiku, June 1992, Tokyo; *Tadao Ando: Beyond Horizons in Architecture*, June 1992, Tokyo.
Lee House
El Croquis, 58, January 1993, Madrid.
Museum of Wood
Shinkenchiku, July 1994, Tokyo; *GA Japan*, 9, July 1994, Tokyo.
Gallery Noda
GA Houses, 37, March 1993, Tokyo; *GA Japan*, 4, July 1993, Tokyo; *Shinkenchiku*, May 1994, Tokyo.
Rokko Housing III
JA Library 3 Tadao Ando Rokko Housing I II III, October 1993, Tokyo.
'Fabrica', Benetton Research Centre
Casabella, 600, April 1993, Milan; *Shinkenchiku*, February 1994, Tokyo; *GA Document*, 36, April 1993, Tokyo.
Installation for 'Tadao Ando Architectural Works' Exhibition
Previously unpublished.

Index of Works

Akabane House 176–179
Art Gallery Complex 96–97
Atelier in Oyodo I 154–155
Atelier in Oyodo II 374–377
Azuma House 56–61

Bansho House and Extension 66–71
Bigi Atelier 172–175
Bigi 3rd 294–295

Chikatsu-Asuka Historical Museum 402–405
Children's Museum 322–327
Children's Seminar House 408–409
Church in Tarumi 420–421
Church of the Light 318–321
Church on Mount Rokko 246–251
Church on the Water 282–287
College of Nursing 396–399
Collezione 296–301

Doll's House Project 190

'Fabrica', Benetton Research Centre 436–439
Festival 158–163
Festival 0 191
Forest of Tombs Museum 388–391
Fuku House 132–133
Fukuhara Clinic 184–185

Galleria Akka 190–293
Gallery for Japanese Screens, Art Institute of Chicago 362–363
Gallery Noda 432–433
Garden of Fine Arts, Expo 90, Osaka 350–351
Garden of Fine Arts, Kyoto 410–411
Guest House for Hattori House 238–239

Hata House 232–235
Hirabayashi House 62–65
Hiraoka House 38–39
Horiuchi House 112–117

I Gallery Project 338–339
I House 274–277
Ishihara House 102–109
Ishii House 168–171
Ishiko House 356–357
Installation for 'Tadao Ando Architectural Works' Exhibition 440–441
Ito House 340–343
Iwasa House and Extension 192–195
Izu Project 332–333
Izutsu House 186–189

Japanese Pavilion, Expo 92, Seville 380–383
Jun Port Island Building 218–221

Kaguraoka Apartment Block 302–303
Kaneko House 204–205
Kara-za Mobile Theatre 270–273
Kidosaki House 198–203
Kitano Alley 92–95
Kitano Ivy Court 122–123
Kitayama Apartment Bock 268–269
Kojima Housing 164–167
Konan University Student Centre 416–417
Koshino House and Extension 144–151
Koto Alley Project 82–83
Kyoto Station Reconstruction Project 412–413

Lee House 424–427

Manabe House 78–81
Matsumoto House Project 86–91
Matsumoto House 118–119
Matsutani House and Extension 124–127
Melrose 196–197
Minolta Seminar Building 370–371
Miyashita House 392–393
Modern Art Museum and Architecture Museum, Stockholm Project, The 400–401
Mon Petit Chou 230–231
Morozoff Studio 304–305
Mount Rokko Banqueting Hall Project 317
Museum of Literature 352–355
Museum of Wood 428–431

Nakanoshima Project I – Osaka City Hall 156–157
Nakanoshima Project II – Space Strata and Urban Egg 334–337
Nakayama House 226–229
Naoshima Contemporary Art Museum 344–349
Nara Convention Hall Project 418–419
Natsukawa Memorial Hall 328–331
Noguchi House 260–261

Ogura House 206–209
Okamoto Housing Project 84–85
Okusu House 110–111
Old/New Restaurant 252–255
Onishi House 120–121
Osaka Station Area Reconstruction Project 34–35
Otemae Art Center 372–373
Oyamazaki Museum 414–415
Oyodo Tea Houses 262–267

Port Island Project 44–45

Raika Headquarters 310–315
Rin's Gallery 142–143
Rockfield Factory 378–379
Rokko Housing I 134–141
Rokko Housing II 278–281
Rokko Housing III 434–435
Rokko Island 364–365
Rose Garden 74–77

Sasaki House 236–237
Sayoh Housing 366–369
Shibata House 42–43
Shibuya Project 258–259
Shinto Shrine Project 316
Soseikan–Yamaguchi House and Extension 46–53
Step 98–101
Sun Place 152–153
Suntory Museum 422–423

Taiyo Cement Headquarters 240–241
Tanaka Atelier 256–257
Tatsumi House 40–41
Temporary Theatre for Photography 394–395
Tezukayama Tower Plaza 72–73
Theatre on the Water 288–289
Time's I 210–213
Time's II 214–217
Tomishima House 36–37
TS Building 242–245
Twin Wall Project 54–55

Ueda House and Extension 128–131
Umemiya House 180–183

Vitra Seminar House 358–361

YKK Seminar House 406–407
Yoshida House 306–309
Yoshie Inaba Atelier 222–225

Water Temple 384–387

Photographic Credits

Many thanks to Tadao Ando Architect & Associates for kindly providing the pictorial material for this publication, as well as to:

Tadao Ando 37, 39, 41, 43, 47, 57, 58 (top left), 63–65, 69, 70, 73, 75–77, 80, 85 (top right), 93–95, 97 (top right), 100 (top left), 108, 109, 111, 117 (top), 119, 121–123, 133, 137, 138 (left and bottom right), 139, 141–143, 147, 155, 159, 160 (right), 161, 167–175, 177–179, 188, 192, 193, 196, 197, 201 (top left), 204, 205, 210–212, 219, 230–237, 239, 246, 253, 254 (right), 256, 257, 261, 268, 269, 275 (bottom), 276, 278, 286 (top right and left), 287, 292, 293 (top left), 302, 303, 304 (top right), 305, 307–309, 313 (right), 315 (bottom), 337, 349, 356, 357, 361 (bottom), 364, 365, 370, 371, 374–378, 391, 404, 405, 409, 421, 435, 437 (left), 440, 445 (bottom), 451, 459, 463 (bottom)

Masao Araki 89–91, 186, 189

Hiroyuki Hirai 275 (top), 277, 293 (bottom right)

Hiroshi Kobayashi 151, 226–229

Mitsuo Matsuoka 49–53, 58 (right), 60, 61, 71, 81, 92, 99, 100 (right), 101, 104, 105, 107, 115, 116, 117 (bottom), 124–127, 129–131, 145, 146, 149, 152, 153, 160 (left), 162, 163, 181–183, 194, 195, 198, 200, 201 (top right), 202, 203, 206–209, 213, 220, 221, 223–225, 240, 241, 243–245, 247–251, 254 (left), 255, 264–267, 283–285, 286 (top centre), 289 (top left), 291, 293 (top right and bottom left), 295, 296, 298–301, 310, 311, 312, 313 (left), 314, 315 (top), 318–321, 323, 325–331, 341–343, 350, 353, 355, 359, 362, 363, 368, 369, 380, 382, 383, 385, 392, 393, 395, 396, 398, 399, 400, 407, 417, 422, 424–427, 445 (top), 455 (bottom), 464

Shigeo Ogawa 410, 411, 429–431

Taisuke Ogawa 136, 138 (bottom right), 140, 164–166

Tomio Ohashi 54, 55, 85 (left), 97 (left), 259, 289 (bottom), 332, 336, 440, 413, 415, 419, 423, 436, 437 (right)

Yoshio Takase 185

Hiroshi Ueda 214, 216, 217, 280, 281, 347, 348, 360, 361 (top), 372, 373, 384, 386, 387, 389, 390, 432, 433, 463 (top), 466